The Encyclopedia of Money

The Encyclopedia of Money

SECOND EDITION

Larry Allen

A B C · C L I O

Santa Barbara, California • Denver, Colorado • Oxford, England

Library of Congress Cataloging-in-Publication Data

Allen, Larry, 1949-
   The encyclopedia of money / Larry Allen. — 2nd ed.
     p. cm.
   Includes bibliographical references and index.
   ISBN 978-1-59884-251-7 (hard copy : alk. paper) — ISBN 978-1-59884-252-4 (ebook)
  1. Money—Encyclopedias. 2. Monetary policy—Encyclopedias. I. Title.
   HG216.A43 2009
   332.403—dc22   2009035247

13   12   11   10   2   3   4   5

This book is also available on the World Wide Web as an eBook.
Visit www.abc-clio.com for details.

ABC-CLIO, LLC
130 Cremona Drive, P.O. Box 1911
Santa Barbara, California 93116-1911

This book is printed on acid-free paper ∞

Manufactured in the United States of America

Contents

List of Entries

Preface to the Second Edition

The 2008–2009 financial crisis holds implications for the subject of money that make a new edition of *The Encyclopedia of Money* timely. A decade has elapsed since the first edition of *The Encyclopedia of Money* came off the press. In that decade, the set of money-related issues and problems underwent drastic change. The last century drew to a close with the widespread perception that inflation remained public enemy number one where money was concerned. The decade of the 1970s had not only seen the United States suspend the convertibility of dollars into gold, but it had also seen rampant inflation. Keeping inflation corralled became the preoccupation of monetary authorities around the world. The proper management of fiat monetary systems as a path to price stability became the central concern of economic research.

Experience with inflation exerts subtle influences on public policy. Inflation makes it easier to resell things at higher prices than were originally paid for them. As households and businesses find it easy to sell things at a profit, they acquire greater confidence in free markets. Because government regulation is the greatest enemy of free markets, households and business are ready to do away with it. Government regulation becomes something that might hold a price below a market price, or subtract from the profits earned when assets are sold for a profit. Government regulation comes to be viewed as a relic of Depression-era economics, as something that should be safely dismantled or ignored. Deflation has the opposite effect. Under deflation, few people want to be left to the mercy of a market. Instead of seeing the market as their friend, households and businesses are more likely to view markets as the playground of clever and sometimes unscrupulous intermediaries that know how to buy cheap and sell dear. Deflation leads to the perception that government regulations are needed to protect the less informed from the better informed.

As governments around the world exalted free markets, a less conspicuous trend was also making itself felt. The worldwide average rate of inflation gradually subsided in the 1990s. It was as if the war against inflation had succeeded all too well. By the mid-1990s, Japan was reporting deflation. In 2008, U.S. monetary authorities gave free reign to monetary growth, trying to prevent a recession from evolving into a trend of deflation. If fear of deflation replaces fear of inflation, the idea of policing markets with government regulations may rise from the ashes and enjoy new prestige. The absence of inflation removes some of the fears of regulations and weakens confidence in free markets. A wave of failures in financial institutions suggests a need for stricter and more conscientious regulation.

Whether deflation develops in the United States remains to be seen. Certainly, fear of depression has led the U.S. monetary authorities to embrace Depression-era monetary policies.

In a nutshell, the focus of money-related issues shifted from the concerns associated with rising inflation to the concerns associated with shrinking inflation, and from the concerns associated with shrinking inflation to the concerns associated with deflation. This new edition of *The Encyclopedia of Money* addresses these new issues in transparent language.

Introduction

Money serves four basics functions in an economic system. It acts as (1) a medium of exchange, (2) a unit of measure, (3) a store of value, and (4) a standard of deferred payment.

As a medium of exchange, money must be universally accepted in exchange. It must be something always accepted in trade. In prisoner-of-war camps, cigarettes have served as a medium of exchange, and in the northern reaches of the earth, furs have circulated as a medium of exchange. Livestock and precious metals have a long history of service as mediums of exchange.

Money must also act as a unit of measure, comparable to yards, gallons, tons, cubic feet, or any other measure. British pounds sterling, U.S. dollars, Japanese yen, German marks, and French francs all serve as units of measurement. A consumer can buy 10 gallons worth of gasoline or $10 worth of gasoline. The Hudson Bay trading posts in Canada measured sales and profits in terms of beaver pelts, and Virginia colonists priced goods in terms of pounds of tobacco.

Anything meeting all of the demands placed on money must be satisfactory as a store of value. That is, it must preserve its value over a length of time. Perishable commodities rarely serve as money because wealth stored in perishable commodities is doomed to extinction. Precious metals such as gold and silver, known for resistance to corrosion and natural deterioration, are the most prized as monetary commodities and have few rivals as commodities that preserve value over time. Livestock reproduce, allowing them to preserve value over time, and even earn a form of interest. Inflation is the chief enemy of paper money because it renders the paper money useless as a store of value.

Money should also furnish society with a standard of deferred payment, enabling debtors and creditors to negotiate long-term contracts. Creditors want assurance that debtors cannot legally discharge debts with money possessing less purchasing power than the money originally borrowed. An unanticipated depreciation of the currency shortchanges creditors and gives debtors a windfall gain, arbitrarily redistributing income from creditors to debtors.

On the other hand, if money becomes unusually abundant, debtors easily find the means to repay debts, and creditors find the money repaid to them is worth less. Debtors are at risk if currency unexpectedly appreciates, increasing what debtors have to repay creditors in real terms. Unexpected currency appreciation redistributes income in favor of creditors over debtors. Because those who need to borrow money are usually worse off than those who have money to lend, an income redistribution favoring creditors is likely to cause hard feelings among those who already feel they get less than their share of income. Monetary issues are the focal point of a not-so-secret war between debtors and creditors.

Money falls within two broad categories, commodity money and fiat money. Commodity money makes use of some commodity, such as tobacco, rice, gold, or silver, that has an intrinsic value, or market value independent of any government decree sanctioning the commodity as legal tender for payment of private and public debts. Commodity monetary standards may make use of tokens or paper circulating money, but the circulating money can always be redeemed in a monetary commodity at an official rate. Under the gold standard, the United States government committed itself to selling gold for $35 per ounce. Fiat money has no intrinsic value; that is, it has no market value independent of a government decree establishing it as legal tender for private and public debts. Modern monetary systems are called inconvertible paper standards, because the fiat money issued by these systems cannot be converted into a commodity at an official rate. Fiat money has value because governments give themselves a monopoly on the privilege to issue fiat money, enabling them to limit its supply, and governments use their power to adjudicate disputes to make the money legal tender for all debts. By limiting the supply and creating a need, the government confers value on paper money that has little or no intrinsic value.

Two commodities, gold and silver, have been promoted as the aristocrats of commodity money. Until the 19th century, silver usually prevailed as the predominant form of commodity money, punctuated by intervals of bimetallism, which made use of both gold and silver and established a fixed ratio that set the value of each metal in terms of the other. Aside from the Byzantine period, when gold reigned supreme, the hegemony of silver lasted from the time of Alexander the Great until the 19th century.

Historically, precious metals have had a funny way of showing up and disappearing as civilizations waxed and waned. The silver mines of Laurium helped finance the golden age of Greece, and the decline of the Roman Empire coincided with the exhaustion of the silver mines in Spain and Greece. The stagnation of Western Europe during the Middle Ages may be explained by the virtual disappearance of precious metals during that era. The economic expansion of Europe that led to the eventual world dominance of European civilization in the 19th century followed the European discovery of vast precious metal deposits in the New World.

The much-vaunted gold standard, the demise of which is still mourned by a few true believers, actually represents a relatively late development in monetary history. The gold standard is a recent upstart compared to silver and bimetallic standards. Only in the 50 years preceding World War I (1914–1918) did gold become the sole standard of purchasing power, completely eclipsing the role of silver in the world's monetary system.

The fascination with gold may be a relic of the awe that surrounded money in some primitive societies. The word "taboo" originated from the sacred character and atmosphere of mystery that surrounded primitive money in islands of the South Pacific. In the Fiji Islands, sperm whale teeth, called "tambua," (of which "taboo" is a variant), acted as money and conferred social status on their owners. The power of a whale tooth guaranteed compliance with any request that accompanied it as a gift. On Rossel Island, some of the most valuable units of shell money could only be handled in a crouched position, and many of these units were thought to have been handed down from the beginning of time. In parts of the Philippines, women were not allowed to enter sacred storehouses where rice money was kept.

John M. Keynes, a famous British economist in the first half of the twentieth century, observed in volume two of his *Treatise on Money* (1930) that gold had "enveloped itself in a garment of respectability as densely respectable as was ever met with, even in the realms of sex or religion" (259). Concerning the power that a relatively small amount of gold played in the world's monetary affairs, Keynes wrote in the same work that "[a] modern liner could convey across the Atlantic in a single voyage all the gold which has been dredged or mined in seven thousand years" (259). The world's supply of gold has increased since Keynes wrote these words, but the supply remains small in comparison to the important role it has always played in monetary affairs. Even during Keynes's time, monetary gold lay out of sight in the underground vaults of central banks, and gold transactions were conducted by paper notations (earmarking), rather than physically moving gold to different locations.

The strength of gold as a monetary commodity lay in the hold it commanded on the human imagination, but its weakness lay in its restricted supply, which failed to keep pace with the growth of trade. The gold standard forced the world's economies to struggle constantly against what today would be called a tight money policy. Although fresh supplies of gold occasionally burst forth, furnishing a brief respite from tight money, the long-term trend was one of deflation owing to the limited money supplies.

The world's trading partners severed the connection between domestic money supplies and domestic gold reserves in the 1930s, hoping that more lax monetary policies would reinflate the depression-ridden economies of that era. Under the Bretton Woods system of the post–World War II era, domestic currencies remained convertible into gold at the request of foreign central banks, but not at the request of private individuals. During the Bretton Woods era, gold reserves failed to keep pace with the need for monetary growth, and by agreement of the members of the Bretton Woods system, a form of "paper gold" was created called "standard drawing rights." Standard drawing rights are really only entries in accounting logs, but they act as reserves of gold or foreign currencies.

Since 1971, the world's major trading partners have been on inconvertible paper standards. The United States dollar and other major currencies became strictly fiat money, inconvertible into gold even at the request of foreign central banks.

The burst of inflation of the 1970s may have been due partially to a void in monetary discipline left by the departure from the last vestiges of the gold standard. The experience of Japan between 1999 and 2005, however, cautions against generalizations about the inevitability of inflation under a fiat monetary system. Japan posted consumer price deflation for seven consecutive years. Japan's experience would not have been unusual if Japanese authorities had induced deflation by a restrictive monetary policy and exorbitant interest rates. Before Japan's episode of deflation, the world's monetary authorities had already learned how to restrict the rate of monetary growth to noninflationary levels. By the mid-1990s, inflation had subsided to insignificant levels virtually worldwide. Japan's experience appeared unique because deflation persisted long after short-term Japanese interest rates fell to near zero levels. Japan's deflation existed under conditions of relatively lax monetary policies.

In 2009, the United States is trying to formulate a policy in light of previous experiences with inflation and Japan's recent experience with deflation. The outcome should reveal clues and hints that are even more interesting about the nature of money.

The Encyclopedia of Money

A

ACT FOR REMEDYING THE ILL STATE OF THE COIN (ENGLAND)

In 1696, Parliament enacted the Act for Remedying the Ill State of the Coin, after one of the famous currency debates in history, which pitted those who favored return to a historical currency standard against those who favored ratifying past depreciation.

Toward the end of the 17th century, the old hammered-silver coinage accounted for the bulk of England's circulating coinage. The coinage was worn and clipped, some dating back to Elizabeth I, effectively reducing the silver weight relative to the face value of each coin. Freshly struck milled coins disappeared as fast as they left the mint as Gresham's law played itself out—bad money chasing out good. The milled coins, immune from clipping, enjoyed greater silver value and were far more beautiful.

Once the government committed itself to recoinage, two schools of thought arose about the principles that should guide it. John Locke, the famous philosopher who influenced the American Revolutionaries, stood firmly in favor of maintaining the historical weight standard of English coins. Locke's proposal required that the lost silver content of worn and clipped coins be restored in recoinage, substantially increasing the government's costs. William Lowndes, secretary to the treasury, proposed recoinage at a lower silver content for a given face value, bringing the silver content of freshly minted coins into line with the silver content of worn, clipped coins. Wear and clipping had on average cost the coinage 20 to 25 percent of silver content. Supporting Lowndes's proposal were numerous historical precedents for stabilizing depreciated coins at current levels. Locke described the proposal to reduce the silver content relative to face value as "a clipping done by public authority, a public crime." Locke was also concerned that reducing the silver content enabled the government to repay debt with cheaper money.

Woodcut illustrating the alchemical bonding of gold and silver, from Von dem grossen Stein Uhralten, *Strasbourg, 1651. (Jupiterimages)*

Sir Isaac Newton, another towering figure who was a player in this drama, served as warden of the mint during recoinage. Newton appears to have favored devaluation and apparently foresaw that refusing to devalue would increase the amount of silver each gold coin would buy, increasing the value of gold at home, causing gold to flow in and silver to flow out.

Parliament sided with Locke, and the Act for Remedying the Ill State of the Coin, with minor exceptions, mirrored Locke's views. The cost of the recoinage surpassed all expectations, totaling £2.7 million, more than half of the government's revenue. In the spirit of the Enlightenment, the government enacted a tax on windows to help pay for the recoinage. In addition to the Tower mint, several branch mints were pressed into service, and the recoinage was completed in three years.

The mechanics of the plan for calling in the old coinage caused no small amount of discontent. For a certain period of time, the government accepted at face value worn and clipped coins for the payment of taxes and government obligations. Landowners with property taxes to pay, and merchants with customs' duties to pay, benefited from the plan, buying up worn and clipped coins at a discount and paying their taxes with them. Wage earners and the poor had less need of the money to pay taxes, and often found the soon-to-be discontinued money accepted only at a discount by shopkeepers.

The act struck a blow for upholding the sanctity of a monetary standard, even at great expense, to protect the interest of creditors, especially when government was a major debtor. Newton correctly anticipated, however, that the act would put England on the road to the gold standard. Gold flowed into England, where it could purchase silver cheaply. The silver was then sold abroad at a profit.

See also: Clipping, Great Debasement, Pound Sterling

References

Chown, John F. 1994. *A History of Money.*

Feavearyear, Sir Albert. 1963 *The Pound Sterling: A History of English Money*, 2nd ed.

Horton, Dana S. 1983. *The Silver Pound and England's Monetary Policy since the Restoration, together with the History of the Guinea.*

ADJUSTABLE-RATE MORTGAGES

An adjustable-rate mortgage (ARM) provides for varying interest rates over the life of the mortgage. It forces the borrower to shoulder some of the risks that fixed-rate loans place on the lender. Key to the rationale for ARMs is the almost one-to-one relationship between short-term interest rates and inflation rates. Over the life of a 30-year, fixed-rate mortgage, inflation ranks among the biggest enemies that a lender faces. Increases in the inflation rate reduce the real (inflation-adjusted) rate of interest that a mortgage pays to a lender. Higher inflation reduces the real purchasing power of each monthly payment while pushing up the real operating cost of a lender. If the inflation rate happens to rise above a mortgage interest rate, the lender ends up earning a negative real interest rate.

The high inflation rates of the 1970s taught lenders the damage that inflation can wreak on the interest income earned from mortgages. Lenders began demanding higher interest rates on 30-year mortgages as insurance against a wave of inflation wiping out the profits and capital of mortgage holders. Adjustable-rate mortgages developed as a way to get home buyers into houses without paying the high interest rates attached to 30-year, fixed-rate mortgages.

Under an ARM, the mortgage interest rate at any given time is linked or indexed to a short-term interest rate. Two short-term, benchmark interest rates commonly used for setting ARM interest rates are the London Interbank Offered Rate (LIBOR) and the one-year, constant maturity treasury bond rate. The interest rate on an ARM is adjusted periodically to reflect changes in a benchmark interest rate. The home buyer benefits because short-term interest rates are usually lower than long-term interest rates, since short-term rates have less inflation risk. The disadvantage to the home buyer lies in the risk that short-term interest rates go up, probably because of rising inflation or anti-inflation policies. If short-term interest rates go up, the monthly payments on ARMs go up. With ARMs, the burden of accelerated inflation is born by the borrower instead of the lender. In turn for bearing the risk of accelerated future inflation, the home buyer stands a chance getting by with lower interest rates. If inflation never drives up short-term interest rates over the life of the loan, the home buyer comes out ahead.

Adjustable-rate mortgages come in several varieties. In some mortgages, the monthly payment can change every month, depending on the benchmark interest rate. Other mortgages allow changes in monthly payments as infrequently as every five years. The time frame between rate changes is called the "adjustment period." A mortgage with a one-year adjustment period is called a one-year ARM.

Many ARMs put a cap on the amount that a mortgage interest rate can change from one adjustment period to the next. This provision protects home buyers from large jumps in interest rates and monthly payments. Other contracts put a limit on the amount that monthly payments can increase from one adjustment period to the next. If interest rate adjustments call for a 10 percent increase in monthly payments, but the contract only allows monthly payments to go up 5 percent, then the unpaid interest will be added to the balance of the mortgage. By law, nearly all ARMs have a cap on how high interest rates can go over the life of a mortgage.

One version of the ARM allows the home buyer to pay an initial interest rate well below the benchmark interest rate used for setting an ARM interest rate. The home buyer enjoys the low interest rate, often called a teaser rate,

for an initial period, such as a year. Then the interest rate is adjusted upward according to the indexing formula tied to the benchmark interest rate. If short-term interest rates happen to be rising at the same time that a homeowner is transitioning from the teaser rate to the fully indexed, benchmark rate, then the home owner may experience "payment shock." The large increase in monthly payment may leave a home owner unable to make a house payment. The practice of offering teaser rates contributed to the severity of the subprime mortgage crisis in the United States.

See also: U.S. Financial Crisis of 2008–2009

Reference

Federal Reserve Board. 2009. *Consumer Handbook on Adjustable-Rate Mortgages.*

ALCHEMY

Alchemy was a pseudoscience that flourished during the Middle Ages. Its chief aims were the transmutation of base metals into gold and silver, and the discovery of an elixir of eternal youth. The alchemists searched in vain for the philosopher's stone, a substance that, if properly treated, would allegedly transmute lead, iron, copper, or tin into gold or silver—but particularly gold.

Perhaps it is only coincidental that Sir Isaac Newton, the master of the London mint from 1699 to 1726 and one of the towering intellects in the history of humanity, spent years conducting experiments in alchemy, leaving behind manuscripts of 100,000 words. Between 1661 and 1692, experiments in alchemy accounted for most of Newton's laboratory work. He experimented with alchemy while he was writing his masterpiece, *Philosophiae Naturalis Principia Mathematica (Mathematical Principles for Natural Philosophy)*, also known as the *Principia*.

The origins of alchemy stretch back into the murky recesses of history. One legend suggests that Jason's golden fleece was actually a papyrus manuscript describing the gold-producing secrets of alchemy. Probably a combination of Greek speculation, Eastern mysticism, and Egyptian technology conspired to make Alexandria, Egypt, one of the first centers of alchemical studies in the West. The Roman emperor Diocletian ordered all Egyptian texts on alchemy destroyed after crushing an Egyptian rebellion at the end of the third century. Apparently his action was taken only to punish the Egyptians. Evidence of alchemical studies in China show up as early as the second century BCE, and India also boasts of an ancient tradition of alchemy.

The Arabs inherited both the eastern and western traditions of alchemy, and made advancements in the science of chemistry while practicing alchemy. The greatest of the Islamic alchemists was the Great Geber, regarded in medieval Europe as the father of alchemy. To the Arab alchemists we owe such terms as "alcohol," "alkali," "borax," and "elixir."

The study of alchemy passed from the Arabs into Europe through Spain. In 1181 the University of Montpellier was founded in southern France. It became the birthplace of European alchemy, producing in the 13th century several of the most famous alchemists, including Albertus Magnus and Roger Bacon, the most renowned of the medieval scientists. Another famous graduate, St. Thomas Aquinas, also wrote about alchemy. Like their Arab predecessors, the European alchemists believed that all metals were constituted of varying proportions of two metals, mercury and sulfur. Much of their research centered on the quest for an elusive elementary solvent with which metals could be broken down into these two basic elements and then reconstituted in different proportions, resulting in different metals.

It was with good reason that alchemists were perceived as charlatans promising more than they could deliver, yet at the same time they were suspected of being in league with dark forces and, akin to sorcerers, using black magic and charms.

The European monarchies also suspected alchemists of fraudulent and heretical practices, but were always in a bind for money. Although fearing alchemists as potential counterfeiters, they could not resist the lure of the alchemists' promise to convert lead and other base metals into gold. James II of Scotland is reported to have dabbled in alchemy himself. King Charles II of England inherited a bare treasury and sought a solution to his fiscal problems in the magic of alchemy. He built his own laboratory for alchemical investigations, connected to his bed chamber by a secret staircase. France also turned to alchemists to help finance wars with England, and both countries issued gold-colored currency as soldiers' pay. In the 20th century, Adolf Hitler is reported to have sought the services of scientists engaged in alchemical studies, hoping to bolster Germany's gold reserves.

The famous English philosopher Sir Francis Bacon, in his book *Advancement of Learning* (1605), may have best caught the significance of alchemy when he wrote, "Alchemy may be likened to the man who told his sons that he had buried gold in the vineyard; where they by digging found no gold but by turning up the mold about the roots of the vines procured a plentiful vintage."

See also: Gold

References
Bacon, Sir Francis. 1625/1969. *Advancement of Learning.*
Cummings, Richard. 1966. *The Alchemists.*
Marx, Jennifer. 1978. *The Magic of Gold.*

AMERICAN PENNY

The penny in the United States is a one-cent coin. Presently, the United States Mint strikes about 12 billion pennies annually, accounting for over one-half of all coins struck by the mint. If the pennies struck by the U.S. Mint since its inception were lined up edge to edge, the pennies would roughly circle the earth 137 times (www.penny.org).

Historically, the penny was a copper coin. Copper coinage came slowly to the English-speaking countries, perhaps because of its long association with currency debasement. Early in the 17th century, Spain had debased its silver coin with copper alloy, eventually striking coins that were virtually all copper with face values commensurate with high silver content. The prevailing opinion in England was that only gold and silver met the standard of a monetary metal. A shortage of small change among tavern keepers and tradesmen, however, prompted the introduction of private tokens. To meet the need for small change, the English government in 1613 first struck copper coins. Great Britain struck the first copper pennies for home use in 1797.

In 1681 New Jersey sanctioned as legal tender copper coins called Patrick's pence, after the Irishman who brought the coins to the colonies. In 1722 the British government authorized William Wood to mint pennies and halfpence for Ireland and the colonies. These pennies were a mixture of copper, tin, and zinc, and had a touch of silver. Under the Articles of Confederation, several states established mints that turned out copper coins. The Coinage Act of 1792 established the cent and the half-cent and set the weight of the cent at 264 grains of copper. The act made no provision for the actual coinage of copper, and the legal tender provisions of the act failed to mention copper coins. Congress soon amended the act to provide for the purchase of copper and for necessary arrangements for the coinage of copper cents and half-cents. Congress also began to think of the copper coinage as a fiduciary issue, and authorized the president to substantially reduce the copper weight of the cent and half-cent.

Congress also banned the circulation of foreign copper coins, a restriction that did not apply for foreign gold and silver coins. The Spanish silver dollar circulated as clearly legal tender currency while the legal tender status of the copper cents and half-cents remained in doubt. After President Washington reduced the copper content of the cent to 168 grains, the coinage of cents and half-cents accelerated as a profit-making venture.

In 1857, Congress substantially increased the seigniorage on the copper coins. It abolished the half-cent and reduced the weight of the one-cent coin to 72 grains with 88 percent copper and 12 percent nickel. In 1864, Congress again changed the composition of the cent, raising the copper content to 95 percent with the remaining 5 percent zinc. Congress also made the one-cent coin legal tender.

In 1909, to mark the 100th year since his birth, Abraham Lincoln became the first historical figure to adorn a United States coin. Fifty years later, an image of the Lincoln Memorial appeared on the reverse side, and today both sides of the penny commemorate Abraham Lincoln. In 2009, the U.S. Mint will issue four different one-cent coins to commemorate the 200th anniversary of President Lincoln's birth and the 100th anniversary of the production of the Lincoln cent.

Rising copper prices in the 1970s caused a shortage of pennies, then worth more as copper than as money. Pennies were melted down for copper, and to keep pennies in circulation the government reduced the penny's copper content to 2.5 percent, the remaining 97.5 percent was composed of zinc.

In the first decade of the new century, the penny's future stands somewhat uncertain. Inflated price levels may have made the penny coin obsolete, but proposals to discontinue the penny have not met with widespread approval. State and local governments claim the penny plays a needed role in the collection of sales taxes applied at percentage rates. Consumer groups claim abolishing the penny will mean that prices will be rounded up a nickel instead of a penny, leading to higher prices. Opponents of the penny cite its insignificant purchasing power, and the time and resources that households and businesses put into managing pennies. In 2001 and 2006, bills came up in Congress to stop production of the penny, but the bills failed to pass. The U.S. Mint contends that coinage of the penny is profitable to the government, and other large major industrialized countries, including Great Britain, Canada, Japan, Germany, France, and Italy, have kept the penny, or penny equivalents, in production. Australia and New Zealand have removed their penny equivalent from circulation.

See also: Coinage Act of 1792, Copper

References

Carothers, Neil. 1930/1967. *Fractional Money*.

Gadsby, J. William. 1996. *Future of the Penny: Options for Congressional Consideration*.

Hagenbauch, Barbara. "A penny saved could become a penny spurned." *USA Today*, July 7, 2006.

ANCIENT CHINESE PAPER MONEY

In the second book of *The Travels of Marco Polo,* Chapter 18 is entitled: "Of the Kind of Paper Money Issued by the Grand Khan, and Made to Pass Current throughout His Dominions." In this chapter, Marco Polo, who lived in China from 1275 to 1292, described the paper money system as follows:

> In this city of Kanbulu is the mint of the grand khan, who may truly be said to possess the secret of the alchemist, as he has the art of producing money by the following process. He causes the bark to be stripped from those mulberry-tree the leaves of which are used for feeding silk-worms, and takes from it that thin inner rind, which lies between the coarser bark and the wood of the tree. This being steeped, and afterwards pounded in a mortar, until reduced to a pulp, is made into paper, resembling (in substance) that which is manufactured from cotton, but quite black. When ready for use, he has it cut into pieces of money of different sizes, nearly square, but somewhat longer than they are wide. . . . The coinage of this paper money is authenticated

Banknote from Kublai Khan's first issue of banknotes, 1260–1287. (The Bridgeman Art Library)

happen to be possessed of paper money which from long use has become damaged, they carry it to the mint, where, upon the payment of only three percent, they may receive fresh notes in exchange. Should any be desirous of procuring gold or silver for the purposes of manufacture, such as of drinking-cups, girdles, or other articles wrought of these metals, they in like manner apply at the mint, and for their paper obtain the bullion they require. (Polo, 1958, 153–155)

Marco Polo's account of the paper money system in China may have been a bit optimistic. China had been issuing paper money since 910 CE and had already suffered at least one round of hyperinflation before Marco Polo's visit. Around 1020, inflation and currency depreciation became such a problem that the authorities resorted to perfuming the paper money to make it more attractive. China seemed to have experienced phases of reformed currencies, punctuated with bouts of inflation. By 1448, the Ming note was worth only 3 percent of its face value, and no further references to paper money are found after 1455.

Paper money lost its charm in China owing to inflation, leading to its extinction as a form of state-sponsored money in China until the 20th century. When the Western world saw a renaissance of paper money toward the end of the 17th century, inflation again reared itself as a rock of danger for any paper-money system. Despite the inflation dangers of paper money, however, the societies experiencing the fastest economic development since the beginning of the 17th century have been those that learned to use paper money.

with as much form and ceremony as if it were actually of pure gold or silver; for to each note a number of officers, specially appointed, not only subscribe their names, but affix their signets also; and when this has been regularly done by the whole of them, the principal officer, deputed by his majesty, having dipped into vermilion the royal seal committed to his custody, stamps with it the piece of paper, so that the form of the seal tinged with the vermilion remains impressed upon it, by which it receives full authenticity as current money, and the act of counterfeiting it is punished as a capital offense. . . . nor dares any person, at the peril of his life, refuse to accept it in payment. When any persons

See also: Leather Money

References
Hewitt, V., ed. 1995. *The Banker's Art*.
Polo, Marco. 1958. *Travels of Marco Polo*.

ANNOUNCEMENT EFFECT

Central banks publically announce intentions of maintaining a key policy interest rate at a certain level called the "target rate." The practice of announcing targets is relatively recent, and represents a sharp departure from the confidentiality and secretiveness that was once thought to be a necessary part of monetary policy and open market operations. The "announcement effect" refers to a central bank's ability to control a key interest rate merely by announcing its intentions.

In the United States, the key policy interest rate targeted by the central bank is the federal funds rate, and the central bank is the Federal Reserve System. The federal funds rate is the interest rate at which commercial banks can borrow funds from each other overnight. The federal funds rate reflects the market tightness for these funds. The Federal Reserve can ease tightness in this market by purchasing U.S. government bonds, and can tighten this market by selling U.S. government securities. Buying U.S. government securities injects additional funds into the banking system, allowing banks to increase lending and enlarge the money supply in the process. Central bank purchases and sales of government securities are called "open market operations." In the Federal Reserve System, a policy-making group called the Federal Open Market Committee (FOMC) formulates the policy for open market operations.

Until 1994, the Federal Reserve kept directives involving open market operations a secret until 45 days after an FOMC meeting, keeping current financial market participants unaware of the Federal Reserve's policy stance at a given point in time. In 1976, the Federal Reserve successfully defended itself against an inquiry filed under the Freedom of Information Act to obtain copies of the minutes of FOMC meetings without the 45-day delay. Federal Reserve cited an "announcement effect" that might lead to volatility and uncertainty in financial markets, and maintained that secrecy was a necessary part of monetary policy.

On 4 February 1994, the FOMC, amidst a two-day meeting, announced that it planned to apply slight pressure to commercial bank reserve positions, and that short-term interest rates could be expected to rise, breaking the Federal Reserve's long stance policy of secrecy in these matters. It was an experiment in clearly communicating policy decisions to financial markets, and using public announcements as a method of communication. The experiment had none of the dire consequences that the Federal Reserve cited in its 1976 defense against a Freedom of Information inquiry. The practice of publically announcing policy decisions and targets became a standard part of central banking in the United States and in numerous other countries. What became known as the "announcement effect" enabled central banks to control a targeted interest rate with fewer interventions in the open market. It gave central banks the ability to control a targeted interest rate merely by announcing its intentions and taking little or no immediate action.

See also: Federal Open Market Committee, Open Market Operations

References

Belongia, Michael T., and Kevin Kliesen. "Effects on Interest Rates of Immediately Releasing FOMC Directives." *Contemporary Economic Policy,* vol. 12, no. 4: 79–91.

Demiralp, Selva, and Oscar Jorda. "The Response of Term Rates to Fed Announcements." *Journal of Money, Credit, and Banking,* vol. 36, no. 3 (June 2004, part 1): 387–405.

ARGENTINE CURRENCY AND DEBT CRISIS

Between 2001 and 2002, Argentina underwent an episode of currency devaluation and debt default that rocked international financial markets and offered fresh evidence of the varied economic trends that can lead to crises. The Argentine crisis has been the topic of wide discussion, partly because it was born of circumstances not normally regarded as fertile ground for currency crises. In the 1990s, Argentina boasted of one of Latin America's fastest growing economies and one of its staunches devotees to the gospel of free market reform. Part of the credit for economic prosperity seemed to lie with a successful monetary reform that ended the hyperinflation of the 1980s. This monetary reform established a currency board that fixed the value of the Argentine peso at one peso to a U.S. dollar. One Argentine peso, exchangeable into dollars at any time, equaled one U.S. dollar. Argentine inflation subsided to low single-digit levels, output grew at a fast clip, and the economy seemed resilient to external shocks.

The genesis of the crisis goes back to 1998 when many of Argentina's trading partners saw their currencies depreciate, perhaps because of fallout to the East Asian Crisis and the retreat of foreign capital. The strong demand for U.S. financial assets keep the U.S. dollar strong, which kept all currencies pegged to the dollar, including the Argentine peso, strong. The strong Argentine peso meant that Argentine exports went at higher prices in foreign markets, while Argentine imports saw falling prices. In summery, Argentina-produced goods grew costlier compared to goods produced by Argentina's major trading partners. Cheaper imports allowed Argentina to live beyond its means, while its exports were over-priced in foreign markets. To restore balance, Argentina needed to either devalue its currency as its trading partners had done, or undergo domestic deflation. Argentina did experience some deflation, which is a characteristic that distinguishes the Argentine crises from other crises. More often these types of crises occur after government deficits, financed by monetary growth, lead to inflation.

Government's budget deficits were modest, but were large enough to force a growing reliance on foreign debt financing. A small financial sector may share the blame for a dependence on foreign capital to finance both private sector and public sector spending. The vulnerability of the system arose from the large share of loans and mortgages denominated in dollars while the income generated to service these debts came in the form of pesos. Once deflationary forces surfaced, output shrank, unemployment spiked, government deficits rose, and the government proceeded to pile up foreign debt. In December 2001, the government of Argentina defaulted on its public debt.

After more than three years of recession, in January 2002, the Argentine

Hundreds of Argentines fearing hyper-inflation line up to buy dollars at exchange houses in Buenos Aires on March 21, 2002. Argentina defaulted on its debt obligations in late December and devalued its currency in January. (AP Photo/Daniel Luna)

government, running out of credit, devalued the peso relative to the dollar. At the time, 70 percent of all Argentine bank deposits and 79 percent of all loans were denominated in dollars (*Economist*, March 8, 2003). To avoid throwing many debtors into bankruptcy, the loans were redenominated into pesos at a rate of one peso per dollar, and the bank deposits were redenominated into pesos at the rate of 1.4 pesos per dollar. (*Economist*, March 8, 2003). The peso deposits quickly dropped in value as the peso plummeted to about four pesos per dollar. The action de-dollarized the Argentine economy.

Devaluating the peso reduced the cost of Argentine exports in the world economy, making it possible for Argentina to earn foreign exchange and recover from deep recession. Foreign exchange is necessary to repay foreign debts.

By 2005, the Argentine economy exhibited a strong expansion, helped in part by a worldwide commodity boom, and the government reported budget surpluses. The government offered the holders of defaulted bonds new bonds in a choice of four different currencies. The value of the new bonds equaled about 30 percent of the value of the defaulted bonds (*Economist*, January 15, 2005). Creditors fumed at the rough treatment and predicted that Argentina would meet with difficulty trying to regain the confidence of foreign investors.

See also: Currency Crises, Foreign Debt Crises

References

Economist. "The Americas: Defaulter of Last Resort." March 8, 2003, p. 56.
Economist. The Americas: Grinding Them Down; Argentina's Debt, January 15, 2005, p. 47.
International Monetary Fund, Policy Development and Review Department. "Lessons from the Crisis in Argentina." October 8, 2003.

ASSIGNATS

See: Hyperinflation during the French Revolution

AUTOMATIC TRANSFER SERVICE (ATS)

See: Monetary Aggregates

AYR BANK

The Ayr Bank was a Scottish bank of the late 18th century that caused one of the most famous banking debacles in European history. In part the bank owes its notoriety to Adam Smith, who, in the

Wealth of Nations, devoted a good bit of space to describing its story.

The Ayr Bank, more accurately called the firm of Douglas, Heron, and Company, came into being in November 1769. It was founded along the lines of the land bank schemes suggested by John Law, but unlike Law's schemes, it was a purely private initiative without official backing. As a copartnership, rather than an incorporated business, its owners were fully liable for all the debts of the business. Its founders were landowners of the first order, one of whom, the Duke of Buccleuch, had accompanied Adam Smith on a tour of Europe and had the benefit of the famous economist's advice. Land owned by the founders was the ultimate security for the bank's notes.

The Ayr Bank burst on the scene when the Scottish economy was in a contraction and many observers felt that a shortage of circulating money acted as a drag on the Scottish economy. According to Smith, writing in the *Wealth of Nations:*

> This bank was more liberal than any other had ever been, both in granting cash discounts, and in discounting bills of exchange. With regard to the latter, it seems to have made scarce any distinction between real and circulating bills, but to have discounted all equally. It was the avowed principle of this bank to advance, upon any real security, the whole capital which was to be employed in those improvements of which returns are the most slow and distant, such as the improvements to land. (Smith, 1952, 135)

The liberal lending policy of the bank led to a rapid expansion of bank notes, greater than what the bank's resources could support. The Ayr Bank expansion of credit found its way into speculation in real estate and the London stock market. Bank notes were redeemed with bills of exchange drawn on London banks in amounts that exceeded the bank's London resources. In 1772, a London-Scottish banking house with close connections with the Ayr Bank failed, and the Ayr Bank's house of cards collapsed. Scotland's public banks refused to grant credits to the failing bank. The bank was liquidated, and the income from the land was pledged to the redemption of outstanding bank notes. The founders of the bank lost everything, some of whom were apparently unaware that their liability was unlimited.

The failure of the Ayr Bank was probably due more to mismanagement than to faults in the land bank principle. The bank may have actually spurred the economic development of Scotland, but its failure weakened public confidence in land-banking schemes, leaving gold and silver as the most acceptable security for bank notes. The bank's history shows how easily an expansion of bank notes leads to a speculative bubble that ends in collapse. History has continued to repeat itself, with Tokyo being the last scene of a speculative bubble fed by overly generous credit policy.

See also: Bank of Scotland, Free Banking, Land Bank System, Scottish Banking Act of 1765

References

Checkland, S. G. 1975. *Scottish Banking History: 1695–1973.*

Kroszner, Randy. 1995. *Free Banking: The Scottish Experience as a Model for Emerging Economies.*

Smith, Adam. 1776/1952. *An Inquiry into the Nature and Causes of the Wealth of Nations.*

B

BALANCE OF PAYMENTS

The balance of payments for a country summarizes all the international transactions that involve either an outflow or an inflow of money. It is composed of three major elements: (1) the current account, (2) the capital account, and (3) the official reserves transactions account. The official reserves transactions account reflects the official transactions between central banks that must occur when the combined balance of the current and capital accounts is in either the deficit or surplus column.

Transactions that lead to an outflow of money are registered as a debit in the balance of payments, and are entered with a negative sign. Transactions that lead to an inflow of money are registered as a credit, and are entered with a plus sign. Imports of foreign goods cause an outflow of money, entering with a negative sign in the balance of payments. Exports of domestic goods to foreign buyers lead to an inflow of money, registering as a credit with a plus sign. The balance of trade is total exports minus total imports.

A balance of trade deficit causes a net outflow of money, and a surplus causes a net inflow of money. Income earned from foreign investments, money transferred between citizens of different countries, can also influence the balance of payments. When these types of flows are figured into the balance of trade, the outcome is the balance on current account.

Capital flows between countries show up in the balance of payments on the capital account. When domestic investors purchase financial or nonfinancial assets in foreign countries, capital flows out, and money also flows out, registering with a negative sign on the balance of payments. When U.S. citizens purchase stock on the Tokyo stock exchange, dollars flow out, just as when U.S. citizens purchase a Toyota. When foreign investors purchase financial or nonfinancial investments in the domestic economy, capital flows in, and money flows in, registering as a positive sign in the balance of payments. The sale of U.S. government bonds to Japanese investors causes dollars to flow into the United

States. If a domestic seller exports goods abroad on credit, the sale of goods is entered as a plus sign in the balance of payments, and the grant of credit is a capital outflow, entered with a negative sign.

Capital flows often offset imbalances in the balance of trade, as can be observed in the bilateral relationship between the United States and Japan. U.S. exports to Japan fall well short of U.S. imports from Japan, contributing to a deficit on the balance of trade, and an outflow of dollars. In turn, Japan invests significantly in the United States, building factories, and purchasing real estate and U.S. government bonds. Japan earns dollars by selling goods in the United States, and invests those dollars back in the United States, causing dollars to flow out on the current account and flow in on the capital account.

If the outflow of money exceeds the inflow of money, the central banks must settle accounts by compensating adjustments in holdings of gold, foreign exchange, or other reserve assets. An excess of money outflow over money inflow will draw down the reserves of the domestic central bank, whereas an excess of money inflow over money outflow will build up reserves of the domestic central bank. An excess in the outflow of money leaves foreigners with a claim on domestic resources; excess in the inflow of money has the opposite effect.

Persistent deficits or surpluses on the combined current and capital accounts cause changes in the value of domestic currency in foreign exchange markets. A deficit causes supplies of domestic currency to build up in foreign exchange markets, and the domestic currency will lose value. As the currency loses value, imports become more expensive, and exports become cheaper in foreign markets. Together these forces will remove the deficit. A surplus causes domestic currency to gain value in foreign exchange markets, making imports cheaper and exports more expensive in foreign markets. These forces act to remove the surplus.

See also: Foreign Exchange Markets, Gold-Specie-Flow Mechanism

References

Appleyard, Dennis R., and Alfred J. Field, Jr. 1992. *International Economics.*

Daniels, John D., and David Vanhoose. 1999. *International Monetary and Financial Monetary Economics.*

BANCO DEL PIAZZA DEL RIALTO, IL

See: Bank of Venice

BANK

The term "bank" apparently owes its origin to the bank (or bench) used by the moneychangers during the Middle Ages. Historically, some banks were called banks of deposit, and mainly held deposits of foreign and domestic currencies and arranged payment in foreign trade transactions. The Bank of Amsterdam was a bank of deposit.

Other banks created deposits that acted as a circulating medium of money in a society. One of the earliest banks in this category, the Bank of Venice, was formed when a group of the government's creditors combined and began using government debt as a means of payment in trade. The famous merchant bankers, such as the Rothschilds, acted largely as brokers marketing government and corporate securities to wealthy patrons.

Central banks are bankers' banks, and these banks trace their history from the Bank of England. These banks buy government debt, have a monopoly on the issuance of paper money, and often act as a lender of last resort to commercial banks. In current times, the term "bank" refers to a commercial bank.

Commercial banks in modern capitalist societies act as financial intermediaries, raising funds from depositors and lending the same funds to borrowers. The depositors' claims against the bank, their deposits, are liquid, meaning banks are expected to redeem deposits on demand, instantly. Banks' claims against their borrowers are much less liquid, giving borrowers a much longer span of time to repay money owed banks. Because a bank cannot immediately reclaim money lent to borrowers, it may face bankruptcy if all its depositors simultaneously withdraw all their money. Protecting banks and bank customers from bank failures of this sort is the aim of much government banking regulation.

The principle of fractional reserve banking lies at the heart of the modern commercial banking system. During a given period of time a bank will receive fresh deposits while existing deposits are withdrawn. Normally the fresh deposits and the withdrawn deposits cancel each other out. Despite daily deposits and withdrawals, a bank maintains an average level of deposits that represents funds the bank can largely keep loaned out. For safety, banks hold back a certain fraction of deposits, called "reserves" (thus fractional reserve banking) to cover themselves over periods of time when withdrawn deposits exceed fresh deposits. Because these reserves earn no interest, banks are tempted to cut the margin of reserves a bit thin. If adequate, these reserves enable a bank to weather a crisis of confidence when masses of people suddenly withdraw deposits out of fear.

When a bank fails, the bank's customers, the depositors, suffer as much or more than the bank's owners. This makes the banking industry an excellent candidate for government regulation. Bank lending policy can also aggravate the business cycle. During an economic downswing, banks can become overly cautious, restricting the availability of loans and sending the economy into a steeper downward spiral. On the upswing, however, banks lose their caution, generously granting loans and propelling the economy into an inflationary boom. Government regulation strives to protect bank depositors from bank failures and to encourage banks to become a stabilizing force in the economy.

See also: Bank of Amsterdam, Bank of England, Bank of Venice, Central Bank, Depository Institution Deregulation and Monetary Control Act of 1980, Goldsmith Bankers, Glass–Steagall Banking Act, Medici Bank, Swiss Banks, Wildcat Banks, World Bank

References

Baye, Michael R., and Dennis W. Jansen. 1995. *Money, Banking, and Financial Markets: An Economics Approach.*

Richards, R. D. 1929/1965. *The Early History of Banking in England.*

BANK CHARTER ACT OF 1833 (ENGLAND)

With passage of the Bank Charter Act of 1833, Parliament renewed the Bank of England's charter until 1855. The act also included provisions that strengthened the bank as the prime note-issuing institution in England, an important step toward giving a single institution a monopoly on the privilege of issuing bank notes (paper money).

In 1832, Parliament formed a committee of inquiry to look at various issues from all sides, including the Bank of England's monopoly on joint-stock banking within 65 miles of London. The law forbade incorporated banks with more than six shareholders from engaging in London's banking business. Other joint-stock banks wanted to enter the London market, and existing law seemed to suggest that other banks were free to set up business in London as along as they did not issue bank notes. The Bank of England hotly contested this viewpoint, and Parliament made timely use of the expiration of the Bank of England's charter to review the matter.

One outcome of the inquiry was a recommendation that did not make it into the law, but nevertheless represented an important principle. Horsely Palmer, governor of the bank, formulated the principle that all demand deposits and bank notes, that is "all liabilities to pay on demand," should be backed by gold reserves equaling one-third of such liabilities. The remaining two-thirds could be invested in securities. The gold reserves were necessary to ensure the convertibility of bank notes and other bank liabilities. Parliament failed to act on Palmer's recommendation, but the quantification of a reserve policy remained an important issue in banking.

One provision of the act stated "that any Body Politic . . . consisting of more than six persons may carry on the Trade of Business of Banking in London, or within sixty five miles thereof provided they did not issue notes." The forbidden notes were notes payable on demand or within less than six months. Other banks could open for business in London, but the Bank of England held a monopoly on the privilege of issuing bank notes.

The act also made Bank of England notes for more than £5 legal tender in England and Wales but not in Scotland and Ireland. These notes were legal tender everywhere except at the Bank of England. This provision enabled country banks to hold Bank of England notes as reserves in lieu of gold, reducing the drain on gold reserves in times of contraction, and centralizing gold reserves in the vault of the Bank of England.

Another important provision lifted the 5 percent usury ceiling on bills of exchange payable within three months. This provision was the beginning of the famed "bank rate" that became a powerful policy instrument for the Bank of England. If gold began to flow out, threatening England's gold reserves, the bank raised the bank rate, attracting funds from abroad and ending the outflow.

With the Bank of England's growing power came responsibility for public disclosure of activities. The act required the Bank of England to begin sending weekly statistics on notes issues and bullion reserves to the treasury, and monthly summaries were to be published in the *London Gazette*.

The Act of 1833 was important in the history of money because it made Bank of England notes legal tender during peace time, it effectively made the Bank of England the custodian of England's gold reserves, and it gave the Bank of England the bank rate with which to control the inflow and outflow of gold. It laid in place principles fundamental to the operation of England's 19th-century gold standard, a standard that ruled the monetary world by the end of the century.

See also: Bank Charter Act of 1844, Bank of England, Central Bank

References

Chown, John F. 1994. *A History of Money*.

Roberts, Richard, ed. 1995. *The Bank of England: Money, Power, and Influence, 1694–1994*.

BANK CHARTER ACT OF 1844 (ENGLAND)

The English Bank Charter Act of 1844 represents an important step in the evolution of the Bank of England as a central bank with a monopoly on the issuance of bank notes (paper money), one of the defining characteristics of a central bank. Today all modern economies have central banks with a monopoly on the issuance of bank notes, the Federal Reserve System in the United States being a good example. In the early 1800s a multitude of commercial banks issued their own bank notes in England, France, the United States, and other countries.

Sir Robert Peel, who was prime minister when Parliament passed the Bank Charter Act of 1844, shared with the famous economist David Ricardo the view that the issuance of currency should be a government monopoly with the profits accruing to the government. Peel considered establishing a new system of currency, with a board independent of government but responsible to Parliament, charged with the issue of paper, convertible into gold, and valid as legal tender. In reality, Peel chose a more moderate course that made use of existing institutions. Important provisions in the Bank Charter Act are paraphrased as follows:

1. The note issuing department of the Bank of England became separate and distinct from other departments. The bank removed it to a different building.

2. The Bank of England was required to hold gold bullion equal in value to the volume of its bank notes issued in excess of £14 million. The government debt secured most of the first £14 million.

3. The Bank of England was required to stand ready to redeem its bank notes into gold at the rate of £3 17/9 (3 pounds, 17 shillings, and 9 pence) per ounce of gold.

4. The creation of new banks with the privilege to issue bank notes was prohibited.

5. Banks currently issuing bank notes continued to issue notes as long as their total notes in circulation never exceeded their average for the 12 weeks preceding April 27, 1844.

6. If a bank became insolvent, it lost the right to issue bank notes.

7. If a bank stopped issuing notes for any reason, it could never again put notes into circulation.

8. If two or more banks combined and ended up with more than six partners, the new bank could not issue bank notes.

9. The Bank of England was allowed to issue new bank notes backed by securities up to two-thirds of the value of discontinued country bank notes.

The act had the desired effect. The issuance of bank notes gradually became the exclusive privilege of the Bank of

Robert Peel, prime minister of Great Britain from 1834 to 1846. (Library of Congress)

England, which by World War I had made its monopoly complete. By monopolizing the issuance of paper money, the Bank of England was able to limit the money supply, helping to maintain its value, which is equivalent to avoiding inflation. The act helped bring stable prices, but its restrictions on the issuance of bank notes hampered the Bank of England's ability to act as a lender of last resort.

The government was forced to suspend the convertibility of Bank of England notes into gold during major financial crises. The financial crises of 1847, 1857, and 1866 all saw suspensions of convertibility.

The Bank of France has enjoyed a monopoly on the issuance of bank notes since 1848, and the Federal Reserve System, established in 1914, has always had a monopoly on the issuance of bank notes. With the demise of the gold standard in the 1930s, the practice of maintaining the convertibility of bank notes into gold disappeared, giving central banks more freedom to inject liquidity into a financial system during a crisis.

See also: Bank Charter Act of 1833, Bank of England, Central Bank

References
Davies, Glyn. 1994. *A History of Money.*
Powell, Ellis. 1915/1966. *The Evolution of the Money Market: 1385–1915.*
Roberts, Richard, ed. 1995. *The Bank of England: Money, Power, and Influence, 1694–1994.*

BANK CLEARINGHOUSES (UNITED STATES)

In the United States, bank clearinghouses partially fulfilled the functions of a central bank before the establishment of the Federal Reserve System. Bank clearinghouses facilitated interbank settlement of accounts, a necessary part of check clearing processes. Also, during financial crises, when currency and coin were scarce, bank clearinghouses issued certificates representing claims on bank assets. These certificates replaced cash in the interbank settlement of accounts and infused additional liquidity into the banking system, allowing banks to survive the outflow of currency and coin typical of financial crises. On rare occasions these certificates circulated as currency.

New York City banks established the first clearinghouse in 1853. Two years later, the concept spread to Boston, and soon all the nation's largest cities had bank clearinghouses. The New York clearinghouse remained the most important because of New York's (Wall Street's) strategic role as the financial nerve center of the United States.

Under a bank clearinghouse system, an individual bank, Bank A, presents all its claims against other banks (deposited checks written on other banks) to the clearinghouse each day. The clearinghouse credits Bank A's clearinghouse account accordingly. All other banks that have received deposits of checks written on Bank A will take these checks to the clearinghouse also, and Bank A will find its clearinghouse account debited to pay for these checks. Whatever discrepancy exists between debits and credits is settled with cash. The clearinghouse system substantially reduces the amount of cash that changes hands in the check clearing process.

Banks operate on the principle that, despite daily withdrawals and new deposits, the average level of deposits at a bank remains steady during normal business conditions, and therefore banks can keep the vast proportion (80 to 95 percent) of customer deposits loaned out. Banks keep reserves, such as vault cash, for those periods of time when withdrawals exceed new deposits. Sound banks, however, often fell prey to their own success by loaning out too much of depositors' money and coming up short of reserves to redeem deposits during a financial crisis. Bank clearinghouses help banks resist the temptation to overextend loans by forcing banks to speedily honor checks written on their accounts. Also, the New York clearinghouse required weekly reports from associated banks showing customer deposits, assets, and reserves.

The New York clearinghouse issued certificates against bank assets to substitute for cash in interbank settlements during financial crises when accelerated withdrawals of deposits often left banks without cash reserves. The clearinghouse issued certificates against a bank's assets when a bank put up 100 percent collateral either in bonds, or short-term commercial loans rated at 75 percent of face value. In a financial crisis, a bank experiencing a drain on reserves could use certificates to settle with the clearinghouse. The use of clearinghouse certificates was not legally sanctioned until 1908, but certificates helped ease the strain in every financial crisis from 1873 until 1914. The clearinghouse was essentially serving as a lender of last resort, one of the important functions of a central bank.

Although clearinghouses were strictly private organizations, acting on private rather than public initiatives, they met some of the regulatory needs of the banking system before the United States turned to central banking in 1914 with the establishment of the Federal Reserve System.

See also: Central Bank, Federal Reserve System, National Bank Act of 1864

References

Gorton, Gary. 1984. *Clearinghouses and the Origin of Central Banking in the U.S.*

Hepburn, A. Barton. 1924/1967. *A History of Currency in the United States.*

Myers, Margaret G. 1970. *A Financial History of the United States.*

BANK FOR INTERNATIONAL SETTLEMENTS

The Bank for International Settlements (BIS) acts as a bank for central banks, holding deposits of and providing a broad array of services to central banks. It accepts deposits in currencies and gold, mostly from central banks. By June 1994, 100 central banks kept deposits at the BIS (Siegman, 1994). Central banks can borrow from the BIS. Money market investments account for a large share of BIS assets.

The BIS has also grown into an important forum for facilitating international monetary cooperation, consultation, and exchange of information between central banks. The BIS conducts research on monetary, economic, and financial issues and serves as agent or trustee for international financial settlements. The bank is headquartered in Basel, Switzerland.

The BIS was established in 1930 to handle the coordination of Germany's World War I reparation payments. The term "settlements" came from the role of war reparations in its original mission. Aside from the temporary issue of war reparations, the bank's primary objective from the beginning lay in promoting cooperation among central banks and providing added facilities for international financial operations.

At its inception, the central banks in Europe and the United States were invited to purchase a share of the total capital subscription of BIS. The United States elected not to subscribe to its share, and the Bank of France and the National Bank of Belgium purchased only a portion of the issues representing their share. J.P. Morgan and Company, the First National Bank of New York, and the First National Bank of Chicago purchased the U.S. part of the capital subscription. Private investors also purchased shares originally intended for the Bank of France and the National Bank of Belgium. In 2008, central banks owned 100 percent of BIS stock (www.bis.org).

The United States was slow to recognize BIS as a necessary and useful part of the international monetary order. The United States abstained from participating in the BIS capital subscription on the grounds that German war reparations was strictly a European issue. During World War II, the United States government supported proposals to liquidate the BIS. After the war, the United States played a large role in creating two new international financial institutions, the International Monetary Fund and the World Bank. The United States had no interest in a financial institution that could be a potential rival to these new organizations. After the BIS played a positive role in the implementation of the Marshall Plan, the United States began to accept the BIS as a legitimate institution in the new international monetary system. It was not until 1994 that the Federal Reserve System became a member central bank of the BIS and accepted positions on the board of directors. Both the chair of the board of governors of the Federal Reserve System and the president of the New York Federal Reserve sit on the board of directors.

Fifty-five central banks from around the world are now member banks of the BIS (www.bis.org). Central bank officials hold monthly meetings in Basel hosted by the BIS. Coordinated interest rate cuts by several central banks have occurred within a few days of these meetings.

See also: Central Bank

References
Bradsher, Keith. "Obscure Global Bank Moves into the Light." *New York Times*, August 5, 1995, p. A31.
Siegman, Charles J. "The Bank of International Settlements and the Federal Reserve." *Federal Reserve Bulletin*, vol. 80 no. 10 (October 1994): 900–906.

BANKING ACTS OF 1826 (ENGLAND)

The Banking Acts of 1826 banned the issuance of bank notes of less than £5 and ended the Bank of England's 100-year monopoly on joint-stock banking. On March 22, 1826, the act put an end to notes of less than £5 and required the redemption of the smaller notes by April 5, 1829. Apparently the number of people hanged for the capital offense of forging notes, even small ones, was one thing that moved Parliament to act. Scotland, where £1 notes were highly popular, was exempted from the act. Before the act passed Parliament, the eminent author Sir Walter Scott had written letters to the *Edinburgh Weekly Journal* that ridiculed the abolition of small notes in Scotland. Another prominent Scot, Adam Smith, in the *Wealth of Nations,* had argued against the issuance of small notes in 1776, observing:

> Where the issuing of bank notes for such very small sums is allowed and commonly practiced, many mean people are both enabled and encouraged to become bankers. A person whose promissory note for five pounds, or even for twenty shillings, would be rejected by everybody, will get it to be received without scruple when it is issued for so small a sum as sixpence. But the frequent bankruptcies to which such beggarly bankers must be liable may occasion a very considerable inconveniency, and sometimes a very great calamity to many poor people who had received their notes in payment. (Smith, 1952, 139)

Arguments in favor of small notes cited the conservation of precious metal reserves when precious metal was no longer needed as a circulating medium. Scotland continued to circulate £1 notes throughout the 19th century, while Britain relied on the gold sovereign coin to circulate as the £1 piece. Subsidiary silver coinage gradually replaced the role played by the small notes.

The act of May 26, 1826, ended the Bank of England's monopoly on joint-stock banking. In addition to giving the Bank of England a monopoly on joint-stock banking, an act of 1707 had prohibited banking partnerships with more than six members from engaging in the banking business. Small-scale partnerships dominated English banking in the countryside, while the Bank of England enjoyed a preeminent position within a radius of 65 miles around London. Joint-stock banks were organized as modern corporations, affording the owners (stockholders) the protection of limited liability. Unlike corporations, partnership banks, in the event of bankruptcy, exposed all the personal assets of partners to the demands of creditors. Scotland had pioneered the proliferation of joint-stock banking, but England had tended to reserve to the Bank of England the exclusive privilege of joint-stock banking.

The act of 1826 preserved the Bank of England's monopoly on joint-stock banking within a 65-mile radius of the center of London, but outside the London area it authorized the establishment of note-issuing banking corporations with an unlimited number of partners. To compensate for its loss of privilege, the Bank of England was authorized to set up branches anywhere in England or Wales. The Bank of England promptly opened branches in major cities, and for a while England flirted with the Scottish system of banking that emphasized competition between note-issuing incorporated banks. The Banking Act of 1833, however, made the Bank of England's notes legal tender, and the Bank Charter Act of 1844 marked a sharp shift toward a policy of concentrating note-issuing authority with the Bank of England.

See also: Bank of England, Free Banking, Scottish Banking Act of 1765

References

Checkland, S. G. 1975. *Scottish Banking History: 1695–1973.*

Davies, Glyn. 1994. *A History of Money.*

Richards, R. D. 1929/1965. *The Early History of Banking in England.*

BANKING AND CURRENCY CRISIS OF ECUADOR

In 1999 and early 2000, Ecuador experienced a banking and currency crisis that led to the dollarization of Ecuador's economy. In 1999, Ecuador defaulted on $13.6 billion in foreign debt (*Wall Street Journal*, March 31, 2000). A banking crisis drove the government to take control of 70 percent of the country's banking sector and to freeze deposits. By March 2000, 41.3 percent of the banking system's loans were nonperforming. It is estimated that within little more than a year's time Ecuador's per capital gross domestic product (GDP), measured in dollars, fell by 41 percent. Between December 1998 and March 2000, Ecuador's currency, the sucre, lost 74 percent of its value against the dollar (*Wall Street Journal,* March 31, 2000). The political sphere mirrored the chaos in the economic sphere. When Gustavo

Noboa ascended to the presidency in January 2000, he became the sixth president in six years. In 1997, Ecuador's Congress forced out President Abdala Bucaram after deeming him mentally unfit.

Ecuador owed the beginnings of its economic problems to a 1995 border war with Peru, the El Niño weather phenomenon, and weak commodity prices. Critics laid much of the blame at the feet of an incompetent finance ministry and central bank. In 1999, Ecuador's central bank fueled the crisis by extending loans to shaky banks. A contributing factor may have been an overall climate of corruption. A survey of international investors ranked Ecuador among the world's worst performers when it came to "rule of law." Compiled in 1999 by Political Risk Services, based in Syracuse, New York, the survey covered issues such as quality of bureaucracy, political corruption, probability of government repudiation of debts or expropriation of property. Germany's Transparency International put Ecuador at 82 out of 99 countries rated for corruption (*Wall Street Journal,* March 31, 2000).

Low oil prices diminished foreign exchange earnings and tax revenue. By 1999, government borrowing ran about 7 percent of GDP, and the current account deficit about 9.6 percent of GDP. Inflation stood at 43 percent in 1998 (*Economist,* March 6, 1999). In 1999, inflation climbed further to 60.7 percent (*BusinessWeek*, January 24, 2000.). Ecuador's congress rebuffed proposals to raise taxes. Discontent festered from all sides. Teachers went on strike for a month, angry over pay freezes, and electricity workers suspended maintenance to protest cuts in severance pay.

In January 2000, Ecuador's currency within a week plunged 20 percent

Workers march through the streets of Quito, Ecuador to protest President Jamil Mahuad's recent austerity measures, February 5, 1999. The march was part of a larger national protest, which occurred on Friday and left the country semi-paralyzed. (AP Photo/Dolores Ochoa)

against the U.S. dollar. Thousands of Ecuadorians took to the streets in protest, prompting President Jamil Mahuad to call a state of emergency. It was the fourth time in a year that the government had sent heavily armed riot police to the streets. Since the government had let the sucre float in February 1999, it steadily lost value against the dollar. On January 10, 2000, it traded at 24,750 sucres to the dollar (*Wall Street Journal*, January 11, 2000).

President Mahuad met the currency crisis with a plan for complete dollarization of Ecuador's economy. A new law, the Trolley-Buss Law, stated that all paper sucre would be exchanged for dollars at a rate of 25,000 sucre per dollar. U.S. dollars displaced the Ecuadorian currency as the circulating currency except for small denomination coinage, which would still circulate in the form of sucre.

Dollarization was a bold and unexpected policy move. President Mahuad did not survive the crisis, but his successor, President Gustavo Noboa, enjoyed a longer tenure as economic stability returned to Ecuador. Rising oil prices along with dollarization put an end to the crisis. By 2001, Ecuador saw inflation rates in single-digit territory, and GDP growth among the fastest in Latin America (*Economist,* September 15, 2001).

See also: Dollarization

References

BusinessWeek Online. "Did the IMF Drop the Ball in Ecuador?" January 24, 2000.

Hanke, Steve H. "The Americas: Ecuador Needs More Than a Dollars-for-Sucres Exchange." *Wall Street Journal* (Eastern Edition, New York) March 31, 2000, p. A19.

"The Furies Wait." *Economist,* March 6, 1999, pp. 34–36.

"Squandering an Unlikely Recovery." *Economist*, September 15, 2001, p. 32.

Vogel, Thomas T. Jr., and Michael M. Phillips. "Ecuador Leader Pegs His Political Survival to the Dollar—Currency Plan Follows Plunge and Rising Protests." *Wall Street Journal* (Eastern Edition, New York), January 11, 2000, p. A18.

BANKING CRISES

Banking crises involve exhaustion of all or nearly all of the capital held in the banking system and usually include a panicky run on bank deposits. As inflation rates worldwide began to subside in the 1990s, another form of financial disruption began to occur with rising frequency and severity—the banking crisis. In particular, Latin America, which had tamed several episodes of runaway inflation in the 1980s, saw an outbreak of banking crises. Although Latin America and the Caribbean seems to have borne a disproportionate share of banking crises for countries of similar stages of development, other parts of the world have also seen banking crises. Between 1994 and 2003, banking crises occurred in 30 different countries, averaged a length of 3.7 years, and cost the afflicted countries about 17 percent of gross domestic product (GDP) (Carstens, Hardy, Pazarbasioglu, 2004). Of the 30 banking crises, 23 occurred in what are called emerging market countries, which are considered less developed than the developed countries. The remaining seven banking crises occurred in the developed countries. Banking crises often occur in concurrence with currency crises, but not always. Of the 30 banking crises, 19 coincided with currency crises. Included in the 30 banking crises are crises in Argentina (1995, 2001), Bolivia (1994), Brazil (1994), Columbia (1999), Dominican Republic (2003), Ecuador (1996, 1998), Haiti (1994), Jamaica (1995), Mexico (1994), Nicaragua (2000), Paraguay (1995), Uruguay (2001), and Venezuela (1994).

Some of the country-specific risk factors associated with a high incidence of banking crises include low savings rates, very limited long-term financial relationships, excessive reliance on external financing, high interest rate spreads, dollarization, and a public sector burdened with heavy debt. The country risk factors are much more combustible when deeper problems exist with trust in the financial system. A history of substantially negative real interest rates, real currency depreciations, weak accounting and creditor rights, disincentives to save, and freezing and unfreezing bank accounts, undercut trust in the financial system, making fertile ground for sparking a banking crises. When these conditions exist, deposit withdrawals quickly induce a credit contraction, starving firms of working capital and investment, sending the economy and the banking sector deeper into crisis. Usually a combination of bad banking practices and bad macroeconomic policies trigger the crises. A sharp fall in the demand for a key export can cause domestic currency to lose value, immediately enlarging the real amount of foreign debt. If banks have borrowed foreign capital, currency depreciation can render them insolvent.

The crises can be contagious to other countries linked by geography or trade. Uruguay's banking crisis of 2001 partly reflected the banking crisis in Argentina, which caused Argentines to start a mass withdrawal of cash from their Uruguay bank accounts. Contagious and spillover effects of a banking crisis in one country may operate through a mere reassessment of expectations on the part of foreign investors, darkening investor outlooks in other countries at similar stages of development and with similar industries.

In Latin America, banking crises have often been preceded by a boom in credit to consumers and businesses; wholesale liberalization without a politically independent, effective regulatory framework for banking; and high bank holdings of sovereign government debt.

See also: Banking and Currency Crisis of Ecuador, Troubled Asset Relief Program

References

Carstens, Agustin, Daniel Hardy, and Ceyla Pazarbasioglu. "Avoiding Banking Crises in Latin America." *Finance & Development* (September 2004): 30–33.

Hoelscher, David, and Marc Quintyn. "Managing Systemic Banking Crises." *IMF Occasional Paper 224*, 2003.

BANKING SCHOOL

Between 1819 and 1844, England was the battleground of one of the most important monetary controversies in history: the debate between the banking school and the currency school. The resumption of specie payments following the Napoleonic Wars had not spared England the trauma of periodic financial crises. Financial crises in 1825, 1833, and 1839 became thought-provoking grist for the monetary debating mill.

The currency school found the answer to England's financial turbulence in tighter linkages between domestic money supplies (defined as gold specie and paper money) and domestic gold supplies that varied with the import and export of gold.

The banking school saw domestic money supplies as a much more passive player in the drama of economic boom and crisis, and argued that the currency school's definition of money supplies was narrow and unrealistic. To the banking school a more workable definition of domestic money supplies would, in addition to specie and paper money, include bank deposits and bills of exchange. Banks supplied these forms of money to meet the needs of trade. Part of the thinking of the banking school hinged on the "law of reflux," stating that every bank note or deposit issued on a loan was canceled when the loan was repaid. The "law of reflux," was akin to the "real bills doctrine," of a similar vintage.

The banking school felt it was unrealistic to attribute a close linkage between prices (inflation) and money supplies as narrowly conceived by the currency school, given the obvious importance of other types of money. The banking school further doubted if circulating domestic money supplies, even if totally metallic, would fluctuate in step with international gold flows as the currency school predicted. Rather than altering circulating money supplies, international gold flows might only lead to hoarding and dishoarding gold, especially within the banking community.

At the time of the debate between the banking school and the currency school, hundreds of banks issued their own bank notes. The banking school essentially defended the status quo, arguing that regulating the issuance of bank notes should be left to the wisdom of commercial bankers, subject to the requirement of convertibility. Left to their own discretion, the bankers would provide an elastic currency able to expand and contract to meet the needs of trade.

The Bank Charter Act of 1844 largely followed the recommendations of the currency school, especially in laying groundwork for monopolization of bank note issues by the Bank of England. Nevertheless, consistent with the thinking of the banking school, the act gave the Bank of England some discretion to expand and contract bank notes independently of gold flows.

See also: Currency School, Inconvertible Paper Standard, Real Bills Doctrine

References

Chown, John F. 1994. *A History of Money.*
Spiegel, Henry William. 1971. *The Growth of Economic Thought.*

BANK OF AMSTERDAM

The Bank of Amsterdam, established in 1609, rose to become a major hub of world monetary affairs in the 17th and 18th centuries. As a so-called bank of deposit, the Bank of Amsterdam hardly resembled anything we now call a bank. It rarely even made loans, with the exception of loans to Dutch municipalities and to the Dutch East India Company. The bank held deposits of major currencies and facilitated payment in foreign trade transactions.

The models for the Bank of Amsterdam were banks in the small Italian city-states of Venice and Genoa, where the circulating money consisted of a medley of currencies issued by home governments and neighboring states. Currency that flowed into these areas from trading

partners was often clipped and worn, creating uncertainty about the value of foreign bills of exchange paid in these currencies. To remove this uncertainty, these small city-states required that foreign bills of exchange above a certain amount be paid in transfers between accounts in a bank rather than in domestic currency. Special banks enjoying full government backing were established to handle these transactions.

Before 1609, the prevalence of worn and clipped coins had depreciated the value of Amsterdam's currency by 9 percent below the value of currency fresh from the mint. With Amsterdam's merchants running short of good money to pay bills of exchange, the government created the Bank of Amsterdam as a means of providing a currency of uniform value. The bank was a bank of deposit, accepting deposits of currencies at face value, foreign or domestic, worn, clipped, or freshly minted. Depositors paid a small recoinage and management fee deducted from each deposit. The balance on a depositor's account constituted a form of money called "money of account" or "bank money," and it never suffered any kind of debasement. Its value remained the same as if it were fresh from the mint. Along with the establishment of the bank came the legal requirement that foreign bills of exchange drawn on Amsterdam, equal to or greater than 600 guilders, be drawn for payment in bank money.

The Bank of Amsterdam also took deposits of bullion, giving each customer a receipt valued in bank money for a deposit of bullion, and crediting the customer's account of bank money in an amount equal to the value of the bullion deposit. The receipt entitled the customer to buy back the bullion with bank money at the price stated on the receipt. The customer paid a modest fee to the bank for storage of the bullion, and if the customer defaulted on the storage fee, the bank took possession of the bullion and sold it as part of the bank's profit. The bank money was much more convenient to handle than bullion and just as good in the eyes of European bankers. Vast deposits of coin and bullion made the Bank of Amsterdam an important holder of the reserves of the European monetary system, putting the bank in a position to play a regulatory role.

Because the Bank of Amsterdam was not a lending institution, it stored all the currency and bullion deposited with it in readiness to redeem its outstanding bank money. Bank money was superior to currency, and merchants were willing to pay a premium for it, enabling the bank to earn income by selling its bank money at a premium.

In the 1780s, wartime difficulties forced the bank to underwrite loans to merchants in difficulty, and the bank saw its reserves drop substantially relative to the deposits of bank money owed to the public. The public turned cautious, and when the French invaded in 1795, caution turned to panic. Unable to redeem all the deposits of coins and bullion, the bank closed down. In 1802, a forced loan allowed the bank to reopen its doors, but it was not successful; in 1820, the Bank of Amsterdam was liquidated.

See also: Bank of Deposit, Bank of Venice, Bills of Exchange, House of St. George

References

Braudel, Fernand. 1984. *Civilization and Capitalism.* Vol. III.

Davies, Glyn. 1994. *A History of Money.*

Israel, Jonathan I. 1989. *Dutch Primacy in World Trade: 1585–1740.*

Smith, Adam. 1776/1952. *An Inquiry into the Nature and Causes of the Wealth of Nations.*

Van Houte, J. A. 1977. *An Economic History of the Low Countries: 800–1800.*

BANK OF DEPOSIT

From the 15th through the 18th centuries, banks of deposit flourished in European cities with heavy traffic in international trade. Banks of deposit accepted deposits of domestic and foreign currency and held them as 100 percent reserves, as opposed to using the deposits to finance loans. This policy of retaining possession of the deposits maximized the safety of depositors' money. Records of each merchant's deposits were kept in account books, and funds were shifted from one depositor's account to another's account without coinage leaving the bank. These deposits constituted so-called bank money, which is a form of money that changes ownership by bookkeeping entries, without any coinage or receipts changing hands. This bank money became the principle circulating medium in commercial transactions.

When Italian banks of deposit first emerged in the 14th century, they required the payer and the payee to appear in person to transfer money in the bank's account books from one account to another. Later, it became possible for the payer and payee to meet elsewhere if a notary was present. In 1494, Fra Luca Pacioli, a Renaissance mathematician and friend of Leonardo da Vinci, published a book famous for including the first written treatment of double-entry bookkeeping. In the tract on double-entry bookkeeping, he gave the following description of banks of deposits:

It is common practice to deal directly with a transfer bank, where you can deposit your money for greater security or for the purpose of making your daily payments to Piero, Giovanni, and Maratino through the bank, because the registration of the transferred claim is as authoritative as a notarial instrument since it is backed by the government ... Now suppose you are a banker ... performing a transfer: If your creditor, without withdrawing cash, orders payment to another party, in your journal you debit that depositor and credit the assignee. Thus you make a transfer from one creditor to another, while you yourself remain debtor. Here you function as an intermediary, a witness and agent of the parties and you justly receive a commission. (Lane & Mueller, 1997, 5)

Adam Smith, in a famous digression in the *Wealth of Nations* (1776), described the class of banks called "banks of deposit." He identified the banks of Venice, Genoa, Amsterdam, Hamburg, and Nuremberg as institutions founded as banks of deposit. According to Smith, the currency of small states was made up almost exclusively of the coinage of neighboring states, leaving a small state virtually no control over the quality of its circulating medium. These foreign currencies, becoming worn and clipped, traded at a discount in foreign exchange markets, acting as a hindrance to merchants in the small states. Because small states could not reform domestic currencies, which was mostly foreign, they established public deposit banks as a substitute. Banks of deposit accepted deposits of all currency, new and worn, and exacted a discount of perhaps 5 percent for currency depreciation from wear and tear. The government of the state guaranteed the value of the bank deposits. These deposits, which changed ownership only by means of bookkeeping entries in the bank, represented a uniform quality and, for that reason, often traded at a premium over metallic coinage. According to Smith, the premium on the bank money of the Bank of Hamburg was 14 percent over the clipped, worn, and otherwise diminished currency that poured in from surrounding states.

Aside from the state's commitment to maintain its integrity, bank money had several advantages over metallic currencies of varying consistencies. According to Smith in his *Wealth of Nations:*

> Bank money, over and above its intrinsic superiority to currency, and the additional value which this demand necessarily gives it, has likewise some other advantages. It is secure from fire, robbery, and other accidents; the city of Amsterdam is bound for it; it can be paid away by a simple transfer, without the trouble of counting, or the risk of transporting it from one place to another. (Smith, 1952, 205)

Perhaps the growth of paper money during the Napoleonic era put an end to banks of deposit. Unlike coins, paper money could not be debased by "clipping" bits off of it. Thus, the problem of coins with varying degrees of wear and tear was no longer an issue after the advent of paper money. The Bank of Hamburg inherited the precious metal trade from the Bank of Amsterdam and

Adam Smith, 18th-century Scottish economist. (Jupiterimages)

remained active in that trade until 1814, when the Bank of Hamburg was converted into the Netherlands Bank, a different type of institution.

See also: Bank of Amsterdam, Bank of Venice, House of St. George

References

Kindleberger, Charles P. 1984. *A Financial History of Western Europe.*

Lane, Frederic C., and Reinhold C. Mueller. 1997. *Money and Banking in Medieval and Renaissance Venice.*

BANK OF ENGLAND

The Bank of England is the central bank of the United Kingdom. It acts as the government's bank, regulates the money stock growth rate and the availability of credit, and serves as a banker's bank for commercial banks, making loans and holding deposits. Like all central banks, it holds the exclusive privilege to issue bank notes (paper money). Sometimes referred to as the Old Lady of Threadneedle Street, the Bank of England sits at the center of the London financial center.

The English Parliament granted the Bank of England a corporate charter in 1694 when England was waging a costly war with France. The government needed money, and the Bank of England began as a plan to help raise funds for the government. Parliament imposed a tax on shipping tonnage, and earmarked the proceeds to go to such persons as should voluntarily advance money to the government.

The government planned to borrow £1.2 million at a moderate 8 percent interest. To attract funds on the scale needed at that interest rate, Parliament granted the subscribers to the loan the privilege of pooling their funds and incorporating themselves under the name of the Governor and Company of the Bank of England. The debate in Parliament over this act raised quite a howl, including predictions that the bank would encourage fraud, gambling, and the corruption of national morals.

Initially, Parliament granted the Bank of England a charter for 10 years. This charter authorized the bank to trade in gold, silver, and bills of exchange, and to issue bank notes equal in amount to its capital. It prohibited the bank from selling merchandise, excepting what had been held as security for unpaid loans. The charter put the management of the Bank of England in the hands of a governor, deputy governor, and 24 directors, elected yearly by the stockholders.

Parliament continued to renew the bank's charter, usually in return for loans to the government, often at lower interest rates. Parliament renewed the bank's charter in 1709 and added a provision that no other joint-stock company with more than six partners could issue bank notes, a provision that eventually gave the Bank of England a dominant position in the issuance of bank notes. In 1751, the bank took over the administration of the national debt, and by 1780 the bank had a virtual monopoly on the issuance of bank notes in London. The Bank of England began to wear the aspect of a central bank as smaller banks began the practice of keeping funds on deposit with it.

Originally conceived to raise money to fight a war, the bank underwent a particularly innovative period of development during the wars with revolutionary France and Napoleon. Over the protests of the bank's directors, the bank was forced to accommodate the financing needs of the government for unlimited amounts. The bank began issuing notes in much smaller denominations, and in 1797 the bank, with approval from Parliament, suspended the convertibility of its bank notes into specie. Government borrowing had weakened the bank's reserve position, and bank note holders were making a run on the bank. Although they were now inconvertible, the value of Bank of England bank notes stood up well because the government accepted them at par value in all payments and, in 1812, made them legal tender. Country banks began to hold Bank of England notes as reserves for their own bank notes.

After resuming convertibility of its bank notes into specie in 1821, the Bank of England saw its bank notes grow in acceptability relative to gold. The country banks found the notes just as useful as gold for managing cash drain, and began to look to the Bank of England as a place to borrow funds in a liquidity crisis. In 1833, the British government again declared Bank of England notes legal tender for sums above £5 so long as the notes remained convertible. As Bank of England notes replaced gold as the circulating medium, the bank became the major holder of gold reserves.

At first the Bank of England resisted the pressure to become a lender of last resort in financial crises, still seeing itself as a bank competing with other banks, rather than a source of succor to competing banks in a financial crisis. The bank discovered, however, that adjusting its bank rate of interest to compete with other banks destabilized markets. After the crash of 1847, the bank began accepting its role as a lender of last resort and using adjustments in its bank rate of interest to stabilize money markets.

The years preceding World War I saw the Bank of England become the custodian of the gold standard, and develop methods of using the bank rate of interest and open market operations to regulate interest rates, and the inflow and outflow of gold. During World War I the government outlawed the export of gold, and after the war the bank became a strong voice favoring restoration of the gold standard, notwithstanding the high interest rates required to prevent an outflow of gold reserves. The high interest rates needed to maintain the gold standard were out of step with the needs of the time, and in 1931 Parliament passed the Gold Standard (Amendment) Act, suspending the gold standard. The bank was never quite the

Bank of England, 18th century engraving. (Jupiterimages)

same after the loss of the gold standard, and the government gave the bank very little guidance as to what policies to follow after the suspension.

During the years between the two world wars, the Bank of England's policies came under closer scrutiny and drew more criticism. In particular, the Macmillan Committee in Parliament inquired into the full range of activities of the bank and criticized it for not being more committed to the methods of monetary management by central banks—perhaps because of the bank's loyalty to the outmoded gold standard.

The success of the government-directed war economy led a new Labor government in Parliament to embark on a program of nationalization of major industries after World War II. Controversy over the policies of the Bank of England before the war made it an obvious target. It was nationalized in 1946 and brought under the authority of the Exchequer, or British treasury. With elected officials exerting much more influence over monetary policy, the Bank of England lost some of its reputation for financial probity. During the inflation-ridden 1970s, Britain suffered much higher inflation rates than Japan, the United States, and West Germany. During the 1980s, tight monetary policies brought down inflation, and by the late 1990s there was talk of again privatizing the Bank of England.

The Bank of England is represented on the General Council of the European Central Bank, but so far the United Kingdom has opted not to participate in the introduction of the euro, the all-European currency. The euro replaced the German mark, the French franc, and the currencies of other participating European countries.

See also: Bank Charter Act of 1833, Bank Charter Act of 1844, Bank of France, Banking Acts of 1826, Central Bank, Federal Reserve System, Pound Sterling

References

Bank for International Settlements. 1963. *Eight European Central Banks.*

Clapham, Sir J. 1970. *The Bank of England.*

Roberts, Richard, ed. 1995. *The Bank of England: Money, Power, and Influence, 1694–1994.*

Sayers, R. S. 1976. *The Bank of England: 1881–1944.*

BANK OF FRANCE

Before the establishment of the European Central Bank, the Bank of France was the central bank in France. It compared to the Bank of England or the Federal Reserve System in the United States, and was responsible for regulating the money stock, interest rates, and credit conditions in France.

When Napoleon assumed the reins of power in 1799, he knew the French government had lost all credibility as a borrower, a factor that had helped spark the French Revolution. His government needed to raise money, but selling government bonds was not a practicable means to do so as there was no market for discredited government debt at the time. In 1800, Napoleon created the Bank of France to help with this problem. It was initially capitalized at 30 million *livres*. Three years later livres were replaced by the new currency, *francs,* making the capitalization 30 million francs. Openly calling the new institution a bank was itself a bold move. After the disaster of John Law's bank in 1720, the very term "bank" had fallen into disrepute in France and disappeared from the names of French financial institutions.

The financial capital for the Bank of France came partly from the capital of the Caisse des Comptes Courants, a Paris discount bank issuing bank notes (paper money) that dissolved and merged into the new institution. Other capital for the bank was raised from public subscriptions, and an additional sum came from the government. The Bank of France was organized as a corporation, the stockholders of which elected a governing committee.

In 1803, the government granted the Bank of France the exclusive privilege to issue bank notes in Paris. The other main note-issuing bank in Paris, the Caisse d'Escompte du Commerce, had been merged unwillingly with the Bank of France in 1802. Other note-issuing banks in Paris were required to withdraw their bank notes before a certain date. Any new note-issuing banks in the provinces had to have the approval of the government.

From the beginning, Napoleon wanted the Bank of France to purchase government bonds at the lowest possible interest rates and pay for the bonds with bank notes. In 1804, the bank caved to government pressure and issued too many bank notes amid rumors that Napoleon had shipped the metallic reserves to Germany for military purposes. A crisis forced the bank to partially suspend convertibility of its bank notes into specie, and the notes depreciated 10 to 15 percent, while the bank—rather than the government—took the blame for the crisis.

In 1806, the governance of the bank underwent a major overhaul. A government-appointed governor and two deputy governors replaced the committee elected by the stockholders. Another partial suspension of convertibility came in 1814.

Napoleon emphasized low interest rates as a means of softening the blow of his continental blockade. He pressured the bank to keep its discount rate (central bank interest rate to borrowers) in the 4 to 5 percent range, a practice the bank continued until the mid-19th century. He also encouraged the bank to act as a lender of last resort.

The Bank of France took advantage of its authorization to set up branch banks in the provinces. However, these branch banks were unsuccessful at first, even in places where they had regional monopolies on the issuance of bank notes. A few private banks opening in the provinces were also unprofitable at first, mainly because of strict government regulation. However, by 1840 private banks began to be a threat in the provinces. After 1840 the government refused to grant charters for new private banks with authority to issue bank notes. Between 1841 and 1848, the Bank of France opened 15 branch banks in the provinces.

In the political crises of 1848, the French government counted on the Bank of France for financial support. The public, remembering the worthless *assignats* of the Revolution, began to convert bank notes into specie and hoard it. The government responding by declaring Bank of France bank notes legal tender throughout the nation, and putting a limit on the number of bank notes the Bank of France could issue. The Bank of France now achieved a clear advantage over the private provincial banks, whose bank notes were only legal tender in their respective regions. The private provincial banks then merged with the Bank of France, and the Bank of France acquired a nationwide monopoly on the issuance of bank notes.

The Bank of France kept its discount rate fairly constant until the 1850s, when it began the practice of adjusting its discount rate to regulate the flow of specie. An increase in the discount rate could halt a specie outflow. In 1857, the bank became exempt from the usury law setting a 6 percent ceiling on interest rates.

By 1900 the Bank of France had an office in 411 French towns, and had as many as 120 full branches, substantially more than the eight branches that the Bank of England had in Britain. The Bank of France played a much greater role in the French money and banking system than the comparable Bank of England played in the British system. The tight control that the Bank of France held over the development of banking in France may have inhibited French economic growth in the 19th century. During World War I and World War II, the French government relied heavily on the Bank of France to buy government bonds with the issuance of bank notes as a measure of war finance. Bank notes increased 400 percent between 1940 and 1945, but controls suppressed inflation until 1944. The government nationalized the Bank of France in 1945. Inflation grew to acute levels in the 1950s.

On August 4, 1993, the Bank of France won its independence from political authorities in a piece of landmark legislation. With its newly won independence came a renewed commitment to price stability as its top priority regardless of domestic political pressures.

In 1998, the Bank of France joined the European System of Central Banks, which on January 1, 1999, assumed responsibility for implementing a single monetary policy for all member states of the European Monetary Union. The governor of the Bank of France sits on the Governing Council of the European Central Bank and the Bank of France shares in the implementation of monetary policy. Monetary policy in the European system is determined by the Governing Council of the European Central Bank.

See also: Bank of England, Central Bank, Deutsche Bundesbank, Federal Reserve System, First Bank of the United States, Monetary Law of 1803, Second Bank of the United States

References

Davies, Glyn. 1994. *A History of Money*.

Kindleberger, Charles P. 1984. *A Financial History of Western Europe*.

Wilson, J. S. G. 1957. *French Banking Structure and Credit Policy*.

BANK OF JAPAN

Japan was the first non-Western country to intentionally transform its economy into a developed capitalist system. In 1882, the Japanese government established the Bank of Japan on the European model of central banks. This was three decades before the United States created the Federal Reserve System and occurred at a time when feudalism was still a fresh memory in Japan.

After the Meiji Restoration in 1868, the government launched Japan on an intensive program of Westernized economic development. The new government found gold, silver, and copper coins circulating alongside paper money issued by feudal lords and merchants. Like previous revolutionary governments, including the Continental Congress of the United States, the Meiji Restoration government turned to the issuance of inconvertible paper money to finance government spending. Inconvertible paper money is paper money not convertible into any type of precious metal. In 1877, the government issued another round of inconvertible paper money to suppress a rebellion. This touched off an inflationary surge from 1877 to 1881.

The Japanese government learned from European and U.S. models. In 1872, Japan adopted a system of national banks patterned after the national banking system in the United States. Like their counterparts in the United States, these banks held government bonds as collateral for bank notes. The government's inconvertible paper currency was redeemable in government bonds, but the system broke down after the government allowed national banks to issue inconvertible bank notes in the late 1870s.

In 1881, the Japanese minister of finance visited Europe to study central banking systems. The National Bank of Belgium had been created in 1850 and appeared to the Japanese as the most advanced institution of its type. The United States had no central bank, and the Bank of England had evolved over nearly two centuries without a written constitution.

The Bank of Japan Act of 1882 provided for the establishment of the Bank of Japan. The bank was organized as a private joint-stock company. The government furnished half of the capital. Government officials not only appointed the governor of the bank and other bank officers, but also supervised the policies and administration of the bank. The bank held a monopoly on the issuance of bank notes, and served as a lender of last resort to other banks.

The Bank of Japan was set up to serve as the fiscal agent of the government, to stabilize seasonal and regional fluctuations in the flow of funds, to finance international trade, and to hold specie reserves. The Japanese treasury exerted strong influence on the operations of the bank. In 1897, Japan went on the gold standard, making the bank notes of the Bank of Japan fully convertible into gold.

In 1868, precious metal specie accounted for 75 percent of the money supply. By 1881, that percentage had decreased to 20 percent. Bank deposits accounted for 7 percent of the money supply when the Bank of Japan was formed. By 1914, this percentage had grown to 44 percent. Japan's economy became highly monetized, complete with bank notes and bank deposits.

In June 1997, the Japanese Diet enacted new legislation, the Bank of Japan Law, which provided that the autonomy of the Bank of Japan be respected. In 1998, the Bank of Japan began a major reorganization aiming at streamlining operations and reducing unnecessary holdings, such as surplus real estate.

The process that led to the formation of the Bank of Japan reveals something of the method that lies behind the Japanese economic miracle. Today, Japanese commercial banks are among the largest in the world.

See also: Bank of England, Central Bank, Bank of France, Federal Reserve System, Yen

References
Davies, Glyn. 1994. *A History of Money.*
Cameron, Rondo. 1967. *Banking in the Early Stages of Industrialization.*

BANK OF SCOTLAND

The Bank of Scotland claims the honor of being the first incorporated bank owned exclusively by private shareholders and devoted exclusively to the business of meeting the banking needs of the private sector. The Scottish Parliament chartered the Bank of Scotland in 1695, and it remains the only surviving institution created by that body. The life of the Scottish Parliament came to a close in 1707 when England and Scotland merged.

In 1695, the larger continental states of France, Prussia, and Austria depended solely on private bankers, such as the famous Fugger family of bankers who

held sway in the 15th and 16th centuries. These countries remained strangers to public banks. Italy, Holland, England, and Sweden had founded public banks, but they all had strong connections to governments. The Bank of Amsterdam was founded in 1609, the Bank of Sweden in 1656, and the Bank of England in 1694. The Bank of England was closest in character to the Bank of Scotland, but Parliament chartered it mainly to raise money for the government. Some of the Italian public banks were little more than societies of government creditors. The Bank of Scotland was expressly forbidden in its charter to make loans to the monarchy.

The Bank of Scotland began as a pure corporation, entailing limited liability for its shareholders and the same standing as an individual in the eyes of the law. The Scottish Parliament gave the Bank of Scotland a monopoly for its first 21 years and made its dividends free from taxation for that period. Anyone could purchase stock in the bank, including foreigners. Edinburgh was headquarters for the bank, but branch offices were opened in Glasgow, Aberdeen, Dundee, and Montrose.

Over the protest of the Bank of Scotland, the British Parliament in 1727 chartered a second public bank in Scotland, the Royal Bank of Scotland. Intense rivalry existed between these two banks from the outset. By 1745, Scotland had a highly developed banking system, and notes of these banks were an important means of payment. In 1746, a third public bank, the British Linen Company, received a charter.

By 1730, the Bank of Scotland on three separate occasions had suspended payment on its bank notes. In that year, its directors approved the insertion of the so-called optional clause on its bank

Interior of the National Bank of Scotland in Glasgow, 19th century. (Jupiterimages)

notes. The optional clause committed the bank to either redeeming its bank notes on demand or suspending redemption for six months, paying a specified interest rate during the interval of suspension. The British Parliament banned the optional clause in the Scottish Banking Act of 1765.

The Act of 1765 also opened up Scotland to "free banking," rendering it easier to organize banks that issue notes. Under Scotland's system of free banking, the Bank of Scotland took the lead in policing the issuance of bank notes by the smaller, provincial banks. In 1776, Adam Smith heaped high praise on the Scottish banking system, writing that "the business of the country is almost entirely carried on by means of the paper of those different banking companies. . . . Silver very seldom appears . . . and gold still seldomer."

In the 19th century, Parliament began to concentrate the note-issuing authority in the hands of the Bank of England. In 1833, the Bank of England's notes became legal tender in England, a status not enjoyed by other bank notes. In 1844, Parliament restricted the further issuance of bank notes by any other bank than the Bank of England. As the Bank of England assumed the role of Britain's central bank, the Bank of Scotland lost its position of leadership in Scottish banking. Mergers between Scottish banks in the 19th and 20th centuries periodically rearranged the rankings of Scottish banks in terms of size, but the Bank of Scotland has remained one of the largest banks in Scotland. A 1989 survey by the *Economist* found the Bank of Scotland to be the bank most admired by its peer bankers.

See also: Bank of England, Royal Bank of Scotland, Scottish Banking Act of 1765

References

Checkland, S. G. 1975. *Scottish Banking History: 1695–1973.*

Colwell, Stephen. 1859/1965. *The Ways and Means of Payment.*

Davies, Glyn. 1994. *A History of Money.*

BANK OF SPAIN

See: Spanish Inconvertible Paper Standard

BANK OF VENICE

The history of the Bank of Venice reveals something of the forces that led to the evolution of central banks. In 1171, the government of the Republic of Venice extracted forced loans of specie from wealthy citizens. The government kept a record book that showed the amounts it owed individual citizens, but otherwise issued no bonds, promissory notes (IOUs), certificates of indebtedness, or other proof of indebtedness. The government's creditors received 4 percent interest per year, but the government did not pay down the principal on the loans. The citizens of Venice began exchanging ownership of these government obligations to transact business, turning these government obligations into a circulating medium of exchange like any other form of money. Money transactions settled by entries in books were much more convenient than coined money transactions, particularly when large amounts were involved. The citizens of Venice soon voluntarily deposited specie with the "bank" in return for book entry deposits that could be transferred to other depositors in any amount.

In 1587, the Venetian government established the Bank of Venice as the Banco del Piazza del Rialto. As early as 1374 a committee of scholars had proposed the formal organization of a public bank, but no action was taken for over two centuries. By the late 1500s, other Italian cities had already established public banks, costing Venice claims of priority in the history of banking. The credit for the first beginnings of modern banking practices, however, belongs to Venice.

The Venetian practice of banking on the security of government loans survived into the modern period. Today in the United States, the Federal Reserve System issues Federal Reserve Notes and deposits at Federal Reserve Banks, holding government bonds as securities against these notes and deposit liabilities.

See also: Bank of Amsterdam, Bank of Deposit, House of St. George, Medici Bank, Venetian Ducat

References

Kindleberger, Charles P. 1984. *A Financial History of Western Europe.*

Knox, John Jay. 1903/1969. *A History of Banking in the United States.*

Lane, Frederic C., and Reinhold C. Mueller. 1997. *Money and Banking in Medieval and Renaissance Venice.* Vols. 1–2.

BANK RATE

See: Bank Charter Act of 1833, Gold Standard

BANK RESTRICTION ACT OF 1797 (ENGLAND)

The Bank Restriction Act of 1797 began England's first experience with inconvertible paper currency—that is, paper currency that was not convertible into precious metal at an official rate. From 1797 until 1821, roughly coinciding with the Napoleonic Wars, the Bank of England suspended payments, meaning that bank notes were no longer redeemable in specie or cash. During this era, England managed a system of inconvertible paper currency that met the needs of trade without triggering a destructive episode of hyperinflation.

Prior to the suspension of payments, banks in England, Ireland, and Scotland issued bank notes that circulated as paper money, and these banks stood ready to redeem bank notes into gold and silver specie, assuring the acceptability of bank notes in trade. Beginning in 1793, banks had difficulty maintaining sufficient specie reserves to satisfy all requests for redemption of bank notes. Heavy government borrowing, coupled with subsidies to foreign allies and military expenditures, caused a major outflow of gold, draining the gold reserves of the Bank of England. The memory was still fresh of the financial debacle that followed John Law's attempt to multiply without limit the paper money in France in 1720. Rumors of a French invasion of Ireland sparked a run on banks, further drawing down gold reserves at the Bank of England. The Privy Council at an emergency meeting on February 26, 1797, decided that the Bank of England should suspend payments, and on May 3, 1797, Parliament confirmed the action with enactment of the Bank Restriction Act. The suspension of payments, advanced as a temporary measure, was continually renewed, lasting six years after the end of the Napoleonic War in 1815. It dominated discussions of monetary issues in Parliament for 24 years.

Measures of inflation during the suspension of payments period were not available because the science of index numbers was still in its infancy. The values of gold and foreign currencies, priced in British pounds, were the main indicators that gauged the value of the paper pound. The Irish pound dropped significantly on foreign exchange markets in 1801, sparking serious discussion. In 1809, the other monetary shoe fell when the British pound dropped significantly on the Hamburg foreign exchange market. The House of Commons appointed a committee, the Select Committee on the High Price of Gold Bullion, to investigate the monetary situation and report to Parliament. The report of this committee, the Bullion Report, fastened the blame on excessive issue of bank notes and recommended the return to convertibility within two years. Thomas Malthus and David Ricardo, famous economists of the time, supported the Bullion Report, whereas most businessmen and bankers, particularly officials of the Bank of England, defended the suspension policy, arguing that banking policy had no effect on foreign exchange rates. In hindsight, the Bullion Report represented sound monetary economics, surprisingly advanced for its time, but the exigencies of war forced England to remain on an inconvertible paper standard. The issues were summed up with the saying that the bankers turned out to be bad economists, and the economists bad politicians.

Two factors seemed to have spared England the ravages of a paper money system out of control. First, England had a developed capital market for long-term financing of government debt. Second, Parliament enacted an income tax that became effective in

1799. The government's use of taxation and long-term borrowing lifted much of the pressure on the monetary system to pay for the war printing by bank notes.

When the war ended in 1815, contrary to expectations, the Bank of England still faced a drain on its gold reserves, and Parliament postponed the resumption of cash payments. In 1819, Parliament passed the Resumption of Cash Payments Act, calling for the resumption of payments by 1823. The Bank of England's reserve position improved faster than expected, and full convertibility into gold was restored in May 1821. The Resumption of Cash Payments Act also put England squarely on the gold standard, which England had been moving toward during the 18th century.

See also: Bank of England, Inconvertible Paper Standard, Liverpool Act of 1816, Pound Sterling

References

Chown, John F. 1994. *A History of Money.*
Clapham, Sir J. 1970. *The Bank of England.*
Fetter, F. W., and T. E. Gregory. 1973. *Monetary and Financial Policy in Nineteenth-Century Britain.*

BARBADOS ACT OF 1706

In 1706, the colonial assembly of Barbados, an English colony, enacted legislation that led to one of the more unusual monetary experiments in history, creating a fiat domestic currency that was virtually legal tender. The legislation sparked a strong protest from merchants, slave traders, and other English traders, the creditors in the economy of Barbados. The British Board of Trade acted to force the redemption of the paper money, but the episode reveals the secret war between debtors and creditors that often surfaces when monetary institutions are evolving.

Sir Bevill Granville, the lieutenant-governor at the time, favored a party of debt-ridden planters in the colonial assembly. With Granville's patronage, the planter party, controlling leadership positions in the assembly, successfully sponsored the legislation, which passed in the lower house by a vote of ten to nine. The planters clothed their proposal in arguments citing the shortage of coin as a contributing factor to the declining state of trade. To assure the successful execution of the plan, the assembly adopted the Triennial Act, which extended its own life for three years.

This proposal to create a locally issued paper money allowed each planter to receive "bills of credit" equaling in value to one-fourth the planter's estate. The institution issuing these bills was a bank, and the bank manager was called the holder. Among other duties, the holder had sole responsibility for appraising the estates of the planters, one of the many objections of the creditors. The legislation called for the acceptance of the bills at face value in all domestic transactions, and required creditors to forfeit half of a debt for refusing to accept the bills in payment. Planters had to redeem the bills in one year, or renew them. Renewed bills remained in circulation. When the planters who first drew the bills failed to redeem them or were unable to pay the interest and renew them, they faced something like a foreclosure sale on that part of their property pledged as security for the bills.

The major flaw of the bills in the eyes of the creditors was that they paid no interest to their holders. The planters paid 5 percent interest on the bills, which went to the bank to cover the administrative cost of issuing, redeeming, and renewing the bills. The merchants and traders who received the bills in payment earned no interest while they held them, a factor that assured the rapid depreciation of the bills in value.

The Royal African Company, a slave-trading company, was among the major critics of the law, and vigorously objected, with other merchants and traders, to the British Board of Trade. The British government recalled Granville, and sent as a replacement Mitford Crowe, an individual in good standing with the merchants. The British government ordered Barbados to redeem the bills held by creditors involuntarily. Meanwhile leadership in the assembly lost confidence in the new bills, and, failing to persuade the assembly to take action, dissolved it, calling for new elections. The new election became a battleground for a clash between creditors and debtors, and the creditors came out on top. The new assembly passed the Relief Act of 1707, which forced planters to redeem their paper bills in one year or face foreclosure auctions.

The experience of colonial Barbados illustrates the difficulty of developing a fiat money standard acceptable to creditors, who bear the burden when money loses its value. Perhaps there is a lesson in the fact that the same New World that flooded the Old World with an influx of precious metals, was also inventive in coming up with new variants of paper money.

See also: Land Bank System, Sugar Standard of West Indies

References

Brock, Leslie V. 1975. *The Currency of the American Colonies, 1700–1764.*

Nettels, Curtis P. 1934/1964. *The Money Supply of the American Colonies before 1720.*

BARTER

Barter is a rude form of exchange, based on directly swapping goods for goods without the intermediary of money. Exchange becomes more important as individuals specialize in the production of goods and services. Money considerably facilitates exchange because everyone accepts it in trade. In a money economy, individuals devoting all their energies and skills to the production of one commodity, such as cattle, can trade cows for money, and use money to buy groceries, televisions, automobiles, and so on. In an economic system based on barter, a cattle rancher must find someone who wants to trade cows for everything else he or she may want to acquire. To buy a television, the cattle rancher would have to find someone with more televisions than he or she needs for personal use, and who is in need of a cow. The cattle rancher, having more cows than needed for personal use, will trade a cow for a television. Economists call this conglomeration of circumstances a double coincidence of wants.

Barter exchange is necessarily time consuming and inefficient. It is hard to imagine someone working in a propeller shop, making propellers for airplanes, receiving pay in a bundle of propellers, and then trading propellers for everything they need. Money simplifies exchange and results in a constant ratio in the exchange rate between propellers, and, say, televisions.

Historically, barter exchange precedes the use of money, but it has experienced resurgence at times. During the Middle Ages, metallic coinage became scarce in Europe, and barter exchange began to play a larger role. Serfs paid manor lords in certain hours of labor, and a noble

Vendors at the Rizhky market in Moscow barter their personal belongings, 1991. (Shepard Sherbell/Corbis)

would make payment in military service. In the American colonies, barter flourished because of a shortage of metallic currency. During the 1970s in the United States, barter again grew in popularity as a means of avoiding income taxes. Individuals with goods to sell, or services to be rendered, formed bartering organizations, with lists of goods that could be bartered.

In the 1990s, an antiquated system of barter appeared in Russia just at the time that Western observers expected the emergence of a market economy. Some estimates suggest that as high as 70 percent of the transactions in Russia involve barter. City taxes may be paid in the form of clothes for policemen. Farmers bring food to factories in exchange for sheet metal, paint, and other useful items, and the factories pay workers in the food supplied by the farmers. Workers may be paid in kind: Workers at a timber factory received a bundle of plywood on payday.

About 50 percent of industrial sales take the form of barter. A cannery trades its finished product, 12-ounce cans of meat, for livestock to slaughter, aluminum to make the cans, canning machinery, electricity, and cardboard boxes suitable for shipping canned meat.

In a country such as Russia, barter emerges only after a complete breakdown of the currency. Companies must arrange deals involving several other companies to pay their own suppliers. They must find out what goods their suppliers will accept in payment, then set out to trade what they have to some other company that will accept these goods in order to get what their suppliers need. All kinds of imbalances develop. A police department might receive a large shipment of woolen socks but no new shoes.

Despite the obvious advantages of money exchange over barter exchange, metallic coinage, the most acceptable medium of exchange, was not freely embraced by ancient societies. Complaints against money were perhaps best expressed by the Chinese scholar Gong Yu (ca. 45 BCE), who favored the abolition of coinage. He wrote:

> Since the appearance of the uruzhu coins over seventy years ago, many people have been guilty of illicit coining. The rich hoard housefuls of coins, and yet are never satisfied. The people are restless. The merchants seek profit. Though you give land to the poor, they must still sell cheaply to the merchant. They become poorer and poorer, then become bandits. The reason? It is the deepening of the secondary occupations and the coveting of money. That is why evil cannot be banned. It arises entirely from money. (Williams, 1997, 155)

Ancient Chinese scholars were not alone in voicing skepticism about money. The New Testament has the now often-repeated refrain that the "love of money is the root of all evil." The ancient Spartans legislated that only huge round metal discs could serve as money, hoping to discourage the accumulation and carrying of large sums of money. Metallic coinage was often blamed for the vices associated with the large seaport cities.

Despite reservations about money use, economies based upon money exchange rather than barter exchange support a much higher level of specialization among individuals, businesses, and regions, and this specialization fosters productivity. Greater specialization requires greater exchange, and money facilitates exchange. Economies using money are more efficient and productive, eclipsing economies based on barter exchange.

See also: Commodity Monetary Standard, Spartan Iron Currency

References

Baye, Michael R., and Dennis W. Jansen. 1995. *Money, Banking, and Financial Markets: An Economics Approach.*

Higgins, Andrew. "Twilight Economy: Lacking Money to Pay, Russian Firms Survive on a Deft System of Barter." *Wall Street Journal,* August 27, 1998, A1:1.

Paddock, Richard C. "Russians Bank of Bartering." *Los Angeles Times,* December 28, 1998, A1:1.

Williams, Jonathan, ed. 1997. *Money: A History.*

BEER STANDARD OF MARXIST ANGOLA

During the late 1980s, imported beer became a medium of exchange on the black market in Angola. By that time, the economy of Marxist Angola was beginning to break under the strain of a 13-year war against rebels supported by the United States and South Africa. Inflation from wartime finance left the official currency of Angola, the kwanza, trading on the black market for 2,000 kwanzas per dollar, compared to the official rate of 30 kwanzas per dollar. As goods disappeared from the shelves of the state-operated stores, a black market arose right in the middle of the garbage dump of Luanda, the capital of Angola. At the black market, consumers purchased all kinds of goods with imported beer. The depreciating kwanzas were pegged to the price of beer.

Initially, the government tried to squelch the black market, which continued to grow as the state-owned industry ground to a halt. The state economists began to visit the black market to get ideas for Angola's economy, which caught the same distemper as the other socialist economies of that era. The government learned to tolerate the black market as it sought to decentralize its own bureaucratic economy, which was suffering shortages of raw material and manpower arising from the war effort. Government officials turned to studying the black market as a crash course in capitalism. Soon, the policemen at the black market were there only for crowd control. The black market had a name, the *Roque Santeiro,* the title of a popular Brazilian soap opera played in Angola, a former Portuguese colony.

Consumers acquired imported beer in one of two ways. If they had dollars, they went to one of the government-owned hard currency stores and bought a case of imported beer—Heineken, Beck's, or Stella Artois—for $12. Only the middle classes, however, were likely to have dollars, which they acquired from foreign travel. Workers often got on the beer standard through their employers, who often paid them partially in coupons that they could spend in company-owned stores. These stores were owned by the multinational corporations that had employees in Angola. Workers could go to one of these stores, buy a case of imported beer, take it to the black market, sell it for 30,000 kwanzas, and then fill their grocery list by shopping at the black market or even buy a plane ticket to Lisbon. The plane ticket cost about two cases of imported beer. The black marketeer would break up the case of beer and sell it for about 2,000 kwanzas per can, turning a nice profit of 12,000 kwanzas.

The debasement of Angola's currency amidst civil war sounded a very familiar note in history. Hyperinflation attended the War of Independence of the American colonies, one example of many that could be cited. The adoption of imported beer as a medium of exchange appeared, however, to have no precedent, and seemed a bit comical. It may have been a reaction to the tendency of socialist economies to emphasize austerity in the production of consumer goods, even in peacetime. The free market that rose up from the ash heap of Angola's Marxist economy adopted as a monetary standard a symbol of Western variety and luxury in consumer goods—imported beer.

See also: Commodity Monetary Standard, Liquor Money

Reference

"In Marxist Angola, Capitalism Thrives, Using Beer Standard," *Wall Street Journal,* September 19, 1988, p. 1.

BELGIAN FRANC

See: Belgian Monetary Reform: 1944–1945

BELGIAN MONETARY REFORM: 1944–1945

The Belgian monetary reform, although not radical, was among the most thorough in post–World War II Europe. Numerous European countries, freshly liberated from Germany, found themselves awash in currency that had been spent lavishly to pay soldiers and finance military expenditures. Monetary reform aimed at soaking up a flood of currency was common in the liberated countries, including France and Italy, in an effort to avoid the hyperinflation debacles that followed World War I.

The Belgian government-in-exile returned to Brussels in September 1944 with plans in hand to reform the Belgium currency. In the course of the war, the Belgian money supply had climbed 250 percent without commensurate increases in price levels, creating a situation ripe for a round of runaway inflation. Bank notes were up 350 percent and bank account money was up 125 percent. Either the money stock needed to decrease rapidly, or prices would soar.

Few European countries thought in terms of returning to prewar exchange rate parities, and Belgium was no exception. Before the war, the Belgian franc had traded at 145 francs to the pound sterling and 30 francs to the U.S. dollar. The postwar Belgian authorities aimed to maintain an exchange rate of 176.6 francs to the pound sterling and 43.70 francs to the U.S. dollar.

The Belgian government had new currency printed in England. In October 1944, all Belgian notes over 100 francs were frozen. In five days a census of circulating cash was completed, and the process of distributing the new currency began. Each family could exchange 2,000 of the old francs for the new francs on a one-to-one basis. More exchange took place, up to certain limits, to replace old francs in notes, bank accounts, and post office accounts. Up to 60 percent of these funds were blocked, unavailable for conversion into new francs. These blocked funds could be used for certain purposes, such as special taxes, including war-profiteering taxes, which ran as high as 100 percent for German collaborators.

Noncollaborators paid war-profiteering taxes up to 80 percent.

The immediate result of these actions was the reduction of note circulation from 300 billion Belgian francs to 57.4 billion. By December 1944, the Belgian money stock had grown to 75 billion, and it grew rapidly in the following year as British and U.S. troops used Belgium as a base.

Belgium's gold holdings had been moved to France for safe keeping, which, however, did not prevent the Germans from capturing them. The Belgian government sued the French government in U.S. courts, charging French negligence in securing Belgium's gold. The U.S. courts ruled in favor of Belgium and awarded Belgium compensation out of French gold reserves held in the United States. Later, all gold that the Germans confiscated from allied governments was recovered, allowing France to recoup its payment to Belgium.

With heavy British and U.S. expenditures in Belgium, coupled with the recovery of its gold reserves, Belgium emerged from the war with an abundance of monetary reserves, sufficient to support a stable currency.

See also: Deutsche Mark, French Franc, Swiss Franc

References

Dupriez, Leon H. 1946. *Monetary Reconstruction in Belgium.*
Kindleberger, Charles P. 1984. *A Financial History of Western Europe.*

BILLON

See: Byzantine Debasement

BILLS OF EXCHANGE

Bills of exchange developed during the Middle Ages as a means of transferring funds and making payments over long distances without physically moving bulky quantities of precious metals. In the hands of 13th-century Italian merchants, bankers, and foreign exchange dealers, the bill of exchange evolved into a powerful financial tool, accommodating short-term credit transactions as well as facilitating foreign exchange transactions.

The invention of the bill of exchange greatly facilitated foreign trade. The mechanics of this can be seen in the following example: Assume that a merchant in Flanders sold goods to a Venetian merchant and accepted in payment a bill of exchange drawn on the Venetian merchant promising to pay an agent of the Flemish merchant in Venice at a certain date in the future and in a certain currency. The bill of exchange allowed the Venetian merchant to accept delivery on the goods from Flanders, sell them, and take the proceeds to redeem the bill of exchange in Venice, probably in Venetian currency.

Bills of exchange were also instruments for foreign exchange transactions. Merchants in Italy and major trading centers in Europe bought bills of exchange payable at future dates, in other places, and different currencies. In the example above, the Flemish merchant could sell the bill of exchange to an exchange dealer for currency of his own choosing. In turn, the exchange dealer could sell the bill of exchange to a Flemish merchant engaged in buying goods in Venice. When the bill came due for payment in Venice, the Flemish merchant would use it to buy goods in Venice where the bill of exchange was

paid. Although this process seems complicated, it substantially reduced the transportation of precious metals. In our example, a Venetian merchant bought goods from Flanders, and a Flemish merchant bought goods from Venice, without any foreign currency leaving Venice or Flanders.

Bills of exchange gave cover to bankers evading usury laws by hiding interest charges in exchange rate adjustments that governed foreign exchange transactions. A Florentine bank could advance a sum to an Italian merchant and receive a bill of exchange payable at a future date to an agent of the Florentine bank in a foreign market. When the bill of exchange matured, the Florentine agent in the foreign market would draw another bill of exchange on the Italian merchant, payable at a date in the future at the Florentine bank that drew the first bill of exchange on the Italian merchant. The Italian merchant would be borrowing the use of money for the time it took for these transactions to be completed, and the interest would be embedded in the fees for handling the bills of exchange. Bills of exchange drawn only to grant credit were called dry bills of exchange.

Credit transactions involving bills of exchange are difficult to untangle, even challenging the talents of Adam Smith, who cited the difficulty of the subject of bills of exchange as credit instruments in the *Wealth of Nations*:

> The practice of drawing and redrawing is so well known to all men of business that it may perhaps be thought unnecessary to give an account of it. But as this book may come into the hands of many people who are not men of business, and as the effects of this practice are not

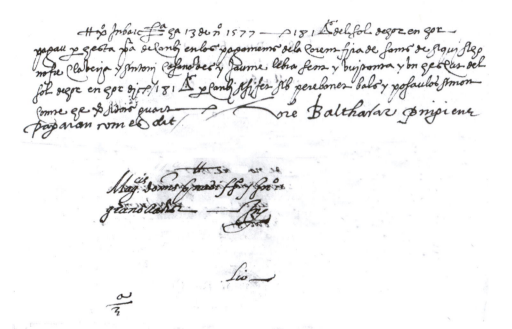

Bill of exchange from Lyons, France, 16th century. (Photo12/The Image Works)

perhaps generally understood even by men of business themselves, I shall endeavor to explain it as distinctly as I can. (Smith, 1952, 133)

Smith goes on to describe a process by which bills of exchange are drawn and then redrawn with interest charges added, turning the bill of exchange into a form of long-term credit.

Bills of exchange circulated as money substitutes, partially playing the role of paper money, and economizing on the need to move specie between countries. When London became the financial center of world during the 18th century, bills of exchange became less important as credit instruments. Uninfluenced by church doctrines toward usury, the London financial markets developed financial instruments that clearly stated what interest rate was paid.

See also: Medici Bank

References

Davies, Glyn. 1994. *The History of Money.*

Homer, Sidney. 1977. *A History of Interest Rates,* 2nd ed.

Kindleberger, Charles P. 1984. *A Financial History of Western Europe.*

Roover, Raymond de. 1966. *The Rise and Decline of the Medici Bank: 1397–1494.*

Smith, Adam. 1776/1952. *An Inquiry into the Nature and Causes of the Wealth of Nations.*

BIMETALLISM

Under a bimetallic standard, a unit of money, such as a dollar, is defined in terms of two metals, usually gold and silver. The United States started out on a bimetallic standard that defined a dollar as equal to either 371.25 grains of silver or 24.75 grains of gold, fixing the relative value of silver to gold at 15 to 1. Bimetallic monetary standards date to the ancient world, and after the 12th century, they are well documented in European history. The use of two metals instead of one appeared as a reasonable means of supplementing money supplies.

A bimetallic monetary standard owes its complexity to the relationship between the price of metals fixed at a mint and the freely fluctuating market price of metals. A bimetallic system functions smoothly in the rare instance in which the market price and the mint price remain equal.

The true nature of a bimetallic standard is best examined when mint prices and market prices vary. If the mint ratio of silver to gold is 15 to 1, and the free market ratio is 16 to 1, citizens have an incentive to take silver to the mint for coinage, convert the silver coins into gold coins, and exchange the gold coins for a larger amount of silver on the free market. According to the theory of bimetallism, the actions of the mint in buying silver will lift the value of silver in the free market, reducing from 16 units to 15 units the amount of silver equal to a unit of gold in the free market. In 19th-century Genoa and Florence, a bimetallic system appeared to work according to the theory that market prices will gravitate toward mint prices.

Subsequent experience suggested that bimetallic systems do not work as the bimetallic theory suggested. Between 1792 and 1834 in the United States, the mint ratio of silver to gold was 15 to 1, while the free market ratio was 15.5 to 1. This discrepancy between mint prices and market prices led to the disappearance of gold from circulation, because no one had an incentive to take gold to the mint for coinage. Valued in

silver, gold was worth more on the open market than at the mint. When Congress tried to remedy the situation by boosting the mint ratio to 16 to 1, above the free market ratio of 15.5 to 1, gold replaced silver as circulating money. Gold rather than silver was taken to the mint for coinage, and the United States began moving toward a gold standard. Under a bimetallic system, experience taught that the metal overvalued at the mint, compared to the free market, tended to drive the other metal out of circulation as predicted by Gresham's Law.

The last half of the 19th century saw a vigorous rivalry develop between bimetallism and the gold standard. The United States and France were the strongest supporters of bimetallism, and the United Kingdom championed the cause of the gold standard. The difficulties of keeping mint prices and market prices in line were a severe drawback to bimetallic standards, and the major trading partners of the world turned to the gold standard toward the end of the century.

See also: Coinage Act of 1792, Crime of '73, Free Silver Movement, Gresham's Law, Latin Monetary Union, Monetary Law of 1803, Symmetallism

References

Chown, John F. 1994. *A History of Money*.

Klein, John J. 1986. *Money and the Economy*, 6th ed.

Kindleberger, Charles P. 1984. *A Financial History of Western Europe*.

BISECTED PAPER MONEY

Cutting notes into two or more pieces has seemed the answer to monetary and financial difficulties in more than one situation. Immediately following World War II, the government of Finland, strapped for resources, bisected notes in denominations of 500, 1000, and 5,000 markkaa. The left halves of the notes continued to circulate at a half of the original face value, without any type of government overstamp, and the right halves became a forced loan to the government.

Greece implemented a similar expedient on two occasions. In 1915, the 100-drachma note was cut into a 75-drachmai and 25-drachmai note, mainly to meet a shortage of small change. In 1925, the Greek government bisected notes as a means of raising a forced loan. Similar to the Finnish episode, the Greek government bisected circulating notes, letting one half of each note circulate at a half of its original face value and holding the other half as a loan certificate. These bisected notes also circulated without a government overstamp or overprint signifying their new value.

In 1944, Colombia faced a shortage of small change because people were hoarding coins to sell to tourists at inflated prices and to convert into buttons. The Banco de la Republica de Columbia withdrew 1-peso notes dated 1942 and 1943, bisected the notes, overprinted each half note as now equal to a half peso, and recirculated the half pesos.

Toward the close of World War I, officials of the Ottoman Empire cut 1-livre banknotes into quarters, each equaling one-quarter of a livre. New denominations and signatures were overprinted on each note. The one-quarter livre notes were apparently needed to meet the need for small change.

With the onset of World War I, Australia faced difficulty shipping currency to the 740 or so Fanning Islands. Virtually everyone on the islands was in the employ of Fanning Island Plantation Limited, a company engaged in exporting coconuts. The local manager of the plantation, with the aid of the U.S. military, arranged to have £1 "plantation notes" printed in Hawaii and delivered to the islands. At the end of the war, Australian currency again circulated on the island, and most of the plantation notes were withdrawn, but some were bisected and used as movie tickets. The left half bore a 1-shilling mark and the right half bore a 2-shilling mark, reflecting the cost of attending movies on the islands.

The Bank of England has bisected notes as a security measure. After 1948, the new state of Israel sent bisected bank notes to the Bank of England for redemption. The notes were bisected and sent in two separate shipments, as protection against robbery.

The common theme in the history of bisected paper money is the exigencies of war. Bisected notes either replace disappearing small coinage or enable the government to arrange a forced loan on the government's terms. The bisection of notes as protection against robbery does not affect money in circulation. It therefore is not a tool of monetary policy, but only a detail of handling banking operations.

See also: Greek Monetary Maelstrom

References

Beresiner, Yasha. 1977. *A Collector's Guide to Paper Money.*

Freris, A. F. 1986. *The Greek Economy in the Twentieth Century.*

BLAND–ALLISON SILVER REPURCHASE ACT OF 1878

The Bland–Allison Silver Repurchase Act of 1878 reaffirmed the status of the silver dollar as legal tender, and provided for the limited coinage of silver dollars. The Coinage Act of 1873 made no provision for the coinage of silver dollars, and dropped the silver standard from the definition of the dollar. It left preexisting silver dollars as legal tender—though none were in circulation at the time—but an amendment to coinage laws in 1874 made silver coins legal tender only for debts up to $5. The Act failed to establish so-called free silver; that is, it did not commit the government to mint all the silver brought to the mint. Silver coinage was limited and gold coinage was unlimited. Congressman Richard P. Bland of Missouri introduced the bill in the House of Representatives, and Senator William B. Allison of Iowa guided the bill through the Senate. The act provided:

> That there shall be coined, at the several mints of the United States, silver dollars of the weight of four hundred and twelve and a half grains troy of standard silver, as provided in the Act of January 18, 1837, on which shall be the devices and superscriptions provided by said act; which coins together with all silver dollars heretofore coined by the United States, of like weight and fineness, shall be legal tender at their nominal value, for all debts and dues public and private, except when otherwise provided by contract.

The bill that passed the House of Representatives provided for the free coinage of silver. It read that "any owner of silver bullion may deposit the same with any United States mint or assay office, to be coined into such dollars for his benefit upon the same terms and conditions as gold bullion is deposited for coinage under existing laws." The Senate amended the bill, substituting the free silver provision with a limit on the coinage of silver to not less than $2 million or more than $4 million per month. An amendment making the silver dollars convertible into gold failed, as did an amendment that forbade the use of silver dollars in payment for interest on the public debt. Measures to increase the silver content of silver dollars also failed.

Also, the act directed the president of the United States to invite European nations to "join the United States in a conference to adopt a common ratio between gold and silver, for the purpose of establishing internationally the use of bimetallic money, and securing fixity of relative value between those metals." This provision led to the International Monetary Conference of 1878, in which the United States urged the adoption of a gold-silver bimetallic standard, but the European nations were not interested.

President Rutherford B. Hayes vetoed the Bland–Allison Act, citing the deterioration in the value of silver and the injustice to creditors receiving payment in silver. The Senate voted 46 to 19 to override Hayes's veto, and the House voted 196 to 73 to override the veto, making the Bland–Allison Act the law of the land.

President Hayes had vowed to veto a free silver bill, and he attached little significance in the Bland–Allison bill to the provision that limited the coinage of silver. The silver advocates were not happy, and the push for free silver took on the aura of a populist movement as the century progressed. The government apparently kept its silver purchases to the minimum allowed of $2 million per month. The coinage of silver continued until 1890, when the Sherman Silver Act required the government to almost double its silver

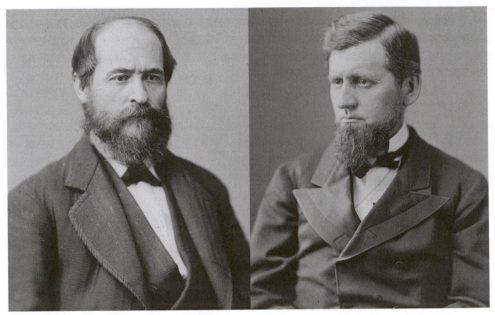

Representatives Richard Bland (left) and William Allison, authors of the Bland–Allison Silver Repurchase Act of 1878. (Library of Congress)

purchases, but substituted the issuance of treasury notes for the coinage of silver. After the enactment of the Sherman Silver Act, concern over the future of the gold standard in the United States sparked a financial panic and Congress repealed it in 1893. The government discontinued the purchase of silver under the Bland–Allison and Sherman acts.

See also: Bimetallism, Crime of '73, Free Silver Movement, Sherman Silver Act of 1890, Silver

References

Friedman, Milton. 1992. *Money Mischief: Episodes in Monetary History.*

Laughlin, J. Laurence. 1896/1968. *A History of Bimetallism in the United States.*

Meyers, Margaret G. 1970. *A Financial History of the United States.*

Nugent, Walter T. K. 1968. *Money and American Society: 1865–1880.*

BRETTON WOODS SYSTEM

From 1946 until 1971 the Bretton Woods System governed foreign exchange rate policies in the world economy. The foreign exchange rate is the rate at which one country's currency can be converted into another country's currency. The system took its name from Bretton Woods, New Hampshire, the 1944 site of the international conference of monetary officials who created it.

For an individual country, foreign exchange rates determine the cost of imported products to domestic consumers and the price of domestic exports to foreign buyers. For example, the foreign exchange rate between British pounds and U.S. dollars determines the cost of a British pound if purchased by a

U.S. dollar, and conversely, the cost of a U.S. dollar if purchased by a British pound. Therefore, this exchange rate will determine the cost in dollars of British goods sold in the United States, and the cost in pounds of U.S. goods sold in Britain. Thus, foreign exchange rates determine the competitiveness of a country's goods and services in the world market. Economies rise and fall with changes in foreign exchange rates.

Before World War I, the world economy was on a gold standard, which fixed the value of each country's currency in terms of a fixed weight of gold, thereby setting exchange rates between currencies in the process. After World War I, governments returned to the gold standard, but the result was unsatisfactory. The same governments abandoned the gold standard during the Great Depression, leaving foreign exchange rates free to float with varying degrees of government involvement.

The Bretton Woods System proposed to combine the stability of fixed exchange rates with the flexibility of floating exchange rates in a system of so-called adjustable peg exchange rates. Under an adjustable peg system, each country declared a par value of its currency in terms of gold and committed itself to buying and selling foreign currency and gold reserves to maintain this par value in foreign exchange markets. An individual country could not change the pegged value of its currency more than 10 percent without permission of the International Monetary Fund, a permanent international institution created by the Bretton Woods System.

In 1971, the Bretton Woods System came to an end because the United States needed to devalue its currency. The United States experienced a large outflow of dollars relative to inflow because of foreign expenditures from the Vietnam War and other obligations in foreign countries. By that time, however, most countries kept their currencies pegged to the value of the dollar rather than the value of gold, a practice that crept into the Bretton Woods System because gold monetary reserves were in short supply. In an effort to save the Bretton Woods System, the United States devalued its dollar relative to gold, but the outflow of dollars remained excessive. In 1973, the world economy went on a system of flexible exchange rates.

The Bretton Woods System kept alive a vestige of the gold standard when gold monetary reserves were inadequate to support the growth in world trade and money stock. It also provided stable exchange rates that reduced the risk and uncertainty associated with foreign trade, a factor that might have helped world trade recover from the disruption of world war. Perhaps its greatest accomplishment was the cooperation it fostered among trading partners in an important area of common interest.

See also: Balance of Payments, Gold Bullion Standard, Foreign Exchange Markets, International Monetary Fund, World Bank

References

Acheson, A. L. K. 1972. *Bretton Woods Revisited.*

De Vries, Margaret Garritsen. 1987. *Balance of Payments Adjustment, 1945–1986: The IMF Experience.*

Snider, Delbert. 1975. *Introduction to International Economics*, 6th ed.

BRIDE MONEY

See: Ivory, Pig Standard of New Hebrides, Whale Tooth Money in Fiji

BRITISH GOLD SOVEREIGN

During the 19th century, the British gold sovereign coin was the pride of the British Empire, the last coin to achieve significant international stature before the era of paper money superseded metallic coinage. It was probably the most successful coin ever turned out by the English mint. Toward the latter part of the nineteenth century it became the foremost coin on the stage of international trade, contributing to London's status as a financial capital of the world.

Lord Liverpool's Coinage Act of 1816 had established gold as the sole standard measure of value for English coinage, and had provided for the coinage of a 20-shilling gold piece containing 123.3 grains of gold. Under the Carolingian system, which survived in Britain until 1971, £1 equaled 20 shillings, which equaled 240 pence. The new coin was called the sovereign. Over a span of approximately 100 years, the sovereign lived up to Lord Liverpool's dictum that gold coins should be made as perfect and kept as perfect as possible.

The sovereigns were popular in foreign countries and many left England permanently. Sometimes fluctuations in exchange rates made it profitable to melt down sovereigns, and resell the gold bullion to the English mint, where it was recoined. England did not directly feel a special duty to provide coins for foreign governments. The burden of keeping the world supplied with coins, however, seemed worth bearing in light of the advantage that a sound international coin afforded English commerce. Sovereigns were also struck in Sydney, Australia, and Bombay, India.

The United Kingdom continued to mint sovereigns until 1914, when gold coinage ceased to circulate domestically. During the interwar period, the United Kingdom returned to a gold bullion standard, but gold coins were not minted. During the post–World War II era, sovereigns were minted intermittently and sold as a hedge against inflation, but not as circulating currency.

The famous historian Arnold Toynbee, in Volume 7 of his *Study of History,* cited evidence that famous coins, such as the Athenian owls continued to circulate in out-of-the-way parts of the world long after the disappearance of the government that issued them. According to Toynbee, "it may be anticipated that the English gold 'sovereign,' of which Englishmen saw the last in A.D. 1914, might still be circulating in Albania for generations, and in Arabia for centuries after that portentous date" (Toynbee, 1954, 317)

The British pound sterling was the preeminent international currency during the 19th and early 20th centuries, comparable to the U.S. dollar in the post–World War II era. The pound sterling, however, was the last international currency, the prestige of which was dependent on a precious metal coin of unquestioned weight and purity.

See also: Gold Standard, Pound Sterling

References

Challis, C. E., ed. 1992. *A New History of the Royal Mint.*

Feavearyear, Sir Albert. 1963. *The Pound Sterling: A History of English Money*, 2nd ed.

Toynbee, Arnold. *A Study of History.* Vol. 7. London: Oxford University Press, 1954.

BYZANTINE DEBASEMENT

In the 11th century CE, the Byzantine Empire began debasing its gold coinage. For seven centuries Byzantium had maintained the purity of a gold coinage inherited from the reforms of the Roman emperor Constantine I.

Until the 11th century, Byzantine gold coins show a gold content ranging between 22 and 24 carats fine, probably the highest standard of purity obtainable with the technical processes of the time. The Byzantine emperor Michael IV (r. 1034–1041) had practiced the money-changing profession before his elevation to emperor, and under his rule the Byzantine mints turned out coins varying between 12 and 24 carats. The purity of the gold coins continued to decline. Under Nicephorus III Botaneiates (r. 1078–1081), gold coinage averaged about 8 carats. By 1090, gold coins consisted of an alloy containing a bit of gold, more silver, and much more copper.

In 1092, Alexius I (r. 1081–1118) introduced a reformed coinage based on four metals. A standard gold coin was struck with a fineness of 20.5 carats, a silver/gold alloy coin was struck with a fineness of 5 and 6 carats, a billon coin was struck containing 6 to 7 percent silver with the remainder of copper, and two copper coins were struck. This system provided the Byzantine Empire with a stable coinage throughout the 12th century.

In 1204, Constantinople fell to Latin crusaders in the Fourth Crusade, and the gold coinage of Byzantium began a downward slide toward debasement. In 1253, William of Rubruck recorded an incident that occurred when the Tartars of Crimea were handed Byzantine gold

Byzantine gold solidus of Constantine VII, 945. (Werner Forman Archive)

coinage. He reported that the Tarters rubbed the coins with their fingers and then held their fingers to their noses to test by smell whether the coins were made of copper or gold. Apparently, the Tartars were trying to detect a sour smell associated with copper, and the Byzantines debased their gold coinage with copper. It was said that India produced a copper that was bright, clean, corrosion resistant, and virtually indistinguishable from gold. Supposedly, Darius had drinking cups of gold and of copper, and these cups could not be distinguished except by their smell.

In 1261, the Byzantine Empire was restored under a new dynasty, but the new government continued to strike debased gold coinage. In the 14th century, debased gold coins ranged between 11 and 15 carats, and a reformed silver coinage began to displace gold coins. The final blow to Byzantine gold coinage came when Constantinople fell to the Turks in 1453. The Emperor ordered that the sacred churches be stripped of precious metal vessels and objects and that these vessels and objects be melted down and struck into coin. The Emperor needed the coin to pay the soldiers, ditch-diggers, and others working to defend the city.

Byzantium's monetary disorder mirrored the deterioration of Byzantine society. Travelers and diplomats at the time noted the palaces, churches, and monasteries that were in ruins, and the destroyed houses and neglected fields.

The Byzantine shift from a gold coinage to a silver coinage marked a geographical shift in metallic coinage. Between the 7th century and the 12th century, the Eastern world depended primarily on a gold-based coinage, and the Western world depended on a silver-based coinage. During the 13th and 14th centuries, a reversal occurred, with the Eastern world shifting to a silver-based coinage and the Western world to a gold-based coinage.

See also: Gold

References

Durant, Will. 1957. *The Reformation*.

Hendy, Michael F. 1985. *Studies in the Byzantine Monetary Economy*.

Williams, Jonathan, ed. 1997. *Money: A History*.

C

CAISSE D'ESCOMPTE

The Caisse d'Escompte performed some of the functions of a central bank in pre-Revolutionary France. After the hyper-inflationary fiasco of John Law's Banque Royale in the 1720s, the term "bank" acquired a negative connotation in France, and it was not used until the founding of the Bank of France in 1800. Despite its name, the Caisse d'Escompte was a bank.

The failure of John Law's Banque Royale thoroughly soured the French people on banks that issued bank notes, thus retarding the continued development of French banking for several decades. In 1767 a so-called Caisse d'Escompte was established to purchase commercial paper and government securities, paying 4 percent interest (5 percent during war) and charging a 2 percent commission. The Caisse d'Escompte also enjoyed a monopoly on the issuance of coinage.

The first Caisse d'Escompte failed, but Finance Minister Turgot established by government decree another Caisse d'Escompte in 1776. This institution was empowered to discount bills of exchange and commercial paper at 4 percent, buy and sell gold and silver, and act as the government's bank. It could accept deposits from the public, but could not borrow funds at interest, or accept any debt that was not payable on demand. It could issue bank notes, because they paid no interest and were payable on demand, but could not issue less liquid assets, such as interest-bearing bonds. At first, the bank notes were not legal tender. Perhaps as a lesson learned from the Banque Royale, the Caisse d'Escompte could not engage in any commercial or maritime enterprise, including insurance.

By 1783, the French government was already inching toward the abyss of bankruptcy that would provide the spark for the French Revolution. The Caisse became overly generous issuing bank notes to purchase government debt, and public confidence suffered. The government, however, was able to float a lottery loan and repay its debt to the Caisse. Also, the capital of the Caisse was increased from 12 million to 15 million livres, the term of discounted commercial paper was restricted to 90 days, and the minimum coin reserve against bank notes was raised to 25 percent. The interest rate on commercial paper maturing past 30 days was increased to 4.5 percent. With these reforms, the Caisse won a reprieve from public distrust.

By 1783, the fiscal crisis of the ancien régime had deepened, and the Caisse and its stockholders became captives of the French government. In February of that year, the Caisse was granted a privilege to issue bank notes for 50 years in return for a loan of 70 million livres to the French government. Now the state absorbed virtually all the financial capital of the Caisse. In August public confidence crumbled, panic erupted, and the Caisse had to redeem 33 million livres in bank notes before the panic subsided. The governing council of the Caisse refused a government offer to make the bank notes legal tender, but did request that the government repay the 70 million livre loan. The government was in no shape to meet such a request, as that money would never be seen again. Public confidence continued to wane, mainly because of the close association between the Caisse and government. Panic broke out again in August 1788, draining the Caisse's coin reserves from 50 million to 25 million livres, and convertibility was suspended. Although repayment of the 70-million-livre loan was out of the question, the government came to the aid of the Caisse by making its bank notes legal tender. It also authorized the redemption of bank notes in discounted commercial paper.

The Caisse advanced more funds to the government before revolution broke out in July 1789. The revolutionary government continued to receive advances as the National Assembly debated proposals to transform the Caisse into a national bank. The National Assembly issued its own paper money, the infamous assignats, and the Caisse received payment in these inconvertible, legal tender notes. The Caisse wobbled on, still making advances to the government, until August 1793 when the revolutionary government took over its assets.

The first two French experiments with public banking, the Banque Royale and the Caisse d'Escompte, ended in hyperinflation, a reminder of the importance of discipline in note-issuing banks. England had a much more successful experience with the Bank of England. Despite two unhappy experiences with public banks, France under Napoleon established the Bank of France, and the organization of the Bank of France strongly influenced the design of the Federal Reserve System in the United States.

See also: Bank of France, Hyperinflation during the French Revolution, Law, John

References

Kindleberger, Charles P. 1984. *A Financial History of Western Europe.*

Wilson, J. S. G. 1957. *French Banking Structure and Credit Policy.*

CALDERILLA

See: Vellon

CAPITAL CONTROLS

Capital controls restrict the ability of households and businesses to hold assets denominated in foreign currency. Capital controls can restrict either the inflow of capital or the outflow of capital. Restrictions on the inflow of capital can include bans on foreign-owned deposits in domestic banks and thrifts, foreign purchase of domestically issued stocks and bonds, and foreign purchase of tangible capital such as land and plant and equipment. Restrictions on the outflow of capital can prevent citizens from holding foreign currency deposits in foreign banks and thrifts, purchasing stocks and bonds issued in foreign countries, and purchasing land, plant, and equipment in foreign countries.

Governments have various motives for imposing capital controls. In the 1970s, Germany imposed restrictions on the inflow of foreign capital out of concern for the competitiveness of its exports in foreign markets (Allen, 2001, 228). Foreigners purchasing German bonds tended to bid up the value of Germany's currency in foreign exchange markets. As the value of a country's domestic currency climbs in foreign exchange markets, its exports become costlier in foreign markets. Germany banned interest payments on large bank accounts held by nonresidents and nonresident purchase of bonds. Germany lifted these restrictions in 1981. Japan, another country concerned about the competitiveness of its exports abroad, banned foreign ownership of Japanese assets until 1980. In 1984, Japan lifted remaining capital controls (Allen, 2001, 228).

Governments more concerned about currency depreciation are more likely to impose restrictions on the outflow of capital. Currency depreciation can unleash a wave of inflation. It makes foreign imports costlier. The United Kingdom enforced restrictions on capital outflows until 1979. France and Italy restricted capital outflows until 1986 (Allen, 2001, 228). Developing countries may restrict capital outflows because they want to keep capital at home to finance domestic economic development. They may allow their citizens to convert domestic currency into U.S. dollars if the dollars go toward the purchase of a tractor or other piece of capital equipment. They may not allow their citizens to convert domestic currency into U.S. dollars to hold a bank account in a Miami bank.

The United States has been among the countries most inclined to allow the unrestricted inflow and outflow of capital. In the 1960s, however, the United States levied an "interest rate equalization tax" that removed the incentive of U.S. citizens to purchase foreign interest-bearing assets (Allen, 2001, 228). The tax lasted into the 1970s. The North American Free Trade Agreement (NAFTA) provides for the free movement of capital between Canada, Mexico, and the United States with a few exceptions. The United States prohibits foreign ownership of radio stations, and limits the percent of a U.S. airline that can be owned by foreign investors. Mexico prohibits foreign investment in its domestic oil business. In 2005, China make a takeover bid for Unical, a large U.S. oil company. Although Chinese purchase of Unical did not strictly violate U.S. law, China dropped the takeover bid after strong opposition arose in Congress. Opponents of the takeover bid were concerned about the national defense repercussions of letting China own a large stake in the U.S. oil industry.

Part of the trend toward globalization has been the removal of all capital controls by both developed and developing countries. Capital controls as economic policy have now largely lost favor. Some exceptions include cases where national defense may be at risk.

See also: Currency Crises, Hot Money

References

Allen, Larry. 2001. *The Global Financial System*.

Allen, Larry. 2005. *The Global Economic System Since 1945*.

CAPITAL FLIGHT

Capital flight usually denotes massive shifts in money from investments in one country to investments in another country. It happens when investors shun country-specific risks out of fear of currency depreciation, inflation, or political instability. Capital flight can refer to movements of money from one industry to another to escape volatility or poor returns, but that species of capital flight is less likely to threaten economic stability.

Capital flight ordinarily does not refer to the flight of human capital, which can be another problem for some countries. Sudden, massive outflows of financial capital from a specific country can shake up the entire global financial system.

A wholesale exodus of foreign capital typically indicates an expectation of domestic currency depreciation in the near future. In a currency crash, investors can easily watch foreign investments fall in value between 20 and 30 percent overnight. Out of self-defense, foreign investors and currency traders keep their fingers on the pulse of macroeconomic fundamentals in the countries where they have investments and hold currencies. Countries are good candidates for speculative attacks and currency crashes if they have

Traders at a Moscow investment firm, concerned about the flight of capital from Russia, work the phones to keep abreast of Russia's financial developments, July, 1999. (AP Photo/Alexander Zemlianichenko)

large current account deficits, large public debts, slow economic growth, and low foreign exchange reserves.

Capital flight is not limited to the activities of foreign investors. With the rise of oil prices between 2004 and 2007, Venezuela enjoyed double-digit economic growth and a large inflow of foreign currency. Under these conditions, a speculative attack on the currency and currency depreciation remained unlikely. Nevertheless, Venezuela experienced capital flight because of distrust of one person, Hugo Chavez, the president of Venezuela. The citizens of Venezuela feared that the government under his leadership might resort to confiscating their bank accounts and businesses. One economist estimated that over three years Venezuela lost one billion dollars per month because of Venezuelans protecting their capital by shifting to foreign investments (Katz, 2007). South Florida was the safe haven for much of the Venezuelan capital flight. Venezuelan bank deposits in Miami banks went by the term "CD dollars," meaning Chavez-driven. Real estate agents in Florida also saw an inflow of Venezuelan capital to purchase condominiums and other real estate.

Fear of inflation is another factor that often drives domestic investors to safeguard their capital by favoring investments in other countries. In addition, domestic investors often suspect that a debt-ridden government will default on domestic debt holders before it defaults on foreign debt holders.

Capital flight can be a serious problem for developing countries. These countries often do not generate enough domestic savings to finance economic development. They in effect have a capital shortage, which becomes worse if the available domestic capital flees to another part of

the world. One study claims that Africa is a net creditor to the rest of the world (Cera, Rishi, Saxena, 2005). The external debt that Africa owes to the rest of the world is less than the private assets Africans hold abroad when the private assets are measured by accumulated capital flight. At the same time that one of the poorest continents is a net creditor to the world, one of the richest countries, the United States, is a net debtor.

See also: Currency Crises

References

Cerra, Valerie, Meenakshi Rishi, and Sweta C. Saxena. "Robbing the Riches: Capital Flight, Institutions, and Instability." *IMF Working Paper* (WP/05/199), October 2005.

Katz, Ian. "Capital Flight South Florida." *Business Week,* June 25, 2007, p. 46.

CAROLINGIAN REFORM

Around 755 CE the Carolingian Reform established the European monetary system, which can be expressed as:

1 pound = 20 shillings = 240 pennies. Originally, the pound was a weight of silver rather than a coin, and from a pound of pure silver 240 pennies were struck. The Carolingian Reform restored the silver content of a penny that was already in circulation and was the direct descendant of the Roman denarius. The shilling was a reference to the solidi, the money of account that prevailed in Europe before the Carolingian Reform. The solidi money of account originated from the Byzantine gold coin that was the foundation of the international monetary system for more than 500 years. The shilling acted to bridge the new monetary system to the old, an important

role because debts contracted prior to the Reform were defined in solidi.

For three centuries following the reform, the only coin minted in Europe was the silver penny. Shillings and pounds were ghost monies—convenient shorthand for keeping accounts, but not actual coins. Rather than writing down "2,400 pennies," it was easier to write or say "10 pounds," and rather than write or say "12 pennies" it was easier to write or say "one shilling." The silver penny was the linchpin of the Carolingian system, but major transactions required unwieldy numbers of pennies, counting into the tens or even hundreds of thousands, and the pound and shilling were handy measures of pennies.

The Carolingian Reform was the work of Pepin the Short (r. 751–768), the first king of the Carolingian dynasty and father of Charlemagne. In addition to establishing the Carolingian monetary system, the Reform also reduced the number of mints, strengthened royal authority over the mints, and provided for uniform design of coins. All coins bore the ruler's name, initial, or title, signifying royal sanction of the quality of the coins.

Charlemagne spread the Carolingian system throughout Western Europe. The Italian lira and the French livre were derived from the Latin word for "pound." Until the French Revolution, the unit of account in France was the livre, which equaled 20 sols or sous, which in turn equaled 12 deniers. During the Revolution, the franc replaced the livre, and Napoleon's conquest spread the franc to Switzerland and Belgium. The Italian unit of account has remained the lira, and in Britain the pound-shilling-penny relationship survived until 1971.

Even in England the pennies were eventually debased, leaving 240 pennies representing substantially less than a pound of silver, and the concept of a pound as a money unit of account became divorced from a pound-weight of silver.

After the breakup of the Carolingian Empire, pennies debased much faster, particularly in Mediterranean Europe, and in 1172 Genoa began minting a silver coin equal to four pennies. Rome, Florence, and Venice followed with coins of denominations greater than a penny, and late in the 12th century Venice minted a silver coin equal to 24 pennies. By mid-13th century, Florence and Genoa were minting gold coins, effectively ending the reign of the silver penny (denier, denarius) as the only circulating coin in Europe.

See also: English Penny, Ghost Money, Pound Sterling, Silver

References
Chown, John F. 1994. *A History of Money*.
Cipolla, Carlo M. 1956. *Money, Prices, and Civilization in the Mediterranean World*.

CASE OF MIXT MONIES

At the turn of the 17th century, the *Case of Mixt Monies* (1601), one of the most famous legal-tender cases in English history, upheld the principle in English-speaking countries that sovereign governments command the prerogative to confer legal-tender status on a monetary unit.

On April 23, 1601 Elizabeth Brett purchased £200 of wares from a London merchant. Brett paid £100 up front and committed herself to pay in September another £100 in current and lawful money of England. The September payment was also to be paid in Dublin, Ireland. An important complication occurred on May 24, when Queen Elizabeth sent to Ireland certain "mixt monies" from the Tower Mint, with official stamps and inscriptions, and proclaimed that the mixed money would be the lawful and current money of Ireland, at rate of a shilling for a shilling, and a sixpence for a sixpence, and that none should refuse it. The Queen also proclaimed that after July 10 other money in Ireland would be valued only as bullion, and not as current money. The mixed money was of a baser alloy than England's coinage and was not current and lawful money in England. On the day of payment, Brett tendered payment in £100 of the mixed money, which, according to proclamation of the English crown, was current and lawful money in Ireland.

The London merchant protested, not wanting to accept the baser currency when the original contract specified sterling, and brought the dispute to court. The issue at hand was whether a time contract among parties required payment in the money that was current and lawful at the time the parties entered into the contract, or the money that was current at the time in the future when the contract specified that payment be made. The court found in favor of Brett, firmly sanctioning the right of the sovereign power to endow a monetary unit with legal-tender status.

The Constitution of the United States did not expressly confer on Congress the power to endow a monetary unit with legal tender status, and forbade the states from declaring any money as legal tender other than gold and silver coins. In 1883, the Supreme Court upheld the right of Congress to make a paper money issue legal tender, citing, among other things, that historically such a right belonged with the prerogatives of sovereignty.

See also: *Juilliard v. Greenman,* Legal Tender

References

Breckinridge, S. P. 1903/1969. *Legal Tender: A Study in English and American Monetary History.*

Dunne, Gerald T. 1960. *Monetary Decisions of the Supreme Court.*

CATTLE

A Gothic translation of the Bible (340–388 CE) made use of the Gothic term for cattle, *faihu,* to stand for "money." The English word "fee" is a descendant of the German word for cattle, *Vieh.* In the language of the Anglo-Saxons, *Vieh* evolved into the word *feoh,* which referred to cattle, property, treasury, price, reward, levy, tribute, and money. *Feoh* became "fee" in modern English, a reminder of the importance of cattle as money in early England. Likewise, the English word "pecuniary" stems from the Latin word for cattle, *pecos.* The modern monetary unity of India, the rupee, evolved from the Sanskrit word for cattle, *rupa.*

At some point in history, cattle have filled a niche in the money supply in virtually every geographical area of the globe, from the most northern Asiatic people of Russia, to the southernmost people of Africa. The Europeans brought cattle to the New World, where they again played the role of money in remote areas.

Homer's *Iliad* and *Odyssey* make numerous references to the use of oxen as a standard of value. A big tripod, the first prize in a competition, was worth 12 oxen, and a woman with many skills

Illustration from an 18th century edition of Virgil's Georgics, *written in 29 BCE. In the foreground, a horse and cow are assessed by farmers. (Jupiterimages)*

was worth four oxen. An unfired caldron was valued at one ox. When two opposing heroes held a friendly exchange of arms in the midst of battle, one set of arms was valued at 100 oxen, and the other at only nine oxen. A son of Priam, king of Troy, was captured and sold into slavery for 100 oxen, and Priam ransomed him for 300 oxen. In the *Odyssey*, one of the suitors who invaded Odysseus' house during his absence sought to appease him, offering to give him bronze and gold equal in value to 20 oxen, suggesting that oxen were a standard of value but not a medium of exchange.

One of the most advanced cattle monetary standards could be found in medieval Iceland. Icelandic law fixed the standard unit of value as a cow of three to ten winters in age. The cow had to fall within a medium size, be unblemished

and horned, have given birth to fewer than three calves, and be giving milk. A cow meeting these standards was called a *kugildi*, the standard monetary unit of medieval Iceland. According to the law, values ranged from two-thirds of a kugildi for a sterile cow to one and one-fourth kugildi for a five-year-old ox, one and one-half kugildi for a six-year-old ox, and so forth. The law also fixed the value of horses, rams, ewes, goats, and pigs in terms of kugildi.

Cattle monetary standards have survived into the modern era, particularly in Africa. In some of these areas cattle have become an ecological problem. They are overstocked because they are a prestigious form of wealth that is valued beyond the bounds of economic practicality. The excess numbers of cows have overgrazed the land, eroding the soil. Traditionally, tribal raids killed off excess supplies of cattle, helping to hold the cattle population in check. Now, a growing cattle population is an unwanted side effect of the demise of tribal warfare. Government authorities search for ways to introduce modern money as a means of reducing the cattle population and sparing the ecology. One proposal in a report of the Kenya Agricultural Commission suggested that the government issue coins bearing images of cows or goats, and provide special tokens shaped in the image of livestock and convertible into money.

Cattle were close to the ideal monetary medium in the earlier stages of economic development of many societies. They were a source of food and clothing, a store and symbol of wealth, and objects of religious veneration. Well-formed and unblemished cattle were in demand as religious sacrifices. They were movable and reproduced, earning a crude form of interest. They could fulfill all the basic roles of money, acting as a medium of exchange, a store of value, or a standard of value.

See also: Commodity Money, Commodity Monetary Standard, Goat Standard of East Africa

References
Davies, Glyn. 1994. *A History of Money.*
Einzig, Paul. 1966. *Primitive Money,* 2nd ed.

CELTIC COINAGE

The coinage of the Celtic tribes in Northern Europe and Great Britain has often been little more than a footnote in the history of the vast coinage of Greece and Rome, perhaps because some of the Celtic coins were imitations of Macedonian and Roman coins. Nevertheless, hundreds of thousands of Celtic coins have been discovered, sometimes in hoards of up to 40,000 pieces. These coins tell more about the life and thought of the Celts than any other artifacts found from this society that left few written records. Certain Celtic rulers are known to history only because of their representation on coins.

The earliest dated coins found in Britain are the golden *staters* struck by Philip II of Macedon, and imitations of this stater are among the earliest Celtic coins found in northwestern Europe. Philip's golden stater found its way to the Celts either through Celtic mercenaries in the pay of Alexander the Great, through the migration of peoples, or through a trickling trade between Britain and the eastern Mediterranean. Between the first century BCE and the first century CE, the Celts struck imitations of the Macedonian golden stater. In addi-

tion, the Celts minted coins from silver, bronze, and a mixture of tin and copper called *potin.* The potin coins were cast rather than hammered or struck and passed as everyday token money. As Celtic coinage evolved beyond the imitation stage, it abandoned the Greek images, displacing them with images of things that reflected the pastoral life of the Celts—horses, boars, or stalks of wheat, among other things.

As Rome pushed the frontiers of its empire northward and across the channel to England, indigenous Celtic coinage disappeared in favor of Roman coinage. After the disintegration of the Western Roman Empire in the fifth century CE, all coinage disappeared in the former Celtic countries for nearly 200 years. During the sixth and seventh centuries, the Merovingian Gauls began minting gold and silver coins, and the winds of trade carried these coins to Anglo-Saxon England. During the seventh century, these gold coins were progressively debased with silver.

Evidence of Anglo-Saxon gold coinage appears in the seventh century. The prime denomination of these coins was the *thrysma,* a reference to one-third of a gold solidus. These coins also succumbed to debasement, leaving silver as the principle monetary metal. Silver coins were often debased with copper or brass, until the eighth century, when full-weighted silver coins again appeared, and the English silver penny began its long history, lasting 1,000 years.

See also: English Penny

References
Allen, D. F. 1980. *Coins of the Ancient Celts.*
Davies, Glyn. 1994. *A History of Money.*
Van Arsdell, Robert D. 1989. *Celtic Coinage of Britain.*

CENTRAL BANK

Central banks are banks that serve as banker's banks, holding deposits of commercial banks and making loans to commercial banks. Typically, a central bank also acts as the government's banker, and holds a monopoly on the issuance of paper money. Commercial banks can turn to a central bank as a lender of last resort in financial crises. The Federal Reserve System in the United States, the Bank of England, the Bank of France, and the Bundesbank of Germany rank among the worlds leading central banks.

Monetary systems regulated by a central bank became the preferred form of monetary regulation in the latter part of the 19th century. The alternative to central bank regulation is what is called "free banking," pioneered by Scotland in the late 18th century. In the high tide of 19th century laissez-faire capitalism, central banks were not fully evolved, and free banking became a trend in the United Kingdom and the United States. The United States abandoned the Second Bank of the United States and turned to a form of free banking. Free banking was a system composed of a multitude of competing commercial banks, each of which issued its own bank notes. Under the free banking system, no one bank commanded a monopoly on the issuance of bank notes, which is the position that a central bank enjoys.

Free banking denotes a banking system in which note-issuing banks are established according to the same principles that govern the establishment of any other new business enterprise. The ability to start a new bank requires sufficient financial capital and public confidence to make the new bank notes acceptable to the public and to help the new bank reach a profit-making scale of operation. A new bank need not clear any legal hurdles, such as charters or grants that require a special act of government. Each bank issues its own bank notes that it converts on demand into an acceptable medium of exchange—often, but not necessarily—gold. None of the banks issue notes bearing the legal status of legal tender, or in any way favored by the government. A bank's refusal to redeem its bank notes into an acceptable medium of exchange is equivalent to a declaration of bankruptcy.

A system of independent commercial banks can cause instability in the economy. In an economic upswing, banks have an incentive to make as many loans as possible, and the loans stand an excellent chance of being repaid. This expansion of loans can turn an economic upswing into an overheated boom and inflationary spiral. In an economic downswing, on the contrary, banks find extending loans more risky, and curtail lending activities accordingly. This restriction on credit and money can push the downswing over the precipice into a depression. Individual banks, driven by the profit motive in a free banking system, add to the severity of cyclical fluctuations.

Central banks seek the public interest rather than strive to maximize profits. In the downswing, central banks supply more credit to the system rather than less. In the upswing, central banks restrict the supply of credit. The monopoly on the issuance of bank notes and commercial bank reserve deposits gives the central bank control over the money supply, interest rates, and credit conditions. These can be adjusted to counter the cyclical swings in order to smooth out these economic fluctuations.

In the 20th century, the preference for central banking over free banking is dogma. Nearly all the discussion weighing the relative merits of these two systems took place in a 50-year interval in the 19th century.

See also: Bank of England, Bank of France, Bank of Japan, Deutsche Bundesbank, Federal Reserve System, Free Banking

References

Broz, J. Lawrence. 1997. *The International Origins of the Federal Reserve System.*

Mittra, Sid. 1978. *Central Bank Versus Treasury: An International Study.*

Smith, Vera C. 1936/1990. *The Rationale of Central Banking and the Free Banking Alternative.*

Solomon, Steven. 1995. *The Confidence Game: How Unelected Central Bankers are Governing the Changed Global Economy.*

Timberlake, Richard Henry. 1978. *The Origins of Central Banking in the United States.*

CENTRAL BANK INDEPENDENCE

An independent central bank is one that is free from short-term political control. Central banks bear responsibility for controlling money stock growth, interest rates, and credit conditions. It is widely believed that political and electoral pressures favor an inflationary bias on monetary policy. Government officials often want to finance public deficits at bargain interest rates, and prefer easy money and low interest rates in months leading up to elections. Easy money policies usually bring temporary reductions in unemployment rates before kindling inflation, making easy money an attractive option right before an election. In the worst cases, where central bank independence is completely lacking, central banks automatically purchase government bonds at requests of treasuries and ministries of finance. When a central bank purchases government bonds, it enlarges domestic money stocks. Inflation correlates almost one to one with money stock growth. Governments are often content to accelerate inflation because inflation represents a tax that can be levied without approval of legislative or parliamentary bodies. Key to the rationale of the independent central bank is insistence that central banks should have one policy mission that stands above all others, and that policy mission is the maintenance of price stability, zero or near zero inflation. Other goals often mentioned in central bank charters included full employment, economic growth, and cooperation with public finance.

In the last decades of the 20th century, economists developed quantitative measures of central bank independence and employed these measures or indexes to test for correlation between central bank independence and inflation rates over a range of countries. These studies reported that inflation rates were lower in countries where central banks boasted high degrees of independence (Alesina and Summers, 1993).

Among the countries registering the highest levels of central bank independence were Germany, Switzerland, and the United States. In Germany, the independence of the central bank is strongly anchored in the law that created the central bank. In the United States, the legal basis for central bank independence is not as robust, but a strong, well-developed financial sector demands that the central bank enjoy political independence.

In the last decade of the 20th century, central bank independence became a measure of a country's commitment to inflation containment and currency stability. Other countries moved to reform central bank law and grant their central banks greater legal independence from political authorities. The European Monetary Union required as a condition of membership that its members confer legal independence on their central banks. Japan enacted new central bank legislation that gave greater autonomy to the Bank of Japan. The new law became effective in April 1998 (Ueda, 1999). It prohibited the Minister of Finance from issuing orders regarding the Bank of Japan's general business or from dismissing bank executives for opinions on policy. Critics charged that Japan's reform did not go far enough, since it allowed two government representatives to sit in on board meetings. The government representatives do not have voting rights, but they can request postponement of a vote.

Central banks argue that independence increases their credibility, which makes it easier for them to achieve their goal of price stability. Anti-inflation monetary policies often throw economies into recession. If households and businesses believe that the central bank will succeed in an anti-inflation policy, the recession will be shorter and shallower. A tight money policy induces greater loss in output and jobs if households and businesses believe that political pressure will force a central bank to ease up before the battle against inflation succeeds. So far, research has not proven the argument that central bank independence decreases the economic pain of disinflation policies (*Economist*, 1999).

See also: Central Bank

References

Alesina, Alberto, and Lawrence Summers. "Central Bank Independence and Macroeconomic Performance." *Journal of Money, Credit, and Banking* (May 1993): 151–162.

"There was an old lady . . ." *Economist,* November 20, 1993, pp. 94–97.

"Born Free." *Economist,* February 27, 1999, p. 76.

Ueda, Kazuo, *Wall Street Journal* (Eastern Edition, New York), April 8, 1999, p. 1.

CERTIFICATE OF DEPOSIT

Certificates of deposit (CDs) are interest-bearing receipts for funds deposited with banks or other depository institutions. Depositors purchase CDs in fixed denominations ($1,000, $10,000, etc.) and for a fixed time to maturity, which typically ranges between six months and five years for CDs of less than $100,000. At maturity, the owner of a CD receives the original purchase price of the CD plus interest. A purchaser of a one-year, $1,000 CD bearing 5 percent interest would receive at the end of a year $1,000, plus $50 interest. Certificates of deposit in denominations less than $100,000 are not negotiable and cannot be sold in a secondary market. Also, the issuing institution imposes a substantial penalty for early withdrawal. Since the deregulation of interest rates, CDs pay interest rates slightly higher than the treasury bill interest rates.

Negotiable certificates of deposit come in denominations of $100,000 and up. The most common denomination is $1 million, and time to maturity is usually six months or less. These CDs are sold mainly to corporations, state and local governments, foreign central banks and governments, wealthy individuals, and financial institutions. They can be can be sold in a secondary market before maturity if the owner needs cash, but most negotiable CDs are held to maturity. In 1961, First National City Bank of New York, now Citibank, first offered the large denomination CDs to its largest customers. Large CDs grew rapidly in popularity, and by 1973 the Federal Reserve Bank had lifted all interest rate ceilings on these large-denomination, negotiable CDs.

Negotiable CDs quickly became a financial instrument for the Eurodollar market. Eurodollar CDs are CDs denominated in dollars but issued by foreign banks, or foreign branches of U.S.-owned banks. Eurodollar CDs first appeared in 1966 and owed their success to the high interest rates paid by institutions beyond the reach of U.S. banking regulations and interest ceilings. In 1968, U.S. and British banks began issuing sterling pound CDs.

The small denomination CDs (less than $100,000) came into being in the late 1970s and were intended to give small savers the advantages of market interest rates. The Federal Reserve Bank includes CDs of less that $100,000 in the calculation of M2, a monetary aggregate often regarded as the best measure of the money supply. The larger CDs are included in the calculation of M3, the most broadly defined monetary aggregate.

Negotiable CDs enable banks to attract deposits that they can count on having for a fixed period without losing to withdrawal, and the owners of negotiable CDs may always sell them for cash, albeit at a sacrifice of part of the interest yield. In contrast to demand deposits, which allow depositors to withdraw funds on demand, CDs assure the bank that deposits will be left with the bank for a while, taking some pressure off the bank. For thrift

institutions, CDs are a powerful tool for raising funds, but at the price of higher interest rates for small savers.

See also: Monetary Aggregates, Money Market Mutual Fund Accounts, Negotiable Order of Withdrawal Accounts

References
Klein, John J. 1986. *Money and the Economy,* 6th ed.
Rose, Peter S. 1986. *Money and Capital Markets,* 2d ed.

CHECK

A check (or "cheque" in Britain) is a written order for a bank to pay money. The term "check" seems to have evolved from orders for payment called "Exchequer orders" that were drawn on the Exchequer, the British treasury. The British Exchequer got its name from the checkered cloth that covered the tables in the rooms where cash payments were counted, or *checked*. The cloth was either black lined with white, or green with redlined squares. Government officials, pensioners, or whoever had a claim on government revenue received written orders that authorized an Exchequer official, or teller, to pay cash in the amount owed.

Checks were not called "checks" when they first came into use in the last half of the seventh century, but were called "drawn notes." These notes, an innovation of the British goldsmith bankers, allowed an individual to order his or her goldsmith banker to make a payment of gold to a third party. In 1686, a young nobleman wrote the following drawn note on his father's banker:

> Pray do mee the favor to pay his bird-man four guineas for a paire of parakeets that I had of him. Pray

don't let anybody either my Ld or Lady know that you did it and I will be sure my selfe to pay you honestly againe. —Arthur Somerset. (Nevin & Davis, 1970, 20)

Early English checks always began with "pray" or "pray pay."

Checks grew in popularity in the 19th century. In England, the Bank Charter Act of 1844 pushed banks toward deposit banking with checks and away from the issuance of bank notes. During the Civil War, the U.S. federal government put a tax on bank notes issued by state banks, forcing the state banks to take up deposit banking with checks. In 1865, France simplified its law on the use of checks, and deposit banking with checks became widespread.

Checks are now the most common means of payment in the developed countries. They circumvent the need to carry large sums of cash and can be written for any amount. Checks are usually less acceptable than cash, but cashier's checks and certified checks are on par with cash as an acceptable means of payment. A cashier's check is issued by a bank against itself and bears the signature of a bank officer. A certified check is a check guaranteed by the bank on which the check is written. Checks are negotiable, meaning they can be transferred to another person by endorsement.

See also: Bank, Goldsmith Bankers, Promissory Notes Act of 1704

References

Davies, Glyn. 1994. *A History of Money*.
Nevin, Edward, and E. W. Davis. 1970. *The London Clearing Banks*.
Richards, R. D. 1929/1965. *The Early History of Banking in England*.

CHILEAN INFLATION

Few countries have suffered sustained inflation rates lasting for more than 100 years, often in the double-digit and occasionally triple-digit ranges, but that has been a fact of economic life in Chile. For a country that has persistently succumbed to the temptations of paper money excesses, Chile was slow to accept the idea that paper could circulate as money. Paper money was rarely observed in circulation before 1860, and Chileans were known for an abhorrence of paper money that only began to soften after 1850. From the colonial period until 1879, Chile remained on a bimetallic standard.

In 1879, Chile began its long inflationary career when Chilean banks stopped redeeming bank notes in specie, turning Chilean bank notes into inconvertible paper money. A fall in export prices precipitated the crisis, and the War of the Pacific (1879–1882) pitted Chile against Peru and Bolivia for control of the nitrate mines in the Atacama Desert.

During the 19th century, countries on a bimetallic or gold standard often suspended convertibility during war, but Chile never permanently returned to convertibility, although abortive efforts were made in 1887, 1895 through 1898, and 1925 through 1931. Although success in the War of the Pacific gave Chile control over the nitrate mines, Chile's exports continued to fall. Between 1878 and 1915, Chile's share of the world's copper production declined from 44 percent to less than 5 percent. The decline in export earnings, coupled with heavy foreign debt and internal inflation, crippled Chile's effort to reassert monetary order.

Between 1879 and 1904, inflation registered an average annual rate of 2 percent, a modest inflation rate but significant in light of the worldwide trend of deflation during that period. Annual inflation averaged 7 percent between 1904 and 1931. By 1914, prices were growing 10 percent a year. From 1931 until 1955, despite the depression decade, price increases averaged 20 percent. In 1931, inflation stood at 8.5 percent, rose to 15.1 percent by 1940, and crested at 47.8 percent in 1952.

From the 1950s through the 1960s, annual inflation rates fluctuated in the 20 to 40 percent range. In 1971, inflation, repressed by wage and price controls, fell to 20 percent, but in 1972 inflation soared to 178 percent. As inflation accelerated in 1973, General Pinochet led a military coup that overthrew the democratically elected socialist president, Salvador Allende, and established a military dicta-

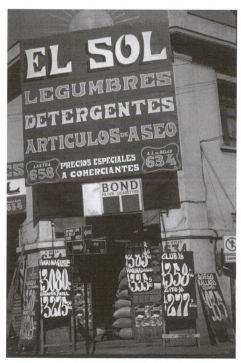

High prices at a market in Santiago, Chile reflect inflation, 1981. (Robert Nickelsberg/Time Life Pictures/Getty Images)

torship noted for brutality and violations of human rights.

As inflation accelerated in the 1970s, rising to 374 percent in 1974, the right-wing military dictatorship used its power to enforce a strict monetarist anti-inflation policy, relying on restricted monetary growth rather than price controls to tame inflation. Monetarists argue that inflation is solely a function of excessive monetary growth rate, and the optimal economic policy is a constant, predictable 3 to 5 percent annual growth rate in the money supply. The Chicago school of economics, a leader in monetarist economic theory, had become influential in Chilean universities, and the Chilean war against inflation became a test case of the monetarists' anti-inflation policy.

Despite the strict monetarists' diet of slow money growth, inflation subsided slowly in Chile. By 1981, the inflation rate stood at a hefty 35.1 percent, but it fell below the 10 percent level the following year. A major economic slowdown in 1982 led the government to ease up on its unforgiving monetary policy and inflation began to creep up. Toward the end of the decade, inflation was in the 30 percent range. Chile began the 1990s faced with an inflation problem of moderate proportions by its own historical standards. Between 1990 and 1999, inflation in Chile averaged 11.5 percent (International Monetary Fund, 2008). Between 2000 and 2008, annual inflation in Chile remained below 5 percent until 2008, when inflation rose to 8.9 percent (International Monetary Fund, 2008).

See also: Hyperinflation in Argentina, Hyperinflation in Brazil, Hyperinflation in Bolivia, Hyperinflation in Post–World War I Germany, Inflation and Deflation

References

Behrman, Jere R. 1976. *Foreign Trade Regimes and Economic Development: Chile.*

International Monetary Fund. 2008 *World Economic Outlook,* October 2008.

Valdes, Juan Gabriel. 1995. *Pinochets' Economists.*

CHINESE SILVER STANDARD

By the early 20th century, China and Mexico were the only large countries remaining on a silver standard, and China was by far the largest. As the world's major trading partners abandoned the gold standard in the early 1930s, China found itself in the clutches of worldwide monetary turmoil and abandoned the silver standard.

After the discovery of vast silver deposits in the New World, silver flowed to the Far East, sometimes directly from Latin America and Mexico, and became the metallic currency of choice in that area. After the opening of China to European trade in the mid-19th century, and the subsequent influx of foreign investment, China ran a balance of trade surpluses. Excesses of exports over imports brought in a steady stream of silver, which became the basis of China's currency.

Silver bullion circulated in different weights and shapes. Silver dollars, some minted in China and others in foreign countries, such as the United States, Mexico, or the United Kingdom, circulated along with subsidiary silver coins and copper coins. In 1895, the United Kingdom, itself on the gold standard, began issuing silver dollars, called "trade dollars," specifically for trade with the Far East. British trade dollars bore inscriptions in English, Chinese, and Malay-Arabic. Briefly during the latter 19th century, the United States issued a special trade dollar designed specifically to compete with the Mexican dollar in Far Eastern trade. The Chinese called these various silver dollars *yuan,* meaning "round things," and yuan became the standard monetary unit in China and modern Taiwan.

At the end of the 19th century, Chinese banks reintroduced bank notes into China, and banks held silver as reserves. The public demanded that banks maintain the convertibility of bank notes into silver, and banks that suspended convertibility saw their bank notes depreciate rapidly. In 1916, Yuan Shih-kai, president of the Republic of China, tried to enforce a regime of inconvertible paper money, instructing banks to cease redemption of bank notes and directing the public to accept notes at par relative to silver coinage. Yuan Shih-kai wanted to seize the silver reserves in government banks and divert those resources to help make himself emperor. The public put up a strong resistance and the effort failed. Provincial governments met with similar resistance to issues of inconvertible bank notes. When the Bank of Three Eastern Provinces could not redeem its notes in silver, the Manchurian government decreed the death penalty for anyone who circulated these notes at less than par. Nevertheless, irredeemable bank notes circulated at heavy discounts.

By 1922, the government banks had retrieved their irredeemable bank notes, and the public's confidence in bank notes strengthened. Banks began publishing reports of their reserve positions and by the eve of the worldwide depression of the 1930s, sound bank notes had virtually displaced inconvertible bank notes issued by provincial banks.

At the beginning of the depression, prices—including the price of silver—fell precipitously in the gold standard countries, making China's exports much more attractive in foreign trade, but making imported goods more expensive in China. China experienced a mild boom while most of the world slid into depression. As the world's major trading partners abandoned the gold standard and began reinflating their economies, China began to feel some of the effects of the depression. The Japanese invasion of Manchuria in 1931 reinforced the forces of depression, causing them to be felt in China. When the United States abandoned the gold standard in 1933 and began reinflating its economy, the price silver began to rise significantly, and China's silver standard began to change from an advantage to a disadvantage. The rising price of silver meant that Chinese-produced goods were more expensive to the rest of the world, and foreign goods imported into China were cheaper.

The crowning blow to China's silver standard came with the enactment by the U.S. Congress of the Silver Purchase Act of 1934. This law authorized the U.S. government to purchase large amounts of silver, sufficient to significantly raise the market value of silver. As the market value of silver rose, Chinese silver was melted down and exported, decreasing the Chinese money supply. Also, the high price of silver made Chinese goods expensive in foreign markets, sharply cutting into Chinese exports. To avoid the deeper ramifications of a deflationary spiral, China officially abandoned the silver standard in 1935. With the abandonment of the silver standard and the Japanese invasion in 1937, China began a descent into a hyperinflation debacle.

See also: Balance of Payments, Hyperinflation in China, Silver, Silver Purchase Act of 1934

References

Chang, Kia-Ngau. 1958. *The Inflationary Spiral: The Experience in China: 1939–1950.*

Friedman, Milton. 1992. *Money Mischief: Episodes in Monetary History.*

CLIPPING

Clipping was a form of grassroots coinage debasement that flourished in the Middle Ages and the early modern period. Clipping occurred when private citizens removed (or clipped) small bits of precious metal from the circumference of coins and then passed the clipped coins on at face value. It required a certain amount of judgment to know how much metal could be removed without rendering a coin unacceptable in payment for goods and debts. Moneychangers, merchants, and other private individuals engaged in clipping accumulated valuable stores of gold and silver bullion. The law dealt harshly with clippers and counterfeiters, both of whom often met their fate at the gallows. The adoption of milled-edge coinage in the seventh and eighth centuries was intended to make clipping more easily detected, and therefore more difficult.

A variation of grassroots debasement, equal in effect to clipping, was known as sweating. Sweating was performed by putting gold or silver coins in a leather bag and shaking the bag violently, removing gold and silver from the coins

Cut farthing of Edward "the Confessor," minted in England, Anglo-Saxon, 1042–1066. (British Museum/Art Resource, NY)

in a process that more closely resembled the natural wear and tear that coins sustained from jingling in pockets and purses over several years of circulation. It was an accelerated process of natural wear and tear and captured small but valuable amounts of gold and silver.

The activities of clippers and sweaters, coupled with natural wear and tear, would eventually lead to the complete breakdown of a coinage system. If a freshly minted coin contained 20 grains of silver, but the typical coin circulating at face value averaged only 18 grains, then the 20-grain coins in circulation would be culled out and melted down for bullion or shipped to foreign countries, where they would be sold at a premium. Under these conditions, governments would stop striking new coins until all the clipped coins were called in under a program of recoinage, perhaps minting new coins at a lower weight that the original coins.

The growth of paper money, bank deposits, milled-edge coins, and token coinage rendered the methods of the clipper obsolete, and clipping ceased to be an issue faced by monetary authorities.

See also: Act for Remedying the Ill State of the Coin, Milled-Edge Coinage

References
Challis, C. E. 1978. *The Tudor Coinage.*
Chown, John F. 1994. *A History of Money.*

CLOTH

From the Far East to Europe and Africa, cloth has surfaced as a medium of exchange and a unit of measurement. During the second millennium, silk cloth passed as money in China, circulating in pieces of a uniform size. The Chinese word *pu* began as a word referring to cloth, but came to denote "money," reflecting the importance of silk cloth as money. Silk money survived the advent of metallic coinage in China. In 460 BCE, the government formed three separate boards for management of currency, one for gems, one for gold, and one for coins and silk.

Northern Europe furnishes numerous instances of cloth money during the medieval era. The Baltic Slavs used linen as a means of payment in commercial transactions, and small strips of thin textiles circulated as coin. In the language of the Northern Slavs, the word *platni* meant "linen," and the word for "to pay" was *platiti*. Up to the 14th century, Sweden made use of a hand-woven woolen cloth currency called *wadmal*. Creditors had to accept wadmal in the payment of money debts, and coined money and wadmal were linked in a fixed exchange ratio. Medieval Iceland also called its hand-woven woolen cloth money wadmal. Iceland's wadmal met the need for a general standard of value, circulated as money, and even in modern times parts of Iceland valued land in units of wadmal. Certain districts of medieval Norway accepted cloth as legal-tender currency, and a district of medieval Germany had a cloth standard that set a certain length of cloth to *Reilmark,* or *Gewandmark,* predecessors of the modern day German mark. In pre-Christian Prussia, pieces of cloth adorned with bronze rings passed as money.

Cloth also enjoyed wide acceptance as money, lasting in some cases into the early 20th century, in several areas of Africa. In Zambia, calico found favor as currency and was used in wages and marriage dowries. On the west coast of Africa, a unit of money called a *long* served as a unit of account. Originally, a long referred to a length of cloth, but later evolved into an abstract unit of account used only for setting and quoting the prices. White shirts of the sort commonly worn for everyday dress circulated as money in parts of equatorial Africa. In the Congo, barter transactions were conducted on the basis of prices set in pieces of cloth. A piece was 12 yards of standard quality cloth. In districts of the Sudan, the unit of account for pricing moderately priced goods was a bundle of 20 cotton threads.

Certain tribes in the Philippines used European cloth as a monetary standard. A monetary unit of cloth was a piece of

cloth as long as the spread of a man's arms. The natives priced jars, glassware, gongs, and perishable items in terms of cloth, and fines were paid in cloth. An adulterer paid a fine of 215 meters of cloth. In Borneo, standard rolls of cloth were a sort of legal tender of money.

In the 19th century, cloth passed as money on Button Island of the Indonesian archipelago. The cloth money was called *kampuna,* meaning the "head cloth of a king," and it was woven on official looms, which validated its use as currency. Ordinary cloth bore no special value as currency and was traded only for its utility.

See also: Commodity Monetary Standard

References

Einsig, Paul. 1966. *Primitive Money,* 2nd ed.
Quiggin, A. Hingston. 1949. *A Survey of Primitive Money.*
Williams, Jonathan, ed. 1997. *Money: A History.*

COCOA BEAN CURRENCY

At the time of the Spanish conquest, cocoa bean currency in the commercially active economy of the Aztec empire ranked above gold dust as the principal form of money. The Aztecs kept cocoa beans in bags holding 24,000 beans. Columbus met with a Yucatan ship hauling goods to trade for cocoa. One early observer of the Aztec society, Peter Martyr, noted regarding Aztec money: "Oh, blessed money which yieldeth sweete and profitable drinke for mankinde, and preserveth the possessors thereof free from the hellish pestilence of avarice because it cannot be long kept hid underground" (Einzig, 1966, 175). The Aztecs also used copper hatchets as money, and Cortez, in a letter to the King of Spain in 1524, referred to a copper hatchet as worth 8,000 cocoa beans. During the 18th century, reports from Mexico indicated that the cultivation of cocoa beans was restricted to maintain the value of cocoa beans as money. Cocoa bean currency was not even spared the episodes of debasement that haunted the early history of precious metal currencies. Debasement of cocoa bean currency was accomplished simply by removing the stone of the cocoa bean and replacing it with dirt.

Girolamo Benzoni, writing in 1572, said that the Spanish inhabitants of Guatemala held their wealth in the form of cocoa. Henry Hawks, a merchant who spent five years in Central America, writing in the same year, claimed that in Guatemala cocoa "goeth currently for money in any market or faire, and may buy any flesh, fish, bread or cheese, or other things" (Einzig, 1966, 177). When Thomas Cavendish landed at Aguatulco in 1587, he found 400 bags of cocoa beans stored in the Customs House, "every bag whereof is worth ten crownes." Master Francis Petty, who accompanied Cavendish, wrote, "These cacaos goe among them for meate and money. For a hundred and fifty of them are in the value of one rial of plate" (Einzig, 1966, 177). To preserve the local supply of money, Guatemala enacted an ordinance banning the export of cocoa unless payment was in coin. Cocoa bean currency stretched into Latin America. In 1712, a royal decree in Brazil listed cocoa, cloves, sugar, and tobacco as commodities that legally circulated as money, and troops were paid in these commodities. In 19th-century Nicaragua, 100 cocoa beans bought a serviceable slave.

The use of cocoa beans as money continued into the 19th century, and remote Indian tribes in Mexico and Central America continued to make small change with cocoa beans into the 20th century. Within these tribes, the smallest silver coin equaled 40 cocoa beans.

The history of cocoa beans as money stands as a reminder that money evolves in a social context. Money is something that everyone will accept in exchange. Any product that holds up as universally acceptable to everyone necessarily has social significance, whether it be cocoa beans among the Aztecs, or cigarettes in a prisoner-of-war camp. Cocoa beans were perishable and bulky to transport in large quantities—serious drawbacks as a form of money. Aztecs, however, placed an important ceremonial value on a bitter cocoa bean drink, the precursor to hot chocolate. Montezuma, the Aztec ruler of Mexico, always drank one of these drinks before visiting his harem.

See also: Commodity Monetary Standard

References
Berdan, Frances F. 1982. *The Aztecs of Central Mexico: An Imperial Society*.
Einzig, Paul. 1966. *Primitive Money,* 2nd ed.
Weatherford, Jack. 1997. *The History of Money*.

COINAGE ACT OF 1792 (UNITED STATES)

The United States Constitution, in Article I, Section 8, conferred on Congress the power "to coin Money, regulate the Value thereof, and of foreign Coin." The first legislation Congress passed under this authority granted by the Constitution was the Coinage Act of 1792. The act was based on a report that Alexander Hamilton made to Congress a year earlier.

The act provided for the establishment of a mint, including naming the officers, specifying their duties, and setting their compensation. The act called for what was known as free coinage, indicating that anyone could bring gold or silver bullion to the mint for coinage at no cost to the owner. The gold and silver coins struck at this mint were legal tender for all debts, public and private.

The act also provided "that the money of account of the United States should be expressed in dollars or units, dismes or tenths, cents or hundredths, and milles or thousandths, a disme being a tenth part of a dollar, a cent the hundredth part of a dollar, and a mille the thousandth part of a dollar." The dollar was intended to be same in value as the Spanish milled dollar that was then in circulation in the former colonies. The act called for the minting of eagles, equivalent to $10; half-eagles, equivalent to $5; and quarter-eagles, equivalent to $2.50. The eagles were gold coins. Coins minted in smaller denominations were made of silver

David Rittenhouse, first director of the U.S. mint. (Library of Congress)

and included dollars, half-dollars, quarter-dollars, dismes, and half-dismes. The act also called for minting cents and half-cents from copper. The act held out the threat of the death penalty to discourage any employee of the mint from secretly debasing the coins (reducing the precious metal content) for personal gain or embezzling precious metals or freshly minted coins.

President Washington placed responsibility for the operation of the mint under the secretary of state, much to the disappointment of Alexander Hamilton, who was then secretary to the treasury. Hamilton later made his disappointment known, and Washington moved control of the mint to the treasury department. David Rittenhouse, an eminent scientist and philosopher from Philadelphia, became the first director of the mint.

Imperfections in the system soon made themselves apparent. The act had established an official exchange ratio between gold and silver at 15 pounds of silver to one pound of gold. It turned out that gold was worth more than 15 pounds of silver in world markets, causing gold to leave the United States. The overvalued silver coins should have stayed in the United States, but the freshly minted U.S. dollars were more attractive than the Spanish dollars that actually contained more silver. Therefore, the U.S. dollars tended to disappear. The Coinage Act of 1793 made some foreign coins legal tender in the United States, and the Spanish dollar circulated as legal-tender money in the United States until 1857.

Although much of the culture and the social institutions of the early United States came from Great Britain and France, the dollar is one institution borrowed from the Spanish, a descendent of the Spanish-milled dollar that circulated in the American colonies. *Milled* referred to the corrugated edge, now universal among coins, that made evident any clipping or other efforts to remove precious metal from the edges. Alexander Hamilton, a strong admirer of British political institutions, recommended the dollar to Congress as the money of account in the United States, citing the fact that the Spanish dollar had been in actual use in all the states and that the decimal system was superior to the duodecimal of England.

See also: Coinage Act of 1834, Dollar

References

Chown, John F. 1994. *A History of Money.*

Hepburn, A. Barton. 1924/1967. *A History of Currency in the United States.*

Watson, David K. 1899/1970. *History of American Coinage.*

COINAGE ACT OF 1834 (UNITED STATES)

The Coinage Act of 1834 put the United States on the monetary path that led to the adoption of the gold standard. By increasing the official value of gold, the act caused gold to flow to the mint for coinage because its mint price exceeded its free market price. Holders of silver found it advantageous to convert silver into gold at free market prices, and take gold to the mint, rather than to take silver directly to the mint. Thus the flow of silver to the mint vanished.

The Coinage Act of 1792 had overvalued silver relative to gold. According to official values fixed by the act of 1792, 15 ounces of silver equaled one ounce of gold. In the free market,

one ounce of gold purchased nearly 16 ounces of silver, meaning gold was worth more on the free market than at the mint. Holders of gold could obtain a larger value of coinage in face value by first purchasing silver on the free market and taking silver to the mint for coinage, rather than taking gold directly to the mint. Therefore, only silver arrived at the mint for coinage, and gold coins disappeared from circulation as gold coinage came to a standstill. The overvaluation of silver in the act of 1792 was unintentional and—in the eyes of many observers—cost the states their prosperity.

Senator Thomas Hart Benton, one of the staunchest supporters of gold in United States history, apparently wanted to attract Latin American gold to the United States. In the book Benton wrote of his 30 years in the United States Senate, *Thirty Years' View,* he put the issue in crystal clear terms:

> Gold goes where it finds its value, and that value is what the laws of the great nations give it. In Mexico and South America, the countries which produce gold, and from which the United States must derive their chief supply, the value of gold is 16 to 1 over silver; in the island of Cuba it is 17 to 1; in Spain and Portugal, it is 16 to 1; in the West Indies it is the same. It is not to be supposed that gold will come from these countries to the United States, if the importer is to lose one dollar in every sixteen that he brings; or that our gold will remain with us, when an exporter can gain a dollar upon every fifteen that he carries out. Such results would be contrary to the laws of trade, and therefore we must place

the same value upon gold that other nations do, if we wish to gain any part of theirs, or regain any part of our own. (Hepburn, 1924, 58).

Congress enacted the Coinage Act of 1834 on June 28 with only 36 representatives and seven senators voting against the legislation. Another piece of legislation, passed on the same day, gave Spanish dollars minted in the newly independent states of the former Spanish colonies the same legal-tender status enjoyed by the Spanish dollars minted in Spain.

The Coinage Act of 1834 decreased the grains of pure gold in the *eagle,* a $10 gold piece, from 247.4 grains to 232 grains, a decrease of 6.26 percent. The gold content of the two other gold coins minted by the treasury, the half-eagle and quarter-eagle, were decreased proportionately. The act left the silver content of silver coinage untouched. The increase in mint value of gold raised the official ratio of silver to gold from 15 to 1 to 16 to 1, essentially making an ounce of gold more valuable in terms of a fixed weight of silver.

By 1834, the United States was on a de facto silver standard, and term contracts were written under the expectation that payment would be made in silver dollars, a factor that might account for the interest in keeping silver a part of the monetary standard. Proponents of the Coinage Act of 1834 saw clearly, however, that the provisions of the act pushed the United States toward a de facto gold standard. The passage of the Coinage Act of 1834 marked the first time that the U.S. Congress debated monetary questions, and it revealed that the majority opinion in the United States favored a gold standard over a silver standard, a view that was in step with future world trends. The California gold discoveries of the 1840s further depressed the market value of gold relative to the mint price, further adding to gold showing up at the treasury for coinage, and the sight of a silver dollar became a rarity.

See also: Coinage Act of 1792, Free Silver Movement, Gold Standard

References

Hepburn, A. Barton. 1924/1967. *A History of Currency of the United States.*

Nettels, Curtis P. 1962. *The Emergence of a National Economy.*

Schwarz, Ted. 1980. *A History of United States Coinage.*

COINAGE ACT OF 1853 (UNITED STATES)

The Coinage Act of 1853 nudged the United States closer to a single monetary standard based on gold. It provided for the coinage of subsidiary silver coins to support small transactions without endangering the precedence of gold as the preeminent monetary metal.

The conditions that spurred Congress to approve the Coinage Act of 1853 grew directly out of the Coinage Act of 1834. That act had decreased the gold metal content of gold coins relative to face value, drawing gold to the mint for coinage at the expense of silver. At United States mint prices, 16 ounces of silver matched in value an ounce of gold, more ounces of silver than was needed to purchase an ounce of gold on the free market. The flow of silver to the mint fell to a trickle, and speculators melted down silver coins and sold them for bullion.

The proponents of the act of 1834 had foreseen that the act would lift gold to preeminence as the primary monetary standard, and that overvalued gold coins would drive undervalued silver coins out of circulation. They did not anticipate that the disappearance of the small denomination silver coinage would impose a hardship on retail businesses. Under the pre–Civil War coinage system, the mint struck the gold eagle, gold half-eagle, and gold quarter-eagle in face values of $10, $5, and $2.50, respectively. In silver coinage, the mint struck the silver dollar, the half-dollar, the quarter, the dime, and half-dime. Ten dimes had the same silver content as a silver dollar. As speculators sold silver coinage for bullion, merchants and consumers stood without the coinage to settle minor transactions.

The Coinage Act of 1853 reduced the silver content of the half-dollar, the quarter, the dime, and half-dime, but left the silver content of the silver dollar untouched. The silver content of a silver dollar remained at 371.5 grains of pure silver, but a dollar's worth of half dollars, quarters, dimes, and half-dimes, dropped to only 345.6 grains of pure silver, about a 7 percent reduction. The treasury continued to stand ready to accept unlimited amounts of silver for coinage into silver dollars, but the act authorized the treasury's purchase of only limited amounts of silver to mint subsidiary coinage, that is, half-dollars, quarters, dimes, and half-dimes. The act gave the treasury the authority to decide the amount of silver to purchase for subsidiary coinage, an amount that would necessarily be less than holders of silver would want to bring to the treasury at overvalued prices. The purpose of the act was to maintain gold as the primary monetary metal while furnishing the public with a subsidiary silver coinage. Theoretically, the United States remained on a bimetallic standard because silver dollars enjoyed a legal-tender status, but in practice no silver dollars were coined.

The act provided that subsidiary coinage was legal tender for amounts up to $5, raising issues that would surface later when the government made paper money legal tender. A flavor of how antagonistic feelings ran on this issue is echoed in the remarks of the bill's major opponent, Andrew Johnson, later vice president, and then president upon the death of Lincoln.

> I look upon this bill as the merest quackery—the veriest charlatanism—so far as the currency of the country is concerned. The idea of Congress fixing the value of currency is an absurdity, notwithstanding the *language* of the Constitution—not the meaning of it . . . If we can by law make $107 out of $100, we can by the same process make it worth $150. Why, Sir, of all the problems that have come up for solution, from the time of the alchemists down to the present time, none can compare with that solved by this modern Congress. They alone have discovered that they can make money—that they can make $107 out of $100. If they can increase it to that extent, they can go on and increase it to infinity, and thus, by the operation of the mint, the government can supply its own revenues. (Watson, 1970, 110)

The Coinage Act of 1853 achieved its purpose. Small coinage increased in circulation, and after 1857 foreign coins were no longer legal tender in the United States. After the outbreak of the Civil War, all metallic coinage went into hiding, and the United States turned to an inconvertible paper standard. In the last quarter of the 19th century, the battle between gold and silver was fought anew before the United

States settled firmly on a gold standard, without even the pretence of a bimetallic standard based on gold and silver.

See also: Bimetallism, Coinage Act of 1792, Coinage Act of 1834, Free Silver Movement, Gold Standard

References

Chown, John. 1994. *A History of Money.*

Hepburn, A. Barton. 1924/1967. *A History of Currency of the United States.*

Laughlin, J. Laurence. 1896/1968. *A History of Bimetallism in the United States.*

Schwarz, Ted. 1980. *A History of United States Coinage.*

Watson, David K. 1899/1970. *History of American Coinage.*

COINAGE ACT OF 1965 (UNITED STATES)

The Coinage Act of 1965 removed all silver content from dimes and quarters, and cut the silver content of half-dollars from 90 to 40 percent.

Two separate trends conspired to substantially reduce the use of silver coinage. First, a coin shortage was making itself felt despite a triple increase in mint output of coins from mid-1959 to mid-1964. The rapid growth in vending machines, pay telephones, parking meters, and sales taxes fueled a corresponding increase in the demand for small change, including dimes, quarters, and half-dollars. Also, collectors may have been absorbing coins at a faster clip. By mid-1964, merchants were facing difficulty making change, and some banks were rationing dimes and nickels.

Second, world demand for silver exceeded world production, and the U.S. treasury had been filling the gap by selling off silver reserves. By mid-1965 the treasury faced a serious depletion of its silver reserves, and the market price of silver was rising, raising the specter that the price of silver might exceed the trigger price of $1.3824, at which point the silver content of small change would exceed the face value. Once the price of silver rose above $1.3824, silver coins would be worth more melted down and sold as bullion, leading to a disappearance of silver coins from circulation.

The treasury proposed the complete removal of all silver from coinage, preferring to completely circumvent the threat that the price of silver would rise high enough to make melting down silver coins profitable. The role of silver in the monetary affairs of the United States, however, has been a politicized issue for over a century, and Congress compromised by maintaining a 40 percent silver content in half-dollars. The act provided for the coinage of dimes and quarters composed of a cupronickel plating over a copper core. Cupronickel is a copper and nickel alloy.

See also: Free Silver Movement, Silver, Silver Purchase Act of 1934

References

Jastram, Roy W. 1981. *Silver, the Restless Metal.*

Rickenbacker, William F. 1966. *Wooden Nickels, Or the Decline and Fall of Silver Coins.*

Schwarz, Ted. 1980. *A History of United States Coinage.*

COMMODITY MONETARY STANDARD

Under a commodity monetary standard, a medium of exchange and unit of account is either a commodity or a claim to a commodity, and the commodity is a good that would have value even if it were not used for money. Put differently, the commodity has an intrinsic value, in contrast to the paper money of an inconvertible paper standard that has value only by government fiat and is called fiat money for that reason.

In the purest form of commodity money, the commodity itself may change hands. History furnishes numerous examples of livestock, necessary staples, stones, shells, metals, and so on, that have acted as a medium of exchange, a unit of account, a standard of deferred payment, and a store of value. The most famous and enduring commodity standard in history is the gold standard, but silver can boast of a history as a monetary standard that almost rivals the history of gold.

In more sophisticated commodity standards, paper claims to the commodity change hands in exchange, while the commodity itself is stored in warehouses or vaults. The gold standard of the 19th and early 20th centuries perhaps offers the best example of a commodity standard in which paper claims to the commodity replace the commodity itself as the circulating medium. Less-developed countries of the world operated silver standards on the same principle, until inconvertible paper standards replaced all precious metal commodity standards in the 20th century.

Although gold, and to a lesser extent silver, have been the most widely embraced commodities to act as the basis of the more sophisticated commodity standards, they do not stand alone. The colonists of Virginia stored tobacco in warehouses and issued tobacco notes representing titles of ownership to the tobacco. The colonists quoted prices in tobacco, and tobacco notes exchanged hands instead of tobacco itself. The colonists could freely convert tobacco notes into tobacco as needed. In the 18th and 19th centuries, Japan operated a similar system based on rice. Rice notes circulated as money, and even the value of gold and silver coins was expressed in terms of rice. In 1760, the Japanese government specifically forbade landowners from issuing rice notes in excess of the amount of rice they had stored, a common abuse in all commodity systems using paper claims to a commodity. Although in practice gold and silver have dominated commodity standards, in theory a whole range of commodities could serve the same purpose.

Under a commodity standard, the value of money is the price, determined by supply and demand, of a commodity that is costly to produce. A government agency sets the price at which it stands ready to buy and sell the commodity, and production of the commodity will expand to a level necessary to stabilize prices. If the official price of gold is $35 per ounce, as it was for a number of years under the U.S. gold standard, gold production expands to the point at which an ounce of gold costs just under $35 to produce. If gold is not profitable to produce at $35 per ounce, gold production contracts, reducing the world money supply and causing prices to fall. The average level of prices continues to fall, reducing the cost of producing gold, until gold becomes profitable to produce at $35 per ounce, at which point the world money supply (and prices) stabilize. If gold is highly profitable to produce at $35 per ounce, the gold production expands, adding to the world's money stock, and prices rise, increasing the costs of producing gold relative to its selling price. Theoretically, gold production expands and contracts to keep price stable, creating a self-correcting mechanism for maintaining price stability. Although governments have more experience with the gold standard than other commodity standards, in theory the same principles work regardless of the commodity.

More complicated commodity standards can be devised using more than one commodity. The bimetallic standard that figured prominently in nineteenth-century monetary history was a commodity standard based on gold and silver. The inflation surge of the 1970s renewed interest in commodity standards among monetary economists. One idea that surfaced was a variable commodity standard based on a composite commodity. A composite commodity is a weighted combination of several commodities. Thus a variable commodity standard makes a currency convertible into a weighted basket of several commodities.

See also: Bimetallism, Commodity Money, Gold Standard, Rice Currency, Symmetallism, Variable Commodity Standard, Virginia Tobacco Act of 1713

References

Bordo, Michael D. "The Classical Gold Standard: Some Lessons for Today." *Monthly Review* (May 1981): 2–17.

Fisher, Irving. 1911. *The Purchasing Power of Money.*

Yeager, Leland B. "Stable Money and Free-Market Currencies." *Cato Journal* 3 (Spring 1983): 305–326.

COMMODITY MONEY (AMERICAN COLONIES)

Stable commodities produced in the American colonies often filled the gap in the colonial money supply left by the outflow of most hard specie for European goods. Colonial assemblies sanctioned commodity money as legal tender and set the price of commodities for the retirement of public debts.

Typical of colonial assembly legislation sanctioning the use of commodity money was an act of the South Carolina assembly adopted in 1687. This act read:

> that all debts, accounts, contracts, bargains and judgments, and executions thereupon . . . which are not made expressly for silver or money or some other particular commodity att a certain price shall and may bee paid and discharged by Corne att two shillings the bushel, Indian Peas at two shillings six pence the bushel, English Peas at three shillings sixpence the bushel, Pork at twenty Shillings per cwt., Beefe at twopence the pound, Tobacco at two pence the pound, Tar at eight shillings per barrell. (Brock, 1975, 9)

Around the same time New York allowed pork, beef, and winter wheat to serve as money, and east New Jersey included wheat, Indian corn, butter, pork, beef, and tobacco as commodity money. New Hampshire's list of commodities serving as money for the years 1701 through 1709 had eight kinds of boards or staves and four kinds of fish, as well as pork, beef, peas, wheat, and Indian corn. The Caribbean colonies often made use of sugar as a medium of exchange, and tobacco dominated the commodity money supply in Maryland and Virginia. Curtis P. Nettels quotes a statement from the Virginia House of Burgesses regarding the salaries of the clergy, which states that "[f]or every marriage by license the laws give them twenty shillings or two hundred pounds of tobacco . . . and if at a private house they marry any person they have for it one hundred pounds of tobacco at least" (Nettels, 1934, 217). The difference between a marriage by license and a marriage at a private house is unclear, but tobacco was an important means of paying clergy.

Colonial assemblies set legal prices for all public payments, such as taxes, but prevailing market prices often set the rate for all private payments. Colonial assemblies invariably set the legal prices for public payments above the market prices, often chafing public officials who received income in commodity money at legal prices. The higher the legal price of a commodity relative to its market price, the smaller would be the quantity of the commodity received by the public official.

One of the problems with the use of commodity money is that commodities often vary substantially in quality. Creditors and government officials in jurisdictions that allowed commodity money often found themselves pressured to accept low-quality commodities in payment. To address this problem, the colony of New Haven (later absorbed into Connecticut Colony) in 1654 required that on:

> every plantation . . . there shall be a viewer of corn, that in case of difference may judge, whether it be well dressed and merchantable or no, which man is to be chosen by each plantation, and shall be under oath to judge faithfully when called to it, and is to be paid for his

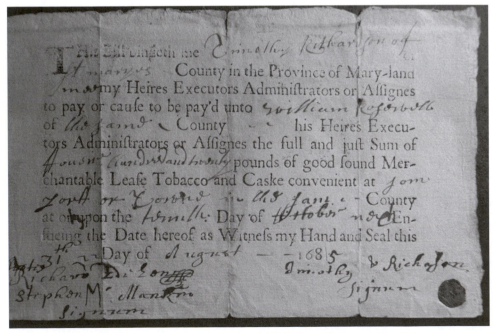

Tobacco note from St. Mary's City, Maryland, dated 1685. (Lowell Georgia/Corbis)

time spent and pains therein by him whose corn is faulty, or who unnecessarily occasions the trouble. (Nettels, 1934, 212)

Connecticut adopted a similar measure for both grains and pork. In Virginia and Maryland a debtor presenting tobacco to a creditor who refused to accept it could ask for two impartial judges. If these judges declared the tobacco good and merchantable, and the creditor still refused to accept it, the debt was counted as paid.

Another problem associated with commodity money is the expense and difficulty of transporting it. In the Massachusetts Bay Colony, the general court said that in the case of cattle driven to Boston for payment of taxes:

> if they be weary, or hungry, or fall sick or lame, it shall be lawful to rest and refresh them for a competent time in any open place, that is not corn, meadow or inclosed for some particular use. (Nettels, 1934, 220)

The widespread use of commodity money reveals the severity of the shortage of coins and other forms of money in the American colonies. It shows that forms of money will develop from the ground up when governments fail to infuse economies with sufficient money to finance trade.

See also: Commodity Monetary Standard, Virginia Tobacco Act of 1713

References

Brock, Leslie. 1975. *The Currency of the American Colonies, 1700–1764*.

Galbraith, John Kenneth. 1975. *Money, Whence It Came, Where It Went*.

Nettels, Curtis P. 1934/1964. *The Money Supply of the American Colonies before 1720*.

COMMODITY PRICE BOOM

An era of booming commodity prices followed the global recovery from the economic sluggishness and recession of 2001. Commodity prices started edging up in 2002 and continued to climb every year. By 2006, a global boom in commodity prices had become a major factor in shaping the growth and evolution of the global economy and its structure. Perhaps the most glaring case of commodity price escalation occurred in the crude oil market. In 1999, the *Economist* magazine ran a cover story forecasting that the price of oil might be headed for $5 per barrel. Instead, the price turned upward. In 2002, West Texas Intermediate Crude traded in the $20 per barrel range. The price skyrocketed, reaching the $60 per barrel range in 2006, and soaring past $100 per barrel in the first months of 2008.

Not many commodity markets saw prices escalate as fast as the oil market, but oil is only a more glaring case of what happened over a wide swath of commodity prices. By the early months of 2008, the average prices of several commodities had doubled over their average prices in 2006. Commodities that saw prices double in less than two years included coal, soybeans, palm oil, and wheat (www.indexmundi.com/ commodities). Over the same time frame, the price of coffee jumped 65 percent, and the price of iron ore jumped 81 percent. Between 2002 and early 2008, gold went from trading in the $350 range to trading above $900.

Economists disagree over what causes booming commodity prices. The blame for sharp price escalations for individual commodities often seems to lie with conditions specific to each market. Political tensions and wars are often credited for interrupting supplies of crude oil, causing prices to spike. High oil prices can lead to high corn prices if part of the corn crop goes to the manufacture of ethanol. Mad cow disease and avian flu bear blame for higher meat prices. Wheat production suffered from multiyear droughts in key wheat-producing nations, and coffee production suffered from too much rain in Brazil. Sometimes tight supplies are attributed to labor-management clashes.

Explanations that focus on unique conditions in individual markets cannot account for a pattern of broad-based commodity price inflation. Therefore, some economists seek a common explanation that explains why prices are rising in a wide range of commodities. One explanation cites the rapid growth in China and, to a lesser extent, India. China doubled its number of steel factories between 2002 and 2008 (Kraus, 2008). Between 2003 and 2005, China bore responsibility for 31 percent of the total rise in global demand for crude oil, 64 percent of the total rise in the global demand for copper, 70 percent for aluminum, and 82 percent for zinc (Krauss, 2008). As billions of people around the world grow wealthier, they consumer more of their own commodities instead of exporting them to the United States.

Another explanation lays the blame for commodity price inflation at the feet of easy monetary policies and low interest rates. The commodity price boom began after a phase of very low interest rates and easy money conditions. Some economists argue that high interest rates quicken the pace of extraction of commodities like oil

and metals and low interest rates have the opposite effect. They also argue that high interest rates encourage firms to minimize inventory holdings, and low interest rates have the opposite effect. Last, they argue that low interest rates encourage speculators to shift out of short-term government bonds and into spot commodity contracts. All three forces cause the prices of mineral commodities to rise as interest rates fall. Falling interest rates cause rising commodity prices by reducing the incentive for extraction, reducing the carrying cost of holding inventories, and encouraging speculators to shift into commodity contracts.

See also: Inflation

References

Frankel, Jeffrey. 2007. "The Effect of Monetary Policy on Real Commodity Prices," in *Asset Prices and Monetary Policy,* John Campbell, ed.

Krauss, Clifford, "Commodities Relentless Surge," *New York Times,* January 15, 2008, pp. C1–8.

COMPOSITE CURRENCY

A composite currency is a weighted combination or basket of two or more currencies. A composite currency ordinarily would not circulate as a medium of exchange, as does the U.S. dollar or Japanese yen, but it can serve as a unit of account and store of value. Service as medium of exchange, store of value, and unit of account are the three basic functions of money.

The European Currency Unit (ECU) was the most successful composite currency until it was officially formalized as one currency in the form of the euro. According to the weight given each currency on September 1989, the Deutsche mark accounted for roughly 30 percent of the value of the ECU, the French franc accounted for about 19 percent, the British pound sterling about 13 percent, and the Italian lira for about 10 percent (*Journal of Accountancy,* 1994). The Dutch guilder, Belgian franc, Spanish peseta, Danish krona, Irish punt, Greek drachma, Portuguese escudo, and Luxembourg franc accounted for the remaining value of the ECU at various fixed percentages. The percentages contributed by each currency equaled 100 percent. Before the introduction of the euro, European banks accepted deposits in ECU, made loans in ECU, and European corporations issued bonds in ECU. Private acceptance of the ECU paved the way for the euro.

The Special Drawing Rights (SDRs) created by the International Monetary Fund represents another example of a composite currency. At first, 16 major currencies defined the value of SDRs. In 1981 the International Monetary Fund reduced the number of currencies to five, the U.S. dollar, the Deutsche mark, the French franc, the yen, and the pound sterling. After the introduction of the euro, the number of currencies fell to four, the U.S. dollar, the yen, the euro, and the pound sterling. Some observers saw the makings of an ideal international currency in SDRs. The private sector gave lukewarm reception to SDRs. At one time, the Bank for International Settlements reported 13 bond issues worldwide that were denominated in private SDRs (Dammes, McCauley, 2006).

From the viewpoint of foreign investors, composite currencies provide a means of diversifying currency risk. If one currency in the basket loses value relative to the dollar or the investor's base currency, the damage is limited to the currency's share in the basket. A disadvantage of composite currencies arises because the weights that make up a composite currency are usually set by an official agency. Private sector use of composite currencies require complicated contracts explaining what happens if the official weights change before a bond matures or long-term contract expires.

Composite currencies provide one solution to a problem in comparing the performance of global corporations. Assume two global corporations, one headquartered in the United States, and the other headquartered in Switzerland. Further, assume that these two companies have identical asset holdings worldwide. One of these companies could report a gain and the other company a loss if the currency of one country strengthened and the currency of the other country weakened. This discrepancy in earnings would occur even if the performance of the two companies was roughly even.

The success of the ECU has led to suggestions that East Asian countries should establish a composite currency based on a basket of regional currencies. Proponents argue that a composite currency based on a weighted basket of East Asian currencies would be less vulnerable to speculative attacks. In the East Asian Crisis of 1997, speculative attacks on one currency led to speculative attacks on other currencies.

See also: European Currency Unit, Special Drawing Rights

References

Asian Development Bank. "ASEAN+3 Regional Basket Currency Bonds." *Technical Assistance Report,* Project Number 40030, August 2006.

Dammes, Clifford, and Robert McCauley. "Basket Weaving: The Euromarket Experience with Basket Currency Bonds." *BIS*

Quarterly Review, March 6, 2006, pp. 79–92.

"What's a Frozen ECU?" *Journal of Accountancy,* vol. 177, no. 4 (April 1994): 14.

CONSUMER PRICE INDEX

See: Value of Money

COPPER

After gold and silver, copper has the longest and most varied history as a monetary metal. Resistant to corrosion and malleable, copper was used by ancient peoples to make utensils, hammers, knives, and vessels of great beauty. As early as 5000 BCE, ancient Egyptians buried copper weapons and tools in graves for use in the afterlife. The Chinese epic *Shu Ching* makes references to the use of copper around 2500 BCE.

In the Mediterranean world, Cyprus was a major producer and the sole supplier of copper to the Romans, whose first metallic monetary system was based on a copper or bronze standard. The Romans called it *aes cyprium,* later shortened to *cyprium.* The English word "copper" stemmed from the word *cuprum,* a corrupted form of *cyprium.* The chemical symbol for copper, Cu, comes from the first two letters of the Latin name.

The ancient Egyptians operated on a copper monetary standard. The standard unit of weight was an *uten* or *deben* of copper, and it was subsided into the *kit* or *kedet.* Some writers contend that the copper units were mainly used to value goods for barter, but others claim that copper rings, equal to multiples or fractions of the copper unit of weight circulated as a medium of exchange.

Copper ingots on display at the Heraklion Archaeological Museum on the island of Crete. Copper, which can combine with tin to yield the useful alloy bronze, was a scarce and valuable commodity in Mediterranean communities during the Bronze Age. (Cascoly Software)

Copper or bronze remained the monetary standard of Rome until the end of the Roman Republic in 30 BCE. The Latin word for copper also denotes bronze, leaving some confusion about Rome's monetary system. Bronze is copper alloyed with tin, and is a tougher metal than either copper or tin separately.

Copper had many practical uses for shaping weapons and tools, but ancient cultures never seemed to have invested copper with the religious significance that enveloped silver and particularly gold in a cloak of reverence. The Old Testament makes only one reference to copper (Ezra 8:27), but makes countless references to gold and silver, beginning in Genesis. Nevertheless, a certain Father Allouez, traveling through the area of Superior

Bay (also called Allouez Bay) on Lake Superior in the 1660s observed:

> There are often found beneath the waters of Lake Superior pieces of copper, well formed and of the weight of 20 pounds. I have seen them in the hands of Indians; and, as the latter are superstitious, they keep them as so many divinities, or as presents from the gods beneath. (Del Mar, 1968, 30)

Before the Spanish Conquest, copper was more valuable than gold in North America, Mexico, and Peru. In modern European history, copper has clearly been a second-class monetary metal. In the 16th century, Spain debased its silver currency with copper alloy. The currency was called *vellon*, and by 1599 it was virtually pure copper. Copper money was sometimes called black money because when mixed with a bit of silver it blackened quickly. In the 17th century, Sweden, which had vast copper deposits, adopted a copper monetary standard that lasted over a hundred years. During the Napoleonic era, the French government tried to make copper legal tender in the settlement of debts in amounts up to one-fourth of the amount owed, but the effort fizzled. In August 1800, the government instructed the Bank of France to pay no more than one-twelfth of the government's debt service in copper.

In the 19th century, the demand for small change created a new demand for copper as a monetary metal. In 1797, England began issuing penny and two-penny coins made of copper. The first coinage legislation of the newly constituted United States authorized the coinage of cents and half-cents made of copper. Copper coinage in the United States

continued into the 1970s, when the high price of copper made pennies more valuable melted down and sold by weight.

The three metals that have served as money in the Western world are gold, silver, and copper. Although copper was not as valuable as gold or silver as a unit of weight, it filled a niche in the monetary system. A person planning to purchase a house would find it very difficult to transport the amount of copper needed to make the payment. For large commercial transactions, gold was ideal, because of its high value per unit of weight. For the purchase of a soft drink, however, the amount of gold needed would be a very small quantity, too small to be easily measured and handled. Silver was preferable for intermediate transactions, but for small retail transactions, copper was most suitable.

See also: American Penny, Sweden's Copper Standard

References
Del Mar, Alexander. 1899/1968. *The History of Money in America*.
Kindleberger, Charles P. 1984. *A Financial History of Western Europe*.
Williams, Jonathan, ed. 1997. *Money: A History*.

CORE INFLATION

Core inflation seeks to measure the underlying, or core, inflation, the persistent trend in the inflation numbers. The concept of core inflation addresses the problem of uncovering which price increases are permanent and which are transient. Put differently, core inflation aims to be a better predictor of the future inflation rate than the actual inflation rate. The most common measure of core inflation equals the growth rate of the Consumer Price Index or Personal Consumption Expenditure Index after the food and energy components have been subtracted. As use of the concept of core inflation has spread, the term "headline inflation" has come to refer to the actual inflation rate. Advocates of the concept of core inflation claim it more effectively signals what the headline inflation rate will be in the medium to long term, and that the long-term average of the more volatile headline inflation rate will roughly equal the core inflation rate.

The CPI index for 2005 shows that headline inflation in the United States registered 3.5 percent, whereas core inflation posted a mere 2.1 percent. The tendency of the core inflation rate to mirror long-term trends shows up when inflation rates are averaged over longer spans of time. Between 1996 and 2004, headline CPI inflation in the United States averaged 2.42 percent, whereas core CPI inflation measured 2.23 percent.

The idea is that food and energy prices are more volatile. Over time, changes in the prices of these commodities either subside or work their way into core inflation. Food and energy prices are volatile because supplies are exposed to onetime shocks. In the case of food, a onetime shock could take the form of drought or pestilence. In the case of energy, high concentration of world crude oil reserves in politically volatile areas lead to onetime interruptions in supply.

The concept of core inflation rarely came up in economic discussions before the 1970s. The Economic Report of the President (1971) advanced the concept of the CPI less mortgage interest and food prices, but the term "core inflation" was not mentioned. The idea of removing mortgage interest did not become part of the concept of core inflation. After the mid-1970s, the term "core inflation" came into use and economists subjected the

concept to systematic and rigorous analysis. In 1978, the Bureau of Labor Statistics began reporting versions of both the CPI and the Producer Price Index that excluded food and energy. In 1981, well-known economist Otto Eckstein published the book *Core Inflation*. Eckstein defined core inflation in terms of weighted growth in unit labor and capital costs, but the concept of core inflation remained largely associated with measures of inflation that excluded food and energy.

Economists have questioned whether the exclusion of food and energy gives the best measure of core inflation. One possibility for calculating core inflation involves subjecting inflation series to a time-series smoothing process that spreads over time the effects of volatile components. Another possibility involves the calculation of a weighted median inflation rate. The weighted median inflation rate is the inflation rate for a chosen product. The chosen product is the one for which half of expenditures go to pay for products whose prices are rising just as fast or faster, and half of expenditures go to pay for products whose prices are rising just as slowly or more slowly. The chosen product exhibits the median inflation rate. Studies suggest that other measures of core inflation work just as well in forecasting inflation.

The practice of excluding food and energy from inflation measures draws criticism from observers who cite the importance of food and energy in the cost of living for wage earners. For this reason, other measures of core inflation may eventually displace the familiar measure based on the exclusion of food and energy.

See also: Inflation

References
Arestis, Philip, John McCombie, and Warren Mosler. "New Attitudes About Inflation."

Challenge, vol. 49, no. 5 (Sept/Oct 2006): 33–52.

Rich, Robert, and Charles Steindel. "A Comparison of Measure of Core Inflation." *Economic Policy Review,* vol. 13, no. 3 (Dec 2007): 19–38.

CORSO FORZOSO (ITALY)

The famous *Corso Forzoso,* "forced circulation," refers to the suspension of convertibility of Italy's paper lira from 1866 to 1881, which put Italy on a paper standard inconvertible into a precious metal. Before the Corso Forzoso, Italy was on a gold and silver bimetallic standard, and holders of Italian bank notes could redeem notes in gold and silver specie.

The origin of the Corso Forzoso can be traced to costly wars waged to unify Italy, disorderly public finances arising from consolidation of budgets and taxation systems of separate Italian governments, and heavy public works expenditures in the name of industrialization. Between January 1, 1862, and January 1, 1867, the public debt grew from 3.131 billion lire to 6.929 billion lire. The debt was financed by short-term treasury bonds, a third of which were held by foreign investors sensitive to crises of confidence and expecting bond redemption in gold and silver. The end of the U.S. Civil War, bringing cancellation of war contracts, demobilization, and renewed competition from cheap U.S. cotton, sent the economic tremors that pushed Italy over the monetary precipice. The price of Italian bonds on the Paris Bourse tumbled from 80 percent to 36.44 percent of par value, and Italian bondholders and Italian correspondents of foreign bondholders asked for redemption in gold, causing a shortage of gold and a crisis of confidence in the banking system.

A run on the banks forced the government's hand, and on May 1, 1866, the government, with prior approval from the legislature, decreed the inconvertibility of bank notes—the Corso Forzoso.

Notwithstanding the Corso Forzoso, the National Bank of Italy avoided the runaway issuance of bank notes that brought to ruin many past experiments with paper money. The index of wholesale prices rose modestly from 0.897 in 1866 to 1.051 in 1873. The gold price index rose from 1.046 to 1.137 over the same time period.

Defenders of the policy of Corso Forzoso argue that the consequent depreciation of the lira in foreign exchange markets made Italian exports cheaper in foreign markets, and foreign goods expensive in Italian markets, together acting as a powerful boost to Italian industry. Also the Corso Forzoso accustomed the Italian people to the acceptance of bank notes. In 1865, only one-tenth of the circulating money had consisted of bank notes. Critics of the policy point to the fear that Corso Forzoso struck in the minds of potential foreign investors at a time when Italy badly needed foreign capital.

After achieving a balanced budget early in the 1870s, the Italian government began taking steps to restore convertibility of the lira. As the government paid off its debts to the National Bank of Italy in gold, the bank was able to restore convertibility, and on April 7, 1881, the Corso Forzoso came to an end.

The Corso Forzoso ranks among the more successful early efforts to circulate fiat money, or money not supported by precious metals or other commodities. During the Napoleonic Wars, the United Kingdom maintained control over its monetary affairs despite the adoption of an inconvertible paper standard. Before the Corso Forzoso, however, the more normal consequence of inconvertible paper money had been a whirlwind of inflation. France lamented two disastrous experiences with inconvertible paper, John Law's paper money, and the French Revolution's assignats, both of which caused runaway or hyperinflation.

See also: Bank Restriction Act of 1797, Inconvertible Paper Standard

References

Chown, John F. 1994. *A History of Money.*
Clough, Shepard B. 1964. *The Economic History of Modern Italy.*

COUNTERFEIT MONEY

Counterfeit money is mostly forged or faked paper money, sometimes referred to as "funny money." Counterfeit paper money is almost as old as paper money, and the practice of counterfeiting money survives into our own day as governments strive to remain one technological step ahead of counterfeiters.

Counterfeiting became a flourishing activity early in the 19th century because of the proliferation of banks issuing their own bank notes. Great Britain was one country that did not spare the rod in handing out justice to counterfeiters. Between 1805 and 1818, the Bank of England successfully brought 501 counterfeiters to the bar of justice, and 207 met their fate at the gallows. Not only was it illegal to counterfeit money but having a forged note in one's possession was illegal, and ignorance was no defense. A public outcry arose against savage sentences meted out to people who accidentally came into possession of forged notes. In 1819, the Society of the Arts, concerned about the hanging of

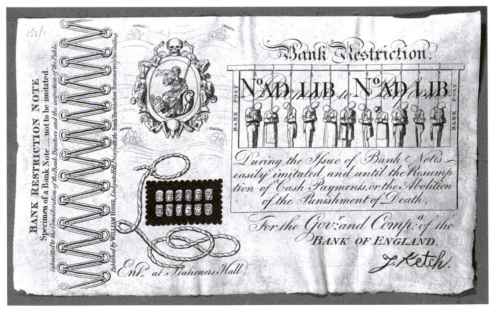

This cartoon, entitled "Bank Restriction Note," by George Cruikshank refers to the British policy of hanging anyone caught passing counterfeit currency, 1818. (Bank of England, London/Heini Schneebeli/The Bridgeman Art Library)

innocent people, published its *Report on the Mode of Preventing the Forgery of Bank Notes*. The report found fault with the Bank of England for issuing bank notes too easily counterfeited, and proposed a distinct set of copper plates and employment of highly skilled artists to design notes and engrave plates.

The sight of two women hanged for passing forged notes led George Cruikshank, cartoonist and political satirist, to produce an antihanging note. His "Bank Restriction Note" bore an image of Britannia with a skull instead of a head, set against a background of despairing figures and highlighting 11 individuals hanging from scaffolds. The note also bore the signature of Jack Ketch, a notorious public hangman. Cruikshank's note sparked riots in London, and the government appointed a royal commission to find ways of producing notes that could not be imitated. The commission turned to the U.S. firm of Murray, Draper, Fairman and Company, which had revolutionized bank-note printing using a siderographic transfer process and highly complicated background patterns. The siderographic process facilitates the exact duplication of engraved steel plates by using alternating hardened and softened steel cylinders to pass on imprints. An employee, Jacob Perkins, inventor of these processes, offered his services to the Bank of England, won a contract, and the firm of Perkins Bacon became the premier producer of postage stamps and paper money worldwide during the 19th century.

Counterfeiting is sometimes a state-sponsored activity, with the object of producing confusion and social unrest in enemy countries. The Bank of England counterfeited vast numbers of assignats, the famous French paper money of the French Revolution that touched off a wave of hyperinflation. One of the largest counterfeiting schemes in history was Operation Bernhard, the code name for Nazi Germany's vast program for counterfeiting Bank of England notes. Apparently, the Soviet Union also resorted to counterfeiting as a weapon in the arsenal of revolution.

Thanks to an international conference held in Geneva in 1929, counterfeiting laws are relatively uniform among various countries. Counterfeiting either domestic currency or foreign currency is illegal, and counterfeiters are subject to extradition. Printing counterfeit money is invariably a felony offense drawing a prison sentence, but incidental offenses, such as owning counterfeiting equipment, or possessing counterfeit money usually draw lesser sentences.

The development of high-quality color copying machines and sophisticated offset printing operations presented new challenges to the problem of combating counterfeiting. The United States now impresses a thin polyester thread into its Federal Reserve notes. The thread runs vertically to the left of the Federal Reserve seal, and can be seen when the note is held up to a light. The notes also have the words "United States of America" microprinted in letters that can only be read with magnification.

The advances in technology have forced the Treasury to regularly add new security features to the currency. The treasury introduced a new currency design in 1996 and again in 2004. The new series introduced in 2004 is called the "New Color of Money" design because of its introduction of subtle background colors.

Despite these innovations, counterfeiting remains a major problem in and for the United States.

In 2005, it came to light that the government of North Korea was operating a large counterfeiting operation of U.S. currency. North Korea's counterfeiting involved foreign banks, Chinese underworld gangs, and the Irish Republican Army. The U.S. government found it difficult to press North Korea over the issue due to the larger issue of nuclear proliferation (Fackler, 2006).

See also: Operation Bernhard

References

Angus, Ian. 1974. *Paper Money*.

Beresiner, Yasha. 1977. *A Collector's Guide to Paper Money*.

Dacy, Joe. "How to Spot Bogus Bills." *Nations Business,* vol. 81, no. 7 (July 1993): 30.

Fackler, Martin. "North Korean Counterfeiting Complicates Nuclear Crisis." *New York Times,* January 29, 2006, p. 3.

CREDIT CRUNCH

A credit crunch refers to a sharp reduction in the availability of credit. It could refer to a sharp increase in interest rates but often it involves a significant shrinkage in supplies of lendable funds. It likely shuts out some subset of borrowers from access to credit. The term came into use in the 1960s when the home mortgage industry began experiencing periodic credit crunches. By 2000, financial innovations and markets for wider ranges of financial assets minimized the possibility that one or two economic sectors would bear the full brunt of a credit crunch. Nevertheless, the credit crunch of 2007–2008 began in the home mortgage industry, and residential construction was the hardest hit economic sector.

The home mortgage industry experienced credit crunches in 1966 and again in 1969, 1973, and 1974. These episodes of credit crunches occurred over a span of years roughly coinciding with the Vietnam War, a time when defense related expenditures of the Cold War put the maximum strain on the financial resources of the United States. In addition to heavy government borrowing, a piece of banking law called "Regulation Q" banned payment of interest on checking accounts and limited the payment of interest rates on savings accounts to the 5 percent range. At the time of these first credit crunches, a type of financial institutions called savings and loans dominated the home mortgage industry. These institutions raised funds by offering savings deposits to depositors, and these funds were lent to home buyers in the form of home mortgages. As inflation and government borrowing exerted upward pressure on interest rates, savers began removing funds from savings and loan deposits. Instead, they invested in 90-day treasury bonds, which paid a substantially higher interest rate. The flow of funds out of savings and loan institutions and into the bond market was called "disintermediation." An increase in short-term interest rates prompted disintermediation, forcing savings and loan institutions to curtail lending, and residential home builders to cut back on construction.

The development of secondary mortgage markets eased the squeeze of these early credit crunches. It severed the link that forced mortgage lending and residential construction to move in step with the flow of deposits in and out of thrift type institutions. The secondary mortgage market allowed the institutions that had expertise in evaluating borrowers and establishing customer relationships to continue to originate mortgages. Instead of financing mortgages out of savings deposits, thrifts sold mortgages to third parties as an investment.

In 2007 and 2008, another type of credit crunch, the subprime meltdown, shut out borrowers from access to credit. A wave of defaults on mortgages negotiated with subprime borrowers shook the secondary market for mortgages, forcing originators of mortgages to greatly raise the bar of creditworthiness. Subprime borrowers are borrowers who paid higher interest rates to compensate for weak credit ratings. A contraction in home mortgages led to a contraction in the housing industry, raising the specter of recession. Lenders, stunned by high mortgage defaults and expecting a recession, began tightening credit standards for a wide range of loans, including automobile loans and other types of consumer credit. As the Federal Reserve slashed interest rates to ward off recession, lenders made it harder for individuals to qualify for loans, arousing fears that the anti-recession monetary policy might not succeed.

See also: U.S. Financial Crisis of 2008–2009

References

Bradley, Michael G., Stuart Gabriel, and Mark Wohar. "The Thrift Crisis, Mortgage-Credit Intermediation, and Housing Activity." *Journal of Money, Credit, and Banking,* vol. 27, no. 2 (May 1995): 476–497.

Kim, Jim. "Credit Crunch Moves Beyond Mortgages: Individuals See Higher Rates, Harsher Terms on Credit Cards and Other Consumer Loans." Wall Street Journal (Eastern Edition, New York), August 22, 2007, p. D1.

CREDIT RATINGS

A credit rating aims to determine before a loan is made whether an individual, corporation, or country is willing, able, and likely to repay a debt. Lenders are the main users of credit ratings, but insurance companies have used credit ratings to determine insurance premiums, and employers have used credit ratings in evaluating job applicants. Utility and leasing deposits can also vary in amount according to credit ratings. Those with poor credit ratings end up either borrowing at high interest rates or unable to borrow at all. The main pieces of information that go into credit ratings are financial history and current assets, liabilities, and income. Financial history includes obvious warning signs such as instances of bankruptcies and defaults, but it also includes late payments by borrowers who otherwise have clean credit histories. In the United States, credit bureaus such as Experian, Equifax, and TransUnion assign credit scores for individuals. Credit rating agencies such as Moody's and Standard and Poor's assign credit ratings for corporations and sovereign governments.

Credit ratings are a relatively new development in the history of financial markets. They appeared after financial markets achieved a high level of development in the United States. The wide expanse of the United States, with its railroads and telegraphs, multiplied the number of business transactions between individuals who were otherwise strangers. The mid-1800s saw the rise of mercantile credit agencies in the United States. These credit agencies assessed the credit worthiness of merchants. In 1909, John Moody began furnishing credit ratings on railroad bonds, and a year later extended his rating service to include utility and industrial bonds. Poor's Publishing Company and Standard Statistics Company issued their first ratings in 1916 and 1922, respectively. In 1941, Standard Statistics Company and Poor's Publishing Company merged to form Standard and Poor's, one of the most widely known credit ratings agencies for securities. Fitch Publishing Company began rating bonds in 1924. In 1982, Duff and Phelps began providing ratings for a wide range of companies.

As capital markets displaced banking institutions as the main mechanism for channeling international capital flows, the demand for credit rating agencies grew outside the United States. The last decades of the 20th century saw Moody's open offices in Tokyo, London, Paris, Sydney, Frankfurt, and Madrid. Standard and Poor's opened offices Tokyo, London, Paris, Melbourne, Toronto, Frankfurt, Stockholm, and Mexico City. Duff and Phelps entered into joint ventures in Mexico and several Latin American countries. U.S. credit rating agencies have the strongest presence in the global market for creditable security ratings, followed by credit rating agencies in Japan, Canada, and the United Kingdom.

Originally, the sale of publication and related material provided the revenue to pay for the rating service, and the companies who were the object of the credit ratings incurred no charges. After the default of Penn Central in 1970, investors discovered that a company with a household name was not necessarily a good investment risk. Other companies began having trouble rolling over their commercial paper. Companies began seeking ratings from credit rating agencies to reassure jittery investors. Fitch and Moody's both started charging companies for ratings in

1970; Standard and Poor's started charging soon after. By 1987, 80 percent of Standard and Poor's revenue came from fees charged the firms who were rated (Canter and Packer, 1994). The practice of depending on the rated companies for revenue has raised questions about whether the rating agencies have an incentive to award high ratings to keep its customers happy. The subprime mortgage crisis of 2008 put the spotlight on the rating agencies and the role they had played in assigning investment grades to securities that were backed by risky home mortgages. Critics charged that the credit rating agencies such as Standard and Poor's were paid handsome fees for complicity in the crisis.

See also: U.S. Financial Crisis of 2008–2009

References

Cantor, Richard, and Frank Packer. "The Credit Rating Industry." *Quarterly Review,* vol. 19, no. 2 (Summer/Fall 1994): 1–26.

Lowenstein, Roger. "Triple-A Failure." *New York Times Magazine,* April 27, 2008, pp. 36–42.

CREDIT UNION SHARE DRAFTS (CUSD)

See: Monetary Aggregates

CRIME OF '73 (UNITED STATES)

The Coinage Act of 1873, a piece of legislation that caused hardly a political ripple in Congress, subsequently acquired the odious title of the "Crime of '73." The act rather informally dropped the bimetallic standard in the United States in favor of the gold standard, an action that incurred the wrath of debtors and western farmers as deflationary trends gathered force in the late 1800s. Since the days of Alexander Hamilton, the United States had been on a bimetallic standard combining gold and silver in a fixed ratio. The Crime of '73 made it into the folklore in the United States, including references in the famous book, *The Wizard of Oz*.

A movement of economic and social protest lifted William Jennings Bryan to the leadership of the Democratic Party, and inspired his famous "Cross of Gold" speech, which compared the gold standard to the crucifixion of mankind on a cross of

Caricature of William Jennings Bryan in the September 14, 1896, edition of Judge *magazine attacking Bryan's "Cross of Gold" speech delivered at the Democratic National Convention on July 8, 1896. In the speech, Bryan advocated the unlimited coinage of silver by the U.S. government, a policy he believed would bring relief to debtors in the economic depression then gripping the nation. (Library of Congress)*

gold. Debt-ridden farmers and unemployed workmen quite rightly pointed the finger of suspicion to the unforgiving discipline of the gold standard, and saw something sinister in quietly removing silver from the monetary standard without the airing of a public debate. With vast holdings of silver in western states, coinage of silver could have infused additional monetary reserves in the economy, raising prices and easing pressure on debtors.

The offensive portion of the act downgraded the silver dollar to subsidiary coinage of the same proportional weight and fineness as the half-dollar, quarter, and dime. These silver dollars were legal tender in amounts up to $5, but in 1877 the treasury discontinued minting the silver dollars, due to a lack of interest.

Before the act, silver owners could sell silver to the mint for $1.292 per ounce, but the market value of silver was $1.298 per ounce, creating an opportunity to melt down minted silver and sell it for a profit, causing silver dollars to disappear from circulation. The high market value of silver in 1873 probably accounts for the lack of public controversy at the time Congress passed the Coinage Act of 1873. The discovery of additional silver reserves in the western states, coupled with deflationary trends, pushed the market price of silver below the mint price. As deflationary trends made themselves felt, culminating in the depression of the 1890s, the silver interests missed the treasury market for silver, and depressed regions saw silver coinage as the answer to economic woes.

Abandonment of the bimetallic standard and cessation of silver as a monetary standard of value were in step with international currents at the time. Europe was rapidly turning to a gold standard that was associated with Great Britain's commercial success. The failure of William Jennings Bryan to win a presidential bid ensured that the United States would remain on a gold standard, which became official with the Gold Standard Act of 1900. The discovery of new sources of gold relieved the monetary tightness of the late 1800s, effectively defusing the silver protest, and letting the Crime of '73 fade into political oblivion.

See also: Bimetallism, Bland–Allison Silver Repurchase Act of 1878, Free Silver Movement, Gold Standard Act of 1900, Sherman Silver Act of 1890, *The Wizard of Oz*

References

Friedman, Milton. 1992. *Money Mischief: Episodes in Monetary History.*
Myers, Margaret G. 1970. *A Financial History of the United States.*
Nugent, Walter T. K. 1968. *Money and American Society: 1865–1880.*

CUPRONICKEL

See: Coinage Act of 1965, Liverpool Act of 1816

CURRENCY ACT OF 1751 (ENGLAND)

The Currency Act of 1751 sought to restrict the issuance of fiat paper money and to ban its use as legal tender for the settlement of private debts in the New England colonies. The beginning of the 18th century saw several New England colonies, led by Massachusetts, issue fiat paper currency. They turned to paper currency partly because of the financial pressures of wars involving the French and the Indians and partly as a measure to relieve domestic shortages of acceptable mediums of exchange for financing business activity. Colonial governments issued paper currency on the condition that they would accept the currency as payment for taxes at a future time, perhaps within a year or possibly as long as seven years later. When governments issued more paper currency than they reclaimed in taxes, the paper currency lost value relative to British currency, and colonial prices inflated. British merchants who had claims of debt against the colonists suffered because the depreciated currency they had to accept in repayment had less value than the credit they had extended.

The Act of 1751 opened by citing the failure of previous acts of Parliament to stem the tide of depreciating paper currency in New England, and by observing that because of the legal-tender status of this paper currency "all debts of late years have been paid and satisfied with a much less value than was contracted for, which hath been a great discouragement and prejudice to . . . trade and commerce."

The Act provided that:

1. Effective September 29, 1751, governors, councils, or assemblies in Connecticut, Massachusetts Bay, New Hampshire, or Rhode Island were forbidden to enact legislation authorizing the issuance of additional bills of credit (paper currency), and could not extend the period of outstanding bills of credit. Any actions along these lines were "declared to be null and void, and of no force or effect whatsoever."

2. Colonial governments were required to retire all outstanding bills of credit at the scheduled date.

3. Colonial governments could issue bills of credit to finance current government expenditures if sufficient taxes were levied to retire the bills within two years.

4. In the event of unusual public emergencies, such as war or invasion, bills of credit could be issued in excess of what the government would reclaim in taxes within two years. These extra bills had to pay interest and be reclaimed by a tax fund within five years.

5. None of the bills issued after September 29, 1751, were to be legal tender in private transactions, and none of the bills then in circulation should be legal tender.

The act allowed governments to continue to issue bills of credit as an instrument of government finance, but prohibited the attachment of the legal-tender sanction for settling private debts. The Currency Act of 1751 was followed by the Currency Act of 1764, which applied the same principles to the remaining colonies. The latter act sought to deny the legal-tender status of paper currency even in the payment of public debts. This was a confusing point, however, and the colonial governments continued to issue paper currency that could be used in payment of taxes. The Currency Act of 1773 clarified the issue by specifically allowing colonial governments to issue paper currency that was legal tender for the payment of public debts. The 1773 act allowed the use of paper currency as legal tender for the payment of taxes but, in deference to British creditors, not for private debts.

The Currency Act of 1751, and its sister act, the Currency Act of 1764, contributed to a shortage of circulating money in the American colonies, adding to the discontent that led up to the American Revolution. The American colonies were not blessed with the abundance of gold and silver mines found in the Spanish colonies. The hard specie that was won by exporting goods to Europe had to be used to import the numerous European goods needed in the American colonies. Entrepreneurs in the American colonies enjoyed practically unlimited supplies of natural resources, but harnessing these resources required a rapidly growing domestic money supply, with opportunities for borrowing money as the need arose. Because the availability of money fell far short of the business opportunities afforded by such a land, the colonists tried to find ways to invent their own money supply. The failure of the British to appreciate the need for an elastic money supply in a land of boundless resources contributed to the tension that resulted in revolution.

See also: Currency Act of 1764, Land Bank System, Massachusetts Bay Colony Paper Issue

References

Brock, Leslie V. 1975. *The Currency of the American Colonies: 1700–1764.*

Ernst, Joseph Albert. 1973. *Money and Politics in America, 1755–1775.*

CURRENCY ACT OF 1764 (ENGLAND)

The Currency Act of 1764 removed the authority of colonial governments in the middle and southern American colonies to issue legal-tender paper money for either private or public debts. The act passed Parliament following the French and Indian War (1754–1763), when colonial governments, particularly Virginia, freely turned to the issuance of paper money to defray military expenditures.

Parliament first acted to restrict the issuance of colonial paper money in the Currency Act of 1751. That act circumscribed the ability of New England colonies to issue paper money and banned the circulation of paper money as legal tender for private debts. The Act of 1751 enabled governments to declare paper money legal tender for public debts—that is, taxes—but not for private debts. England's Board of Trade moved to extend the provisions of the Act of 1751 to colonies south of New England, but the French and Indian War intervened, and the Board of Trade tended to wink or look away as colonial governments issued paper money to finance war expenditures. British merchants, however, saw the issuance of legal-tender paper money as a conspiracy of American debtors to defraud British creditors by repaying debts in depreciated paper money. They lobbied the Board of Trade and Parliament to stop the colonies' issuance of legal-tender paper money. To be sure, the paper money invariably depreciated relative to British pounds, reducing its value to British merchants.

Unlike the Currency Act of 1751, the Currency Act of 1764 did not restrict the authority of colonial governments to issue paper money, but did ban the designation of any paper money as legal tender for the payment of either private or public debts, thus making the issuance of paper money impractical. The prohibition on the issuance of paper money as legal tender for public debts put colonial governments in a financial crunch. These governments issued paper money and then levied taxes payable in the paper money, automatically providing for the retirement of the paper money issues, and preventing paper money from depreciating in value. Government treasuries rather than monetary authorities, contrary to current practice, issued this paper money. In addition, the issuance of this paper money helped relieve a shortage of coinage that hampered economic activity in colonial economies. Therefore, the Currency Act of 1764 was the equivalent of England enforcing a tight money policy in the colonies in the aftermath of the French and Indian War.

The legal-tender provisions of the act seemed perplexing and ambiguous to the colonists, who found it difficult to understand how a government could issue paper money and not accept it as taxes. Also, several colonies operated loan offices that issued paper notes against the security of real estate. The Act of 1764 seemed to suggest that loan offices could not accept in repayment the notes they had issued. The colonial governments appear to have worked around the act and continued to accept their own paper money in payment for taxes, but the colonists lobbied with Parliament to have the legal-tender restriction on public debts lifted. The colonies needed the paper money to supplement domestic money supplies, which were limited and thus acted as a brake on domestic economic growth. The restrictions on the issuance of paper money added to the tension between the colonies and the British government. With the Currency Act of 1773, Parliament amended the Currency Act of 1764 and lifted the ban on paper money as legal tender for public debts.

See also: Currency Act of 1751, Virginia Colonial Paper Currency

References

Brock, Leslie V. 1975. *The Currency of the American Colonies: 1700–1764.*

Ernst, Joseph Albert. 1973. *Money and Politics in America, 1755–1775.*

CURRENCY ACT OF 1773 (ENGLAND)

See: Currency Act of 1751, Currency Act of 1764

CURRENCY CRISES

A currency crisis occurs when the value of a currency crashes in foreign exchange markets, when holders of a currency stampede to sell it in foreign exchange markets out of fear that the currency is headed for lower values in the future. Foreign exchange markets determine the rate or price at which one currency can be purchased with another currency. An exchange rate of $1 per 10 Mexican pesos tells how many pesos it takes to purchase a dollar and how many dollars it takes to purchase a peso. While exchange rates are subject to market forces, certain groups have vested interests in exchange rate stability. One such group would be U.S. investors who have purchased Mexican peso bonds issued by the Mexican government. Bondholders who purchased Mexican bonds with dollars when the exchange rate stood at 10 pesos per $1 will experience a windfall loss if the Mexican peso depreciates to 20 pesos per $1. When they sell the Mexican bonds and convert the pesos back into dollars, they will receive roughly half as many dollars as they originally invested. Therefore, if holders of Mexican bonds expect the peso to depreciate in the future, they will try to sell their Mexican bonds for pesos, and convert the pesos back into dollars before the depreciation occurs. If large numbers of investors try to sell pesos for dollars all at once, the value of the peso in the foreign exchange market will crash.

Speculators may trigger a currency crisis if they think a currency is vulnerable to a sudden crash. If speculators think the peso may depreciate in the future, they will borrow pesos and sell them for dollars. If speculators borrow pesos to buy dollars when the exchange rate is 10 pesos per $1, then they can repay their loans and reap a profit if the peso depreciates to 20 pesos per $1. Speculative attacks can turn mere expectations that a currency will depreciate into a self-fulfilling prophecy.

The common denominator behind all currency crises is a current account deficit. A current account deficit most likely indicates that outflows of domestic currency from imports exceed inflows of domestic currency from exports. As long as outflows of domestic currency approximately balance inflows of domestic currency, the foreign exchange rate tends to remain stable. If the outflow of currency outruns the inflow of currency on the current account, then foreign investors must either be willing to hold financial assets denominated in the domestic currency, or the central bank responsible for the domestic currency must buy back the excess outflow with its holdings of other foreign currencies. Central bank holdings of other foreign currencies are called foreign exchange reserves. The more foreign exchange reserves a central bank holds, the less likely a domestic currency will suffer a currency crisis. A current account deficit and the associated excess outflow of currency lead to currency depreciation if the central bank does not buy back the excess currency outflow and if foreign investors do not find financial assets denominated in the domestic currency attractive. If, for instance, Mexico has a currency account deficit and the Banco de Mexico does not hold sufficient reserves of U.S. dollars to buy back the excess outflow of pesos, then excess supply of pesos will build up in foreign exchange markets and one of two possibilities are left. One possibility is that foreign investors will purchase the excess supply of pesos and use the pesos to purchase bonds and other investments in Mexico. If foreign investors are afraid of investing in Mexico, or find Mexican interest rates too low, then there will be pesos in foreign exchange markets that nobody wants, and the Mexican peso will depreciate.

Countries that run persistent current account deficits tend to run out of foreign exchange reserves. Speculators are prone to launch speculative attacks on countries with current account deficits and low foreign exchange reserves. If the attack is successful, the currency crashes.

A current account deficit usually indicates a large government budget deficit, but it can indicate a high level of domestic investment spending relative to domestic savings. Either way, the country is importing foreign capital. A currency crisis usually occurs when a country that has been experiencing a foreign capital inflow suddenly starts experiencing a foreign capital outflow, perhaps because foreign investors have lost confidence.

See also: East Asian Financial Crisis, Current Account, Mexican Peso Crisis of 1994

References

Bordo, Michael, and Anna J. Schwartz. "Why Clashes between Internal and External Stability Goals End in Currency Crises, 1797–1994." *Open Economy Review,* vol. 7 (suppl): 437–468.

Fontaine, Thomson. "Currency Crises in Developed and Emerging Market Economies: A Comparative Empirical Treatment." *IMF Working Paper* (WP/05/13), January 2005.

CURRENCY–DEPOSIT RATIO

The currency–deposit ratio equals the total circulating currency divided by checkable bank deposits. Checkable bank deposits are deposits that are used in transactions. Also called "demand deposits," checkable deposits represent claims on currency that the public can exercise freely and with minimal delay. The total circulating currency counts only currency held by the nonbank public. It excludes currency held as vault cash at banks. Both currency and checkable deposits act as a form of money.

The currency–deposit ratio reflects public preferences for holding currency relative to bank deposits. It undergoes some seasonal variation. During the Christmas shopping season, the ratio tends to rise as the public carries more currency. The public can raise the currency–deposit ratio by withdrawing currency from banks, and it can reduce the currency–deposit ratio by depositing currency in bank accounts.

The currency–deposit ratio is important because currency is part of what economists call "high-powered money." High-powered money includes circulating currency and bank reserves. It is called high-powered money because a banking system expands deposits by some multiple of bank reserves. Bank reserves are either vault cash or commercial bank deposits with Federal Reserve Banks. Since circulating currency deposited in a bank account becomes part of bank reserves, banks can expand bank deposits by some multiple of the amount of a new deposit of currency. When bank lending multiplies bank deposits, the money stock expands accordingly. A mass withdrawal of currency from banks will cause a contraction in bank deposits several times greater than the amount of currency withdrawn.

A sudden shift in the public's preferences for holding currency as opposed to bank deposits can induce a change in the money stock independent of actions by official monetary authorities. During the early 1930s, the United States saw the public suddenly increase its preference for currency over deposits (Boughton and Wicker, 1979). The public was reacting to a large increase in the numbers of bank failures. At the beginning of the 1930s, the United States had not established deposit insurance, and when a bank failed, depositors lost their money. An outbreak of bank failures persuaded many people that they would rather keep their money stashed in mattresses or buried in coffee cans. The mass withdrawal of currency from banks not only added to the number of bank failures but also caused the money stock to contract. When an economy is sinking into recession or depression, it needs an increase in the money stock to stem the tide of economic retrenchment. To regain depositor confidence, banks started holding larger reserves relative deposits, further reducing the amount of bank lending. Between depositors withdrawing currency from banks, and banks trying to bolster reserve holdings, the money stock contracted significantly even though the Federal Reserve increased the amount of high-powered money. To ease the crisis, the United States government established the Federal Deposit Insurance Corporation. By mid-1934, 97 percent of all commercial bank deposits were protected by deposit insurance (McCallum, 329). Bank failures subsided, and the currency–deposit ratio began a steady decline.

See also: High-Powered Money

References

Becker, William E. Jr. "Determinants of the United States Currency-Demand Deposit Ratio." *Journal of Finance,* vol. 30, no. 1 (March 1975): 57–74.

Boughton, James M., and Elmus R. Wicker. "The Behavior of the Currency–Deposit Ratio during the Great Depression." *Journal of Money, Credit, and Banking*, vol. 11, no. 4 (Nov 1979): 405-18.

McCallum, Bennett T. 1989. *Monetary Economics: Theory and Policy*.

CURRENCY SCHOOL

The currency school emerged as an important body of monetary thinking following England's resumption of specie payments after the Napoleonic Wars in 1821. England had suspended specie payments from 1797 to 1821 because of the financial stress of wars with France. The fundamental principle of the currency school lay in the concept of a money supply composed of coin and paper money acting just as if all money was entirely metallic.

Before the development of paper money, domestic supplies of metallic currency fluctuated with the ebb and flow of foreign trade. Buying goods from foreigners caused metallic currency to flow out, and selling goods to foreigners caused metallic currency to flow in. A net outflow of metallic currency depressed domestic prices, rendering domestic goods more competitive at home and abroad, and a net inflow of metallic currency lifted domestic prices, rendering domestic goods less competitive at home and abroad. Economic competition between countries ensured monetary stability.

The resumption of specie payments—that is, the return to convertibility of the pound in 1821—had not ended fits of monetary and financial disorder and adherents of the currency school saw variations in the money supply as the culprit. England had suffered major crises in 1836 and 1839, a mere three-year interval that many regarded as a wake-up call. According to the thinking of the currency school, domestic money supplies were fluctuating, not with the ebb and flow of international trade, but with variations in bank notes issued by banks. Everyone agreed that banks could expand or contract the supply of bank notes within a wide range without endangering their ability to convert bank notes into specie.

The currency school argued that fluctuations in money supplies were the major cause of economic swings, an idea that is commonplace now, and that banks were causing these fluctuations. The solution to the problem lay in establishment of a state authority exercising a monopoly privilege on the issuance of bank notes, a practice that is universal in modern monetary institutions. Unlike current monetary arrangements, however, the currency school contended that the issuance of bank notes should be kept strictly proportional to domestic metallic currency and bullion. A loss of gold to other countries should cause domestic bank notes to decrease an equivalent amount, putting downward pressure on domestic prices. A gain in gold from other countries worked in reverse. At that time in Great Britain, hundreds of banks issued bank notes without coordination, and the principle of convertibility had not ensured that gold flows would drive domestic money supplies.

Opposed to the arguments of the currency school was the banking school.

The banking school argued that bank notes expanding and contracting with the needs of trade were not a source of instability and that an elasticity of currency was needed to pave the way for economic expansion. The banking school preferred leaving the management of bank notes to bankers whose discretion was tempered by the requirement of convertibility.

The Bank Charter Act of 1844 was a great victory of the currency school over the banking school. The act included provisions that would ultimately give the Bank of England a monopoly on the issuance of bank notes. The act also separated the Bank of England's note-issuing authority from its other banking business. In a departure from the principles laid down by the banking school, the act left the Bank of England with some discretion to regulate the issuance of bank notes independent of changes in gold reserves.

The currency school shares with the modern-day monetarist school the idea that the money supply should be managed by fixed rules rather than left to the discretion of bankers and policy makers. Modern-day monetarists would agree with the currency school that management of the money supply is the foundation of macroeconomic policy. Imbedded in the thinking of both the currency school and the monetarist school was skepticism about the wisdom of government policy makers, and a preference for policies founded on fixed principles rather than subjective judgments made in the midst of economic disturbances.

See also: Bank Charter Act of 1844, Bank of England, Banking School, Central Bank, Monetarism

References

Chown, John F. 1994. *A History of Money*.

Spiegel, Henry William. 1971. *The Growth of Economic Thought*.

CURRENCY SWAPS

A currency swap allows two parties to exchange equivalent amounts of different currencies initially, followed by exchanges in the series of interest payments that must be paid on each series. The swap is concluded at a future date when the initial trade in different currencies is reversed. A basic currency swap involves transactions in three separate cash flows. First, two parties exchange or swap equivalent amounts of two different currencies, perhaps yen for dollars. One party might be a U.S.-based corporation selling computers in Japan. The company generates revenue in yen, which it needs to convert into dollars to pay dividends to its stockholders. The other party could be a Japan-based corporation selling cameras in the United States. This Japan-based company generates revenue in dollars, which it needs to convert into yen to pay dividends to its stockholders. In essence, these two companies initiate the swap by loaning each other equal sums of cash in their home currencies. The U.S.-based company loans dollars to the Japan-based company, and the Japan-based company loans an equivalent amount of yen to the U.S.-based company. Second, these two companies make interest payments to each other for the duration of the swap contract. The U.S.-based company receives interest payments in dollars from the Japan-based company earning dollar revenue in the United States. The Japan-based company receives interest payments in yen from the U.S.-based company earning yen revenue in Japan. Last, the two companies complete the swap by re-exchanging the exact sums of cash originally borrowed from each other. In the transaction, the two companies have protected themselves from adverse changes in exchange rates between the currencies of their home countries.

Currency swaps are a method of hedging foreign exchange risk over long spans of time. Foreign exchange risks have to do with risks associated with unanticipated changes in the rate at which a sum of money in one currency can be translated into a sum of money in another currency.

Currency swaps can be useful in a variety of situations. Take a U.S.-based company that plans to raise funds by selling bonds. Assume this company can issue bonds in Switzerland denominated in Swiss francs at a lower rate of interest than it can issue bonds in the United States. denominated in U.S. dollars. The risks of selling Swiss franc–denominated bonds arises from the possibility that the U.S. dollar might depreciate relative to the Swiss franc, leaving the U.S. company unable to generate enough dollars to pay off its Swiss bonds. To protect itself from exchange rate depreciation the U.S.-based company could enter into a currency swap agreement with a European bank. Suppose the U.S.-based company raised 100 million Swiss francs by selling Swiss franc–denominated bonds. In a currency swap agreement with a European bank, the U.S.-based company exchanges its 100 million Swiss francs into an equivalent amount of U.S. dollars. The European bank pays interest on the Swiss francs to the U.S.-based company. The U.S.-based company pays interest in dollars to the European bank. The U.S. bank will receive the

Swiss franc interest payments on the same day that it owes interest payment on the Swiss franc bonds. When the Swiss franc bonds mature, the U.S.-based company will exchange dollars for Swiss francs with the European bank. The exchange rate for the final transaction would be part of the original swap agreement. The U.S.-based company will use the Swiss francs to redeem the bonds.

Central banks also engage in swap agreements with other central banks. During the subprime financial crisis of 2008, the Federal Reserve entered into a swap agreement with the European Central Bank. The European Central Bank needed dollars to meet the liquidity needs of some European banks that had liabilities denominated in dollars.

See also: Foreign Exchange Markets

References

Goswami, Gautam, Jouahn Nam, and Milind Shrikhande. "Why Do Global Firms Use Currency Swaps?: Theory and Evidence." *Journal of Multinational Financial Management,* vol. 14, no. 4/5 (October 2004): 315–334.

Ziobrowsky, Alan, Brigitte Ziobrowsky, and Sidney Rosenberg. "Currency Swaps and International Real Estate." *Real Estate Economics,* vol. 25, no. 2 (Summer 1997): 223–252.

CURRENT ACCOUNT

The current account summarizes transactions that fall within the categories of imports or exports of good and services, income earned abroad, domestically generated income belonging to foreigners, and unilateral transfers. The common denominator behind all these transactions is the involvement of an inflow or outflow of currency. Unilateral transfers include foreign aid and gifts of money from residents of one country to family members living in another country. Cross-country investments, such as buying and selling foreign stocks and bonds, also involve currency inflows and outflows, but are summarized in another account called the capital account. A third account, the official reserves transactions account, summarizes central bank transactions that involve an inflow or outflow of currency and that change official reserve holdings. A Federal Reserve purchase of gold with dollars is an example of the type of transaction covered by the official reserves transactions account. These three accounts make up the balance of payments.

The current account balance is considered a significant indicator of the economic and monetary health of a country. It is among the handful of indicators that the *Economist* magazine reports for major countries of the world. The *Economist* reports the current account balance both in absolute numbers and as a percent of gross domestic product (GDP).

On the current account, transactions that involve an outflow of currency are a debit item, and transactions that involve an inflow of currency are a credit item. Exports of goods and services are a credit and imports are a debit. The foreign expenditures of a U.S. family visiting Greece count as an export on the U.S. current account. The interest income that a resident earns on a foreign bond counts as a credit. The interest income that a domestic bond pays to a foreign owner is a debit. Money residents send to family members living abroad counts as a debit. If the money value of the debits outweighs the money value of the credits, then the outflow of currency outruns the inflow of currency, and a country has a current account deficit. If the credits exceed the debits, the country has a current account surplus.

Persistent current account deficits is often regarded as an indication that a currency is overvalued and therefore faces a heightened risk of future depreciation. The largest component in the current account balance is net exports (exports minus imports). A current account deficit is nearly always an indication that imports exceed exports. As the value of a country's currency goes up in foreign exchange markets, foreign imports into that country become less costly while exports from that country become costlier in foreign markets. An excess of imports over exports suggests that a domestic currency is too strong and likely to weaken in the future. A current account deficit indicates that the currency outflow on the current account exceeds the inflow. If the excess outflow of currency from a current account deficit is not offset by an excess inflow on a capital account surplus, a currency will depreciate unless a government is able and willing to take action. Governments usually hold sufficient official reserves to defend domestic currencies against speculative attacks, but not against long-term downward trends driven by market forces.

Currencies can remain strong in foreign exchange markets for extended periods of time in situations where a large current account deficit is offset by a large capital account surplus. A capital account surplus indicates that the inflow of foreign capital exceeds the outflow of domestic capital to foreign countries. A net inflow of capital equates to a net inflow of currency. Countries with per-

sistent current account deficits often maintain elevated interest rates. The high interest rates encourage the inflow of foreign capital, offsetting the tendency of a current account deficit to undermine the value of a currency.

Even with strong capital inflows, a current account deficit is regarded as a risk factor in foreign exchange markets. The components in the current account are not tightly linked to the volatility and varying psychology of financial markets whereas capital flows are tightly linked to conditions in financial markets. Capital flows are much more sensitive than exports and imports to changes in expectations, and can therefore be more volatile. A net capital inflow can quickly change to net capital outflow, leading to almost certain currency depreciation and crashing financial markets for a country with a current account deficit. Currency speculators are always closely watching countries using elevated interest rates to sustain current account deficits offset by capital account surpluses. If these speculators see signs that elevated interest rates are pushing a country with a current account deficit into recession, they will dump the currency of that country. The value of the currency will crash in foreign exchange markets, domestic financial markets will crash, and the country will likely undergo a full-blown economic collapse.

For several years, the United States has been able sustain current account deficits with little difficultly. That is because the United States holds a reputation as a safe haven for foreign capital. United States' investments are considered among the safest in the world. Over the last 30 years, however, the Japanese yen has gained strength relative to the dollar, reflecting the fact that Japan usually has current account surpluses and the United States usually has current account deficits.

See also: Balance of Payments, Currency Crises, Foreign Exchange Markets

References

Abel, Andrew B., Ben S. Bernanke, and Dean Croushore. 2008. *Macroeconomics,* 6th ed.

Daniels, Joseph, and David VanHoose. 2004. *International Monetary and Financial Economics,* 3rd ed.

D

DE A OCHO REALES (PIECES OF EIGHT)

Toward the end of the 16th century, Spanish coins, particularly the *de a ocho reales,* had become the international currency and held that position until they were eclipsed by the British pound sterling in the 19th century. The pieces of eight was the immediate forerunner of the U.S. dollar.

The pieces of eight, called "Spanish dollar" in the United States, was equal to eight *reales,* a Spanish monetary unit. "Reales" was a word for "royal" in Spanish. Today, the monetary unit of account in Saudi Arabia is called the *riyal,* and in Oman and Yemen the monetary unit is the *rial,* both derivatives of the *real.* Spanish coins dominated Far Eastern trade, Mediterranean trade, and trade with the New World.

The Spanish real, a silver coin, came into existence in 1497 with the monetary reform of Ferdinand and Isabella, the Spanish monarchs who financed Columbus's voyage to the New World. Originally, the real consisted of one-sixty-seventh of a mark of silver and

was coined in multiples, quadruples, and octuples (the piece of eight reales), and in fractions of a real. The real was sometimes called a "bit." The pieces of eight were eight bits. A fourth of a real equaled two bits, a half real equaled four bits, and three-fourths of a real equaled six bits. The division of the dollar into bits lives on in the cheerleading yell heard at many high school sporting events: "Two bits, four bits, six bits, a dollar, all for the [name of team] stand up and holler." Ferdinand and Isabella's monetary reform set out to provide Spain with a unified coinage system. Charles V popularized the pieces of eight, equal to the Bohemian or Saxon *thaler,* which gave its name to the United States dollar.

Mints in Mexico City and Peru turned out vast quantities of Spanish reales. Mexico City boasted of the largest mint in the world, and minted a pieces-of-eight coin called the "pillar dollar," because a symbol on the obverse side denotes the Pillars of Hercules, the strait that opens the Mediterranean into the Atlantic Ocean. The modern dollar sign

Obverse view of a rare Spanish Empire silver coin from 1743. This coin, worth eight reales, was minted during the reign of King Ferdinand VI. (Hoberman Collection/Corbis)

($) may have originated from this symbol of the Pillars of Hercules, with the "S" portion a reference to a banner hanging from a pillar.

Mexico, after winning independence from Spain in 1821, minted its own *peso* with a bit more silver than the old Spanish pieces of eight. The new Mexican peso was called the "Mexican dollar" in Far Eastern trade, where it was the most popular coin throughout the 19th century, competing with the U.S. silver trade dollar and a British silver trade dollar. Spanish pieces of eight and Mexican pesos were legal tender in the United State in much of the pre–Civil War era. Mexico remained on a silver standard while most of the world adopted the gold standard, and Mexican silver pesos remained important in Far Eastern trade. During the Great Depression of the 1930s, Mexico abandoned the silver standard, just as the United States abandoned the gold standard.

With the loss of Mexican silver, and the European shift toward the gold standard after 1875, Spanish coinage receded into the background as international currency.

See also: Dollar, Silver

References
Braudel, Fernand. 1972. *The Mediterranean and the Mediterranean World in the Age of Phillip II,* vol. I.
Hamilton, Earl J. 1947. *War and Prices in Spain, 1651–1800.*
Hamilton, Earl J. 1965. *American Treasure and the Price Revolution in Spain, 1501–1650.*
Weatherford, Jack. 1997. *The History of Money.*
Vives, Jaime Vicens. 1969. *An Economic History of Spain.*

DEBIT CARD

Debit cards, similar in shape and size to credit cards, substantially advanced the replacement of coins, paper money, and checks with electronic money. These plastic cards with a magnetic strip on one side enable individuals to convert bank deposits into instant cash or to pay for purchases by electronically shifting money from a buyer's bank account to a seller's bank account. The development of the debit card may rank with coinage, printed paper money, and checks as one of the great innovations in money, creating a new monetary era that supplants the era of paper money.

The debit card burst on the world in 1971 when a banker in Burbank, California, connected the idea of money with the idea of a vending machine. A vending machine dispensing cash would free customers from the rigor of fixed banking hours, enabling customers to withdraw cash 24 hours a day, seven days a week. Thus, the automated teller machine (ATM) came into being.

The next important step in debit card development occurred in 1974 when the First Federal Savings and Loan of Lincoln, Nebraska, installed debit card reading machines at the cash registers of the Hinky Dinky supermarket. Rather than withdrawing cash, these machines enabled customers to transfer funds from their own bank accounts to the supermarket's bank accounts, ending the need to carry cash or a checkbook to the supermarket. Debit card transactions take less time than check transactions and eliminate the need for protection against bad checks.

Debit cards have not been an unmixed blessing. There have been numerous instances in which unauthorized individuals have used debit cards to empty someone's bank account. The use of debit cards at ATMs usually requires a personal identification number, which makes unauthorized use more difficult. Some of the debit cards that double as credit cards may be used at some retail outlets without personal identification numbers, and these cards have the greatest potential for fraudulent misuse.

Debit card transactions require an intricate telecommunications network that is most cost effective in grocery stores, department stores, and other large retail outlets that handle large volumes of sales. Small transactions that take place at small retail stores and even vending machines still depend heavily on coins and paper money. A new debit card, sometimes called the smart card, removes the need for an expensive telecommunication network, making it feasible for use with vending machines and small retailers. The smart card has an embedded computer chip that allows the card to be programmed for a fixed amount of money. The smart card can be used to make purchases up to a fixed or approved amount without a telecommunication network that connects a card-reading machine with a bank computer. The smart card can be used at isolated retail sites, or at vending machines, without the necessity for correct change.

The latter part of the 20th century saw smart cards develop along lines that could have put an end to circulating cash. Under the Mondex system, a machine transfers money from a customer's card to a merchant's card, without going through the intermediary of a bank. The merchant then passes on the electronic money from his or her card to the card of another person. The Mondex system allows blips of electronic money to change hands without going through a bank. The Mondex system seemed to hold the promise of ending the use of coins and paper money. The United States Congress held hearings to learn whether digital money would displace coinage and paper money.

Futuristic visions of a cashless society, however, turned out be very premature. Too much shopper resistance and too many technological glitches existed. Smart cards continued to develop along different lines. In one application, utility customers can buy a certain amount of credit from a local utility company, receiving a card with information that could be downloaded into a home utility meter. Electronic displays installed in the kitchen show how much of the credit is left on the meter. Utility customers say this method makes it easier for them to conserve on utility costs.

In a bid to replace cash and checks, credit card companies experimented with using key chains, wristwatches, and armbands for payment devices. These devices have not caught on, but the "contactless" smart card is catching on. This card has an embedded computer chip that allows the allows an electronic reader to read the card when the user holds the card in front of it. This saves swiping the card through a reader. The contactless cards seemed to be preferred over the traditional cards.

References

Becket, Paul. "Banking: Glitches Trip Up Real-Life Test of Plastic Cash." *Wall Street Journal* (Eastern Edition, New York) October 8, 1998, p. B1.

Bray, Nicholas. "Future Shop: No Cash Accepted." *Wall Street Journal*, July 13, 1995.

Sidel, Robin. "American Express Drops High-Tech Payment Device." *Wall Street Journal* (Eastern Edition, New York) March 31, 2008, p. B1.

Weatherford, Jack. 1997. *The History of Money*.

DECIMAL SYSTEM

The decimal system, a number system based on the number 10, became a distinguishing characteristic of currency systems during the 19th and 20th centuries. The currency system of the United States offers a typical example of a decimal currency system, with one dime equal to one-tenth of a dollar, and one cent equal to one-tenth of a dime, or a one-hundredth of a dollar.

From the ninth century until the end of the 18th century, the Carolingian currency system held sway in Europe. Under the eighth-century Carolingian reform, instituted by Charlemagne's father, King Pepin, 12 pence equaled one shilling, and 20 shillings made one pound.

The Carolingian reform established a new silver coinage in which 240 *denarii* (pennies) equaled a livre, or pound weight of silver. The Norman Conquest brought the Carolingian system to England, where it survived until 1971.

The Russians deserve credit for giving the modern world the decimal system of currency. By 1535, the Russians were trading in a Novgorod ruble, and a smaller unit, the *denga,* equal to a one-hundredth of a ruble. Under Peter the Great, the denga became the *kopek,* but otherwise Russia's decimal currency system has remained intact to the present day.

The Russian decimal system met with a cold reception in the courts of Europe, which had elaborated on the Carolingian system into currency systems susceptible to manipulation because of a multiplicity of coins that could be selectively debased. Also, the royal courts of Europe were not impressed with innovations from countries such as Russia, which were mired in economic backwardness.

The American revolutionaries, eager to depart from the practice of European monarchies, found no charm in coins called "crowns" and "sovereigns," bearing portraits of British monarchs. The Spanish milled dollar was a popular coin in the American colonies, but the Spanish dollar was subdivided into eight reales. In 1782, Robert Morris, U.S. superintendent of finance, sent a report to the Congress of Confederation recommending that the states coin their own money as a substitute for the medley of foreign coins then circulating, and that the state coinage systems uniformly follow a decimal system. The reasons for preferring the decimal system were:

> that it was desirable that money should be increased in the decimal

Ratio, by that means all calculations of Interest, exchange, insurance and the like are rendered much more simple and accurate, and of course, more within the power of the mass of people. Whenever such things require much labor, time and reflection, the greater number, who do not know, are made the dupes of the lessor number who do. (Watson, 1970, 10)

Thomas Jefferson forwarded the idea that the hundredth part of the dollar be called a "cent," after the Latin word for "one hundred," and that the tenth of the dollar be called a "dime," which means "tenth" in Latin. Alexander Hamilton incorporated these ideas into his *Report on the Establishment of a Mint,* and the Coinage Act of 1792 called for the adoption of a decimal currency system in the United States. Because the Russian currency system made use of coins outside the decimal system, the United States can boast of the first completely decimal currency system.

The arguments favoring the decimal system impressed the revolutionary imagination of France, and on October 7, 1793, the French revolutionary government replaced the coinage system of the Bourbon dynasty with a decimal currency system. In 1795, the French revolutionary government changed the name of the livre to the franc, which equaled the sum of 100 centimes. The conquest of Napoleon helped launch the decimal system in Europe, where it spread rapidly during the 19th century. Great Britain held out until 1971, becoming one of the last countries to adopt a decimal currency system. A pound now equals 100 pence, instead of 240 pence.

See also: American Penny, Carolingian Reform, Coinage Act of 1792, Dollar, Monetary Law of 1803

References

Chown, John F. 1994. *A History of Money.*
Watson, David K. 1970. *History of American Coinage.*
Weatherford, Jack. 1997. *The History of Money.*

DENARIUS

See Carolingian Reform, Florentine Florin, French Franc, Roman Empire Inflation

DEPOSITORY INSTITUTION DEREGULATION AND MONETARY CONTROL ACT OF 1980 (UNITED STATES)

In 1980, Congress passed the Depository Institutions Deregulation Monetary Control Act (DIDMCA), the most important piece of banking legislation in the United States since the Glass–Steagall Banking Act of 1933. The DIDMCA signaled a marked shift in government banking policy in the direction of a deregulated banking system. This was a sharp contrast to the banking legislation of the 1930s, which had added to the regulation of the banking industry.

One of the more important provisions of the DIDMCA authorized all depository institutions to offer negotiated order of withdrawal (NOW) accounts. These accounts are interest-bearing savings accounts with check-writing privileges that depositors basically treat as checking accounts. The banking legislation of the 1930s had forbidden banks from paying interest on checking accounts. In the 1970s, thrift institutions, faced with an outflow of funds and hoping to make their savings accounts more attractive, received permission from banking regulators to let thrift depositors write checks on savings accounts. Before the DIDMCA, only savings and loans (S&Ls), credit unions, and other thrift institutions offered NOW accounts. In practical terms, the DIDMCA enabled all depository institutions, including commercial banks, to pay interest on checking accounts. The DIDMCA also removed interest-bearing deposits from the restrictions of state usury laws.

A related provision of the DIDMCA made automatic transfer accounts legal, further lifting restrictions on interest-bearing checking accounts. These accounts let commercial banks automatically transfer unused checking account funds into interest-bearing savings accounts. Because checking accounts could not pay interest before the DIDMCA, the ability to switch funds from checking to savings as needed gave checking accounts some of the advantages of interest-bearing accounts.

By the mid-1970s, technology had made switching an inexpensive procedure, but the courts had ruled that automatic transfer accounts violated the law against the payment of interest on checking accounts. Therefore legislation was necessary to remove the prohibition on automatic transfer accounts.

The DIDMCA called for the formation of a Depository Institutions Deregulation Committee charged with overseeing the removal of interest-rate ceilings on all deposits, except business

deposits at commercial banks. This committee was composed of the heads of the Treasury Department, the Federal Reserve Board, the Federal Depository Insurance Corporation, the Federal Home Loan Bank Board, and the National Credit Union Administrator. The Comptroller of the Currency served as a nonvoting member.

The DIDMCA freed from state usury ceilings residential mortgages and agricultural and business loans in excess of $25,000 and extended partial exemption to other loans made by state-chartered banks, savings and loan institutions, and credit unions. States had the option to reinstate state usury ceilings on these loans, but action had to be taken by April 1, 1983.

The DIDMCA gave federally chartered S&Ls permission to make consumer loans, and invest in commercial paper and corporate debt securities. Up to 20 percent of a savings and loan's assets could be committed to these uses. The DIDMAC also added credit cards, trusts, and fiduciary services to the range of services offered by S&Ls. In a nutshell, the S&Ls now compete with commercial banks in a wider range of services.

The DIDMAC authorized mutual savings banks with federal charters to enter the market for business loans. These institutions could invest up to 5 percent of their assets in these loans, and the business borrowers could not receive checking privileges associated with these loans.

The DIDMAC put all federally insured depository institutions under the reserve requirements imposed by the Federal Reserve System. Before the DIDMAC, the Federal Reserve System set reserve requirements of federally chartered commercial banks. (Reserve requirements set the percentage of checking and savings deposits that must be retained in the form of vault cash or a deposit at a Federal Reserve Bank.) Reserve requirements protect depositors (or the FDIC) by making bank assets more liquid and less risky, but they also leave bank assets less profitable because reserves pay no interest. State laws had invariably set lower reserve requirements, as a percentage, for state-chartered banks. The DIDMAC increased the power of reserve requirements as a tool of monetary regulation, and leveled the playing field between federally chartered institutions and state-chartered institutions.

The consumer is the clear beneficiary of competition in most industries, but when a bank fails, the bank's customers suffer as much as the bank's owners. Depression-era legislation reduced competition between banks to stem the tide of bank failures. The DIDMCA took an important step toward restoring competition to the banking industry.

See also: Federal Reserve System, Glass–Steagall Banking Act of 1933

References

Baye, Michael R., and Dennis W. Jansen. 1995. *Money, Banking, and Financial Markets: An Economics Approach.*

White, Lawrence J. 1986. "The Partial Deregulation of Banks and other Depository Institutions." In *Regulatory Reform: What Actually Happened?* Ed. Leonard W. Weiss and Michael W. Klass.

DEUTSCHE BUNDESBANK

The Deutsche Bundesbank is the central bank of Germany. Before the establishment of the European Central Bank, it was comparable to the Federal Reserve System in the United States. A relatively young addition to the ranks of European central banks, the Deutsche Bundesbank gained a position of preeminence among European central banks during the post–World War II era.

The Reichsbank, the central bank of Nazi Germany, came to an end in 1948. In West Germany, the allied occupation authorities established a new currency, the Deutsche Mark, and organized a regional system of autonomous central banks, called *Landeszentralbanken*. At the apex of this system stood the Bank Deutscher Länder. This bank had the exclusive privilege to issue banknotes and acted as a lender of last resort. It was a two-tier structure, the lower layer composed of legally independent entities, and the structure may not have been organizationally efficient.

The Bundesbank Act of 1957 reorganized West Germany's central banking system, merging the independent Landeszentralbanken and the Bank Deutscher Länder. The act incorporated these entities as the Deutsche Bundesbank, a corporation wholly owned by the West German government. The head office remained at Frankfurt am Main, and each of the 11 Länder central banks operated its own system of branch banks. In 1990, the state banking system of East Germany was integrated with the Bundesbank, and the latter assumed the responsibility for monetary policy in the unified Germany. The system is spread out into more branches than the Federal Reserve System in the United States; one of the Länder central banks may oversee as many as 50 branch banks.

The distinguishing characteristic of the Bundesbank is its independence from government officials. The German people, having suffered through two

Deutsche Bundesbank in Hamburg, Germany. (Stephan Mosel)

episodes of hyperinflation in the 20th century, were committed to establishing a central bank that would protect the integrity of its currency. The law creating the Bundesbank conspicuously ignored any economic goals other than price stability. In the words of the statute:

> The Bundesbank, making use of the powers in the field of monetary policy conferred upon it under this Law, shall regulate the money circulation and the supply of credit to the economy with the aim of safeguarding the currency and shall ensure the due execution by banks of payments within the country as well as to and from foreign countries. (Bank for International Settlements, 1963, 59)

The supreme policy-making body of the Bundesbank is the Central Bank Council, composed of a president, vice president, up to eight additional members of a directorate, and the presidents of the 11 Länder central banks. The president of the Federal Republic of Germany appoints the members of the directorate, each serving eight-year terms. The president of the directorate is appointed for an eight-year term, and is highly secure in that appointment. The president of the Federal Republic appoints the presidents of the Länder central banks upon the recommendation of the directorate of the Central Bank Council.

Because of its independence from government officials, the Bundesbank could concentrate solely on controlling inflation during the post–World War II era when other central banks, less independent of government authorities, pursued policies aimed at reducing unemployment. During the 1970s, when most Western countries were racked by inflation, West Germany kept inflation to modest levels, and the Bundesbank rose to become the most influential central bank in Europe. In 1993 the European Monetary Institute, the precursor to a European central bank, was set up in Frankfurt, symbolizing the European Union's commitment to sound monetary policies.

With the establishment of the European Central Bank in 1998, the Bundesbank became a member of the European central bank system. The president of the Bundesbank serves on the Governing Council of the European Central Bank. The European Central bank sets monetary policy for all countries in the euro area, which includes Germany. The Bundesbank shares in implementing the European Central Bank's monetary policy.

See also: Bank of England, Bank of France, Central Bank, Federal Reserve System

References

Bank for International Settlements. 1963. *Eight European Central Banks.*

Kennedy, Ellen. 1991. *The Bundesbank: Germany's Central Bank in the International Monetary System.*

Padoa-Schioppa, Tommaso. 1994. *The Road to Monetary Union in Europe.*

DEUTSCHE MARK

Before the introduction of the euro, the Deutsche Mark, or German mark, was the currency unit of Germany, comparable to the dollar for the United States. After the collapse of the Bretton Woods system in 1973, the U.S. dollar, no longer convertible into gold and subject to depreciation from inflation, lost some of its position as an international currency. As the U.S. dollar lost ground as an international currency, the German mark began to play the same role in the European economy as the U.S. dollar played in the world economy.

Compared to the British pound sterling, which can boast of a 1,300-year history, the history of the German mark is a bit short in light of the prestige that it commanded in international trade before it was superseded by the euro. In the immediate aftermath of World War II, the Reichsmark, the currency of Nazi Germany, no longer functioned as a medium of exchange. Trade took place on a black market, outside the system of German price controls, and commodities such as cigarettes and coal acted as mediums of exchange. Barter also flourished; city dwellers walked to the countryside with whatever goods they had and traded them for food.

The victorious Allies originally planned to introduce monetary reform in 1946, but an agreement between France, the Soviet Union, Britain, and the United States to treat Germany as single economic unit broke down, delaying monetary reform from May 1946 to June 1948. Part of the difficulty was that France, Britain, and the United States did not want to entrust the Soviet Union with plates to print currency, fearing that the Soviets would print up extra currency to impose an inflation tax on Germany. As the rift between the Western occupation powers and the Soviet Union widened, the decision was made to print the currency in the United Kingdom. The plan to replace the Reichsmark with a new currency, the Deutsche Mark, was a closely guarded military secret, given the code name Operation Bird Dog.

On June 20, 1948, the Western powers issued to every inhabitant in the three Western zones 40 Deutsche Marks in exchange for 40 Reichsmarks. Two months later, another 20 Deutsche Marks were exchanged for 20 Reichsmarks. Aside from the per capita distribution, Deutsche Marks replaced the Reichsmarks on a 1:10 basis, one Deutsche Mark equaling 10 Reichsmarks. All debts were written down at this ratio, including government debt, mortgages, bank loans, and insurance policies. Bank deposits and balance sheets of businesses were adjusted on the same basis, deflating the asset side and the liability side to one-tenth of their original amounts. The authorities decreed that all new debts had to be contracted in Deutsche Marks. A central bank, patterned somewhat after the Federal Reserve System, was created from the branches of the Reichsbank. It was called the Bank of Deutscher Länder (Bank of German States), and in 1957 it was transformed into the Deutsche Bundesbank.

All price controls were lifted on June 24, 1948. With the new currency, goods suddenly showed up at stores where shelves had been empty for years. Apparently many goods had been hiding in the underground economy.

The Soviet authorities were forced to follow the example of currency reform in order to keep the Reichsmarks no longer useable in the Western zones from flooding the Soviet zone. The Soviets issued the *Deutsche Mark East* and for a while the western Deutsche Mark circulated side by side with the Deutsche Mark East at equal value. By the end of July 1948, the Deutsche Mark East traded at about half the value of the Deutsche Mark, a factor that contributed to the political separation of East and West Germany.

A noted economist, Charles Kindleberger (1984), wrote, "I regard the German monetary reform of 1948 as one of the great feats of social engineering of all time" (418). The Deutsche Mark evolved into the most prestigious currency in Europe. During the inflation-ridden 1970s, West Germany kept inflation to modest levels, and in the 1980s, West Germany led Europe in the disinflation process. As Europe moved toward economic integration, the Deutsche Mark played a major role in the monetary affairs of Europe. In the 1990s, economic turmoil from combining the two Germanys cost the Deutsche Mark a bit of its reputation for stability. Also, France began to rival Germany in reputation for price stability.

On January 1, 1999, the European System of Central Banks launched a new European currency, the euro, that replaced the national currencies of participating countries. The euro replaced the Deutsche Mark, the French franc, and several other European currencies. Banknotes and coins in Deutsche Marks, French francs, and other superseded currencies continued to serve in hand-to-hand circulation until January 1, 2002.

See also: Hyperinflation in Post–World War I Germany, Gold Mark of Imperial German, Rentenmark

References

Kindleberger, Charles P. 1984. *A Financial History of Western Europe.*

Padoa-Schioppa, Tommaso. 1994. *The Road to Monetary Union in Europe.*

Stolpher, Gustav. 1967. *The German Economy: 1870–Present*.

DISSOLUTION OF MONASTERIES (ENGLAND)

Between 1534 and 1540, King Henry VIII, showing the same hasty, thoughtless stubbornness that marked his quest for a son, dissolved most of the English monasteries and confiscated their property.

Early in the 16th century, England's enemy was Charles V, emperor of the Holy Roman Empire, which Voltaire later described as "neither holy, nor Roman, nor an empire." The Catholic world looked to Charles V to champion the cause of Catholicism against the impious king of England, and precious metals from the New World poured in to Charles, enlarging his vision of possibilities.

The dissolution of the monasteries occurred against the backdrop of the Reformation, the 16th-century religious movement that began as an effort to reform the Catholic Church and ended with the establishment of the Protestant churches. Thus the forces of the Reformation in England made monasteries a clear and open target. In addition, expenses for public works impelled Henry VIII along a course that ended in the confiscation of vast holdings of ecclesiastical properties. Aside from extravagant court expenditures, Henry VIII financed a major enlargement of the English navy, and a significant improvement of England's harbors and ports. Paying for these public expenditures with more taxes was not workable. Taxes were already high and any increase would have prompted tax evasion, perhaps increasing collection costs as much as revenue. Henry VIII resorted to currency debasement, the worst such episode in English history, and to the confiscation of ecclesiastical properties. Monasteries had large landholdings that generated income and were also storehouses of gold and silver candlesticks, crosses, plate, and other precious metal objects.

Legislative action began in 1534 with the Act for the Suppression of the Lesser Monasteries. This law covered all monasteries with annual incomes of less that 200 pounds, accounting for about two-thirds of all the monasteries in England. In 1538, Henry expanded the policy of dissolution to friaries and, in 1539, expanded it to the larger monasteries.

The monasteries were stripped and sometimes destroyed. About 75,000 pounds sterling in gold and silver was sent to London from dissolved monasteries. Bells were melted down and recast as cannon, and lead from roofs and gutters was exported. By 1540, nearly all ecclesiastical orders had ceased to exist, although a few survived until Henry's successor, Edward VI, dissolved them in 1547, thus completing Henry's policy.

The abbots of targeted monasteries resorted to various stratagems to hide precious metals when the king's agents came to dispose of monastery property. Some abbots placed gold and silver objects with private individuals in hopes of getting them back later. Some objects were hidden in secret vaults and walls, and some were sold for money, converting ecclesiastical property into private property. Nevertheless, the king's agents were tenacious, and uncovered much property that had been concealed or secretly sold.

King Henry VIII of England, one of Europe's notable absolute monarchs, instituted a series of changes within England that had a dramatic impact on the nature of English government and indelibly altered the relationship between the English Crown and the church. (Library of Congress)

Where possible, gold and silver were coined directly, but in some cases embedded jewels, wood, or other materials had to be extracted and separated. Gold and silver either went straight to the mint or ended up at the goldsmiths.

The sanctity of religious temples, churches, and monasteries had always enabled these facilities to accumulate larger quantities of gold and silver than private individuals could safely shelter. During the Reformation, the Catholic institutions lost some of their inviolability in countries destined to be predominately Protestant, and governments pressed for funds tended to expropriate the precious metals for their own use.

See also: Great Debasement, Silver Plate

References
Challis, C. E. 1978. *The Tudor Coinage.*
Davies, Glen. 1994. *A History of Money.*

DOLLAR

"Dollar" is the official name for the U.S. currency, the closest approximation to a world currency, and is also the name for numerous other national currencies.

The term "dollar" is apparently a variation of the term "thaler," a common term for coins in Germany and Eastern Europe that may have been derived from a valley named Joachimsthal, where coins were minted in the 16th century. The coins were called *Joachimsthalergroschen,* soon shortened to *thaler,* and later to *taler.* In the 16th century, the Scots adopted the term "dollar" to distinguish their currency from that of the English. The Scots were not always compliant subjects of the English crown, and from the outset the term "dollar" bore an anti-English and antiauthoritarian connotation. Scottish emigrants brought the term "dollar" to the British colonies.

Although England forbade its colonies to mint coins, Spain put no such prohibition on its colonies, which were rich in precious metals. Mexico boasted of one of the world's largest mints. Spanish coins were the most readily accepted worldwide, including in the British colonies, but the colonists called the coins "dollars" rather than their Spanish names of *reales* and *pesos.* The Spanish pieces-of-eight coins had a face value of eight reales, and in the United States the phrase "two bits" is still used to refer to a quarter, one-fourth of a dollar.

The most common Spanish coin circulating in the British colonies was sometimes called the "pillar dollar" because the obverse side bore an image of the Eastern and Western hemispheres with a large column on each side. The columns represented the Pillars of Hercules, and the words "plus ultra," meaning "more beyond," embellished a banner hanging from one of the columns. The coin was apparently a means of publicizing the discovery of America. The dollar sign probably evolved from the pillar dollar, with the two vertical parallel lines representing the columns, and the "S' shape representing the banner.

The dollar had established itself as the primary money unit of account in the 13 colonies, and the Congress of the new republic declared on July 6, 1785, that the "money unit of the United States of America be one dollar" (Weatherford, 1997). In 1794, the United States began minting silver dollars containing 371.25 grains of silver, an amount based on the average weight of Spanish dollars circulating in the United States. Spanish and Mexican dollars remained legal tender during the early days of the Republic.

Popular usage made dollars, whether United States, Spanish, or Mexican, the accepted currency in the New World. Canada created an official currency, the Canadian dollar, pegged at a one to one exchange rate with the United States dollar. Among the British colonies in the Caribbean, dollars became the official currency in Anguilla, Saint Kitts and Nervis, Antigua and Barbuda, Montserrat, Dominica, Saint Lucia, Saint Vincent, Guyana, the Bahamas, Belize, Barbados, the Cayman Islands, the British Virgin Islands, Trinidad and Tobago, the Turks and Caicos Islands, and Jamaica. Most Latin American countries adopted as their official currency the peso, which shares with the dollar a common ancestor, the Spanish real.

Spain also popularized the use of dollars in the Pacific basin. In the late 19th century, Mexican dollars dominated Pacific basin trade but both the United States and Britain issued so-called trade dollars for foreign trade with the area. The Chinese called silver dollars "yuan," meaning "round things," and yuan became the standard currency in China and Taiwan. The Japanese shortened "yuan" to "yen" and established a yen currency. Initially 1 yen approximately equaled 1 dollar.

The term "dollar" became the name of the official currencies in Australia, New Zealand, Fiji, the Cook Islands, Kiribati, Brunei, Singapore, Hong Kong, the Solomon Islands, Pitcairn, Tokelau, Tuvalu, the Marshall Islands, and Western Samoa. By 1994, the "dollar" denoted the official currencies in 37 countries and autonomous territories. Europe, the birthplace of the original dollar, is one of the few places in the world where "dollar" is not a designation for an official currency. In 1991, the newly independent country of Slovenia, part of the former Yugoslavia, adopted "tolar," a variation of "dollar," to denote its official currency. Zimbabwe, among the latest African countries to join the ranks of independent nations, named its official currency the "dollar."

See also: Coinage Act of 1792, De a Ocho Reales, *Taler*

References

Nussbaum, Arthur. 1957. *A History of the Dollar*.
Weatherford, Jack. 1997. *The History of Money*.

DOLLAR CRISIS OF 1971

In August 1971, the United States government suspended the convertibility of dollars into gold for foreign official holders of dollars, marking the final break with the gold standard in the world economy. Uneasiness about the dollar reached crisis levels in 1971 as the rest of the world became increasingly aware that the United States did not own enough gold to redeem all the foreign-owned dollars. The drain on its gold reserves also concerned the U.S. government. Before the suspension, foreign official holders of dollars (foreign central banks and foreign governments) had been able to convert dollars into gold at the rate of $35 per ounce. (Domestic holders of dollars had been unable to convert dollars into gold since the 1930s.) Gold has remained an important component of international monetary reserves, but currencies are no longer convertible in gold at a fixed, official rate.

The Bretton Woods system, created in 1944, established a world gold standard for international purposes, requiring each country to define a par value of its currency in terms of a fixed weight of gold. A shortage of world gold reserves, however, led countries to define domestic currencies in terms of U.S. dollars, and the United States stood ready to redeem dollars into gold at the official rate for foreign official holders. The redemption of dollars into gold drained the U.S. gold stock from $25 billion in 1949 to $12 billion in the early 1970s.

Largely because of worldwide military and political obligations, the United States ran what are called balance of payments deficits after World War II, infusing additional dollars into a world economy hungry for monetary reserves. A balance of payments deficit occurs when the outflow of dollars from U.S. imports and investment abroad exceeds the inflow of dollars from U.S. exports and foreign investment in the United States. The consequence in 1971 was an increase in the number of foreign-owned dollars that the United States was committed to redeeming in gold. After the mid-1960s, the U.S. balance of payments deficits grew at a faster tempo because of military involvement in Vietnam and heavy investment abroad. The rest of the world saw that the U.S. gold stock was insufficient to redeem all foreign-held dollars in gold. In August 1971, President Nixon announced that the United States would no longer convert dollars into gold for foreign official holders. Between August 1971 and May 1973, world governments endeavored, without success, to save the Bretton Woods system with a dollar devalued in terms of gold.

After 1973, the value of the dollar was no longer defined in terms of a fixed weight of gold, and other currencies were no longer defined in terms of dollars. The exchange rates between currencies floated freely and were based on supply and demand. Today, governments manage the floating exchange rates, but currencies are not tied to each other in fixed exchange rates.

Historically, the suspension of convertibility of paper money into precious metal has occurred during wartime— the Civil War and the War of 1812 being prime examples in the United States. The suspension of the convertibility of the dollar in 1971 occurred when the United States was engaged in the expensive Cold War with the Soviet Union, coupled with a lengthy effort in Vietnam. Some observers attribute the inflation of the 1970s to the collapse of the gold standard and the loss of the discipline that the gold standard had imposed on monetary growth. As control over monetary growth brought inflation down in the 1980s, however, a connection between the gold standard and price stability seemed less necessary.

See also: Balance of Payments, Bretton Woods System, Dollar, Gold Standard

References

De Vries, Margaret Garritsen. 1987. *Balance of Payments Adjustment, 1945 to 1986: The IMF Experience.*
Snider, Delbert A. 1975. *Introduction to International Economics.*

DOLLARIZATION

Dollarization occurs when a foreign currency either officially replaces or unofficially displaces domestic currency as the primary means of payment and unit account. The term suggests situations where the U.S. dollar as the major world currency fulfills the roles of a domestic currency in other countries, but the term is applied in a broader sense to situations where other foreign currencies take precedence or replace a domestic currency. The euro serves as currency in Kosovo, and the Swiss franc in Liechtenstein. Examples of dollarization using the U.S. dollar include Ecuador and San Salvador. Ecuador officially adopted the U.S. dollar as legal tender domestic currency in 2000, and San Salvador in 2001 (Quispe-Angnoli, Whisler, 2006). One of the oldest instances of permanent dollarization using the U.S. dollar is found in Panama, which adopted the U.S. dollar in 1903. Unofficial dollarization occurs when the spontaneous use of the U.S. dollar or other foreign currency surfaces alongside a country's domestic currency. Full dollarization occurs when the U.S. dollar or other foreign currency completely replaces the domestic currency.

Dollarization can bring monetary stability to a country gripped by runaway inflation. In these cases, dollarization is likely to develop spontaneously if the government does not officially enact it. Ecuador is an example of a government that turned to dollarization to meet a crisis of monetary and inflationary chaos.

As a global, free-market economy has developed, full dollarization as an attractive policy has drawn strong interest, even in countries not rocked by monetary and economic stability. Countries haunted by a past history of rampant inflation often find that fears of a recurrence of inflation keep interest rates elevated long after the inflation subsides. High interest rates act as a deterrent to economic growth and development in emerging economies. One method of bringing down interest rates is to adopt as legal tender domestic currency a foreign currency with a history of price stability. A closely related reason has to do with the attraction of foreign capital.

When foreign investors from a developed economy contemplate investing in an emerging economy, one risk they have to weigh is the risk of currency crisis and depreciation in the country receiving the investment. Dollarization removes one element of risk that foreign investors face and helps ease the flow of foreign capital into an emerging economy. Fears of currency crisis and depreciation can spark capital flight and speculative attacks, even when the fears are unfounded. Globalization and freer markets have increased the mobility of capital between countries. The enhanced mobility of foreign capital has brought in its wake a higher incidence of currency crises triggered by sudden and expected outflows of capital. Dollarization is one approach to taming what at times seems an epidemic of currency crises. The global economy stands to benefit from dollarization since currency crises tend to spread to trading partners, causing contagion.

In the case of the U.S. dollar, the U.S. government does not object to a country adopting the dollar as legal tender domestic currency, but dollarization does involve some disadvantages to the country adopting the dollar. First, all governments generate a certain percent of revenue from printing money, a practice called "seigniorage." Revenue from seigniorage is given up when a country opts for dollarization. Second, dollarization takes away from governments the power to pursue an independent monetary policy. A country enduring persistent high unemployment may need to depreciate its currency to make its goods cheaper in other countries, an option unavailable to a country that has embraced dollarization. In summary, dollarization has costs and benefits as an official policy and is still being studied.

References

Schuler, Kurt. "Some Theory and History of Dollarization." *Cato Journal,* vol. 25, no. 1 (Winter 2005): 115–125.

Berg, Andrew, and Edwardo Borensztein. "The Dollarization Debate." *Finance & Development,* vol. 37, no. 1 (March 2000): 38–42.

Quispe-Angnoli, Myriam, and Elena Whisler. "Official Dollarization and the Banking System in Ecuador and El Salvador." *Economic Review* (0732183), vol. 91. no. 3 (3rd Quarter 2006): 55–71.

E

EAST ASIAN FINANCIAL CRISIS

In 1997, a financial crisis threw the East Asian economies into a financial chaos that threatened to derail the East Asian economic miracle and engulf the global financial system. In the 1990s, East Asia had become the scene of a new group of economic miracles. From the mid-1990s until the outbreak of financial crisis, East Asian countries such as Thailand, Singapore, Indonesia, South Korea, and Malaysia posted real gross domestic product (GDP) growth rates in the 8 percent range or higher (International Monetary Fund, 1997).

Until the East Asian financial crisis, currency crises were often the domain of countries suffering from high inflation, slow growth, large government budget deficits, low savings, and political instability. Unlike the usual candidates for currency crises, the East Asian countries had what economists call "sound macroeconomic fundamentals." They had high savings rates, low public debts, fast growth and low inflation—the very qualities that win the confidence of foreign investors.

One crack in the foundation involved the structure of corporate finance. Enterprises had relied too heavily on debt financing as opposed to stock issuance. Enterprises do not face bankruptcy when the value of company stock plunges, but they do face bankruptcy when they cannot pay debts. An equally important vulnerability stemmed from the balance sheets of East Asian banks. These banks borrowed foreign capital on a short-term basis to underwrite long-term loans. The short-term nature of the foreign capital inflows left these banks open to a sudden and unexpected reversal from a foreign capital inflow to a foreign capital outflow. A sudden reversal of foreign capital flows made these banks and enterprises illiquid. Much of the foreign debt was denominated in dollars. When the exchange rates of local currencies fell, the real value of foreign debt in local currencies skyrocketed.

The baht, currency of Thailand. (Jupiterimages)

The East Asian countries practiced an economic policy that pegged the value of their local currencies to a basket of currencies in which the U.S. dollar played a highly dominate role. The rate at which a local currency could be converted into dollars remained almost constant. This policy shared in making East Asia an attractive haven for foreign capital, but it also was the undoing of these economies. In the late 1990s, the value of the U. S dollar went up, probably because of strong global demand for U.S. financial assets. As the value of the dollar climbed, the values of currencies linked to the dollar, such as the East Asian currencies, also climbed. The appreciation of a country's currency leaves the exports of that country more expensive in foreign markets. It also makes foreign imports into that country less costly. Falling exports and rising imports left the East Asian economies with current account deficits that needed to be financed by an inflow of foreign capital. East Asian companies began to feel the pain as sales fell off in foreign markets, and domestic sales faced greater completion from imports. In addition, East Asian central banks raised interest rates to increase the attraction for foreign capital. The policy of keeping the local currency exchange rates pegged to the dollar required that current account deficits be financed by foreign capital inflows. Otherwise, the value of the local currency relative to the dollar would sink.

The economic and financial situation in Thailand sparked the crisis. Many currency traders believed that the baht, Thailand's currency, traded too high, higher than the central bank of Thailand could support.

Thailand's economy was already suffering from double-digit interest rates and depressed stock prices. Currency traders launched billions of dollars of sell contracts on the baht. Fears of currency depreciation excited a broad outflow of foreign capital, putting more pressure on foreign exchange reserves. In a single day, the central bank spent $500 million dollars of its dollar reserves to keep the baht from falling below its pegged level (Daniels and VanHoose, 1999, 441). In 1997, Thailand's central bank let the baht float, free to depreciate, which it did.

The depreciation of the baht triggered foreign capital outflows from other East Asian economies. By the end of 1997, Thailand, Indonesia, and South Korea had watched local currencies depreciate about 40 percent relative to the U.S. dollar (Daniels and VanHoose, 1999, 36).

See also: Currency Crises

References

Daniels, Joseph, and David VanHoose. 1999. *International Monetary and Financial Economics.*

International Monetary Fund. 1997. "Crisis in Asia: Regional and Global Implications." *World Economic Outlook: Interim Assessment,* December 1997.

Islam, Azizul, 1999. "The Dynamics of the Asian Economic Crisis and Selected Policy Implications." in *Global Financial Turmoil and Reform,* ed. Barry Herman, pp. 49–74.

Masahiro, Kawai. "The East Asian Currency Crisis: Causes and Lessons." *Contemporary Economic Policy,* vol. 16, no. 2 (April 1998): 157–173.

ENGLISH PENNY

The English silver penny circulated for at least 1,100 years, first appearing in the eighth century and remaining in circulation until 1820, setting a record of longevity for a circulating coin that has probably never been matched.

At the opening of the eighth century, small silver coins circulated, known to modern scholars as *sceattas,* and mentioned in the laws of Ine, a local English ruler, as *pennies.*

The clearest point of departure for a history of the penny begins about 760 CE with King Offa, ruler of Mercia, an Anglo-Saxon kingdom in central England. King Offa enjoys the added distinction of being the only English King ever to strike coins bearing the name and bust of his consort. He minted over a million pennies—by some estimates several millions—and he surpassed all of his predecessors in the quality of his coinage, as well as its quantity. Beginning with King Offa's coinage, the penny remained the only English coin in circulation for 500 years. Initially 240 silver pennies weighed one pound, beginning the history of the English sterling pound.

The weight of the penny probably varied. In 1266, the English government defined a silver penny to be the weight of "thirty-two wheat corns in the midst of the ear." In 1280, the English government fixed the weight of the penny equal to 24 grains, setting the precedent that makes a pennyweight today equal to 24 troy grains. The 32 grains of wheat were comparable to 24 grains. During the 13th century, a penny was worth a day's wages or could buy a sheep. The value of the penny was sufficiently high that the government turned to minting halfpenny coins in the 14th century, and three-halfpenny coins in the 16th century. The weight of the penny steadily fell until silver pennies struck in 1816 weighed 7.27 troy grains.

In 1257, Henry III minted gold pennies that were worth 20 silver pennies. Per unit of weight, gold was 10 times as valuable as silver, and Henry III's gold pennies weighed twice as much as the silver pennies. The issue of gold coins failed, being too valuable to meet the needs of the English economy.

The word "penny" may have originated from the word "pending," which was the name of a coin issued by Penda, a king who ruled Mercia in the second quarter of the seventh century. Nevertheless, linguistic forms of "penny" are widely spread with equivalents in Dutch and Friesian. The Danish word for money is still *Penge*, resembling *penig*, the old English word for "penny." Variants of the word "penny" may have evolved from an old Danish word for the pans that were used to coin money.

The smallest denomination of coins minted in the United States are called "pennies." They are token coins, but were formerly minted from copper. The purchasing power of the U.S. penny is a bit modest to justify the phrase, "a pretty penny," referring to a large sum of money. Sixpenny nails now denote nails of a certain length, but originally denoted nails that sold for six pennies per 100.

See also: American Penny, Copper

References

Davies, Glyn. 1994. *A History of Money*.

Feavearyear, Sir Albert. 1963. *The Pound Sterling: A History of English Money*, 2nd ed.

EQUATION OF EXCHANGE

The equation of exchange identifies the exact mathematical relationship that exists between the money supply, the price level, and the volume of economic activity. The economist Irving Fisher (1867–1947) first formulated the equation of exchange, and his version took the following form:

$$MV + M'V' = PT$$

Here, M stands for the stock of currency in a given year, V stands for the velocity or number of times a dollar bill changes hands during a year, M' measures the quantity of checkable deposits, and V' the velocity of checkable deposits. P stands for the price involved in a typical transaction, and T represents the number of transactions.

Contemporary economists make use of a simplified equation of exchange that takes the following form:

$$MV = PY$$

Here, M stands for a measure of the money stock that includes, at a minimum, currency in circulation plus checkable deposits. Time deposits and other highly liquid assets may also be included. V stands for the income velocity of money, defined as being equal to the money value of income and output divided by the money stock. P stands for the price level, and Y stands for real output. In practice, PY stands for gross domestic product (GDP) unadjusted for inflation, called "nominal GDP," and Y stands for GDP adjusted for inflation, called "real GDP." P is a factor standing for the price level and is calculated by dividing nominal GDP by real GDP. Velocity is calculated by dividing nominal GDP by the money stock.

Nominal GDP divided by M equals V, which can be converted to the form $MV =$ nominal GDP. Furthermore, nominal GDP divided by real GDP (Y) equals the price index (P), which is mathematically equivalent to saying that nominal GDP $= PY$. Therefore $MV = PY$ is what is called an "identity" in mathematics, true by definition.

The equation of exchange is often converted to a percentage change form, expressed as:

$$\% \text{ change in } M + \% \text{ change in } V = \% \text{ change in } P + \% \text{ change in } Y$$

A school of economists called "quantity theorists" assumes that velocity is relatively stable, suggesting that the percentage change in V is always zero. They also assume that the percentage change in Y is at the long-term growth rate of real GDP, approximately 3 percent. With these assumptions, the inflation rate (percentage change in P) will always be 3 percent less than the growth rate of the money stock (percentage change in M). If the money stock grows at 10 percent a year, the inflation rate will be 7 percent a year. Therefore, inflation is an exact mathematical function of the money stock growth rate, and the equation of exchange furnishes us with a theory of inflation.

Empirical evidence bears out the close correspondence between money stock growth and inflation, but there is still room for some economists to argue that increases in the inflation rate force authorities to increase monetary growth, instead of the other way around. These issues stand to benefit from further study.

See also: Monetarism, Velocity of Money

References

Mankiw, N. Gregory. 1996. *Macroeconomics,* 3rd ed.

Klein, John J. 1986. *Money and the Economy,* 6th ed.

EURO CURRENCY

On May 3, 1998, leaders of the European Union (EU) concluded an agreement to establish a European Monetary Union (EMU) and, on January 1, 1999, to launch a common EMU currency, called the "euro." The new European currency made its debut in two phases. The first phase lasted between January 1, 1999, and January 1, 2002. During this phase, the banknotes and coins of the traditional national currencies such as the French francs and Deutsche Marks continued to circulate and the euro only existed as a "virtual currency." The second phase began on January 1, 2002. In the second phase, banknotes and coins in euro superseded the banknotes and coins of the traditional national currencies.

Initially, 11 countries agreed to adopt the euro, Germany, France, Italy, Spain, Portugal, Belgium, Luxembourg, the Netherlands, Austria, Finland, and Ireland. Later, Greece, Cyprus, Malta, and Slovena joined the euro zone. For now, Britain, Sweden, and Denmark plan to retain their own national currencies. Some economists have named the new monetary zone "Euroland."

The historic agreement to form the EMU provides that responsibility for management of monetary policy in Europe falls to a newly established European Central Bank (ECB). Central banks regulate money supplies, interest rates, and credit conditions, and currently each member of the EMU has its own central bank to share in the implementation of the ECB's monetary policy. The major challenge facing the ECB is the formulation of a monetary policy that can meet the needs of such diverse economies as Germany and Portugal. A single European monetary policy means a single interest rate all across Europe, regardless of economic conditions in each country.

The president of the ECB normally serves an eight-year term. To ease tensions, the first president, Dutchman Wim

Euro in various denominations. (Jupiterimages)

Duisenberg, kept his promise to step down after four years in favor of Frenchman Jean-Claude Trichet. Frenchman Christain Noyer served as the first vice-president of the ECB. The first president, vice-president, and a four-member board, with representatives from Germany, Italy, Spain, and Finland, oversaw the management of the ECB during its first years. Reaching an agreement on the leadership of the ECB was the last major hurdle to finalizing the agreement.

A common European currency renders transparent differences in wages, labor costs, and prices among European countries, forcing high-cost countries to enact reforms to improve efficiency and lower costs. Uncompetitive countries no longer have the option of devaluing domestic currencies, making their exports cheaper to foreigners and their imports more expensive compared to domestic goods. The new currency system, by increasing competition between European national economies and coming on line amid an inflation-free recovery, suffered fears of currency weakness that might be expected to undercut a new currency without a track record. To bolster the euro, EMU countries had five times more gold and currency reserves than did the United States.

By increasing cross-border competition and trade, the EMU economically strengthened Europe in the global economy. European leaders envision that the euro, supported by an economic bloc with more inhabitants than the United States, is well positioned to challenge the dominance of the dollar in the global market place.

Nevertheless, the introduction of the euro was not met with universal applause. Europe suffered from high unemployment rates—in some countries the highest since the 1930s—and much of the blame was pinned on the economic integration of Europe. The introduction of the euro was seen as a further step down the road of economic integration, forcing companies to undertake more streamlining to remain competitive by laying off more workers.

The euro was introduced in 1999 at a value of 1 euro = $1.16. To the embarrassment of the European Central Bank, the currency had lost nearly one-fourth of its value by January 2002, equaling much less than one U.S. dollar. After the introduction of euro banknotes and coins in January 2002, the euro began to gain strength. On June 3, 2009, the euro stood at 1 euro = $1.41.

See also: Latin Monetary Union, Wendish Monetary Union

References

Karouf, Jim. "Start the Presses: Euro Set to Debut." *Futures,* vol. 27, no. 9 (September 1, 1998): 30.

Wall Street Journal. "Economic Climate Looks Good for Launch of New Currency." May 4, 1998, A17–18.

EURODOLLARS

Eurodollars come into existence when the ownership of dollar deposits in U.S. banks passes into the hands of foreign banks. The dollar deposits, more commonly called "demand deposits" or "checking accounts," remain in U.S. banks, but the owners of the deposits are foreign banks, or foreign branches of U.S. banks. Individuals in foreign countries have dollar deposits in U.S. banks, but these deposits do not count as Eurodollars. Dollar deposits owned by foreign banks count as Eurodollars because these banks conduct a business of attracting dollar deposits and making dollar loans. Eurodollar deposits in foreign banks are interest-paying time deposits, usually of large amounts, and borrowers of dollars can turn to these foreign banks for dollar loans.

In the late 1950s, European banks first began holding deposits denominated in dollars, and borrowing and lending in dollars. The probable cause of the growth of the Eurodollar market lay with interest rate ceilings in the United States. Regulation Q, promulgated by the Federal Reserve Board, put a legal ceiling of less than 6 percent on interest rates that time deposits could pay in U.S. banks. The payment of interest rates that exceeded the legal interest rate ceiling in the United States constituted one of the major attractions of Eurodollar deposits. When interest rates soared in the 1970s, foreign banks, not subject to U.S. banking regulations, were able to pay much higher interests on time deposits, and make dollar loans

on favorable terms. In the 1980s, the deregulation of U.S. banking took away some of the competitive advantage of Eurodollars, but the Eurodollar market had already established itself. From 1976 until 1992, Eurodollars grew from $14 billion to $56 billion.

The growth of multinational corporations, major customers in the Eurodollar market, may have contributed to the expansion of Eurodollars. Growth was further facilitated because the Eurodollar market made dealing in dollars a daytime affair in European time zones. Large United States banks also have borrowed funds in the Eurodollar market, and during the Cold War, the Soviet government kept dollar deposits in European banks to prevent the U.S. government from freezing Soviet assets in a political dispute.

London is the headquarters for the Eurodollar market, but Eurodollar transactions take place worldwide. Banks in the Bahamas, Cayman Islands, Canada, Hong Kong, and Singapore hold dollar deposits and lend dollars.

Eurodollars are a subspecies of Eurocurrencies, all of which have extraterritorial markets such as the Eurodollar market. Other important Eurocurrencies are Japanese yen, German marks, British pounds, French francs, and Swiss francs. Luxembourg is headquarters for Euromark deposits, and Paris and Brussels for Eurosterling deposits.

See also: Euro Currency, European Currency Unit

References

Daniels, John D., and Lee H. Radebaugh. 1998. *International Business*, 8th ed.

Terrell, Henry S., and Rodney H. Mills. "International Banking Facilities and the Eurodollar Market." *Staff Study no. 124*, August 1983.

EUROPEAN CENTRAL BANK

The European Central Bank (ECB) is not only the newest but also one of the most important central banks in the world. It bears responsibility for the conduct of monetary policy within the euro area, setting interest rates and money stock growth across all countries that use the euro as domestic currency. The mission statement of the European Central Bank underscores the goals of price stability and safeguarding the value of the euro. Headquartered in Frankfurt, Germany, the bank came into being on June 1, 1998, as mandated by treaty. The bank did not wield its full powers until the introduction of the euro on January 1, 1999. The bank holds the exclusive privilege to authorize the issuance of euro banknotes. Individual governments of euro countries can issue euro coins, but the amount must be authorized in advance by the European Central Bank.

The German Bundesbank furnished the model that shaped the design of the European Central Bank. Like the German Bundesbank, the European Central Bank enjoys substantial independence from political authorities. The treaty calling for the establishment of the European Central Bank prohibits it from taking orders from politicians.

Responsibility for monetary policy and oversight of the European Central Bank resides with a governing council. The council usually meets twice a month. Two groups compose the council, an executive board and the governors of the national central banks for each of the fifteen countries within the euro area. The executive board consists of the president, the vice-president, and four other members. The heads of state or governments of the coun-tries within the euro area appoint the members by common accord. The members of the executive board, including the president and vice-president, serve eight-year terms. The terms are nonrenewable, giving the members less incentive to accommodate political pressure. The executive board bears responsibility for implementing policies decided on by the governing council.

The governing council establishes a target inflation rate of 2 percent. It aims at maintaining this inflation rate by adjustment in three key interest rates. In press releases regarding monetary policy, the governing council announces the minimum bid rate on the main refinancing operations, the interest rate on the marginal lending facility, and the interest rate on the deposit facility. The minimum bid rate on the main refinancing operations is the interest rate that is closest to the Federal Reserve System's targeted federal funds rate. The main refinancing operations involve a weekly auction of two-week repurchase agreements. In these repurchase agreements, the ECB, through the central banks of each euro country, provides reserves to banks in exchange for securities, and then reverses the transaction two weeks later. The main refinancing operations are the ECB's counterpart to the Federal Reserve's open market operations. The interest rate on the marginal lending facility is the interest rate that commercial banks pay on overnight loans from the ECB. This interest rate is usually above the minimum bid rate on the main refinancing operations. The interest rate on the deposit facility is the interest rate that commercial banks receive for putting excess reserves on overnight deposit with the ECB. This interest rate is usually substantially below the minimum bid rate of the main refinancing operations.

which dated back to the 1950s and was used for official transactions between countries. The ECU was similar in concept, and but it experienced a totally unforeseen growth in private sector use, suggesting that there might be a strong demand for an international currency. The initials, ECU, were consciously devised as a reference to the ancient French coin, *ecu*, which was equal to three French *livres*.

The ECU acts as a unit of account for keeping books and defining the terms of contracts, but does not circulate in the form of a paper currency. The European Monetary Fund kept its funds designated in ECUs. The ECU was an intermediate step toward a common European currency that European Union countries launched in mid-1998.

At its first introduction, an ECU consisted of specified amounts of the following currencies:

West German mark 0.828

French franc 1.15

Belgian franc 3.66

Luxembourg franc 0.14

Italian lira 109.00

Danish krone 0.217

Dutch guilder 0.286

Irish pound 0.00759

British pound sterling 0.9885

Later, the ECU basket incorporated the currencies of Spain, Portugal, and Greece. As various currencies were devalued or revalued, the weights were reconfigured accordingly.

ECUs could be expressed in terms of single ECU units or in terms of equivalent amounts of separate national currencies. Member countries of the

The European Central Bank, based in Frankfurt, Germany, sets monetary policy for the European Union. (Alexander Mironov)

See also: Central Bank

References

Moutot, Philippe, Alexander Jung, and Francesco Mongelli. "The Workings of the Eurosystem: Monetary Policy Preparations and Decision Making-Selected Issues." *Occasional Paper Series,* no. 79, 2008.

Scheller, Hanspeter K. 2006. *The European Central Bank: History, Role, and Functions.*

EUROPEAN CURRENCY UNIT

The European Currency Unit (ECU) began in 1979 as what is called a "basket currency," a composite currency based on a weighted average combination of European currencies. It had a predecessor in the European Unit of Account (EUA),

European Monetary System cooperated to maintain desired exchange rates between individual national currencies and the ECU.

The ECU began as a basket currency, but it soon took on characteristics of an independent currency. A market for ECU-denominated assets developed independently of the market for assets denominated in component currencies, and ECU deposits earned interest, which was often different from a weighted average of interest rates paid on deposits of component currencies. By 1985, ECU transactions in Paris ranked third, after the U.S. dollar and the German mark, and by 1987 ECU futures on the Chicago Mercantile Exchange approached 3 million transactions. Financial assets denominated in ECUs included certificates of deposit, commercial paper, bank loans, and fixed rate and variable rate bonds. Central banks created ECUs for settling payments between individual countries, and private banks bundled individual currencies to create ECU financial instruments as needed.

The ECU represented an important step in the development of a European currency. Presumably with the introduction of the euro in 1998, a European basket currency such as the ECU will no longer serve a purpose.

See also: Euro Currency, Snake, The

References

Kenen, Peter B. 1955. *Economic and Monetary Union in Europe*.

Padoa-Schioppa, Tommaso. 1994. *The Road to Monetary Union in Europe*.

EUROPEAN MONETARY UNION (EMU)

See: Euro Currency

EXCHEQUER BILLS

See: Exchequer Orders to Pay

EXCHEQUER ORDERS TO PAY (ENGLAND)

Exchequer orders of payment, which appeared during the 17th century, were the first paper money issued by the English government. The orders were what might be called "state notes," in contrast to banknotes, which completely displaced state notes as circulating money in England, and later the United States. State notes are issued by government treasuries to finance government spending. Banknotes are liabilities of banks and are secured by the assets and investments of the issuing bank. Virtually all paper money today is banknotes issued by central banks.

In 1667, Parliament authorized Charles II to issue paper orders, or assignments of revenue, to whoever advanced cash or supplied goods to the government. A record book kept a list of the Exchequer orders according to their order of issuance. As tax revenue poured in, the Exchequer redeemed in cash the orders in the same sequence as they were issued. The first order issued was the first redeemed and so on. At first, the government assigned revenue from a particular tax to redeem an issue of orders, but later the government issued orders for redemption out of general revenue.

The Exchequer orders supplemented and eventually replaced tallies, which were the notched wooden sticks split into matching parts. Tallies served the same purpose as the orders but were not as amendable to written endorsements, and therefore were not as suitable as currency. The orders, like the tallies, were negotiable; that is, they were transferable to another party with a written endorsement. This rendered them serviceable as a medium of exchange.

The government issued Exchequer orders to department heads who either paid for supplies with orders or discounted orders to goldsmiths in return for cash. As a loan to the government, orders bore interest, sometimes as high as 8 to 10 percent, a handsome interest rate to goldsmiths who paid depositors as much as 6 percent interest to attract funds for discounting orders. The goldsmiths made a ready market for the orders, rendering them liquid and even more acceptable as money. The orders supplemented the scarce coinage in the English economy and offered an interest-bearing investment in small denominations (20 pounds or so) for the small investor.

In late 1671, the market for Exchequer orders became saturated, even at the high interest rates, and the goldsmiths stopped discounting orders for the government. On January 2, 1672, Charles II issued a proclamation, the infamous Stop of the Exchequer, suspending the redemption of the orders. The goldsmiths were left with vast holdings of unredeemable orders, and many went bankrupt. Interest payments were suspended until 1677. The money owed by the government later became part of the British public debt, but the credit of the British crown was seriously impaired, and the issuance of Exchequer orders came to an end.

In 1696, the English government began issuing Exchequer bills. These bills paid interest, were acceptable in payment of most taxes, transferable by written endorsement, and convertible into cash on demand at the Bank of England. The popularity of these bills as a form of currency allowed the government to drop the interest rate to as low as 1.5 percent per annum. Private banks complained that the bills competed with their own banknotes.

Later, in the 18th century, the government's financing requirements outgrew the small denomination Exchequer bills, around 20 pounds, that were payable on demand. The government opted for bills paying higher interest rates and payable after a fixed time period. These bills were not suitable as a medium of exchange, and banknotes became the only paper money circulating in England.

The experience with the Exchequer orders struck a hard blow against the credibility of state paper money in England. If the Exchequer orders had turned out to be a successful experiment in paper money, England might have developed a monetary system based on state paper money, rather than banknotes.

See also: Bank of England, Stop of the Exchequer, Tallies

References

Davies, Glyn. 1994. *A History of Money.*

Feavearyear, Sir Albert. 1963. *The Pound Sterling: A History of English Money,* 2nd ed.

Nevin, Edward, and E. W. Davis. 1970. *The London Clearing Banks.*

Richards, R. D. 1929/1965. *The Early History of Banking in England.*

F

FEDERAL DEPOSIT INSURANCE CORPORATION (FDIC)

See: Glass–Steagall Banking Act of 1933

FEDERAL OPEN MARKET COMMITTEE (FOMC)

The Federal Open Market Committee (FOMC) is the chief policy-making group within the Federal Reserve System. It makes the key decisions for monetary policy in the United States. Monetary policy has to do with interest rates, credit conditions, and growth in the money supply.

The FOMC consists of 12 members. All seven members of the board of governors of the Federal Reserve System serve on the FOMC. The president of the Federal Reserve Bank of New York is also a permanent member of the FOMC. The presidents of the 11 other regional Federal Reserve Banks hold the remaining four seats on a rotating basis. The seven presidents of regional Federal Reserve Banks who do not hold a seat attend meetings of the FOMC as nonvoting members. The chair of the board of governors of the Federal Reserve System also serves as chair of the FOMC. The president of the Federal Reserve Bank of New York serves as vice-chair. The seven members of the board of governors wield a powerful sway over monetary policy. They hold the majority of the voting seats on the FOMC and are permanent members. FOMC decisions are made either by consensus or near consensus.

The president of the Federal Reserve Bank of New York owes his precedence over the other presidents to the special role played by the Federal Reserve Bank of New York. The Trading Desk at this bank carries out the day-to-day operations required to implement the policies decided by the FOMC. The account manager for the FOMC is the chief supervisor of the New York bank's Trading Desk. That person is in daily contact with members of FOMC subcommittees. Normally, the FOMC meets eight times per year to assess monetary policy and make adjustments. If developments in the economy warrant quicker action, the FOMC holds additional meetings either in person or by conference call. Immediately after a meeting, the FOMC announces its decisions to an eagerly awaiting Wall Street and financial media. Financial markets often react within minutes of an announcement from the FOMC. Financial markets may react right before a meeting as speculators try to make money by betting on what action the FOMC will take.

The wording of the formal instructions to the New York Trading Desk is decided at the FOMC meeting. Once the FOMC decides to change policy, the new policy is implemented immediately. The policies are implemented through the purchase and sale of U. S government securities. The Federal Reserve's trading in U.S. government securities are called "open-market operations." The New York Trading Desk decides the amount of securities to buy or sell to carry out the instructions handed down by the FOMC.

The main interest rate the FOMC aims to influence is the Federal Funds Rate, which is the rate of interest commercial banks charge each other for overnight loans. The FOMC decides on a target for the Federal Funds Rate and instructs the New York Trading Desk to conduct the open-market operations necessary to maintain the targeted rate. To ease monetary policy, the FOMC lowers the targeted rate, and to tighten monetary policy, the FOMC raises the targeted rate.

See also: Announcement Effect, Open Market Operations

References

Meade, Ellen E. "The FOMC: Preferences, Voting, and Consensus." Review, Federal Reserve Bank of St. Louis, March 2005, pp. 93–101.

Thornton, Daniel L. "When Did the FOMC Begin Targeting the Federal Funds Rate? What the Verbatim Transcript Tells Us." Working Papers, 2004-015, Federal Reserve Bank of St. Louis, 2005.

FIAT MONEY

See: Inconvertible Paper Standard

FEDERAL RESERVE SYSTEM

The Federal Reserve System is the central banking system for the United States, established by the Federal Reserve Act of 1913. Most countries have only one central bank, such as the Bank of England, or Bank of Japan. Several countries in Europe share the European Central Bank. The Federal Reserve System makes up a system of 12 regional central banks. Central banks are bankers' banks, holding deposits of commercial banks, making loans to commercial banks, and serving as lenders of last resort to commercial banks in an economic downturn. The Federal Reserve System also acts as a bank for the U.S. government, and has a monopoly on the issue of banknotes, called Federal Reserve Notes. The term "reserve" in the title refers to the role central banks play in determining the liquidity of commercial banks. The Federal Reserve System regulates the money supply, interest rates, and credit conditions in the United States.

The United States was slow to adopt the concept of central banks as systems of monetary control. The early years of the Republic saw the creation of the First Bank of the United States in 1791, but Congress failed to renew its charter in 1811. Congress chartered the Second

The Federal Reserve System is headquartered in the Eccles Building on Constitution Avenue in Washington, D.C. The building is named for Marriner Eccles, chair of the Federal Reserve from 1934 to 1948. (iStockPhoto.com)

Bank of the United States in 1816, but President Jackson vetoed the renewal of its charter in 1832. These two banks, similar in structure, were early experiments in central banking, but were unpopular. The U.S. government's control over the management and policies of these banks was limited to the voting rights of a minority stockholder. Fear of East Coast domination of the banking industry helped undermine support for the Second Bank of the United States.

The decentralized and unregulated banking system of the latter 1880s constantly buffeted the country with money panics and financial crises, leading public officials to see the necessity for overcoming the political objections to a central bank. Political objections came from several angles, including government officials who felt that the banking industry could not be trusted to regulate itself, and

leaders in banking who felt that elected politicians lacked the necessary knowledge to regulate banking and were often irresponsible in financial matters. In addition to the distrust between leading bankers and elected politicians, there was distrust between regions of the country. Many regions presumed that a central bank would be located in New York City, subjecting the country to Wall Street domination. These contending forces helped shape the Federal Reserve Act of 1913 that created the Federal Reserve System.

To diffuse the fear of Wall Street domination of banking, the Federal Reserve Act created a system of 12 regional central banks. The Federal Reserve Bank of New York is the most important for policy purposes, but there are Federal Reserve Banks in Boston, Philadelphia, Atlanta, Cleveland, St. Louis, Kansas City (Mo.), Richmond, Dallas, San Francisco, Chicago, and Minneapolis.

Like the First and Second Bank of the United States, the Federal Reserve Banks are privately owned. Private ownership helped appease the banking community's arguments that knowledgeable bankers can best regulate the banking industry. Commercial banks in each district that are members of the Federal Reserve System own the stock in the regional Federal Reserve Bank. The Federal Reserve Act requires all banks with national charters to be members of the Federal Reserve System.

The final authority for monetary policy lies with the Board of Governors of the Federal Reserve System. The president of the United States makes appointments to this seven-member board, subject to the approval of the Senate. The seven board members serve 14-year terms that are staggered so that one member's term expires every other year. This constant rotation on the board dilutes the power of any one president to bias the board politically. One of the board members acts as chairman of the board of governors, and the president—with the approval of the Senate—appoints that person. The chairman serves a four-year term that is renewable. Congress organized the board of governors to be independent of either the banking industry or the elected politicians.

Despite the trend toward deregulation in banking, Congress has not limited the authority of the Federal Reserve System, except in certain areas such as fixing interest rates on savings accounts. The Depository Institution Deregulation and Monetary Control Act of 1980 gave the Federal Reserve System the authority to set reserve requirements for state-chartered banks in addition to its existing authority to set reserve requirements for national chartered banks. (The reserve requirement is the percent of money deposited in checking and savings accounts that a bank has to retain in the form of vault cash and deposits at Federal Reserve Banks.)

Because the Federal Reserve System's governing board is composed of unelected officials who are somewhat immune to political pressure, the Federal Reserve System often bears the brunt of the responsibility for combating inflation in the United States. Anti-inflation policies are often accompanied by high unemployment, rendering these policies unpopular with elected officials, who like to earn credit for reducing unemployment rather than increasing it. Therefore the elected officials often defer to the unelected officials that compose the board of governors the responsibility for slowing down the economy and taming inflation.

Amid the U.S. financial crisis in 2008, the Federal Reserve put aside, at least temporarily, its concern about inflation and broadened its role as a lender of last resort. Customarily, only depository institutions enjoyed the privilege of borrowing funds at the discount window of the Federal Reserves. Even banks in financial difficulty could borrow as long as they put up good collateral. In the rescue of investment bank Bear Stearns, the Federal Reserve accepted as collateral securities backed by subprime mortgages of unknown risk and market value. The Federal Reserve agreed to grant loans against the mortgage-backed securities as part of a deal for JPMorgan Chase & Co. to purchase Bear Stearns. The Federal Reserve justified its action of the grounds that the failure of Bear Stearns put the entire financial system at risk. The Federal Reserve also gave other investment banks and primary dealers in U.S. government securities the same access to discount window lending that is ordinarily reserved for depository commercial banks.

See also: Bank of England, Bank of France, Central Bank, Deutsche Bundesbank, First Bank of the United States, Second Bank of the United States

References

Board of Governors of the Federal Reserve System. 1984. *The Federal Reserve System: Purposes and Functions*.

Broz, J. Lawrence. 1997. *The International Origins of the Federal Reserve System*.

Greider, William. 1987. *Secrets of the Temple: How the Federal Reserve System Runs the Country*.

Timberlake, Richard Henry. 1978. *The Origins of Central Banking in the United States*.

FINANCIAL SERVICES MODERNIZATION ACT OF 1999 (UNITED STATES)

The Financial Services Modernization Act of 1999 (FSMA) repealed the provisions of the Glass–Steagall Act of 1933 and the Bank Holding Act of 1956 that kept commercial banks, securities firms, and insurance companies organized into separate, noncompeting businesses. Before passage of the FSMA, deposit-holding commercial banks could not engage in the underwriting and brokerage activities of an investment bank, and neither a commercial bank nor an investment bank could engage in the insurance business. Congress put together the legislation after Citicorp and Travelers Group announced plans to merge. Citicorp was a large U.S. international bank, and Travelers a large U.S. insurance company.

The heart of the FSMA repealed the provision in the Depression era Glass–Steagall Act that prohibited commercial banks from providing investment banking services such as underwriting, brokerage, and holding stock in nonfinancial corporations. The FSMA allows commercial banks to form financial holding companies that can offer a full range of financial services, including holding deposits, granting personal and commercial loans, underwriting and brokering securities, and providing insurance. Holding companies do not sell goods and services themselves, but only own a controlling interest in stock of other companies.

Proponents of the FSMA argued that it brought U.S. banking regulation more into line with banking regulation of other advanced, industrialized countries, creating a level playing field for U.S. banks. Before passage of the act, foreign subsidiaries of U.S. banks could provide insurance and underwriting services in foreign banking markets. Foreign banks, evolving under easier regulations, had grown larger and more diverse than U.S. banks, and some feared more resilient and competitive. After passage of the FSMA, the United States, along with Japan, still has the strictest regulations on the ability of commercial banks to mix deposit banking with insurance and securities businesses. The least restrictive regulations are found in the United Kingdom, the Netherlands, and Switzerland. Most other countries do not require the holding company structure. Foreign banks usually conduct the securities business within the bank and provide insurance services through a subsidiary.

The FSMA paved the way for the consolidation of firms in the banking, brokerage, insurance business. Amid the financial crisis of 2008, the Financial Services Modernization Act (FSMA) allowed JPMorgan Chase to acquire Bear Stearns, and Bank of America to acquire

Merrill Lynch. Before 2008, the rate of consolidation had been relatively slow. The difficulties of investment banks such as Bear Stearns, Merrill Lynch, Goldman Sachs, and Lehman Brothers may have stemmed in part from the severe competition posed by the large, diversified universal banks such as JPMorgan Chase. These large banks were not possible before the enactment of the FSMA.

Under the financial holding company arrangement, the ability of a commercial bank to use depositors' money to finance investment-banking operations in an affiliate is severely restricted. Under the pressure of the financial crisis of 2008, the Federal Reserve System granted a temporary suspension of these rules. The suspension of these rules made it easier for Bank of America to purchase Merrill Lynch.

In addition, the FSMA opened the path for two ailing investment banks, Goldman Sachs and Morgan Stanley, to reorganize as bank holding companies and create affiliated commercial banks. These commercial banks are able to attract retail deposits as an added source of funds.

One of the provisions of the FSMA requires financial service companies to furnish customers written disclosure of privacy policies and practices. This disclosure must be made at the beginning of a banking relationship and repeated once a year. The disclosure must indicate what nonretail affiliates of a bank will have access to customers' data, and the range and kind of customer data. Customers also have a choice to prohibit such sharing of information.

See also: Glass–Steagall Banking Act of 1933, Universal Banks

References

Akhigbe, Aigbe, Melissa B. Frye, and Ann Marie Whyte. "Financial Modernization in U.S. Banking Markets: A Local or Global Event." *Journal of Business Finance & Accounting,* vol. 32, no. 7 (2005): 1561–1585.

Enrich, David, and Damian Palaetta. "The Financial Crisis: Walls Come Down, Reviving Fears of a Falling Titan." *Wall Street Journal* (Eastern Edition, New York) September 23, 2008, p. A6.

Knee, Jonathan A. "Boutique vs. Behemoth." *Wall Street Journal* (Eastern Edition, New York) March 2, 2006, p. A14.

FIRST BANK OF THE UNITED STATES

The First Bank of the United States (1791–1811) met the needs of a central bank in the early years of the Republic. It helped regulate the issuance of banknotes by state banks and acted as the bank of the United States government. The First Bank received its charter from the national government in 1791, when President George Washington signed the bill authorizing its incorporation.

The First Bank of the United States was a brainchild of Alexander Hamilton, who saw such a bank as a means of raising short-term capital for the government and handling bills of exchange needed for making payments to foreign holders of the national debt. Hamilton patterned the First Bank after the Bank of England, and got many of his ideas from the role the Bank of England played in the English economy and government finances. He also promoted the bank as a means of increasing the circulation of banknotes, which was needed at that time because of a shortage of specie.

Hamilton's *Report on a National Bank* went to Congress in December 1790. The proposal drew fire from critics concerned that the bank was a

Bank of the United States in Philadelphia at the turn of the 19th century. (Library of Congress)

monopoly sanctioned by Congress. As the debate on this issue waned, constitutional questions arose that were to haunt the bank for the duration of its existence. The Constitutional Convention of 1787 had chosen not to give Congress the power to grant charters of incorporation and the Constitution itself was silent on the subject.

The bill for the bank's charter passed by a 2–1 vote in the House and by a majority vote in the Senate, but Washington balked at signing it, partly at the urging of such luminaries as Thomas Jefferson. Washington signed the bill chartering the bank after Hamilton wrote a very able paper in its defense. The First Bank made Philadelphia its headquarters and, over Hamilton's opposition, set up branches, one as far away as New Orleans.

The charter authorized a capital stock of $10 million. The U.S. government purchased one-fifth of the stock, paid for by a loan from the First Bank, and the remaining four-fifths was opened for public subscription. The bank was fully capitalized within an hour after shares became available to the public. Public subscribers could pay one-fourth in specie and four-fifths in government obligations, and foreigners eventually held much of the stock. The charter prohibited the bank from trading in anything besides bills of exchange, gold and silver bullion, and goods held as security for defaulted loans. The total debt of the First Bank could not exceed its capital and money held on deposit. The bank needed congressional approval before it could make loans in excess of $100,000 to the U.S.

government, any state government, or to purchase any of the public debt.

Commercial loans accounted for most of the bank's lending, and the bank served some of the functions of a central bank. At that time bank loans were paid out in banknotes, convertible into specie on demand. The bank held other commercial banks accountable by presenting to them their banknotes for redemption in specie. The First Bank's role in controlling the issuance of banknotes won the support of the large commercial banks. The bank particularly helped control the over-issuance of banknotes by country banks, often the source of inflationary pressures.

When the charter for the First Bank came up for renewal in 1811, it failed by one vote in the House. Constitutional issues and foreign ownership cost the First Bank much of its support in Congress. The vote in the Senate was a tie, and the vice president broke it by voting against the First Bank.

Congress soon missed the First Bank and, in 1816, chartered the Second Bank of the United States, but that bank lost its charter in 1832. The Federal Reserve System, established in 1913, was the first central bank in the United States to establish itself in the confidence of the voters.

See also: Bank of England, Central Bank, Free Banking, Federal Reserve System, Second Bank of the United States

References

Myers, Margaret G. 1970. *A Financial History of the United States.*

Timberlake, Richard Henry. 1978. *The Origins of Central Banking in the United States.*

FISHER EFFECT

The "Fisher effect" refers to the tendency for the nominal interest rate and the inflation rate to march in step with each other. The nominal interest rate is the quoted market rate and is not adjusted for inflation. The linkage between the nominal interest rate and the inflation rate is one-to-one. A 1-percent increase in the inflation rate causes a 1-percent increase in the nominal interest rate. The relationship gets its name from Irving Fisher, an influential U.S. economist of the early 20th century.

Fisher developed his hypothesis to solve what was called "Gibson's paradox," a positive correlation between interest rates and the price level that was highly evident during the period of the classical gold standard. John Maynard Keynes named this correlation "Gibson's paradox" and called it one of the most completely established empirical facts in quantitative economics. It was considered a paradox because there was no reason for it to exist in theory. Irving Fisher pointed out that although there was no reason for a positive correlation between the nominal interest rate and the price level, there was strong reason for positive correlation between nominal interest rate and the rate of change in the price level, meaning the inflation rate. Fisher also observed that a weighted moving average inflation, with recent inflation rates having larger weights, correlated highly with the price level. Fisher concluded that in Gibson's paradox the price level in effect acted as a proxy for weighted moving average of the inflation rate. In summary, inflation raises nominal interest rates, but not immediately. Over time, however, a steady and fully anticipated inflation rate is eventually fully reflected in nominal interest rates.

Fisher developed an equation that became the basis of his theory:

nominal interest rate =

real interest rate + expected inflation

According to this equation, in a zero-inflation economy, the nominal interest rate equals the real interest rate. The real interest rate is determined by the productivity of capital and the thriftiness of savers. The productivity of capital creates a demand for lendable funds, the thriftiness of savers creates a supply of lendable funds, and the real interest rate adjusts to keep the two in balance. Inflation enters the picture on both the demand side and the supply side. On the demand side, inflation creates an incentive to beat inflation by borrowing funds and buying capital goods before prices rise. Borrowers are willing to pay a higher interest rate because borrowing funds allows them to buy before prices go up. On the supply side, inflation means that money used to repay a loan has less purchasing power than the money that was loaned out. Therefore, lenders must demand a higher rate of interest to compensate for inflation. In an inflationary economy, lenders demand a higher interest rate, and borrowers have an incentive to pay a higher interest. To keep the supply and demand for lendable funds in balance the nominal interest rates has to change on a one-to-one basis with the expected inflation rate.

The Fisher effect is highly evident in short-term interest rates, such as those earned by three-month treasury bonds. For short-term interest rates, the actual inflation rate acts as a reasonable proxy for the expected rate of inflation. For longer-term interest rates, the Fisher effect becomes difficult to test because expected inflation is not subject to direct measurement.

See also: Interest Rate, Inflation and Deflation

References

Fisher, Irving, *The Theory of Interest*. New York: Macmillan, 1930, pp. 399–451.

Gibson, W. E., "Interest Rates and Inflationary Expectations," *American Economic Review*, vol. 62, no. 5, pp. 854–865.

FLOAT

Float is the money available to households or businesses because checks that they have written have not yet been withdrawn from their bank accounts. Banks have gradually whittled down the number of days that it takes to clear a check. Before the age of modern transportation and electronic check clearing, households and businesses had an incentive to hold deposits in distant banks to increase the amount of float. High interest rates particularly encouraged this practice. Many checks are still cleared in back-office batch processes, and it can take between two or three days and sometimes weeks to clear a check. The time can vary with disruptions in transportation. After the September 11, 2001, terrorist attacks on the United States, unprocessed checks piled up in U.S. banks because air traffic stood at a standstill, leaving banks unable to process checks.

Writing checks on accounts with insufficient funds with plans to deposit money in the account before the checks clear represents another way of exploiting float. A survey conducted during January and February of 2005 indicated that 23 percent of bank customers occasionally wrote checks without sufficient funds in the accounts to cover the check (Credit Union National Association, 2005). The customers usually do not let the checks bounce, but they may end up covering the check by racing to the bank to make a last-minute deposit. Individuals in their thirties and earning no more than $40,000 were among the likeliest offenders. This type of float decreased substantially after Congress enacted the Check Clearing for the 21st Century Act, which became effective in October 2004. Enacted to hasten the adoption of electronic check clearing, the act allows banks to clear checks by sending electronic images of checks instead of hard copies. The use of electronic images can subtract several days from the time taken to clear nonlocal checks.

With the dwindling ability to use float to manage their money, some consumers may switch to credit cards. Credit cards can defer payment much longer than check float, often up to 30 days before interest charges are added.

Commercial banks often hold deposited funds from checks for a length of time before making the funds available for customer withdrawal. If a commercial bank holds the deposited funds for a longer length of time than it takes the checks to clear, the bank enjoys a form of float. It can earn interest on the funds before it allows a depositor to make withdrawals. The Check Clearing for the 21st Century Act did not require banks to give depositors quicker access to funds from checks deposited in bank accounts. Banks can hold deposited funds from local checks for up to two days before making them available to depositors. Nonlocal checks can be held up to five days and checks above $5000 up to 11 days. Although the adoption of electronic check clearing decreases the amount of float available to bank customers, it may increase the amount of float available to banks. Money comes out of customer accounts quicker but does not necessarily go in quicker. In time, competition or regulation will probably force banks to speed depositor access to deposited funds.

Check-kiting schemes make use of float to defraud financial institutions of vast sums of money. In a check-kiting scheme, a bank customer writes a check on one bank account in which there is not enough funds on deposit to cover the check. To cover the insufficient funds, the customer deposits a check written on an account at another bank. This second check is also an insufficient funds check. There can be several banks involved in a check-kiting scheme. By writing checks to cover checks written on other accounts, an individual creates artificially inflated bank balances, which are then used to purchased goods and services from outside parties. Once the scheme is exposed, one or more banks will be left holding large negative balances in check-kiting accounts. In 1997, a Michigan bank lost $2.5 million dollars to a check-kiting scheme (Kline, 1998).

Federal Reserve float is a type of float that occurs in the Federal Reserve's check-collection process. It can briefly inflate the amount of money in the banking system. Commercial banks hand over deposited checks to a Federal Reserve Bank. The Federal Reserve Bank credits the commercial banks' Federal Reserve accounts by the amount of the checks. A prearranged schedule determines how soon the commercial banks' accounts will be credited after the checks are presented to the Federal Reserve Bank. Usually the accounts are credited after one or two business days. The banks on which the checks are written will pay the Federal Reserve Bank after they receive the checks from the Federal Reserve Bank. It may take more than one or two days for the Federal Reserve Bank to receive payment, in which case Federal Reserve float is created. Before the advent of electronic check clearing, Federal Reserve float could be a significant amount, sometimes requiring the use of open market operations to offset it. Since the 1980s, it has been continually declining.

References

Blackman, Andrew. "Family Finances: Farewell to the Float: Checks will Clear in an Instant." *Wall Street Journal* (Eastern Edition, New York) August 1, 2004, p. 4.

Kline, Alan. "Bank in Michigan Says Check-Kiting Scheme Could Cost It $2.5 Million; '97 Profits Slashed." *American Banker,* vol. 163, no. 48 (March 12, 1998): 8.

Credit Union National Association, Point for Credit Union Research & Advice. "Will Consumers Turn to Plastic to Regain Float." April 1, 2005.

FLORENTINE FLORIN

The Florentine florin was the first European gold coin to achieve the status of an international currency after the disappearance of European gold coinage in the eighth century. Florence first issued the florin in 1252. It weighed 3.53 grams or 72 grains of fine gold and took its name from the fleur-de-lis, the iris flower whose image adorned one side of the florin. The florin preceded the era of milled coins with corrugated edges that protected coins against the clippers. To circumvent the clippers, florins circulated in leather bags sealed by the mint. The seal was intended to vouch for the integrity of the coins inside. Thus, anyone who wished to clip coins also had to be able to counterfeit the seal.

The florin did not burst on the world without European rivals. Genoa also commenced gold coinage in 1252, but Genoa's coins never commanded the international stature of the florin.

Frederick II of Sicily may have struck gold coins a few years earlier than Florence, but his coinage was a descendant of Moslem and Byzantine coinage, despite its popularity in Europe.

Originally, Florence struck the florin as a gold pound, equal to 20 *soldi* or shillings, or 240 *deniers,* or pennies. The Florentine version of the Carolingian system soon broke down amid fluctuating exchange rates between gold and silver, and an imaginary money of account developed based on a pound *affiorino,* in which 20 florins equaled 29 affiorinos. A separate silver standard evolved that set the value of the silver pound equal to 20 silver soldi, or 240 silver deniers. Market forces overrode government efforts to establish official exchange ratios between gold and silver such as existed with the European bimetallic system in the 19th century.

From the outset, Florence groomed the florin to play the part of an international currency. Florentine law provided that only international merchants of the Calimala Guild, the moneychangers, the cloth and silk manufacturers, the grocers, and furriers, could keep books and conduct business in florins. Silver currency was used in retail trade, payment of wages, and small transactions. Wholesale prices were often quoted in florins, whereas retail prices were quoted in silver currency.

San Antonino (1389–1459), archbishop of Florence, complained of the government debasing the silver currency used by the lower classes, while maintaining the purity of the gold currency used by the wealthier classes. The employer-controlled government of Florence could effectively reduce real wages by debasing silver coins used to pay wages while maintaining the purity of gold florins in which wholesale goods were priced. Separate gold and silver standards, with separate prices, exposed one segment of the population to the ravages of inflation through debasement, while another segment remained untouched by inflation. From 1252 until the beginning of the 15th century, the florin rose in value 700 percent relative to silver coinage, largely reflecting debasement of silver.

In the second half of the 13th century and the first part of the 14th century, the Florentine florin rose to become the equivalent of the modern day dollar in international trade. As often happens in currencies, the florin was unable to dodge the pitfalls of success. Foreign governments minted florin imitations from lighter metal, and at the beginning of the 15th century Florence minted florins of a lighter weight. The florin may have owed part of its success to the strength and expansion of the Florentine economy. During the 15th century, the Venetian *ducat* displaced the Florentine florin as the international currency par excellence.

See also: Carolingian Reform, Gold, Venetian Ducat

References

Chown, John. 1994. *A History of Money*.

Goldthwaite, Richard A. 1980. *The Building of Renaissance Florence: An Economic and Social History*.

FOOD STAMPS

Food stamps are coupons redeemable for food at stores. The government allots food stamps to low-income families to assure that minimal nutritional needs are met. Because they are redeemable for food, food stamps have circulated as money in ghetto areas. Although the food stamp program is a federal program, supervised by the United States Department of Agriculture, the process of identifying qualified families and issuing food stamps is left to the individual state governments.

The first food stamp program grew out of the contradictions of the Great Depression of the 1930s in which agricultural surpluses mocked the problems of rising unemployment, hunger, destitution, and falling farm incomes. The government's initial response of destroying agricultural commodities seemed unreasonable in light of growing poverty and hunger. The first food stamp program began in 1939 and continued until 1943, when the wartime boom had solved the unemployment problem, and agricultural surpluses were no longer accumulating.

The food stamp program was revived in the 1960s, partly because President Kennedy, when campaigning in West Virginia, had observed schoolchildren taking home leftovers from school lunches. Various pilot programs were put into operation until Congress enacted the Food Stamp Program Act of 1964. Later in the 1960s and early 1970s Congress increased the benefits and eased the eligibility requirements. At first, food stamp recipients had to pay for the stamps, but in the 1970s the stamps became free.

To qualify for food stamps families must fall below certain income levels, after allowances are made for housing costs, childcare, etc. The lower a family's income, the more food stamps the family can receive.

In the 1970s and early 1980s, food stamps became a sort of second-class currency in low-income neighborhoods. Although food stamps could legally be used only to purchase food, some

Food stamps are vouchers that the poor and otherwise distressed can use, much like money, to purchase food. (PhotoDisc, Inc.)

merchants fudged and sold alcohol and other grocery store items for food stamps. On the streets, foods stamps traded for cash, but at steep discounts. Individuals traded food stamps for cash and used the cash to purchase items that could not be purchased with food stamps.

Partly because of the fraudulent use of food stamps, the federal government during the Reagan years cut back on food stamp expenditures. The program remained in place, however, and the 1990s saw many states implement electronic benefit transfer programs that substituted a debit card for coupons. The use of the cards requires identification, rendering the transfer of food stamp benefits to parties other than the cardholder almost impossible. Since 2004, all 50 states have had electronic benefit transfers. Given that food items such as livestock, rice, corn, and many others have historically emerged as

mediums of exchange, it should not be surprising that coupons redeemable for food would wear the aspect of money and circulate accordingly. Presumably, food stamp money will disappear in time because it involves an illegal use of food stamps, and the government will work to improve its regulation of the program.

See also: Commodity Money

References
Berry, Jeffrey, M. 1984. *Feeding Hungry People*.
Weatherford, Jack. 1997. *The History of Money*.
Weinstein, Steve. "True Benefits." *Progressive Grocer*, vol. 77, no. 5 (May 1998): 80–86.

FORCED SAVINGS

"Forced savings" refers to the use of money creation and inflation to divert resources into the production and acquisition of capital goods. A government that prints money, as opposed to levying taxes or selling bonds, to pay for the construction of a hydroelectric generation facility is pursuing a policy of forced savings. Less-developed countries, particularly in Latin America, turned to forced savings policies in the post–World War II era as a means of financing economic development. At least some of the inflation in Latin America has its roots in economic development strategies based on forced savings.

The mechanics of forced savings operates through the medium of inflation. The government prints money to purchase capital goods, attracting resources into the production of capital goods at the expense of consumer goods. Consumer goods production falls relative to demand, and consumer goods prices increase, reducing the amount of consumer goods that households can afford. This forced reduction in consumer goods acquisition translates as forced savings. Consumers still spend the same amount of money, it just does not stretch as far as it did before inflation. Thus, the consumers do not come out with any more savings, but society does, because society is extracting resources for the production of capital goods. The forced reduction in consumer goods production is the key to forced savings.

Savings always involve a reduction in current acquisition of consumer goods. Ordinarily, households elect to divert a share of income away from consumption expenditures, and set that share of income aside as savings. Financial institutions and stock and bond markets channel these savings into businesses that need financing to purchase capital goods. Savings are always at the expense of consumption expenditures, but normally savings are a voluntary choice of households. Societies must save, that is, depress current consumption, to make resources available for the production of capital goods.

Economists and policy makers have advanced several arguments in favor of forced savings as an attractive vehicle for financing economic development. First, vast portions of the populations of less-developed countries live at the margin of subsistence, too poor to voluntarily engage in much saving. Second, many less-developed countries do not have the financial institutions necessary to mobilize the small savings of individual households. Third, wars have shown that governments can print up money to finance major public undertakings without destroying economic systems. The same effort that goes into financing a war can theoretically be tapped to finance industrialization.

Notwithstanding arguments favoring forced savings, the anti-inflation bias in current economic thinking emphasizes the downside of any policy that can only be activated with inflation. There has been no evidence of a correlation between inflation and growth, and many countries, such as the United Kingdom and the United States, experienced rapid economic development in the 19th century without inflation. Also, inflation disrupts society and the burden of inflation is not evenly shared. Unionized workers can often strike and gain wage increases that compensate for inflation, and some businesses may receive government aid that compensates for inflation. Other groups in society, those on fixed incomes or living on past savings, are likely to bear the bulk of the inflation burden. Inflation encourages households to invest voluntary savings in hedges against inflation such as land, buildings, jewelry, gold, silver, or stocks of grocery and household necessities. Investment in hedges against inflation diverts voluntary savings away from the purchase of capital goods such as factories, machinery, and so on. After inflation has become expected, creditors extort high interest rates as inflation protection, further discouraging risk-bearing entrepreneurs from accessing sources of borrowed funds.

In countries that insist on printing money to finance government expenditures, forced-savings strategies may make more sense than the acquisition of military goods, or the construction of lavish government buildings and monuments. Nevertheless, forced savings, because of its inflationary effects, entails major complications for the efficient operation of the economy and seems to hold little charm for contemporary policy makers.

See also: Inflation and Deflation

References

Friedman, Milton. 1972. *Money and Economic Development.*

Hogendorn, Jan S. 1987. *Economic Development.*

FOREIGN DEBT CRISES

Economies and governments can accumulate debt to external creditors, meaning creditors from other parts of the world. External financing for productive investments can expand opportunities for economic development and accelerate economic growth. Just as households and businesses can sink too deeply into debt, countries and individual economies can accumulate debt to the point that external debt obligations cannot be met. Measures of indebtedness compare the amount of debt with income. A household with a moderate amount of debt can double its debt if its income doubles and remain only moderately in debt. If a country's gross domestic product (GDP) doubles, it can double its external debt without increasing its debt burden. A country that is able to meet its external debt obligations is said to be able to "service" its debt.

Analysis of an individual country's debt to the rest of the world takes on a macroeconomic perspective because it involves converting one currency into another currency. In addition to an individual borrower's ability to repay, in the case of foreign borrowing there are aggregate credit conditions that must be met by the whole economy. Exceeding aggregate credit limitations can lead to sharp adjustments in domestic interest rates or exchange rates. Often a foreign debt is denominated in a foreign currency. In that case, a country must be able earn enough foreign currency in exports and capital inflows to service the debt. If a country's debt is denominated in its own currency, it still needs to service its debt without upsetting exchange rates. A country can in effect default on its external or foreign debt by suspending convertibility of its domestic currency into foreign currencies. If a country is unable to earn sufficient foreign currency from exports and capital inflows to service its foreign debt, it can increase capital inflows by increasing domestic interest rates. These higher interest rates will be a burden on the economy and can force an economy into recession.

The debt that a sovereign government owes to external creditors is called "sovereign debt." When a government defaults on obligations to external creditors, it is called a "sovereign debt crisis." Russia, Ecuador, and Argentina furnish examples of outright debt default. Ukraine, Pakistan, and Uruguay avoided outright default through debt restructuring. Mexico, Brazil, and Turkey averted default with the help of large-scale support from the International Monetary Fund. Some debtor governments are more cooperative than others in resolving default situations. Uncooperative governments can harm the ability of private domestic corporations to access international debt markets. Risk of foreign debt default or restructuring appears to be lowest when total external debt as a percent of GDP is less than 49.7 percent, short-term debt as a percent of foreign currency holdings is less than 130 percent, public external debt is less than 214 percent of fiscal revenue, and the exchange rate not over appreciated above 48 percent (Manasse and Roubini, 2005, p. 40).

Economists have developed indicators to measure a degree of a country's indebtedness. For poor, debt-laden countries, some type of debt restructuring is likely to occur when net present value of debt exceeds 200 percent of exports. For other, nonindustrial countries, it appears that the risk of debt exposure starts to rise when external debt as a percent of GDP rises above 40 percent (Daseking, December 2002). Countries can sustain higher debt ratios if exports are growing rapidly, or if exports represent a large proportion of GDP, or if a large share of external debt is denominated in domestic currency.

The United States is a debtor nation, but its debt ratios are well below the threshold levels that signal a possible foreign debt crisis. Given the role of the U.S. dollar as a world currency, it is not clear if the same debt–ratio threshold levels apply to the United States. The rise of foreign debt in the United States is worrisome to some observers. Easy access to foreign credit sometimes allows countries to delay painful but inevitable reforms.

References

Daseking, Christina. "Debt: How Much Is Too Much?" *Finance and Development*, vol. 39, no. 4 (December 2002): 12–15.

Manasse, Paolo, and Nouriel Roubini. "'Rules of Thumb' for Sovereign Debt Crises." IMF Working Paper, WP/05/42, International Monetary Fund, March 2005.

Mandel, Michael. "After The Binge, Who Should Suffer?" *Business Week,* October 13, 2008.

FOREIGN EXCHANGE MARKETS

Foreign exchange markets are markets in which national currencies are bought and sold with other national currencies. In a foreign exchange market, U.S. dollars may purchase British pounds, German marks, French francs, Japanese yen, and so on.

Prices of foreign currency are expressed as exchange rates, the rate at which one currency can be converted into another currency. On March 12, 1997, it took $1.59 to purchase a British pound in foreign exchange markets, or, alternatively 0.6256 British pounds could purchase one U.S. dollar. Exchange rates are reported daily in large metropolitan newspapers and financial papers such as the *Wall Street Journal*.

Foreign exchange markets are as old as coinage itself. In the ancient world, religious temples were a popular site of foreign exchange markets because the sacredness of the grounds acted to safeguard treasuries of coin. The modern term "bank" evolved from the money-changers' bench of the Middle Ages. Today, modern communication and computers have made possible a world-wide integrated foreign exchange market where trades are conducted electronically 24 hours a day during the business week. The big players in the foreign exchange markets are the large commercial banks with foreign branches.

Under the current international monetary system, foreign exchange markets are highly competitive and exchange rates can change daily. (Between 1946 and 1971, the world was on a fixed exchange rate system, and exchange rates were pegged at certain levels by governments.) A supply of U.S. dollars is created in foreign exchange markets when Americans buy goods or make investments in foreign countries where dollars are not accepted. A demand for U.S. dollars is created in foreign exchange markets when the rest of the world wants to buy U.S. goods, or make U.S. investments, which require payment in dollars. Exchange rates fluctuate to balance supply and demand, clearing the market for U.S. dollars as foreign exchange. Markets for other currencies emerge in a similar fashion.

Exchange rates can exert strong influences on domestic economies. If the market value of the dollar appreciates relative to the Japanese yen—meaning it takes fewer dollars to purchase a yen—Japanese goods become cheaper to U.S. consumers, increasing the importation of Japanese goods and reducing demand for domestic goods in competition with Japanese goods. If the market value of the dollar depreciates relative to the Japanese yen—meaning it takes more dollars to purchase a yen—Japanese goods become more expensive to U.S. consumers, diminishing the importation of Japanese goods and making domestic goods more competitive. In summary, a depreciation of the dollar increases the demand for U.S. goods, and an appreciation of the dollar decreases the demand for U.S. goods.

Foreign exchange rates are quoted in spot rates and forward rates. The spot rate is the rate at which foreign currency can be purchased for delivery within two business days. A forward rate is the rate at which a foreign currency can be purchased for delivery after a length of time, such as 90 days. A forward market enables a U.S. importer to strike a deal to import French goods and purchase French francs to pay for the goods when they arrive at some date in the future, protecting the importer from fluctuations in exchange that could make the goods much more expensive than expected.

Unless the world adopts a common currency, foreign exchange markets will remain a vital part of the international trade framework, the connecting link that allows trade between countries with different currencies. On January 1, 1999, Europe launched the euro, a European currency that eventually replaced German marks, French francs, Swiss francs, and other European currencies, and abolished the need for foreign exchange markets to establish rates for the convertibility of one European currency into another. If the world follows the path of economic integration taken in Europe, then a world currency could become a reality. On the upside, a world currency would remove the risk and uncertainty of exchange-rate fluctuations that can disturb the flow of international trade, and promote trade between the regions of the world. On the downside, a world currency would preclude the use of localized monetary policies to help specific areas. In the 1990s, Japan struggled against a decade-long period of stagnation. The Bank of Japan was free to expand the Japanese money supply to stimulate the Japanese economy. If the world had been on a worldwide currency system, and Japan was the only country suffering stagnation, world monetary authorities could not have expanded the money supply worldwide just to help Japan, and increasing the money supply worldwide might not have helped Japan.

See also: Balance of Payments, Gold-Specie-Flow Mechanism

References

Baye, Michael R., and Dennis W. Jansen. 1995. *Money, Banking, and Financial Markets.*

Daniels, John D., and Lee H. Radebaugh. 1998. *International Business*, 8th ed.

Daniels, John D., and David Vanhoose. 1999. *International Monetary and Financial Monetary Economics.*

FORESTALL SYSTEM

The Forestall system of Louisiana banking regulation, established in the middle of a depression in 1842, was one of the most successful and influential systems of state banking regulations, establishing principles that became standard in banking regulation.

The Panic of 1837 threw the U.S. economy into a deep depression that lasted until 1843. The depression was sparked by President Andrew Jackson's Specie Circular, requiring that only gold and silver specie (coinage) be used to pay for land purchased from the government. The Specie Circular put the brakes on a land boom. Banks across the United States, including Louisiana, suspended payments, meaning they could no longer redeem their banknotes with specie. At

that time, each bank issued its own banknotes, in contrast to the current practice of issuing checking accounts. Louisiana boasted of nine commercial banks when the Forestall system was put in place. All nine banks had suspended payments.

Among the detailed regulations of the Forestall system was the requirement that customers' deposits could be loaned out only for 90 days. The capital contributed by bank owners was exempt from this limitation. These short-term loans could not be renewed, and the law required that banks publish the names of borrowers requesting renewals.

The Forestall system also forced banks to maintain specie reserves equal to 30 percent of their bank-note and deposit liabilities. The remaining 70 percent had to be backed by short-term commercial loans.

Amid the Panic of 1857, an epidemic of payment suspensions spread through the United States. Thanks to the Forestall system, however, Louisiana banks were among the few banks that continued to make specie payments. Other state legislatures, noting the panic-proof resilience of the Louisiana banks, began to insist on cash reserves. The reserve policy of Louisiana banks enabled them to continue to make remittances to their New York correspondents long after the Civil War had started.

The success of the Forestall system created a predilection for cash reserves in U.S. banking regulation that remains an important element of national banking regulation today. Commercial banks in the United States are required to hold reserves either in the form of vault cash or deposits at a Federal Reserve Bank. Deposits at another financial institution, government bonds, or other forms of seemingly safe assets are not acceptable as legal reserves. The Federal Reserves System usually requires commercial banks to hold reserves that range between 10 to 20 percent of demand deposits.

See also: Federal Reserve System, Free Banking, New York Safety Fund System, Suffolk System

References

Cameron, Rondo, ed. 1972. *Banking and Economic Development: Some Lessons of History.*

Davis, Lance E., Jonathon Hughes and Duncan M. McDougall. 1969. *American Economic History.*

FORT KNOX

Fort Knox, a United States Army post, is the location of the largest U.S. gold bullion depository. Located about 31 miles southwest of Louisville, Kentucky, Fort Knox began as a post for army maneuvers in 1918 and was called Camp Knox. Its name was changed to Fort Knox in 1933. The post covers about 110,000 acres and is home to 57,000 residents. In addition to guarding the gold bullion depository, Fort Knox is famous for training armored divisions in the United States Army. Construction of the Fort Knox Bullion Depository was finished in 1936. Because of the security surrounding the depository, which lies in the middle of the military base, Fort Knox has become a universal symbol of an impregnable store of wealth. No tourists are allowed on the military base.

Early in the Great Depression of the 1930s, the United States nationalized privately owned gold, and devalued the dollar from $20.67 per ounce of gold to $35 per ounce of gold. The rise in the price of gold triggered an inflow of gold into the United

Often referred to simply as Fort Knox, the U.S. Bullion Depository holds most of the nation's gold. It was built at the Fort Knox military base in 1936 for maximum security. (Library of Congress)

States, and by 1939 the United States had swept into its vaults over half of the world's gold stock. The United States Treasury built the new gold depository at Fort Knox to help store its newly acquired gold treasure.

The Fort Knox Bullion Depository is a granite building constructed from 16,000 cubic feet of granite, 4,200 cubic yards of concrete, and 750 tons of steel for reinforcement. The legend "United States Depository," engraved in gold, adorns a marble-lined entry, along with the gold seal of the Treasury Department.

Today, the depository holds approximately 4,600 tons of pure gold with a market value of approximately $58 billion. The gold is stored in bars of 1,000 ounces each. Because gold does not deteriorate, gold in the vaults of Fort Knox could be hundreds of years old, probably including gold seized from the Aztecs and the Incas. Some of the gold that flowed into the United States from France in the 1930s was still in the wrappings that held the gold when the Jefferson administration had sent the gold to France to pay for the Louisiana Purchase. The United States government maintains smaller gold caches at West Point and in Denver.

The world's largest hoard of gold is not stored at Fort Knox. The Federal Reserve Bank of New York maintains an air-conditioned vault about 80 feet below street level in the bedrock of Manhattan Island, New York. This Federal Reserve vault holds about 11,000 tons of gold at a market value of about $176 billion, accounting for about a third of the gold reserves in Western economies. The gold mostly belongs to foreign governments and foreign central banks that store the gold in New York as a matter of convenience. Some of this gold was shipped over on the eve of World War II for security, but much of it was purchased by European

governments from the United States during the 1950s and 1960s, but kept in the United States to spare shipping costs. In 1971, the United States stopped redeeming dollars presented by foreign governments into gold.

See also: Gold, Gold Exchange Standard, Gold Reserve Act of 1934, Gold Standard

References
Green, Timothy. 1981. *The New World of Gold.*
Marx, Jennifer. 1978. *The Magic of Gold.*
Weatherford, Jack. 1997. *The History of Money.*

FRACTIONAL RESERVE SYSTEM OF BANKING

See: Bank, Monetary Multiplier

FRANKLIN, BENJAMIN (1706–1790)

In addition to filling the roles of diplomat, newspaper publisher, inventor, scientist, and signer of the Declaration of Independence, Benjamin Franklin, perhaps the most American of the American revolutionaries, was a tireless advocate of paper money in the American colonies. As early as 1729, he wrote a pamphlet, *A Modest Enquiry into the Nature and Necessity of a Paper Currency*, and continued to advance proposals for paper money as an answer to economic ills that afflicted the colonies. Perhaps the same practical turn of mind that led Franklin to invent the lightning rod, bifocal glasses, and the Franklin stove, also led him to take up the currency problems of the colonies, and seek answers in paper money schemes. By the time of Franklin's death, and owing partly to his efforts, North America had experimented with more paper money issues than any other part of the world up to that time. Even today, the U.S. $100 bill bears an engraved portrait of Benjamin Franklin, symbolizing his long association with paper money in the United States.

The young Franklin apprenticed himself to the trade of printer, and in later years was publisher of the *Pennsylvania Gazette*. Franklin's pamphlet on paper currency helped secure approval of a proposal continuing the issuance of paper money in Pennsylvania, paving the way for Franklin to receive the task of printing the paper money, which he described as "a very profitable job, and a great help to me." Franklin's involvement in the printing business may have favorably disposed him toward paper money.

The Colony of Pennsylvania had created a land bank that issued paper money as loans against real estate and precious metal plate. In 1765, British government officials asked for proposals to raise revenue from the American colonies in the least objectionable way. Parliament enacted the infamous Stamp Act to help service wartime debt and pay part of the expense of defending the colonies. Franklin argued forcibly with the British government for his "paper money scheme," which would generate income from loans and at the same time supply the American colonies with a continental currency. Franklin wanted the British government to establish a loan office that would make loans secured by real estate. The interest-paying loans would be taken out as paper money issued under the authority of the British government, infusing the American colonies with much-needed money and raising revenue for the British government. According to Franklin, an annual interest rate would act as a general tax, but not "an unpleasing one." This paper money would have been legal tender for public debts, including repayment of loans to the land bank. If Great Britain had adopted Franklin's plan rather than the Stamp Act, perhaps history would have taken a different turn.

Franklin was noted for conservative philosophy in financial matters, and famous for sayings such as "A penny saved is a penny earned," and "Early to bed and early to rise makes a man healthy, wealthy, and wise," and "God helps them that help themselves." That Franklin's philosophy of thrift, honesty, and commerce could embrace the concept of paper money should have been taken as unerring signal that paper money was the wave of the future. Nevertheless, history has held up many examples showing that the abuses of paper money are harmful of the virtues that Franklin preached.

See also: Land Bank System

References

Ernst, Joseph Albert. 1973. *Money and Politics in America, 1755–1775*.

Weatherford, Jack. 1997. *The History of Money*.

FREE BANKING

Free banking was a trend toward a highly decentralized monetary system that originated in Scotland and in the early 19th century, appeared on a modest scale in England, and developed on a wider scale in the United States, beginning in 1838 and ending with the National Banking Act in 1864.

Before the era of free banking, bank charters were granted for political favors, regarded as matters of political patronage. Rising inflation from 1834 to 1837, followed by a money panic and a rash of bank failures, elevated public concern about privilege and political corruption in the banking system. New York acted first with the Free Banking Act of 1838. This act allowed any person or group of persons to obtain a bank charter who could meet capitalization criteria requiring that banknotes be 100 percent backed with mortgages and state bonds, plus an extra 12.5 percent in gold and silver specie. The reserves of gold and silver specie enabled bank customers to count on redemption of banknotes in gold and silver, and when banks failed, the state sold the mortgages and state bonds to compensate bank customers.

About 18 states adopted free banking laws similar to the New York act. They usually allowed anyone, without political connections, to deposit suitable financial securities with a state banking authority, receive a bank charter, and make loans and discount bills by issuing their own banknotes.

Free banking was not the only solution to the crisis of confidence in banks. In 1845, the fledgling state of Texas completely outlawed banks in its first constitution, and by 1857, four other states had enacted similar legislation.

The success of the free banking system depended on a delicate balance of state regulation and freedom of enterprise. A certain amount of chaos ensued. Banknotes circulated from defunct banks, and "wildcat" banks established in remote areas issued banknotes that would never be redeemed in specie. Some scholars argue that by the eve of the Civil War, state regulation had begun to shape the free banking system into a workable and orderly system.

Free banking aroused fears of inflation because there was no one entity regulating money supplies, and the perplexing assortment of banknotes, trading at different discounts, hampered trade between regions.

The development of the national banking system during the Civil War ended the free banking era in the United States.

During the 1970s, the slow progress of the monetary authorities toward taming inflation brought a renewed interest and attention to the free banking system. Under a properly regulated free banking system, banknotes remain convertible into a precious metal currency, but there is no central bank regulating the total national money supply. In the 1970s and 1980s, scholars developed theoretical models of free banking systems that maintained convertibility of banknotes into commodities such as gold and silver. These modes functioned without a central bank and much of current banking regulation. These scholars saw the free banking system as preferable to the so-called stop-and-go policies of the Federal Reserve System. The interest in free banking faded as the Federal Reserve showed more progress combating inflation.

See also: Central Bank, National Bank Act of 1864, Second Bank of the United States, Wildcat Banks

References

Rockoff, Hugh. 1975. *The Free Banking Era: A Reexamination.*

Rolnick, Arthur J., and Warren E. Weber. "New Evidence of the Free Banking Era." *American Economic Review*, vol. 73, no. 5 (December 1983): 1080–1090.

Dowd, Kevin. 1996. *Competition and Finance: A Reinterpretation of Financial and Monetary Economics.*

FREE SILVER MOVEMENT

The free silver movement was a populist movement in the United States during the last quarter of the 19th century. "Free silver" meant that silver could be brought to the mint and struck into coins without a seigniorage charge; that is, without taking any of the precious metal to pay mint expenses. Also, the amount of silver that could be brought to the mint was to be unlimited. Before 1873, anyone who brought 3.7125 grains of silver to the mint could receive a legal-tender silver dollar, and the campaign for free silver fought for a return of these conditions.

Between the mid-1830s and 1873, the market price of silver exceeded the mint price of $1.29 per ounce; therefore, very little silver found its way to the mint. Silver dollars had largely disappeared from circulation when Congress enacted the Coinage Act of 1873, an act that made no provision for the coinage of silver, and put the United States on an unofficial gold standard. Proponents of free silver later condemned the Act as the "Crime of '73."

The deletion of the silver dollar drew little attention at the time, but the United States was already in the clutches a deflationary downswing that would last three decades. From 1870 until 1896, prices plunged 50 percent, a deflationary wave that hit hard at farmers in the West and South, where debt incidence stood at high levels. These groups quite rightly saw that a return to free and unlimited coinage of silver would raise the domestic money stock, raise prices, and reduce their debt burden. Much of the populist flavor of the free silver movement came from the hopes it lifted among large numbers of low-income farmers.

Silver prices felt an added deflationary force because the world was rushing toward a gold standard that left little role for silver as a monetary metal. Major silver discoveries in the U.S. West further depressed the market for silver. From 1850 until 1872, the market price of an ounce of silver stood above $1.32, clearly above the mint price, but the price had slipped to $1.24 by 1874, and from there it tumbled to $0.65 by 1895. Silver-mining interests in the United States saw free silver as a way of increasing the demand for silver, and putting a floor under silver prices. They would have been delighted to sell silver to the U.S. Treasury for $1.29.

The free silver proponents achieved limited success in Congress. On February 28, 1878, Congress enacted, over a presidential veto, the Bland–Allison Act, which required the treasury to coin between $2 and $5 million worth of silver per month. The bill had begun as a free silver bill but had been amended to restrict the amount of silver the treasury purchased. In 1890, the Sherman Silver Act required the treasury to purchase $4 million of silver per month and issue silver certificates. The Sherman Silver Act was blamed for sparking a crisis of confidence in the U.S. monetary system, and Europeans began withdrawing gold from the United States. President Cleveland, a staunch advocate of the gold standard, prompted Congress to repeal the silver purchase provisions of the Sherman Silver Act.

The silver controversy loomed as a major issue in the presidential election of 1896, coinciding with the nadir of the 30-year deflationary wave. William Jennings Bryan won the Democratic nomination after his famous "Cross of Gold" speech, denouncing the gold standard, and defining himself as the free silver candidate. Bryan lost the election, and in 1900, the United States went squarely on the gold standard. About this time, the book *The Wizard of Oz* came out as a monetary allegory of the issues raised by the free silver

Cover of Judge *magazine entitled "The Silver Candle and the Moths," July 25, 1898. The illustration shows proponents of the free silver movement, including Cleveland and Bland, as moths flying around the flame of a candle labeled "free silver" and dying. (Library of Congress)*

movement. Bryan ran for president again in 1900, but prices were inflating, and the silver issue was losing its punch. Bryan lost again, and he would run again in 1908 without success.

The free silver movement died out with the return of prosperity at the turn of the century. The silver-mining interests, however, continued to exert a disproportionate share of power into the 20th century. Until the 1960s, dimes, quarters, and half-dollars contained 90 percent silver. Treasury silver stocks fell as the industrial demand for silver grew, and by 1970, the half-dollar was silverless.

See also: Bimetallism, Crime of '73, *The Wizard of Oz*

References

Friedman, Milton. 1992. *Money Mischief: Episodes in Monetary History*.

Nugent, Walter T. K. 1968. *Money and American Society, 1865–1880*.

FRENCH FRANC

Before the introduction of the euro, the French franc was the monetary unit of account in France, just as the U.S. dollar is the monetary unit of account in the United States. It was the first decimalized currency system in Europe, except for the Russian ruble.

French francs were first coined in 1803. Before the decimalized franc was introduced, the French currency system was based on the Carolingian system, in which 1 livre equaled 20 *sols*, which in turn equaled 240 *deniers*. In 1793, the French revolutionary government decided to replace the Carolingian system with a decimal system. In 1795, the livre was replaced with a franc equaling 100 *centimes*. These changes meant little amid revolutionary chaos, but Napoleon's government began striking francs based on the new system in 1803.

The French Monetary Law of 1803 put the franc on a bimetallic system with the silver to gold ratio, per unit of weight, equal to 15.5 to 1. Coin pieces of 5 francs and less were struck in silver, and gold coins came in denominations of 20 francs and 40 francs. One franc equaled 5 grams of silver. The smallest denomination coin authorized by the act was a quarter franc. During the wars of the French Revolution and Napoleon, France imposed its new currency system on conquered states. In 1798, France reorganized the freshly conquered Switzerland as the Helvetian Republic with a unified currency system in which 1 Swiss franc equaled 10 *batzen*, which in turn equaled 100 *rappen*. With the downfall of Napoleon, the Swiss threw off their imported currency system, but in 1850, they readopted the French system voluntarily. The Netherlands had also seen the French system imposed from without, but abandoned it in 1814. When Belgium won its independence from the Dutch in 1830, the Belgians reestablished the French System. Italy adopted the French system in 1861, but named its money of account the "lira" rather than the franc. One lira equaled 1 franc. Under different names, the French system became the basis of currencies in Greece, Spain, Rumania, Bulgaria, and Finland. Although the British pound sterling dominated international trade in the 19th century, the French franc was the most influential currency in Western Europe.

By the beginning of the 19th century, France had acquired a horror of inflation from two firsthand experiences. The hyperinflation of the French Revolution was still a fresh memory, further bolstering French resolve to maintain the stability and integrity of the franc. The French maintained the metallic content of the franc for 125 years. During the Napoleonic Wars, the franc experienced milder fluctuations than the pound sterling, perhaps because Napoleon's war indemnities helped supply the gold and silver to maintain the franc's parity. France suspended convertibility of the franc in the Revolution of 1848 and during the Franco-Prussian War of 1870–1871. Following the Revolution of 1848, convertibility was resumed in 1850, and during the whole episode, the franc had only depreciated mildly. After the Franco-Prussian War, France was burdened with heavy war reparations and the political situation was clouded by the episode of the Paris Commune, which put Paris under the control of working-class revolutionaries. Nevertheless, the franc fluctuated only within a narrow range, and convertibility was resumed in 1878.

In 1865, France, Italy, Switzerland, and Belgium formed the Latin Monetary Union, which fought to preserve a unified, bimetallic monetary system in the face of the growing prestige of England's gold standard. Declining silver prices made the bimetallic standard untenable, and France abandoned silver in 1873. By 1878, France was officially on the gold standard.

Under the gold standard, the franc lost a bit of its reputation for soundness. The French authorities were hesitant to allow an outflow of gold and insisted on their right to pay out badly worn 10-franc gold coins and 5-franc silver coins. All European countries effectively suspended the gold standard during World War I, but the franc emerged from the war weaker than the pound sterling and suffered speculative attacks. In 1926, the franc stabilized at about one-fifth prewar parity. From 1927 until 1931, the franc was undervalued and the pound sterling overvalued, putting an end to speculative attacks on the franc. With the onset of the Great Depression, England, Japan, and the United States devalued their currencies, leaving the franc overvalued. The Gold Bloc countries, mainly consisting of members of the old Latin Monetary Union, clung to the gold standard, and France, the leading member, remained on the gold standard until 1936. After World War II, the franc went through a series of official devaluations under the Bretton Woods fixed-exchange regime, the last occurring in 1968.

During the post–World War II era, the West German mark rose to become the preeminent European currency, partly because West Germany, compared to England and France, kept inflation subdued. In the 1990s, France tamed its inflation and the German mark was buffeted by the turmoil of merging the two Germanys. As a consequence, the French franc regained some lost ground as one of the leading European currencies. In May 1998, members of the European Union announced plans to launch a European currency, called the *euro,* to replace the individual national currencies, including the French franc and the German mark. During a period of transition between January 1, 1999, and January 1, 2002, French franc banknotes and coins continued to circulate while the euro functioned as a "virtual currency." In 2002, euro banknotes and coins replaced the French franc and other European currencies as the circulating currency in the euro area countries.

See also: Decimal System, Deutsche Mark, Dollar, Monetary Law of 1803, Pound Sterling, Swiss Franc

References

Caron, Francois. 1979. *An Economic History of Modern France.*

Einzig, Paul. 1970. *The History of Foreign Exchange,* 2nd ed.

Kindleberger, Charles P. 1984. *A Financial History of Western Europe.*

Weatherford, Jack. 1997. *The History of Money.*

FRENCH LIVRE

See: Bank of France, Carolingian Reform, French Franc, Hyperinflation during the French Revolution

G

GDP DEFLATOR

See: Value of Money

GENERALIZED COMMODITY RESERVE CURRENCY

A generalized commodity reserve currency is a currency issued with the backing of several commodities. It bears a resemblance to the gold and silver standard, but it is based on a wide range of commodities, and it does not presume to keep the price of any one commodity constant. Under the precious metal standards, the price of a precious metal remained constant. A generalized commodity reserve currency resembles the bimetallic standard in that it is based on more than one commodity. Again, under the bimetallic standard the price of gold and silver remained constant. Symmetalism bears a closer kinship to a generalized commodity reserve currency in that it can include a wide range of commodities. Under symmetalism, a composite commodity is created by combining two or more commodities in fixed proportions. Under symmetalism, one-tenth of an ounce of gold and five-tenths of an ounce of silver might be equivalent to one monetary unit such as the dollar. A generalized reserve currency does not combine commodities in fixed proportions. The proportions are free to change. The gold standard, the silver standard, the bimetallic standards, and symmetalism may be regarded as special cases of a generalized commodity reserve currency. Like symmetalism, a generalized commodity reserve currency has only been examined in theory and never been put into practice.

A generalized commodity reserve currency can best be understood in the context of a simple, primitive society. This primitive society is composed of individuals producing goods that they desire to trade. Assume that one member of this society undertakes the role of banker and monetary authority. This banker issues currency or script in exchange for the various goods that the individuals in this primitive society produce. This banker would not be acting much different than a trading-post that pays for various good in script and stands ready to redeem the script in a wide range of goods and not just gold or silver. The members of this primitive society sell their goods to the banker for script and later redeem the script for merchandise of their choice from the banker's inventories. This script or piece of currency can be interpreted as a receipt for goods stored in a warehouse. The total currency in circulation equals the value of the goods society has stored up with the banker. The banker's warehouse would become empty the day the last piece of script was redeemed for goods. The banker may keep only the most popular commodities on hand, but the script will become a generally accepted medium of exchange for all goods and services. Individual goods can be bought from and sold to the banker without restriction. The system can be expanded to allow the banker to buy commodity futures. To complete the picture the banker raises the price of scarce items and cuts the price of abundant items in such a way that he always has the chosen commodities in stock. Although individual prices go up and down, the value of the script always equals the value of the goods stored. The script in some sense retains its value, and inflation cannot occur.

The operation of a generalized commodity reserve currency involves some complications such as storage cost that might render it unpractical in the modern world. Whether it represents a realistic alternative to the current fiat money system is still open for debate.

See also: Gold Standard, Symmetallism

References

Luke, Jon C. "Inflation-free Pricing Rules for a Generalized Commodity-Reserve Currency." *Journal of Political Economy*, vol. 83, no. 4 (1975): 779–790.

Weber, Warren. "The Effect of Real and Monetary Disturbances on the Price Level under Alternative Commodity Reserve Standards." *International Economic Review*, vol. 21, no. 3 (October 1980): 673–690.

GHOST MONEY

During the late medieval period, money units of account arose that did not correspond to real or tangible pieces of money or coin. Some historians have labeled as "ghost" money units of account without real counterparts. Some of the ghost money owed its origin to coins that were minted in the past, but were no longer minted or found in circulation. Two important units of account, however, the pound and the shilling began as ghost money.

King Pepin the Short of France, father to Charlemagne, decreed that a pound weight of silver be struck into 240 pennies. He also introduced the shilling as a unit of account equal to 12 pennies, comparable in value to the popular Byzantine *solidus*. In the Carolingian system, one pound equaled 20 shillings or 240 pennies. The only coin that was actually minted for several centuries, however, was the penny, and the pound and shilling remained only money units of account or ghost money. Rather than recording 2,400 pennies in a ledger, or pricing a good at 2,400 pennies, merchants found it much easier to write 2 pounds. The silver weight of pennies dropped in time, but a pound remained the equivalent of 240 pennies, losing all connection with a pound in weight of silver. The shilling was also a money unit of account for several centuries. England minted its first shilling during the 1500s.

In 1252, Milan began minting gold florins equivalent to 120 pennies. Perhaps because of the debasement of pennies, the value of the florin rose to 384 pennies and remained at that value for 60 years. A ghost florin emerged that was equal to 384 pennies, meaning that a florin came to signify 384 pennies. Later, the value of the real florin rose to 768 pennies, leaving a real florin at twice the value of the ghost florin. Venice and Genoa developed ghost money in a similar fashion.

In Florence, the florin also established itself, after a period of stability, at a rate of 384 pennies, another ghostly multiple unit of account. The Florentines, however, kept the real florin as a unit of account, and made the penny a ghost penny equal to 1/384 florin, and the shilling, also a ghost, 1/29 florin.

The subject of ghost money touches on an issue always important to debtors and creditors—the stability of the purchasing power of a unit of money. Debtors invariably prefer contracts expressed in depreciating units of account, whereas creditors prefer contracts expressed in a stable coin. Put differently, debtors in Milan preferred to pay off debts in ghost florins rather than real florins. Creditors wanted to receive payment in real florins. Depreciating units of money and ghost monies created the same divergence of interest of debtors and creditors as found in modern societies suffering inflation.

See also: Carolingian Reform

References

Chown, John F. 1994. *A History of Money*.
Cipolla, Carlo M. 1956. *Money, Prices, and Civilization in the Mediterranean World*.
Evans, A. 1931. Some Coinage Systems of the Fourteenth Century. *Journal of Economics and Business History*, p. 3.

GLASS–STEAGALL BANKING ACT OF 1933 (UNITED STATES)

The Glass–Steagall Banking Act, more than any other piece of banking legislation, shaped the development of the current banking system in the United States. One of the numerous acts of economic reform passed in the first 100 days of Franklin Roosevelt's administration, it sought to revive confidence in the banking system and reduce bank competition for depositors' money.

In 1931, the position of banks in the United States caught the attention of the eminent economist John Maynard Keynes, who described it as the weakest element in the whole situation. Suspensions of deposit redemptions by banks had been averaging about 634 banks per year before the Depression, already a high level. The banking crisis deepened with the onset of the economic crisis. Depositors pulled money out of banks, sometimes sending it abroad, sometimes hoarding it in homes. Gold reserves declined. From 1929 to 1933, over 5,000 banks suspended redemption of deposits. One-third of all U.S. banks failed during the Depression. President Hoover saw the banks as a victim of a crisis in confidence. To prevent panic from spreading, President Roosevelt in March 1933 ordered all banks to close for a week.

On June 16, 1933, the Glass–Steagall Banking Act became the law of the land. To help restore confidence in banks, the act banned deposit banks from engaging in investment banking. Investment banks buy newly issued stocks and securities from corporations and resell them to the public for a profit, playing a key role in marshalling capital corporations. After

On June 16, 1933, Franklin D. Roosevelt signs the Banking Act of 1933, a part of which established the Federal Deposit Insurance Corporation. At Roosevelt's immediate right and left are Carter Glass of Virginia and Henry Steagall of Alabama, the two most prominent figures in the bill's development. (Federal Deposit Insurance Corporation)

the stock market crashed, banks that had invested depositors' money in stocks had no way to recover their investment and were forced into bankruptcy. The ban on investment banking remained in until 1999. Innovations in the organization of the banking industry had weakened the act, and many people in Congress thought it should be repealed. This divorce between deposit banking and investment banking had never existed in many countries, including Germany, France, and Switzerland.

The Act also gave the Federal Reserve System the power to regulate interest rates on savings and time deposits. This provision, known as Regulation Q, helped keep the cost of funds down for financial institutions. Another provision of the Glass–Steagall Banking Act prohibited interest-earning checking accounts. The payment of interest on checking accounts increased bank competition for deposits. This added competition might have driven some banks into bankruptcy. The deregulation of financial institutions in the 1980s phased out Regulation Q and removed the ban on checking accounts that pay interest.

The Federal Deposit Insurance Corporation (FDIC) owes its existence to the Glass–Steagall Banking Act. This corporation insures deposits from bank failure up to a maximum limit. All banks that are members of the Federal Reserve System must buy deposit insurance from the FDIC. Today virtually all commercial banks insure deposits with the FDIC. After the savings and loan crisis in the 1980s, the FDIC took over responsibility for furnishing deposit insurance to the thrift institutions. Deposit insurance helps maintain the public's confidence in the banking system.

Large numbers of bank and thrift failures during the 1980s showed that financial institutions remained vulnerable to disinflation and recession. The Glass–Steagall Banking Act went a long way toward instilling resiliency and public confidence in the banking system. Support for Glass–Steagall, however, gradually waned with rising confidence in deregulation of markets. In 1999, Congress overhauled banking regulation with the passage of the Financial Services Modernization Act of 1999. This act repealed the provisions in Glass–Steagall requiring separation of deposit banking and investment banking. The U.S. financial crisis of 2008 raised questions about the wisdom of repealing the ban against combined deposit and investment banking within one company.

See also: Depository Institution Deregulation and Monetary Control Act of 1980, Federal Reserve System, Financial Services Modernization Act of 1999.

References

Baye, Michael R., and Dennis W. Jansen. 1995. *Money, Banking, and Financial Markets: An Economics Approach.*

Schlesinger, Arthur M., Jr. 1960. *The Age of Roosevelt.*

Wall Street Journal (Eastern Edition, New York). "Many Cooks Had a Hand in Repealing Glass–Steagall in '99." September 26, 2008, p. A13.

GLOBAL DISINFLATION

The decade of the 1990s saw world inflation subside from around 30 percent to around 4 percent. More exactly, world inflation averaged 30.4 percent between 1990 and 1994 and averaged 3.9 percent between 2000 and 2004. It was a decade of disinflation (Rogoff, 2003). Inflation decelerated at a rate sufficient to arouse fears of deflation. Alan Greenspan, chair of the board of governors of the Federal Reserve System from August 1987 to January 2006, felt the need to address the prospects of deflation in December 2002. In a speech to the Economic Club of New York City, he commented that it was vital to "ensure that any latent deflationary pressures were appropriately addressed before they became a problem" (Kumar, 2003, 16).

Regardless of stage of economic development or geographical location, countries around the world watched inflation rates recede. For the years between 2000 and 2004, industrialized countries experienced inflation averaging 1.8 percent, less than half of an average inflation rate of 3.8 percent that the same countries posted between 1990 and 1994 (Rogoff, 2003). The most dramatic reduction in inflation occurred in the transition economies, referring to the economies switching over from socialism to capitalism. These countries saw inflation melt away, averaging a mere 13.4 percent between 2000 and 2004, compared to an average of 363.2 percent between 1990 and 1994 (Rogoff, 2003). Latin America boasted similar success in the war to corral inflation. Starting at an average inflation rate of 232.6 percent for the years between 1990 and 1994, Latin America saw inflation rates slip to an average of 7.9 percent for the years between 2000 and 2004 (Rogoff, 2003). For the same time frame, developing countries around the world reported average inflation falling from an average of 53.2 percent to an average of 5.6 percent (Rogoff, 2003). In Africa, average inflation fell from 39.8 percent to 11.0 percent for the same time frame (Rogoff, 2003).

If the trend toward disinflation had gone on uninterrupted, the world economy at some point would have tipped over to deflation. The thin edge of the wedge of deflation had already made inroads in Japan, where inflation averaged a –0.8 percent between 2000 and 2003 (Rogoff, 2003). A minus sign on inflation numbers indicates prices are falling. Hong Kong also saw deflation, posting an inflation rate of –2.5 percent for the 2000 to 2003 time frame (Rogoff, 2003). Deflation in Japan sparked fears that deflation would spread to other countries, particularly since China and Germany were flirting with deflation. China reported inflation of 0.1 percent, and Germany 1.7 percent for the years between 2000 and 2003 (Rogoff, 2003).

The onset of world deflation would almost certainly herald the beginning of world recession. Businesses are hesitant to invest in plant and equipment if they see the prices of their output falling. Consumers are likelier to postpone spending decisions when they learn that the longer they wait, the lower the prices that they pay for consumer goods. Japan's deflation episode coincided with a highly stagnated economy.

Several factors may have played a role in the deceleration of inflation rates around the world. First, governments around the world have yielded more independence to central banks, shielding them from electoral pressures. Central banks in both the United Kingdom and Japan won legal independence. In the same vein, central bankers have become more adept at applying tight money policies with less cost in terms of unemployment. Another factor is a technology-driven rise in productivity around the world, increasing output and decreasing business costs. Last, globalization and increased emphasis on

markets and competitiveness may have diminished any positive role that inflation plays in maintaining high economic performance. In a world where prices are rigid downward, inflation helps to maintain balances in markets where prices are free to rise at different rates, but prices are not free to fall. In such situations, market equilibriums can be achieved by some prices rising faster than others, rather than some prices rising and other prices falling. With more markets having downward price flexibility as well as upward price flexibility, monetary authorities are less tempted to elevate inflation in a bid to restores macroeconomic balance.

By 2008, a worldwide boom in commodity prices put an end to fears of world deflation. On the contrary, inflation seemed on the rise. It will be interesting to see if the current uptick in inflation rates around the world is only a temporary reprieve from a longer-term trend toward deflation.

See also: Central Bank, Inflation

References

Kumar, Manmohan S. "Deflation: the New Threat." *Finance and Development*, vol. 40, no. 2 (June 2003): 16–19.

Rogoff, Kenneth. "Globalization and Global Disinflation." *Economic Review*, vol. 88, no. 4 (4th quarter 2003): 45–78.

GOAT STANDARD OF EAST AFRICA

John Maynard Keynes, in volume 1 of his *Treatise on Money*, published in 1930, says that:

> A district commissioner in Uganda today, where goats are the customary native standard, tells me that it

is a part of his official duties to decide, in cases of dispute, whether a given goat is or is not too old or too scraggy to constitute a standard goat for the purposes of discharging a debt. (11)

Often goats shared with cattle the role of currency, a store of value, and standard of deferred payment in Uganda well into the 20th century. Like many livestock standards, the rate at which goats and cattle could be traded for each other was fixed. The goats circulated more easily in subsistence economies and were often used to buy weapons and salt. Goats could be loaned out for interest; a chief might send a herd of goats to be kept by his subjects, and receive every third kid born to the herd as interest. The government also fixed fines payable in goats.

In Tanzania, 25 goats were equivalent to one cow or ox, and one goat equaled one hoe. The exchange rate between goats and oxen varied between districts. The Masai rated one ass at five goats, an iron spear at two goats, and a big cattle bell or a small ax at one goat. They also paid bride money in goats.

In equatorial Africa, goats often served as a store of value and a standard of deferred payment, but not a medium of exchange. Bride money was paid in goats and sheep; in order for a man to marry, he had to be able to borrow goats and sheep.

Societies living closer to the threshold of survival found food items useful as money because food was what everyone needed, and a large share of each individual's activity was devoted to securing food. Therefore, food items were an obvious choice as a readily acceptable medium of exchange. The problem with much food, such as grain, was that it was perishable, hampering its usefulness as a store of value, one of the important functions of money. Livestock not only made excellent food, but also reproduced, solving the problem of perishability, and even earning a crude form of interest. Therefore, livestock could serve both as a medium of exchange and a store of value. Because livestock could be counted on to maintain its value, creditors preferred to define debts in terms of livestock. Livestock shared with other commodities one important defect as a medium of exchange. The quality of livestock varied because of age and heath, and people invariably sought to repay debts with inferior animals, creating conflicts of the sort referred to in the quotation from John Maynard Keynes. Also, livestock are often bulky and difficult to transport.

Livestock money is not necessarily a symptom of primitive economics and culture. Remote areas often suffer shortages of coins and other forms of money and turn to commodities as a medium of exchange. The American colonies resorted to commodities as money at a time when the world economy was flush with supplies of precious metals from the New World. The Massachusetts Bay Colony enacted a law for cattle being driven to Boston for payment of taxes, providing "if they be weary, or hungry, or fall sick, or lame, it shall be lawful to rest and refresh them for a competent time in any open place, that is not corn, meadow, or inclosed for some particular use" (Nettels, 1934, 220).

See also: Cattle, Commodity Monetary Standard

References
Einzig, Paul. 1966. *Primitive Money.*
Nettels, Curtis P. 1934. *The Money Supply of the American Colonies Before 1720.*

GOLD

Gold, the most enduring, highly valued, and universally accepted monetary metal, is a chemical element represented by the symbol "Au" on the periodic table. A lustrous yellow metal, soft and malleable, gold does not tarnish or corrode, and is found in nature in a relatively pure form. From earliest times up to the present, the search for gold in nature has remained a never-ending quest. Man's earliest chemical researches were inspired by a desire to find a means of converting other metals into gold.

Because it did occur in pure form, gold was one of the first metals that drew man's attention, but it was too soft to be a practical metal for making weapons and farming tools. As a metallic medium for artistic work, however, gold had no rivals and elaborate artistic productions in gold rank among the most prized relics of antiquity.

Gold's role as a monetary metal probably has its roots in the perception, widespread in ancient cultures, that gold was a divine substance. That gold suffered no deterioration with time and that its color resembled the color of the sun may have encouraged the belief that gold was a sacred substance. Gold adornments were a necessary part of religious temples, further underlining the connection between gold and the gods.

The ancient Egyptians held gold to be sacred to Ra, the sun god, and vast quantities of gold went into the tombs of the divine pharaohs. A religion of ancient India taught that gold was the sacred semen of Agni, the fire god, and Agni's priests accepted gold as a gift for priestly services. The Incas of South America saw gold and silver as the sweat of the sun and the moon, and these precious

Gold bullion from the 1622 wreck of the Spanish galleon Nuestra Señora de Atocha *on the Florida coral reef. (Library of Congress/Jay I. Kislak Collection/Rare Books and Special Collections Division)*

metals adorned the walls of their religious temples. After the Spaniards took the Indians' gold and silver, the natives substituted foil paper, and threw gold and silver-colored confetti into the air. The Maya of the Yucatan threw gold, silver, and jade sacrifices into their gods' cenotes (deep pools of water formed when a limestone surface collapsed).

The legend of El Dorado propelled Spain into one of the greatest searches in history, ending with the exploration and conquest of much of the Americas. El Dorado was the name of an Indian who ruled a town near Bogota, Columbia. According to legend, El Dorado celebrated festivals by plastering his body with gold dust, and plunging himself into Lake Guatavita at the end of the festival to wash off the gold, and make the gold a gift to the gods. His subjects also threw gold and other valuables into the lake. The legend of El Dorado grew, and the

Spanish, Portuguese, and German explorers went in search of the golden Eldorado, a city in a land fabulously rich in gold. El Dorado himself was never found, but Eldorado came to mean a land of gold populated by several cities rich in gold. The English explorer Sir Walter Raleigh went in search of one of these cities.

Because gold was always in demand as a religious donation or sacrifice, it had an unlimited demand and was always valued. It was an excellent store of value because it did not tarnish or corrode, and it was divisible into units of any size, making it useful for exchanges of varying magnitudes, and making change. The high value of gold per unit of weight made gold more transportable than other commodities that might serve as money. For these reasons, gold became the basis for the most famous commodity standard in history, the gold standard, a monetary standard that dominated the world monetary system from the 1880s until 1914.

See also: Fort Knox, Gold Dust, Gold Rushes, Gold Standard

References

Green, Timothy. 1981. *The New World of Gold*.

Marx, Jennifer. 1978. *The Magic of Gold*.

Weatherford, Jack. 1997. *The History of Money*.

GOLD BULLION STANDARD

Under a gold bullion standard, countries hold reserves of gold in the form of bars rather than coins, removing gold from monetary circulation in the form of coinage. Instead, each country establishes an official price of a fixed weight of gold in terms of its own currency. The United States was on a gold bullion standard from the 1930s until 1971, and the official United States price of gold was $35 per ounce, committing the United States Treasury to selling gold at that price.

The gold bullion standard was a means of stretching existing supplies of gold, which were not sufficient to support the international monetary system at prevailing price levels. The famous British economist David Ricardo had first suggested the idea after the Napoleonic Wars.

Under a gold bullion standard, private citizens can only hold gold for industrial purposes, such as dentistry, or jewelry manufacture. Monetary gold is owned by the government and is used solely to settle international transactions. Countries without substantial gold reserves can function on a gold exchange standard, whereas countries with significant gold reserves remain on a gold bullion standard.

The world began to move toward a gold bullion standard after World War I, when the world's trading partners sought to return to a version of a gold standard. With the complete breakdown of the gold exchange standard in the 1930s, the world moved toward a gold bullion standard. The gold bullion standard allowed countries to manage domestic currency supplies somewhat independently of international gold flows, giving governments more flexibility to meet the crisis of depression.

At the end of World War II, the world's trading partners established the Bretton Woods system, putting most nations on a gold bullion standard. The United States emerged from World War II owning most of the noncommunist world's gold. Under the Bretton Woods system, the United States defined the value of the dollar in a fixed weight of gold. The United States agreed to buy and sell gold at a rate of $35 per ounce, and most other nations set the value of their own unit of money equal to a certain value in U.S. dollars.

The post–World War II gold exchange standard came to an end in 1971 when the United States stopped converting dollars into gold. By 1971, foreign central banks held more dollars than the United States could redeem in gold without substantially devaluing the dollar.

See also: Bretton Woods System, Gold Exchange Standard, Gold Reserve Act of 1934

References

De Vries, Margaret Garritsen. 1987. *Balance of Payments Adjustment, 1945–1986: The IMF Experience.*

Kindleberger, Charles P. 1984. *A Financial History of Western Europe.*

GOLD DUST

During the Alaskan gold rush, gold dust became a circulating currency in parts of Alaska. Silver coinage and other small coinage was nonexistent, so in its place little packets of gold dust, sealed in writing paper similar to medicine powders, passed as current money. The packets contained a fixed weight of gold dust, and the value of the enclosed gold was written on the outside of each packet. The packets came in popular denominations, such as $1 or $2 denominations, and some of the packets were known to circulate for two years.

The Alaskan gold dust currency demonstrates how societies will identify a medium of exchange when nothing else is available, but gold dust currency has a long history. In the 10th century, the Japanese began circulating bags of gold dust. Later Japanese merchants began wrapping gold dust in small paper packets. The units were the *ryo*, the *bu*, and the *shu*. The bags of gold dust equaled about 10 *ryo*. After learning that a certain amount of gold dust seeped from the opened end of the bag, the Japanese began melting down the gold dust into gold bars. In the 19th century the people of Tibet used as currency gold dust by weight.

For part of the 19th century, gold dust was virtually the only metallic money in Ghana. A farthing's worth of gold could be scooped up on the tip of a knife, and an ounce of gold dust equaled three to four British pounds. The government received taxes in gold dust and employed special weighing scales that gave an advantage to the government.

In the eighteenth and nineteenth centuries, gold dust by weight circulated as money in the islands in and around the Indonesian Archipelago. As early as the 16th century, gold dust acted as currency in the Philippines. The gold-producing districts of Siam made use of gold dust as currency into the 20th century. In 19th-century Siam, a tube of gold dust, 10 centimeters long and the diameter of a thumb, could purchase a buffalo. Some Malayan tribes packed gold dust of uniform weight in pieces of cloth, and circulated these cloth packets as coins.

Africa also furnished examples of gold dust by weight circulating as currency. In Arguin of Spanish Sahara, on the west coast of Africa, an ancient Arabic unit of weight, the *mitkhal*, survived as a unit of weight of gold dust. The mitkhal was a monetary unit of account, but it does not appear that gold dust circulated as money on a significant scale. For a while, gold dust by weight was the

Illustration from Harper's Weekly *shows miners bringing in gold dust to the bank for weighing, 1866. (Library of Congress)*

favored medium of exchange in the Ivory Coast.

See also: Gold, Gold Rushes, Gold Standard

References
Einzig, Paul. 1966. *Primitive Money*.
Stuck, Hudson. 1932. *Ten Thousand Miles with a Dog Sled*, 2nd ed.

GOLD EXCHANGE STANDARD

Under a gold exchange standard, a nation's unit of money is convertible at an official rate into a unit of money of a pure gold standard nation—that is, a nation that maintains the convertibility of its unit of money into gold at an official rate.

A gold exchange standard became a popular monetary standard after World War I when many nations could not marshal the gold reserves to support a gold standard. In 1922, Britain proposed at a Genoa conference the adoption of an international monetary system organized with major nations holding reserves only in gold and the remaining nations holding reserves in foreign currencies. Governments (or central banks) would hold reserves to redeem domestic currencies at official rates as a means of guaranteeing currency value. Although the adoption of an international monetary system failed to materialize from the Genoa conference, many countries individually went on a gold exchange standard. Nations of the British Commonwealth often defined their currencies in terms of the British pound. Other nations defined their currencies in terms of the currencies of nations they were dependent on politically. The gold exchange standard of the post–War World I era ended when the world's major trading partners abandoned the gold standard early in the 1930s.

Critics of the gold exchange standard following World War I and World War II contend that it encouraged dominant nations to incur balance of payments deficits as a method of infusing the rest of the world with additional monetary reserves. Britain ran balance of payments deficits in the post–World I era and the United States ran balance of payments deficits under the Bretton Woods system. A balance of payments deficit allows a nation to buy goods and investments from the rest of the world with payment in domestic currency never used to claim domestic goods. Historically, the gold exchange standard helped the world maintain the discipline of a gold standard when world supplies of gold were not keeping pace with the need for international monetary reserves.

See also: Gold Standard, Gold Standard Act of 1925, Gold Standard Amendment Act of 1931

References

Kindleberger, Charles P. 1984. *A Financial History of Western Europe.*

McCallum, Bennett T. 1989. *Monetary Economics: Theory and Policy.*

GOLD MARK OF IMPERIAL GERMANY

The gold *mark* of imperial Germany, the ancestor to the Deutsche Mark, burst on the world in 1871 with the adoption of the gold standard in imperial Germany.

Before "iron and blood" (Keynes, 1920) forged the German Reich in 1871 from 30 loosely confederated independent states, Germany was split into seven separate currency areas. Six of the areas were on a silver standard, and one was on a gold standard. Soon after the Zollverein, the German customs union, first began to emerge in 1818, pressures arose for a unified German coinage and monetary system. In 1837, southern members of the Zollverein established the *gulden* or *florin*, equivalent to 1/24.5 Cologne mark of silver, as a common monetary unit. Northern members in 1838 responded with the adoption of the Prussian *thaler*, fixed in value at 1/14 Cologne mark of silver, as a common unit of currency. The Dresden convention fixed the exchange ratio at 4 thalers to 7 gulden. In 1857, the members of the Zollverein and Austria formed a coinage union that replaced the Cologne mark of silver with a *Zollpfund* (customs union pound) of 500 grams. The Zollpfund was equivalent to 30 thalers, 52.5 South German florins, or 45 Austrian florins, with each currency unit convertible to the other at the fixed ratio. Austria dropped out in 1866, leaving two rival monetary units, the thaler and the gulden, competing for the monetary hegemony of the members of the Zollverein. German commercial interests continued to push for a unified monetary system based on one currency rather than multiple currencies trading at fixed exchange rates.

Following the formation of the Reich in 1871, the German government enacted monetary reform that put Germany on the road to the gold standard, and establishment of the mark as the money unit of account. The mark had been a money of account on the Hamburg exchange, equivalent to 1/3 Prussian thaler. On December 4, 1871, the German Reichstag enacted monetary legislation, the first three sections of which read:

> Sec. 1. There shall be coined an imperial gold coin, 139 1/2 pieces

of which shall contain one pound of pure gold.

Sec. 2. The tenth of this gold coin shall be called a "mark" and shall be divided into one hundred "pfennige." Sec. 3. Besides the imperial gold coin of 10 marks (Sec. 10) there shall be coined imperial gold coins of 20 marks, of which 69¾ pieces shall contain one pound of pure gold. (Laughlin, 1968, 137)

On July 9, 1873, the Reichstag took action that officially put Germany on a gold standard. The first section of the act read: "Sect. 1. In place of the various local standards now current in Germany, a national gold standard will be established. Its monetary unit is the 'mark,' as established in Sec. 2 of the law dated December 4, 1871" (Laughlin, 1968, 138).

A war indemnity that Germany extracted from France after the Franco-Prussian war helped furnish the gold reserves that enabled Germany to adopt the gold standard. Germany also began selling silver to bolster its gold holdings. Either Germany correctly saw the coming of the gold standard, and was only acting in step with the times, or perhaps the commercial success of England had elevated the prestige of the gold standard in the eyes of Germany.

At the time of Germany's monetary reform, England and Portugal were the only countries on a gold standard, which is why Germany's action was of an extraordinary nature. The gold standard became virtually universal in Europe between 1875 and 1880. The United States went on a de facto gold standard in 1879, Austria-Hungary adopted the gold standard in 1892, and Russia and Japan in 1897. The era from 1875 until 1914 is regarded as the golden era of the gold standard.

The mark of imperial Germany lasted until the monetary reform that followed Germany's episode of post–World War I hyperinflation. In 1923, the *Rentenmark* replaced the mark at a rate of 1 rentenmark to 1,000 million marks. In 1924, Germany enacted another monetary reform that replaced the rentenmark with the *Reichmark*, and after World War II the reichmark was abolished in favor of the deutsche mark. In the post–World War II era, the deutsche mark of the Federal Republic of Germany became the strongest currency in Europe. The new European currency, the euro, launched January 1, 1999, eventually replaced the German mark, the French franc, and other major European currencies.

See also: Gold, Gold Standard

References

Chown, John F. 1994. *A History of Money*.

Keynes, John Maynard. 1920. *Economic Consequences of Peace*.

Kindleberger, Charles P. 1984. *A Financial History of Western Europe*.

Laughlin, J. Laurence. 1968. *The History of Bimetallism in the United States*.

GOLD RESERVE ACT OF 1934 (UNITED STATES)

The Gold Reserve Act of 1934 nationalized all monetary gold in the United States. Only the U.S. Treasury could own gold and buy and sell gold. The act also limited the power of the president to reduce the gold weight equivalent of a dollar, and the day after the passage of the Gold Reserve Act President Roosevelt fixed the gold equivalent of the dollar at $35 per ounce of gold, where it remained until 1971.

The act also established a stabilization fund of $2 billion, put at the disposal of the secretary of the treasury, to support the purchase and sale of foreign currencies as needed to stabilize the value of the dollar.

The groundwork for the enactment of the Gold Reserve Act began with the banking crisis in March 1933 that led President Roosevelt to suspend banking operations for four days. Before banks were reopened, the government required that all commercial banks turn over to the Federal Reserve System all gold and gold certificates and furnish lists of all persons who had withdrawn gold or gold certificates since February 1. The Federal Reserve issued Federal Reserve Notes in exchange for gold and gold certificates. The export of gold and speculation in foreign exchange was banned, and one month later individual ownership of gold and gold certificates was likewise banned. The treasury purchased privately held gold in the United States at a price of $20.67 per ounce, the price that had prevailed with few fluctuations for 100 years. The value of the dollar on foreign exchange markets depreciated 15 percent when the U.S. dollar was no longer redeemable in gold.

The World Economic and Monetary Conference, held in London during June and July 1933, sought to forge an agreement for the stabilization of international currencies and the eventual return to an international gold standard. Even members of the United States delegation could not agree among themselves, and President Roosevelt undermined the conference by announcing that the United States would manage its monetary policy to meet the needs of its domestic economy rather than fulfill conditions set for international monetary cooperation.

Abandonment of the gold standard in the United States aroused fears of inflation, inspiring references to the French Revolution and post–World War I Germany. Nevertheless, there were voices of support. Winston Churchill, responding to the United States severance from the gold standard, called the action "noble and heroic sanity." On July 3, 1933, John Maynard Keynes responded to Roosevelt's announcement in an article (with the headline "President Roosevelt is magnificently right"), referring to the new law as a "challenge to us to decide whether we propose to tread the old unfortunate ways, or to paths new to statesmen and to bankers but not new to thought. For they lead to the managed currency of the future" (Schlesinger, 1959, 223).

Churchill later observed, perhaps overstating the case:

> The Roosevelt adventure claims sympathy and admiration from all . . . who are convinced that the fixing of a universal measure of value not based on rarity or abundance of any commodity but conforming to the advancing powers of mankind, is the supreme achievement which at this time lies before the intellect of man. (Schlesinger, 1959, 224)

The treasury began, through the New Deal–era Reconstruction Finance Corporation, to purchase gold, at first domestically and later in international markets, driving up the price of gold in dollars, which effectively devalued the dollar in terms of gold. As the price of gold was rising, Roosevelt fixed the price officially at $35 per ounce. The increase in the dollar price of gold substantially increased the value of the government's gold holdings, creating a windfall profit for the government that supplied funds for the treasury's stabilization fund and later for the U.S. contribution to the World Bank and International Monetary Fund.

In the 1970s, the United States government stopped selling gold to foreign central banks at $35 per ounce, ending the fixed exchange rate between dollars, gold, and foreign currencies. The price of gold was allowed to fluctuate freely, and the ban on the domestic ownership of gold was lifted.

See also: Bretton Woods System, Gold, Gold Standard, Gold Standard Amendment Act of 1931

References

Chandler, Lester V. 1971. *American Monetary Policy, 1928–1941.*

Myers, Margaret G. 1970. *A Financial History of the United States.*

Schlesinger, Arthur M., Jr. 1959. *The Coming of the New Deal.*

Schwartz, Anna J. "From Obscurity to Notoriety: A Biography of the Exchange Stabilization Fund." *Journal of Money, Credit, and Banking*, vol. 29, no. 2 (May 1997): 135–153.

GOLD RUSHES

Nineteenth-century gold discoveries sparked gold rushes—manias that rival, if not eclipse, the major speculative crazes that periodically rock financial markets. England adopted the gold standard following the Napoleonic Wars, and the United States was on a de facto gold standard after 1834. The discovery of gold in California in 1848 and in Australia in 1851 increased the world's monetary gold reserves from 144 million pounds sterling in 1851 to 376 million pounds sterling in 1861, a increase of 161 percent over a 10-year period. The gold discoveries enabled the United States to become an official gold standard country, and supplied the monetary reserves for the world to adopt the gold standard in the last quarter of the 19th century. Following the gold discoveries, a silver monetary standard became the mark of a low-income country.

On January 4, 1848, James W. Marshal found gold on land in California owned by a Swiss man named Sutter. The discovery occurred nine days before the United States signed a treaty with Mexico making California, New Mexico, Arizona, Nevada, and Utah part of United States territory. The secret soon leaked out—not in time to prevent the signing of the treaty—and gold fever infected the residents of San Francisco and Monterrey, most of whom went straight to the gold mines, leaving their houses empty. Workers left employers, and employers decided to join their workers mining for gold. Soldiers deserted, and ship captains were afraid to make port for fear that sailors would leave for the gold mines. Some ships lay stranded in harbors, deserted by sailors who took up prospecting. The population of California had increased to 92,560 by June 1850, a sixfold increase. By November 1852, the population stood at 269,000, and by 1856, the population had topped half a million. Wages at unheard-of levels lured immigrants, who were content to leave the actual mining to others and take jobs as cooks or fill other skilled positions. Of course, the price of life's necessities also soared.

The repercussions of the Australian gold discoveries were a bit mild compared to the California experience. An emigrant who had already prospected in

The Bullfinch gold mine in western Australia, 1910. (The Illustrated London News Picture Library)

California began in 1851 searching for gold in the Northern Bathurst region of Australia, an area geologists believed to contain gold. Gold was discovered, but the mines were scattered, a factor that—coupled with a well-established sheep industry—blunted the demographic effects of the strike.

Something of the effect of these gold discoveries can be gleaned from the words of Karl Marx, who in 1859 mentioned in the preface to his *Contribution to the Critique of Political Economy* that the gold discoveries were a factor encouraging him to continue his studies of capitalism. He wrote:

> The enormous material on the history of political economy which is accumulated in the British Museum; the favorable view which London offers for the observation of bourgeois society; finally, the new stage of development upon which the latter seemed to have entered with the discovery of gold in California and Australia, led me to the decision to resume my studies from the very beginning and work up critically new material. (Vilar, 1976, 322–323)

The late 1890s saw another round of gold discoveries. The monetary gold stock of the United States more than doubled between 1890 and 1900, thanks to discoveries in Alaska and northeast Canada, South Africa, and Australia. A new cyanide process for extracting gold from low-grade ores also added to gold production.

In 1896, gold was discovered in the Klondike area of Canada, along the Yukon River, on a scale comparable to the California gold discoveries. Twelve dollars worth of gold could be separated in a dish full of sand. Thirty thousand prospectors, crossing a mountain range in

Arctic conditions, arrived after a heroic trial of endurance that could match the hardships of any expedition or human migration in history. Dawson City was born, where miners held out against disease and starvation, and salt fetched its weight in gold. Gold was found in other provinces, and Canada became the world's third-largest gold producer.

Under the gold standard, a shortage of monetary gold stocks led to falling prices between 1875 and 1895, making gold that much more valuable. As prices fell, the scramble for gold increased in intensity. Gold discoveries eased monetary tightness, allowing prices to rise, reducing the value of gold and the intensity of the search for gold.

See also: Gold, Gold Dust, Gold Standard

References

Benton, Pierre. 1954. *The Golden Trail.*
Green, Timothy. 1982. *The New World of Gold.*
Littlepage, Dean. 1995. *The Alaska Gold Rush.*
Vilar, Peter. 1976. *A History of Gold and Money, 1450–1920.*

GOLDSMITH BANKERS

The goldsmiths of 17th-century London developed banking in its modern form. In one business enterprise goldsmiths united functions such as: maintaining safe storage of gold, silver, and deposits of money; loaning out deposits of money (as well as their own money); transferring money holdings from town to town or person to person; trading in foreign exchange and bullion; and discounting bills of exchange. Before the goldsmith bankers, these activities were scattered, often as sidelines or by-products of other trading activities. Around 1633, goldsmith banking arose as an indigenous form of banking in England. Before the goldsmiths, banking in London was the province of Italians, Germans, and particularly the Dutch.

The first step in the goldsmith evolution toward banking began when some goldsmiths became dealers in foreign and domestic coins. Goldsmiths who specialized as coin dealers became known as exchanging goldsmiths as opposed to working goldsmiths. The seizure of the mint in 1640 and the outbreak of civil war in 1642 sent people to goldsmiths in search of safety for jewelry, gold, silver, and coins. The civil war interrupted the normal goldsmith business of forging objects from gold and silver. Instead, goldsmiths developed facilities to store gold and silver deposits in safety. The goldsmiths maintained a running account of each depositor's holdings. They also conducted a profitable business loaning out depositors' gold, silver, and coins to government and private customers. To meet the demands from borrowers, goldsmiths turned to paying interest on deposits and offering time deposits.

The paperwork and record keeping of these activities laid the foundation for important innovations in banking. The banknote (paper money) evolved out of receipts for deposits at goldsmiths. The depositor got a receipt with the depositor's name and the amount of the deposit. These receipts soon became negotiable like endorsed bills of exchange. Modern banking began when these receipts were issued not just to those who had deposited money but also to those who borrowed money. Instead of bearing the name of a particular depositor or borrower, soon the receipts were issued to the "bearer." Thus the modern banknote came to life. The Promissory Notes Act of 1704 ratified the practice of accepting notes in exchange.

The goldsmiths were thus the first to develop checks. The British word "cheque" came from *exchequer*, the British term for "treasury." The cheques were named after the Exchequer orders to pay. The first cheques evolved out of bills of exchange and were called notes or bills. The courts confirmed the negotiability of endorsed bills and notes in 1697.

The paper records of credit transactions and transfers of funds evolved into a considerable supplement of the metallic money supply. By the time Adam Smith's *The Wealth of Nations* was published in 1776, banknotes in circulation exceeded metallic coins. The money supply of the capitalist economic system was no longer limited to the supply of precious metals.

See also: Bank, Check, Seizure of the Mint, Stop of the Exchequer

References

Challis, C. E. 1978. *The Tudor Coinage.*
Davies, Glyn. 1994. *A History of Money.*

GOLD-SPECIE-FLOW MECHANISM

David Hume (1711–1976), one of the most famous philosophers in Western civilization, was the first to give a thorough and complete explanation of the gold-specie-flow mechanism, which is the automatic adjustment mechanism that balances the inflow and outflow of gold under an international gold standard.

On a gold standard, a country's money supply, including paper money, is

David Hume, 18th-century Scottish philosopher. (Library of Congress)

directly proportional to domestic gold holdings, including bullion and gold specie. When a country imports goods from abroad, making payment causes gold to flow out of the importing country. When a country receives payment for goods exported abroad, gold flows into the country. In addition, investments in a foreign country cause gold to flow out, destined for the country receiving the investment. When a country attracts foreign investment, gold flows in to pay for the investment.

David Hume addressed the problem of what happens when the outflow of gold, owing to imports and investments in foreign countries, is unequal to the inflow of gold from exports and foreign investment attracted from abroad. He developed the gold-specie-flow mechanism to explain the forces that bring the outflow of gold into balance with the inflow of gold, stabilizing domestic money supplies.

If gold outflows exceed gold inflows, domestic money supplies dwindle, putting downward pressure on domestic prices. As domestic prices fall, domestic goods become cheaper relative to imported goods, decreasing gold outflows from imports. Also, falling domestic prices lower the prices of domestic goods in export markets, increasing gold inflows from exports. Therefore, imports decrease and exports increase, closing the gap between the gold outflows and gold inflows.

If gold inflows exceed gold outflows, domestic money supplies balloon, putting upward pressure on domestic prices. Rising domestic prices render domestic goods less competitive in export markets, decreasing gold inflows from exports. Also, rising domestic good prices lift the price of domestic goods relative to imported goods, increasing gold outflows from imports. Therefore, imports increase and exports decrease until the gap between gold inflows and gold outflows has closed.

Hume's theory of the gold-specie-flow-mechanism helped supply the theoretical foundation of the gold standard as a stabilizing force in monetary affairs.

See also: Balance of Payments, Foreign Exchange Markets, Gold Standard

References

Hume, David. 1955. *Writings on Economics.*

Hume, David. 1963. *Essays, Moral, Political, and Literary.*

Fausten, Dietrich K. "The Humean Origin of the Contemporary Monetary Approach to the Balance of Payments." *Quarterly Journal of Economics*, vol. 93, no. 4 (November 1979): 655–673.

GOLD STANDARD

Under a gold standard, the value of a unit of currency, such as a dollar, is defined in terms of a fixed weight of gold, and banknotes or other paper money are convertible into gold accordingly. Although the monetary systems of individual countries have been based on the gold standard at times, all the economically advanced countries of the world were on the gold standard for a relatively brief time—roughly from 1870 to 1914, sometimes called the period of the classic gold standard.

The coinage of gold dates back to 700 BCE in the Mediterranean world, and it continued during the Roman Empire. Gold coinage disappeared from Europe during the Middle Ages, but during the 13th century Florence popularized gold coinage among Italian cities. The influence of the Italian cities seems to have brought the practice of gold coinage to England, where it caught on, particularly after the mid-14th century. In 1663, Charles II introduced a new English gold coin called a "guinea." From England gold coinage then spread to the rest of Western Europe.

At the opening of the 19th century, no European country was on a gold standard or had developed a gold standard system. England and other countries coined both gold and silver and set the conversion ratio at which gold could be exchange for silver. England was still officially on a sterling silver standard, but in the 18th century the English government overvalued gold relative to silver, causing an outflow of silver and an inflow of gold and lifting gold to a position of preeminence in England's monetary system.

In normal times, banks redeemed paper money out of reserves of specie (precious metal coinage), but during the wars with revolutionary France and Napoleon, the Bank of England suspended the redemption of its banknotes in specie. After Napoleon's defeat in 1815, Parliament turned its attention to the resumption of specie payments, and passed the Coinage Act of 1816. This act placed England definitely on the gold standard, whereas the rest of Europe remained on a silver or bimetallic standard. In 1819, Parliament passed the Act for the Resumption of Cash Payments, which provided for the resumption by 1823 of the convertibility of Bank of England banknotes into gold specie. By 1821, the gold standard was in full operation in England. Except for England, most countries operated bimetallic systems until the 1870s. Under a bimetallic system both gold and silver coins circulated as legal-tender mediums.

The English banking system evolved toward the use of Bank of England banknotes as reserves for commercial banks, and the Bank of England became the custodian of the country's gold reserves. The Bank of England learned to protect its gold reserves by adjustments in interest rates, using its bank rate and open market operations to raise interest rates and stem an outflow of gold. Higher interest rates attracted foreign capital that could be converted into gold, and lower interest rates had the opposite effect. Low interest rates were the natural results of a gold inflow.

By the end of the 1870s, France, Germany, Holland, Russia, Austro-Hungary, and the Scandinavian countries were on the gold standard. The bimetallic system became awkward because official conversion ratios between gold and silver often differed from the ratio that existed in the precious metals market. Gold discoveries in California and Australia flooded markets for precious metals, and

gold began to replace silver as the circulating medium in France and other European countries. The wars and revolutions of the mid-19th century again forced governments into issuing inconvertible paper money. Governments often restored convertibility by establishing the gold standard. If the gold standard had a golden age, it was between 1870 and 1914, when it acted as a brake on the issuance of paper money. If prices in Country A rose faster than prices in Country B, residents of A would start buying more goods from Country B. Gold would flow out of Country A into Country B, increasing the money supply in Country B and decreasing it in Country A. These money supply changes lowered prices in Country A and raised prices in Country B. These adjustments restored equilibrium, eliminating the need for further gold flows, and stabilizing prices at an equilibrium level.

World War I brought an end to the gold standard, partly because the export of gold was not feasible after 1914, and partly because governments wanted the freedom to print extra paper money to finance the war effort. The end of World War I set the stage for an international scramble for gold as countries tried to reestablish national gold standards. Britain and France kept their currencies overvalued in terms of gold, hurting the competitiveness of their export industries in foreign markets and causing recessions at home.

The economic debacle of the 1930s spelled the end of the gold standard for domestic economies. Governments wanted the freedom to follow cheap money policies in the face of severe depression. The United States Gold Reserve Act of 1934 authorized the United States Treasury to buy and sell gold at a rate of $35 per ounce of gold in order stabilize the value of the dollar in foreign exchange markets. This legislation laid the foundation for the world to return to the gold standard for international transactions after World War II. The value of the dollar was fixed in gold, and the value of other currencies was fixed in dollars. The system only became fully operational after World War II, when most countries lifted bans on the exportation of gold. This gold exchange standard for international transactions remained in effect until 1971.

In 1971, the United States, after experiments with devaluation, suspended the conversion of dollars into gold as the only means of stemming a major outflow of gold. Abandonment of the gold standard preceded the strong worldwide surge of inflation in the late 1970s, and critics attributed the inflation to the loss of discipline provided by the gold standard. The inflation of the 1970s can be attributed to many factors, such as shortages of important commodities, powerful unions, monopolistic pricing, and undisciplined monetary growth.

Most economists see the gold standard as a relic of history. In the absence of the gold standard, governments and monetary authorities enjoy more flexibility to adjust domestic money stocks to meet the needs of domestic economies. The experience of the 1980s and 1990s suggests that countries can control inflation without the gold standard.

See also: Dollar Crisis of 1971, Gold Standard Act of 1900, Gold Standard Act of 1925, Gold Standard Amendment Act of 1931

References

Bordo, Michael D., and Forrest Capie. 1993. *Monetary Regimes in Transition.*

Davies, Glyn. 1994. *A History of Money.*

GOLD STANDARD ACT OF 1900 (UNITED STATES)

The Gold Standard Act of 1900 put the United States for the first time explicitly on the gold standard, removing all traces of the bimetallic standard based on gold and silver. The United States remained on a gold standard until 1933.

The world's major trading partners had been moving toward the gold standard since the United Kingdom adopted the gold standard in 1821. Portugal adopted gold as its standard in 1854, even making British sovereigns legal tender, and Canada went on the gold standard in 1867. After Germany adopted a gold standard in 1873, silver began to lose ground as a monetized commodity. The United States and France ended free minting of silver soon after Germany acceded to a gold standard. Austria-Hungary adopted a gold standard in 1892, and Russia and Japan did so in 1897.

In 1873, the United States ended free minting of silver in legislation that provoked no controversy at the time, but later social protest and silver interests kept the United States on a limited bimetallic standard. The uproar inspired a book, *The Wizard of Oz*, a monetary allegory of the advantages of monetized silver. The proponents of silver wanted to return to the free minting of silver, meaning that the treasury stood ready to buy silver at $1.29 per ounce, above the then-prevailing world market price of silver. A return to a policy of free minting of silver would have increased domestic money supplies and eased the burden of a world trend of deflation that was making itself felt in the United States. At the Democratic Convention in

U.S. Democratic Party politician William Jennings Bryan was a tireless advocate of reform and a staunch anti-imperialist. He served in Congress and as secretary of state, and he was a presidential candidate in three elections. (Library of Congress)

1896 William Jennings Bryan, referring to the enemies of silver and proponents of a gold standard, exclaimed: "You shall not press down on the brow of labor this crown of thorns, you shall not crucify mankind upon a cross of gold."

Bryan lost the presidential election to William McKinley, who favored a gold standard but was slow to take action, knowing that feelings ran high on the issue. The Spanish-American War galvanized public support for McKinley and shifted the issues that held the attention of the voting public. On March 14, 1900, five days before the next Democratic Convention, McKinley signed the Gold Standard Act. Bryan, renominated as the presidential nominee of the Democratic Party, launched a vigorous campaign, again favoring free minting of silver, but lost a second time. McKinley's reelection seemed to ratify the adoption of the gold standard in the United States.

It is probable that increased world production of gold, and particularly increased United States gold reserves, accounts for the United States becoming the most powerful convert to the gold standard. Early in the 1890s, the United States exported gold to the rest of the world, but late in the 1890s, an excess of exports over imports changed the United States to an importer of gold. A substantial increase in tariffs on imported goods may have caused the trade surplus, coupled with a general revival of the world economy. Also, world supplies of gold rose significantly, partly due to new discoveries in Alaska, Africa, and Australia and partly due to a new cyanide process that made lower-grade ores a profitable source of gold. The annual world output of gold grew from 5,749,306 ounces in 1890 to 12,315,135 ounces in 1900, and the U.S. monetary gold stock doubled over the same interval.

The act unequivocally defined the value of the dollar in terms of gold alone, without reference to another metal. The dollar was defined as equal to "twenty-five and eight-tenths grains of gold nine-tenths fine." Responsibility for maintaining parity fell to the secretary of the treasury. No gold certificates were to be issued under $20, and silver remained as a subsidiary coinage and currency, with 90 percent of silver certificates remaining under $10.

The act also set up a system of reserves for national banks and substantially reduced the amount of capital needed to establish a national bank. These measures had the expected effect of increasing the quantity of banknotes in circulation, which rose from $349 million in 1901 to $735 million in 1913. These measures were also intended to make the supply of banknotes more elastic as the needs of trade varied. The elasticity of the currency, or lack thereof, remained a source of economic instability, leading to the establishment of the Federal Reserve System in 1913.

The United States remained on the gold standard until 1933 when the United States government, facing the debacle of the Great Depression, needed more flexibility in its handling of monetary matters. Like many governments around the world at that time, the United States government felt that a domestic money supply, completely uncoupled from domestic gold supplies, could be adjusted as needed by the Federal Reserve System to meet the needs of trade.

See also: Gold Standard, Gold Reserve Act of 1934

References

Davies, Glyn. 1994. *A History of Money.*

Hepburn, A. Barton. 1924. *A History of Currency in the United States.*

Myers, Margaret G. 1970. *A Financial History of the United States.*

GOLD STANDARD ACT OF 1925 (ENGLAND)

The Gold Standard Act of 1925 returned the United Kingdom to the gold standard after the disruption of World War I, signaling the beginning of a new gold standard era that lasted until 1931.

Great Britain's commercial supremacy and financial leadership had secured the gold standard as the international monetary standard between the 1870s and 1914, the years of the classic gold standard. If there was a headquarters for the international gold standard, it was England, and the return of England to gold after World War I was anxiously awaited.

Great Britain had not officially gone off the gold standard during World War I, but the risk of transporting gold under wartime conditions effectively put an end to the convertibility of pounds into gold. After April 1919, the export of gold was strictly prohibited except for freshly mined gold imported from other parts of the Empire.

To study the financial aspects of postwar reconstruction the British government in 1918 had appointed a committee, soon called the Cunliffe Committee after its chairman, Lord Cunliffe, governor of the Bank of England. Nine of the 12 members of the committee were traditional bankers, perhaps accounting for the deflationary recommendations of the committee. From the outset, the Cunliffe Committee assumed that Great Britain should return to the gold standard, and that the value of the pound should be fixed at its prewar value. The recommendations of the committee were phased in over a 10-year period, including the return to the gold standard in 1925.

Wartime inflation had continued at the war's end, lifting the 1920 price level threefold higher than the 1913 price level. In 1920, however, the postwar boom hit the skids, and by 1922 prices were less than twice the 1913 price level. The bout of deflation was temporary but prophetic, and the Cunliffe Committee would have done well to heed the warning.

With the help of loans from the Federal Reserve Bank of New York and a United States banking syndicate, Great Britain returned to the gold standard. The ban on the export of gold was lifted, and the Gold Standard Act of 1925 made the pound convertible into gold at prewar parity. Unlike the classic gold standard of the prewar years, gold coins no longer circulated domestically, and the public could only convert Bank of England banknotes into gold bars. To meet the needs of international finance, the Bank of England could have gold minted into gold coins, but the British public could not demand the convertibility of banknotes into gold coins.

Perhaps the fateful mistake of the act was the return of the pound to its prewar value. The pound needed to depreciate to enhance the competitiveness of British exports in foreign markets, and to diminish the competitiveness of imported goods in British markets. Great Britain's industry could not compete with German industry and industry from other parts of the world. England's economy settled into a sluggish recession, marked by militant labor-management clashes, struggling along until the more devastating collapse occurred in the 1930s.

The Bank of England had to keep domestic interest rates up to make the pound valuable in foreign markets, restricting the desire to convert pounds into gold, and keeping Great Britain in possession of its gold reserves. But domestic economic problems limited the ability of the Bank of England to raise domestic interest rates to protect its gold reserves. A conflict between the need to improve domestic economic conditions and the need to support the pound put the Bank of England in a difficult position. In 1931, the conversion of pounds accelerated, causing a drain on British gold reserves. The government suspended its gold standard with the Gold Standard Amendment Act of 1931. Great Britain and the world's trading partners never returned to domestic gold standards after the debacle of the 1930s. Later in the 1930s, a gold standard for international transactions was established, lasting until 1971.

See also: Gold Exchange Standard, Gold Standard, Gold Standard Amendment Act of 1931, Gold Reserve Act of 1934

References

Feavearyear, Sir Albert. 1963. *The Pound Sterling: A History of English Money*, 2nd ed.

Kindleberger, Charles P. 1984. *A Financial History of Western Europe*.

Moggridge, D. E. 1969. *The Return to Gold, 1925*.

GOLD STANDARD AMENDMENT ACT OF 1931 (ENGLAND)

The Gold Standard Amendment Act of 1931 is a rather euphemistic title for an act that marked the end of the international gold standard. The gold standard had provided the world with a stable monetary system from the 1870s until 1914, and was regarded as the ideal monetary system in the aftermath of World War I. In the pre–World War I era, Britain had been the major proponent and custodian of the gold standard, and the departure of Britain from the gold standard permanently removed the world from the gold standard.

Despite the interruption of World War I the world had by the mid-1920s returned to a gold standard that combined elements of a gold bullion and gold exchange. Countries held international reserves to redeem national currencies at official rates, and these reserves took the form of gold or leading foreign currencies, mainly British pounds and U.S. dollars, which were "as good as gold." The United States held gold reserves well in excess of what was needed to satisfy foreign claims, but in

Britain foreign claims exceeded domestic gold reserves, making Britain vulnerable to an international liquidity crisis.

After World War I, Britain not only committed itself to returning to the gold standard, but also sought to fix the pound at its pre–World War I value, which was equivalent to $4.86 in the United States. In 1925, Britain returned to the gold standard with the pound at pre–World War I parity in terms of gold and foreign currencies, leaving the pound overvalued in the new international order. The overvaluation of the pound made British exports more expensive in foreign markets and foreign imported goods less expensive in British markets, increasing the supply of goods in Britain relative to demand. Deflationary effects of overvaluation in Britain caused strikes, unemployment, and recession, and forced on the British government added social spending, leading to larger budget deficits. The Bank of England kept interest rates high to attract foreign capital, and discourage withdrawal of foreign funds, together minimizing pressure to redeem pounds into gold. High interest rates also helped keep the British economy depressed.

With the onset of the Great Depression of the 1930s, many smaller countries lost export markets and began to draw on reserves of foreign currencies to pay for imports. Bank failures in Austria and Germany weakened confidence in foreign currencies, encouraging redemption of foreign currencies into gold. France, perhaps sensitive to the feeling that the leading powers held reserves in gold and that secondary powers held reserves in foreign currency, took every opportunity to convert its holding of pounds and dollars into gold.

Britain first negotiated loans with the central banks of France and the United States, seeking to bolster its reserves and weather a mounting crisis of confidence in the pound. Later, the British government arranged another loan from private sources, but only after restricting government deficit spending, and curbing expenditures on unemployment compensation and wages of government workers. The loans however were only stopgap measures, and the drain on Britain's gold reserves continued.

On Saturday September 19, 1931, the British government decided to suspend gold payments, effective the following Monday, September 21. The act was rushed through Parliament on September 21 and read, "Until His Majesty by Proclamation otherwise directs subsection 2 of section one of the Gold Standard Act of 1925 shall cease to have effect." The Gold Standard Act of 1925 had returned Britain to the gold standard.

Australia, New Zealand, Brazil, Chile, Paraguay, Uruguay, Venezuela, and Peru had already suspended gold payments. Within a few weeks, most of the world's trading partners abandoned the gold standard or restricted foreign currency transactions. By the end of 1932, only the United States, France, Belgium, Switzerland, and the Netherlands remained on the gold standard and maintained freedom of transaction in foreign currencies. The United States abandoned the gold standard in 1933, followed by the remaining European countries in 1936.

See also: Gold Reserve Act of 1934, Gold Standard, Gold Standard Act of 1925

References
Chandler, Lester V. 1971. *American Monetary Policy: 1928–1941.*
Chown, John F. 1994. *A History of Money.*

Feavearyear, Sir Albert. 1963. *The Pound Sterling: A History of English Money*, 2nd ed.

GREAT BULLION FAMINE

Fifteenth-century Europe encountered a severe shortage of precious metals—particularly silver—that scholars have named the Great Bullion Famine. The worst years of the bullion famine lasted from 1457 until 1464. Evidence of price levels are scanty, but E. J. Hamilton, author of a well-known study of the 16th-century price revolution, found evidence that prices in Valencia and Aragon dropped as much as 50 percent in gold equivalents, and 25 percent in silver equivalents from 1400 to 1500. Interest rates that ranged between 4.875 and 8.375 percent during the first half of the 14th century in Italy, rose to a range between 6 percent to over 10 percent 100 years later.

The reasons for the bullion famine lay in the depletion of silver mines located in what are now Germany, Austria, the Czech Republic, and Slovakia, and a European trade deficit with countries of the Middle and Far East. Diminished European silver production began with the depopulation caused by the Black Death epidemic of the 14th century, and continued into the 15th century. A contributing factor to the bullion famine was the strong tendency to hoard precious metals in plate, cups, jewelry, and treasures of coin. Falling prices rendered hoarding precious metal a productive investment and hoarding was also a means of protection against coinage debasement.

A European trade deficit with the Middle and Far East existed because exotic goods from China and India—spices, silks, cotton, and others—were highly prized in Europe, but European products—such as woolens from England—were not valued in Eastern countries. Even falling European prices could not erase the trade deficit. Precious metals, particularly silver, were strongly valued in the Eastern countries, and European precious metals sent to the East in payment for goods never returned in payment for exported European goods. Precious metals were a European export, and Eastern countries became a sinkhole for those metals. The Eastern countries exhibited the same strong propensity to save that now is associated with Japan, causing Japan to export goods to the United States without buying a comparable volume of U.S. goods.

Mints closed down all across Europe. A lack of bullion forced mints in the Rhineland to close one after another between 1440 and 1443. The English mint at Calais shut down permanently in 1442, and at one point the Tower of London housed the only mint in northwestern Europe that remained active. As early as 1392, the minting of silver in France had dropped to a trickle, and about the same time Sweden ended minting silver for 20 years. At the height of the bullion famine, mints closed down in Flanders, Holland, Hainaut (southwestern Belgium), Dordrecht, and Valenciennes.

The bullion famine was one of the not-so-secret causes of the Age of Discovery. Portuguese explorations down the coast of Africa opened up new routes to sub-Saharan gold. Christopher Columbus, in his diary of his first voyage, mentions gold 65 times. After the mid-16th century, the discovery of silver in Latin America put an end to the bullion famine,

Europe entered an era of rising prices, and trade with the Eastern world reached a higher level of intensity.

See also: Ghost Money, Price Revolution in Late Renaissance Europe, Silver Plate

References

Davies, Glyn. 1994. *A History of Money*.
Day, J. 1978. The Great Bullion Famine of the Fifteenth Century. *Past and Present*, p. 79.
Spufford, Peter. 1988. *Money and its Use in Medieval Europe*.

GREAT DEBASEMENT

The Great Debasement (1542–1551) refers to the English crown's policy of coinage debasement during the reigns of Henry VIII and Edward VI. Coinage debasement occurred when governments replaced to a significant degree the gold or silver content of coinage with a base metal such as copper. By reducing the value of gold or silver content relative to face value, governments extracted useable revenue from domestic money stocks. This stratagem was called debasement because each coin was worth less in terms of its precious metal content.

Normally, the face value of the coined money exceeded its production cost, including the cost of the precious metals. This difference, which the crown earned as a profit, was called seigniorage. The crown of England, like many governments, held an exclusive monopoly on the privilege to coin money from precious metals, and used the profits of seigniorage to help pay for government expenditures.

During the Great Debasement, the English crown's profits from debase-

ment rose to unreasonable levels. In March 1542, the value of the silver content of each English coin averaged 75 percent of each coin's face value. By March 1545, the value of the silver content had fallen to 50 percent, and by March 1546 to 33.33 percent. The value of each coin in silver content fell to only 25 percent of face value by the time the debasement had run its course in 1551.

During a period of coinage debasement, a mechanism called Gresham's law comes into play. Gresham's law is sometimes expressed as bad currency drives out good currency. Households and businesses will hoard the good (or undebased) coinage, and use the debased coinage to pay for goods and services. The result is that only the debased currency remains in circulation, and the good currency goes into hiding or is spent on goods from foreign countries where the debased currency is not legal tender and therefore not accepted.

In 1551, the English government under Elizabeth I instituted a plan to retire the debased currency and replace it with currency the face value of which corresponded with its precious metal content. Because of Gresham's law, retiring the debased currency was a tricky affair because households and businesses tend to hoard good coinage and pay debts with debased coinage. To retire the debased currency the government enacted laws forbidding the outflow of good coinage to foreign markets, and ending the legal-tender status of the debased coinage beyond certain date.

During the gold standard era, governments achieved the same purpose as debasement by increasing the paper money in circulation relative to the gold bullion held in reserves. Debasement, like printing excess paper money, was a secret form of taxation that monarchs could impose, often without receiving the approval of representative bodies such as Parliament. The secret tax made itself felt by increasing prices relative to measures of wages and other incomes.

An apologist for the debasement policies of the English crown might point to the need to build up the English navy and finance other public defense expenditures. Critics would answer that Henry VIII was fond of building palaces. Whatever the driving force of debasement, the public gradually lost faith in the ability of governments to manage money supplies without oversight from private financial sectors that are affected by monetary mismanagement. In the United States, a quasi public-private agency, the Federal Reserve System, regulates the money supply, largely independent of the executive and legislative branches of government. Studies have shown that in the 1970s countries with independent monetary authorities experienced lower inflation rates than countries with monetary authorities dominated by government authority.

See also: Byzantine Debasement, Dissolution of Monasteries, Gresham's Law

References

Glyn Davies. 1994. *The History of Money.*

Gould, J. D. 1970. *The Great Debasement.*

GREEK MONETARY MAELSTROM: 1914–1928

Between 1914 and 1928, Greece saw annual inflation rates vary from 85 percent to 11 percent, and monetary experiments that rank among the strangest in history.

The seeds of Greece's monetary disorder were sown in the middle to late 19th century, when the National Bank of Greece, founded in 1841, gradually acquired a virtual monopoly on the prerogative to issue banknotes and became the primary creditor of the government of Greece. The bank was founded as a private bank whose principle stockholder was the government, and it dominated the monetary affairs of Greece, acting as a central bank until the establishment of a genuine central bank in 1928. The bank also made loans to the private sector.

Originally, the government conferred on the National Bank the privilege to issue banknotes as long as the bank stood ready to convert its banknotes into gold. The government, however, suspended convertibility on four separate occasions: right after the 1848 revolutions, again from 1868 to 1870, from 1877 to 1884 when the government borrowed heavily, and last from 1885 to 1928.

Inflation reared its head during the prolonged era of suspended convertibility, but never reached the frenzied hyperinflation levels that characterized post–World War I Germany, Austria, Hungary, and Poland. Between 1914 and 1928, the cost of living index rose 868 percent, perhaps reflecting the threat of losing access to foreign capital that may have helped Greece keep a tight rein on its monetary affairs. Between 1895 and 1910, international financial pressure put Greece on a stricter monetary discipline, requiring the government to withdraw and burn 2 million drachmas in banknotes each year. This pressure came from imperialistic powers with vast financial resources, such as Britain, and served some of the same functions now performed by the International Monetary Fund. The Allies lifted these controls during World War I and even granted credits to Greece, allowing Greece to substantially increase the issuance of banknotes. The credits were never realized, further adding to the supply of unsecured banknotes in circulation.

The government budget of Greece was clearly in the surplus column at the opening of World War I, but by 1918 red ink had shown up in the deficit column. The costs of the war in Asia Minor sent the budget deficit soaring, and by 1922, the government was unable to raise additional revenue either from taxation or borrowing from traditional sources.

Under the duress of a deficit-ridden budget, the government of Greece carried out one of the most fantastic pubic finance schemes in history. On March 25, 1922, the government ordered all citizens to physically cut in half banknotes in their possession. One half of each banknote was to be retained by its owner and could continue to circulate at half of its face value. The owner was to surrender the other half to the government and receive in exchange a 20-year loan at 6.5 percent interest.

The National Bank of Greece exchanged with the government fresh notes for the canceled halves, making the whole process a means of raising a loan for the government. The government enacted a similar measure again on January 23, 1926, this time putting three-fourths of the value of the note in the hands of the owner, and the remaining one-fourth the government took in exchange for a 20-year loan at 6.5 percent

interest. Despite, or because of, these unorthodox financing measures, inflation, after reaching a peak of 85 percent in 1923, steadily subsided until the end of the decade, even dipping into the negative range in 1930. The establishment of the Bank of Greece, a genuine central bank, began monetary rehabilitation, helping Greece to experience monetary stability during the decade of the Great Depression.

See also: Bisected Paper Money

Reference
Freris, A. F. 1986. *The Greek Economy in the Twentieth Century.*

GREENBACKS (UNITED STATES)

Greenbacks were the fiat money that the United States government issued during the Civil War. Fiat money, or inconvertible paper money, is money that cannot be converted or redeemed into a precious metal such as gold or silver. By the close of the Civil War, greenbacks and related U.S. government notes accounted for about 75 percent of the money in circulation, largely displacing banknotes of state banks, the principle currency in circulation before the Civil War.

The United States government was not the first to issue inconvertible paper money during the Civil War, but was preceded by commercial banks. The secretary of the treasury of the new Lincoln administration, Salmon Portland Chase, who came to that office without financial experience, possessed a naïve faith in "hard money." The government borrowed heavily from banks to finance

Sheet music from an 1863 song entitled "Greenbacks: New Song for the Times." The song lyrics lampooned the greenback currency that was issued by the federal government under President Abraham Lincoln during the Civil War. (Library of Congress)

the difference between $6 million in tax revenue and $25 million in expenditures. When the government took out bank loans, it demanded payment in specie, and the specie was not redeposited in banks, but was removed from the banking system. Fears about the ultimate success of the war led the public to hoard specie. On December 30, 1860, banks in New York suspended specie payments on banknotes and deposits, and banks in other parts of the country soon followed. The government began issuing "demand notes" and the country was effectively put on an inconvertible paper standard.

On December 30, 1860, Congress entertained the first proposal for issuing legal-tender notes (fiat money) to defray government expenses. Bankers raised a howl about the government issuing fiat

money and dispatched a delegation to advise the secretary of the treasury and Congress on ways to finance the war. This delegation urged a program of heavy taxation and borrowing in long-term capital markets to finance government spending as an alternative to the issuance of fiat money.

Government officials weighed the alternatives: the issuance of legal-tender fiat money, or an issue of long-term government bonds. Given the poor credit reputation of the government, the paper money was bound to depreciate in value, but bonds would have to pay high interest rates to attract buyers. The government chose the issuance of fiat money, and the only remaining question for debate was whether Congress would clothe the fiat money with the legal status of legal-tender money.

On February 25, 1862, Congress adopted an act providing for the issuance of notes that were lawful money and legal tender in payment of all debts public and private. The government issued $150 million of these notes, $50 million of which went to retire demand notes the government had already issued. The new notes were called greenbacks. The legal-tender provision contained two noteworthy exceptions. The government demanded payment of import duties in gold coin, and the government committed itself to paying in gold coin the interest earned from government bonds.

To dampen inflationary pressures, the government devised means of diverting greenbacks from the spending stream. The greenbacks could be used to buy treasury bonds paying 6 percent interest redeemable after five years and maturing after 20 years. Also, the treasury accepted deposits of greenbacks, paying

5 percent interest, and redeemable with 10 days notice. The option of converting greenbacks to Treasury bonds was removed in subsequent bills that authorized the issuance of additional greenbacks.

Prices more than doubled during the Civil War. In June 1864, Congress set a limit of $450 million on the issuance of greenbacks, a limit that was never exceeded. After the Civil War, various interest groups dreaded the deflation that would likely follow the reduction of the supply of fiat money in circulation.

It was 1879 before the federal government began redeeming greenbacks with specie, and joined the world's major trading partners on a worldwide gold standard. The greenback experience was prophetic in light of the 20th century's widespread adoption of inconvertible paper money.

See also: Legal Tender, Pacific Coast Gold Standard

References

Barrett, Don C. 1931. *The Greenbacks and Resumption of Specie Payments: 1862–1879.*

Nugent, Walter T. K. 1968. *Money and American Society, 1865–1880.*

Ritter, Gretchen. 1997. *Gold Bugs and Greenbacks: the Antimonopoly Tradition and the Politics of Finance in America.*

GRESHAM'S LAW

Gresham's law is often stated in a simplistic and aphoristic form as "bad money drives out good money." It means in practice that if two coins are in circulation, perhaps one silver and one gold, the public always wants to hoard the coin that has a face value equal to or less than the market value of the coin's precious metal value. In turn, the public will use coins with a face value greater than their market value as precious metal to pay off debts and pay for goods and services. Coins with a face value less than the market value as precious metal can always be melted down and sold for a profit, causing these coins to disappear. The "bad money," sometimes called "debased money," is the money with a face value greater than the market value of its precious metal content, and it becomes the medium of circulation. The "good money" is the money whose face value is comparable to the market value of its precious metal content, and holders of good money are reluctant to give it up. In a country with debased money circulating alongside good money, the latter tends to flow into the hands of foreigners, domestic hoards, or goldsmiths' melting pots, leaving only bad money in circulation, thus the phrase "bad money drives out good money."

Gresham's law owes its name to Sir Thomas Gresham, the foremost financial wizard of the Elizabethan era, who acted as a councilor to Elizabeth I and as the royal agent in European financial markets. England was on the silver standard, and during the mid-16th century, the silver value of England's silver coinage had dropped from 75 percent of face value to 25 percent. Only three ounces of silver was in a coin that had a face value equivalent to 12 ounces of silver. Elizabeth I inherited the confusion and monetary disorder of the debasement policies of her predecessors, who had practiced debasement to build up England's military defenses. Sir Thomas Gresham formulated Gresham's law to explain the difficulty of introducing good money in a monetary environment dominated by bad money, explaining how bad money would drive out the good money. Gresham explained that the government ran the risk of coining full-valued money that would only end up in the hands of foreigners and the goldsmiths while the bad money remained in circulation. Gresham devised a policy based on a quick recall, revaluation, and recoinage of debased money combined with severe legal penalties for melting down or exporting the new coinage.

Although Gresham received the credit for formulating a law still discussed in modern economic textbooks, he was not the first to put the law into words. Aristophanes, the great comedic playwright of ancient Greece, writing in 405 BCE, remarked concerning Athens, "In our Republic bad citizens are preferred to good, just as bad money circulates while good money disappears" (Angell, 1929, 98). A French theologian, Nicholas Oresme (*c.* 1320–1382) wrote a book, *A Treatise on the Origin, Nature, Law, and Alterations of Money*, in which he explained the operation of Gresham's law as one of the consequences of debasement.

In the modern world inflation of paper money has replaced debasement of coinage as a means of extracting more revenue for financially strapped governments. Gresham's law can sometimes be seen in operation in countries where domestic currencies are depreciating from inflation, and United States dollars are hoarded as a preferred currency.

See also: Great Debasement

References

Angell, Norman. 1929. *The Story of Money*.
Chown, John F. 1994. *A History of Money*.
McCallum, Bennett T. 1989. *Monetary Economics*.

GUERNSEY MARKET HOUSE PAPER MONEY

Guernsey Island, second largest of the Channel Islands, home to the famous Guernsey dairy cows, boasts of one of the more interesting paper money experiments in monetary history. The parliament of Guernsey Island, called the States, hit on the scheme of issuing paper money to pay for the construction of public facilities, and in turn reclaiming the paper money in payment for rent on the use of the finished facilities.

In April 1815, the Guernsey States appointed a committee to investigate a proposal for enlarging the Guernsey meat market. The committee recommended the issuance of 1-pound state notes, beginning with a 3,000 pound issue. These 1-pound notes were earmarked to pay the costs of material and wages for construction of the enlarged Guernsey meat market. According to the plan, those who used the building would have to pay rent in these 1-pound notes. As these notes fell into the hands of the government of Guernsey as payment for rent, they would be destroyed, and therefore canceled. According to the committee report:

> Thus at the end of ten years, all the Notes would be cancelled and the States would be in possession of an income of 150 pounds per annum, which would be a return to the 3,000 pounds spent by them. Looked at from all sides, the scheme shows nothing but the greatest advantage for the public and for the States. (Angell, 1929, 267)

In 1820 and 1821, the Guernsey States issued over 4,000 pounds in 1-pound notes to pay off its public debt. In 1826, the States authorized another paper issue of 1-pound notes to pay for Elizabeth College and parochial schools. This authorization set a limit of 20,000 pounds on notes in circulation.

In 1827, the States authorized another issue of 11,000 pound notes to pay for improvements to Rue de la Fontaine, a street adjoining the market. Again the rents related to the project would reclaim the notes, leading to their cancellation. Other note issues were approved.

In 1828, the States appointed the Finance Committee "to replace the used and worn-out Notes by new Notes, payable at the same time as the destroyed notes would have been." In 1829, a member of the Finance Committee observed that the volume of notes in circulation had risen to 48,183.

The Guernsey States experiment with paper money is one of the most interesting in history. It was a successful and productive use of a paper money issue that commanded value independent of a gold standard. It never climaxed in an inflationary finale that seemed to be the outcome of a merciless logic inherent in all the early issues of paper money. One important characteristic that distinguished the Guernsey paper money experiment from other early experiments was this: Unlike earlier paper money, often inspired by wartime expenditures, the Guernsey paper money issue went to pay for the production of durable, income-earning wealth. Therefore the nongold wealth of the community kept pace with the growth in paper money even though the amount of gold in the community may have declined.

Reference
Angell, Norman. 1929. *The Story of Money*.

H

HIGH-POWERED MONEY

High-powered money is sometimes called the "monetary base." It includes all cash, even vault cash at commercial banks, and commercial bank deposits at Federal Reserve Banks, which are redeemable in cash. These assets are called "reserves" because commercial banks hold them to honor checking account withdrawals during times when withdrawals exceed new deposits. New loans are also made out of reserves in the sense that a bank with no reserves would have no funds to loan out. The term "high-powered" is a reference to the fact that a $1 increase in the volume of high-powered money will cause the most narrowly defined measure of the money stock to increase by about $2.50.

High-powered money is important because it represents net wealth to the private sector. In contrast, checking account money, called demand deposits, represents an asset to the owner of the checking account, but represents a liability from the perspective of the bank, which owes that money to a customer on demand. The liability cancels out the asset, leaving a net effect of zero on the net wealth of the private sector. Commercial bank deposits at a central bank represent a liability to the central bank. However, a central bank is a government or quasi-government agency that is not considered part of the private sector.

The narrowest definition of the money stock, called M1, includes checkable deposits and circulating currency, but not vault cash at commercial banks. Because M1 includes checking deposits and excludes vault cash, it is possible for the supply of high-powered money to change without a change in a money stock measure such as M1. Normally, a 1 percent increase in the supply of high-powered money will lead to a 1 percent increase in M1, the most narrowly defined measure of the money supply in the United States.

The concept of high-powered money is important because central banks directly control high-powered money and exert only indirect control over measures of the money supply, which are influenced by the willingness of commercial banks to make loans out of reserves.

See also: Bank, Central Bank, Legal Reserve Ratio, Monetary Aggregates, Monetary Multiplier

References

Baye, Michael R., and Dennis W. Janise. 1995. *Money, Banking, and Financial Markets: An Economic Approach.*

McCallum, Bennett T. 1989. *Monetary Economics: Theory and Practice.*

HOT MONEY

The term "hot money" in an economic or financial context refers to money that quickly shifts between financial markets in search of the highest short-term interest rate or rate of return. "Hot money investors" are investors who jump into and out of short-term investments, sometimes driven to act in mass by a seemingly herd mentality. The term does crop up in criminal investigations where it refers to marked bills or new currency with consecutive serial numbers. Such currency bears the name "hot money" because it can be easily identified and linked to a specific crime.

In today's world of globalization and financial liberalization, the term "hot money" in the popular media usually refers to the use of the term in an economic or financial context. Even from the economic and financial perspective, "hot money" can carry different shades of meaning. Banks often think of deposits from foreign and institutional investors as being hot money because these deposits are large and may be suddenly and unexpectedly withdrawn. Questions about a bank's solvency or higher interest rates in other places can cause a mass exodus of these deposits. To a buffer against the volatility of hot money, banks may cultivate a large base of consumer and household deposits.

As trading strategies of investors and speculators have grown in complexity, the influence of hot money has been felt in markets normally outside the sphere of risky speculation. In 2006, observers expressed concern about the influx of hot money in to the U.S. municipal bond market, one of the drabber and quieter financial markets (Pollock, 2006). Usually investors in these bonds are U.S. investors because the interest rate paid by these bonds, although lower that the interest rate paid on other bonds, is exempt from federal taxation. Foreign investors began investing in these bonds after they found a way to place leveraged bets on a divergence between the prices of municipal bonds and non–tax-exempt bonds. Some investors feared that than a mass exodus of foreign investors would cause the market for these bonds to plummet.

In 2005, some analysts and investors saw hot money behind a large run up of oil prices and the greater volatility in oil prices (Sesit and Reilly, 2005). They blamed hedge funds making use of large computer programs, organizations that unlike airlines and utilities had no direct need to purchase oil.

Hot money is often cited as a disruptive factor in international capital flows, allowing sudden shifts that can spark contagious financial crises. In 2008, Chinese officials expressed concern about the excess inflow of hot money (McMahon, 2008). Foreign investors depositing money in China gained in two fronts. First, Chinese interest rates stood nearly twice U.S. levels. Secondly, between January and May of 2008, Chinese currency gained in value 4.2 percent relative to the U.S. dollar. Observers had credited hot money for drastic fluctuations in China's booming stock market and real estate market. Unlike many countries, China has strict controls on foreign capital movements that should restrain inflows and outflows of hot money, but foreign investors have found ways to get around the controls. One way of getting around the controls involves inflating receipts of legitimate trade and investment transactions. Chinese officials have no way of knowing exactly how much hot money has entered China. China's case is interesting in that it shows that controlling movements of hot money can be difficult.

See also: Capital Flight

References

Karmin, Craig. "Can Asia Control the 'Hot Money'?; Even Some Investors Endorse Cash Controls to Fight Speculators." *Wall Street Journal* (Eastern Edition, New York) April 5, 2007, p. C1.

McMahon, Denis. "World News: China Vows to Crimp 'Hot Money' Flows." *Wall Street Journal* (Eastern Edition, New York) March 10, 2008, p. A6.

Pollock, Michael. "Welcome to a Changed Muni World; Foreigners, Hedge Funds Are Among the Newcomers; One 'Hot Money' Scenario." *Wall Street Journal* (Eastern Edition, New York) April 4, 2006, p. C13.

Sesit, Michael R., and David Reilly. "Going Global: 'Hot Money' Helps Drive Oil Volatility." *Wall Street Journal* (Eastern Edition, New York) July 14, 2005, p. C1.

HOUSE OF ST. GEORGE

The House of St. George was a Genoese public bank, one of the first organized. It is regarded as a direct ancestor of the modern central banks, acting both as a state treasury and a private bank. During the 16th and 17th centuries, the banking industry would briefly lift Genoa to the leadership of the capitalist world, with Genoese merchant bankers conducting business throughout Europe, making loans and transferring funds.

In a war with Venice during the 14th century, the city of Genoa had raised money from citizens in return for promissory notes. At the end of the war, Genoa pledged the customs dues from its port to redeem the notes. In 1407, the creditors organized themselves into a bank, the Casa di San Georgio, or House of St. George, appointed eight directors to watch after their investments, collected taxes, and made loans to the state. The bank's Renaissance palace can still be seen in the Piazza Caricmento.

The House of St. George was what Adam Smith called a "bank of deposit." Coins from all parts of the world were deposited with the bank. The ownership of the deposits, called "bank money," changed hands by book-keeping entries at the bank in the presence of a notary, similar to the Bank of Amsterdam or Bank of Hamburg. Shares of stock in the bank also acted as a medium of exchange and changed hands through book-keeping entries. The Genoese government paid interest on the public debt in three-year installments, and accounts of accrued interest that were payable also exchanged ownership in the capacity of money.

The House of St. George is credited with being the first bank to issue banknotes, not in specific denominations such as 100 or 1,000, but on an individual basis for large deposits. Each note was written out in hand, and the ownership could be passed on by endorsement. These handwritten notes could represent either a deposit of gold or silver, or shares of stock in the bank.

Genoa's control of European finances was brief. Repeated bankruptcies of the

Spanish crown may have scared the Genoese bankers, or perhaps the Dutch and English demanded more involvement in the shipment and distribution of the precious metals from the New World. By 1647, Dutch ships carried Spanish silver directly to the Low Countries.

See also: Bank of Deposit, Bank of Venice, Bills of Exchange

References

Colwell, Stephen. 1965. *The Ways and Means of Payment.*

Homer, Sidney. 1977. *A History of Interest Rates*, 2nd ed.

HYPERINFLATION DURING THE AMERICAN REVOLUTION

On June 22, 1775, the First Continental Congress, struggling to finance the Revolutionary War effort without power to tax or borrow, authorized the issuance of $2 million in bills of credit. These bills of credit, soon to be known as "continentals," were issued with the understanding that individual states would redeem them according to an apportionment based on population. The Congress had considered, but rejected, another option that would have assessed to each state a sum of money to be raised by the issuance of state notes on the authority of each state government.

Congress issued an additional $4 million in continentals before the year was out. These were scheduled for redemption between the years 1779 and 1986, and, contrary to a suggestion from Benjamin Franklin, paid no interest. The plan for each continental to bear the signature of two members of Congress fell by the wayside, and Congress hired 28 individuals to sign the bills. Congress continued to run the presses, authorizing the issuance of $241,552,780 in bills of credit before voting to limit circulation to $200 million in bills of credit toward the end of 1779. After 1779, Congress ceased the issuance of continentals.

Congress issued the continentals because the states did not want to levy taxes to finance a war that was partially sparked by anger over English taxation of the colonies. Desiring to tread lightly on taxes, the individual state governments issued $210 million of their own notes between 1775 and 1780, further fanning the flames of inflation.

Although the states shied away from levying taxes to redeem continentals, they complied with the request from Congress to declare continentals legal tender. To reinforce the state action, Congress passed resolutions to shame people into accepting continentals in payment for goods. After hearing of one instance of an individual refusing to accept continentals, Congress resolved (November 23, 1775): "That if any person shall hereafter be so lost to all virtue and regard for his country as to refuse. . . , such person shall be deemed an enemy of his country." Until the end of 1776, price inflation remained relatively tame, but then inflation began to gather momentum, becoming runaway in 1779 when the ratio of continentals to specie in face value increased from 8:1 to 38:1.

In December 1776, the New England states held a price convention in Providence, Rhode Island, that called for less paper money and more taxation, and that developed a recommended set of prices for farm labor, wheat, corn, rum, and wool. The New England states enacted these price recommendations into law,

The American colonies began circulating their own currencies prior to independence. States issued their own currency, with Continental dollars coming a few months later. The issuances were initially unregulated, which caused a loss of market value and extreme inflation. Following the war, Secretary of the Treasury, Alexander Hamilton, was charged with establishing a national bank to standardize and control the currency system. (Library of Congress)

and Congress urged other states to do the same. Congress also gave its blessing for states to assume the authority to confiscate hoarded goods. Citizens held mass meetings denouncing price increases, and irate women raided shops that reportedly were hoarding goods. Merchants had to defend themselves in court. Philadelphia protesters hanged in effigy a specie dollar to protest dealers refusing to accept paper money.

In 1778, a second price convention set forth a list of recommended prices, and Congress seemed ready to legislate, calling for a price convention in 1780. Congress also asked the states to formulate price recommendations on the assumption that

prices were 20 times higher than they were in 1774. Congress gave up on the idea of fixing prices, however, and in March 1780, Congress asked the states to remove punitive legislation against those refusing to accept continentals.

After 1779, the depreciation of continentals continued, the face value ratio of continentals to specie raising to 100 to 1 by January 1781. The ratio of 100 to 1 became the official ratio at which Congress converted continentals into interest-bearing, long-term bonds under the funding act of 1790.

The experience of the continentals became a lesson in the evolution of paper money—a lesson that had to be relearned many times. The issuance of inconvertible paper money became the accepted practice worldwide as governments learned to maintain its value by restricting its supply.

See also: Hyperinflation in the Confederate States of America, Hyperinflation during the French Revolution, Hyperinflation in Post–World War I Germany, Inconvertible Paper Standard, Hyperinflation during the Bolshevik Revolution

References

Bezanson, Anne. 1951. *Prices and inflation during the American Revolution, Pennsylvania, 1770–1790.*

Hepburn, A. Barton. 1967. *A History of Currency in the United States.*

Myers, Margaret G. 1970. *A Financial History of the United States.*

Paarlberg, Don. 1993. *An Analysis and History of Inflation.*

Stabile, Donald R. 1998. *The Origins of American Public Finance: Debates over Money, Debt, and Taxes in the Constitutional Era, 1776–1836.*

HYPERINFLATION DURING THE BOLSHEVIK REVOLUTION

In the aftermath of the Bolshevik seizure of power (1917), Russia experienced a bout of hyperinflation comparable to the hyperinflation of the French Revolution, sending prices to levels more than 600 million times higher than 1913 levels.

The imperial Russian Government resorted to inflationary finance to sustain itself through World War I. On the eve of World War I, Russia boasted of the largest gold reserves in Europe, which backed 98 percent of the Russian banknotes in circulation. The treasury held large gold reserves to back paper rubles. Tax revenue from taxes levied on the manufacture and sale of alcohol, one-fourth of the treasury's revenue, fell because of a newly enacted law against alcohol consumption. Tariff revenue also dropped significantly with the onset of war. Instead of direct taxes and internal war bond financing, the government turned almost exclusively to paper money and foreign loans to finance the war.

On July 27, 1914, the government suspended specie payments on paper rubles. The gold reserve requirement for the issuance of banknotes also came to an end. The government doubled the supply of paper money at the beginning of the war when it issued an additional 1.5 billion rubles. The issuance of paper money continued until the supply had increased fourfold by January 1917. The issuance of paper money increased 100 percent in France and 200 percent in Germany over the same time frame.

This wartime finance led to monstrous price increases, and set a precedent that the Bolsheviks would continue to accelerate the revolution. Inflation forces remained dormant through the first half of 1915 because the war blocked exports, which increased domestic supplies. Toward the end of 1915 inflation began to accelerate rapidly, and by the end of 1916 prices were four times higher than their 1913 levels. From 1913 to October 1916, the price of wheat flour rose 269 percent, buckwheat by 320 percent, salt by 500 percent, meat by 230 percent, and shoes and clothes by 400 to 500 percent. The cost of living grew two or three times faster than wages, and food and fuel shortages were common in urban areas. Workers formed cooperatives to purchase food and other necessities at lower prices. The government helped maintain order by threatening to induct into the army anyone who caused trouble.

Worker discontent became the political base that drove the revolution. Long lines of people waited to buy bread, and by the time workers were off work the shops no longer had bread on the shelves. The anger of the workers mounted as food and fuel became scarce, and strikes erupted in Petrograd, the largest industrial center.

In 1917, the revolution began in earnest. Nicholas I abdicated in March 1917, followed by the Bolsheviks' seizure of power in October 1917. Throughout 1917, prices rose more rapidly, topping 7.55 times their 1913 level by October 1917. The supply of rubles in circulation rose to 19.6 billion, compared to 2.4 billion in the first half of 1914. After the October coup, the tax system fell apart and the new government counted on the printing presses to finance government spending. In 1918, notes were printed in denominations up to 10,000 rubles. By October 1918, prices had grown to 102 times their 1913 level, and to 923 times in October 1919.

In May 1919, the government completely unleashed the supply of paper money. The only restriction on printing of fresh paper money was the supply of ink and paper. The government used gold holdings to buy printing supplies abroad. Nearly 50 percent of the treasury's budget went for the cost of printing paper money. In 1919, the supply of paper money in circulation grew to 225 billion. In 1920, it reached 1.2 trillion and doubled again in the first half of 1921. In 1921, notes were issued with face values up to 100,000 rubles. By 1923, prices were 648,230,000 times their 1913 level.

In 1922, a new ruble was introduced that was equal to 10,000 of the old rubles. This currency reform did not halt inflation, and in 1923, a newer ruble was introduced that equaled 1,000,000 of the 1922 rubles. Also, the government introduced a parallel currency called the *chervonetz* that was linked to gold. This currency remained in circulation until 1928.

Revolutions are often attended with episodes of hyperinflation. The French Revolution, the American Revolution, the Bolshevik Revolution, and the Communist Revolution of China were attended with episodes of hyperinflation.

See also: Hyperinflation during the American Revolution, Hyperinflation during the French Revolution, Hyperinflation in Post–World War I Germany, Inflation and Deflation

References

Paarlberg, Don. 1993. *An Analysis and History of Inflation.*

Pipes, Richard. 1991. *The Russian Revolution.*

Hasegawa, Tsuyoshi. 1981. *The February Revolution: Petrograd, 1917.*

HYPERINFLATION DURING THE FRENCH REVOLUTION

The famous English economist John Maynard Keynes, commenting on an observation of Lenin, wrote:

> Lenin is said to have declared that the best way to destroy the Capitalist System was to debauch the currency. . . . Lenin was certainly right. There is no subtler, no surer means of overturning the existing basis of society than to debauch the currency. The process engages all the hidden forces of economic law on the side of destruction. And does it in a manner which no one man in a million is able to diagnose. (Keynes, 1920, 236)

No doubt Lenin and Keynes were familiar with the role of inflation during the French Revolution.

In October 1789, the French National Assembly found itself in a desperate situation. Tax revenue fell far short of expenses, and the government survived day by day with advances from the Bank of Discount, a bank that largely loaned funds to the government. The bank declared itself out of funds, and the Assembly needed resources to complete the revolution. The Assembly met the financial crises with two important and interrelated measures. It confiscated church lands, and it created an "extraordinary treasury" charged with raising 400 million *livres* by selling *assignats*, which were certificates of indebtedness bearing 5 percent interest. The government announced its intention to sell the church property and take assignats in payment. The church property in effect served as collateral for the assignats.

The assignats met with less than a hearty reception, because it was not clear which lands would be sold to creditors. In August 1790, the Assembly turned assignats into banknotes and added an extra 800 million livres to the issue. The decree specified that the total number of assignats in circulation should never exceed 1,200 million livres. The new assignats bore no interest and could be acquired by anyone, whereas the first issue was available only to creditors of the government. Instead of just liquidating the national debt, the government took to issuing assignats to pay for deficit spending.

By mid-1792, the inflation horse was definitely out of the barn; prices rose 33 to 50 percent while wages lagged far behind. In January 1793, a mob stormed stores in Paris, and in February, a

scarcity of soap sparked further riots. Mobs also obstructed grain shipments. In 1794, the government implemented a system of price controls known as the Law of the Maximum. People who refused to accept assignats in payment or accepted them (or paid them) at a loss, could be fined 3,000 livres and imprisoned six months for the first offense. The fine and imprisonment could be doubled for the second offense. Speculation in specie and assignats could bring six years' imprisonment, and forestalling was punishable by death. A forestaller was a person who withheld necessary commodities from circulation. Nevertheless, farmers and manufactures hoarded goods, and the specter of famine rose up for the spring. In December 1794, the government abandoned price controls, prices soared, and assignats fell to less than 3 percent of their face value.

The Convention, the governing body at that stage of the revolution, acknowledged the fall of the assignats in June 1795. The nominal value of each successive issue was reduced according to a scale of proportions. In July of the same year, the Convention ordered in-kind payments for half of the land tax and rents. Peasants stopped bringing produce to market to avoid accepting assignats. Speculation became rampant, while inflation ruined creditors and savers. As prices outpaced wages and workers suffered, speculative profits created a new class of ostentatious rich who stood in stark contrast to the destitution of the lower classes. Inflation reached its peak as the Directory took power. Each day saw prices rise hourly, and each night paper money came off the press for issuance the following day. Paper money issues doubled in four months, for a total of 39 billion livres in assignats.

In February 1796, the Directory discontinued the assignats. It tried an issue of land warrants, which were good for the purchase of national property at an estimated price without competitive bidding. The sale would be to the first taker. The public had lost faith in paper money, however, and in July 1796, the government decided to return to specie. Inflation continued to ravage the economy until the advent of Napoleon in 1799. Apparently, his wars brought in more than they cost, and his government improved the efficiency of taxation, ending the government's need to promiscuously print paper money.

Since the experience of the French Revolution, hyperinflation has been associated with revolutionary change. It played a role in the rise of Hitler to power in Germany, the Communist Revolution in China, and the Bolshevik Revolution in Russia. The American Revolution also had a hyperinflationary episode.

See also: Hyperinflation during the American Revolution, Hyperinflation in Post–World War I Germany, Inflation and Deflation, Hyperinflation during the Bolshevik Revolution

References

Harris, S. 1930. *The Assignats.*

Keynes, John Maynard. 1920. *The Economic Consequences of Peace.*

Lefebvre, Georges. 1964. *The French Revolution.*

Paarlberg, Don. 1993. *An Analysis and History of Inflation.*

Thiers, M. A. 1844. *The History of the French Revolution.*

HYPERINFLATION IN ARGENTINA

Between 1988 and 1991, Argentina saw the climax of more than a half century of inflation, sending runaway annual inflation rates into four-digit territory.

Unlike Chile, Argentina was no stranger to paper money in the early 19th century. In 1822, the Bank of Buenos Aires issued banknotes that traded at a premium, but war with Brazil in 1826 led to the suspension of convertibility of these notes into gold. The notes depreciated significantly before resumption of convertibility in 1867. Convertibility was suspended again in 1876, and Argentina's peso depreciated by more than 50 percent.

In 1899, Argentina adopted the gold standard and began an era of price stability that, aside from the interruption of World War I, lasted until Argentina and the world abandoned the gold standard early in the depression of the 1930s. Argentina's wholesale price index (based on 1943 prices equaling 100) stood at 31.6 in 1907, rose to 38.3 in 1914, and climbed steadily—reaching 68.0 in 1920. Then Argentina saw prices decline steadily until reaching a trough of 42.1 in 1933.

From 1934 until 1990, prices rose and inflation fluctuated with a long-term upward trend. Inflation averaged over 50 percent between in 1940 and 1950, and then subsided to an average slightly over 23 percent between 1961 and 1965. Inflation began to creep upwards and really took off in the early 1970s, averaging nearly 109 percent between 1973 and 1976. Inflation finished the decade of the 1970s in the 170 percent range, and approached 400 percent in the mid 1980s. By 1989, the annual inflation rate exceeded 3,000 percent. Inflation exceeded 2,000 percent in 1990 and declined to 84 percent 1991. By the mid-1990s Argentina had tamed inflation to well within the single-digit range and had become a model of monetary stability.

Money is printed in Argentina in 1989, fueling inflation. (Diego Goldberg/Sygma/Corbis)

The root cause of the inflation originated in isolationist foreign trade policies, political instability alternating between military dictatorships and civilian governments, interventionist domestic economic policies emphasizing subsidies, and the failure of the tax system to fund public expenditures. The unfortunate episode of the Falklands war in 1982 may have helped put Argentina on the road to bankruptcy and collapse. Between 1980 and 1990, real wages fell 20 to 30 percent. Between 1973 and 1990, per capita income fell 26 percent. Tax revenue as a percentage of the gross national product (GNP, a measure of total national output and income, comparable to the gross domestic product in use today) fell in the 1980s, and the public debt surpassed 100 percent of GNP. Printing money became a substitute for taxation.

Dissatisfaction with economic chaos helped bring a democratic revival in Argentina, and early in the 1990s, a democratic government brought inflation under control, a feat that had eluded military governments. Worldwide inflation in the 1970s had led some observers to doubt the ability of democratic governments to face up to the disease of inflation.

In March 1991, the Argentine legislature enacted the Law of Convertibility, creating a new Argentine peso convertible into one U.S. dollar. The new monetary base was backed by 100 percent of reserves in gold, dollars, or other foreign currencies. United States dollars were also accepted as a currency for domestic transactions. The value of the peso was pegged at 1 dollar, and the central bank maintained convertibility between pesos and dollars. This currency reform not only broke the back of inflation, but made Argentina's monetary system a model for other developing countries. Monetary reform coincided with a capitalist revolution in Argentina, emphasizing privatization, less government intervention, and openness to foreign trade.

Between 1995 and 2001, Argentine inflation remained below the 4 percent range. In 2002, Argentine inflation jumped to 25.9 percent. By 2007, it had settled down to single-digit ranges, between 8 and 9 percent (International Monetary Fund, 2003, 2008).

See also: Hyperinflation in Bolivia, Hyperinflation in Brazil, Chilean Inflation, Hyperinflation during the French Revolution, Hyperinflation in Post–World War I Germany, Inflation and Deflation

References

De la Balze, Felipe A. M. 1995. *Remaking the Argentine Economy.*

International Monetary Fund, *World Economic Outlook*, April 2003 and April 2008.

Meiselman, David. 1970. *Varieties of Monetary Experience.*

HYPERINFLATION IN AUSTRIA

After the close of World War I, Austria, one of the states that emerged from the division of the Austro-Hungarian Empire, experienced an episode of soaring hyperinflation, registering an annual inflation rate of 10,000 percent between January 1921 and August 1922. A legacy of food shortages and high unemployment after World War I helped send Austria on a monetary path of economic insanity. The creation of new states, coupled with the scarcities of war, disrupted traditional flows of trade, and Austria, a loser in the struggle, owed war reparations.

The government of Austria met the crisis by incurring large expenditures on food relief and unemployment relief.

From 1919 until 1922, the Austrian government collected less than 50 percent of public expenditures in taxes and financed the remainder selling treasury bills to the Austrian section of the Austro-Hungarian Bank, which paid for the treasury bills with fresh banknotes, denominated in Austrian crowns. From March 1919 until August 1922, the Austro-Hungarian Bank multiplied Austrian banknote circulation by a factor of 288, increasing the supply of banknotes in circulation from the equivalent of $4.7 million to over $1.3 billion. Aside from public borrowing, the bank continued to make private sector loans at favorable interest rates.

As inflation mounted, Austrians began a "flight from the crown." They spent the banknotes sooner after receiving them and Austrian crowns held as a form of wealth were spent. Austrians put wealth in foreign exchange or real assets, minimizing holdings of Austrian currency. Contemporary economists might describe the flight from the crown as an increase in the velocity of money, meaning money is spent more frequently on goods and services. The government instituted exchange controls in a rather ineffective effort to stop Austrians from converting Austrian crowns to foreign exchange. The value of Austrian crowns in the New York foreign exchange market dropped sharply. In January 1919, one U.S. dollar bought 17.09 Austrian crowns, and in August 1922 one U.S. dollar bought 77,300 Austrian crowns.

The flight from the crown caused prices to rise faster than the money supply growth rate. Between January 1921 and August 1922, retail prices rose by a factor of 110, whereas banknote circulation rose by a factor of only 39.

The depreciation of the crown in foreign exchange markets stopped abruptly in

August 1922, and the upward spiral in retail prices ended the following month. The League of Nations arranged for the Austrian government to receive a loan of 650 million crowns. In return, the Austrian government had to end deficit spending and establish a central bank independent of the government. The mere spread of knowledge of the agreement was sufficient to stabilize retail prices and the crown in foreign exchange markets.

The central bank of Austria continued to rapidly infuse banknotes into the Austrian economy, but inflation subsided, appearing to defy the laws of economics. These banknotes, however, were backed with gold, foreign assets, or commercial paper, rather than government securities. The change in the composition of the assets of the central bank accounted for the end of the monetary disorder.

At the end of 1924, long after the inflation subsided, Austria issued a new unit of currency, the shilling, worth 10,000 crowns.

See also: Hyperinflation in Post–World War I Germany, Hyperinflation in Post–World War I Hungary, Hyperinflation in Post–World War I Poland

References

Sargent, Thomas J. 1993. *Rational Expectations, and Inflation*, 2nd ed.

Wicker, E. "Terminating Hyperinflation in the Dismembered Hapsburg Monarchy." *American Economic Review*, vol. 76, no. 3 (1986): 350–364.

HYPERINFLATION IN BELARUS

After becoming independent from the Soviet Union on August 25, 1991, the Republic of Belarus entered into an economic phase of declining output and hyperinflation. As a transition economy, Belarus faced the task of undertaking the necessary reforms to transform its economy from central planning to one based on market mechanisms. Runaway inflation afflicted all the new transition countries created after the dissolution of the Soviet Union, but in most cases, inflation subsided to single-digit territory by 1997.

Belarus is unique in that the problem of moderate to hyperinflation lasted for nearly a decade. Between 1992 and 2001, inflation never dropped below the 50 percent range. Belarus may have owed the stubborn persistence of inflation to its greater reluctance to embrace market reforms. According to the International Monetary Fund's World Economic Outlook Database for May 2001, the trajectory of Belarus's inflation unfolded as follows: In 1993, Belarus posted an average annual inflation rate of 1,190 percent and in 1994 an average annual inflation rate of 2,434.11 percent. By 1995, the worst of the hyperinflation was over, with inflation subsiding to the 700 percent range. In 1996, Belarus appeared well on the road to price stability with annual inflation numbers in the 50 percent range. After 1996, annual inflation started climbing again until it reached an annual rate of 293.7 percent in 1999. After 1999, the government, by substantial monetary tightening, again showed progress in corralling inflation. By 2001, average annual inflation stood in the 75 percent range.

Under the Soviet Union, Belarus boasted of one of the more industrialized areas, including a strong concentration of defense industries. It imported raw materials from and exported manufactured goods to other areas in the Soviet Union. At independence, it inherited a pattern of trade that largely reflected its role in the Soviet economy. Russia remained its main trading partner in its post-independence phase. After the election of Aleksandr Lukashenko to the presidency on July 20, 1994, the pace of economic reform became highly uneven. He launched the country on a path of "market socialism" which reimposed some administrative controls over prices and exchange rates. The government ended subsidies on staples, such as bread, milk, beef, housing, and utilities, but imposed ceilings on producers' profit margins to soften the blow to consumers. Even so, milk prices soared 20 fold and beef prices tripled.

The slow progress in containing inflation may have reflected some confusion over the cause of the inflation. For a small, open economy highly dependent on imported raw materials, it is possible to make the case that inflation is imported from abroad in the form of higher commodity prices. Also, Belarus saw real wages increase between 1996 and 1999 because of indexation and discretionary wage adjustments (Bogetic and Mladenovic, 2006). Some observers felt increases in real wage bore some of the blame.

Economists emphasize the role of the money supply in situations of hyperinflation. Between 1996 and 1999, the local currency money stock in Belarus grew at an average annual rate of 124 percent. (Bogetic and Mladenovic, 2006). A main goal of Belarusian monetary policy during this period was to provide cheap credit to state enterprises and privileged sectors such as agriculture. In addition, central bank credit to the government expanded at an annual rate of 65 percent in 1996, 289 percent in 1998, and 200 percent in 1999 (Bogetic and Mladenovic, 2006). Inflation in Belarus mainly mirrored excessive monetary growth.

Other factors such as rising import prices and real wages may have encouraged the monetary growth.

See also: Hyperinflation in Post-Soviet Russia

References

Bogetic, Zeljko, and Zorica Mladenovic. "Inflation and the Monetary Transmission Mechanism in Belarus, 1996–2001." *International Research Journal of Finance and Economics*, no. 1 (2006): 1–20.

International Monetary Fund. *World Economic Outlook*, May 2001.

HYPERINFLATION IN BOLIVIA

During the 1980s, Bolivia experienced an episode of hyperinflation that reached annual rates of 24,000 percent during the peak years of 1984 and 1985. Cups of coffee sold for 12 million pesos. A 1-million-peso note that was equivalent to $5,000 in 1982 was worth only 55 cents by 1985. During the period of raging hyperinflation, the Bolivian peso depreciated 40,000 percent, sometimes losing 1 to 2 percent per hour.

Paper pesos were counted in bundles of identical bills, and sometimes pesos were measured by the height of stacks of bills. In some cases, paper pesos were weighed. A university professor received pay in a stack of bills about 19 inches in length. A secretary received a stack of bills from 9 to 10 inches in length.

Despite the shortcuts in counting money, an airline desk clerk would spend 30 minutes counting the 85 million pesos charged for an airline ticket. Small-denomination bills became nearly worthless and were often seen blowing in the wind, piling up in muddy clumps alongside sewage ditches and in bushes on vacant lots.

The Bolivian government had to rely on foreign countries to print its paper pesos on the scale needed to satisfy the hunger of a hyperinflationary economy. Paper pesos measured in thousands of tons were flown in from Germany, Brazil, and Argentina, arriving at the La Paz airport on pallets.

Checking account and credit card transactions lost favor, because the clearance process took up valuable time as the inflation clock ticked away. Banks had no money to finance mortgages for households and businesses, which paid for construction on a pay-as-you-build basis.

The United States dollar became the de facto, unofficial standard of value in Bolivia during the hyperinflation. Bolivia's bustling cocaine trade with the United States supplied the Bolivian economy with dollars that fed a black market in currency. Currency traders walked the streets, offering to buy and sell dollars and pesos. Consumers came to town with dollars, traded the dollars for pesos before entering a store, then made their purchases with the pesos. The shopkeeper owner hardly received the pesos before going out on the street and converting the pesos back into dollars. Legally, transactions had to be conducted in pesos, but no one kept pesos longer than necessary. According to an article in the *Wall Street Journal* describing the Bolivian hyperinflation,

> Civil servants won't hand out a form without a bribe. Lawyers, accountants, hairdressers, even prostitutes have almost given up working to become money-changers in the streets. . . . "We don't produce anything. We are all currency speculators," a heavy equipment dealer in La Paz says. "People don't know what's good and bad anymore. We have become an immoral society." (*Wall Street Journal*, 1985, 1)

The blame for the Bolivian inflation has to be put at the feet of government finance. Tax revenues covered only 15 percent of the Bolivian government's expenditures, and the government's budget deficit equaled 25 percent of the country's annual output. As late as 1990, the annual inflation rate was still 7,000 percent, well below the levels of the mid-1980s, but still high. In the 1990s, the inflation rate began to subside substantially as the government reduced deficit spending. In 2002 Bolivia posted an inflation rate below one percent. In 2007, Bolivia reported inflation of 11.3 percent, the first time Bolivian inflation had risen above ten percent since 1996 (International Monetary Fund, 2003, 2008).

See also: Hyperinflation in Argentina, Hyperinflation in Brazil, Chilean Inflation, Hyperinflation in Post–World War I Germany, Inflation and Deflation

References

International Monetary Fund, *World Economic Outlook*, April 2003 and April 2008.

Wall Street Journal. "Precarious Peso— Amid Wild Inflation, Bolivians Concentrate on Swapping Currency." August 13, 1985, p. 1.

Weatherford, Jack. 1997. *The History of Money.*

HYPERINFLATION IN BRAZIL

Between 1989 and 1994, Brazil saw inflation soar into hyperinflation dimensions, registering annual inflation rates from 1,600 to 2,500 percent.

Brazil can boast of a long history with inconvertible paper money. Notes of the Bank of Brazil appeared no later than 1808, and copper displaced gold and silver as the only metallic currency in circulation. In 1833, the government took over the issuance of paper notes, and in 1835 these notes were made legal tender. The currency system was reformed several times, but periods of monetary disorder became part of economic life in Brazil, although they never reached hyperinflation proportions until 1989.

Brazil shared an inflationary trend with the rest of the world during the post–World War II era, but with greater intensity. Between 1948 and 1965, the inflation rate in Brazil averaged 2 percent per month, lifting prices by a factor of 79 over the same time period. Annual inflation rates finished the decade of the 1960s in the 20 percent range. During the decade of the 1970s, when worldwide inflation gathered momentum, Brazil saw annual inflation rates reach 77 percent by 1979.

The dynamics of inflation seem to require that inflation persistently rise above the expected range. Brazilian inflation rose above 110 percent in 1980, and in 1988 entered four-digit territory. The year 1989 saw annual inflation exceed 1,700 percent. Inflation subsided to the three-digit range before soaring to 2,500 percent annually in 1993. The government began anti-inflation policies in earnest, cutting the inflation rate by half in one year. Annual inflation then dropped rapidly, reaching the 4 to 5 percent range in 1997. Between 1997 and 2007, inflation in Brazil remained below 10 percent except for one episode in 2002 and 2003 when Brazilian inflation briefly rose slightly above 14 percent *(International Monetary Fund, 2003. 2008)*.

Unlike other famous examples of hyperinflation, the blame for Brazilian hyperinflation cannot be pinned on wartime expenditures or war reparations. Brazil did bear a heavy debt burden, and much of the debt was owed to foreigners. Brazil's central bank was a buyer of last resort of short-term government bonds, which was the immediate cause of the inflation.

Before inflation reached hyperinflation levels, Brazil had adopted a system of indexation, making inflation more bearable to average citizens. Under indexation, government bonds, wages, and other long-term contracts were automatically revised upwards to adjust for inflation. The system of indexation contributed additional inertia to inflation, and initially may have slowed the rate of acceleration of inflation.

Supermarket in Rio de Janiero updates prices as Brazil transitions to a new currency under Fernando Henrique Cardoso's plano real, *1994. (Julio Pereira/AFP/Getty Images)*

Taming inflation required deep and substantial economic reforms. Brazil underwent a capitalist revolution, emphasizing discipline in government spending, privatization, trade liberalization, and stringent monetary control. Brazil also phased in a new currency, and when the old currency was extinguished, prices stabilized. The new currency was tied to the United States dollar, and backed by foreign exchange reserves, including dollars.

See also: Hyperinflation in Argentina, Hyperinflation in Bolivia, Chilean Inflation, Indexation, Inflation and Deflation

References

International Monetary Fund, World Economic Outlook, October 2008.

Pereira, Luiz Carlos Bresser. 1996. *Economic Crisis and State Reform in Brazil*.

Wachter, Susan M. 1976. *Latin American Inflation*.

HYPERINFLATION IN BULGARIA

Between 1996 and 1997, Bulgaria faced a daunting macroeconomic crisis, posting an average annual inflation rate of 500 percent for January 1997 (Gulde, 1999). For March 1997, the average annual inflation rate soared above 2000 percent (Gulde, 1999). Bulgaria owed the rapid acceleration of inflation to large liquidity injections for propping up the country's weakening banking system, to central bank financed budget deficits, and to a loss of confidence in the Bulgarian lev, reducing demand for that currency. Deeper problems involved Bulgaria's reluctance to embrace market-based institutions that ease the way for bankruptcies and liquidations and encourage effective corporate governance.

The banking crisis began bubbling up in 1995. By 1996, 9 out of 10 state-owned banks reported negative capitalization, and more than half of the portfolios of these banks were nonperforming. The 10 state-owned banks accounted for more than 80 percent of banking sector assets (Gulde, 1999). Half of the private banks, including the largest and best known, fell into the technically bankrupt category. Several runs on banks erupted amid rumors of the banking situation.

The Bulgarian National Bank closed banks to restore confidence. The first round of bank closures occurred in May of 1996. It was too narrow in scope, only closing banks widely known to be in trouble. Confidence in the banking system continued to vex the economy. In September 1996, the Bulgarian National Bank announced another round of banking closings. Total bank closures accounted for about one-third of Bulgaria's banking system. The National Bank of Bulgaria announced that there would be no further bank closures and committed itself to keeping the remaining banks open. As conditions continued to deteriorate in the banking sector, the National Bank of Bulgaria kept its promise of not closing more banks and met the growing crisis by injecting added liquidity into the banking system and repurchasing government bonds. This policy fueled the inflation.

Another side of the problem had to do with falling tax revenues. Real output shrank by 10 percent in 1996 (Gulde, 1999). Falling output translates into lower income, which reduces tax revenues tied to income. In addition, Bulgaria faced a mounting problem with tax evasion. Tax revenues as a percent of gross domestic product (GDP) fell from 40 percent to 14.7 percent (Gulde, 1999). The government financed the growing budget deficit by issuing treasury bills with shorter maturities and higher interest rates.

Bulgaria recovered more rapidly than most countries from the hyperinflation and macroeconomic crisis. By 1998, hyperinflation had effectively erased the real value of the public debt. Lower interest rates also helped with the debt burden of the government's deficit. The government beefed up tax collection and scaled back social spending, effectively balancing its budget by 1998. The East Asian financial crisis may have helped Bulgaria by creating global deflationary forces. By the end of 1998, the inflation had fallen to 1 percent, and the basic interest rate of the Bank of Bulgaria had fallen to 5.2 (Gulde, 1999). At the height of the crisis, this key interest had stood at 200 percent.

The cornerstone in Bulgaria's stabilization plan was the establishment of a currency board to replace central bank management of monetary policy. The currency board went into operation on July 1, 1997. A currency board guarantees that all of a country's outstanding circulating currency is supported by equivalent amounts of an anchor currency. Bulgaria chose the deutsche mark as the anchor currency.

See also: Hyperinflation in Yugoslavia

References

Organization for Economic Cooperation and Development. "OECD Economic Surveys: Bulgaria." Vol. 1999, no. 9 (April 1999): 1–111.

Gulde, Anne-Marie. "The Role of the Currency Board in Bulgaria's Stabilization." *Finance and Development*, vol. 36, no. 3 (1999): 36–40.

HYPERINFLATION IN CHINA

From 1937 until 1949, China experienced a bout of inflation no less spectacular and no less fraught with social and political consequences than the hyperinflation of post–World War I Germany. The inflation began in Free China, the part of China not invaded by the Japanese, and continued until the communist government solidified control of the mainland in 1949 through 1950.

Chinese inflation falls into three eras. Between 1937 and 1939, the early war years, prices did not fully give way to inflationary pressures. Between 1940 and 1945, the war years, the Chinese people began to loose confidence in currency, and inflation accelerated. The end of World War II saw a brief lull in inflation before inflation rose to stratospheric heights, ending in the collapse of the currency system just before the nationalist government fled to Taiwan.

Japan's invasion of China left Free China robbed of 90 percent of its industrial capacity, and the Chinese government bereft of the tax revenue of the wealthiest provinces of China. Japan's blockade of ports serving Free China also reduced supplies of imported goods. The Chinese government sought to finance a military resistance and an industrialization of Free China without recourse to significant taxes, instead relying on voluntary sacrifices and foreign aid. The government ran up massive deficits and expanded bank credit for industrial expansion. However, good harvests kept the prices of consumer goods down and wholesale prices increased 200 percent between December 1937 and December 1939, a modest increase in light of the inflationary pressures.

During the war years, 1940 through 1945, Japan tightened its noose around China, blocking virtually all imports into China, and crop failures further reduced the supplies of goods. China's archaic tax system, in which revenue rose with the number of transactions rather than prices, failed to produce added revenue commensurate with the rate of inflation. Government expenditures rose with inflation, but tax revenue tended to stand still, causing the budget deficit to increase fourfold from 1939 to 1941. Prices rose nearly 600 percent between December 1939 and December 1941. Between December 1941 and December 1945, the government budget deficit increased over 100-fold, and prices increased 10,000 percent. The public lost confidence in the currency, and the velocity of circulation increased, further fueling the inflation. The government made a half-hearted effort at price controls, but China had neither the administrative apparatus nor the statistical information to carry out a plan for fixing prices.

The end of the war brought a stabilizing influence to prices, which actually fell from August to December 1945. In 1946, peace negotiations with the communists broke off, and the nationalist Chinese government continued heavy military expenditures and deficit spending. In 1946, government expenditures increased threefold, and revenue covered only 37 percent of the expenditure. Between June 1946 and August 1948, prices rose 146,772 percent in Shanghai. In August 1948, the government discounted the old currency, issued a new currency at a rate of one unit of the new currency to 3 million of the old. The government also imposed price controls. Inflationary pressures burst through the price ceilings, and prices continued to rise at a feverish pitch. From August 1948 until April 1949, prices rose 112,390 percent. The communists occupied Shanghai in May 1949, the nationalist government was in confusion, and the compilation of price information was

suspended. As the communists consolidated control of Mainland China, the nationalists' currency became completely unacceptable.

The Chinese inflation experience adds further corroboration for Lenin's comment that the surest way to overthrow the capitalist system was to debase the currency. The rapid inflation was probably a major factor causing the climate of cynical corruption in the nationalist government, and helped contribute to its demise.

See also: Hyperinflation during the American Revolution, Hyperinflation during the French Revolution, Hyperinflation in Post–World War I Germany, Inflation and Deflation, Hyperinflation during the Bolshevik Revolution

References

Chang, Kai-Ngau. 1958. *The Inflationary Spiral: The Experience in China, 1939–1950.*

Chou, Shun-Hsin. 1963. *The Chinese Inflation, 1939–1949.*

Friedman, Milton. 1992. *Monetary Mischief: Episodes in Monetary History.*

Paarlberg, Don. 1993. *An Analysis and History of Inflation.*

HYPERINFLATION IN GEORGIA

One of the worst cases of hyperinflation on record occurred in Georgia between 1992 and 1995. Georgia had declared its independence from the Soviet Union in April 1991 and quickly sank into civil conflict and political turmoil. The breakdown in law and order enfeebled the government's authority, while the dissolution of the Soviet Union buffeted Georgia's economy with severe economic shocks. The government of Georgia met the economic difficulties with slack financial policies.

The breakdown of trade and capital flows within the former Soviet Union accounted for the external shocks. The worst trade shock came between 1992 and 1993, when the prices of Georgia's key energy imports, gas and refined oil products, leaped up fourfold and 21-fold respectively (Wang, 1999). Georgia also lost capital inflows and transfers that in the past it had received from the central government of the Soviet Union.

Civil conflict and wars undercut the government's ability to collect taxes. Tax revenue measured 22 percent of gross domestic product (GDP) in 1991, 8 percent in 1991, and only 2 percent in 1993 (Wang, 1999). Expenditures as a percent of GDP changed slightly on the upside at 36 percent of GDP between 1992 and 1993 (Wang, 1999).

While Georgia remained in the ruble zone, its monetary policy was controlled by the Central Bank of Russia. Georgia faced a cash crisis after the Central Bank of Russia stopped supplying ruble banknotes to the National Bank of Georgia in late 1992. In April 1993, the government introduced a Georgian currency, the "coupon," to circulate at par with the Russian ruble. At the direction of the government and parliament, monetary and credit polices became highly accommodative, allowing the currency in circulation to increase 152-fold between the end of March 1993 and the end of August 1994 (Wang 1999). Direct or indirect loans extended to the government by the National Bank of Georgia accounted for most of the growth in the money stock.

The excess supply of coupons quickly spilled into the foreign exchange market. The coupon depreciated in step with each increase in central bank credit extended to the government. A dual economy sprang up composed of a coupon-based official economy and an unofficial but much larger economy based on the ruble and other foreign exchange. The coupon-based economy consisted almost totally of government transactions.

Between 1992 and 1994, inflation stampeded to loftier and loftier levels, posting 887 percent in 1992, 3,125 percent in 1993, and peaking at 15,606 percent in 1994 (Branco, 1996). Real output mirrored the economic chaos, shrinking 44.8 percent in 1992, 25.4 percent in 1993, and 11.4 percent in 1994 (Branco, 1996).

In March 1994, the Georgian government opened serious discussions with the International Monetary Fund (IMF) and agreed to a strategy for stopping hyperinflation as first step in qualifying for IMF financing. The steps included (1) curbing central bank financing of budget deficits and commercial bank access to overdraft privileges at central bank, (2) removing consumer subsidies on bread, electricity, and gas consumption, (3) curtailing government expenditures and government subsidies to state-owned enterprises, (4) lifting foreign exchange restrictions, (5) allowing free floating of the coupon in foreign exchange markets, and (6) improving tax collection and raising tax rates. The measures were painful. Without government subsidies, the price of bread went from 700 coupons per kilogram to 200,000 coupons per kilogram (Wang, 1999).

Inflation subsided rapidly after 1994, posting 162.7 percent in 1995, 39.4 percent in 1996, and 7.1 percent in 1997 (International Monetary Fund, 1999). The Georgian authorities issued a new currency on September 25, 1995. The new currency was called the "lari." The conversion to the new currency was conducted on a no-questions basis at a uniform rate of one million coupons per one lari. The new currency became legal tender on October 2, 1995.

See also: Hyperinflation in Post-Soviet Russia

References

Branco, Marta de Castello. "Georgia: From Hyperinflation to Growth." *IMF Survey*, September 23, 1996.

International Monetary Fund. "IMF Approves Augmentation and Extension of Georgia's EASF Loan." Press Release no. 99/34, 1999.

Wang, Jian-Ye. "The Georgian Hyperinflation and Stabilization." International Monetary Fund, IMF Working Paper no. 99/65, May 1999.

HYPERINFLATION IN PERU

For August 1990, Peru saw its inflation rate peak at 12,378 (Reinhart and Savastano, 2003). The 12 previous years Peru had not seen inflation rates below 40 percent. Between 1960 and 1969, annual inflation in Peru averaged 9.8 percent, between 1970 and 1979, it averaged 26.5 percent, and between 1980 and 1985, it averaged 97.3 percent (Cardso, 1989). Between 1986 and 1987, inflation in Peru subsided slightly before it took off in 1988 to an average annual rate of over 1,700 percent. For every year except three between 1971 and 1990, Peru experienced current account deficits on the balance of payments.

In August 1985, new president, Alan Garcia, came to power and launched an economic policy that limited external debt service to 10 percent of exports, imposed price controls, and fixed the exchange rate. With the help of fixed exchange rates and government subsides, the Peruvian economy briefly experienced high growth, moderating inflation, rising employment, and rising real wages. Peru hoped it had found a way to combat inflation without sacrificing growth and employment, without undergoing the "tight money, fiscal austerity" cure advanced by the International Monetary Fund.

The apparent policy success was short-lived. The limit on external debt service triggered a flight of foreign capital. By 1988, Peru faced shortages of basic foods like milk, sugar, and bread. Fiscal deficits as a percent of gross domestic product (GDP) hovered in the 7 to 7.4 percent range (Reinhart and Savastano, 2003). Inflation reared up precipitously when controlled prices had to be adjusted upwards. Real wages fell. Output shrank 20 percent in two years, foreign exchange reserves slipped into the negative column, and inflation had pared tax collection to 3.5 percent of national income (*Economist*, November 1990).

On June 10, 1990, Alberto Fujimori won Peru's presidential election by waging a campaign against a policy of brutal contraction to corral inflation, but in office, realities forced his hand. In August 1990, the new government raised the price of gasoline by 30-fold, and raised by fourfold the state-controlled prices of stable foods (*Economist*, August 1990). Peru burst into chaos. For days, fear of looting and rioting kept shops and markets closed, and transport buses off the roads. Thieves left street vendors denuded of goods to sell, and small farmers near the city pillaged crops.

The new government committed itself to spending only what it received in taxes. Half of the increase in gasoline prices went into the treasury. The government also scrapped tariffs and import quotas, exposing Peru's manufacturers to competition from less expensive imports. When the government abandoned the fixed exchange rate, the value of Peru's currency, the inti, sank to 300,000 intis per U.S. dollar (*Economist*, August 1990).

The austere policies steadily broke the back of inflation. Peru posted an inflation rate of 409.5 percent in 1991, 73.5 percent in 1992, and 48.6 percent in 1993 (Reinhart, Savastano, 2003). In 2000, Peru posted 3.7 percent inflation and in 2001, Peru posted deflation of 0.1 percent (International Monetary Fund, 2004). Inflation edged up after 2001, but remained in single-digit territory.

References

Cardoso, Eliana, A. "Hyperinflation in Latin America." *Challenge*, vol. 32, no. 1 (Jan–Feb 1989): 11–19.

Economist. "Dearer Still and Dearer." August 18, 1990, pp. 2–3.

Economist. "Inflation Unbeaten." November 3, 1990, p. 52.

International Monetary Fund, Public Information Notice (PIN) no. 04/62, May 28, 2004.

Reinhart, Carmen M., and Miguel A. Savastano. "The Realities of Modern Hyperinflation." *Finance and Development*, vol. 40, no. 2 (June 2003): 20–23.

HYPERINFLATION IN POST-SOVIET RUSSIA

In 1992, Russia saw an inflation rate of 1,528.7 percent (Rock and Solodhov, 2001). The exact number may be in doubt since the International Monetary Fund did not start reporting inflation rates for Russia until 1993. The other post-Soviet republics also posted spectacular inflation rates that year. Of these countries, Latvia posted the lowest inflation rate for the year at 951.2 percent (Rock and Solodhov, 2001).

The Russian government opened the year with the liberalization of price controls on most products at the wholesale and retail level. The government took that initiative in January 1992. Price controls remained in effect for a handful of key commodities: bread, milk, residential rents and utilities, electricity, natural gas, and retail gasoline. The new Russian reformers held high hopes for the transition to capitalism, including the prospect that massive Western aid would flow into Russia. They gave scant attention to the prospect that the political and economic disintegration unfolding in the former Soviet Union would play havoc with the short-run outcomes of liberalization. Between 1992 and 1993, the economy of the former Soviet Union went from having one central bank and one monetary policy to having 15 different central banks with 15 different monetary policies (Rock and Solodhov, 2001). The one economy became 15 separate but tightly linked economies. The need for collaboration on monetary policies, tariff policies, and tax policies went unnoticed.

As prices leaped up, the Russian government directly felt budget pressure, partly because hyperinflation erased the earning power of government salaries, pensions, enterprise budgets, and social expenditures, and partly because state tax revenues evaporated. Output shrank, Russian enterprises needed funds to carry on operations, and non-Russian republics need funds to finance trade deficits with Russia. The Russian government and its central bank met the crisis by channeling "centralized" loans to Russian enterprises through commercial banks, and "technical" loans to non-Russian enterprises through local republican authorities. Much of the proceeds from these loans were diverted to the purchase of dollars in the recently liberalized Russian foreign exchange market, causing the ruble to depreciate, which increased the cost of imports and added to the inflation.

With zero-interest funds available from the central bank, commercial banks in Russia had little incentive to attract individual retail deposits and savings accounts. In addition, as the crises progressed, the Russian government temporarily froze withdrawals on bank accounts at state-banks. The Russian people took to storing purchasing power and saving in the form of non-ruble assets, such as U.S. dollars stuffed in a sock. By 1993, most individuals and enterprises were buying U.S. dollars whenever possible (Rock and Solodhov, 2001).

Between 1993 and 1995, a new kind of financial institution sprang up in Russia. A new banking law went so far as to allow individual nonbank businesses to attract deposits and other financial businesses. Some of the new financial institutions were no more than Ponzi-pyramid schemes and promised depositors returns as high as 45 percent per month payable in dollars (Rock and Solodhov, 2001).

A Russian pensioner sells cigarettes in downtown Moscow in order to raise some extra money for living expenses in the face of the country's financial crisis, June 5, 1998. (AP Photo/Ivan Sekretarev)

The new financial institutions mainly speculated in the foreign exchange market for dollars. Many citizens went so far as to collateralize their newly won private property to invest in these schemes. In July 1995, the government successfully curbed ruble fluctuations within the range of a managed float, severely undercutting the ability of the new financial institutions to earn speculative profits in the foreign exchange markets. In addition, by this time, inflation was subsiding and those who had taken out high interest ruble loans found themselves unable to repay these loans in a disinflation environment. With defaulting borrowers and fewer opportunities for speculation, the new financial institutions quickly crumbled. A central banker, Tatyana Paramonova, was credited for imposing the tight monetary policies that subdued inflation and stabilized the ruble. In November 1995, President Boris N. Yeltsin dismissed her in a bid to appease the Russian parliament.

Russian inflation steadily subsided after reaching a peak in 1992, falling to 874.7 annual percent in 1993, 307.4 in 1994, 197.4 in 1995, 47.6 in 1996, 14.7 in 1997, and 27 in 1998 (International Monetary Fund, May 2000). On January 1, 1998, the Russian government knocked off three zeros from the ruble. After the Russian default in 1998, inflation again soared into double-digit territory, reaching 85.7 percent in 1999. It again subsided, posting a level of 10.9 percent in 2004 (International Monetary Fund, May 2006). As of 2008, rising commodity prices seem to have frustrated efforts to push the inflation rate clearly into single-digit territory.

References

International Monetary Fund, *World Economic Outlook*, May 2000 and April 2006.

Rock, Charles P., Vasiliy Solodhov. "Monetary Policies, Banking, and Trust in Changing Institutions: Russia's Transition in the 1990s." *Journal of Economic Issues*, vol. 35, no. 2 (June 2001): 451–459.

Lewis, Michael. "The Capitalist; Ruble Roulette." *New York Times Magazine*, August 13, 1995, p. 622.

Oomes, Nienke, and Franziska Ohnsorge. "Money Demand and Inflation in Dollarized Economies: The Case of Russia." IMF Working Paper (WP/05/144), June 2005.

HYPERINFLATION IN POST—WORLD WAR I GERMANY

The German hyperinflation of the early 1920s stands as a constant reminder of the monetary insanity lurking beneath the surface of modern systems of money and banking. The German money supply grew during and after World War I. In June 1914, the German marks in circulation stood at 6,323 million, but by December 1918 the number of marks in circulation had grown to 33,106 million. Prices over the same time span more than doubled. Germany had financed the war largely by monetizing government debt rather than raising taxes or borrowing in capital markets.

After the armistice in 1918, German marks in circulation continued to expand, and by December 1921, German currency in circulation stood at 122,963 million marks. Prices then were slightly over 13 times the 1914 level. Prices now began to catch up with money growth. By June 1922, German marks in circulation had risen to 180,716 million, but prices were now over 70 times the 1914 level. The Reichsbanks abandoned all pretense of monetary control as marks in circulation rose to 1,295,228 million by

Bundles of German mark notes double as children's building blocks, 1923. (The Illustrated London News Picture Library)

December 1922. By June 1923, the number had increased to 17,393,000 million.

After June 1922, price increases broke into runaway inflation. By December 1922, prices stood at 1,475 times their 1914 level, and prices stood 19,985 times their 1914 level by June 1923. Prices were rising so fast that workers were paid at half-day intervals and rushed to spend their wages before they lost their value. Customers at restaurants would negotiate prices in advance because prices could change before the meal was served. Grocery shoppers rolled to the store wheelbarrows laden with sacks of money, which was also bailed up and used for fuel. Prices continued to rise into November 1923. A newspaper that sold for 1 mark in May 1922 rose in price to 1,000 marks in September 1923. By November 17, 1923, the same newspaper sold for 70 million marks.

In December 1923, the money supply and prices stabilized. The German government reformed its monetary affairs, issuing a new unit of currency called the *rentenmark*, equal to 1 trillion marks. The new currency was issued by the Rentenbank, which replaced the Reichsbank as the note-issuing bank. The only asset of the new bank was a mortgage on agricultural and industrial land, and the paper money issue of the new bank was strictly limited.

The inflation began with the stress of wartime finance. After World War I, Germany needed to restock its warehouses with imported raw materials and pay war reparations. This led to an outflow of German marks and a depreciation of the German mark in foreign exchange markets. This depreciation caused inflation in the prices of imports, and the inflation spread to the rest of the economy. The Reichsbank kept the money supply rising faster than prices to ward off unemployment. The French occupation of the Ruhr aggravated the matter considerably. The German government encouraged passive resistance, banned reparation payments, and printed money to pay striking miners. The French blockaded the area, and Germany lost the tax revenue.

The German experience with hyperinflation was the most spectacular the world had seen. Since World War II, Germany can boast of one of the best records for controlling inflation of any advanced industrialized country. In the book *Economic Consequences of Peace* (1920) John M. Keynes saw the inflation trends and commented:

> By a continuing process of inflation, the governments can confiscate, secretly and unobserved, an important part of the wealth of their citizens. . . .

While the process impoverishes many, it actually enriches some. The sight of this arbitrary rearrangement of riches strikes not only at security, but at confidence in the equity of the existing distribution of wealth. (235)

Many observers blame the episode of German hyperinflation for creating the political conditions that led to Hitler's rise to power. Partly because of the German experience, modern societies consider price stability an important ingredient of social stability.

See also: Hyperinflation during the American Revolution, Hyperinflation during the French Revolution, Inflation and Deflation, Hyperinflation during the Bolshevik Revolution

References

Paarlberg, Don. 1993. *An Analysis and History of Inflation.*

Parsson, Jens D. 1974. *Dying of Money: Lessons from the Great German and American Inflations.*

Webb, Steven B. 1989. *Hyperinflation and Stabilization in Weimar Germany.*

HYPERINFLATION IN POST—WORLD WAR I HUNGARY

In the aftermath of World War I, Hungary, one of the successor states to the Austro-Hungarian Empire, saw inflation advance into a hyperinflationary stage, multiplying prices by a factor of 263 between January 1922 and April 1924.

In addition to owing war reparations, Hungary inherited an economy facing shortages and uprooted from traditional trading relationships. The erection of new national barriers restricted trade between regions of the former Austro-Hungarian

Empire. To complicate the economic turmoil, a Bolshevik revolution threw Hungary into monetary confusion; the revolutionaries seized the plates for 1- and 2-crown Austro-Hungarian banknotes and ran the printing presses liberally in support of their cause. A right-wing regime supplanted the Bolsheviks, but through 1924 the government continued to finance between 20 and 50 percent of government expenditures with issues of paper money.

The Hungarian section of the Austro-Hungarian bank was spun off as the State Note Institute, a note-issuing bank under the authority of the minister of finance. The State Note Institute exchanged its notes, the Hungarian *krone*, for the notes of the Austro-Hungarian bank, and even the notes issued by the Bolshevik government.

Total notes and deposit liabilities of the State Note Institute grew by a factor of 85 from January 1922 until April 1924, the time frame over which prices increased by a factor of 263. The percentage growth in prices exceeded the percentage growth in the money supply, reflecting the effects of the flight from the krone. As prices escalated, Hungarian residents sought to spend krones before they lost value, raising the velocity of circulation, adding further fuel to the inflationary spiral. To restrict Hungarians from using krones to buy assets denominated in more stable foreign currencies, the Hungarian government established the Hungarian Devisenzentral as part of the State Note Institute. This agency was responsible for making it difficult or illegal for Hungarians to own foreign currency.

The end of the inflationary episode in Hungary came when the League of Nations arranged an international loan for Hungary conditioned on government policies committed to balanced budgets and a central bank independent of government authorities. The reparation committee also gave up its claim on Hungary's resources. The broad outlines of the reconstruction of Hungary's finances mirror closely the Austrian experience. The new central bank, the Hungarian National Bank, was able to continue increasing the supply of paper krones, but these krones were now backed by gold, other foreign assets, and commercial paper.

Inflation stabilized in December 1924, and the krone ended its slide on the New York foreign exchange market.

The Hungarian inflation experience underlines the importance of expectations in monetary affairs. The assurance of a return to responsible government policies was sufficient to bring a quick halt to inflationary momentum.

See also: Hyperinflation during the American Revolution, Hyperinflation in Austria, Hyperinflation during the French Revolution, Hyperinflation in Post–World War I Germany, Inflation and Deflation, Hyperinflation in Post–World War I Poland

References

Sargent, Thomas J. 1993. *Rational Expectations and Inflation*, 2nd ed.

Wicker, E. "Terminating Hyperinflation in the Dismembered Hapsburg Monarchy." *American Economic Review*, vol. 76, no. 3 (1986): 350–364.

HYPERINFLATION IN POST–WORLD WAR II HUNGARY

From July 1945 until August 1946, hyperinflation raged in Hungary on a scale more spectacular than Germany's hyperinflation experience following

World War I. When the German hyperinflation was stabilized in 1923, the government issued a new mark equivalent to 1 trillion of the depreciated marks. On August 1, 1946, Hungary replaced its depreciated *pengo* with the *florint* at a rate of one florint to 400 octillion pengos. Although Germany's hyperinflation crisis lasted a bit short of two years, Hungary's post–World War II hyperinflation crisis ran its course in slightly less than a year.

Hyperinflation was not new to Hungary, which had shared in the hyperinflation frenzy that had afflicted Germany, Poland, and Austria at the end of World War I. Like its post–World War I experience, Hungary's post–World War II hyperinflation episode fit a familiar pattern in the history of hyperinflation. Episodes of hyperinflation usually occur during or immediately after a war, when the government is financing huge budget deficits, and supplies of goods have been disrupted. During Hungary's second hyperinflation experience, government revenue covered only 15 percent of government expenditures. The following schedule shows the increase of banknotes by the National Bank of Hungary that fueled the hyperinflation:

December 31, 1945: 765,400

January 1, 1946: 1,646,000

February 28, 1946: 5,238,000

March 31, 1946: 34,002,000

April 30, 1946: 434,304,000

May 31, 1946: 65,589,000,000

June 30, 1946: 6,277,000,000,000,000

July 31, 1946: 17,300,000,000,000,000,000

Hungary's first effort to tame the inflation came in December 1945 when the government announced that notes of 1,000 or more pengos were banned unless special stamps were affixed to them. The stamps had to be purchased from the government at a cost of three times the face value of the notes. The owner of four 1,000-pengo notes had to give up three notes to buy a stamp to make the one note valid. The stamp requirement effectively reduced the number of notes in circulation by three-fourths. Inflation halted, and prices even fell for a few days, but by the end of December, prices were rising so fast that employees hardly received their pay before they rushed to spend it.

On January 1, 1946, the government took an innovative approach to the inflation problem and created a new money of account, called the tax pengo, ostensibly to protect the government's tax revenue from an inflation loss between the time taxes were levied and the time of collection. The tax pengo equaled the regular pengo multiplied by a daily price index that measured the ratio of current prices to prices on January 1, 1946. Soon business transactions were paid in tax pengos, and on January 10, commercial banks began offering tax pengo deposits. With tax pengo deposits, a customer deposited regular pengos in a bank. When the deposit was withdrawn the customer received the amount of regular pengos multiplied by the ratio of prices on the withdrawal date to prices on the date of deposit. Multiplication by a price index ratio adjusted the pengo for loss in purchasing power. On June 1, 1946, the government issued tax pengo notes that circulated as paper money with values depending on daily price ratio calculations. At this point, the tax pengo had become a new indexed currency—indexed to the rate of inflation. The regular pengo rapidly depreciated in value relative to the tax pengo, but prices quoted in tax pengo remained stable until mid-April 1946.

In April, prices began to escalate in tax pengo, and beginning on June 20, the depreciation accelerated rapidly. On August 1, 1946, the government issued the new florint, the convertibility into dollars of which was assured with reserves of gold, foreign currencies, and foreign securities. At that point, Hungary's hyperinflation crisis ended. Hungary's official documents do not make it clear where these reserves originated.

The Soviet Union contributed to Hungary's hyperinflation crisis, probably in an effort to destroy Hungary's economy. In 1945, the Soviet army issued in Hungary the highest denomination banknote ever printed, a 100-quadrillion-pengo note.

Hungary's second hyperinflation experience suggests that the only remedy for inflation is monetary discipline, restraint of monetary growth. Hungary's indexed currency failed because banknote circulation continued to race ahead.

See also: Hyperinflation in Austria, Hyperinflation in Post—World War I Germany, Hyperinflation in Post—World War I Hungary, Inflation and Deflation, Hyperinflation in Post—World War I Poland

References

Bomberger, W. A., and G. E. Makinen. "The Hungarian Hyperinflation and Stabilization of 1945–1946." *Journal of Political Economy*, vol. 91, no. 5 (1983): 801–824.

Nogaro, Bertrand. "Hungary's Recent Monetary Crisis and It's Theoretical Meaning." *American Economic Review* (September 1948): 526–542.

Paarlberg, Don. 1993. *An Analysis and History of Inflation*.

Siklos, P. L. "The End of the Hungarian Hyperinflation of 1945–46." *Journal of Money, Credit, and Banking*, no. 2 (1989): 132–147.

HYPERINFLATION IN POST—WORLD WAR I POLAND

In January 1921, the Polish wholesale price index stood at 25,139, indicating that prices were over 251 times their level in 1914, the base year in which the index equaled 100. By February 1924, the index had risen to 248,429,600, an increase of 988,223 percent in a bit over three years. That growth rate in prices is equivalent to a 50-cent newspaper rising in price to nearly $5,000. In the aftermath of World War I, Poland was a country newly formed from territories formerly belonging to Germany, Austro-Hungary, and Russia.

The Polish episode of hyperinflation was born of large government deficits incurred by the fledgling Polish government freshly constituted following World War I. Germany's economic rape of Polish machinery and raw materials would have put even the most foresighted economic policy to the test. Furthermore, the armistice of 1918 left Poland locked in a costly war with the Soviet Union, a struggle that continued until the fall of 1920. Aside from heavy claims on scarce Polish resources, the Polish government fell heir to a grab bag of currencies—Russian rubles, crowns of the Austro-Hungarian bank, German marks, and Polish marks issued by the Polish State Loan Bank, an institution Germany established to regulate Poland's monetary affairs. Under these circumstances, hardly any government could turn away from the temptation to run the printing presses.

Between October 1918 and February 1924, circulating banknotes grew 60,090,040 percent, and the Polish mark steadily decreased on foreign exchange markets. The Polish government took command of the Polish State Loan Bank, which financed the government's budget deficits by issuing banknotes.

Unlike Austria and Hungary, Poland reformed its finances without help from an international loan, although an international loan was granted in 1927 to prop up the Polish mark in foreign exchange markets. In January 1924, the government invested the minister of finance with broad power to balance the government's budget. The minister of finance established the Bank of Poland, replacing the Poland State Loan Bank, as an independent central bank issuing notes secured with reserves in gold or foreign assets denominated in stable currencies that equaled 30 percent of the value of the notes. Whereas the government budget deficit in 1923 accounted for over 50 percent of government expenditures, in 1924 the government reported a balanced budget. The government also created a new currency, the gold *zloty*, worth 1.8 million paper marks.

The Polish wholesale price index stabilized early in 1924, and the Polish mark stabilized in foreign exchange markets about the same time. The rather quick adjustment of inflation to responsible monetary and fiscal policies affirms the power that expectations wield over monetary affairs. Late in 1925, a lax central bank policy led to another spurt of inflation and currency depreciation that lasted a year before the central bank pulled in the monetary reins.

See also: Hyperinflation in Austria, Hyperinflation in Post–World War I Germany, Hyperinflation in Post–World War I Hungary, Inflation and Deflation

References

League of Nations. 1946. *The Course and Control of Inflation.*

Sargent, Thomas J. 1993. *Rational Expectations and Inflation*, 2nd ed.

HYPERINFLATION IN THE CONFEDERATE STATES OF AMERICA

From October 1861 to March 1864, price increases averaged 10 percent per month in the states of the Confederacy, putting the Confederate price index when General Robert E. Lee surrendered at 92 times its prewar base. In the history of the United States, only the hyperinflation during the American Revolution compares in intensity with the hyperinflation of the Confederacy.

Like the revolutionaries that spearheaded the American Revolution, the leaders of the Confederacy faced a populace that was in no mood to pay additional taxes. Southerners felt that the present generation bore the burden of a war that would primarily benefit future generations, and as much of the expense as possible should be passed to future generations. Union blockades of Confederate ports precluded any effort to implement a revenue tariff on imports, the main source of federal government tax revenue. The Confederate government enacted a property tax but lacked the machinery to collect it in the face of uncooperative state governments. By October 1864, tax revenue accounted for less than 5 percent of all revenue that found its way to the Confederate treasury.

The Confederacy met with slightly more success in trying to finance public expenditures with bonds. In May 1861, the Confederate Congress approved a $50 million bond issue. The bond issue faltered on a depressed cotton market that resulted from the use of cotton as a bargaining chip with European governments whose recognition the Confederacy needed, leaving angry planters unable or unwilling to subscribe to bonds on the scale needed. By October 1864, bond sales had raised less than 30 percent of all revenue that had entered the Confederate treasury.

The remaining source of revenue was Confederate money. On March 9, 1861, the Confederate Congress authorized printing notes in an amount not exceeding $1 million, but the treasury department over four years printed $15 million of notes. Treasury employees at the note-signing bureau rose from 72 in July 1862 to 262 in July 1863. As printers, paper, and engravings became scarce, the Confederate government granted credit for counterfeit bills, which were stamped valid and reissued. From July 1, 1861, to October 1, 1863, the paper money column of the Confederate treasury ledger accounted for 68.6 percent of all government revenue.

Surprisingly, private banks in the Confederacy were restrained in the issuance of banknotes. The uncertainties of war encouraged private banks to hold large quantities of vault cash, which actually tempered the inflationary thrust of the excess paper money.

Much of the Confederate currency bore the option to buy interest-bearing Confederate bonds up to a certain date, after which that option expired. As inflation gathered force early in 1864 the Confederate Congress enacted a currency reform that brought a lull in the inflation rate. The reform provided that all currency in bills greater than $5 could be converted into 4 percent bonds, dollar for dollar. Currency not converted into bonds by April 1, 1864, had to be exchanged for new currency at a rate of three for two. Inflation subsided until December 1864, when the Confederate government again had to turn to the printing presses.

From the first quarter of 1861 until January 1, 1864, prices in the Confederacy rose 28-fold whereas the money supply rose only 11-fold. Prices rose even faster than the money supply because of wartime disruptions in the supply of goods, and the phenomenon of velocity. Velocity is the average number of times per year that a dollar is spent, and in a hyperinflationary environment, recipients of money rush to spend it before it loses its value. An increase in the velocity of money has the same effect on the economy as an increase in the money supply.

The experience of the Confederacy shows what happens when the supply of money exceeds what is demanded by the normal transactions of business and the desire for liquidity. When the supply of money exceeds the demand, the value of money falls, meaning it buys less because of price increases.

See also: Hyperinflation during the American Revolution, Inflation and Deflation, Velocity of Money

References

Lerner, Eugene M. 1956. "Inflation in the Confederacy, 1861–1865." In *Studies in the Quantity Theory of Money*, ed. Milton Friedman.

Myers, Margaret G. 1970. *A Financial History of the United States.*

Slabaugh, Arlie. 1998. *Confederate States Paper Money*, 9th ed.

HYPERINFLATION IN UKRAINE

Between 1991 and 1994, Ukraine posted the ugliest inflation record of any former Soviet Republic. From the beginning of 1992 until the mid 1994, Ukrainian prices soared at an average monthly rate of 33 percent (Kravchuk, 1998). The immediate cause of the inflation was growth in the money stock, which grew in the range of 74–75 percent per quarter between 1992 and 1994 (Kravchuk, 1998). Ukraine declared its independence from the Soviet Union on August 24, 1991.

Rapid money stock growth stemmed from the budget deficits of the Ukrainian government. During the hyperinflation years, the government's budget deficit ranged between 10 and 14 percent of gross domestic product (GDP) (Kravchuk, 1998). In 1992, off-budget subsidies and cheap credits to industrial and agricultural enterprises roughly equaled 16 percent of GDP (Kravchuk, 1998). In 1993 and 1994, the government mandated that the financial sector provide vast amounts of nearly zero-interest credits to enterprises.

To finance a deficit, a government must borrow domestically, borrow abroad, or create new money. The Ukrainian domestic securities market remained too undeveloped for government mobilization of domestic capital. In addition, the Ukrainian government had limited ability to borrow abroad. The remaining alternative required the creation of new money to finance a government deficit. Borrowing only accounted for roughly 20 percent of Ukraine's fiscal deficit and the remainder was financed by money stock growth (Kravchuk, 1998).

The cost of energy helped send Ukraine down the path of hyperinflation. Ukraine imports vast amounts of oil and gas. Under the Soviet system of central planning, energy-using industries enjoyed large subsidies, a practice that began in the 1970s amid escalating oil and gas prices. After the break-up of the Soviet Union, Russia began raising the prices of oil and gas and demanded payment in hard currencies. Rising energy prices sent consumer prices soaring and evoked cries of protest from farmers and miners. To avert a strike, the government promised a vast payment to miners equal to half its expected tax revenue for the year (*Economist*, July 1993). The government printed the money to pay the miners, causing the money stock for June 1993 to increase by 40 percent (*Economist*, August 1993).

Ukraine was known to have inherited nuclear weapons from the Soviet Union, making the threat of civil unrest in that country a matter of worldwide concern. In addition, Ukraine held a sizable contingent of the Soviet Union's defense industry, and the firms making up Ukraine's defense industry no longer had a market for their output.

Beginning in 1994, Ukraine negotiated a series of agreements with the International Monetary Fund. The agreements were conditioned on progress in deficit reduction. The massive depreciation of the Ukrainian currency left it less useful as a means of financing deficits. Some observers felt the government had no choice but to reign in its deficits. The currency had depreciated to the point that households and businesses refused to hold it. In summary, the government brought deficit spending under control and inflation subsided.

In September 1996, Ukraine took advantage of a lower inflation to reform its currency, introducing a new currency, the hryvna, to replace the old currency, the karbovanet. By 1996, everyday transactions took millions of karbovanet, requiring huge wads of cash. Recording transactions had become difficult, time-consuming, and prone to error. The new currency effectively erased five zeros from all prices.

See also: Hyperinflation in Belarus, Hyperinflation in Georgia, Hyperinflation in Post-Soviet Russia

References

Economist. "Galloping Towards the Brink." July 3, 1993, p. 49.

Economist. "Ukraine Over the Brink." August 4, 1993, pp. 45–46.

Kravchuk, Robert S. "Budget Deficits, Hyperinflation, and Stabilization in Ukraine, 1991–96." *Public Budgeting & Finance*, vol. 18, no. 4 (Winter 1998): 45–70.

HYPERINFLATION IN YUGOSLAVIA

The history of hyperinflation offers few cases that can rival the stampeding, runaway inflation that Yugoslavia lived through between 1992 and 1995. Yugoslavia owed the hyperinflation to the government's practice of paying for budget deficits by printing money. The problem was compounded because state-owned enterprises held substantial foreign liabilities, and residents held foreign exchange deposits in government banks. As the dinar depreciated, these liabilities became too costly to pay off, and residents withdrew foreign exchange deposits until the government put an end to the practice.

In terms of the multiplicative climb of prices, Yugoslavia's inflation ranks second only to the Hungarian hyperinflation of 1946–1947. In terms of the time it took to run its course, it ranks second only to the Russian hyperinflation of 1922–1924. In hard numbers, Petrovic and Mladenovic (2000) give the following scenario of Yugoslavia's inflation: In 1991, inflation in Yugoslavia gathered momentum, hitting 50 percent per month

by February 1992. The beginning of 1993 saw inflation raging at 200 percent per month. By June and July of 1993, the monthly inflation rate had doubled to 400 percent per month. August and October of 1993 saw monthly inflation on the order of 2000 percent. November 1993 posted monthly inflation of 20,000 percent. Then prices really went wild, climbing at a monthly rate of 180,000 percent in December, and 58 million percent in January 1994. The last figure is based on black market exchange rate depreciation and is below the officially reported rate of 313 million percent per month.

The government levied price controls in an effort to stop the inflation, but inflation continued. Soon the government mandated prices that producers were receiving too low to be any kind incentive for production. In October 1993, the bakers stopped baking bread. All government-owned gasoline stations closed for lack of gasoline to sell. Gasoline could only be purchased from roadside dealers who sold gasoline from a plastic container conspicuously sitting on the hood of a parked car. The roadside gasoline went for the equivalent of about $8.00 per gallon (Lyon, 1996). Most people gave up driving personal cars. Buses became so overcrowded that ticket collectors could not climb aboard to collect fares. In November 1994, 87 patients in a large psychiatric hospital died after going without heat, food, and medicine (Lyon, 1996). Pensioners waited in line at post offices where government pensions were paid. Without government funds to pay the pensions, the postal workers took whatever money they received when someone mailed a letter or package and gave the money to pensioners, who stood in line knowing that each minute they waited their pension would buy less. They were afraid to go home and come back the next day because within a mere day inflation would eat up a pension's value.

In October 1993, the government launched a new currency, a "new" dinar equal to one million of the "old" dinars, equivalent to removing six zeroes from the old currency. Early in January 1994, the government launched another new currency, a *new* "new" dinar, equal to one billion of the old "new" dinars. On January 24, 1994, the government unveiled the "super" dinar equal to 10 million of the new new dinars. The super dinar was pegged to the German mark at one dinar to one mark, and residents could exchange dinars for marks at government banks. In 1998, the inflation rate was 29.5 percent, and then it edged up to around 91 percent in 2001 (International Monetary Fund, 2002). Inflation subsided significantly for 2002. In 2002, the IMF approved a line of credit for the Federal Republic of Yugoslavia based on a stabilization plan submitted by the government.

See also: Hyperinflation in Belarus, Hyperinflation in Georia, Hyperinflation in Ukraine

References

International Monetary Fund. "IMF Approves US$64 Million Tranche Under Stand-By Credit and US$829 Extended Arrangement for the Federal Republic of Yugoslavia (Serbia/Montenegro)" Press Release no. 02/25, May 13, 2002.

Lyon, James. "Yugoslavia's Hyperinflation, 1993–1994: A Social History." *East European Politics and Societies*, vol. 10, no. 2 (March 1996): 293–327.

Petrovic, Pavle, Zorica Mladenovic. "Money Demand and Exchange Rate Determination under Hyperinflation: Conceptual Issues and Evidence from Yugoslavia." *Journal of Money, Credit, and Banking*, vol. 32, no. 4 (November 2000): 785–806.

HYPERINFLATION IN ZIMBABWE

In 2008, Zimbabwe boasted the highest inflation rate in the world, another case of hyperinflation reminiscent of the post–World War I hyperinflation of Germany. As of February 2007, the inflation rate stood at an annual rate of 1,281 percent (Wines, February 2007). It had remained above the 1000 percent level since April 2006, causing prices to double every three to four months. Zimbabwe had finished 2005 with inflation in the 500 percent range, but that was before the government in February 2006 printed up $21 trillion in Zimbabwean dollars to purchase U.S. dollars (Wines, May 2006). The U.S. dollars went in payment to the International Monetary Fund (IMF) to cover a debt in arrears. The IMF had threatened to oust Zimbabwe from the membership in the IMF for debt delinquency.

It is hard to find the beginning point for Zimbabwe's inflation. According to IMF data in the yearly *World Economic Outlook* issue, Zimbabwean inflation in the 1990s remained in double-digit territory. It fell from an annual rate of 22.2 percent in 1994 to 18.8 percent in 1997, rising to 31.7 percent in 1998. Between 1997 and 1999, inflation nearly tripled, reaching 58.57 percent in 1999. By 2000, it had slacked to 55.9 percent. The seeds for the current hyperinflation go back to 1999 when the IMF suspended its aid programs to Zimbabwe, citing a lack of fiscal restraint owed partly to a costly two-year military intervention in the Congo. The government compounded the situation in 2000 when it seized white-owned commercial farms. Foreign capital took flight and manufacturing output hit the skids. Capital flight strained foreign exchange reserves, restricting supplies of imported goods. Rising prices of scarce imported goods sparked an escalation of the inflation rate. In September 2001, the IMF declared Zimbabwe ineligible to use the IMF's general resources or to use resources available through the IMF's Poverty Reduction and Growth Facility program. In 2003, the IMF suspended Zimbabwe's voting rights, citing a failure to cooperate with IMF in areas of policy implementation and a debt that had been in arrears since February 2001. By 2003, the inflation rate had climbed to an annual rate of 365 percent.

As the crisis unfolded, Zimbabwe's central bank cast aside all thought of stabilizing prices, unleashing unbridled monetary growth to meet the credit needs of grossly inefficient, government-owned corporations that mainly served as a job source for political patronage.

The inflation rate had vaulted to an annual rate of 10,000 percent by June 26, 2007, when President Robert Mugabe announced a decree that ordered businesses to roll back prices by 50 percent (Wines, August 2007). President Mugabe defended the price roll back on the grounds that profiteering businesses were part of a Western conspiracy to bring back colonialism. Since the cost of producing goods exceeded government-imposed sale prices, business shut down production. Mobs seized basic dietary staples such as bread, sugar, and cornmeal, leaving store shelves naked.

In February 2007, Zimbabwe's central bank declared inflation illegal and that anyone who raised prices or wages between March 1 and June 30 would face arrest and punishment. Gangs of price inspectors patrolled shops and factories for violations of price caps, and 4,000 business people suffered arrests, fines, and incarceration (Wines, August 2007). Trade union officials met with beatings at the hands of police. Many Zimbabweans survived with the help of relatives who fled to other countries and sent food to the relatives who remained behind. Doctors report a rising incidence of diseases associated with poverty, such as tuberculosis and malnutrition, including among the whites who where once part of the wealthier classes.

By the time President Mugabe and his ZANU-PF faced reelection on March 29, 2008, the inflation had soared to an annual rate of 150,000 percent and his government was facing major opposition (*Wall Street Journal*, 2008).

See also: Hyperinflation in Belarus, Hyperinflation in Georia, Hyperinflation in Post–Soviet Russia

References

Wall Street Journal (Eastern Edition, New York). "Amid Zimbabwe's Economic Collapse, Desperate Investors Send Market Soaring." September 15, 2000, p. A17.

Wall Street Journal (Eastern Edition, New York). "Freedom for Zimbabwe." March 21, 2008, p. A13.

International Monetary Fund, *World Economic Outlook*, September 2002 and October 2008.

Wines, Michael. "How Bad Is Inflation in Zimbabwe?" *New York Times* (Eastern Edition, New York) May 2, 2006, p. A1.

Wines, Michael. "Caps on Prices Only Deepen Zimbabweans' Misery." *New York Times* (Eastern Edition, New York) August 2, 2007, p. A1.

Wines, Michael. "As Inflation Soars, Zimbabwe Economy Plunges." *New York Times* (Eastern Edition, New York) February 7, 2007, p. A1.

I

INCONVERTIBLE PAPER STANDARD

An inconvertible paper standard is a monetary standard based on paper money, either banknotes or government currency that cannot be converted into any commodity or precious metal at an official rate. Inconvertible paper money is called "fiat money" and it bears a face value that may or may not be expressed in metallic terms.

The inconvertible paper standard evolved directly from precious metal standards. Originally, paper money circulated as something resembling warehouse receipts representing titles to ownership of gold or silver safely secured with a goldsmith or bank. Exchanging titles of ownership was less risky and costly than physically transporting precious metals. From those warehouse receipts evolved banknotes, ancestors to the contemporary Federal Reserve Notes and other banknotes of modern central banks.

War and other national emergencies often forced governments to put heavy claims on domestic gold and silver reserves, and in turn governments granted banks the privilege to suspend convertibility of banknotes into precious metal. The United Kingdom suspended convertibility during the Napoleonic wars, and the United States suspended convertibility during the War of 1812 and the Civil War. Suspended convertibility was invariably attended with some currency depreciation, but often the patriotic fervor of war helped maintain some monetary order. Government assurances of return to convertibility at war's end also helped protect currency values from a wave of inflation.

Two famous paper money fiascoes occurred toward the end of the 18th century, the hyperinflations of the American and French revolutions. France had already had one paper money disaster early in the 18th century with the episode of John Law's bank. The memory of these episodes acted as a constant reminder of the monetary insanity lurking beneath the surface of an inconvertible paper money standard, and encouraged governments to accept inconvertibility only as a temporary measure.

Between 1866 and 1881, Italy apparently made good use of inconvertible paper money to assist in the financing of economic development. The episode was called *Il Corso Forzoso,* or "forced currency," and it was accompanied by a modest depreciation of the lira by 10 to 16 percent. Nevertheless, a new government felt the need to promise a return to convertibility, which was accomplished in 1881.

By the beginning of World War I, the world was on a gold standard. Countries banned the export of gold, suspending convertibility for international trade, and the right of domestic convertibility was rarely exercised. At the end of the war, returning to an international gold standard became an important goal of the world's major trading partners.

The world was on a gold standard in the early 1930s when worldwide depression shook the foundations of the international monetary system. It was during this era that inconvertible paper standards became virtually universal among the world's major trading partners. These countries went on inconvertible paper standards for domestic purposes but remained on a gold bullion standard for international purposes. In the United States, private citizens could no longer convert dollars into gold, and private ownership of gold for anything but industrial purposes was illegal. The United States and other countries continued to redeem domestic currency into gold at the request of foreign central banks. After 1971, the world's major trading partners went on inconvertible paper standards for international as well as domestic purposes, severing the last ties with convertibility.

See also: Gold Reserve Act of 1934, Gold Standard, Gold Standard Amendment Act of 1931

References
Chown, John F. 1994. *A History of Money.*
McCallum, Bennett T. 1989. *Monetary Economics.*

INDEPENDENT TREASURY (UNITED STATES)

From the 1840s until 1863, the Independent Treasury, as it was called, divorced the government's fiscal operations from private sector banks. It accepted payment for public obligations—taxes—only in gold and silver specie and treasury notes, and operated its own depositories around the country. The Independent Treasury did not accept banknotes and did not hold deposits in commercial banks. Its own depositories were separate from state banks

The Independent Treasury was born of the freewheeling banking environment that flourished after the demise of the Second Bank of the United States. At first, the treasury tried to supply a modicum of regulatory discipline by holding treasury deposits in state banks and requiring special specie reserves for those deposits. The treasury found, however, that its own deposits could be held hostage to overly aggressive lending policies of state banks, and on occasion the treasury could not withdraw its funds. During this time, gold and silver specie commanded a reverence in the eyes of a public that distrusted banks, banknotes, and even corporations themselves. Large segments of the public saw banknotes as a sham scheme of the "moneyed interests" to exploit the unwary, and the proponents of the Independent Treasury were "hard currency" people who wanted the government's business separated from banks and corporations.

The Sub-Treasury Act of 1840 became law during the presidency of Martin Van Buren, a staunch advocate of the hard currency policies that marked the presidency of his predecessor, Andrew Jackson. Daniel Webster stood flatly opposed to the bill, remarking on March 12, 1938, that "[t]he use of money is in the exchange. It is designed to circulate, not to be hoarded. . . . to keep it that is to detain it . . . is a conception belonging to barbarous times and barbarous governments" (Chown, 1994). Opponents of the bill saw it turning the treasury into a hoarder of gold and silver, and throwing the private sector into a deflationary spiral. Banks held gold and silver specie to act as reserves for the redemption of banknotes. If the government began absorbing

Campaign print issued in support of Democratic incumbent Martin Van Buren's 1840 presidential bid. Designed to appeal to the workingman, the print invokes the recent history of Democratic support of labor interests, including Van Buren's support of the Independent Treasury Bill, passed in July, 1840. (Library of Congress)

gold and silver specie, banks would be forced to contract the supply of circulating banknotes.

After heated political combat, Congress enacted the Sub-Treasury Act on June 30, 1840. It provided that in the first year one-fourth of public obligations, that is, taxes, should be paid in specie, and by 1843, 100 percent of public obligations should be paid in specie. In 1843, Congress repealed the first Sub-Treasury Act.

In 1846, Congress enacted a second Sub-Treasury bill. This bill required that government offices accept only gold and silver specie and treasury notes (nonlegal-tender paper money issued by the treasury) in payment of public obligations. The Independent Treasury System lasted in some form until 1920. As early as 1863, however, the treasury began to hold deposits in commercial banks.

In its pre–Civil War phase, the Independent Treasury proved that the fears of some of its critics were well founded. Problems arose because treasury tax collections did not coincide with government expenditures. When tax collections rose above government payments, specie left private banks and entered treasury depositories, forcing banks to contract banknote circulation. When government payments overtook tax collections, specie flowed into the banking system, and banks issued more banknotes. The ebb and flow of specie from treasury depositories imparted a cyclical motion to the supply of circulating banknotes, and acted to destabilize the economy. After the treasury was allowed to maintain commercial bank deposits, the treasury learned to conduct the government's fiscal operations without rocking the banking system.

The Independent Treasury System represents another episode in the paper money drama that would eventually define the terms on which the public would come to accept paper money. It represented a phase in which societies had come to accept precious metal coins, something that could not be taken for granted in ancient societies. Despite the acceptance of precious metal coins, feelings about paper money ran high, and suspicion about paper money gained ground quickly in hard times. Distrust of paper money left a social seam, often hidden, but always threatening to rip open and become a power force in political life.

See also: Free Banking, Specie Circular, Treasury Notes

References

Chown, John F. 1994. *A History of Paper Money.*

Hammond, Bray. 1957. *Banks and Politics in America from the Revolution to the Civil War.*

INDEXATION

Indexation is a method of controlling the income-redistributing effects of inflation. Inflation is a decrease in the purchasing power of a unit of money. Households and businesses that supply commodities, credit, and raw materials under long-term contracts have revenues and incomes that are fixed regardless of what is happening to other prices. In an inflationary environment, revenues from long-term contracts diminish in real terms, that is, in real purchasing power.

Redistributive effects of inflation significantly harm important players in the economic system. With inflation, savers and lenders find their wealth losing value while in the hands of other households and businesses. The real

losses to savers and lenders occur because their wealth is defined in terms of a unit of money that steadily, perhaps rapidly, buys less. Debtors stand to gain windfall profits from inflation that can reduce the value and burden of a debt, or, under hyperinflation, even eliminate a debt in practical terms.

Governments are suspected of generating inflation as a means of canceling vast public debts too large to service. In the aftermath of World War I, the German government, shouldering a vast public debt from wartime expenditures coupled with war reparations, fueled an episode of hyperinflation that rendered its pubic debt null and void. The U.S. government emerged from World War II with a sizable public debt, perhaps removing government incentive to aggressively combat an inflation problem that continued until the early 1980s.

A system of indexation protects households and businesses whose wealth and income are at risk from inflation. Under indexation, escalator provisions automatically administer inflation adjustments to sources of income and assets fixed in money terms by contract. In the United States, Social Security benefits automatically receive inflation adjustments geared to the Consumer Price Index, a limited application of the principle of indexation. Under a full-blown system of indexation, checking accounts, savings accounts, long-term and short-term bonds, mortgages, wages, and long-term contracts receive periodic adjustments to keep pace with inflation.

Some economists propose limited forms of indexation, applying only to government bonds and taxable income. This limited indexation automatically increases the maturity value of government bonds at a rate equivalent to the inflation rate, and withholds from government tax revenue paper profits due only to inflation. With limited indexation, government is spared the temptation to generate inflation as a means of canceling public debt, and levying a hidden tax.

As inflationary momentum increased during the 1970s, prominent economists, such as Nobel Prize winner Milton Friedman, proposed that the United States adopt a system of indexation. Brazil implemented a broad system of indexation, and Israel and Canada adopted indexation systems on smaller scales. Proponents of indexation felt it would lift the burden of forming accurate inflationary expectations and moderate economic fluctuations caused by discrepancies between actual and expected inflation. Strong anti-inflation policies often induce a bout of high unemployment because expected inflation remains high after the actual inflation rate has fallen. Indexation should moderate the high unemployment that often accompanies disinflation. Critics feel that the adoption of a system of indexation is equivalent to giving up the fight against inflation and observe that inflation has often accelerated in countries practicing indexation. The United States never adopted indexation, and as other countries enacted market-oriented reforms, systems of indexation began to lose favor as another form of government interference.

See also: Hyperinflation in Brazil, Inflation and Deflation, Tabular Standard of Massachusetts Bay Colony

References

Fellner, William. 1974. "The Controversial Issue of Comprehensive Indexation." In *Essays on Inflation and Indexation*, pp. 63–70.

Friedman, Milton. "Using Escalators to Help Fight Inflation." *Fortune Magazine*, July 1974.

Weaver, R. Kent. 1988. *Automatic Government: Politics of Indexation.*

INDIAN RUPEE

See: Cattle, Indian Silver Standard, Mughal Coinage

INDIAN SILVER STANDARD

During the last quarter of the 19th century, when the world was abandoning bimetallism in favor of the gold standard, India adapted its silver standard to a modified gold system that held gold reserves to maintain the value of an entirely silver coinage.

The Indian currency system had always attracted the curiosity of the British. In 1772 the eminent economist Sir James Steuart advanced a recommendation to the East India Company "for correcting the DEFECTS of the present CURRENCY." John Maynard Keynes wrote his first book, *Indian Currency and Finance*, after serving on a committee studying India's monetary system.

A bit of the impression India's 19th-century monetary system left on contemporary British observers may be gleaned from a quotation of A. J. Balfour, later prime minister of Great Britain:

> What is the British system of currency? . . . You go to Hong Kong and the Straits Settlements, and you find obligations are measured in silver; you go to England, and you find that obligations are measured in gold; you stop half way, in India, and you find that obligations are measured in something which is neither gold nor silver—the strangest product of

monometallist ingenuity which the world has ever seen—a currency which is as arbitrary as any forced paper currency which the world has ever heard of, and which is as expensive as any metallic currency that the world has ever faced, and which, unhappily, combines in itself all the disadvantages of every currency which human beings have ever tried to form. (Chown, 1994, 100)

Between 1835 and 1893, India practiced what in the United States was called "free silver," a silver standard that allowed anyone to bring silver to the Indian mint for coinage. Only two coins were struck, the silver *rupee* and the silver half-rupee, and only silver coins were legal tender. Gold was not legal tender, and the mint did not strike gold coins.

As long as the European bimetallic system remained a viable monetary system, preserving a constant ratio of silver to gold of about 15.5 to 1, the Indian system functioned with a stable exchange rate between the silver rupee and Britain's gold pound sterling. India's silver rupee equaled 22.39 pence under Britain's gold standard. After Western trading partners began shifting over to the gold standard in the 1870s, the value of silver fell, adversely affecting the terms of trade of countries on the silver standard, mainly China, India, and Japan. Prices of both domestic and foreign goods rose in India, putting a squeeze on the household budgets of civil servants and other groups on fixed incomes.

In an effort to raise the value of the silver rupee, the government suspended the private coinage of silver in 1893, hoping to manage the supply of silver currency and maintain its value in gold. The value of the silver rupee modestly climbed relative to gold to a rate of 1 shilling and 4 pence per rupee, or 15 rupees per British sovereign. The government stood ready to redeem silver rupees and paper rupees in gold at an official rate of 1 shilling and 4 pence in gold per rupee. The silver coinage now wore the aspect of a token coinage whose value was supported in the same manner as the value of paper rupees was supported. India became a gold standard country, but its only circulating coinage was silver.

The limitation on Indian coinage of silver, coupled with high Indian interest rates needed to support the rupee internationally, depressed economic conditions in India and led to further calls for currency reform. In 1898, another government commission studied the problem and recommended that India bolster its gold reserves and issue gold coinage. These new reforms failed to bring monetary relief to India, and in 1912, the British government formed the Royal Commission on Indian Currency and Finance, including among its members John Maynard Keynes, who would later become the most famous economist of the 20th century. Keynes wrote a book on Indian currency in which he recommended that India remove gold coins from circulation and concentrate gold holdings in a state bank that would use the gold as reserves to support banknotes.

See also: Bimetallism, Gold Standard, Silver

References
Carter, Martha L. 1994. *A Treasury of Indian Coins.*
Chown, John F. 1994. *A History of Money.*
Keynes, John Maynard. 1913. *Indian Currency and Finance.*
Laughlin, J. Laurence. 1968. *The History of Bimetallism in the United States.*

INFLATION AND DEFLATION

Inflation presents itself as an overall rise in the general price level, meaning that the average level of all prices is rising, rather than the prices of a select few goods and services. A closer examination suggests that inflation is a decrease in the value (purchasing power) of a unit of money, perhaps because of an increase in the supply of money relative to demand. Deflation is the reverse—a fall in the average level of prices. History appears to be inflationary, although episodes of deflation are numerous.

Inflation is measured by the growth rate in price levels calculated as weighted averages of prices of a spectrum of goods and services. In the United States, the gross domestic product deflator (GDPD) measures the price level for all goods and services, including factory equipment and other goods bought by businesses, luxury goods, and goods bought by the government. Another index, the consumer price index (CPI), measures the price level for goods and services that are associated with the basic cost of living, including food, gasoline, utilities, housing, clothes, and so on.

Wartime government expenditures can nearly always be counted on to create inflationary pressures, as happened in the United States during World War II. At that time, the U.S. government enacted wage and price controls to contain inflation. The price controls were lifted at the end of World War II, but inflation remained a problem throughout the Cold War era. Inflation tends to become a problem whenever governments do not want to levy the taxes sufficient to support government expenditures.

Economists often see controlling inflation as a problem in maintaining the value of money, which rises in value as the money supply is restricted. In the 1980s, a prolonged reduction in the growth of the money supply ended the inflationary inertia in the U.S. economy.

A slow steady rate of inflation that is easily anticipated causes less disruption than high inflation rates showing substantial volatility. Inflation in the range of 300 percent annually or higher is called "hyperinflation." This brand of galloping or runaway inflation is often associated with the complete breakdown of society.

The last quarter of the 19th century saw deflation in the United States and several European countries. Deflation puts a burden on debtors, who find it harder to earn money to repay debts that remain fixed in value as wages and

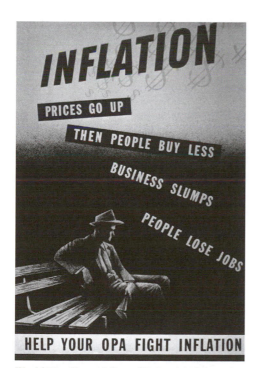

World War II-era Office of Price Administration poster lays out the basics of inflation. (National Archives)

profits fall. In the late 19th century, debtor hardship attributable to deflation fueled a populist revolt in the United States that nearly propelled William Jennings Bryan to the presidency. Bryan decried the gold standard as "crucifying" mankind on a cross of gold. The supply of gold was not keeping pace with rapid increases in production due to technology, causing the supply of goods to increase faster than the supply of money. Prices fell, and Bryan proposed to increase the coinage of silver, adding to the money supply and easing deflationary pressures.

See also: Hyperinflation during the American Revolution, Hyperinflation during the French Revolution, Hyperinflation in Post–World War I Germany

References

McCallum, Bennett T. 1989. *Monetary Economics: Theory and Policy.*

Sargent, Thomas. 1993. *Rational Expectations and Inflation*, 2nd ed.

Weintraub, Sidney. 1978. *Capitalism's Inflation and Unemployment Crisis.*

INFLATIONARY EXPECTATIONS

Inflationary expectations are what households and businesses think the inflation rate will be in the future. Inflation is a rise in the general or average level of prices, a decrease in the purchasing power of a unit of money. Economic decisions involving long-term contracts, interest rates, and purchases of capital goods entail added complications, partly because households and businesses do not know what future inflation rates will be. If households and businesses expect prices of durable goods to rise in the future, they will speed up the purchase of these goods to beat inflation. If lenders expect higher inflation in the future, they will increase interest rates, particularly on long-term loans. Certain economic decisions force households and businesses to form opinions about what inflation rate to expect in the future.

Economists theorize that at any time there is a general, or census, rate of expected inflation. This expected inflation rate influences economic decisions and is directly linked to interest rates on a one-to-one basis. A 1 percent increase in expected inflation leads to a 1 percent increase in interest rates.

A difference between expected inflation and the inflation that actually materializes has real repercussions in the economy. Creditors gain when actual inflation comes in lower than was expected. In that case, the high interest rates that creditors charged to protect themselves against inflation turn into a windfall gain. Debtors gain and creditors lose when actual inflation comes in higher than was expected. In that case, creditors fail to protect themselves adequately against inflation, and debtors are able to borrow funds at low interest rates to buy durable goods before the prices of these goods go up. In summary, an excess of expected inflation above actual inflation redistributes income in favor of creditors, and an excess of actual inflation above expected inflation redistributes income in favor of debtors.

The adverse effects of inflation are largely minimized when actual inflation and expected inflation are equal, that is, when inflation is accurately anticipated. Shoe-leather costs and menu cost are two costs that inflation imposes on an economy even if the inflation is perfectly anticipated. "Shoe-leather costs" refer to the cost and inconvenience of the added number of financial transactions households and businesses undertake to avoid costs of inflation. Inflation, even if perfectly anticipated, erodes the value of cash holdings. In an inflationary environment, households and businesses reduce cash holdings and keep a larger proportion of wealth in the form of assets that offer some protection against inflation. This reallocation entails more trips to financial institutions to convert other assets into cash as cash is needed to finance daily transactions. The cost of these trips is called "shoe-leather cost." "Menu costs" refer to the cost of updating menus and price catalogues more often to reflect current pricing. In addition to these costs, even inflation that is perfectly anticipated imposes some drag on efficiency. Relative prices between goods and services exhibit some added volatility because of differences in the frequency at which various firms and industries change prices. The case of equality between actual inflation and expected inflation is theoretically possible but unlikely in practice.

Unlike other economic indicators, there is no ready gauge of expected inflation. An important step forward in measuring expected inflation came after the U.S. government began issuing inflation-indexed bonds. The difference in interest rates between an inflation-indexed government bond and a regular government bond gives a measure of expected inflation at least among participants in the government bond market. Economists have also tried to measure expected inflation by surveying households and businesses and by extrapolating past inflation rates. It is likely that extrapolations and moving averages of past inflation rates are a major determinate of expected inflation. Attitudes toward current government budgetary and monetary policy may also influence expected inflation.

One of the most difficult economic situations occurs when deflation is expected. Deflation gives households and businesses an incentive to postpone purchases of durable goods, knowing these goods will be less costly in the future. Under deflation, holding on to cash becomes attractive because its purchasing power goes up daily. If expectations of deflation are strong enough, increases in the money supply will fail to increase spending or arrest falling prices.

See also: Fisher Effect, Inflation

Reference

Abel, Andrew B., Ben S. Bernanke, and Dean Croushore. 2008. *Macroeconomics*, 6th ed.

INFLATION TAX

An inflation tax is a tax on cash. Inflation reduces the real purchasing power of cash. After inflation, holders of cash can buy less with that cash. The decrease in what can be purchased with a fixed amount of cash is the tax paid on that cash.

Like all taxes, the inflation tax is a tax imposed by government and the proceeds go to pay for government expenditures. A government initiates an inflation tax by printing money to pay for goods and services instead of raising sufficient revenue through taxation or borrowing. As the money stock grows relative to the production of goods and services, prices rise, leaving households and businesses poorer to the extent that they hold cash balances representing less purchasing power. If the inflation rate is 10 percent, then an individual holding $1000 cash for a year is taxed at a rate of 10 percent on that cash.

Like any property tax, households and businesses can avoid the inflation tax by not holding cash. Economists theorize that there is an optimum inflation rate at which the tax revenue from the inflation tax reaches a maximum. Inflation rates beyond the optimum rate cause cash holdings to shrink to the point that tax revenue from the inflation tax contracts in terms of real purchasing power. At lower inflation rates, households and businesses are more willing to pay the inflation tax, regarding it as a necessary expense to enjoy the convenience of holding cash.

The inflation tax can generate government revenue in other ways. By pushing taxpayers into higher tax brackets, the inflation tax brings in additional tax revenue. In addition, inflation reduces the real, inflation-adjusted amount of debt that a government owes. Usually, no additional tax collectors and mechanisms are needed to collect the inflation tax.

Critics observe that the inflation tax is taxation without consent. Without any kind of legislative approval or even public announcement of a tax increase, the government increases the tax burden on citizens. Critics also cite the numerous negative effects of inflation.

Economists seemed to have known about inflation tax for several centuries but paid it little attention until the 20th century, when paper money begin to dominate monetary systems. The famous 20th-century economist John Maynard Keynes credited Rome with discovering the power of taxation through currency depreciation. In 1922, Keynes gave the first full treatment in English of the inflation tax. In his article, "Inflation as a Method of Taxation," Keynes hinted that the Soviets preceded him in regarding inflation as an instrument of taxation. Evgeni Alexeevitch Preobrazhensky (1886–1937), a Soviet economist, wrote the book *Paper Money in the Epoch of Proletarian Dictatorship,* published in Russian in 1920, predating Keynes's article. Preobrazhensky argued that inflation was a highly effective policy for diverting resources from the private to the socialized sector and for expropriating the money capital of the bourgeoisie. One often quoted line from Preobrazhensky's book on paper money referred to the printing press as "that machine gun which attacked the bourgeois regime in the rear."

The idea of inflation as a tax on cash balances caught on rapidly in the United States following World War II. It gave a rationale for a government that seemed a bit complacent in combating inflation. The Nobel Prizing economist Milton Friedman broached the subject first in his book *Essays in Positive Economics,* published in 1953. By the 1980s, the idea had entered into political debate, and "inflation tax" became a household phrase.

See also: Forced Savings, Seigniorage

References

Abel, Andrew B., Ben S. Bernanke, and Dean Croushore. 2008. *Macroeconomics.*

Kleiman, Ephraim. "Early Inflation Tax Theory and Estimates." *History of Political Economy,* vol. 32, no. 11 (2000): 265–298.

INTEREST RATE

The interest rate can be regarded as the cost of money, expressed as a percentage. If the annual interest rate is 10 percent, an individual borrowing $100 for a year pays $10 interest.

Decimalized currency systems substantially facilitated the calculation of interest. This is one reason countries rapidly adopted decimalized currency systems during the 19th century.

Theoretically, interest rates adjust to a level at which the interest earned on $100 invested in financial assets (for example, corporate bonds) equals the income earned from the ownership of a $100 worth of capital goods (for example, tools, machinery, buildings). During the recovery phase of the business cycle, interest rates tend to rise as capital goods become more productive, and in the recession phase, interest rates tend to fall as capital goods lose productivity.

During early European history, religious authorities regarded charging interest as a sinful means of earning income. Governments either banned interest or put a legal ceiling on interest rates. In the United States, state usury laws limiting interest rates were common as late as the 1970s. Most of them have now been repealed.

Historically, the highest peaks in interest rates have occurred during wartime. Interest rates reached historic levels during the Napoleonic Wars and during World War I. Wars are often the occasion for heavy government borrowing and high inflation, both of which are enemies to low interest rates. The legacy of the Depression and wage and price controls helped keep a lid on interest rates during World War II, but the era of the Cold War, from 1946 to 1983, saw the longest upswing in interest rates since the beginning of the 18th century.

Governments may act purposely to reduce interest rates as an antidote to depression. In 1998, the Federal Reserve System in the United States acted to lower interest rates to prevent a global financial crisis from spreading to the United States. Again in 2008, the Federal Reserve pushed its benchmark interest rate from 5.25 percent to almost zero (Hilsenrath and Evans, January 7, 2009) That is the lowest interest rate on record for the federal funds rate.

See also: Usury Laws

References

Barro, Robert J. "Government Spending, Interest Rates, Prices, and Budget Deficits in the United Kingdom, 1701–1918." *Journal of Monetary Economics* no. 20 (September 1987): 221–248.

Hilsenrath, Jon, and Kelly Evans. "Fed Outlook Darkens on Economy." *Wall Street Journal* (Eastern Edition, New York) January 7, 2009, p. A1.

Homer, Sidney. 1977. *A History of Interest Rates.*

INTEREST RATE TARGETING

Interest rate targeting is the most widely practiced method and strategy that central banks use for the implementation of monetary policy. Large, highly developed economies have central banks that bear responsibility for monetary policy. Regulation of the money supply, interest rates and credit conditions is monetary policy. In the conduct of monetary policy, central banks aim to achieve ultimate goals, such as low or no inflation, full-employment, and an overall prosperous and stable economy. A central bank, however, cannot directly affect the inflation rate, unemployment rate, or other economic indicators that measure the achievement of these ultimate goals. It is true that statistical correlations between inflation rates and money stock growth rates indicate a strong linkage between the two, but the linkages between central bank actions and money stock growth is not that tight. Central banks have policy measures that can affect money stock growth, but central bank control over monetary stock growth is far from absolute. Although setting targets in terms of money stock growth may seem a more direct approach to controlling inflation, in practice most central banks opt for setting interest rate targets instead.

Under interest rate targeting, a central bank selects an interest rate that it can easily and precisely control. It will be a short-term interest rate because the long-term rates are less controllable. The Federal Reserve System in the United States targets the federal funds rate. Commercial banks pay that interest rate when they borrow reserves from each other overnight. It is an unsecured loan. By buying and selling government bonds, the Federal Reserve System can peg the federal funds rate at a certain level. Control over the federal funds rate is much tighter than control over money stock growth.

The idea behind interest rate targeting is that there is some neutral interest rate. At that neutral interest rate, the economy will operate at full-employment without inflation. At an interest rate below the neutral rate, households and businesses become too aggressive in borrowing funds, which can be inflationary. If banks expand lending at full-employment, the money stock grows faster, the demand for goods outruns the supply, and inflation rises. At an interest rate above the neutral rate the reverse happens. Higher interest rates slacken household and business demand for bank loans. Banks

contract lending, leading to slower money stock growth. With less money in circulation, the demand for goods weakens relative to the supply, causing falling inflation and rising unemployment.

The practice of interest rate targeting evolved over time. In 1995, the Federal Reserve began to publically announce a specific target for the federal funds rate. The Federal Open Market Committee fixes the target rate, and rarely changes it more than a quarter of a percentage point at each meeting. If the Federal Open Market Committee feels that inflation is the primary risk facing the economy, it will raise the targeted federal funds rate. If unemployment and recession appears the primary risk, the Federal Open Market Committee lowers the targeted federal funds rate.

The practice of interest rate targeting has drawn some critical fire for having an inflationary bias. Critics argue that interest rates are one of the stabilizing variables in the economy. An excessive demand for credit exerts upward pressure on interest rates. If interest rates are allowed to go up, they will moderate the excessive demand for credit, decreasing the chance that an expansion of credit will fuel an inflationary spiral. If a central bank prevents interest rates from going up in this scenario, it gives unwitting support to inflationary forces. In summary, holding interest rates constant in the face of fluctuations in the demand for credit may interfere with the stabilizing role of interest rates. Part of the problem is that no one knows exactly how to gauge the neutral interest rate. There is no way to measure it, and it does change (Wu, October 21, 2005, 2).

Despite criticisms, interest rate targeting has become the favored strategy of monetary policy. During the 1970s, rising inflation discredited the practice of interest rate targeting. In 1979, facing double-digit inflation, the Federal Reserve adopted the practice of targeting non-borrowed reserves. Changes in non-borrowed reserves change the ability of commercial banks to extend credit and change the money stock. Proponents of non-borrowed reserve targeting argued it gave the central bank tighter control over the money stock growth. It turned out that targeting non-borrowed reserves led to greater volatility in money stock growth and interest rates. In 1982, the Federal Reserve abandoned the practice of targeting non-borrowed reserves. It introduced another policy that worked out in practice to be similar to interest rate targeting. In the 1990s, the Federal Reserve reverted to a more explicit policy of practicing interest rate targeting. The Federal Reserve had been explicitly following a policy of interest rate targeting for well over a decade when the U.S. financial crisis erupted in 2008. In December 2008, the Federal Reserves took the unprecedented step of pushing its targeted interest to almost zero, well below one percentage point (Hilsenrath and Evans, 2009).

See also: Federal Open Market Committee

References

Davis, Richard G. "Intermediate Targets and Indicators of Monetary Policy." *Quarterly Review*, vol. 15, no. 2 (1990): 71–83.

Hilsenrath, Jon, and Kelly Evans. "Fed Outlook Darkens on Economy." *Wall Street Journal* (Eastern Edition, New York) January 7, 2009, p. A1.

Wu, Tao. "Estimating the 'Neutral' Real Interest Rate in Real Time." *FRBSF Economic Letter*, no. 2005–27 (Oct 21, 2005).

INTERNATIONAL MONETARY CONFERENCE OF 1878

The International Monetary Conference opened in Paris on August 10, 1878. The Conference was called at the request of the United States, which wanted to push for an international bimetallic monetary system. It utterly failed to live up to expectations. On July 23, 1878, the *New York Times* had printed an editorial with the heading, "Promoting the Federation of the World," suggesting that the Conference would lead to the establishment of an international gold metric coinage unit and the new coinage unit would inculcate "true notions of the nature and purposes of money" (Nugent, 254). The idea of an international coinage unit lingered in the background of the conference, partly as a pretext for some countries to attend the conference, but it never surfaced as a goal to be reached.

The seeds for the Conference were sown with the passage of the Bland–Allison Act in the United States. This act began in Congress as a free silver act, but passed Congress, over a presidential veto, as an act requiring the treasury to coin silver up to a fixed amount and asking the government to call an international conference to negotiate a world bimetallic standard. A world bimetallic standard would fix worldwide an official ratio of gold to silver. The United States hoped that if all governments set the same official ratio of gold to silver, the official world ratio would dominate the free market ratio, arresting the plunge of silver values in the free market.

The United States, possessing vast silver deposits, wanted to retain silver as a monetary metal, but the wealthier nations were rapidly shifting to a gold standard.

The United Kingdom practiced "imperial bimetallism," maintaining herself on a gold standard, and India on a silver standard. Germany was selling off silver reserves after the adoption of the gold standard in 1871, and refused to attend the conference. The Latin Monetary Union countries, the largest being France, had ceased the coinage of silver because of its plunging value and were not favorably disposed toward resuscitating silver.

The representatives of the United States, isolated from the outset of the conference, found no crack in the diplomatic armor of the forces arrayed against a revival of bimetallism. A Dutch delegate suggested that the United States might look for monetary allies among the less-developed world (Latin America, Asia, etc.), hinting that the United States might belong with the less-developed countries itself and prompting a U.S. delegate to ask for a clarification. The European conference delegates offered to let the United States save face by turning the Conference into a series of sessions on coinage and bullion practices around the world, but the United States remained unswerving in its commitment to an international bimetallic standard.

On August 28, 1878, the conference delegates recessed for 45 minutes to let the European delegates reach an agreement on an answer to the U.S. proposal. The European delegates flatly turned down the proposal, saying that each nation, governed by its special situation, should set its own monetary standard.

The Conference of 1878 dropped the curtain on bimetallism, and by 1880, the world was squarely on a gold standard. The United States, the staunchest supporter of silver among the monetary powers, stood against the adoption of a bimetallic standard unless it was part of an international agreement.

The idea of an international monetary unit surfaced in the latter 19th century, and it is an idea that may yet be realized. Adoption of an international monetary unit would encourage international trade by reducing the risk of changing exchange rates between currencies and facilitating cost comparisons between goods produced in different countries. Europe has already launched a European currency, the euro, to replace national currencies in Europe, and the growth of international trade may push the world toward the adoption of an international monetary unit. Presently, the U.S. dollar fulfills some of the roles of an international monetary unit.

See also: Bimetallism, Latin Monetary Union

References

Bordo, Michael D. 1994. *Monetary Regimes in Transition,* ed. Forrest Capie.

Nugent, Walter T. K. 1968. *Money and American Society, 1865–1880.*

Willis, Henry Parker. 1901. *A History of the Latin Monetary Union.*

INTERNATIONAL MONETARY FUND

The International Monetary Fund (IMF), is a supranational lending institution whose primary mission lies in furnishing short-term credit for countries suffering balance of payments deficits. Balance of payment deficits occur when a country's outflow of money from transactions with foreign countries exceeds its inflow. Like its sister institution, the World Bank, the IMF was born of the Bretton Woods Conference. That 1944 meeting of international monetary officials put foreign exchange markets under a system of fixed exchange rates—a system that lasted until 1971. The IMF began operations in 1946 and in 1964 it founded its headquarters in Washington, D.C. Although the mission of the World Bank lay in financing development and reconstruction projects, the IMF bore responsibility for loaning foreign currency reserves to countries on a short-term basis.

An excess of imports and investment in foreign countries relative to exports and domestic investment financed by foreign investors causes an excess outflow of a country's currency. This leads to currency depreciation in foreign exchange markets unless some type of market intervention occurs. A country can prevent currency depreciation by borrowing foreign currencies from the IMF and using these foreign currencies to purchase its own currency in foreign exchange markets, increasing the demand for its own currency and arresting its depreciation.

The funds of the IMF come from subscriptions of member countries, which contribute on the basis of such variables as national income and foreign trade. In 1946, member countries numbered 35, but by 1998, the number had grown to 182 countries. Soviet bloc countries did not join the IMF until after their transition to market countries. The United States has the largest quota of contributions and in 1998 contributed about 18 percent of all IMF funds. Each country contributes sums of its own currency, which serve as the IMF's lending capital. Out of these funds, the IMF might make foreign currency loans to countries that use the proceeds to buy up excess amounts of their own currency in foreign exchange markets. The

Headquarters of the International Monetary Fund in Washington, D.C. (International Monetary Fund)

borrowing country puts up its own currency as collateral for such a loan.

Perhaps the greatest economic innovation of the IMF during the period of fixed exchange rates was the development of Special Drawing Rights (SDRs), sometimes referred to as "paper gold." By international agreement, the SDRs are exchangeable for other currencies just as gold reserves.

Under the fixed exchange rate system, the IMF loaned funds to countries that needed to intervene in foreign exchange markets to maintain the values of their currencies at the fixed rates. Under the floating exchange rate system, the industrially developed countries had little need of the resources of the IMF. The IMF turned its attention to the less-developed countries, making longer-term loans to finance balance of payments of deficits, and granting soft loans to the poorest of the world's countries. These balance of payments deficits allowed these countries to import capital.

The oil price revolution of the 1970s not only pushed the fixed exchange rate system to the breaking point, but also put a heavy burden on the less-developed countries of the world, which responded by incurring large amounts of debt to foreign lenders. During the 1980s, high interest rates increased the cost of servicing this debt, and reduced exports to the recession-ridden United States, decreasing the inflow of dollars needed to service this debt. Many of the less-developed countries also turned to inflationary policies at home, further endangering the investments of foreigners. Under these conditions, the IMF assumed the thankless task of requiring these countries to follow responsible monetary and fiscal policies as a condition for receiving additional IMF credit. The IMF usually requires policies of high interest rates, depreciated currencies, and smaller budget deficits, translating as less social spending. Private lenders often refuse credit to countries that fail to follow IMF adjustment programs.

The decade of the 1990s kept the IMF unusually busy. The decade opened with Soviet bloc countries making the transition to market economies and needing domestic currencies convertible into hard currencies at stable exchange rates. The IMF provided expertise on the organization of central banks and supplied loans of hard currencies such as U.S. dollars to help these countries stabilize their currencies at stable exchange rates. In 1995, Mexico fell victim to a severe financial crisis, prompting the IMF to extend a record loan of over $17 billion to that country. Toward the end of the decade, global financial crisis was placing heavy demands on the resources of the IMF. By the end of 1998, Russia had received over $20 billion in loans, and $35 billion was committed to Korea, Indonesia, and Thailand to assist with the Asian financial crisis.

The U.S. financial crisis of 2008 left the IMF with little role to play. Recapitalizing banks stood outside its authority. With crisis lending to developing countries down, the IMF faced a budget deficit. In April 2008, it reduced its workforce by 15 percent to cut costs (Economist, 2008).

See also: Bretton Woods System, Dollar Crisis of 1971, World Bank

References
Economist. "Finance and Economics: Selling the Family Gold; The IMF." April 12, 2008, p. 84.

Polak, Jacques J. 1994. *The World Bank and the International Monetary Fund: A Changing Relationship.*

Myers, Robert J., ed. 1987. *The Political Morality of the International Monetary Fund.*

ISLAMIC BANKING

Islamic banking operates in accordance with Islamic principles, which absolutely ban the payment or receipt of interest. Islamic principles also prohibit banks from furnishing capital to firms providing immoral goods and services, such as pornography. Compliance with prohibitions against interest in financial transactions is the core difference between Islamic banks and their Western counterparts. For the purpose of banking and finance, the key point in Islamic principles is that paying or receiving interest is forbidden, but earning profits is permissible. A fixed or predetermined rate of return represented by interest violates Islamic principles, but an uncertain rate of return represented by profits raises no ethical issues under Islam. The growth of Islamic banking began to gain momentum in the last half of the 1970s as oil revenue began flowing into the Middle East.

Forms of Islamic banks can vary between countries but follow a general line. These banks hold two forms of deposits, transactions deposits and investment deposits. The transactions deposits bear a strong resemblance to the demand deposits held by Western commercial banks. These deposits earn no interest and act as a medium of exchange. The bank guarantees the nominal value of the deposit against loses. Investment deposits provide the bulk of the Islamic banks' funds. These funds do not pay interest or a fixed rate of return, and the bank does not guarantee the nominal value of these funds. Investment deposits bear a stronger resemblance to Western style shares of corporate stock than to the time and savings deposits of Western banks. Like shareholders, investment depositors receive a share of the profit and losses earned by the bank. The bank only guarantees that the profits and losses will be distributed between the bank and a depositor in a certain proportion. The proportion cannot be changed during the life of a contract.

Islamic banks finance business activity by acquiring profit-sharing assets. Rather than pay interest, an entrepreneur promises to pay the bank a predetermined share of the profits. The bank bears all the financial loss in the case of unprofitable ventures. Large and long-term ventures usually involve more than one financial contributor. A predetermined share of the profits are distributed to the various contributors according to the relative size of their respective contributions. This system works similar to an equity market in Western capitalism in that shares in an investment project can be acquired by the public, banks, central banks, or the government.

In financial arrangements where there are no profits to be shared, Islamic banks have other methods. Zero return loans can be made to individuals. On these loans, the bank can charge an administrative fee as long as the fee is a fixed amount and does not vary with the value or length of the loan. In the case of installment purchases, the bank can buy a product on the borrower's behalf, and sell it to the borrower at a higher price. The borrower pays a higher price but can pay the higher price out in an installment plan. Some contracts are set up as lease-purchase agreements, in which the bank leases the product to the borrower. Part of each lease payment goes toward final purchase of the good when the lease expires. Manufacturers and farmers borrow working capital by selling the finished product or commodity to the bank, with the condition that the bank will take delivery at some specified date in the future, perhaps at the end of harvest season.

See also: Bank

References

Economist. "Banking Behind the Veil." April 4, 1992, p. 49.

Khan, Mohsin, and Abbas Mirakhor. "Islamic Banking: Experiences in the Islamic Republic of Iran and in Pakistan, *Economic Development and Cultural Change,* vol. 38, no. 2 (January 1990): 353–376.

Kowsmann, Patricia, and Karen Lane. "Islamic Banking Moves Into Singapore; City-State Stakes Claim in Growing Sector; DBS, Mideast Investors Capitalize New Firm." *The Wall Street Journal* (Eastern Edition, New York), May 8, 2007, p. C7.

ISLAMIC COINAGE

See: Ottoman Empire Currency

ITALIAN LIRA

See: Carolingian Reform, Corso Forzoso, Quattrini Affair

IVORY

The tusks of elephants are composed of ivory, a substance much in demand throughout history for its durability and beauty. The demand for ivory has nearly become the downfall of elephants, which have been decimated in large numbers for the sake of their tusks.

The role that ivory has played as money is rather limited, in spite of the fact that its aesthetic qualities and durability give it some of the same attraction as precious metals. In mountain villages on the island of Ili Mandriri in the Indonesian archipelago, islanders used ivory as a store of value and mark of social status. An individual's social standing was a function of the number and size of ivory tusks that he or she owned. It appears that not too far in the past ivory also served as a medium of exchange. In the post–World War II era, the islanders still used ivory as the main form of bride money.

Men pose with ivory tusks in Dar Es Salaam, Tanganyika, the economic center of German East Africa during the 19th century. (Frank and Frances Carpenter Collection)

Before the arrival of Arabian traders, tribes in Uganda cut ivory discs that served as a favored form of money. Although anyone was free to cut ivory discs, no one could kill elephants or possess ivory without the king's permission, and cutting ivory discs required special skills possessed only by a few people. In effect, the king had a monopoly on the supply of ivory discs.

During the time of German colonization of equatorial Africa, fines were set in ivory, eventually leaving the colonial administration with a large stockpile. There is also evidence of an ivory monetary unit in Gabon. In Loma, a 100-pound chunk of ivory represented a monetary unit for large transactions, but it was a fictitious unit, in reality representing an assortment of European goods. In the Nama tribe of southwest Africa, ivory represented a stable export and acted as a medium of exchange.

Ivory has functioned as money primarily in Africa. Famous African explorer, John H. Speke, who discovered Lake Victoria as the source of the Nile, mentioned the use of ivory as money in his book, *The Discovery of the Source of the Nile.* Henry M. Stanley, in his book, *In Darkest Africa,* tells of treasuries of ivory and his own use of ivory to pay for services rendered by tribes. He also wrote of raiding parties that captured slaves mainly to exchange the slaves for ivory. Ivory might have acted as money on a grander scale if it had commanded more religious significance for the Africans, or if the foreign ivory demand had not been so high relative to the domestic demand.

See also: Commodity Monetary Standard

References
Einzig, Paul. 1966. *Primitive Money.*
Speke, J. H. 1864/1906. *The Discovery of the Source of the Nile.*
Stanley, Henry M. 1890. *In Darkest Africa.*

J

JAPANESE DEFLATION

Between 1999 and 2005, Japan experienced deflation (International Monetaray Fund, 2003, 2008). That is, on average, prices fell. Between 1985 and 1994, Japan experienced an average inflation rate of 1.4 percent, a relatively low inflation rate by world standards. A slowing economy brought the inflation rate down to negative territory in 1995. It rebounded and climbed to the 2 percent range in 1997, before falling again, sinking into negative territory by 1999. The inflation rate of consumer prices stood at zero in 2007. The inflation rate of consumer prices edged into positive territory in 2008.

The economic deceleration that marked the beginnings of deflation began when an asset bubble burst. In 1986, the Nikkei Index of the Tokyo stock market stood in the 12,000 range (www.finance.yahoo.com). The market took off, reaching the dizzy height of roughly 39,000 in 1989. Then the market began unwinding, sinking to the 15,000 range in 1992. The market never recovered its previous high. In October 2008, the Tokyo stock market sank to 6994.9.

In monetary systems managed by modern central banks, unwanted and uncontrolled deflation poses a puzzle in the eyes of many observers. In the past, central banks were limited in the amount of paper money they could issue by a gold standard. Today, central banks can issue as much money as is consistent with stable prices. If a country is caught in a deflationary spiral, the central bank is free to augment domestic circulating money stocks until prices stop falling. The concept that printing more money leads to inflation is standard economic doctrine.

The trend toward deflation marked the end of a spectacular phase of economic development in Japan. Between 1960 and 1973, economic growth in Japan averaged 9.8 percent annually, over twice the rate of most developed countries. Between 1973 and 1980, economic growth in Japan slipped to 3.9 percent, still a relatively high growth rate for that period. The United States averaged 2.1 percent growth for the same period. Nearly all countries experienced a substantial deceleration of growth for that time frame. Between 1980 and 1988, growth converged closer to the average of other developed countries, averaging annual growth of 3.6 percent. The United States averaged growth of 3.3 percent for this same period. These comparisons are based on data in Summers and Heston (1991). In the 1990s, Japan went from above average growth to below average growth, averaging less than 1 percent between 1992 and 2002 (Bank for International Settlements, 2005).

In Japan, the overnight interest rate is the main index of monetary policy, comparable to the federal funds interest rate in the United States. Monetary laxness shows up as lower interest rates. To arrest the deflation and stimulate economic growth, the Bank of Japan dropped the overnight interest rate. In 1995, the Bank of Japan changed the rate from over 8 percent to less than 0.5 percent (International Monetary Fund, 2003). The easy money policy failed to stem the tide of deflation. As inflation slipped into the negative column, the Bank of Japan pushed the overnight interest rate to ranges measured in one thousandths of a percentage point. For 1999, the International Monetary Fund reports an average overnight interest rate of zero. The average rose to 0.2 percent for 2000, and then sank back to zero for the years 2001 through 2005. The International Monetary Fund reports an average rate of 0.2 percent for 2006. In February 2007, the average rate stood at 0.5 percent.

The development of deflationary expectations became a major complicating factor. Expectations of inflation persuade consumers and businesses to borrow money and buy goods before prices go up. Inflation encourages buying goods and capital equipment sooner rather than later. Expected deflation has the opposite effect. Consumers and businesses are hesitant to buy goods and equipment with borrowed money if the goods and equipment are selling for prices higher than what they will sell for in the future. With expected deflation, businesses require a higher expected rate of return before borrowing funds to purchase capital equipment.

Many economists believe Japan in the 1990s entered into a liquidity trap. In a liquidity trap, money is in high demand because of the expectation that all other assets can be purchased on more favorable terms in the future. The strong demand for money as a financial asset frustrates efforts to increase spending by increasing the money supply.

See also: Liquidity Trap

References

Bank for International Settlements. "Japan's Deflation, Problems in the Financial System and Monetary Policy." BIS Working Paper no. 188, November, 2005.

Economist. "Wading in the Yen Trap." July 24, 1999, pp. 71–74.

Economist. "Seeking the Right Medicine." June 21, 2003, p. 70.

International Monetaray Fund, *World Economic Outlook,* September 2003, April 2007, April 2008.

Summers, Robert, and Alan Heston. "The Pen World Table (Mark 5): An Expanded Set of International Comparisons, 1950–1988." *Quarterly Journal of Economics,* vol. 106, no. 2 (May 1991): 327–369.

JUILLIARD V. GREENMAN (UNITED STATES)

In the case of *Juilliard v. Greenman,* 110 U.S. 421 (1884), the United States

Supreme Court ruled that Congress had the right to issue notes to be legal tender for the payment of public and private debt. Legal-tender notes are treasury notes or banknotes that, in the eyes of the law, must be accepted in the payment of debts.

Under the Legal Tender Act of February 25, 1862, Congress authorized the issuance of U.S. notes as legal tender for all debts public and private, excepting custom duties and interest on the public debt, which were payable in coin. The United States Constitution had not explicitly conferred on Congress the right to issue legal-tender notes, or other legal-tender paper money, and many doubted if legal-tender legislation was constitutional. The Constitution was framed while the memory of the hyper-inflation episode of the Continental currency was still fresh.

Hepburn v. Griswold, 75 U.S. 603 (1870), was the first Supreme Court case to test the constitutionality of legal-tender notes. The Court found that the issuance of legal-tender notes amounted to an impairment of contracts without due process of law, which was forbidden by the Constitution and therefore unconstitutional. Contracts were abridged because a creditor had to accept depreciated notes rather than coin. Interestingly, Chief Justice Chase, who wrote the majority opinion, was secretary of the treasury when the notes were issued at his strong urging. Some observers felt that Chase changed his mind to improve his chances for a presidential bid.

The Hepburn decision did not stand long. In *Parker v. Davis,* 79 U.S. 457 (1871), the Court—enlarged with two new appointees—ruled in favor of Congress's power to issue legal-tender notes, but the decision drew heavily on

the exigencies of war and left in doubt the constitutionality of the issuance of legal-tender notes in peacetime.

In 1878, Congress repealed an earlier act providing for the retirement of outstanding legal-tender notes (greenbacks) and provided for the reissuance of these notes. Because these notes where reissued in peacetime, the constitutional authority of Congress to maintain their legal-tender status remained in doubt.

When *Juilliard v. Greenman* came before the Supreme Court in 1884, the Court held that Congress had the authority to issue legal-tender notes even in peacetime. The majority opinion argued that Congress had the authority to issue legal-tender notes under its constitutional power "to raise money for the public use on a pledge of the public credit," including the power "to issue, in return for the money borrowed, the obligation of the United States in any appropriate form of stock, bonds, bills, or notes . . . adapted to circulation from hand to hand in the ordinary transactions of business" (110 U.S. at 432). The majority opinion also argued that the power to confer legal status on money derived from the rights of sovereignty as understood when the Constitution was framed.

The decision of *Juilliard v. Greenman* settled the question of the authority of Congress to provide a national currency for the United States.

See also: Case of Mixt Monies, Legal Tender

References

Breckinridge, S. P. 1969. *Legal Tender*.

Dunne, Gerald T. 1960. *Monetary Decisions of the Supreme Court*.

Hepburn, A. Barton. 1924/1967. *A History of the Currency of the United States*.

Myers, Margaret G. 1970. *A Financial History of the United States*.

L

LABOR NOTES

Labor notes, a unique monetary experiment in the United Kingdom in the early 19th century, bore a face value equivalent to a certain number of hours of work. The notes were the brainchild of Robert Owen (1771–1858), a successful textile manufacturer in the United Kingdom, who rose to fame as a utopian socialist reformer at the beginning of the industrial age. He is famous in the United States for involvement with New Harmony, Indiana. In 1825, Owen purchased 30,000 acres of land in Indiana and launched New Harmony as a cooperative society, a project that would cost him 80 percent of his fortune before he abandoned it.

In 1832, Owen was publishing a penny journal, *The Crisis,* in which he publicized his plan to form an association for the exchange of all commodities on the principle of the numbers of hours of labor embodied in each commodity. All commodities that required the same amount of labor to produce were to be

Robert Owen, English utopian socialist. (Jupiterimages)

traded evenly, and other commodities were to be exchanged at ratios ruled by the number of hours of labor required to produce each one. If it took two hours of labor to produce product A and one hour of labor to produce product B, then it took two units of product B to purchase one unit of product A. Owen adapted his plan from the labor theory of value, a widely accepted concept among 19th-century economists, which held that all value comes from labor.

To carry out his plan, Owen opened the Equitable Labor Exchange on September 3, 1832, at a building called the Bazaar on Gray's Inn Road, London. Producers and manufacturers brought goods to the exchange and received in return labor notes equal to the amount of labor required to produce the goods. The labor notes could be used to buy other goods at the exchange, which were priced based on the hours of labor that went into producing each good. Exchanges opened in different regions; one of the largest was in Birmingham, where two series of labor notes were issued in denominations of 1, 2, 5, 10, 50, and 80 labor-hours.

The exchanges were short lived. It was a utopian idea that could not compete with a market system that incorporates all the available information that affects the prices of goods and services. Owens closed down the London exchange in March 1834 and paid off a £2,000 deficit the exchange had run up.

References
Angell, Norman. 1929. The Story of Money.
Beresiner, Yasha. 1977. *Paper Money*.
Birchall, Johnson. 1994. *Co-op: the People's Business*.

LAND BANK SYSTEM (AMERICAN COLONIES)

During the first half of the 18th century, land banks infused paper currency into the economies of the American colonies, helping to relieve the shortage of money that hampered trade and industry. Aside from two short-lived exceptions, these were public banks, functioning under the auspices of colonial governments.

Land banks loaned paper money to citizens who put up collateral in the form of some sort of real estate, such as farm land or houses in town. Borrowers ran the risk of forfeiting their property in the event of default, although the land banks, as public institutions, enjoyed reputations for extending the terms for debtors in difficulty. The real estate nevertheless stood as security maintaining the value of the paper money, and foreclosure was a legitimate weapon. When foreclosure failed to produce sufficient revenue to redeem the paper currency, then governments were usually obliged to make good the paper money. The borrowers paid interest on the loans, which in most colonies went to pay governmental expenses. Often a local public board of property-owning citizens acted as a loan board, approving and disapproving loans as it saw fit. In other cases, provincial officials at a higher level made these decisions. These boards or officials received an allotment of paper currency for issuance in a given locality.

During the 17th century, several proposals were floated for organizing private land banks in the American colonies, particularly in Massachusetts, but invariably the colonial assemblies refused to grant charters for these private ventures. In 1712, South Carolina led the way in the land bank movement when it established the first public land bank in the American colonies. Other colonies quickly followed the example set by South Carolina. Massachusetts founded a land bank in 1714, Rhode Island in 1715, New Hampshire in 1717, New Jersey and Pennsylvania in 1723, North

Carolina in 1729, Maryland in 1731, Connecticut in 1732, and New York in 1737.

The British government viewed all colonial paper money as a threat to British creditors who faced severe losses if colonists sought to wipe out debts with a round of inflation. In 1720, royal governors in America received orders from London to suspend the operation of any land bank, pending approval from the Privy Council. Both American and British officials, however, were slow to take action. The land bank in Massachusetts remained in operation until 1730, and the land banks in the other colonies until 1740.

The saga of the land banks is another chapter in the struggle of the American colonies to fill the vacuum in the colonial money supply left by the outflow of hard specie in payment for European imports. Great Britain aggravated the money shortage by squashing efforts to mint coins in the colonies and severely restricting the authority of colonial governments to issue paper money. After the American Revolution, the Articles of Confederation granted state governments authority to establish mints and issue paper currency. The United States Constitution gave Congress sole authority to coin money and regulate the money supply.

See also: Franklin, Benjamin, Massachusetts Bay Colony Paper Issue

References

Chown, John F. 1994. *A History of Money.*

Ernst, Joseph Albert. 1973. *Money and Politics in America.*

Thayer, Theodore. "The Land-Bank System in the American Colonies." *Journal of Economic History*, vol. 13, no. 2 (1953): 145–159.

LATIN MONETARY UNION

One of the early efforts to establish a uniform and universal coinage, equally acceptable in all countries, led to the formation of the Latin Monetary Union. The union itself came to life through the work of a conference held in Paris, France, in 1865. In addition to France, three other countries, Italy, Switzerland, and Belgium, participated in the conference, all three of which were on the French bimetallic system. This conference was the first international meeting on monetary affairs.

Under a bimetallic system, silver and gold coins circulated as money and the government set the value of silver relative to gold at a fixed ratio. Before the conference, the value of silver was rising, causing holders of silver to buy gold and leading to the disappearance of silver. Switzerland debased the value of its silver coins to address the problem, and France responded by banning the acceptance of Swiss coins in public offices. The immediate technical problem facing the conference participants was the overvaluation of silver. Under the bimetallic system of the Latin Monetary Union, 15.5 ounces of silver stood equal to one ounce of gold in all member countries.

The conference participants saw the treaty creating the Latin Monetary Union put into effect on August 1, 1866. The States of the Church (the lands in central and north central Italy that were ruled by the pope) joined the Union later in 1866, followed by Bulgaria and Greece in 1867. Member countries minted gold pieces in denominations only of 100, 50, 20, 10, and 5 francs. They also minted silver pieces in denominations of 5, 2, and 1 francs and 50 and 20 silver *centimes*. Each country minted coins that were made legal tender and circulated throughout the union.

In 1867, France called another conference to discuss the establishment of a uniform world monetary system. Hopes of expanding French influence and prestige may have supplied the motive that pushed Louis Napoleon to call the conference. The need to keep the bimetallic monetary standard alive and working in the face of competition from the United Kingdom's gold standard may also have been a contributing factor.

The United States accepted the concept of a world monetary union and made a case for France to begin minting a 25-franc gold piece. Spokesmen for United States, whose arguments for the 25-franc piece fell on deaf ears in France, observed that:

> Such a coin will circulate side by side everywhere and in perfect equality with the half eagle of the United States and the sovereign of Great Britain. These three gold coins, types of the great commercial nations, fraternally united and differing only in emblems, will go hand in hand around the globe freely circulating through both hemispheres without recoinage, brokerage, or other impediments. This opportune concession of France to the spirit of unity will complete the work of civilization she has had so much at heart and will inaugurate that new monetary era, the lofty object of the international conference, and the noblest aim of the concourse of nations, as yet without parallel in the history of the world. (Chown, 1994, 87)

The conference ended without reaching an agreement, only passing a resolution to meet again. The United Kingdom had refused to support the plan for a world monetary union, but did establish a Royal Commission on International Coinage to study the findings of the conference. The commission acknowledged the advantages of an international currency, citing that:

> Small manufacturers and traders are deterred from engaging in foreign transactions by the complicated difficulties of foreign coins . . . by the difficulty in calculating the exchanges, and of remitting small sums from one country to another. Anything tending to simplify these matters would dispose them to extend their sphere of operations. (Chown, 1994, 89)

Nevertheless, the commission cited numerous practical considerations that stood in the way of forming an international currency.

The commercial success of Great Britain persuaded the major trading partners of the world that the gold standard was the wave of the future. The fate of the bimetallic system of the Latin Monetary Union was sealed when France lost the Franco-Prussian War and had to pay war reparations to Germany. The war reparations enhanced Germany's gold reserves, giving Germany the wherewithal to follow Britain's example and adopt the gold standard. The value of silver dropped sharply, and the members of the Latin Monetary Union had to restrict the coinage of silver. The union wobbled on until the 1920s, when the strains of war and diverging gold and silver prices put an end to the system.

The idea of a European monetary union, complete with a European central bank, became a reality on January 1, 1999, when the European Central Bank launched the euro in a non-physical form. It functioned as a money of account. Euro banknotes and coins first entered into circulation on January 1, 2002, replacing major European banknotes and coins in German Marks and French francs. This monetary union with its uniform currency ended the risk of fluctuations in foreign exchange rates and the inconvenience of converting domestic money into foreign exchange, thus easing the path for the growth of international trade.

See also: Bimetallism, Euro Currency, International Monetary Conference of 1878

References

Davies, Glyn. 1994. *A History of Money*.
Chown, John F. 1994. *A History of Money*.
Willis, Henry Parker. 1901. *A History of the Latin Monetary Union*.

LAW, JOHN

In the *Wealth of Nations* (1776), Adam Smith observed that "[t]he idea of the possibility of multiplying paper money to almost any extent was the real foundation of what is called the Mississippi scheme, the most extravagant project of banking and stock-jobbing that perhaps the world ever saw." John Law was the author of the Mississippi scheme. He was a Scottish financier who felt that Scottish industry languished from a lack of money. He conceived the notion that a bank could issue paper money equal in value to all the land in a country. The Scottish Parliament was not interested, but the new regent of France, Philippe

John Law, 18th-century monetary theorist. (Guizot, Francois Pierre Guillaume, A Popular History of France From The Earliest Times, 1878)

d'Orleans, saw Law's theories as a way out of the bankrupt finances of France. Philippe authorized Law to establish the Banque Generale (1716). Among other things, this was the first bank to issue legal-tender paper money. It accepted deposits, paid interest, and made loans. The value of its paper money was defined in terms of a fixed weight of silver. In April 1717, taxes were made payable in the bank's paper money.

In 1717, Law secured a royal charter to launch the Mississippi Company. This was a trading company organized to exploit the Mississippi basin. Law sold 200,000 shares of this new company to the public. The price stood at 500 livres per share, but three-fourths of the payment could be made with government notes at face value. These government notes were then worth one-third of their face value. The shares found a ready market in holders of depreciating government notes eager for a piece of a profit-making enterprise. Law became bolder with success and instructed his bank to buy the royal tobacco monopoly and all French companies devoted to foreign trade. These companies he combined with the Mississippi Company for the complete monopolization of French foreign trade.

In 1718, Law's bank was reorganized as the Banque Royal, and the government made the bank's paper money legal tender. By 1720, the combination of trading companies known as the Mississippi Company was amalgamated with the bank. The Banque Royal bought up the national debt by exchanging it for shares in the Mississippi Company. Turning the national debt into shares of the Mississippi Company set the example that was soon copied by the South Sea Company in Great Britain. The prices of the shares in the Mississippi rose to fantastic heights on a wave of speculative frenzy. Law's bank continually increased the supply of paper money, much of which was used to bid up the shares in the Mississippi Company. When prices of commodities rose 100 percent and wages 75 percent between 1716 and 1720, the public lost faith in the value of paper money.

In the meantime, things were not going well for the Mississippi Company. There were no precious metals to be found, and no attraction could induce families to emigrate to the Mississippi basin. Profits fell far short of expectations.

In 1719, the price of the stock peaked and the downward spiral began. Those in the know sold their stock at the peak and redeemed their bank paper money with gold. As the sell-off gained momentum, Law's bank issued paper money to buy the shares of stock. Holders of paper money besieged the bank, demanding silver or gold, and several people were killed in the confusion. Law himself was forced to leave France, passing his declining years as a professional gambler in Venice.

The Mississippi bubble left a deep distrust of paper money and big banks in the mind of the French people. Nearly a century elapsed before France was willing to try paper money again. Learning the pitfalls of paper money has been a slow process in modern capitalist countries. Angola, Argentina, and Bolivia rank among the countries that have experienced hyperinflation in the post–World War II era.

See also: Caisse d'Escompte, Hyperinflation during the French Revolution

References
Minton, Robert. 1975. *John Law: The Father of Paper Money*.
Murphy, Antoin E. 1997. *John Law: Economic Theorist and Policy Maker*.
Schumpeter, Joseph. 1939. *Business Cycles*, vol. I.
Spiegel, Henry Williams. 1971. *The Growth of Economic Thought*.

LAW OF ONE PRICE

The Law of One Price states that identical goods sold at different geographical locations will sell for identical prices when the prices are expressed in a common currency. The law assumes that traders and arbitragers would exploit price differences between the same good at different locations. They will purchase the good at the cheapest location and resell it in the location with the highest price. The activity of traders exploiting price differentials guarantees that the prices of identical goods sold at different geographical locations will converge to one price. The differences between prices of identical goods at different geographical locations should only reflect different transportation cost and trade barriers.

The Law of One Price explains why on any given day the price of gold in U.S. dollars in London is nearly equal to the price of gold in New York. The theory does not work quite so well for other goods. Since 1986, the *Economist* has published a "Big Mac Index" showing the prices of McDonald's Big Mac sandwiches around the world. According to the Law of One Price, if a Big Max cost $3.00 in the United States and $1 equals 100 yen in foreign exchange markets, then a Big Mac should cost $3, or 300 yen, in Japan. According to the Big Mac Index reported in the May 25, 2006, issue of the *Economist,* a Big Mac cost $3.10 in the United States and $2.23 in Japan. The same issue reported that in China a Big Mac only cost $1.31 in U.S. currency.

The Law for One Price works best for highly tradable and homogeneous goods such as steel, copper, and agricultural commodities. Houses are not tradable goods, and house prices are known to vary substantially within regions inside the United States. Departures from the Law of One Price may reflect either overvalued or undervalued exchange rates. In the above example, a Big Mac went for an unusually low price in China at a time when it was known that China's currency was undervalued in foreign exchange markets. The low price of a Big Mac in China could have been interpreted as indicating that China's currency would appreciate in the future, which it did.

Studies have shown that disparate regional prices of a tradable good tend to converge to one price. Disparate regional prices within a single country tend to converge faster than disparate prices for the same good between two separate countries. Within the United States, distance between cities appears to be the major determinant of the magnitude of price differences for the same good between cities.

References

Economist. "Finance and Economics: Sizzling; The Big Mac Index." July 7, 2007, p. 82.

Fan, C. Simon, and Xiangdong Wei. "The Law of One Price: Evidence from the Transitional Economy of China." *Review of Economics and Statistics,* vol. 88, no. 4 (November 2006): 682–697.

LAW OF THE MAXIMUM

See: Hyperinflation during the French Revolution, Wage and Price Controls

LEATHER MONEY

Leather money should perhaps be regarded as the most immediate precursor of paper money. It was usually issued as an emergency measure under the stress of war. The extinct city of ancient Carthage issued leather-wrapped money before the wars with Rome. The leather wrapping was sealed, and the substance inside the wrapping remained a mystery.

Better documentation exists for the use of leather money in France and Italy as an emergency measure. In Normandy, Philippe I (1060–1108) used as money pieces of leather with a small silver nail in the middle. Leather currencies also appeared under Louis IX (1266–1270), John the Good (1350–1364), and Charles the Wise (1364–1380). It is not clear whether these leather currencies bore an official stamp. Foreign ransoms had impoverished France of its metallic currencies, necessitating the development of an inferior substitute.

In 1122, Doge Domenico Michaele, ruler of Venice, financed a crusade by paying his troops and fleets in money made of leather with an official stamp. In 1237, the emperor Frederick II of Sicily, one of the first European monarchs to reestablish gold coinage after the long hiatus of the Middle Ages, paid his troops in stamped leather money during the sieges of Milan and Faventia. In 1248, at the siege of Parma, he again paid troops in leather money. Frederick's money was converted into silver at a later date.

Leather money bearing an official stamp bore a close kinship to modern paper money. English history furnishes a few references to leather money. In a speech to Parliament in 1523, Thomas Cromwell commented in referring to the expenses of sending an expedition to France:

> Thus we should soon be made incapable of hurting anyone, and be compelled, as we once did to coin leather. This, for my part, I could be content with; but if the King will go over in person and should happen to fall into the hands of the enemy—which God forbid—how should we be able to redeem him? If they will naught for their wine but gold they would think great scorn to take leather for our Prince. (Einzig, 1966, 286)

Reports exist of leather money on the Isle of Man during the 16th and maybe 17th centuries. A description of the Isle of Man published in 1726 states that leather currency had a history on the Island of Man, and that men of substance were allowed to make their own money up to a limit.

See also: Siege Money

References

Einzig, Paul. 1966. *Primitive Money*.

Quiggin, A., and A. Hingston. 1949. *A Survey of Primitive Money*.

LEGAL RESERVE RATIO

A legally required reserve ratio is one of the important central bank instruments for changing the stock of money in circulation. The reserve ratio is the fraction of customer deposits banks hold in the form of assets that satisfy a legal definition of reserves. In the United States, only vault cash or deposits at a Federal Reserve Bank may legally serve as reserves. A reduction in the legally required reserve ratio, allowing banks to loan out more depositor funds, leads to an expansion of the money stock. Raising this ratio reduces the money stock.

Commercial banks accept deposits of funds from customers. On a given day, the fresh deposits approximately offset withdrawals from earlier deposits, leaving the bank with an average level of deposits available for loans to customers. Banks keep a fraction of these deposits as reserves to keep the bank solvent during those intervals when fresh deposits fall short of withdrawals. Without government regulation of reserve requirements, banks often fall prey to the temptation to trim reserves too thinly and come up short of funds if depositors suddenly place heavy demands for cash withdrawals. Because reserves are funds that are not invested, and therefore not earning income, banks have an incentive to hold reserves to a minimal level.

In the United States, the Banking Act of 1935 authorized the board of governors of the Federal Reserve System to vary the legally required reserve ratio within prescribed limits. Before the Act of 1935, legal reserve ratios were set by statute. From 1935 until 1980, the board of governors could change the reserve requirements of commercial banks that were members of the Federal Reserve System, which included all commercial banks with national charters. State banks remained subject to state statutory reserve requirements until 1980. The Depository Institution Deregulation and Monetary Control Act of 1980 gave the board of governors authority to set reserve requirements for all depository institutions. The legal reserve ratio is usually set well below 20 percent. In 1992, the board of governors reduced the ratio from 12 to 10 percent.

If the level of deposits in a bank rises by $1,000, and the legal reserve ratio is 10 percent, the bank has to retain only $100 as reserves and can loan out the other $900. If the reserve ratio is cut for all banks, each bank can immediately loan out more funds. Furthermore, as deposits at each bank grow from the lending at other banks, each bank can loan out a share of new deposits. The cumulative effect of these actions on the ratio of customer deposits to vault cash

and deposits at the Federal Reserve Banks can be dramatic. If the legal reserve ratio decreased from 20 percent to 10 percent, the ratio of customer deposits to vault cash and deposits at the Federal Reserve Banks could double. Because bank deposits account for the lion's share of money supply measures, a reduction in the legal reserve ratio can sharply increase the money stock. An increase in the legal reserve ratio can have an equally blunt impact on the money stock in the opposite direction.

Significant controversy arose out of one of the early policy actions using legal reserves requirements. In 1936, commercial banks were flush with reserves, representing a potential for substantial increase in lending and monetary growth. The U.S. economy was still inching out of the Depression, but the banking system brimming over with reserves aroused inflationary fears. The board of governors virtually doubled reserve requirements to mop up excess reserves. In 1937, the recovery stalled out, nosing the economy over into another recession, and many observers put the blame at the feet of the improper use of legal reserve requirements by the board of governors.

Today, legal reserve ratios are one of the less important means of regulating monetary growth. Small changes in legal reserve ratios have powerful effects and create management difficulties for banks. Open market operations have become the most important means of regulating the money stock in the United States. Open market operations have to do with central bank purchases and sale of government bonds. When a central bank purchases bonds with new funds, the money stock increases.

See also: Bank, Central Bank, Federal Reserve System, Monetary Multiplier, Open Market Operations

References

Baye, Michael R., and Dennis W. Jansen. 1995. *Money, Banking, and Financial Markets.*

Klein, John J. 1982. *Money and the Economy,* 6th ed.

LEGAL TENDER

Money is legal tender when creditors are legally obliged to accept it in payment of debts. "This note is legal tender for all debts, private and public," appears on all Federal Reserve Notes, meaning that these notes are acceptable in payment of taxes or other obligations owed to the government and also that creditors must accept the notes in payment of all private debts.

In the expression "legal tender," the word "tender" means "offer," as when an individual tenders his resignation. The term "tender," with reference to money, arose out of actions of creditors against debtors in English courts. A debtor could tender to the creditor the amount he or she thought was owed to the creditor. If the creditor thought the sum tendered unacceptable, the debtor could deposit the sum with the court, which would decide if the tender met the debtor's obligation.

The legal-tender quality of a unit of money can be restricted. The American colonies issued paper money that was acceptable for the payment of public debts, but not private debts. The colonial governments committed themselves to accepting the money in payment of taxes, but did not require private creditors to accept it in payment of debts. Currently in the United States, the dime is legal tender for all debts up to $10.

English sovereigns arrogated to themselves the privilege of coining

Seal of the Federal Reserve on a five-dollar bill. (Paul Topp)

money and stipulated penalties for refusing to accept the king's coinage at face value. Orders from the crown went so far as to require the acceptance of pennies that had been halved and demanded that anyone refusing to accept halfpennies should be seized for contempt of the king's majesty, imprisoned, and exposed to public ridicule in a pillory.

Although the English government threw the full weight of its sovereign power behind its coinage, disputes between creditors and debtors continued to raise questions, leaving with the courts the final authority for establishing the legal-tender quality of money. An important court case in 1601, *The Case of Mixt Monies*, set the legal-tender quality of money on firm footing when it demonstrated that creditors had to accept in payment for debts the money that was legal tender when the debt was paid, as opposed to the money that was legal tender when the debt was incurred.

The Constitution of the United States specifies that: "No state shall coin money; . . . make anything but gold and silver coin a legal tender in payment of debts." Prior to 1862, no paper money in the United States commanded the legal-tender status. Nevertheless, the government often accepted banknotes and treasury notes in payment of taxes and public land sales, giving the paper money some legal-tender qualities. In 1862, amid the fiscal crisis of the Civil War, the U.S. government issued paper money that was legal tender for all private debts, and many, but not all, public debts. The power of the government to issue legal-tender paper money was challenged in the courts, but the wartime crisis clouded the issue at first. When

paper money continued to circulate after 1878, the legal-tender issue came before the Supreme Court, and in 1883 the Court ruled in favor of the power of the federal government to issue legal-tender paper money. In 1890, the federal government issued the first paper money that was legal tender in payment of all private debts and all payments owed to the government.

Economists have not always written approvingly of governments using their power to adjudicate disputes to render money legal tender. The famous economist John Stuart Mill wrote in book 3, chapter 7 of his *Principles of Political Economy*:

> Profligate governments having until a very modern period never scrupled for the sake of robbing their creditors to confer upon all other debtors a license to rob theirs by the shallow and impudent artifice of lowering the standard; that least covert of all modes of knavery, which consists in calling a shilling a pound that a debt of a hundred pounds may be canceled by the payment of one hundred shillings. (Mill, 1965, 505)

When governments become major debtors, they have an incentive to change the standard to pay off the debts, and in the 20th century, governments have printed up legal-tender paper money to cancel large public debts, the post–World War I government of Germany being the most notorious case. Despite the latent possibility for abuse, governments worldwide issue legal-tender paper money, which poses no problems as long as the supply is restricted to noninflationary levels.

See also: Juilliard v. Greenman

References

Breckinridge, S. P. 1903. *Legal Tender*.

Dunne, Gerald T. 1960. *Monetary Decisions of the Supreme Court*.

Myers, Margaret. 1970. *A Financial History of the United States*.

Mill, John Stuart. 1965. *Principles of Political Economy*. Vol. 3 of *Collected Works of John Stuart Mill*.

LIQUIDITY

The liquidity of an asset refers to the ease with which that asset can be converted into cash. Two main characteristics enter into the liquidity of an asset. One is the ability to sell the asset on short notice, and the other is the ability to sell the asset without significantly discounting the price. Both of these characteristics must be present for an asset to be considered highly liquid. Money or cash is the most liquid of all financial assets. Ninety-day U.S. Treasury bonds and shares of corporate stock can both be sold on short notice, but the treasury bonds are considered much more liquid. Treasury bonds can be quickly sold at a price close to the price paid for them. The corporate stock can only be sold on short notice at the current market price, which may be significantly below the price paid for the stock. A parcel of real estate is likely to be less liquid than shares of corporate stock. Finding a buyer for a piece of real estate on short notice can be difficult, and the price that buyers are willing and able to pay for real estate varies with economic conditions and interest rates.

The liquidity of an asset does not reflect its soundness. A sales person may find that investing a sizable sum of cash in a nice wardrobe can be a wise investment, one that pays off handsomely in higher sales commissions. If that sales person turns up jobless, however, and needs to sell the wardrobe, that person will likely recover only a small fraction of the original investment. Often highly profitable investments are illiquid.

In the case of financial investments, the liquidity of the asset is not related to the prospects that the investment will pay off. A parent may grant a ten-year loan to a studious, overachieving child with perfect assurance that the loan will be repaid. If the parent, however, tries to discount that loan to a third party for cash, they will find it very difficult. On the contrary, if the parent purchases a ten-year corporate bond, essentially loaning funds to a corporation, that parent can easily sell that bond before it matures. For an asset to be liquid, there has to be a market for it.

Liquidity confers certain advantages. Cash does not earn interest, but it enables its holder to take advantage of bargains and speculative opportunities. Interest earned by financial assets can be interpreted as a reward that must be paid to overcome a preference for liquidity. Usually, but not always, long-term bonds pay a higher interest rate than short-term bonds. The higher interest earned on long-term bonds is partly because liquidity is given up for a longer period of time.

Most business firms face a trade-off between liquidity and profitability. This trade-off is easily seen in the case of banks. If a bank took all of its depositors' money and never loaned it out, the bank would be highly liquid but would report zero revenue. On the other hand, the bank cannot loan out all of depositors' money and remain capable of honoring requests for withdrawals on demand. Banks must strike a balance between liquidity and profit maximization, keeping cash holdings as low as possible without jeopardizing the ability to redeem deposits. Other businesses may have to choose between holding cash and holding inventories. Holding cash guarantees that the business can meet its short-term obligations. A business may increase its profits by trimming its cash holdings to a bare minimum and investing in more inventories. Such a strategy can increase profits, but it also increases the risk that the firm will be left unable to meet its short-term obligations. A firm with relatively large cash holdings has greater chance of remaining solvent in the event of sudden and unexpected adversity.

Reference

Horne, James C. Van, and John M. Wachowicz, Jr., 1997. *Fundamentals of Financial Management*, 10th ed.

LIQUIDITY CRISIS

The liquidity of an asset refers to the ease and quickness with which it can be converted into money or other goods and services. An asset that can be quickly sold for money at low cost is a liquid asset. Money is the most liquid of all financial assets since it can be quickly exchanged for goods and services. Liquidity crises usually indicate difficulty in converting nonmonetary assets, particularly financial assets, into cash either by selling the assets or by using them as collateral.

Individual firms are said to face a liquidity crisis when they cannot obtain short-term financing. A retailer who cannot obtain short-term loans to purchase inventories or obtain goods on credit from suppliers is said to suffer a liquidity crisis. A liquidity crisis for a particular firm indicates that creditors worry about the firm's ability to pay. The failure of an anticipated loan to come through or sudden and unexpected one-time expenditures can leave a firm with a liquidity crisis. For an individual firm, a liquidity crisis may be virtually synonymous with a credit crunch.

The more serious liquidity crises can put an entire financial sector under severe pressure, can have wide macroeconomic dimensions, and usually requires government or central bank action to resolve. In the course of business, financial institutions accept claims against themselves that are liquid. In the case of banks, depositors can withdraw their money any time. The claims that financial institutions accept against themselves are offset by claims that financial institutions accept against others. Financial institutions cannot demand payment on these claims against others as quickly. A bank must redeem a bank deposit on demand but it cannot demand early repayment of loans. A wave of depositors withdrawing money from a financial institution can force that institution into a liquidity crisis even if all its outstanding loans are sound and have an excellent chance of repayment.

In the late 1980s, thrift institutions in Texas went through a severe liquidity crisis that virtually wiped out the savings and loan (S&L) industry. The S&L institutions first encountered difficulty with troubled loan portfolios. The crash in oil prices plunged the Texas real estate market into a deep slump, substantially reducing the value of collateral that S&Ls held against loans. A string of well-publicized failures of Texas S&Ls

caused worried depositors to start pulling their money out. There was never a run on these institutions, probably because S&L deposits had deposit insurance. It was a slow, steady withdrawal. Pension funds and other large customers began pulling money out. Texas S&Ls began accepting deposits put together by brokers at interest rates well above the rates paid by thrifts in other states. Regulators tried to broker funds from stronger thrifts to weaker ones, but the effort was not sufficient. The large number of failures in Texas and elsewhere bankrupted the Federal Savings and Loan Insurance Corporation that insured deposits at S&Ls. Congress enacted a multimillion dollar bailout to meet the claims of deposit insurance.

In 2008, the United States experienced a liquidity crisis that threatened to bring down an entire financial system. Financial institutions were holding mortage-backed securities, including securities backed by mortgages extended to borrowers with credit problems. Financial institutions purchased these mortgages by borrowing short term in credit markets. When the default rate on these mortgages rose above expected levels, the market value of these securities plummeted. Financial institutions were left unable to borrow short term and unable to sell mortgage-backed securities for cash. As an emergency measure, the U.S. central bank, The Federal Reserve System, began granting loans based on other kinds of collateral than government bonds.

References

Apcar, Leonard M. "Thrifts in Texas Scrambling for Funds, Liquidity Crisis Feared, Regulators Say." *Wall Street Journal* (Eastern Edition, New York) June 10, 1987, p. 1.

Paletta, Damian, and Allstair MacDonald. "World News: Liquidity-Crisis Guide Set for an Update." *Wall Street Journal* (Eastern Edition, New York) February 22, 2008, p. A9.

LIQUIDITY TRAP

A liquidity trap is a macroeconomic condition in which injecting additional money and liquidity into an economy exerts very little impact on overall price levels, output, or employment. It is a macroeconomic phenomenon, meaning that it applies to the economy as a whole and not to industries individually. Only an economy at a low point in a business cycle is at risk of developing a liquidity trap. During a recession, a liquidity trap can become a major hindrance to economic recovery, considerably complicating the task of designing an effective economic policy.

The liquidity trap at first seems more of a puzzle than a trap. It seems paradoxical that the money stock can grow without commiserate growth in spending. Theories of inflation assume that money stock growth does lead to comparable growth in spending, and the growth in spending drives inflation. Only economies experiencing deflation or near deflation seem to be at risk of developing a liquidity trap.

A liquidity trap becomes possible because money, particularly bank balances, can act as a substitute for stocks and bonds, and may even become an attractive substitute if interest rates drop to very low levels. Money pays little or no interest, but it is the most liquid of all financial assets. Liquidity confers certain advantages. It puts one in a position to exploit speculative opportunities or handle financial emergencies. To offset the advantages of liquidity, stocks and bonds pay dividends and higher interest. The danger of a liquidity trap occurs when interest rates reach very low levels, probably lower than 1 percent. Unusually low interest rates of this order occurred in the United States during the 1930s, and again in Japan in the 1990s. Extremely low interest rates, coupled with fear of deflation, makes bank balances a highly attractive financial asset compared to much less liquid stocks and bonds. Low interest rates involve the expectation that interest rates will be higher in the future. Investors do not want to lock in a low interest rate by purchasing longer term financial assets when interest rates are low.

The practical significance of a liquidity trap is that it leaves the monetary authority powerless to stimulate the economy by increasing the money supply. The main ingredient of a monetary stimulus is the purchase of government bonds with newly printed money. Called "open-market operations," this action makes the bond market more of a seller's market, meaning bond sellers can sell bonds at lower expected yields. In other words, interest rates fall. In a liquidity trap, the preference for holding bank balances over bonds becomes so strong that open-market operations can no longer reduce interest rates. Falling interest rates no longer accompany above average growth in the money supply.

As a recession unfolds, the market for used capital goods is likely to see severe deflation, which will undercut the prices of new capital goods. Businesses become hesitant to purchase capital goods if they come to expect that capital goods can be purchased at lower prices in the future. Falling demand for finished goods further undermines the willingness to purchase capital goods. With the liquidity trap acting as a floor under interest rates, open-market operations cannot push interest rates low enough to stem the tide of falling investment spending. The economy sinks deeper into recession.

The cure for a liquidity trap involves a high level of government deficit spending to compensate for the absence of business investment spending. In the 1990s, the Japanese government baulked at enlarging the public debt on the scale needed to lift Japan out of the liquidity trap. The Japanese economy languished in recession during much of the 1990s.

See also: Open Market Operations

References

Auerbach, Alan J., and Maurice Obstfeld. "The Case for Open-Market Purchases in a Liquidity Trap." *American Economic Review,* vol. 95, no. 1 (March 2005): 110–138.

Colander, David, and Edward Gamber. 2006. *Macroeconomics.*

Hanes, Christopher. "The Liquidity Trap and U.S. Interest Rates in the 1930s." *Journal of Money, Credit, and Banking,* vol. 38, no. 1 (February 2006): 163–194.

LIQUOR MONEY

Perhaps some measure of the importance of stimulants and depressants to civilization can be seen in the use of these goods as money. Stimulants such as coffee, tobacco, and cocoa beans have served as money, and alcohol—a depressant—has also fulfilled the functions of money in some societies.

During the 19th century, gin circulated as money in Nigeria. A bishop reported that it was impossible to buy food in parts of the Nigerian Delta, unless one could offer gin in payment.

Bottles of gin changed hands for years, eluding human consumption. Members of a commission on native races, visiting the home of a chief in the central province, saw a stockpile of cases of gin, some cases exceeding 30 years of age. Gin functioned as a store of value, with chiefs holding large stocks of gin as a treasure. Gin owed part of its popularity as a form of wealth to the government's practice of steadily raising the taxes on imported spirits, rendering domestic stocks more valuable. Although there is no evidence that prices were fixed in gin, signifying gin as a standard of value, gin served as a medium of exchange and store of value. The government banned the importation of spirits during World War I, ending the use of gin money and opening a period of a silver currency shortage.

In Australia, rum served as the medium of exchange of choice during the late 18th and early 19th centuries, a time in Australian history known as the "period of the rum currency." Metallic currency was in short supply, a common problem among remote colonies, including the American colonies along the eastern seaboard. Adding to the currency shortage in Australia was the thinking among British authorities that a convict colony did not need to be provided with money. Trade brought in a limited number of Spanish dollars that were used to pay for imports, and rum could be found in the cargo of every ship that came into port.

Rum met the need for a domestic medium of exchange in Australia. Farmers sold their produce for rum, workers expected to be paid in rum, convicts performed additional work for payment in rum, and law enforcement authorities offered rewards in rum for the apprehension of criminals. Rum functioned better as a medium of exchange than as a store of value. Its value fluctuated with the size of the last shipment, and its owners often fell prey to the temptation to drink it, rather than save it to buy other goods. Although Europeans accepted rum in payment for goods and wages, there is no evidence that the aborigines accepted rum in payment, unlike the American Indians who were reported to have had a fondness for whiskey.

Beer has found a place among the ranks of currencies. Some tribes in Uganda are reported to have made payments in homemade beer, and tribal workers to have accepted beer in payment of wages. The consecration of a goat or the manufacture of a shield cost a pot of beer, and the barber charged a pot of beer and one chicken. There is no evidence that these tribes used beer as a store of value, but there is some evidence in Angola that during the 1980s imported beer served as a store of value.

Some might expect liquor money to challenge the physical and moral strength of a society in ways that other currencies would not. Many societies have held up objects of reverence as money, such as whales' teeth on the Fiji Islands, or even gold and silver in ancient Western societies. In Angola, the cynicism of war may deserve some credit for the use of imported beer as money. Also, colonial domination by other cultures may be a factor in the use of liquor money in Australia and Nigeria.

See also: Beer Standard of Marxist Angola, Commodity Monetary Standard

References
Einzig, Paul. 1966. *Primitive Money*.

Shann, E. O. G. 1948. *An Economic History of Australia*.

LIVERPOOL ACT OF 1816 (ENGLAND)

The Liverpool Act of 1816 officially put the United Kingdom on the gold standard and provided for a subsidiary silver coinage to complement the gold coinage and banknotes that dominated the British money supply. It gave silver a role to play in a monetary system in which the monetary standard was defined in terms of gold.

During the 18th century, Great Britain was technically on a bimetallic standard, but the market price of silver stood above the mint price for most of that era, and consequently no silver was brought to the mint for coinage. Great Britain had in practice settled into a gold standard, and silver coins were in short supply. After 1785, the market price of silver tumbled, and silver flowed to the mint in large amounts for coinage, threatening to upset an unofficial gold standard that met with the approval of the British government. Parliament hastily enacted legislation that prohibited the mint from purchasing silver for coinage, circumventing the possibility that silver would oust gold as the predominant monetary metal. By 1797, the financial stringencies of war with Revolutionary France had forced Great Britain onto an inconvertible paper standard that lasted until 1821, encompassing the period of the Napoleonic Wars. As pressure mounted for a return to the gold standard, a complementary movement gathered strength to reform the silver coinage.

As early as 1798, the government had appointed the Committee of the Privy Council on the State of the Coinage, but the committee failed to reach quick agreement and chose not to make recommendations until the war ended. In 1816, the committee made its report, recommending the coinage of both gold and silver, but also recommending that the monetary standard be defined in terms of gold only, thus officially ratifying a century-old gold standard. The committee's recommendations left the weight and denominations of gold coins unchanged.

The committee recommended a return to silver coins, but only as a subsidiary coinage. Silver coins were to be regarded as representative coins, legal tender for payments of no more than 40 shillings. The committee recommended that the mint purchase silver for 62 shillings per pound, but coin the silver at a rate of 66 shillings per pound. That is, the face value of the silver coins struck from a pound of silver was equal to 66 shillings. The committee hoped that the slight increase in face value per unit of silver weight would make the melting down and export of silver coins unprofitable. Also, the remaining silver content, which was still significant, would discourage counterfeiters.

The government adopted the committee's recommendations without delay in the Liverpool Act of 1816. This act made silver coins an important component of the British money supply until 1947, when the United Kingdom removed all precious metal content from its "silver" coinage. Beginning in 1947, British silver coinage has been composed of cupronickel alloy, a copper and nickel alloy.

See also: Bank Restriction Act of 1797, Gold Standard

References
Chown, John F. 1994. *A History of Money*.

Feavearyear, Sir Albert. 1963. *The Pound Sterling*.

Jastram, Roy W. 1981. *Silver: The Restless Metal*.

LOMBARD BANKS

Lombard banks were banks that accepted deposits of goods and issued credits on account. These credits could pass from one person's account to another's as a medium of exchange. The term "Lombard" probably came from the importance of Italian bankers in the early history of the London financial market, sometimes referred to as Lombard Street, just as Wall Street signifies the financial center of New York. In early English history, "Lombard" was another name for "Italian." According to *Merriam-Webster's Collegiate Dictionary,* "Lombard," broadly speaking, can refer to a banker or moneylender.

In 1661, Francis Cradocke published a pamphlet, *Wealth Rediscovered,* in which he proposed the establishment of banks secured by things other than precious metals or financial assets. Among the commodities he advanced as possible securities were jewels, "rich pictures or hangings," silks, iron, sugar, wines, tobacco, and land. He recommended dividing the kingdom into a hundred districts, each of which would have a "standing and constant Bank or Registry" that registered all lands, houses, and rents, and granted credit on the basis of land, goods, or pawns.

In 1676, Robert Murray published *A Proposal for the Advancement of Trade,* a proposal for a Lombard banking scheme, in which he argued for the establishment of a "Bank and Lombard united." Under his plan, people would deposit their "dead stock" in magazines, and receive credit on

William Petty, 17th-century British economist. (The Print Collector)

account that could be exchanged as money. He recommended awarding credit on account up to "two-thirds or three-fourths of their value according to the quality thereof." In explaining the credit on account, Murray explained that:

> [N]o more is required than what is already practised in Banks here and abroad, where men deposite Money and obtain the Bank-Credit, which generally passeth in Receipts and Payments without the real issuing of Money, the Money remaining as a Pawn or Ground of Security in the Cash-Chest, or else imployed by the Banker to his own Benefit. (Richards, 1929, 101)

The most famous economist of the era, William Petty, put in a good word for Lombard banks in his *Treatise of Taxes and Contributions* (1662). He wrote, "If public Loan Banks, Lombards, or Banks of Credit upon deposited Plate, Jewel, Cloth, Wooll, Silke, Leather, Linnen,

Mettals, and other durable Commodities were erected, I cannot apprehend how there could be above one-tenth part of the Law-suits and Writings as now there are" (Hull, 1963, 26). Lombard banks were sometime called "Banks of Credit."

In 1682, the city of London established the Bank of the City of London, which acted primarily as a Lombard bank. Despite the noble mission of the bank, which was to pay down the city's debt to the Orphans' Fund, the experiment collapsed suddenly.

Lombard banks were a hybrid of pawnshops and deposit banks. Unlike pawnshops of today, Lombard banks issued credits that could circulate as money, adding to the money supply. Although pawnshops, called "Lombards," had a long history, it is not clear that Lombard banks of the sort proposed in the 17th century ever developed far beyond the theory stage. Nevertheless, the Bank of England, created by an act of Parliament in 1694, was authorized to conduct a pawnbroker's business, reflecting the influence of Lombard banking schemes at the time.

See also: Bank, Bank of England, Land Bank System

References

Hull, Charles Henry, ed. 1963. *The Economic Writings of Sir. William Petty.*

Nevin, Edward, and E. W. Davis. 1970. *The London Clearing Banks.*

Richards, R. D. 1929. *The Early History of Banking in England.*

LONDON INTERBANK OFFERED RATE

The London Interbank Offered Rate (LIBOR) is the interest rate at which large, internationally active banks can borrow funds from other banks in the London interbank market. The British Bankers Association (BBA) reports the rate daily, based on a filtered average of the world's most creditworthy banks' interbank deposit rate for large loans. The LIBOR is the world's main benchmark interest rates, the basis for setting interest rates on short-term interest loans and deposits. It is the lowest rate of interest at which the world's most creditworthy borrowers may borrow funds. Many adjustable-rate mortgages in the United States are tied to the LIBOR.

The LIBOR is set everyday in 10 different currencies and 15 different maturities (Mollenkamp, June 2008). Each currency has a panel of banks whose borrowing costs determine the LIBOR for that currency. The BBA decides the composition of the panel of banks. The LIBOR is fixed each day at 11:00 a.m. London time. Every day, the BBA surveys the members of each panel, asking them the interest rates they must pay for borrowing "reasonable amounts" in a particular currency and maturity at 11:00 a.m. GMT (Michaud and Upper, 2008). The maturities on the unsecured deposits range from overnight to one year. The BBA counts on the banks to supply accurate information. One European central bank, the Swiss National Bank, uses the LIBOR as a target in monetary policy. In May 2008, the Swiss National aimed at maintaining a Swiss franc LIBOR rate of 2.75 percent for a three-month deposit (Wall Street Journal, May 2008).

Payments on $90 trillion in dollar-denominated mortgages, corporate debt, and financial contracts are indexed directly with the LIBOR. Interest payments on this debt fluctuate in step with the LIBOR (Mollenkamp and Whitehouse, May 29).

The LIBOR became a focal point of attention as the subprime crisis deepened in the United States. Normally, the three-month unsecured LIBOR remained barely above the rate at which commercial banks borrow from central banks. In November 2007, the gap between the LIBOR and the U.S. federal funds rate reached half a percentage point, an unusually high gap. The U.S. federal funds rate is a Federal Reserve–managed interest rate at which U.S. commercial banks borrow funds from each other overnight. Not since Y2K had the gaps between the LIBOR rate and central bank-regulated rates grown so large. The stickiness of the LIBOR kept interest rates high on many loans and adjustable-rate mortgages just as central banks were trying to lower interest rates.

As central banks struggled against financial crisis, critics began lodging complaints against the LIBOR. One problem cited asked whether the LIBOR on dollar loans attached too much weight to European banks in light of widespread use of the benchmark rate in the United States. Of the 16 banks composing the LIBOR panel for dollar loans, only three were U.S. banks (Mollenkamp, June 2008). Ten members of the panel were European banks. Another problem cited related to the accuracy of the data supplied by the panel banks. The quoted interest rates received by the BBA are nonbinding. No one expects a credit transaction to take place. Therefore, the banks enjoy some leeway in giving less than accurate quotes to engage in some strategic misrepresentation. The BBA compensates for strategically misleading quotes by ignoring quotes regarded as atypical, removing the highest and lowest quartiles of the quote distribution, and averaging the remaining quotes.

To narrow the gap between the LIBOR rate and the central bank-controlled rates, central banks began loaning more money against a broader range of collateral and against a wider group of financial institutions. Normally, central banks only make loans to commercial banks holding retail deposits, and only accept as collateral government bonds. The tendency of the three-month LIBOR to remain stubbornly high in the face of monetary easing reflected the widespread fear of bank failures. LIBOR deposits are unsecured.

In 2008, the LIBOR rose even higher after the BBA opened an investigation into the possibility that banks were reporting interest rates below what they were actually paying in hopes of appearing stronger than they were (Mollenkamp, June 2008). Among banks, ability to borrow at a low interest rate is a sign of health. It appeared that what observers saw as an elevated LIBOR should have been even higher. To ease concerns, in June 2008, the BBA announced changes to the calculation of the LIBOR. One change increases the number of banks reporting borrowing costs for calculation of the LIBOR. Another change involves plans to police the accuracy of quotes received from banks more carefully. The BBA also announced that it had under consideration a plan to establish new rates that would reflect differences in borrowing cost between European and U.S. banks.

See also: Federal Open Market Committee

References

Forsyth, Randall W. "Calling London: The Fed Takes Aim at Libor." *Barron's*, vol. 88, no. 18, p. M8.

Michaud, Francois-Louis, and Christian Upper. "What Drives Interbank Rates?

Evidence for the Libor Panel." *BIS Quarterly Review* (March 2008): 47–58.

Mollenkamp, Carrick. "U.K. Bankers to Alter Libor to Address Rate Doubts." *Wall Street Journal* (Eastern Edition) June 11, 2008, p. C1.

Mollenkamp, Carrick, and Mark Whitehouse. "Study Casts Doubt on Key Rate; WSJ Analysis Suggest Banks May Have Reported Flawed Interest Data for Libor." *Wall Street Journal* (Eastern Edition), May 29, 2008, p. A1.

Wall Street Journal (Eastern Edition). "Swiss Bank Weighs Its Use of Libor." May 29, 2008, p. A12.

M

MACMILLAN COMMITTEE

See: Bank of England

MARAVEDIS

See: Vellon

MASSACHUSETTS BAY COLONY MINT

The Massachusetts Bay Colony boasted of the first and only mint in the American colonies before the American Revolution. The colonial economies fought against a currency shortage that acted as a brake on economic activity. The largest component of the circulating coin in the colonies was the Spanish dollar or pieces of eight, but all currency tended to leave America faster than it came in because of the huge need for imported products from Europe. There were no local coins per se, and the mint of Massachusetts was erected on the initiative of the Massachusetts colonial government to meet the need for a colonial currency.

The mint was erected in 1652 and remained in operation for 30 years, eventually falling victim to the royal displeasure of the English crown. Apparently, it was subject to the orders of the General Court of Massachusetts. The first order issued on May 27, 1652, said:

> That all persons whatsoeuer have libertie to bring into the mint house, at Boston, all bullion, plate, or Spanish coyne, there to be melted and brought to the alloy of sterling siluer by John Hull, master of the sd. Mint, & his sworne officers, & by him to be coyned into twelue pence, six pence, & three pence peeces. (Watson, 1970, 3)

These silver coins were of small denominations for the time.

The mint house was a square building constructed of wood, measuring 15 feet on each side, and 10 feet high. The coins were legal tender in the area under the jurisdiction of the General Court.

The Massachusetts mint debased its coins about 22 percent relative to the

275

silver content of English coins of the same denominations. The officials of Massachusetts approved of this debasement in an effort the keep the coins from going to Europe in payment for American imports of foreign goods. The European merchants, however, simply raised the prices of their products in Massachusetts coin, and there remained the problem of hard specie leaving the American colonies.

The English government complained about debasement of the coins, contending that coinage should be uniform throughout the empire. To be sure, the English government occasionally changed the silver content of its own coins, but was unwilling that the silver content could vary among colonies. It also objected to the coinage of copper or other inferior metals that would solely support internal trade.

The operation of the mint contributed to the friction that led the English government to revoke the first charter of the Massachusetts Bay Colony in 1684, which was the last year that the mint operated. Other colonies asked for permission to establish mints, but the English government refused. The coins from the mint continued to circulate in the American colonies until after the Articles of Confederation authorized individual states to establish mints. The constraints that a coin shortage placed on the colonial economy helped lift the discontent of the colonists to a revolutionary pitch.

See also: Massachusetts Bay Colony Paper Issue

References

Nettels, Curtis P. 1934. *The Money Supply of the American Colonies before 1720.*

Terranova, Anthony, 1994. *Massachusetts Silver Coinage.*

Watson, David. 1970. *History of American Coinage.*

MASSACHUSETTS BAY COLONY PAPER ISSUE

The colonial government of the Massachusetts Bay Colony has the dubious distinction of being the first to issue paper money in America. The first hesitant steps toward the issuance of paper money occurred in 1676 when the colonial government raised a loan from provincial merchants and issued treasury receipts as an acknowledgment of debt, expecting these receipts to circulate as currency. Public lands secured the loan.

In 1690, the Massachusetts Assembly enacted legislation that authorized the government to issue paper money. The immediate circumstance that forced the hand of the assembly was the need to pay soldiers returning from a war expedition in Canada. Paper money is similar to many other inventions in that pressures of war often serve to speed up its development and acceptance, a theme that can be explored into the 20th century.

Although war expenditures provided the immediate pretext for the paper money issue, broader concerns helped create a political environment receptive to the issuance of paper money. In 1686, the governor's council cited the "great decay of trade and obstructions to manufactures and commerce in this country, and multiplicity of debts and suits thereon, principally occasioned by the present scarcity of coin" (Nettels, 1934). William Penn later commented that "the want of money to circulate trade . . . has put Boston herself upon thinking of tickets to supply the want of coin" (Nettels, 1934). The law of 1690 also mentioned "the present poverty and calamities of the country, and through a scarcity of money, the want of an adequate measure of commerce" (Nettels, 1934).

Historically, paper money has either taken the form of banknotes, precursors to the modern Federal Reserve Note in the United States, or bills issued directly by government treasuries. The Massachusetts paper money was of the latter variety. The government issued the paper money and levied taxes that could be paid with the paper money. As long as the paper money issue was commensurate with the tax levy, the money maintained its value.

The first bills issued by the Massachusetts colonial government were not legal tender for all debts. The legislation of 1692 specified that the bills be accepted "in all payments equivalent to money," effectively making the bills legal tender. Bills issued between 1702 and 1712 were not legal tender, although after 1710 these bills could be used to stay out of debtors' prison until legal-tender currency could be obtained.

The Massachusetts paper money held its value reasonably well until 1713. Bills issued in 1709 were not redeemable in taxes until four years beyond the issue date, and the period of redemption for paper money issued between 1710 and 1712 was postponed for six or seven years. During the interim between issuance and redemption, the bills earned 5 percent interest, but many more bills were issued than were needed to pay taxes. The bills depreciated in value, and hard specie flowed out in foreign trade. In 1716, the assembly established a public bank that issued banknotes secured by land.

In 1748, over two million pounds of paper money were in circulation when Massachusetts received a large reimbursement from Great Britain for war expenses, and used the proceeds to redeem paper money at about 20 percent of its face value. Gresham's law that bad money drives out good money had played out its ruthless logic in Massachusetts as paper money virtually displaced the specie. After 1720, the British government began to restrict the ability of colonial governments to issue paper money with legal-tender status. Experiences of the colonial governments with paper money led members of the Constitutional Convention to endow the Congress of the federal government with the sole privilege to coin money.

See also: Land Bank System, Tabular Standard of Massachusetts Bay Colony

References

Galbraith, John Kenneth. 1975. *Money, Whence It Came, Where It Went.*

Hepburn, A. Barton. 1924/1967. *A History of Currency in the United States.*

Nettels, Curtis P. 1934. *The Money Supply of the American Colonies before 1720.*

MEDICI BANK

The Medici Bank, perhaps the most famous bank of Renaissance Italy, rose to the top rank of European financial institutions during the 15th century. It accepted time deposits, the sum of which was several times larger than the invested capital, and was a lending institution. This was unlike some of the exchange banks of the time that were primarily involved in fund transfers associated with international trade. The Medici Bank was the chief bank for the Curia, and it had branches in the major cities of Italy, as well as London, Lyons, Geneva, Bruges, and Avignon.

In Renaissance Italy, openly charging interest (usury) was prohibited, but interest charges were hidden in bills of exchange through which foreign currency was purchased for delivery at a future date. Profit was at the mercy of the foreign exchange markets. What was called a "dry exchange" involved no transfer of goods or foreign exchange and effectively guaranteed interest to the lender. In 1429, dry exchanges were outlawed in Florence, but the law was suspended at least temporarily in 1435, right after the Medici became the de facto, if not legal rulers, of Florence. The Medici Bank was organized as a partnership with the Medici family being the largest investor in the parent company and the parent company being the largest investor in the branch partnerships. The parent company functioned like a modern holding company. The system of branch banks was organized such that one branch could be declared independent by rearranging accounts. Such arrangements protected the parent bank from the bankruptcy of individual branches due to localized economic difficulties.

Members of the Medici family entered the Florentine banking business in the latter 1300s. In 1393, Giovanni di Bicci de' Medici (1360–1429) took ownership of the Roman branch of a bank owned by one of his Florentine cousins. He removed the headquarters of his bank to Florence in 1397, the official founding date for the Medici Bank. At the time Rome was a source of funds, whereas Florence offered a better market for making loans. By 1402, the Medici Bank had opened a branch bank in Venice, another important outlet of investment opportunities. By then the bank boasted a total of 17 employees at its headquarters in Florence, five of whom were clerks.

In the 14th and 15th centuries, wool and cloth industries were the export mainspring of the Florentine economy. In 1402, the Medici Bank loaned 3,000 florins (nearly one-third of its original capital) to finance a Medici family part-nership to produce woolen cloth. The year 1408 saw the establishment of a second and more successful shop for producing woolen cloth. In addition to banking, the Medici traded wool, cloth, alum, spices, olive oil, silk stuffs, brocades, jewelry, silver plate, citrus fruit, and other commodities, diversifying their risks by investing in a range of ventures.

In 1429, Giovanni di Medici died, passing the management of the bank into the hands of his eldest son, Cosimo. Under Cosimo's leadership, the Medici Bank became the largest banking house of its time. In 1435, the bank opened a branch in Geneva, the first branch beyond the Alps. The Medici opened another woolen cloth manufacturing shop and acquired a silk shop in 1438. The Medici Bank opened a branch in Bruges in 1439, and branches in London and Avignon in 1446. The Milan branch was opened in 1452 or 1453. The Geneva branch was transferred to Lyons in 1464.

When Cosimo died in 1464, the bank had passed its peak. An invalid son, Piero de' Medici, assumed management of the bank. According to Machiavelli, he began calling in loans, causing a contraction in credit and numerous business failures. Piero died in 1469. Piero's son, Lorenzo the Magnificent, was a great statesman. He had a humanistic education without business training or experience. He turned the management of the bank over to managers, and the bank gradually lost ground. On Lorenzo's death in 1492, his son, Piero di Lorenzo, assumed control of the Medici political and business interests in Florence. Piero had neither business nor political acumen, and in 1494 the Medici were ousted from Florence. The bank, already tottering on bankruptcy, was confiscated, and was not successful under its new owners.

See also: Bank of Venice, Florentine Florin, House of St. George, Quattrini Affair

References

Bullard, Melissa M. 1980. *Filippo Strozzi and the Medici: Favor and Finance in Sixteenth-Century Florence and Rome.*

Goldtwaite, Richard A. 1995. *Banks, Palaces, and Entrepreneurs in Renaissance Florence.*

Roover, Raymond de. 1966. The Rise and Decline of the Medici Bank: 1397–1494.

MEXICAN PESO

See: De a Ocho Reales

MEXICAN PESO CRISIS OF 1994

The sharp depreciation of the Mexican peso in December 1994 marked one of the swiftest macroeconomic reversals in the history of developing economies and currency crises. President Ernesto Zedillo had barely been in office three weeks when, on December 19, 1994, his administration asked the Banco de Mexico to undertake roughly 15 percent devaluation of the peso, adjusting the pegged exchange rate from 3.45 pesos per dollar to 4.00 pesos per dollar (Sharma, 2001). It was a modest devaluation, but it undercut the confidence of foreign investors and touched off a wild speculative run against the peso. On December 22, 1994, the Banco of Mexico, unable to defend the peso against stampeding, panic-stricken foreign investors, allowed the peso to float. The peso immediately sank another 15 percent (Sharma, 2001). By February 16, 1995, the peso had depreciated 42 percent against the U.S. dollar (Torres, February 1995). The peso reached its

nadir at 7.65 pesos per U.S. dollar (Sharma, 2001).

The outgoing President Carlos Salinas and the soon-to-be President Zedillo met on November 20, 1994, to discuss the currency situation. The Friday before, Mexico had lost $1.7 billion in a run on the peso. The two leaders agreed that devaluation on the order of 10 percent was needed, but the outgoing officials refused to devalue the currency on their watch (Wessel, July 1995).

The peso crisis caught many observers and investors by surprise. Mexico had become the darling of Wall Street. Mexico's economic policy seemed to have all the right ingredients. It emphasized privatization and deregulation of state-owned enterprises, restrictive monetary and fiscal policies, and a pegged exchange rate relative to the U.S. dollar. The ratification of the North American Free Trade Agreement (NAFTA) in January 1994 opened Mexico's economy to the largest consumer market in the world. Between 1989 and 1994, Mexico's gross domestic product (GDP) growth averaged 3.9 percent (Sharma, 2001). Mexico's inflation rate, which raged as high as 160 percent in 1987, sank to single-digit territory in 1993 (Sharma, 2001). Government indebtedness as a percent of GDP shrank from 15 percent in 1987 to 1 percent in 1992 and 1993 (Sharma, 2001). Between 1987 and 1994, government spending as a percent of GDP shriveled from 44 percent to 24.6 per cent (Sharma, 2001). In February 1994, Mexico's foreign exchange reserves stood at $28 billion, well above the $6.3 billion level held in 1989 (Sharma, 2001). With the dawn of NAFTA, Wall Street saw no limits to Mexico's potential.

In hindsight, one economic statistic signaled trouble. Mexico's current

After the government's announcement that it had effectively devalued the peso, a Mexican man checks the peso exchange rate against the dollar at a Mexico City exchange house on December 20, 1994, in Mexico City. (AP Photo/Jose Luis Magana)

account deficit steadily climbed from $6 billion in 1989 to $20 billion by the end of 1993 (Sharma, 2001). Mexico's imports were growing much faster than its exports. Current account deficits reflect either a high level of government deficit spending, high levels of private investment spending relative to savings, or some combination. In 1994, government deficit spending in Mexico was minimal, and the high level of private investment spending seemed to reflect Mexico's bright future under NAFTA. Foreign portfolio investments in Mexican stocks and short-term bonds made possible the high level of investment spending. It also left Mexico vulnerable to a sudden outflow of foreign capital.

In 1994, foreign investors began to get jittery over the size of Mexico's current account deficit. Mexico tamed inflation, but did not eradicate it. Under a pegged exchange rate, inflation increases the prices of domestic goods, but does not affect the price of imported foreign goods unless the peg is adjusted. Mexico failed to adjust the pegged exchange rate to compensate for domestic inflation, encouraging Mexico's consumers to purchase more imported goods at the expense of domestically produced goods. As long as foreigners exhibited a strong appetite for Mexican stocks and bonds, the Mexican government felt no pressure to devalue its currency. The peso appeared to be in high demand at the current exchange rate.

In 1994, the strong foreign demand for portfolio investments in Mexico began to diminish over worries about Mexico's rising current account deficit. Rising current account deficits often lead to a devaluation of a currency. If a currency depreciates 25 percent, foreign investors immediately see the value of their investment depreciate by 25 percent.

Part of the attraction of Mexican stocks and bonds had to do with low interest rates in the United States. Throughout 1993, the U.S. federal funds rate remained at 3 percent. In 1994, the Federal Reserve System started raising the federal funds rate, pushing it up to 5.5 percent by November 1994 (Sharma, 2001). As interest rates rose in the United States, investors became less willing to chase higher interest rates in developing countries and emerging markets. When the Mexican government announced a devaluation of the peso in December 1994, foreign investors decided it was time to get out of Mexico.

After the peso crisis, Mexico's economy sank into steep recession. Inflation soared as devaluation lifted the prices of imported goods. In the United States, President Bill Clinton put together a nearly $50 billion rescue package (Greenwald and Carney, 1995). Without the rescue package, the Mexican government would have defaulted on a large amount of dollar-denominated government bonds. (In 1994, the Mexican government had started issuing dollar-denomniated bonds to ease investor fears about devaluation of the peso.) The rescue package helped calm markets and limited the damage inflicted on other Latin American countries.

See also: East Asian Financial Crisis, Currency Crises

References

Greenwald, John, and James Carney. "Don't Panic: Here Comes Bailout." *Time*, February 13, 1995, pp. 34–37.

Sharma, Shalendra. "The Missed Lessons of the Mexican Peso Crisis." *Challenge*, vol. 44, no. 1 (January/February 2001): 56–89.

Torres, Craig. "Mexican Markets Are Hit by Fresh Blows—Stock Index Sags as Rates on Treasury Bills Soar; Firm announces Default." *Wall Street Journal* (Eastern Edition) February 16 1995, p. A11.

Wessel, David, Paul Carroll, and Thomas Vogel Jr. "Peso Surprise: How Mexico's Crisis Ambushed Top Minds in Officialdom, Finance—As Pressure to Devalue Rose, Finance Chief Refused; Then It Was Done Badly—The Hot Money Turns Cold." *Wall Street Journal* (Eastern Edition, New York) July 6, 1995, p. A1.

MILLED-EDGE COINAGE

A milled-edge coin has various forms of graining, ribbing, or serration around its circumference. In an Order of Council of May 1661, Charles II, king of England, set forth that all coin was to be struck as soon as possible by machinery, with grained or lettered edges, to stop clipping, cutting, and counterfeiting. As the order reveals, the motivation for the serrated edges lay in the search for a means to discourage clippers, who removed bits of precious metal from the edges of coins, diminishing the metal content of coins without rendering them completely unacceptable in exchange. Hammered coins minted by hand produced coins of irregular shape that invited clipping.

Mechanized minting began in Italy, which may also have been the birthplace of the milled edge. Mechanized minting passed from Italy to France and Germany, and then to Spain and England. In 1553, Eloy Mestrell fled from Paris, where he was engineer to the mint, and arrived in London, bringing knowledge of the methods of a horse-powered mill that turned out uniform blank coins, stamped with uniform images, and a milled-edge circumference. The machine for milling the edge made use of counterrotating hand screws. Mestrell's coins that survived are of impressive quality, but he faced strong opposition from established moneyers. After an inquiry yielded adverse findings, Mistrell was relieved of his duties at the mint, and six years later he was hanged for counterfeiting.

The Paris mint again lost talent to London in 1625 when Nicholas Briot, chief engraver in Paris, left France out of frustration over the opposition of the established moneyers. Between 1631 and 1640, Briot minted silver coins with milled edges, but hammered coins still dominated English coinage. In 1649, Pierre Blondeau, an engineer from the Paris mint, arrived in London. Blondeau had developed an inexpensive and practical method of producing the milled edge, prompting Louis III of France to ban the minting of hammered coins in 1639. In England, Blondeau minted a token quantity of milled-edge coins. Apparently, both Briot and Blondeau returned to France after the Commonwealth government refused to progress beyond the experimental stage with the new methods of coinage.

After the Restoration returned Charles II to the throne, he recalled Blondeau from France and awarded him a 21-year contract to develop and apply methods for making milled and engrained edges. The contract for turning out blanks and stamping fell to three Flemish brothers, John, Joseph, and Phillip Roettier. In 1663, the Tower mint produced a £1 coin that signaled the beginning of mechanized minting in England.

Methods for minting coins with the serrated or corrugated edge also passed from France to Spain. In the English colonies and early United States, the Spanish milled dollar was among the most popular and widely circulated coins, passing as legal tender for brief periods. The Spanish milled dollar established the dollar as the principal unit of currency in the United States.

The practice of milled-edge coinage continues to the present day. In the United States, coins in denominations larger than a nickel have milled edges.

References

Challis, C. E., ed. 1992 *A New History of the Royal Mint.*

Craig, J. 1953. *The Mint: A History of the London Mint from A.D. 287 to 1948.*

Feavearyear, Sir Albert. 1963. *The Pound Sterling: A History of English Money*, 2nd ed.

MISSING MONEY

The case of missing money refers to the fact that more than half of U.S. currency in circulation is held abroad by foreigners. The money is missing in the sense that the currency leaves the United States for foreign destinations through underground and illegal activities.

A study of $100 bills illustrates the magnitude of the missing money. About two-thirds of the outstanding currency in circulation is in $100 bills, yet these bills play a small part in daily transactions. Cash registers do not have a slot for $100 bills, and automatic teller machines (ATM) do not issue them. Instead, $100 bills rank among the important exports of the United States.

In May 2006, the stock of U.S. currency stood at $742 billion, averaging about $2500 per person. By these numbers, each family with two adults and two children should be holding about $10,000 in currency. Surveys have shown that individual holdings of currency average much closer to $100 per person. The amount of missing currency therefore approximates $2,400 per person, no small amount of money (Porter and Judson, 1996). Retailers and other businesses hold currency to conduct daily transactions but only a small fraction of the $2,400 per person that is missing. It is estimated that businesses account for less than $100 per person of the missing money. The underground economy, including the informal transactions aimed at dodging taxes, probably accounts for slightly more than the legitimate business sector. Combining the currency holdings of legitimate businesses and the underground economy still puts the average currency holding at less than $225 per person (Porter and Judson, 1996).

Studies have uncovered that a large share of the missing money is held in foreign countries. Anywhere between 55 and 70 percent of U.S. outstanding currency is held in foreign countries. During the first half of the 1990s, roughly 75 percent of the increase in U.S. currency emigrated abroad (Porter and Judson, 1996).

Residents of foreign countries often see holding U.S. currency as protection against domestic inflation. In the early 1990s, hyperinflation plagued several countries that had been either part of the Soviet Union or a member of the Eastern Bloc. Between 1988 and 1995, about half of U.S. currency that went overseas found its way to Europe, particularly to Russia and the other nations of Eastern Europe (Porter and Judson, 1996). In addition, residents of a foreign country may hold U.S. currency in case they must flee oppression and want to take some of their wealth with them. Before U.S. currency became popular in Russia, Latin America held a large share of U.S. overseas currency. In foreign countries, U.S. currency does not circulate as a medium of exchange or serve as a unit of account, but it does serve as a store of value.

The U.S. government does not regard the large foreign holdings of U.S. currency as a problem. Outstanding currency is a liability on the Federal Reserve System's balance sheet. It is an interest free loan to the Federal Reserve and, indirectly, to the U.S. government. The popularity of the U.S. dollar as a store of value in foreign countries allows the U.S. government to borrow funds interest free. The European Central Bank began issuing 500-euro notes, probably hoping to enjoy some of the advantages the United States receives from the popularity of $100 bills in foreign countries.

References

Brimelow, Peter. "Going Underground." *Forbes*, September 21, 1998, pp. 206–207.

Porter, Richard D., and Ruth A. Judson. "The Location of U.S. Currency: How Much is Abroad?" *Federal Reserve Bulletin*, vol. 82, no. 10 (October 1996): 883–903.

Sprenkle, Case M. "The Case of the Missing Money." *Journal of Economic Perspectives*, vol. 7, no. 4 (Fall 1993): 175–184.

MONDEX SYSTEM

See: Debit Card

MONETARISM

Monetarism is a school of macroeconomic theory emphasizing the causal role of the money stock in aggregate economic fluctuations, and holding that the key to aggregate economic stability lies with a steady, noncyclical growth path in the money supply. The aggregate economic system experiences upswings and downswings manifested in such statistics as the unemployment rate. These cyclical swings are a response to imbalances between the total demand for all goods and services relative to the total supply, as opposed to imbalances between supply and demand in individual markets, such as the market for automobiles.

According to monetarism, the aggregate economic system has strong intrinsic tendencies to gravitate toward a full-employment equilibrium, and these tendencies will assert themselves in the absence of shocks to the money stock growth rate. If the money stock growth rate is stable, the aggregate economic system will mirror that stability. Economists who adhere to the tenets of monetarism are called "monetarists."

In policy terms, "monetarism" means that central bank monetary policy should set target rates of growth of money stock measures and rather single-mindedly pursue those targets. Keynesian monetary policy, the orthodox policy in the 1950s and 1960s, emphasized interest rates as a target of monetary policy, raising interest rates to slow down the economy and reducing interest rates to speed things up. Monetarists contended that the Keynesian policies took the focus off the money stock and replaced it with subjective ideas about what interest rates should be. According to monetarism, financial markets should determine interest rate levels.

Monetarism rose to prominence in the 1970s as inflation began to eclipse unemployment as the most dreaded economic problem. Monetarists contended that the relationship between inflation and money stock growth was virtually a one-to-one relationship, and that money stock growth was feeding the inflation. Monetarists clung to the money stock theory as the sole explanation of inflation, excluding the possible role of government budget deficits, powerful unions, monopolistic corporations, harvest failures, and shortages of key raw materials.

Although restricted money stock growth seemed a plausible antidote against inflation, the first effects of restricted money stock growth were seen in rising unemployment rates rather than falling inflation rates, making the tactic a touchy matter in democratic societies subject to the moods of voters. A president no less conservative than Richard Nixon preferred to give wage and price controls a try rather than put the economy on a prolonged diet of restricted money stock growth.

The decade of the 1980s saw what might be called a monetarist experiment. The governments of Margaret Thatcher in the United Kingdom and President Reagan in the United States imposed strict monetarist policies of restricted money stock growth in an effort to break the back of double-digit inflation. In the United States, the prime interest rate soared to 20 percent, and unemployment reached double-digit levels. Thatcher's policies put the United Kingdom through similar rigors. The tight money policies put these economies through recessions deeper than any economic contraction since the 1930s.

Monetarist policies succeeded in bringing down inflation rates, and unemployment rates began to fall back, suggesting that monetarist policies were succeeding. Nevertheless, in October 1987, stock markets crashed in New York and London, and central banks began increasing money stock growth to reinflate world financial markets. Contrary to monetarists' expectations, the added money stock growth did not trigger another round of inflation. During the 1990s, inflation was less than expected based on money stock growth, casting a bit of doubt on monetarism. Between 1999 and 2005 Japan reported deflation. Japan's deflation persisted in the face of interest rates that stood near 0 percent, further undermining confidence in monetarism.

At the very least it can be said that monetarism brought a stoical quality to economic policy making that was needed to endure the pain of disinflating the economies of the world. Notwithstanding the departure in the 1990s from monetarist policies based on strict, steady growth rates in money stocks, inflation rates have steadily subsided, perhaps reflecting the policy effects of new knowledge gained from the monetarists' theoretical explorations.

See also: Central Bank, Equation of Exchange, Monetary Theory

References

Friedman, Milton. 1969. *The Optimum Quantity of Money, and Other Essays*.

Mankiw, N. Gregory. 1997. *Macroeconomics*, 3rd ed.

McCallum, Bennett T. 1989. *Monetary Economics: Theory and Policy*.

MONETARY AGGREGATES

Monetary aggregates measure the money stock, which is defined as the sum of highly liquid assets that serve either as a medium of exchange, standard of value, or a store of value. Money supply measures in terms of monetary aggregates are necessary because many assets serve the same purpose as currency; for example, checking accounts, savings accounts, and so on. Therefore, operational measures of the money stock must take these assets into consideration.

In the United States, the monetary aggregate denoted "M1" is the most narrowly defined measure of the money stock, and a broader measure, denoted "M2," includes everything in M1 plus additional assets. "M3" is an even broader measure, including everything in M1 and M2 and more.

In the United States, M1 includes all the currency not held by the U.S. Treasury, Federal Reserve Banks, foreign financial institutions, and commercial banks, plus an array of checkable deposits and travelers' checks. Currency included in M1 is the currency circulating as a medium of exchange. Commercial bank vault cash is excluded because it is represented in depositors' accounts, and summing the vault cash with customer checking accounts would be counting those funds twice. The largest share of checkable deposits are called "demand deposits," because the bank owes that money to the depositor on demand, without prior notice or other conditions. Bank customers often call these accounts "checking accounts." Another checkable account is the negotiable order of withdrawal (NOW) account, an interest-bearing account at thrift institutions that resembles a savings account but has checking privileges. Automatic transfer service (ATS) accounts, which automatically transfer funds from an interest-bearing savings account to a checking account as needed, are also included as checkable deposits in M1, as are Credit Union Share Drafts (CUSDs).

Checkable deposits owned by other depository institutions, the U.S. government, foreign banks, and other official institutions are excluded from M1. M1 therefore represents highly liquid assets acceptable as a medium of exchange. Often, cash is preferred over checks for small transactions, but for large transactions checks are preferred over cash.

In the United States, M2 includes everything in M1 plus small repurchase agreements (less than $100,000), money market deposit accounts and money market mutual fund accounts when minimum deposits are less than $50,000, and savings and small time deposits (less than $100,000). A repurchase agreement is an arrangement under which a commercial bank sells a government bond to a large depositor and agrees to buy it back at a higher price in the future, overnight in some cases. It is an underhanded means of paying interest, and grew into prominence when regulations forbade interest rate ceilings on checking accounts. Money market deposit accounts and money market mutual fund accounts require high minimum deposits, pay high interest, and allow only checks written above a certain amount, such as $500. M2 does not include deposits held in tax-exempt retirement accounts, or those owned by the federal government, foreign governments, or commercial banks. M2 embraces assets less liquid than the assets included in M1, but assets that can readily be converted into cash.

The Federal Reserve System ceased reporting statistics on M3 in 2005. Other central banks still report M3 for their currencies. For the United States, M3 included everything in M2 but added large repurchase agreements and time deposits, Eurodollar accounts, large time deposits, and money market mutual fund accounts held by institutions. Eurodollar accounts are accounts owned by U.S. residents at foreign branches of U.S. banks worldwide, and all banking offices in Canada and the United Kingdom. An even broader monetary aggregate is "L." L includes everything in M3 plus short-term treasury bonds, commercial paper, savings bonds, and bankers' acceptances. Commercial paper is an unsecured prom-

ise to pay. It is sold at a discount from a face value and matures in a short time, no more than nine months. Bankers' acceptances, meaning a bank accepts (or guarantees) another firm's promise to pay, provide short-term financing for commercial trade.

See also: Certificate of Deposit, Eurodollars, Federal Reserve System, Money Market Mutual Fund Accounts, Negotiable Order of Withdrawal Accounts

References

Baye, Michael R., and Dennis W. Jansen. 1995. *Money, Banking, and Financial Markets: An Economics Approach.*

Federal Reserve System. 1998 (January). *Federal Reserve Bulletin.*

McCallum, Bennett T. 1989. *Monetary Economics: Theory and Policy.*

MONETARY LAW OF 1803 (FRANCE)

The French Monetary Law of 1803 ratified the franc as the French money of account and established France on a bimetallic system. From the Carolingian monetary reform in the eighth century until the French Revolution, the livre was the money of account in France. Under the Carolingian, system each livre consisted of 20 *sols*, and each sol consisted of 12 *deniers*. These basic provisions of the Law of 1803 were first passed in Calonne's law of 1785, named after a comptroller general of French finances. The chaos of revolution disrupted the implementation of Calonne's law, but on October 7, 1793, France acted on the precedent set by the United States and Russia, and established a decimal monetary system. In 1795, the French revolutionary government changed the name of the money of account from livre, to franc. In 1799, the terms "franc,"

Two-franc coin bearing the likeness of the emperor Napoleon, approximately 1804. (British Museum/Art Resource, NY)

"dixieme," and "centime" replaced "livre," "sol," and "denier" as the official units required in accounting.

The Law of 1803 fixed in law the provisions of Calonne's law, based on a decimal monetary system with the franc as the French monetary unit. The franc had two legal equivalents, one in silver and the other in gold. The law declared that "[f]ive grams of silver, nine-tenths fine, constitute the monetary unit, which retains the name of *franc*." The law also provided that the mint strike silver coins in denominations of a quarter-franc, half-franc, three-quarter franc, 1 franc, 2 francs, and 5 francs.

After declaring the specifications and denominations of the silver franc, the law stated that "[t]here shall be coined gold pieces of twenty *francs* and of 40 *francs*." The 20-franc Napoleon coin weighed 6.45 grams, making a gold franc equal to 0.3225 grams of gold. The defined metal contents of the silver franc and the gold franc established a bimetallic system in which a gram of gold was 15.5 times as valuable as a gram of silver.

Both gold and silver coins were legal tender, and unlike the old livres each coin bore a stamp of its value. Anyone, including a foreigner, was free to bring gold and silver to French mints for coinage. The law specified that:

> The expense of coinage alone can be required of those who shall bring material of gold and silver to the Mint. These charges are fixed at nine francs per kilogramme of gold, and at three francs per kilogramme of silver. When the material shall be below the monetary standard, it shall bear the charges of refining or of separation. (Laughlin, 1968, 313)

Just as the United Kingdom became the headquarters for the gold standard during the 19th century, France became the staunch defender of bimetallism. A bimetallic ratio of between 15 and 16 to 1 continued until the 1870s when the value of silver began to fall significantly, forcing France and other bimetallic countries in Europe off the bimetallic standard in favor of the gold standard. The United State abandoned bimetallism in favor of the gold standard during the same period.

See also: Bimetallism, Decimal System, French Franc, Latin Monetary Union

References

Chown, John. 1994. *A History of Money.*

Laughlin, J. Laurence. 1968. *The History of Bimetallism in the United States.*

Vilar, Pierre. 1976. *A History of Gold and Money, 1450–1920.*

MONETARY MULTIPLIER

The monetary multiplier shows the multiple by which the money stock can expand given an initial infusion of fresh funds into the banking system. A central bank, such as the Federal Reserve System, can infuse additional funds into commercial banks by purchasing government bonds owned by commercial banks or commercial bank customers. The central bank can also loan funds to commercial banks, but purchasing bonds has a more permanent impact.

A customer of a commercial bank sells a bond to the Federal Reserve System, taking the proceeds of the sale and depositing it in an account at the commercial bank. Under a fractional reserve system of banking, the commercial bank has to hold only a fraction of the new deposit, say 20 percent if the legal reserve ratio is 20 percent, and the remainder the commercial bank can lend to a borrowing customer. Whatever amount is loaned out is likely to be deposited in either the bank making the loan, or more likely, in another bank. The bank that receives this second deposit originating from the bank loan only has to keep a fraction of the new deposit, and can lend the remainder. Therefore, a second loan will be made.

The customer that first sold a bond to the Federal Reserve System still has the proceeds of that sale in the form of a bank deposit, and two subsequent bank deposits have been created, causing a magnified expansion of the money supply, the bulk of which is bank deposits. The expansionary process will continue, as the proceeds of a second loan will, in all probability, land in a bank deposit, giving another bank a new deposit from which it can make a loan. Each bank that receives a new deposit must hold a fraction of the new deposits as reserves, and may lend the remainder.

Because each subsequent new deposit is smaller than the previous new deposit, the cumulative expansion of new deposits slows to a halt. The monetary multiplier shows how far bank deposits could theoretically expand under ideal conditions. If the monetary multiplier is five, then an initial infusion of $1,000 of fresh funds into commercial banks could lead to a maximum expansion of bank deposits of $5,000.

The simplest monetary multiplier is calculated by taking the reciprocal of the legal reserve ratio. A legal reserve ratio of 20 percent produces a monetary multiplier of five. This simplest multiplier ignores the possibility that banks may purposely maintain a reserve ratio above the legal reserve ratio, or that some funds loaned out by a bank may leak into circulation, never to be deposited in another bank. In practice, the actual monetary multiplier will be less than the theoretical monetary multiplier based only on the legal reserve ratio. More complicated multipliers incorporate a currency-to-deposit ratio to adjust for the leakage of cash into circulation.

The funds that the Federal Reserve System injects into commercial banks is sometimes called "high-powered money," because a series of commercial banks making loans will multiply that initial injection of funds into a much larger money stock increase. The monetary multiplier also shows that the money supply is not entirely in the hands of the Federal Reserve System, but expands and contracts with the eagerness of commercial banks to make loans, giving the commercial banks as much influence on the money supply as the printing presses at the Bureau of Engraving.

See also: Bank, High-Powered Money, Legal Reserve Ratio

References

McCallum, Bennett T. 1989. *Monetary Economics.*

McConnell, Campbell R., and Stanley L. Brue. 1998. *Economics: Principles, Problems, and Policies*, 14th ed.

MONETARY NEUTRALITY

In economics, the principle of monetary neutrality holds that changes in the circulating money stock leave no lasting impact on the quantity of goods and services produced, unemployment rate, wages measured in real purchasing power, or other indicators of economic prosperity. To understand the concept of monetary neutrality, it helps first to understand what economists mean by real variables. In economics, nominal variables are not adjusted for inflation whereas "real" variables are adjusted for inflation. If the average nominal wage in the United States doubled over a span of time, and prices on average doubled over the same span of time, then economist would say that real wages remained constant. Wages doubled, but prices doubled. The result was that the real purchasing power of wages remained constant, and the standard of living of wage earners saw no change. The same principle applies to other variables. If the money supply doubles, but prices double, the real money supply remains constant. The real wage equals the nominal wage divided by the average level of prices. The real money supply equals the nominal money supply divided by the average level of prices. The "real interest rate" equals the contracted or quoted interest rate minus the inflation rate.

The principle of monetary neutrality claims that even the real money supply will not be impacted by a change in the nominal money supply. If monetary authorities double the money supply, then after a period of adjustment prices will double as a result, and the real money supply will return to its original level. The real money supply is a function of other real variables, such a real output and real interest rates. According to monetary neutrality, real variables are functions of other real variables. There is no causal nexus between changes in the circulating money supply and real economic variables.

The principle of monetary neutrality casts some doubt on the value of monetary policy. All advanced nations have central banks that adjust domestic money stocks to meet the needs of trade and economic activity. If the only impact of a 10 percent increase in the money supply is to increase prices by 10 percent, one might ask whether anything useful is being accomplished. The answer lies in a consensus that the principle of monetary neutrality does not hold in the short run. Changes in the money supply do not directly impact prices, and in the adjustment process, real variables are effected temporarily. The strongest adherents of monetary neutrality tend to favor a nonfluctuating rate of monetary growth that is in line with the overall growth in economic activity.

The principle of monetary neutrality has strong logical and theoretical foundations, but it is difficult to verify empirically. Economic data clearly shows that the principle does not hold in the short run. To test the principle as a long-term concept, the money stock would need to be held constant for a long span of time, giving the economy plenty of time to adjust to the last change in the money stock. Then the economy would have to undergo a one-time, abrupt change in the money stock. With the money stock held constant at the new level, the economy would be given plenty of time to assimilate the new money, allowing ample time for adjustments to work themselves out. These conditions are never met in the real world.

Even with the difficulties of establishing it with unimpeachable proof, the principle of monetary neutrality serves as a warning against the abuse of monetary policy. It shows that increases in the money supply are not a road to permanent increases in prosperity. In a recession, accelerated money stock growth may help bring the unemployment rate back to more normal levels, but cannot permanently peg the unemployment rate at an unusually low rate.

References

Bullard, James. "Testing Long-Run Monetary Neutrality Propositions: Lessons from the Recent Research." *Review*, Federal Reserve Bank of Saint Louis, vol. 81, no. 6, pp. 57–77.

Lucas, Robert E. Jr. "Nobel Lecture: Monetary Neutrality." *Journal of Political Economy*, vol. 104, no. 4 (August 1996): 661–683.

MONETARY THEORY

Monetary theory, an important subarea of macroeconomics, proposes to explain the relationship between the money stock and the macroeconomic system. Macroeconomics is the part of economics concerned with the economy as a whole, as opposed to individual industries or sectors. Fluctuations in the economy as a whole, that is, in aggregate output, cause fluctuations in the unemployment rate, interest rates, and average prices.

Monetary theory analyses the role of money in the macroeconomic system in terms of the demand for money, supply of money, and the natural tendency of the economic system to adjust to a point that balances the supply and demand for money, a point that is called "monetary equilibrium." One sector of the macroeconomic system is conceived as the monetary sector, and the monetary sector has a natural tendency to converge to monetary equilibrium.

A phenomenon such as inflation can be attributed to an excess of the supply of money relative to the demand. Excess money supply causes the value of money to drop, which manifests itself as higher prices, causing each unit of money to buy less. A stock market crash can be attributed to an excess demand for money relative to supply, causing stockholders to sell stocks to raise money. Theoretically, the macroeconomic system converges to equilibrium, and one necessary condition for macroeconomic equilibrium is monetary equilibrium.

Monetary theory usually assumes as a rough approximation that the money supply is fixed by monetary authorities, and can be changed as necessary for the public's interest. The demand for money, however, is outside the control of public officials and is a function of other economic variables, particularly aggregate income, interest rates, the price level, and inflation. Aggregate income determines the amount of money households and businesses plan to spend in the near future. Households and businesses hold money because they plan to buy things in the near future.

Money holdings of households and businesses that will not be needed for purchases in the near future may be invested in long-term assets (stocks and bonds) that earn income. Money holdings earn little or no income. When money holdings are used to purchase stocks and bonds, the demand for money decreases, and the demand for stocks and bonds increases. Rising interest rates decrease money demand as money holdings are drawn into the purchase of bonds. Falling interest rates cause bonds to become less attractive, raising the demand for money.

Like rising interest rates, inflation means that money can be put to better use in other places, perhaps in the purchase of gold, silver, or real estate. Inflation reduces the demand for money, but deflation makes hoarding money an attractive investment, increasing the demand for money. Higher price levels, however, will eventually increase the demand for money, as money is needed to finance more costly transactions. Inflation reduces the demand for money at first, but when the inflation ceases, the demand for money will level out at a higher level than existed before the inflation started.

When monetary authorities change the money supply, the macroeconomic system adjusts to bring the demand for money in line with the supply of money. If the money supply is increased while the economy is in a recession, the extra money will probably flow into the stock and bond markets, stimulating business. As the economy expands, income grows, and the demand for money grows, catching up with the supply of money and restoring monetary equilibrium. If the money supply is increased while the economy is at full employment, the extra money will cause an increase in the demand for goods relative to supply. Prices will go up until the real (inflation adjusted) value of the money supply has fallen sufficiently to stop the inflation.

Monetary theory supplies the theoretical foundation for monetary policy, which has to do with the regulation of the money supply growth rate. Economists disagree as to whether the money supply growth rate should be speeded up and slowed down to meet the apparent needs of the economy, or whether the money supply growth rate should remain at a fixed amount, probably between 3 and 5 percent per year. Many contemporary economists argue that a fixed money supply growth rate is the best guard against inflation and economic instability.

See also: Equation of Exchange, Monetarism, Value of Money, Velocity of Money

References

Mankiw, N. Gregory. 1996. *Macroeconomics*, 3rd ed.

McCallum, Bennett T. 1989. *Monetary Economics*.

MONEYER

Before the mechanization of coinage, mints were staffed by moneyers, who physically struck the coins. In England at least, moneyers seemed to have owned their own tools. In 1484, Robert Hart, an English moneyer, bequeathed to his apprentice "my anvil, 4 hammers, a mallet, a pair of tongs, an hamnekyn, and 2 pairs of shears" (Challis, 1978, 5 footnote).

Moneyer as an organized trade or skill stretches back to the ancient world. In the Roman Empire, moneyers were members of a hereditary profession, recruited mainly from families holding high positions in government. A member of the moneyer caste could not resign without furnishing someone to take his place. In Rome, as in later societies, trust and character were an important qualification for the profession of moneyer. The same skills that allowed a moneyer to strike coins meeting official specifications could be put to work to forge counterfeit coins, or to debase official coinage at a secret profit to the moneyer.

English moneyers organized themselves into a company or guild and elected a leader, the provost, who could call a meeting of the moneyers at any time and impose mild disciplinary penalties. New recruits to the company had to serve as apprentices for seven years and take an oath to serve the company and the crown loyally. The warden of the mint paid the provost, who in turned paid individual moneyers. Mints lay idle portions of the year, and moneyers came to work only when the mint was in operation. The most important mint in medieval England was the Tower Mint, and moneyers from the Tower Mint were assigned to local mints in other parts of England. A few localities provided housing for moneyers while they were engaged at the mint. Some of the moneyers worked for goldsmiths when the mint lay idle, and judging from their debts, moneyers were not poor people.

Codes of law in medieval England regulated the conduct of moneyers. One provision stipulated that a moneyer found guilty of issuing debased or light coin should have the offending hand severed and fastened to the mint. Although the profits from forgery were high, the risks were also substantial. At Christmas in 1124, Henry III summoned all moneyers to Winchester, where, according to the Anglo-Saxon Chronicle, within a period of 12 nights all were mutilated. According to the Margam Annals, 94

were punished. By the close of Henry's reign, 19 out of 30 mints had shut down, probably because of a shortage of moneyers.

In the 17th century, mechanization began to replace the moneyers. Moneyers were now supervisors who oversaw the work of laborers operating machinery. The term "moneyer" does not seem to have been used in the United States. It was still applied to British mint workers into the 19th century, but it fell into disuse in the 20th century. Today there are no craftsmen working at mints who bear the title "moneyer."

See also: Milled-Edge Coinage

References

Challis, C. E. 1978. *The Tudor Coinage*.

Challis, C. E., ed. 1992. *A New History of the Royal Mint*.

Freeman, Anthony. 1985. *The Money and the Mint in the Reign of Edward the Confessor, 1042–1066*.

MONEY LAUNDERING

Money laundering refers to the processes of turning money earned from criminal activity into untainted, innocent money that bears no traces of its illegitimate origin. Laundering money hides untaxed and otherwise illegitimate income from tax collectors and law enforcement. It transforms the profits from crime into legitimate investments. More recently, the term has been applied to money secretly channeled into financing terrorist activity. Money laundering makes it more difficult to trace the origin of terrorist activity.

The age of computer networking and liberalized capital flows opened new opportunities for money launderers. As late as 1989, Columbian police, after shooting dead a Columbian drug lord, unearthed his stash of millions of dollars. He had buried it because sneaking it into the financial system unnoticed was too difficult (*Economist*, July 1997). According to some experts, now it is much easier. Rapid growth in the number of cross-border transfers played into the hands of those needing to hide ill-gotten gain. In addition, the multiplication of sophisticated financial instruments has aided and abetted the work of money launderers. On one case, money launders fabricated a profitable options trade to account for the sudden appearance of a hefty sum of cash in a bank account. Russian crime-lords have gone so far as to buy a whole bank.

Money laundering is service that can be purchased by those who know where to look. By one estimate, the going rate for cleansing drug money is Britain is between 5 and 10 percent (*Economist*, May 2006). Britain has some of the world's toughest laws against money laundering.

About three quarters of laundered money probably originates from the profits of illicit trade. Estimates of the total amount of criminal money cleansed through the global financial system ranges as high as $1.5 trillion per year (*Economist*, April 2001). The total amount of criminal money in the global financial system could easily run into the trillions. Some even suspect that flows of criminal money inflate and deflate financial markets. In the 1990s, both Mexico and Thailand underwent currency crises. Although economic mismanagement existed in each case, it was also true that both countries were centers for money laundering.

Aside from criminals themselves, the main culprits in money laundering are the off-shore banks, particularly the "shell" or "brass-plate" banks. The shell or brass-plate banks have no physical presence in any location. In one case, U.S. investigators discovered that illegal drug money has been wired to a bank account outside the United States. After getting the government in the bank's country to assist in the investigation, investigators discovered that the bank and bank account to which the money was wired actually resided in another country. Officials in this last country discovered that the bank had no buildings or branches. It turned out the shell bank had an account in a correspondent bank in New York. That was where the money was found.

In 1986, the United States enacted the Money Laundering Control Act, the world's first law specifically directed against money laundering. As the War on Terror became a major concern after September 11, 2001, the United States strengthened its stance against money laundering, levying heavy fines against offending banks. In both the United States and Britain, banks are obligated to report suspicious transactions. The problem of money laundering resembles the problem of global warming in that effective action requires cooperation of all countries. So far, an international consensus has not emerged on what bans should exist on money laundering. Some remember the experience of Jews in Germany who violated capital controls to get money out of Germany and into Swiss bank accounts. Bans on money laundering could interfere with the legitimate needs of oppressed people to move assets to a safe haven.

References

Economist. "Cleaning Up Dirty Money." July 26, 1997, p. 13.

Economist. "Special: Through the Wringer." April 14, 2001, p. 64.

Economist. "Britain: In a Spin; Money Laundering." May 27, 2006, p. 35.

Riley, Clint "Help Wanted, Bank Officials to Watch Cash; Compliance Executives Are in Growing Demand As Regulation Increases." *The Wall Street Journal* (Eastern Edition, New York) February 6, 2007, p. C1.

MONEY MARKET MUTUAL FUND ACCOUNTS

Money market mutual fund accounts (MMMFA) arose during the 1970s as a financial innovation designed to circumvent Regulation Q, a federal rule that limited the interest rate payable on checking and savings accounts to less than 6 percent. The high inflation rates of the 1970s put unreasonably low government ceilings on checking and savings account interest rates. Ninety-day treasury bills were exempt from interest rate ceilings, but these bills were only available in denominations of $10,000, outside the reach of the small saver. Other large denomination financial instruments, such as commercial paper and banker's acceptances, were also inaccessible to small savers.

Mutual funds raise capital by selling shares to investors, and invest the capital in an array of assets. They distribute the income from these investments to shareholders, minus management and other fees. Money market mutual funds sell shares to investors, but the value of shares is manipulated to remain at a fixed amount, such as $1 per share. The proceeds from the sale of shares are invested only in safe, short-term assets, such as U.S. Treasury bills, giving small savers access to the high earnings of the high-denomination assets.

Small savers can often open a MMMFA with a small investment, maybe as little as $500 but usually between $2,000 and $4,000. As long as a minimum investment is maintained, the shareholder of a MMMFA enjoys limited check-writing privileges, generally in minimum amounts of $500 against their share holdings. An MMMFA is technically not a deposit subject to the regulations of a depository institution, but the accounts are managed to act as a deposit with check-writing privileges. Although an MMMFA cannot boast of the safety of deposits insured by the Federal Depository Insurance Corporation (FDIC), MMMFAs often invest a high proportion of their capital in U.S. Treasury bills, giving them the same guarantee of the federal government as deposit insurance.

With check-writing privileges, MMMFAs began to serve the same purposes as checking accounts, an important component of the money supply. Between 1976 and 1992, MMMFAs grew from $2.4 billion to $360 billion, due to the movement of deposits from checking and savings accounts. The Federal Reserve System includes MMMFA accounts in M2, a monetary aggregate economists often consider the best operational definition of the money supply.

On December 14, 1982, banks received authorization to offer money market deposit accounts (MMDAs), which offer depositors comparable interest rates on assets similar to MMMFAs and have the added advantage of protection from the FDIC. At first, MMDAs grew rapidly at the expense of MMMFAs, and the depository institutions regained ground lost to MMMFAs. By the 1990s, MMMFAs had established themselves as an important monetary asset, but the volume of MMMFAs remained below the volume of the MMDAs.

See also: Certificate of Deposit, Monetary Aggregates, Negotiable Order of Withdrawal Accounts

References

Baye, Michael R., and Dennis W. Jansen. 1995. *Money, Banking, and Financial Markets: An Economics Approach.*

Klein, John J. 1986. *Money and the Economy*, 6th ed.

MUGHAL COINAGE

The Mughal emperor Jahangir (1605–1627) wrote in his diary of his new coinage bearing signs of the zodiac:

> Previous to this the rule of the coinage was that on the face of the metal they stamped my name, and on the reverse side the name of the place and the year of the reign. At this time, it entered my mind that in the place of the month they should substitute the figure of the constellation which belonged to that month. (Williams, 1997, 96)

One of Jahangir's coins bore a resemblance to himself with a cup of wine in his hands, a significant departure from Islamic coinage practice.

Evidence of Indian coinage prior to Alexander the Great's invasion (329–325 BCE) is scanty, but Indian coinage may have appeared soon after the invention of coinage in Lydia. Whatever the date, early Indian coinage seems to follow Greek models, and Alexander can be credited with spreading the techniques of Greek coinage in India. Indian coinage spread eastward in the wake of Indian culture and religion, and by the 13th century could be seen as far away as Indonesia and the Philippines.

In the 16th century, the Mughals descended on India from the northwest, establishing an Islamic kingdom. Under Islam, a new ruler could expect to have his name mentioned at the daily Mosque prayers and to have the privilege to issue coinage bearing his name.

The money of account of the Mughals was the silver rupee, which also dates back to 16th-century India. To be accepted as money, coins had to bear the name of the current Mughal emperor, a custom that persisted even after the Mughal emperor existed in name only and the Mughal empire had splintered into autonomous kingdoms. Roughly 300 types of rupee circulated when the British reformed India's currency and standardized the rupee early in the 19th century.

Under the Mughal system, money-changers, called "shroffs," played a prominent and necessary role in monetary transactions. All large transactions required the presence of shroffs to count each coin and assign discounts according to the wear of each coin and the time and location that each was struck.

Late in the 18th century, the British introduced mechanical coinage into India. Mechanical coinage had been universal in Europe since 1700. In 1835, the British reformed India's currency and standardized the rupee, ending the multitude of rupees and the need for shroffs. The British continued the practice of issuing coins in the name of the Mughal emperor, a necessary condition to make coins acceptable. Under the prestigious influence of the British Empire, the rupee became the standard unit of currency in the Persian Gulf and southern Arabia, and spread as far south as British East Africa and Natal in South Africa.

See also: Ottoman Empire Currency

References

Carter, Martha L., ed. 1994. *A Treasury of Indian Coins.*

Williams, Jonathan, ed. 1997. *Money: A History.*

N

NAILS

In the most famous book on economics, *Wealth of Nations,* published in 1776, Adam Smith wrote that "there is at this day a village in Scotland where it is not uncommon, I am told, for a workman to carry nails instead of money to the baker's shop or the alehouse" (Smith, 1937, 23).

Smith goes on to speculate why metals have been the money of choice for many countries:

> [M]en seem at last to have been determined by irresistible reasons to give the preference for this employment to metals above every other commodity. Metals can be kept with as little loss as any other commodity, scarce anything being less perishable than they are, but they can likewise, without any loss, be divided into any number of parts, as by fusion those parts can easily be reunited again, a quality which no other equally durable commodities possess, and which more than any other quality renders them fit to be the instruments of commerce and circulation. . . . The man who wanted to buy salt, for example, and had nothing but cattle to give in exchange for it, must have been obliged to buy salt to value of a whole ox, or a whole sheep at a time. . . . If, on the contrary, instead of oxen or sheep, he had metals to give in exchange for it, he could easily proportion the quantity of the metal to the precise quantity of the commodity which he had immediate occasion for. (Smith, 1937, 23)

There is some evidence that nails served as money in one of the 19th-century French coal fields. Nails were perhaps a convenient form of a metallic currency, functioning without the service of a mint, and putting the metal in a form that was equally serviceable as a medium of exchange or as a practical commodity.

See also: Spartan Iron Currency

References

Einzig, Paul. 1966. *Primitive Money.*

Smith, Adam. 1937. *An Inquiry into the Nature and Causes of the Wealth of Nations.*

NATIONAL BANK ACT OF 1864 (UNITED STATES)

The National Bank Act of 1864 gave the United States a uniform currency, universally accepted at par, sparing merchants the necessity to consult banknote detectors to appraise the value of various banknotes received from customers. Banknote detectors were regularly published booklets showing the discount on each banknote.

Before the National Bank Act of 1864, the United States had no permanent and uniform national currency but only a confusing medley of state banknotes trading at various discounts, usually depending on the distance from the issuing bank. The National Bank Act established a system of note-issuing national banks, with national charters, to compete with the state banking system, which was regulated by separate banking regulations in individual states.

The National Bank Act bore a striking similarity to much of the states' free banking regulations, allowing any group of five or more persons meeting certain capitalization requirements to obtain a national charter. Capital requirements varied from $50,000 to $200,000, depending on the size of the city the bank proposed to serve. Larger cities required larger capitalization. A third of the capital, or $30,000, whichever was smaller, had to be held as U.S. government bonds deposited with the comptroller of

Salmon P. Chase conferring with President Lincoln about the National Bank Act of 1864. (Library of Congress)

the currency, a new position created to supervise the national banking system. In exchange for the government bonds, the bank received national banknotes. Aside from other advantages, the new national banking system created a market for U.S. government debt.

The act provided for a hierarchy of reserve banks that led to a pyramiding of reserves in New York, creating an unstable link between the banking system and Wall Street financial markets. Country banks had to meet a 15 percent reserve requirement, three-fifths of which could be deposited in banks located in 18 large cities designated as redemption centers. The act subjected banks in the redemption centers to a 25 percent reserve requirement, half of which could be deposited with New York banks. The reserve requirement was the fraction of outstanding checking accounts or other deposits that a bank had to keep as reserves—vault cash or a reserve deposit at an acceptable institution.

Separate legislation effectively gave national banks a monopoly on the privilege to issue banknotes. In 1862, Congress put a 2 percent tax on the issuance of state banknotes. In 1866, Congress increased the tax to 10 percent, putting an end to the profits of state banknotes, and leaving only national banknotes in circulation. About one-fourth of the state banks in northern states survived the National Bank Act and the tax on state banknotes. In the later 1800s, the substitution of the personal check for banknotes brought a resurgence of the more gently regulated state banks.

The National Bank Act significantly advanced the monetary system in the United States, but it made no provision for a lender of last resort to act as a safety net during financial crises. Concern over recurring financial crises led the United States to further centralize its monetary system with the establishment of the Federal Reserve System in 1913.

See also: Federal Reserve System, Greenbacks

References

Hepburn, A. B. 1924/1964. *A History of the Currency of the United States.*

Myers, Margaret G. 1970. *A Financial History of the United States.*

Selgin, George A., and Lawrence H. White. "Monetary Reform and the Redemption of National Bank Notes." *Business History Review,* vol. 68, no. 20 (Summer 1994): 205–243.

NEGOTIABLE ORDER OF WITHDRAWAL ACCOUNTS

Negotiable order of withdrawal (NOW) accounts are interest-bearing checking accounts offered by banks and, particularly, thrift institutions, in the United States. The so-called M1, the narrowest definition of the money supply in the United States, includes NOW accounts. NOW accounts came about from a process of regulatory evolution rather than consciously thought-out planning for the monetary system.

The Glass–Steagall Act of 1933 banned payment of interest on checking accounts, reflecting the Depression-era thinking that interest-paying checking accounts had contributed to the high incidence of bank failures. Payment of attractive interest rates on checking accounts was one means banks used to attract depositors away from other banks, and banks that lost a large quantity of deposits faced bankruptcy.

Because savings and loan and other thrift institutions were not authorized to issue demand deposits, the zero-interest rate ceiling on demand deposits did not directly affect them. Thrift institutions were authorized to issue passbook accounts and regular savings accounts, which allowed customers to deposit funds or make withdrawals anytime during business hours. Technically, thrift institutions could require a seven-day notice before allowing the withdrawal of funds from these accounts, but in practice this requirement was usually waived.

The first NOW accounts were offered in 1972 by the Consumer Savings Bank in Worchester, Massachusetts, a mutual savings bank. Massachusetts had mutual savings banks, which were insured by a state insurance fund and therefore independent of the regulations imposed on the federally insured depository institutions. By 1970, Massachusetts savings banks were already authorized to waive a 30-day withdrawal notice for regular savings accounts, and depositors could walk into a savings bank and transfer funds to a third party by using counter checks devised for that purpose. The Worchester bank only proposed changing the location at which the third-party draft was written. The idea came before the Massachusetts Supreme Judicial Court, and the court took two years before deciding that the Consumer Savings Bank had a point. After 1972, NOW accounts spread rapidly among mutual savings banks in Massachusetts. Regulatory bodies allowed NOW accounts to penetrate the rest of New England, and then New York and New Jersey. Title III of the Depository Institution Deregulation and Monetary Control Act of 1980, called the Consumer Checking Account Equity Act, authorized the savings and loan industry to offer NOW accounts nationwide. The act also authorized credit unions to issue similar accounts called share drafts. Theoretically, share drafts pay dividends rather than interest, but the practical implications are the same.

Before the introduction of NOW accounts, savings deposits at thrifts fluctuated with opportunities to earn interest in other types of financial investments. A period of rising interest rates was invariably attended with a withdrawal of funds from savings deposits at thrift institutions. The availability of interest on NOW accounts eased some of the pressure on depositors to find investments for their money outside of the thrift institutions. NOW accounts increased the costs of funds to thrift institutions, but also have added stability to savings accounts. From the consumer's stand point, accounts that pay interest are not as vulnerable to inflation, because the interest earned offsets the deterioration in purchasing power from inflation.

See also: Certificate of Deposit, Depository Institution Deregulation and Monetary Control Act, Monetary Aggregates, Money Market Mutual Fund Accounts

References
Rose, Peter S. 1986. *Money and Capital Markets,* 2nd ed.
Woerheide, Walter J. 1984. *The Savings and Loan Industry.*

NEW YORK SAFETY FUND SYSTEM

The New York Safety Fund System represents one of the early efforts to protect the public from bank failures and is an ancestor to the Federal Depositary Insurance Corporation (FDIC) in the United States. The Safety Fund System required that banks chartered by the state of New York contribute to a safety fund to pay for the redemption of banknotes issued by failed banks.

Under the pre–Civil War banking system individual banks issued their own banknotes, which in principle they stood ready to redeem in specie. Banknotes played the role that checking accounts play in the modern banking system. When banks, failed the public could no longer convert the banknotes of failing banks into gold and silver coins. In the modern banking system, bank failures, in the absence of deposit insurance, leave the banking public unable to withdraw bank deposits in cash.

The legislature enacted the New York Safety Fund Act on April 2, 1829, and the system remained in effect until the era of free banking that began in 1838. Some of the public skepticism toward banks at the time can be read in the wording of the act, which referred to a bank as a "monied corporation." The act required that each bank annually contribute 0.5 percent of its capital to a fund until the bank's contribution to the fund equaled 3 percent of its capital. The interest earned on the fund, after allowances for administering the fund, was paid back to the banks. When a bank failed, the safety fund paid the debts of the failing bank, but the fund did not reimburse the owners of the bank for loss of capital. The act put the administration of the fund in the hands of three commissioners, one appointed by the governor, and two by the banking community. The act provided that a bank could be liquidated if the bank was two months behind in its contribution to the safety fund, had sustained a loss of half of its capital stock, had suspended specie payments on its banknotes for 90 days, or had refused access to bank commissioners. The act also required that bank officers pledge an oath that a bank's stock was not purchased with a bank's own banknotes, a common abuse of banking laws at the time.

The safety fund system worked well until 1837, but the crisis of 1837 was more than the fund could handle. The safety fund appears to have remained in existence into the era of free banking, but not on sound footing. In 1842, the act was revised to remove the safety fund from responsibility for bank deposits and debts, but maintained the fund's responsibility for banknotes.

R. Hildreth, writing in 1837 on the banking system, commented on the safety fund, saying: "it does not level the root of the evil; and it has the obvious defect of taxing the honest for the sins of the fraudulent" (Chown, 1994).

See also: Central Bank, Free Banking, National Bank Act of 1864, Suffolk System

References

Chown, John F. 1994. *A History of Money*.

Hepburn, A. Barton. 1924/1964. *A History of the Currency in the United States*.

Myers, Margaret G. 1970. *A Financial History of the United States*.

O

OPEN MARKET OPERATIONS

Open market operations are the most important means of expanding and contracting money supplies in modern monetary systems regulated by central banks. Central banks, such as the Federal Reserve System in the United States, regulate money supplies as a means of maintaining economic stability and price stability.

To infuse additional money into the U.S. economy, the Federal Reserve System purchases U.S. government bonds, paying for the bonds with freshly created funds added to commercial bank deposits at any of the twelve Federal Reserve Banks. Commercial bank deposits at Federal Reserve Banks, coupled with vault cash, make up what is called "high-powered money," because a system of commercial banks, making loans, can expand customer demand deposits by some multiple of the volume of high-powered money.

To withdraw money from circulation in the U.S. economy, the Federal Reserve system sells from its holdings of U.S. government bonds, and withdraws the proceeds of the sales from circulation and the banking system, leading to a contraction of money supplies.

The Bank of England may have been the first to regulate credit markets along the lines of modern open market operations. Late in the 19th century, the Bank of England would borrow funds in the London money market as a means of raising interest rates.

The Federal Reserve System apparently discovered by accident the practice of open market operations as an instrument of monetary control. The Federal Reserve Act of 1913 did not specifically address open market operations but did empower individual Federal Reserve Banks to buy and sell securities along the lines set forth by the rule sand regulations of the the Federal Reserve Board.

An economic slowdown in the 1920s reduced the demand for Federal Reserve Bank loans to commercial banks.

Federal Reserve Banks began buying government securities in the open market as a means of acquiring income-earning assets, compensating for the loss in the discount loan business to commercial banks. At first, individual Federal Reserve Banks separately purchased government securities, occasionally pitting individual banks against each other in bidding for securities. The Federal Reserve Banks collectively decided to coordinate all purchases of government securities through the New York Federal Reserve Bank. In 1922, the then Federal Reserve Board, since renamed the Board of Governors of the Federal Reserve System, established a special committee, composed of board members and officials of the Federal Reserve Banks, to make decisions about open market operations. The comparable committee is now called the Federal Open Market Committee.

The Federal Reserve Banks soon learned the impact of open market operations on money supplies, interest rates, and credit conditions, but the board remained split on the wisdom of open market operations until the 1930s. During the Great Depression of the 1930s, open market operations began to play a larger role in monetary policy. By the end of World War II, open market operations had become the most important tool in the central bank arsenal of monetary controls.

See also: Central Bank, Federal Reserve System

References

Anderson, Clay J. 1965. *A Half-Century of Federal Reserve Policymaking, 1914–1964.*

Baye, Michael R., and Dennis W. Jansen. 1995. *Money, Banking, and Financial Markets: An Economics Approach.*

Klein, John J. 1986. *Money and the Economy*, 6th ed.

OPERATION BERNHARD

The scale of Operation Bernhard dwarfs all other counterfeiting operations in the history of paper money. Nazi Germany counterfeited British £5 banknotes and, later, £50 banknotes to fund its foreign intelligence operations. Operation Bernhard got its name from Bernhard Kruger, who headed a workshop in which Germany's security service forged passports, motor licenses, university degrees, and other personal documents.

Counterfeiting as a weapon of war stretched well back into the 19th century, and at the beginning of World War II, Britain had dropped forged German food and clothing coupons over Germany and had made awkward attempts to counterfeit German marks. Germany's technical mastery of counterfeiting, however, far surpassed all preceding operations.

The decision to counterfeit money went all the way to Adolf Hitler, who approved counterfeiting British pounds in his own handwriting but with the proviso that "dollars, no. We're not at war with the United States" (Pirie, 1962, 6). Germany stuck to counterfeiting Bank of England banknotes even after the United States entered the war, but toward the end of the war German apparently prepared plates to counterfeit French francs and U.S. dollars.

The practical problem of counterfeiting British banknotes was broken down into three separate parts: (1) production of paper identical to paper in British banknotes, (2) construction of plates identical with Bank of England plates, and (3) devising a numbering system.

Example of a counterfeit Bank of England ten-pound note, created by slave laborers at the Sachsenhausen concentration camp during the Nazis' Operation Bernhard. (AP Photo/Florence and Laurence Spungen Family Foundation)

After finding that rags made from Turkish flax produced paper almost identical to Bank of England banknotes, the Germans hit on the expedient of sending the rags to factories to get dirty first, and then cleaned the used rags before using them to make banknote paper. Engravers spent seven months making plates that matched the original prints even when enlarged 20-fold. The numbering problem was the last to be solved. Apparently, the necessity of developing a numbering system that would blend in with the British numbering system posed the most troublesome obstacle. The finished plates were among the most closely guarded secrets in Germany.

Later in the project, the German counterfeiters attacked the problem of making the notes age. As printed notes age, the oil in the printing ink begins to seep into surrounding areas, blurring the quality of the print. German counterfeit notes were not aging properly until the Germans learned to treat their printing ink with chemicals to make it seep into surrounding areas, producing an aging effect.

After the technical problems were solved, the Germans sent an agent to the Swiss, carrying a bundle of counterfeit notes and a letter from the Deutsche Reichsbank asking the Swiss to find out if the notes were forged. When the Swiss replied that the notes were genuine without a doubt, the agent feigned a lingering suspicion and asked the Swiss to check with the Bank of England. The Bank of England also returned a reply that the notes were genuine.

At first, the German government planned to use an infusion of counterfeit notes to ruin the British economy, but efforts to inject large quantities of notes into circulation led to diplomatic embarrassments, and the German government dropped the plan. Then Germany's secret intelligence service decided to use counterfeit notes to finance its operations, and that is how the counterfeit notes were put into circulation.

The Bank of England banknotes were counterfeited at the Sachsenhausen concentration camp. Three hundred prisoners, some of them experts in forgery, took part in the project, and for a time these prisoners produced 400,000 notes per month. About £130 million were counterfeited in banknotes. As the demand for counterfeit money increased, the Germans began to counterfeit £50 notes.

Both the Germans and the Allies kept Operation Bernhard a secret. Because of the circulation of counterfeited banknotes, the Bank of England withdrew all notes of £10 or above in 1943 and changed the paper of the £5 note in 1944. In May 1945, notes from £10 to £1,000 ceased to be legal tender.

Toward the end of the war, the Germans dumped counterfeiting supplies and a vast quantity of notes into the Toplitzee, a lake in Austria. Large numbers of floating notes fueled rumors of the dumping, and the Allies sent divers into the lake, but no banknotes were recovered. The first public knowledge of Operation Bernhard came in 1952 when *Readers Digest* carried an article about it, and gradually more knowledge of the operation came to light. Only in 1959 did divers finally recover the vast quantities of notes and printing supplies. Notes recovered from the lake were indistinguishable from genuine Bank of England notes.

Apparently, some of the notes continued to circulate until 1955, when the Bank of England went to colored notes, and its older notes ceased to be legal tender. Some evidence suggests that as late as 1961 these notes were sold behind the Iron Curtain to people looking for a store of wealth until the communist regimes fell.

See also: Counterfeit Money

References

Beresiner, Yasha. 1977. *Paper Money*.

Burke, Bryan. 1987. *Nazi Counterfeiting of British Currency during World War II: Operation Andrew and Operation Bernhard*.

Pirie, Anthony. 1962. *Operation Bernhard*.

OPTIMAL CURRENCY AREA

In the post–World War II era, economists raised the issue of the optimal currency area, which is that area that stands to gain from an independent currency. The issue grew in importance as Europe made plans to establish an all-European currency, the euro, to replace individual national currencies such as the German mark, French franc, and Swiss franc. Although Europe merged into one large currency area, the break-up of the Soviet Union held out the spectacle of a large currency area splintering into smaller currency areas. New nations such as Ukraine replaced rubles with their own currency.

One theory of optimal currency areas emphasizes the importance of resource immobility. Consider two areas, one with a high unemployment rate and another with a low unemployment rate. If labor is a mobile resource, the unemployed workers will migrate to the area with the low unemployment rate. If labor is not mobile, due to distance, national laws, or language differences, then differences in currency exchange rates between the two geographical areas can serve some of the same purpose, assuming the two areas have their own separate currencies. The area with high unemployment can lower the value of its currency, making its exports cheaper to the area with low unemployment. Also, the lowered currency value will increase the cost of imports to the high-unemployment area, encouraging domestic consumers to buy locally produced goods. Therefore, adjustments in the exchange rate will increase the demand for goods produced in the high-unemployment area, and lower the demand for goods produced in the low-unemployment area, indicating that areas with immobile resources should have their own currency. According to this criterion, Canada is probably too large to have a single currency because of the vast distance between the east coast and west coast, making mobility difficult. Among members of the European Union, reductions in barriers restricting the flow of capital and labor between countries preceded the introduction of the euro in 1999.

Another theory of optimal currency areas looks at the importance of internal trade relative to trade with outsiders. In the case of Europe, this theory looks at the size of trade between European countries, such as France and Germany, relative to the size of trade between Europe as a whole and outsiders, such as the United States. An area that trades a great deal with itself, and not so much with the rest of the world, should qualify as an optimal currency area, and have its own currency. Under this criterion, Canada again would not constitute an optimal currency area if regions in Canada traded largely with the United States, rather than with other regions in Canada. If regions in Canada trade mostly with other Canadian regions, then Canada benefits from having its own currency. This criterion leaves the case of Europe somewhat in limbo, because Europe trades significantly within itself, but also trades significantly with outsiders.

Another criterion for an optimal currency area is that the area must have institutions that can make political and technical decisions for the area as a whole. Nation-states are the most obvious currency areas for this reason. Canada obviously qualifies as an optimal currency area under this criterion. Europe has moved toward political integration, including the election of a European Parliament, making Europe much more suitable as an optimal currency area.

See also: Euro Currency, European Currency Unit, Snake, The

References

McKinnon, Ronald I. "Optimal Currency Areas." *American Economic Review,* vol. 53 (1963): 717–725.

Melitz, Jacques. "The Theory of Optimal Currency Areas." *Open Economies Review*, vol. 7, no. 2 (April 1996): 99–116.

Mundell, Robert A. "A Theory of Optimal Currency Areas." *American Economic Review*, vol. 51 (1961): 637–665.

OPTIONAL CLAUSE

See Bank of Scotland, Scottish Banking Act of 1765

OTTOMAN EMPIRE CURRENCY

At its height, the Ottoman Empire ruled present-day Turkey, the Middle East, North Africa (including Egypt), and southeastern Europe. By World War I, the Ottoman Empire had largely disintegrated, and after the war the core of the empire was organized as the Republic of Turkey. Although the Sunni-Ottoman dynasty dates back to the 13th century, the empire became a power to be reckoned with after the capture of Constantinople in 1453. Perhaps the most famous sultan of the Ottoman Empire was Suleiman the Magnificent (1520–1566), whose conquest in the 16th century gave the Ottoman Empire control of East-West trade.

The prime coins of the Ottoman Empire were the *akce,* silver coins that provided the basis of monetary calculations for prices and wages. Suleiman's architect earned 55 akce per day. A niche for smaller coins was filled by the *dirham*, with its quarter, and the *manghir*, which were copper. The most important gold coin was the *ashrafit*, patterned after the Venetian *ducat.* To compete with Austrian *talers*, which rapidly gained acceptance in areas of the empire, Suleiman III (1687–1691) minted a silver coin known as the *qurush.*

To meet the coinage needs of the empire, the Ottomans purchased blank coins from Austria and the Dutch. Unlike other Islamic coinage, which often bore religious inscriptions, Ottoman coins bore inscriptions of the Sultan's titles. One coin bore an inscription that translates as "sultan of the two lands and lord of the two seas."

Mechanized methods of minting coins first appeared in Turkey in the mid-19th century, two hundred years later than the widespread adoption of these methods in Europe. Iran saw its first mechanized mint established in Tehran in 1876. In the 20th century, European mechanized mints supplied coins for colonized areas of the Ottoman Empire.

Paper money also made its debut in the mid-19th century. The Ottomans led the way with the issuance of notes in Turkey, setting an example that was soon followed by other provinces of the empire. Iran waited until the late 1880s to issue banknotes. Colonial powers often introduced paper money, paving the way for newly independent countries to issue their own paper money. In the 20th century, the paper money issued in countries of the old Ottoman Empire was often printed in European countries. A British firm, De La Rue, printed paper money for Iraq until the invasion of Kuwait in 1990 cut Iraq off from Europe.

See also: Mughal Coinage

References

Ehrenkreutz, A. S. 1992. *Monetary Change and Economic History in the Medieval Muslim World.*

Williams, Jonathan, ed. 1997. *Money: A History.*

P

PACIFIC COAST GOLD STANDARD

California and Oregon remained on a gold standard during the 1862 to 1879 period when the rest of the country transacted business on an inconvertible paper standard. During the Civil War the Confederate government abandoned all monetary discipline and flooded the South with Confederate paper money. In 1862, the North began issuing inconvertible greenbacks, and only in 1879 provided for the redemption of greenbacks in gold and silver specie. During the 1862 to 1879 period, Gresham's law drove all gold and silver coins out of circulation in the eastern United States, but state laws and organized business interests kept gold in circulation on the Pacific coast. The Pacific coast could boast of no less than $25 million of gold and silver coins in circulation during the period when the rest of the country used paper money as a medium of exchange and standard of value.

Before the Civil War, both California and Oregon relied exclusively on gold and silver coins rather than banknotes to circulate as money. When greenbacks were first issued, banknotes accounted for almost half of the circulating money in the East. The constitutions of both California and Oregon banned the issuance and circulation of paper money, and banks were forbidden to create "paper to circulate as money."

Aside from legal barriers to the circulation of paper money, merchants collectively agreed not to accept greenbacks on par with gold. The merchants of San Francisco agreed to neither receive nor make payment in greenbacks at any rate other than the greenback market value in terms of gold. They set prices in gold and accepted greenbacks at whatever discount the market dictated. When leading merchants in Portland agreed to accept greenbacks at the going rate in San Francisco, merchants throughout Oregon enforced the same policy. The merchants in Portland went so far as to circulate an announcement that customers who insisted on paying debts in greenbacks would find their names on a blacklist of the Portland merchants' association. Commercial ostracism awaited any businessperson who paid a business debt in greenbacks, that is, who "greenbacked" a creditor. Banks in California and Oregon refused to accept deposits in greenbacks, and newspapers worked to keep down the circulation of greenbacks.

After the federal government began issuance of greenbacks, the legislatures of both California and Oregon enacted measures allowing people to contract debts in either coin or greenbacks but requiring that payment be made as specified in the contract. The Oregon legislature enacted legislation requiring the payment of state and local taxes in only gold and silver coin, ruling out greenbacks. The California Supreme Court ruled that greenbacks were not acceptable in the payment of state and county taxes.

Organized opposition to greenbacks triggered a bitter debate on the Pacific coast. Critics charged that repudiation of greenbacks was tantamount to refusing to share in the financial burden of the Civil War. Crowding all the greenbacks on to the East Coast caused faster depreciation of the greenbacks, putting a greater burden of inflation on the East Coast. Although prices in greenbacks doubled over the course of the Civil War, Oregon prices in gold increased only 25 percent.

Two factors may help explain opposition to greenbacks on the Pacific coast. First, gold discoveries in California had already given that region a taste of inflation caused by increases in the money supply. A paper issue would only accelerate money growth, contributing to further inflation. Second, as a gold-producing region, the Pacific coast did not want to encourage the use of any other form of money. As abundant gold production drove out silver money, the Pacific coast moved essentially to a gold standard between 1862 and 1879, a unique exception to the paper standard that reigned in the rest of the country.

See also: Gold Rushes, Gold Standard, Greenbacks

References

Greenfield, Robert L., and Hugh Rockoff. "Yellowbacks Out West and Greenbacks Back East: Social-Choice Dimensions of Monetary Reform." *Southern Economic Journal*, vol. 62, no. 4 (April 1996): 902–915.

Lester, Richard A. 1939/1970. *Monetary Experiments.*

Moses, Bernard. "Legal Tender Notes in California." *Quarterly Journal of Economics*, vol. 7 (October 1892): 1–25.

PAPAL COINAGE

The Roman papal court rose to become a significant European financial center in the late Middle Ages, and the papal mint, called the *Zecca*, was a major focus of curial activity. The famous Renaissance artist and architect, Donato Bramante, built a new mint for Pope Julius II. Another Renaissance architect of some renown, Antonio da Sangallo the Younger, later remodeled the mint, his facade remaining on the building to this day. The Renaissance popes needed money to pay soldiers, hire artists, and build monuments and buildings, and the papal mint often furnished the coins to make payment.

The popes minted gold and silver coins. The principle gold coin of the Renaissance era was the gold *ducat of the Chamber*, named after the Apostolic

Silver piastra of Pope Clement X, 1675. (The Trustees of The British Museum/Art Resource, NY)

Chamber that handled the financial affairs of the papacy. The gold ducat was preceded by the gold *florin of the Chamber*, approximately equivalent in value to the ducat. In 1530, the papal mint issued a new coin, the *scudo d'oro in oro*, a coin that in value fell short of the ducat by a small margin. A papal ducat equaled about one-third of a Tudor pound sterling. The papal mint struck silver coins called *carlina*, and later, *giulii*, that equaled approximately one-tenth the value of a ducat.

The papal treasury and Roman treasuries tended to accumulate precious objects, and during times of financial stress, treasures were melted down and minted. Under Innocent III, the opening of a sepulcher of a noble lady of imperial Rome brought to light a golden brocade on her robes, which was promptly sent to the mint and melted down.

The papal court of Rome drew income from benefices across Europe, and the Apostolic Chamber expected payment in its own coinage, partly to protect itself from payments in mixed and depreciated silver money. Princes usually made payments in gold and the lower classes in silver. The combined gold and silver sent to Rome raised the ire of northern Europe, leading to charges that the Roman church was bleeding Europe white.

Papal coinage was noted for its beauty, a trait not surprising in light of the celebrated Renaissance artists who applied their gifts to coinage at the papal mint. The most eminent was Benvenuto Cellini, the Renaissance goldsmith, sculptor, and author of a famous autobiography. Perhaps less known is Francesco Francia, who struck coins so distinguished by their beauty that they became collectors' items and sold at premiums soon after his death. Vasari, in his *Lives of the Most Eminent Painters, Sculptors, and Architects*, says of Francia that he was "so pleasant in conversation that he could divert the most melancholy individuals, and won the affection of princes and lords and all who know him"(Vasari, 1927, 119).

Papal coinage is among the more modern manifestations of a familiar theme in monetary history. Temples and religious institutions usually have had the inside track on the accumulation of gold and silver. Because of the reverence for these institutions, the treasures of these institutions are usually safe from theft and extortion. (This reverence did not keep the papacy from losing much of its treasure during the Sack of Rome in 1527.) The moral leadership of these institutions can also add credibility to the precious metal purity of coinage. Historically, these institutions have often held a stronger claim of trust on the public than kings and princes.

Today the Vatican issues its own paper money, in francs and lire, which is noted for beautiful pictorial and religious themes.

References

Cellini, Benvenuto. 1931. *The Life of Benvenuto Cellini.*

Cellini, Benvenuto. 1967. *The Treatises of Benvenuto Cellini on Goldsmithing and Sculpture.*

Partner, Peter. 1976. *Renaissance Rome, 1500–1599.*

Ryan, John Carlin. 1989. *A Handbook of Papal Coins.*

Vasari, Giorgio. 1927. *Lives of the Painters, Sculptors, and Architects*, vol. 2.

PIG STANDARD OF NEW HEBRIDES

Until the eve of World War II, pigs played the role of money in the New Hebrides. The pig standard of New Hebrides was more than another livestock standard that combined a ready source of food with a store of wealth. In the New Hebrides boar hogs with curved tusks conferred status in a unique economic, political, and social system. On some islands, neutered pigs qualified, if they also grew tusks. The length of the tusks was the crucial quality determining the value of pigs, rather than weight or condition of the animal. Islanders removed two teeth from the upper jaw, causing the tusks to grow longer, adding to the pig's value.

The special role of pigs as sacrificial victims at feasts raised them above the category of a common source of food, endowing them with a special cultural significance that substantially increased their value as a store of wealth. Islanders gauged a man's wealth by the number of boars in his possession, which enabled him to make handsome contributions to sacrifices and feasts. They were too valuable for the small change of everyday transactions, which were facilitated by other exotic forms of money, such as mats, shells, quartzite stone money, and feathers. Pigs were used to buy land, pay workers (including magicians, dancers, and mortuary officials), purchase brides, and pay blood money, ransoms, and fines for violating taboos. Debts were defined in terms of pigs, and a large share of the murders on the islands arose from disputes over pig debts.

The social life of the islanders was dominated by men's clubs or secret societies. To purchase a bride, gain admission to a secret society, or earn promotion within a secret society, young men borrowed pigs, probably from relatives. A young man already in a secret society borrowed pigs from fellow members. A person acquired power by being able to loan pigs to those who needed to borrow them. Interest on debts was paid not by returning to the lender more pigs than were originally borrowed, but by returning pigs with longer tusks. Because pigs became more valuable as their tusks grew, interest on debts was paid by returning to the lender pigs with longer tusks. The rate of interest was determined by the growth of the tusks.

In the 1930s, pigs with quarter-circle tusks fetched 4 British pounds, half-circle tusks 6 pounds, three-quarter-circle tusks between 10 and 15 pounds, and full-circle tusks over 30 pounds. Pigs with tusks extending beyond one circle, perhaps a circle and a half, commanded premium prices.

The pig standard of New Hebrides shows that cultural and religious factors can outweigh utilitarian factors in raising up a commodity to serve as a medium of exchange in universal demand. Livestock standards are founded in the reality that people must find food on a daily basis, rendering them receptive to accepting edible livestock in exchange. Having a large reservoir of livestock, as a source of food, however, can become a status symbol, further enforcing the value of the livestock as money. In the New Hebrides, the length of a pig's tusks bore no relationship to its food value, but the tusks became a status symbol that acquired a cultural life of its own, making tusk length the lynch pin of the monetary standard.

See also: Cattle, Goat Standard of East Africa

References

Cheesman, Evelyn. 1933. *Backwaters of the Savage South Seas.*

Einzig, Paul. 1966. *Primitive Money.*

Humphreys, C. R. 1983. *The Southern New Hebrides: An Ethnological Record.*

PLAYING-CARD CURRENCY OF FRENCH CANADA

The French colonies shared with the British colonies the problem of insufficient money to transact the volume of business that was possible in a land with bountiful resources. French Canada turned to using playing cards as paper money to cope with a currency shortage.

Wheat, moose skins, beaver skins, and wildcat skins are among the commodities that belonged on the list of mediums of exchange in 17th- and 18th-century Canada. In 1713, the British soldiers stationed at Nova Scotia, which France had just ceded to Great Britain, petitioned the British authorities to end the practice of paying soldiers in rum, asking "that they be payd in money, or Bills, & not in Rum or other Liquors, that cause them to be Drunk every days, and Blaspheme the name of God" (Lester, 1935). In 1740, the accounts of a storekeeper in Niagara showed a "deficit by 127,842 *cats*" (Lester, 1935).

In 1685, the colonial authorities faced a cash-flow crisis that led to the issuance of ordinary playing cards as a form of paper money. During that year, the French government ended its practice of appropriating and sending funds to French Canada in advance of a budget period. The funds for 1685 did not reach Quebec until September, leaving the civil and military authorities in Canada to fend for themselves for the first eight months of the year. By June 1685, the authorities saw the necessity of issuing some sort of paper money that they could redeem when fresh funds arrived from France. The absence of suitable paper and printing facilities to produce paper money forced the expedient of using playing cards. Each denomination of paper money was associated with playing cards of a certain color and cut into a certain shape. It was a system easily understood by the generally illiterate population. Also, the colonial agent of the treasurer wrote the denomination on each card and, with the governor general and the intendant, signed each card. As long as the French government sent adequate funds once a year to redeem the playing-card money, prices in the new currency remained steady.

The authorities acted to discourage counterfeiting. In 1690, a surgeon found guilty of counterfeiting was condemned "to be beaten and flogged on the naked shoulders by the King's executioner" (Lester, 1939). He got six lashes of the whip in each "customary square and place." After surviving this ordeal, the surgeon was sold into bondage for three years. Later, the crime of counterfeiting drew the death penalty, often by hanging.

When hostilities broke out between France and England, France stopped sending silver coin to Canada for redemption of playing-card money. Instead, the authorities redeemed playing-card money with bills of exchange drawn payable in silver coin in Paris. The merchants in Canada made use of these bills of exchange to pay for supplies imported from France.

As was the case with many other early experiments with paper money, war proved to be the greatest enemy to the integrity of the playing-card system. The supply of playing-card money stood at 120,000 livres in 1702, when war erupted between England and France. By 1714, one year after the war ended, the supply stood at more than 2 million livres. During the war, France began paying the bills of exchange in paper money rather than silver coin, and prices in Canada entered a spiral of inflation. In 1714, the French government offered to redeem all the playing-card money in silver coin at half its face value. The program of redemption took place over a five-year period, and after 1720, the playing-card money was declared worthless.

From 1730 to 1763, the French government again issued card money in Canada, but the cards were blank cards rather than playing cards. The second issue of card money was again reasonably successful until war put a strain on resources.

The use of playing-card money seems a far-fetched expedient for a New World that had supplied the Old World with an abundance of precious metals for coining money. Unlike the Spanish colonies, however, the French and British colonies were not rich in deposits of precious metals. The episode of playing-card money shows the flexibility, adaptability, and inventiveness of an expanding economic system to raise up something to serve as a medium of exchange. It is also a reminder of the role of culture in identifying a suitable medium of exchange. The sensibilities of the New England Puritans would have been shocked at accepting playing cards as a form of money.

See also: Inconvertible Paper Standard, Siege Money

References

Beresiner, Yasha. 1977. *A Collector's Guide to Paper Money.*

Heaton, Herbert. "Playing Card Currency of French Canada." *American Economic Review* (December 1928): 649–662.

Lester, Richard A. 1939/1970. *Monetary Experiments.*

PONTIAC'S BARK MONEY

Pontiac was an Ottawa Indian chief and intertribal leader who organized the Indian resistance to British control in the aftermath of the French and Indian War in North America. The Indian resistance, known as Pontiac's War (1763–1764), gave rise to one of the first examples of siege money in America.

The French defeat in the French and Indian War had left the Great Lakes area in control of the British, who were less hospitable to the Indians. The Indians also discovered that the British were the thin edge of the wedge of an aggressive settler movement. As friction developed between the British and the Indians, Pontiac organized virtually every Indian tribe from Lake Superior to the lower Mississippi and launched a coordinated and simultaneous assault against 12 British forts in the area. Each tribe attacked the nearest British fort, and Pontiac laid siege to the fort at Detroit.

Pontiac's siege of Detroit lasted from May through October, and, unlike the assaults on most of the other forts, ended in failure. Nevertheless, while the siege was in process, Pontiac had recourse to an interesting experiment in money. In October, Pontiac issued "notes" in payment for supplies his warriors needed to continue the siege. These notes were none other than pieces of birch bark. Each bark note bore two images, an image of the item that Pontiac wanted to purchase with it, and a figure representing the otter, which he adopted as his totem or hieroglyphic signature. Apparently, Pontiac fulfilled his commitment to redeem all the notes after the war, and the notes were withdrawn from circulation, but the details of how this was done are sketchy.

Pontiac's confederation of Indian tribes achieved a momentary success, but in 1766, Pontiac, seeing the inevitable superiority of the British, negotiated a peace treaty. His expedient of bark money probably indicates how far European practices had influenced the Indians rather than the evolution of ancient Indian practices. The French trappers and hunters, who still had strong connections with the Indians, had agitated against the British, and the bark notes bear a striking resemblance to various sorts of token money or inconvertible paper money that governments often issue during wartime. By the time of Pontiac's War, the British colonies had issued vast quantities of paper money to finance the French and Indian War.

See also: Siege Money

References

Del Mar, Alexander. 1899/1968. *The History of Money in America*.

Parkman, Francis. 1899/1933. *The Conspiracy of Pontiac and the Indian War after the Conquest of Canada*.

POSTAGE STAMPS

Postage stamps have served as money in areas as diverse as the United States, Europe, and the Far East. During the U.S. Civil War, merchants, struggling with a shortage of small coins, began the practice of making small change with postage stamps. Daily purchases of stamps increased fivefold in New York City alone, and individual stamps circulated until they became too dirty and tattered for recognition. John Gault, a Boston sewing-machine salesman, proposed the encasement of stamps in circular metal discs with transparent mica on one side showing the face of the stamp. Soon the metal side of the discs was bearing inscriptions of advertisements; one series of encased stamps bore the slogan, "Ayer's Sarsaparilla to Purify the Blood." Denominations of encased stamp money ranged from 1 cent to 90 cents, and one rectangular encasement had three 3-cent stamps, making a 9-cent coin.

The government took up the idea of postage money and begin issuing postage currency in denominations of 5-, 10-, 15-, and 50-cent stamps, and some of the postage currency was even perforated around the edges to resemble stamps. The postage currency soon dropped any association with postage stamps and became simple fractional currency in denominations of 3 cents to 50 cents and bearing the inscription "Receivable for all U.S. stamps."

The British South Africa Company issued stamps affixed to cards bearing the statement, "Please pay in cash to the person producing this card the face value of the stamp affixed thereto, if presented on or after the 1st August 1900. This card must be produced for redemption not later than 1st October 1900" (Beresiner, 1977, 210).

Either during or immediately after World War I, postage stamps circulated as money in Germany, Austria, France, Russia, Italy, Norway, Denmark, Belgium, Greece, and Argentina. Germany and Austria imitated the U.S. practice of encasing the stamps in a circular metal disc with a transparent face, and a reverse side bearing an advertisement. France issued similar discs, but put a numeral on one side indicating the value of the encased stamp. Russia issued stamps on stout cards that bore the inscription "On par with silver currency." The Russian stamps were intended to circulate as money, but could also be used as postage stamps.

During World War II, Ceylon and the Indian state of Bundi issued small change in the form of cards printed with contemporary stamps. In 1942, Filipino guerrillas fighting the Japanese issued 5-peso notes to which stamps of the appropriate amount were affixed.

In both World War I and World War II, the British government declared postage stamps legal tender, but the stamps were never encased for special protection, or affixed to a special card.

Postage stamp money has usually emerged as money for domestic circulation when wartime finance has mobilized hard currency for purchasing military goods abroad.

See also: Shinplasters

References
Angus, Ian. 1975. *Paper Money.*
Beresiner, Yasha. 1977. *A Collector's Guide to Paper Money.*
Coinage of the Americas Conference. 1995. *The Token: America's Other Money.*

POTIN

See: Celtic Coinage

POTOSI SILVER MINES

Potosi, a desolate plateau 12,000 feet above sea level, now in Bolivia, was the site of a virtual "silver mountain," discovered in the 16th century. As a flood of silver poured into Europe, in England and Spain the word "Potosi" became synonymous with "wealth"; in France, the word "Peru" symbolized wealth, because that area of Latin America was then called Peru.

In the aftermath of Columbus's discovery of America, until 1530, Europe imported substantial quantities of readily accessible gold from the New World, but

Pack train of llamas laden with silver from Potosi mines of Peru, 1602. (Library of Congress)

silver was not significantly in evidence. After 1530, silver production in the New World reached significant levels, but still was dwarfed by the gold imports following Pizarro's conquest of the Incas between 1531 and 1541.

Europeans discovered the silver mountain of Potosi in 1545, a time when silver was still a highly favored metal in the Middle and Far East; a unit weight of silver exchanged for twice as much gold in the Eastern world as in Europe. Also, existing silver deposits were playing out, putting silver in strong demand. The base of the silver mountain measured six miles in circumference. The windy, dusty plateau of Potosi nourished a few fields of potatoes amid an otherwise agricultural wasteland. From an uninhabited, desolate plateau, Potosi grew to a sizable city, boasting a population of 55,000 by 1555, and climbing to a peak of 160,000 by 1610. Everything to meet the needs of this population had to be brought in, and a journey to Lima, the capital of Peru, took two and a half months.

Even high wages could not compensate for the prohibitive cost of living and arduous living conditions that the new immigrants faced at Potosi. To supplement a voluntary labor force, the *mita* system of forced labor required Indian villages within a certain radius of Potosi to send a quota of conscripted or drafted young men to work in the mines. The work was harsh, and labor in the silver mines came down through history as a symbol of Spanish oppression of the Indians. One eyewitness tells the following account of the plight of the Indian miners:

The only relief they have from their labors is to be told they are dogs, and be beaten on the pretext of having brought up too little metal, or taken too long, or that what they have brought is earth, or that they have stolen some metal. And less than four months ago, a mine-owner tried to chastise an Indian in this fashion, and the leader, fearful of the club with which the man wished to beat him, fled to hide in the mine, and so frightened was he that he fell and broke into a hundred thousand pieces. (Vilar, 1969, 127)

In 1563, rich mercury deposits were discovered at Huancavelica, located between Potosi and Lima, Peru. Convenient accessibility to mercury enabled the Spanish to employ the mercury amalgam process of silver extraction, substantially increasing the productivity of low-quality silver ore left after the richest veins were mined.

Much of the silver found its way to the East to cover Europe's balance of trade deficit, and some of the silver was shipped directly from the New World to China. China enjoyed an economic boom until silver shipments fell off in the 1640s, plunging China into a depression. In Europe, the infusion of silver fueled the price revolution, the century-long wave of inflation that engulfed Europe from 1540 until 1640.

Spain came to view the flood of silver less as a blessing from heaven and more as the curse of the devil. In the 17th century, Spain entered into a phase of monetary disorder that could rival any of the modern periods of inflation. Spain squandered its newfound wealth on costly wars, royal extravagance, and the growth of churches, convents, and ecclesiastics. By the second half of the 17th century, Spain had reverted to the Bronze Age, its coinage minted from copper.

See also: Great Bullion Famine, Price Revolution in Late Renaissance Europe, Silver

References

Davies, Glyn. 1994. *A History of Money.*

Flynn, Dennis O. 1996. *World Silver and Monetary History in the 16th and 17th Centuries.*

Vilar, Pierre. 1969. *A History of Gold and Money, 1450–1920.*

POUND STERLING

The pound sterling is the currency unit for the United Kingdom and has a longer continuous history than any other currency. For 1,300 years the pound has been the currency unit of England, never replaced by a "new pound" or any other change of name signifying a break with the past. Even the French franc, dating back to 1803, is young compared to the pound sterling. The German Deutsche Mark came into being immediately following World War II.

Around the time of William the Conqueror, the English government began striking coins from a silver alloy containing 925 parts of pure silver per 1,000. Debased coins appeared occasionally, but Norman and English kings always returned to the silver alloy containing over 92 percent pure silver, which came to be known as the "ancient right standard of England." Early in the 12th century, the English called their silver pennies "sterling." The reputation of the English silver coinage for consistent fineness gave rise to the term "sterling silver."

The English currency system traces its ancestry directly to the Carolingian currency reform. Charlemagne's father, Pepin, established a silver standard that made 1 livre (pound) equal to a pound weight of silver. Also, 240 silver *denarii* (pennies) equaled a pound, and 20 shillings equaled a pound. In the English version of the Carolingian system, 1 pound equaled 20 shillings, which equaled 240 pence. The Carolingian system did not remain intact long on the Continent, particularly regarding the silver content of the pound, but it came to England with the Norman Conquest, where it survived longer than anywhere else. Only in 1971 did the United Kingdom decimalize its currency, making 100 pence equal to a pound.

Over the first eight centuries of its existence, the pound lost two-thirds of its silver content, averaging a depreciation of 0.13 percent per annum. After 1696, the silver content of the pound remained steady until 1817 when the United Kingdom officially adopted the gold standard, and silver coinage became only subsidiary. During the 19th century, the pride of the British currency was the gold sovereign, equal to 20 shillings or 1 pound. The sovereign and half-sovereign continued in circulation until 1914.

During the 19th century, the pound sterling began to wear the aspect of an international currency. Although the pound sterling played no special role on continental Europe, the currencies of other European countries financed trade only within colonial empires, leaving the field free for the pound sterling to become the dominant international currency.

After World War I, the United Kingdom made a frantic, and briefly successful, effort to return to the gold standard at the prewar parity, which was 3 pounds, 17 shillings, and 10.5 pence per fine ounce. In truth, the United Kingdom needed to devalue the pound sterling, and failure to do so helped usher in the British Great Depression. In the Gold Standard Amendment Act of 1931, the United Kingdom abandoned the gold standard, and other countries had to decide to keep their currencies tied to the pound sterling, remain on the gold standard, or follow an independent policy. The Commonwealth countries, excepting Canada, the British colonies, Portugal, and the Scandinavian countries, elected to keep their currencies linked to the pound sterling, and these areas became known as the sterling area.

The pound sterling emerged from World War II as second only to the U.S. dollar as an international currency. In the post–World War II era, the prestige of the pound sterling suffered from currency devaluation, and the vast U.S. gold stock, combined with production facilities undamaged by war, gave the U.S. dollar the preeminent position as the international currency.

England's long history of conservatism in monetary matters may explain why the United Kingdom has been slow to participate in the European movement toward monetary union. In May 1998, members of the European Union announced plans to launch a European currency to replace the national currencies of several European countries, including France and Germany. The European Union launched the euro in a non-physical form on January 1, 1999, and on January 1, 2002, euro notes and coins replaced the circulating currencies of several European countries, including Germany and France. As of mid-2009 Britain still refused to adopt the euro and planned to retain its own national currency, the pound sterling.

See also: Act for Remedying the Ill State of the Coin, Bank of England, English Penny, Gold Standard, Gold Standard Act of 1925, Gold Standard Amendment Act of 1931, Liverpool Act of 1816

References

Chown, John F. 1994. *A History of Money.*

Davies, Glyn. 1994. *A History of Money.*

Feavearyear, Sir Albert. 1963. *The Pound Sterling: A History of English Money.*

Horton, Dana S. 1983. *The Silver Pound and England's Monetary Policy Since the Restoration, together with the History of the Guinea.*

POW CIGARETTE STANDARD

A unique form of commodity money surfaced in the Nazi prisoner-of-war (POW) camps during World War II. Cigarettes came to fulfill all the functions of money: a medium of exchange, unit of account, standard of deferred payment, and store of value.

The Red Cross furnished the prisoners with cigarettes along with food, clothing, and other goods. The goods were distributed without precise knowledge of individual needs and taste, giving prisoners an incentive to barter unwanted goods for goods that more closely met their needs. A situation in which trade can considerably raise individual welfare is fertile ground for the emergence of a money commodity, and in the POW camps cigarettes came to play the role of money.

Prisoners set prices in cigarettes. Shirts cost 80 cigarettes, and one prisoner would do another prisoner's laundry for two cigarettes. Even nonsmoking prisoners kept a store of cigarettes to buy other goods and services, and prisoners built up supplies of cigarettes as savings, making cigarettes a store of value— another function of money. Cigarettes met the need for a standard of deferred payment. Debts were also run up in cigarettes, particularly gambling debts, and prisoners bought goods and services on credit, promising to pay out of future allocations of cigarettes.

As a monetary commodity, cigarettes possessed many advantages. Their value was maintained by a strong consumer demand; they were somewhat durable, not perishable; and to make change they could be subdivided from a box to individual packages and even to individual cigarettes.

The history of POW cigarette money furnishes examples of a wide range of monetary phenomenon. Gresham's law could be seen in the tendency for inferior cigarettes to remain in circulation while prisoners hoarded higher-quality cigarettes. Sometimes prisoners debased the currency by removing tobacco in the middle of the cigarette and replacing it with inferior material. A diminished (or expectation of a diminished) influx of cigarettes caused a fall in the velocity of circulation as prisoners hoarded cigarettes, which were becoming more valuable as prices in cigarettes fell. An added infusion of cigarettes, or rumors of an added infusion, brought a rise in velocity, dishoarding, and rising prices in cigarettes. Even banks were established that issued banknotes convertible into cigarettes, but unfortunately the banknotes were often easily forged. Communal stores emerged that were capitalized in cigarettes, and paid dividends in cigarettes.

The history of cigarette money continued after the war. In postwar Germany, a cigarette standard emerged, particularly in transactions between Germans and British and U.S. troops. In the late 1980s in the Soviet Union, packs of Marlboro brand cigarettes served as a medium of exchange in a large underground economy that had lost faith in the ruble.

See also: Commodity Monetary Standard, Gresham's Law

References

Einzig, Paul. 1966. *Primitive Money.*

Radford, R. A. "The Economic Organization of a POW Camp." *Economica* (November 1945): 189–210.

PRICE REVOLUTION IN LATE RENAISSANCE EUROPE

Historians call the wave of inflation that swept Europe during the 16th and 17th centuries the Price Revolution. It is seen as revolutionary in character partly because it followed a long period of stable prices, and partly because the prevailing view at the time was that prices and wages should be matters of fairness and justice rather than functions of supply and demand. By the mid-17th century, the inflation had ceased in most countries, followed by a century of stable or even falling prices.

Economists have mostly ascribed the influx of gold and silver from the New World as the cause of the inflation. An increase in the supply of anything, including money, relative to its demand causes its value to go down. A reduction in the value of a unit of money translates as inflation to the public. Scholars in other areas seem less satisfied with this single explanation. The timing of the beginning, the peak, and the end of the inflation only roughly corresponds with the timing of dates for the influx of gold and silver. The economist Jean Bodin (1530–1596) listed five reasons for the inflation: (1) the abundance of gold and silver, (2) monopolies, (3) scarcity of goods caused by exports and waste, (4) the luxury of kings and nobleman, and (5) the debasement of coin. He regarded the abundance of gold and silver as the principal reason.

The inflation struck Spain the hardest, quadrupling prices within a century. In England from 1580 to 1640, prices of necessities rose 100 percent while wages inched up only 20 percent. England's first series of humane poor laws came into being in the midst of the Price Revolution. The acceleration in prices reached a peak in most countries between 1540 and the 1570s. Wages and rents fell behind prices and profits soared. Entrepreneurs ploughed these profits into new industries and new ventures of trade, speculation, and building, laying the foundation for further economic expansion.

See also: Gold, Inflation and Deflation, Potosi Silver Mines, Silver

References

Flynn, Dennis O. 1996. *World Silver and Monetary History in the Sixteenth and Seventeenth Centuries.*

Hamilton, Earl J. 1934. *American Treasure and the Price Revolution in Spain, 1501–1650.*

PRICE STICKINESS

"Price stickiness" refers to the tendency of prices to adjust sluggishly to changes in the economy. Many economists believe that if wages and prices adjusted freely and quickly, then changes in the money supply should cause only proportionate changes in prices and the rest of the economy would feel no repercussions. With perfectly flexible wage and prices, a doubling of the money stock would double the average level of prices. According to this thinking, if doubling the money stock quickly doubled prices, other important variables such as the unemployment rate and the level of industrial production would remain unchanged.

The level of prices is measured by indices such as the consumer price index (CPI), the gross domestic product (GDP) deflator, and the producer price index (PPI). Because of price stickiness, the level of prices does not quickly mirror changes in the money stock. Therefore, changes in the money stock can bring about at least temporary adjustments in real variables such as the unemployment rate and industrial production.

In some markets, prices are highly flexible. For commodities such as corn and wheat, prices react quickly to changes in supply and demand. In these markets, the sellers have no control over the prices of the commodities they produce and sell. Farmers that grow these commodities are what economists call price takers. They have to take the market price and cannot charge one cent more without all the buyers disappearing. Corn farmers produce a standardized product and one farmer cannot claim that his corn is superior to the corn produced in other markets. Price stickiness does not occur on any appreciable scale in these markets.

It is in markets where producers and sellers set the price that price stickiness occurs. In industries populated with only a handful of sellers, competition becomes personalized rivalry. These sellers become fearful of price competition as a path to destructive price wars. The U.S. automobile industry of the 1950s and 1960s is a good example of an industry that shunned price competition. Instead, the U.S. automobile industry of that era favored competition based on styling, advertising, and gadgetry, unveiling new body styles yearly. In times of falling costs, individual sellers in these types of industries are afraid to cut prices for fear of sparking a price war. In times of rising costs, these sellers are afraid to raise prices out of fear that competitors will not raise prices.

In some industries, firms that set their own prices face a large number of competitors. Restaurants are a good example of this type of industry. The fear of price wars does not loom as large in these industries, but these firms may still find it costly to change prices too often. These firms bear what are called "menu costs." Changing prices involves producing a new menu or catalogue. Menu costs can be as simple as the cost of remarking the prices of goods already on the shelf.

The regulation of prices accounts for some price stickiness. Utility rates for electricity and gas are still set by regulatory authorities. Union contracts make some wages rigid, which may contribute to some price rigidity among unionized employers. In addition, some prices are fixed by long-term contracts.

Economists have studied the frequency of price changes among firms that set their own price. One study found that nearly half the firms in a sample changed prices no more than once a year.

Some economists refuse to accept that price stickiness is the deciding consideration in the relationship between the money stock and real variables such as industrial production. They argue that the general tendency of producers to increase production when prices go up and vice versa leads to a positive correlation between money stock changes and output changes. This positive correlation occurs because producers tend to only see the prices of their own products going up, and are unaware that other prices and costs are increasing at roughly the same rate.

See also: Monetary Neutrality

References

Bils, Mark, and Peter Klenow. "Some Evidence on the Importance of Sticky Prices." *Journal of Political Economy*, vol. 112, no. 5 (October 2004): 947–985.
Blinder, Alan. 1994. "On Sticky Prices: Academic Theories Meet the Real World." In *Monetary Policy*, edited by N. Gregory Mankiw, pp. 117–150.

PRIVATE PAPER MONEY IN COLONIAL PENNSYLVANIA

In 1766, eight Philadelphia mercantile houses issued short-term, interest-bearing promissory notes that circulated as a medium of exchange. The experiment was short-lived but represents the first instance of private money in what was to become the United States.

The colonial economies suffered from a shortage of currency. Parliament forbade the coinage of money in the colonies, and the enactment of the Currency Acts of 1751 and 1764 restricted the authority of colonial governments to issue paper money. In addition, colonial economies invariably faced an excess of imports over exports, and an outflow of metallic currency paid for the extra imports, further leaving the colonial economies impoverished of currency. Colonial governments lobbied for the repeal of the Currency Act of 1764, not because of a need to finance budget deficits, but because a currency shortage was strangling the colonial economies.

By 1766, the shortage of colonial currency led to an appreciation of colonial currency relative to British pounds sterling, putting at a disadvantage export merchants who earned British pounds sterling in exports and had to convert British money back into colonial money to purchase colonial goods for export. The currency appreciation enhanced the incentives for creating fresh supplies of colonial currency that could be used to purchase colonial goods for export to earn British pounds.

Eight Philadelphia mercantile companies saw an opportunity to issue private notes, easing the shortage of a circulating medium of exchange and purchasing domestic produce at good prices for profitable export. These firms issued 30,000 pounds in short-term, interest-bearing promissory notes to pay for "Wheat and other Country Produce." The notes were payable in nine months in British sterling pounds.

A public outcry rose up against the issuance of private paper money for profit. Nearly 200 provincial merchants put an advertisement in the *Pennsylvania Gazette* on December 11, 1766, declaring that they would not accept these notes in payment for goods. A month later the inhabitants of the city and county of Philadelphia petitioned the General Assembly, the Pennsylvania colonial legislature, pleading that the privilege to issue money belonged only to the legislature. Eventually the king's attorney general and solicitor general took up the issue and declared that the notes were probably not illegal, but the notes were withdrawn in the face of a strong negative public reaction.

After the War of Independence private banks began to issue banknotes, but during the colonial period the issuance of paper money remained strictly a government prerogative.

See also: Land Bank System, Currency Act of 1764

References

Ernst, Joseph Albert. 1973. *Money and Politics in America, 1755–1775.*
Yoder, Paton S. 1941. Paper Currency in Colonial Pennsylvania. Ph.D. dissertation, Indiana University.

PRODUCER PRICE INDEX

The producer price index (PPI) for all commodities is an index of the domestic price level that the United States Bureau of Labor Statistics estimates and publishes once a month. It is concerned only with domestic producers and the prices that they receive for their output. The PPI ranks among the oldest economic indicators assembled and reported by the Federal Government. It owes its origins to a resolution passed by the United States Senate in 1891. This resolution authorized the Senate Committee on Finance to look into the impact tariffs had "on the imports and exports, the growth, development, production, and prices of agricultural land manufactured articles at home and abroad."(Senate Committee on Finance, 1893) In 1902, the United States Department of Labor

published a bulletin on the course of wholesale prices between 1890 and 1901, marking the first publication of a U.S. price index. Until 1978, the PPI was called the "wholesale price index." The change in name was intended to emphasize that the PPI aims to measure the prices received by producers from the first buyers.

The PPI for all commodities and the consumer price index (CPI) provide the two main measures of monthly inflation in the United Sates. Whereas the CPI emphasizes the retail prices of goods and services relevant for a family's or household's cost of living, the PPI measures what prices output bring for the producers rather than for the retailers. It includes all kinds of goods absent from the CPI, such as business capital equipment. The PPI includes the price of footwear, but it also includes the prices of leather, hides, and skins. The prices of agricultural and construction equipment are reflected in the PPI, but not in the CPI. The prices of aircraft, ships, and railroad equipment help make up the PPI.

The PPI for all commodities incorporates fifteen different commodity groupings. The groupings are Farm Products; Processed Foods and Feeds; Textile Products and Apparel; Hides, Skins, Leather, and Related Products; Fuels and Related Products and Power; Chemicals and Allied Products; Rubber and Plastic Products; Lumber and Wood Products; Pulp, Paper, and Allied Products; Metals and Metal Products; Machinery and Equipment; Furniture and Household Durables; Nonmetallic Mineral Products; Transportation Equipment; and Miscellaneous Products. Indexes are calculated for each one of these sub-groups, as well as for individual commodities within these subgroups. As a case in point, there is a price index for Fuels and Related Products and Power subgroup. The fuel subgroup is broken down into further subgroups including crude petroleum, refined petroleum products, electric power, and gas fuels. A price index is also reported for each of the subgroups within the Fuel subgroup.

The PPI calculations also make available price indexes for subgroups based on the stage of processing. A finished goods index provides a price index for a class of goods ready to be purchased by final users. They need no further processing and may be either durable or nondurable goods. Finished goods include capital equipment for business firms. Another index measures the cost of intermediate materials, supplies, and components. The intermediate goods undergo some processing before they serve as material and component inputs to other manufacturing and construction activities. Another index measures the cost of crude materials, which are unprocessed goods and raw materials.

In the calculation of the PPI, the Bureau of Labor Statistics make allowances for changes in the quality for products. Suppose the cost of a new automobile rises by $500, but $300 of the price increase is owed to extra safety equipment required by new government regulations. The PPI only counts $200 of the price increase as an increase in the price of automobiles.

References

Bureau of Labor Statistics. June 2008. "Producer Prices." Chap 14 of *BLS Handbook of Methods*.

Senate Committee on Finance, Wholesale Prices, Wages, and Transportation. "The Aldrich Report." Senate Report no. 1394, Part I, 52nd Congress, 2d sess., March 3, 1893.

PROMISSORY NOTES ACT OF 1704 (ENGLAND)

The Promissory Notes Act of 1704 officially established promissory notes as negotiable instruments. A promissory note is negotiable when it can be transferred to a third party by an endorsement, usually in the form of a signature of the recipient of the note. Because the banknote is a direct descendant of the promissory note, the act of 1704 furnished the legal prerequisites for the use of banknotes as a medium of exchange.

In 17th-century England, people deposited gold in the safekeeping of goldsmiths, who in return issued something like a warehouse voucher made out to the owner of the gold. It was a receipt for a deposit of gold. Rather than exchange gold in trade it was much easier to exchange warehouse receipts, giving rise to the custom of making these receipts transferable by endorsement. Promissory notes originated from these receipts. The wording on promissory notes entitled a certain person, or the "bearer," of the note, to a fixed amount of gold on demand. The custom arose of transferring the ownership of promissory notes with signature endorsements. The ownership of these notes might change over and over as long as there was room for more endorsements. With promissory notes changing hands through repeated endorsements, invariably disputes came before the courts involving cases in which someone did not want to redeem an endorsed promissory note, or in which the recipients of endorsed promissory notes did not receive the same consideration as the initial recipients of the notes. For promissory notes to circulate as a medium of exchange, it was necessary that the holders of endorsed notes suffer no disadvantages when demanding that notes be paid in gold. That is, the promissory notes had to be negotiable. The courts waffled on the issue of the negotiability of promissory notes, forcing Parliament to take action.

Parliament named the law "An Act for giving like Remedy upon Promissory Notes, as is now used upon Bills of Exchange, and for the better Payment of Inland Bills of Exchange." The act provided that promissory notes payable to order, or bearer, were legally binding obligations, assignable by endorsement to new holders, and new holders could sue in the courts for enforcement of their rights. Parliament cited the benefits to trade and commerce accruing from the provisions of the act.

The first step toward the evolution of banknotes came when goldsmiths dropped the names of individuals entitled to gold, and instead made the unnamed "bearer" of the note entitled to a fixed amount of gold. The rise of engraved notes completed the transition to banknotes. Indorsed checks also became negotiable instruments by virtue of the act of 1704. With the legal status of notes clarified, banknotes grew in popularity. Adam Smith observed in *The Wealth of Nations*, published in 1776, that bank money had surpassed metallic money in quantity of circulation, marking a turning point in monetary history.

See also: Check, Goldsmith Bankers

References

Beutel, Frederick K. "The Development of Negotiable Instruments in Early English Law." *Harvard Law Review*, vol. 51, no. 5 (1938): 813–845.

Nevin, Edward, and E. W. Davis. 1970. *The London Clearing Banks.*

Rogers, James S. 1995. *The Early History of the Law of Bills and Notes: A Study of the Origins of Anglo-American Commercial Law.*

PROPAGANDA MONEY

As a circulating medium, money has drawn the attention of political organizations looking for a vehicle to spread propaganda. In times of war and social turmoil paper money is particularly susceptible to becoming a medium for bearing revolutionary messages.

In 1967, the Chinese Communist Party instigated riots against the Hong Kong government and put to use the circulating money of Hong Kong to propagate messages discrediting the government. The communists were exploiting a touchy economic situation associated with the devaluation of the pound sterling and subsequent devaluation of the Hong Kong dollar. Hong Kong was a colony of the British government at the time.

The Hong Kong and Shanghai Banking Corporation issued notes in Hong Kong, and the communists took in $10 and $100 notes and overprinted messages calculated to inflame the populace against the government. The top left corner of the overprinted $10 notes bore the famous figure of John Bull with outstretched hands and a gaping mouth. Behind his head in Chinese characters was the message, "He is so greedy that he swallows money." At the bottom of the overprinted $10 notes were two Chinese characters meaning "Devaluation." On the reverse side of the $10 banknotes the communists overprinted a text heavily sprinkled with words such as "imperialism," "banditry," and "fascism," and describing the British exploitation of Hong Kong that led to the devaluation of the Hong Kong dollar.

The communists overprinted the $100 notes with a caricature of a pirate with a sack of protruding $100 notes thrown over his back. Printed on the sack were the words "Open Banditry." In the center of the bill the communists overprinted the message, "Worth only 94.30 dollars after devaluation." On the reverse side the communists overprinted a text ending with the rallying cry, "fellow brothers: in order to survive we must unite together and fight to the end against the British in Hong Kong."

During the Vietnam War, peace protesters in the United States drew peace symbols and slogans on dollar bills. At the height of the peace protests the Federal Reserve Banks withdrew the bills bearing antiwar messages. During World War II, the British authorities overprinted German military notes with propaganda messages derogatory of Adolf Hitler.

Metallic coinage may have begun as a means of advertising seaports, and the use of propaganda money demonstrates that money is a vehicle for communication. Propaganda money defaces a symbol of government—usually images hallowed by time that are typically placed on paper money—and at the same time propagates a message that discredits the government.

See also: Siege Money

Reference
Beresiner, Yasha. 1977. *Paper Money.*

PUBLIC DEBTS

In Montesquieu's *The Spirit of Laws*, published in 1748, one reads that: "Some have imagined that it was for the advantage of the state to be indebted to itself: they thought that multiplied riches by increasing the circulation" (Montesquieu, 183). The reasoning behind this statement had to do with the exclusive use of gold and silver for money. By issuing government bonds that households and businesses were willing to hold instead of hoarding gold and silver, more gold and silver became available to circulate as a medium of exchange. Alexander Hamilton, first secretary of treasury of the United States, also saw advantages in a public debt. He argued that interest-bearing government bonds gave businesses a place to earn interest on capital when it was not in use.

Most national governments of highly industrialized economies have public debt. The degree of indebtedness can be a matter of concern. The main consideration in debt, private or public, is the amount of income available to repay it. Doubling one's debt while doubling one's income, does not raise the debt burden or the chance of default. Economists use the ratio of public debt to gross domestic product (GDP) to measure the degree of indebtedness of a particular government. As long as GDP grows faster than public debt, the ability of a government to pay off its debt is always improving. Below is a list of countries with public debts measured as a percent of GDP.

Public debts often soar significantly during wars. Following the Napoleonic wars, Great Britain's public debt as a percent of GDP stood close to a dizzy 300 percent. It steadily fell, dropping

Public Debt as a Percent of GDP for
Selected Countries in 2007

Australia	15.4
Canada	64.1
France	70.1
Germany	65.5
Italy	113.2
Japan	170.6
Switzerland	48.6
United Kingdom	46.9
United States	62.9

Source: OCED Economic Outlook no. 84, 2008

below the 50 percent range by the eve of World War I (Miles and Scott, 606). By the end of World War II, the United Kingdom's debt had climbed to a lofty level of 250 percent of GDP. The United States finished World War II with a public debt above 100 percent of GDP (Miles and Scott, 266). Inflation helps countries reduce the burden of public debts. In the post–World War II years, inflation helped reduce the public debt burdens of the United Kingdom and the United States. The stress of wartime finance, coupled with war reparations sent post–World War I Germany into a frenzy of runaway inflation.

It is true that a government should never face default if its debt is denominated in its own currency. It can always print up the currency to redeem a debt, but the outcome is likely to be inflation and economic chaos. Governments usually turn to hyperinflation to get out from under a debt only if creditors have lost confidence in the government and are withholding credit. All the U.S. government debt is denominated in U.S. dollars. Governments in developing countries often contract debt denominated in the currency of a foreign government. These governments can face default if they run short of foreign currency reserves.

In the United States, the public debt as a percent of GDP steadily fell from the end of World War II until around 1980 (Miles and Scott, 266). It reached a trough roughly at 25 percent of GDP. In the 1980s, the U.S. public debt as a percent of GDP turned upwards with larger budget deficits, reaching a level of 70 percent of GDP in 1996 (OECD, 2008). The public debt as a percent of GDP steadily fell from 1997 until 2001, and then began climbing. In 2008, the OECD Economic Outlook was expecting the U.S. public debt as a percent of GDP to reach 80 percent in 2010.

The public debt equals the accumulation of past budget deficits. The budget deficit is the annual shortfall in government revenue relative to government spending. A public debt indicates that over a span of years the annual budget deficits outweigh annual budget surpluses. Even if a public debt remains within a moderate range, observers and critics claim that the annual budget deficits have harmful effects. Firstly, these deficits subtract from the amount of credit available to finance house purchases and business capital expansion. Secondly, they elevate interest rates, and create a class of financial assets that pay good interest rates at low risk. Foreign investors in the pursuit of these government bonds bid up the value of the domestic currency in foreign exchange markets. A strongly valued currency in foreign exchange markets makes imports less costly to domestic consumers and home exports more costly to foreign consumers. Critics charge that imports swell while exports shrink, and that the result is fewer domestic jobs.

See also: Foreign Debt Crises

References

Miles, David, and Andrew Scott. 2002. *Macroeconomics: Understanding the Wealth of Nations.*

Montesquieu, Charles De Secondat, Baron de. 1748/1952. *Spirit of Laws.*

OCED Economic Outlook, Number 84, 2008. www.oced.org/publications

Q

QUATTRINI AFFAIR

The *quattrini* was one of the three silver coins that circulated in fourteenth-century Florence. The "quattrini affair" refers to a devaluation of the quattrini in 1371 that set in motion a course of events leading in 1378 to a popular uprising and a brief dictatorship of the proletariat.

The Florentine money of account was the *lira*, originally meaning a pound of silver, and in the Florentine currency system 240 *denarii* equaled 1 lira, 60 quattrini equaled 1 lira, and 8 *grossi* also equaled 1 lira. Florence also minted the *florin*, a gold coin that circulated mainly in international trade and among the wealthiest members of society. The exchange rate between silver coins and florins varied with the silver content of silver coins.

The money stock of a 14th-century Italian city-state consisted of a varying medley of domestic and foreign coins and the rate of coinage depended on the amount of private silver brought to the mint. Private persons took their silver to city-state mints that struck coins with the greatest excess of face value per weight of silver. A city-state such as Florence could debase the silver content of its currency, increasing the face value of its coinage relative to silver content, and attract more silver to its mint. The system encouraged cities to engage in competitive devaluation, and devaluation became a plague that spread from one city to another.

Florentine authorities balked at currency devaluation, and by the mid-14th century the coinage of denarii, quattrini, and grossi came to a halt because no silver was brought to the mint. Currency from Pisa invaded the Florentine economy, driving out Florentine currency in accordance with Gresham's law that bad money drives out good. In 1366, the Florentine authorities gave way and slashed the silver content of the *denaro*, the most overvalued of the Florentine coins, by 36 percent. The authorities also banned the circulation of petty foreign currency, apparently under the expectation that the ban would have no practical significance.

Next, Florentine grossi and quattrini came under pressure as Pisan grossi and quattrini with the same face value but less silver content were exchanged for the Florentine coins. Florentine grossi stood only slightly above Pisan grossi in silver content, and in 1366, Florence debased the grossi by 2.5 percent, a sufficient debasement to bring Florentine grossi into parity with Pisan grossi.

The Florentine quattrini, overvalued relative to Pisan quattrini by a good 18 percent, now came under pressure. The Florentines had sought to avoid devaluing the quattrini because local prices were most often quoted in quattrini and the whole domestic price structure and monetary stability depended on quattrini. The invasion of devalued Pisan currency again forced the hand of the Florentines, and in 1371, the silver content of Florentine quattrini fell by 18 percent and Florentine denarii by 5 percent.

Silver flowed into Florentine mints with the rise in face value relative to silver content, and soon a boom in the coinage of quattrini and denarii was underway. As supplies of quattrini and denarii soared, the forces of currency depreciation made themselves felt with a merciless logic, in time sending a thunderclap through the Florentine economy.

The florin rose in value as the silver content of the silver coinage fell, prices rose faster than wages, and discontent rose to a boiling point among the minor artisans. In 1378, Michele di Lando, a barefoot workingman, led the wool carders in a proletarian revolution against the financial oligarchy that ruled Florence. The revolutionaries dismissed the government officials, established a dictatorship of the proletariat, and set out to reform society, repealing laws against unionization, enfranchising unions of lower-paid workers, imposing a 12-year debt moratorium on debts of wage earners, and reducing interest rates. Businesses fought back by closing down and recruiting outside forces to overthrow the government. The proletarians split into factions between more conservative skilled labors and unskilled labors sympathetic with communistic ideas. An armed force from the countryside overthrew the government in 1381, but not before the government had melted down large quantities of quattrini in an effort to end the pressures for currency depreciation.

The quattrini affair gives some support to Lenin's comment that the best way to destroy the capitalist society is to debauch its currency. Inflation and monetary instability have attended all major revolutions, including the French Revolution, the Russian Revolution, and the Chinese Revolution.

See also: Florentine Florin

References

Cipolla, Carlo M. 1982. *The Monetary Policy of Fourteenth-Century Florence.*

Chown, John F. 1994. *A History of Money.*

Goldthwaite, Richard A. 1980. *The Building of Renaissance Florence: An Economic and Social History.*

R

RADCLIFFE REPORT

In 1957, the British government formed a committee "to inquire into the working of the monetary and credit system, and to make recommendations." In August 1959, this committee issued a report called the Radcliffe Report after the committee chairman, Lord Radcliffe, that played down the importance of keeping the growth of the money stock within strict limits. The report became a symbol of the kind of government views of monetary policy that let inflation accelerate and develop a momentum of its own in the 1970s. According to Glyn Davies (1994), "No official report has ever in British history (nor I believe elsewhere) shown such skepticism regarding monetary policy in the sense of trying to control the economy by controlling the quantity of money" (400).

The report was sprinkled with such exaggerated statements suggesting that banknotes are a relatively unimportant part of the money supply and that the supply of banknotes should respond passively to the needs of trade.

The report cited two main factors that impaired the operational significance of regulated money stock growth. The first factor was the importance of monetary substitutes that were always ready to come forth and fill gaps in the money supply. Obvious examples of money substitutes, or near-monies, were savings accounts and government bonds. The report stressed that it was an individual's liquidity position, rather than money holdings, that shaped that individual's spending decisions. An individual with modest money holdings might nevertheless be in a very liquid position financially.

The second factor hampering the effectiveness of regulated money stock growth was the velocity of circulation. An increase in velocity has the same economic impact as a money stock increase, and changes in velocity can offset changes in money stock growth. The flavor of the report's findings is captured in the following passages:

> If, it is argued, the central bank has both the will and the means to control the supply of money . . . all

will be well. Our view is different. It is the whole liquidity position that is relevant to spending decisions. . . . The decision to spend thus depends upon the liquidity in the broad sense, not upon immediate access to money. . . . *Spending is not limited to the amount of money in circulation.* (400, author's emphasis)

In a highly developed financial system the theoretical difficulties of identifying "the supply of money" cannot be lightly swept aside. Even when they are disregarded, all the haziness of the connection between the supply of money and the level of total demand remains: the haziness that lies in the impossibility of limiting the velocity of circulation (Davies, 1994, 401).

The findings of the Radcliffe Report essentially threw out the control of the money stock in the arsenal of weapons against inflation, a weapon that was sorely needed in the 1970s. The views expressed in the report became economic orthodoxy in the 1960s, and treated as the accepted view in economics textbooks. As inflation mounted in the 1970s, the views of the Radcliffe Report came under increasing criticism, and by the 1980s the quantity theory of money had largely supplanted the views of the Radcliffe Report. The quantity theory of money emphasizes the connection between the quantity of money and inflation.

See also: Bank of England, Deutsche Bundesbank, Equation of Exchange, Monetarism, Velocity of Money

References

Davies, Glyn. 1994. *A History of Money.*

United Kingdom. 1959. *Report of the Committee on the Workings of the Monetary System,* Cmnd. 827.

REAL BILLS DOCTRINE

The real bills doctrine holds that if banks make loans only to finance short-term commercial transactions, the money supply will expand and contract to meet the needs of trade and fluctuations in the money supply will not be a source of economic instability leading to either inflation or deflation. The self-liquidating nature of these loans, and their use to finance the production of goods and services, allegedly checks the rise of inflationary forces. The doctrine found favor with Adam Smith and it has commanded some interest to the present day.

To appreciate the doctrine one must first understand that when banks advance loans, the money supply expands. When banks allow money to build up as vault cash or other forms of reserves, the money supply contracts.

The real bills doctrine first broke into public debate in the United Kingdom during the Napoleonic Wars. Under the stress of wartime finance, Great Britain had suspended the convertibility of banknotes into precious metal, putting Britain on an inconvertible paper standard comparable to inconvertible paper standards in the United States or the United Kingdom today. So-called bullionists argued that the money supply should remain proportional to precious metal reserves, such as gold reserves, to maintain its value and avoid inflation or deflation. Antibullionists defended the suspension of convertibility on the grounds of the real bills doctrine and attributed problems of rising prices and currency depreciation to other causes. After the Napoleonic Wars, the United Kingdom established a gold standard and a new monetary debate developed between the banking school and the currency school.

Both schools supported the gold standard but the banking school felt that banks should have the flexibility to make loans according to the real bills doctrine, allowing the money supply to expand and contract to meet the needs of trade. The currency school made the case that the money supply should remain proportional to gold reserves, and should only change as gold flowed in and out of the country.

In the early stages of development the Federal Reserve System followed the real bills doctrine in practice. During the post–World War II era the real bills doctrine and similar doctrines have lost credibility in favor of proposals to increase the money supply at a fixed rate, such as 3 to 5 percent per year, to encourage the economy to mirror the same stability.

See also: Bank Restriction Act of 1797, Banking School, Currency School, Monetarism, Radcliffe Report

References

Klein, John J. 1986. *Money and the Economy,* 6th ed.

Perlman, Morris. "Adam Smith and the Paternity of the Real Bills Doctrine." *History of Political Economy,* vol. 21, no. 1 (Spring 1989): 77–90.

Spiegel, Henry Williams. 1971. *The Growth of Economic Thought.*

REDENOMINATION

The term "redenomination" refers either to a change in the number of zeros associated with a given currency, or it can apply to the introduction of a new currency. On January 1, 2005, Turkey slashed six zeroes from its currency. One million of the old Turkish lira converted to one of the new Turkish lira (*Economist,* August 2004) Before the redenomination, 1 euro equaled 1.8 million Turkish lira. After the redenomination, 1 euro equaled 1.8 new Turkish lira. In July 2008, Zimbabwe slashed ten zeroes from its currency (US Fed News Service, July 2008). At the time of Zimbabwe's redenomination its currency was trading a 110 billion Zimbabwe currency to one U.S. dollar. When a currency is redenominated, balance sheets, debts, and financial portfolios are adjusted accordingly.

The introduction of the euro can be viewed either as the introduction of a new currency or a redenomination but it raised many redenomination issues. Debts and balance sheets in displaced European currencies had to be redenominated in terms of the Euro. Each government enjoyed certain autonomy in deciding the redenomination process for their own currencies. The French and Italian authorities decided that their debt would not have any decimal places after redenomination whereas German authorities used decimal places. The timetable allowed governments to implement redenomination anytime between 1999 and 2002.

More commonly, redenomination refers the removal of zeroes from a currency. There are several reasons why countries undertake redenomination. One obvious reason is that it simplifies the mathematics of currency transactions. Extra zeros put a burden on accounting and statistical records, data processing software, and payment systems. From political and psychological perspectives, slashing zeroes wipes out evidence of past hyperinflation and monetary chaos, and serves as a commitment from government that uncontrolled inflation is a thing of the

Man in a Harare taxi displays the newly released 50,000 Zimbabwean dollar note on October 13, 2008. Inflation stood at 231 million percent. (AP Photo)

past. Redenomination may represent the finishing touches on tough but successful economic reform measures. Less common is the case where governments use redenomination to confiscate resources. Laos only gave its citizens one day to exchange old currency for new currency in 1976 (Mosely, 2005). The Soviet Union in 1991 and Nicaragua in 1988 only gave citizens three days to swap old currency for new currency (Mosely, 2005). In these situations, some citizens will not succeed in getting their old, worthless currency exchanged for the new currency. The loss to the citizens left holding the old currency becomes revenue to the government.

Between 1960 and 2003, developing and transition economies redenominated currencies on 60 different occasions (Mosely, 2005). In 14 of these cases of currency redenomination, only one zero was removed. In nine cases six zeros were removed. The median redenomination removed three zeros. Nineteen countries redenominated only once, and ten countries redenominated twice. As of 2003, Brazil has redenominated six times, the former Yugoslavia/Serbia five times, and Argentina four times (Mosely, 2005). A few countries have added digits to their currency: South Africa, 1961; Sierra Leone, 1964; Ghana, 1965; Australia, 1966; the Bahamas, 1966; New Zealand, 1967; Fiji, 1969; the Gambia, 1965; Malawi, 1971; and Nigeria, 1973 (Mas 1995). Adding digits makes the currencies more comparable to a key currency such as the U.S. dollar. Triple digit inflation or higher often leads to redenomination, but not always.

Japan has debated redenomination for the yen. In 2008, the yen often traded around 110 yen per one U.S. dollar. The introduction of the euro prompted concern that the yen's stature as an international currency might suffer from new competition. A sluggish Japanese economy in the 1990s encouraged Japanese policy makers to consider the advantages of redenomination. In 1999, the ruling Liberal Democratic Party formed a committee to evaluate the idea of removing two zeros from the yen.

Among highly industrialized countries, Korea has the highest exchange rate with the U.S. dollar. The U.S. dollar is equal to more than 1000 Korean won. South Korean Officials have also discussed the possibility of redenomination.

References

Economist. "Nought to Worry About: Zeroing on Too Many Zeroes." August 28, 2004, p. 67.

Mas, Ignacio. "Things Governments Do to Money: A Recent History of Currency Reform Schemes and Scams." *Kyklos,* vol. 48, no. 4 (1995): 483–513.

Mosley, Layna. "Dropping Zeros and Gaining Credibility? Currency Redenomination in Developing Nations." Conference Paper, American Political Science Association, 2005 Annual Meeting, pp. 1–28.

US Fed News Service. "VOA News: Zimbabwe's Central Bank Snips 10 Zeros in Currency Redenomination." July 30, 2008.

REGULATION Q

See: Eurodollars, Glass–Steagall Banking Act of 1933

REICHMARK

See: Gold Mark of Imperial Germany, Rentenmark

RENTENMARK

The *rentenmark* was the currency that the German government issued in the aftermath of the hyperinflation that occurred in Germany immediately following World War I. Hyperinflation had completely discredited the mark, leaving the price of something as simple as a newspaper at 70 million marks. Toward the end of 1923, the rentenmark replaced the mark as a new, stable currency.

A costly war and heavy war reparations had left Germany virtually bankrupt, and without the gold and foreign exchange reserves needed to support a paper currency. Usually, governments seeking to restore monetary stability had arranged foreign loans that allowed them to issue a new currency convertible at an official rate into gold and foreign exchange. Germany, lacking access to foreign loans, faced the challenge of establishing a new currency that would command the confidence of the public without the backing of significant reserves of gold and foreign exchange.

Germany handled these monetary difficulties in much the same spirit that France handled similar difficulties in the past. Early in 18th-century France, John Law's Banque Royal had issued paper money on the security of land in Louisiana, a financial venture that set the stage for France's first paper money debacle. Later the revolutionary French government issued paper money called "assignats," backed by land confiscated from the church. At first the church land was reserved for sale to owners of assignats, but too many assignats were issued and the plan ended in a storm of hyperinflation.

The Deutsche Rentenbank, a new bank of issue organized to issue rentenmarks, held collateral in the form of agricultural and industrial mortgages. Theoretically, the agricultural and industrial mortgages could have been liquidated and the proceeds used to redeem the rentenmarks, but in practice such a liquidation would have been difficult. One rentenmark was worth 1 billion of the old marks.

In addition to reforming the currency, the German government reformed its fiscal affairs, balancing the budget in terms of rentenmarks and ending government dependence on the central bank to purchase government bonds. The German government, by getting its own house in order, diffused the pressure for inflationary finance. In turn the Rentenbank, by strictly limiting the issuance of rentenmarks, ended the spiral of inflation, showing the world that gold and foreign exchange reserves were not necessary for a stable, noninflationary currency. The experience of the rentenmark underlined the role of government fiscal mismanagement as the force that invariably fuels hyperinflation.

Late in 1924, Germany received a sizable loan under the Dawes Plan, enabling it to reorganize the Reichbank, which had suspended the issuance of banknotes after the formation of the Rentenbank. The Reichbank again took over responsibility for issuing banknotes and the rentenmark was renamed the *reichmark*. The reichmark was convertible into gold but gold coins did not circulate as currency, a system that spread to the rest of the world during the 1930s. Following World War II, the reichmark was discontinued and replaced by the *deutsche mark*.

Although land-secured paper money had twice led France into the chaos of hyperinflation, Germany had embarked on a land-secured system of paper money determined to contain inflationary pressures. Germany's experience with the rentenmark demonstrated that a society may avoid inflation and stabilize the value of a currency by strictly limiting currency supplies. By strict monetary discipline, Germany's experiment succeeded where similar efforts had failed.

See also: Deutsche Mark, Hyperinflation in Post–World War I Germany, Gold Mark of Imperial Germany

References

Davies, Glyn. 1994. *A History of Money.*

Kindleberger, Charles P. 1984. *A Financial History of Western Europe.*

Stolper, Gustav. 1967. *The German Economy: 1870 to the Present.*

REPORT FROM THE SELECT COMMITTEE ON THE HIGH PRICE OF BULLION

The so-called Bullion Report, published on June 8, 1810, ranks with the most famous documents in the history of monetary theory. The report was actually written by Henry Thornton, a prominent banker and economist. Thomas Malthus and David Ricardo, the most famous economists of the day, rallied to support the conclusions of the report, which cited fiat money (money inconvertible into a precious metal at an official rate) as the cause of the high price of bullion. Actually, the first volley had come from the pen of Ricardo, who wrote newspaper articles and pamphlets on the subject, one entitled *The High Price of Bullion* (1810).

During the French Revolution and Napoleonic Wars, the Bank of England suspended convertibility of banknotes into metallic coinage and precious metal, an action that would become common practice during future wars but was then unprecedented. Inflation measures calculated from price indices were unavailable at the time, but the price of gold bullion in British pounds soared and the British pound depreciated relative to other European currencies in foreign exchange markets. Discussions on the high price of bullion and currency depreciation led to the appointment of a select committee to make an inquiry.

The current state of knowledge of monetary theory would have the finger of suspicion immediately turn to the issuance of fiat money, but at the threshold of the 19th century other causes were cited for the high price of bullion and the depreciation of the British pound. To the observation that the high price of gold was due to increased demand for gold to supply French armies, the Report answered:

> Your Committee is of the opinion that in the sound natural state of the British currency the foundation of which is gold no increased demand for gold from other parts of the world however great or from whatever causes arising can have the effect of producing here for a considerable period of time a material rise in the market price of gold. . . . it was to be expected that those who ascribed the high price here to a great demand abroad, would have been prepared to state that there were corresponding high prices abroad. . . . [I]t does not appear that during the time when the price of

Gold bullion was rising here as valued in our paper there was any corresponding rise in the price of Gold bullion in the market of the Continent as valued in their respective currencies. (Chown, 1994, 239)

The select committee was equally unimpressed with theories that attributed the depreciation of the pound to harvest failures, Napoleon's blockade, subsidies of foreign allies, and support of armies in foreign lands. In the words of the report:

> From the foregoing reasoning relative to the state of the Exchanges if they are considered apart, Your Committee find it difficult to resist an inference that a portion at least of the great fall which the Exchanges lately suffered must have resulted not from the state of trade but from a change in the relative value of our domestic currency. But when this deduction is joined with that which your Committee have stated respecting the market price of Gold, that inference appears to be demonstrated. (Chown, 1994, 241)

The report recommended a return to convertibility as soon as possible, but the exigencies of war outweighed the logic of the report and a resumption of convertibility had to wait until 1821.

The bullionist controversy demonstrated the difficulty of pinpointing the causes of currency depreciation and inflation. Often the blame was laid at the feet of shortages, greedy labor unions, monopolies, and speculators, when a more careful examination placed the cause in undisciplined growth in money stocks. The report recommended a return to convertibility as a means of maintaining monetary discipline.

See also: Bank Restriction Act of 1797, Monetarism, Gold Standard, Real Bills Doctrine

References

Chown, John F. 1994. *A History of Money.*
Spiegel, Henry Williams. 1971. *The Growth of Economic Thought.*

REPURCHASE AGREEMENTS

A repurchase agreement is the sale of a security coupled with a promise to buy back the security at a specific price and date in the future. It is called a repurchase agreement but it is actually a loan. The seller receives cash for the security sold. The buyer of the security is loaning cash to the seller, and holding the security as collateral. The seller agrees to buy back the security at a higher price after a certain amount of time has elapsed. By repurchasing the security at a higher price in the future, the seller is in effect paying interest on funds borrowed from the buyer. Typically, the selling price is set equal to the repurchase price plus a negotiated amount of interest. If the borrower fails to repurchase the security at the agreed on date in the future, the lender can sell the security to a third party and recoup the funds lent. If the lender fails to resell the security to the previous owner, the previous owner can use the funds for repurchasing the security to purchase another investment.

Repurchase agreements have long played a role in the U.S. monetary system. As early as 1917, Federal Reserve Banks used repurchase agreements to extend credit to commercial banks. During the 1920s the New York Federal Reserve used repurchase agreements to extend credit to nonbank dealers in short-term credit instruments.

As U.S. inflation led to higher interest rates in the post–World War II era, repurchasing agreements grew in popularity. Nonbank dealers in treasury bonds went searching for less costly financing than what commercial banks, their traditional sources of credit, were offering. At the same time, large state and local governments and nonfinancial corporations discovered that, despite rising interest rates, bank deposits paid zero interest. By being party to a repurchase agreement these institutions could earn interest on funds idly sitting in interest-free bank accounts. Purchasing a treasury bond under a repurchase agreement involved minimal risk, negotiable maturities, and routine mechanics. Treasury bond dealers and institutional cash managers created a market for repurchase agreements. After the 1970s the growth in U.S. Treasury marketable debt and rising short-term interest rates made repurchase agreements attractive to all kinds of creditors, including school districts and other small creditors that could not earn interest on checking accounts (Garbade, 2006). Repurchase agreements became a common vehicle for the short-term investment of surplus cash. Congress lifted the ban on interest-bearing checking accounts in 1980.

The securities most often involved in repurchase agreements are U.S. Treasury and federal agency bonds, but repurchase agreements can be arranged for mortgage-backed securities, and various short-term money market credit instruments, including negotiable bank certificates of deposit.

Repurchase agreements are nearly all short-term agreements. Overnight repurchase agreements are the most common type of treasury bond repurchase agreement. Other standard maturities for repurchase agreements include one, two and three weeks, and one, two, three, and six months. The parties to the repurchase agreement may negotiate flexible terms to maturity.

The purchaser of a security in a repurchase agreement only earns the interest that is agreed on in the contract. A treasury bond in a repurchase agreement will usually remain registered in the name of the seller. The seller in the repurchase agreement will directly receive any coupon payments earned by the bond while the buyer is holding it.

U.S. commercial banks regard repurchase agreements as a close substitute for Federal funds borrowing. The interest rate commercial banks pay on repurchase agreements is usually 25 to 30 basis points below the Federal funds rate (Lumpkin, 1987). The interest rates on repurchase agreements are a bit lower because repurchase agreements are backed by high-quality collateral. Rather than borrow funds in the Federal funds market, a commercial bank may arrange an overnight repurchase agreement with one of its large depositors. Some countries include the repurchase liabilities of depository institutions in the broader measurers of the circulating money stock. The Federal Reserve Bank of New York also arranges repurchase agreements with primary dealers in treasury securities as a part of its open market operations.

See also: Monetary Aggregates

References

Garbade, Kenneth D. "The Evolution of Repo Contracting Conventions in the 1980's." *Economic Policy Review-Federal Reserve Bank of New York,* vol. 12, no. 1 (May 2006): 27–44.

Lumpkin, Stephen. "Repurchase and Reverse Repurchase Agreements." *Economic Review,* Federal Reserve Bank of Richmond, vol. 731 (January 1987): 15–23.

RESERVES

See: Bank, Forestall System, High-Powered Money, Legal Reserve Ratio, Monetary Multiplier, National Bank Act of 1864

RESUMPTION ACT OF 1875 (UNITED STATES)

The principle objective of the Resumption Act of 1875 was to provide for the resumption of specie payments on greenbacks, the fiat paper money born of the Civil War, which was still current in the 1870s.

The act had three important sections. The first section provided for the retirement of the fractional paper currency that been current since the Civil War. The fractional paper currency was in denominations of 10, 25, and 50 cents. The act of 1875 provided for the issuance of subsidiary silver coin to replace the fractional currency. This provision was a bow to the silver interests because only gold coins circulated at the time. The second section got rid of seigniorage, or mint charges, on the coinage of gold, a provision that pleased

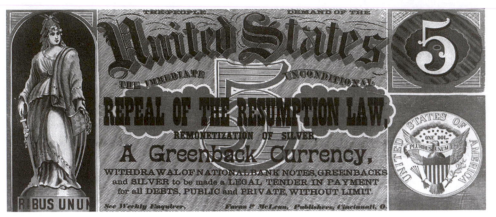

Poster in the form of a "greenback" legal-tender note urges the repeal of the Resumption Act, 1875. (Library of Congress)

the mining interests. The third section of the act removed limitations on the total number of banknotes that national banks could issue, a provision that met the demand for what then was called free banking. The treasury was to retire greenbacks in an amount equal to 80 percent of the increase in national banknotes, until greenbacks in circulation fell to 300 million.

The third section took up the heart of the legislation, the redemption of greenbacks. After January 1, 1879, greenbacks were redeemable in coin when brought to the assistant treasurer at New York in sums no less than $50. The act also authorized the secretary of treasury to "issue, sell and dispose of, at not less than par, in coin" any of the bonds authorized under existing legislation.

A certain amount of pessimism surrounded the Resumption Act of 1875. Many opponents felt that resumption was not feasible, that people would show up in mass to exchange greenbacks for gold, that it would trigger an unbearable contraction of the money supply, and that Congress would not stand firmly in favor of resumption. In 1878 a bill to repeal the Resumption Act failed to pass Congress

by a narrow margin, and Congress did raise from 300 million to 346 million the maximum number of greenbacks that could remain in circulation. Nevertheless, the expected eagerness to exchange greenbacks for gold had been overstated, and resumption took place without difficulty.

The term "coin" in the legislation was generally assumed to refer to gold coins. In 1878, the Bland–Allison Silver Purchase Act made silver legal tender, opening up the possibility that bonds sold to raise coin—gold coin—could be redeemed in silver. Advocates of silver felt that redemption of bonds was legitimate, but the proposal aroused strong opposition. President Hayes in his veto message on the Bland–Allison Act (the act was passed over a presidential veto) cited the large number of bonds the government had sold. He noted that the bonds were sold for gold, and that the bondholders expected the bonds to be redeemed in gold, and would not have bought the bonds otherwise. In the words of his veto message:

National promises should be kept with unflinching fidelity. There is no power to compel a nation to repay its debts. Its credit depends on its honor. The nation owes what it has led or allowed its creditors to expect. (Watson, 1970, 154)

Despite the provisions of the Bland–Allison Act making silver legal tender, the U.S. government maintained its commitment to redeem public bonds in gold.

The Resumption Act of 1875 is one of the important pieces of coinage legislation in U.S. history because it ended an era of fiat money.

See also: Bland–Allison Silver Repurchase Act of 1878, Free Silver Movement, Greenbacks

References

Carothers, Neil. 1930/1967. *Fractional Money.*

Hepburn, A. Barton. 1924/1967. *A History of Currency in the United States.*

Meyers, Margaret G. 1970. *A Financial History of the United States.*

Ritter, Gretchen. 1997. *Gold Bugs and Greenbacks: The Antimonopoly Tradition and the Politics of Finance in America.*

Watson, David K. 1970. *History of American Coinage.*

RETURN TO GOLD: 1300–1350

During the first half of the 14th century, Europe saw gold currency displace silver currency as the primary circulating medium. The Carolingian reform of the eighth century had ended gold coinage in Europe, and for over 400 years Europe had contented itself with minting the silver *denarius*, a small denomination coin, predecessor to the modern penny. A critical development in returning Europe to gold coinage was the discovery of Hungarian gold deposits around Kremnica in Slovakia, which became producing mines around 1320.

In the mid-13th century, Florence and Genoa had introduced gold coinage and Venice followed later in the century with the gold *ducat* to rival the Florentine *florin*. Dependence on African gold restricted the supply of the early Italian gold, limiting its circulation to the Mediterranean area.

After 1320, Hungarian gold grew in abundance, enabling Charles Robert of Anjou, King of Hungary, to began minting gold coins in 1328. These gold coins imitated the Florentine florin and were the first gold coins minted north of the Alps. An exchange of Bohemian silver for Hungarian gold enabled John the Blind of Luxemburg, king of Bohemia, to begin coinage of gold florins coincidentally with the Hungarian coinage as part of a Hungarian-Bohemian monetary cooperation.

Hungarian gold profusely poured into Italy in exchange for Italian goods and services. In 1328, Venice effectively abandoned a silver standard in favor of a gold standard, and coinage of the gold ducat began to vastly outstrip the silver *grossi*.

In the 1330s, France and England borrowed from Italian bankers large sums of gold florins to finance wars. The pope also subsidized France with vast sums of florins, and in 1337, France began minting large quantities of it own gold coin, the *ecu.*

Gold coinage began on a large scale in the Low Countries around the same time. In 1336 the mint of Flanders began striking large quantities of gold coins, and the mints of Brabant, Hainault, Cambrai, and Guelders first struck gold coins in 1336 and 1337.

Most of the German mints striking gold coins during the 14th century were located in the valleys of the Rhine and Main. One important exception, Lubeck, the principle city of the Hanseatic League, received royal permission to mint gold and silver coins in 1340. In 1342, Lubeck began striking gold Lubeck coins.

England had made an abortive effort to coin gold pennies in 1257, roughly coinciding with the appearance of gold coinage in Italy. England's second and more successful effort at gold coinage began in 1344. Edward III engaged Florentine mintmasters and issued a gold coin, the "leopard," which proved unsuccessful because its official value in terms of silver exceeded its market value. After adjustments in metal content, Edward II minted another gold coin, the "noble," valued at 6 shillings and 8 pence. Nobles, half-nobles, and quarter-nobles became important components of English coinage.

Scotland first launched a gold coin in 1357, but the first gold coinage failed, and a successful gold coinage had to wait until the end of the century.

As gold coinage spread silver coinage took on the role of subsidiary coinage suitable for small, local transactions, a role the silver continued to play until alloyed token currency replaced full-bodied metallic currency.

See also: Florentine Florin, Gold, Venetian Ducat

References

Chown, John F. 1994. *A History of Money.*
Spufford, Peter. 1988. *Money and its Use in Medieval Europe.*

RICE CURRENCY

The history of rice currency takes into scope geographical areas as diverse as the Far East and the American colonies, and touches on familiar subjects in the history of money, including debasement, Gresham's law, paper money, and religious associations.

The most developed system of rice currency emerged in feudal Japan. At the opening of the 17th century, Japan added up its wealth, measured in *koku* of rice, and found the country's wealth equivalent in value to 28 million kokus. After the 16th century, copper, gold, and silver circulated alongside rice, but values were expressed in rice, debts were contracted in rice, and taxes were collected partly in rice and partly in metallic money. Workers received rice in payment for work, and the retainers and attendants of feudal lords received stipends in rice.

Large landowners issued rice notes, maintained large storehouses to redeem those notes, and often sought to redeem the notes at harvest season to make room for the new crop. When they discovered that some of the note bearers never claimed the rice, they began, in the manner of the goldsmith bankers, to issue more notes than they could actually redeem in rice. After a rash of abuses, the Tokugawa banned this practice in 1760.

Rice currency shared an inconvenience common to commodity money—it was bulky to transport for large commercial transactions. With the growth of trade, Japan began to supplant rice currency with metallic money, but not without hearing from the political philosophers, who saw metallic money as the opening wedge for all kinds of evil. Perhaps these philosophers echoed the Confucian emphasis on social stability and saw metallic money as a revolutionizing influence. Other ancient societies, including Sparta of ancient Greece, saw metallic money as an immoral influence. Rice currency survived in some of the remote villages of Japan up to the eve of World War II.

In the 19th century, local governments in Burma measured their revenue in baskets of rice. The Burmese ate the good rice and circulated as money the inferior broken rice unsuitable for food or seed, giving history another example of currency debasement and Gresham's law.

Rice was the most important primitive currency in the Philippines. In 1775, the Sultans of Magindan collected taxes from the Philippines in unthreshed rice. The prime monetary unit was a handful of unthreshed rice, called *palay*. A scale of denominations of palay rose from 1 handful to 1,000 handfuls. A day's wage of a mountain wood gatherer was 5 handfuls. Some of the Philippine tribes endowed rice with religious significance. No women could enter a rice storehouse, and men had to perform certain religious rituals before entering.

In 1739, the colony of South Carolina enacted a law that made rice an acceptable means for paying taxes. The following year the colonial government collected 1.2 million pounds of rice. The government issued "rice orders" to public creditors, which were redeemable after taxes were collected in rice at a rate of 30 shillings per 100 pounds of rice. These rice orders circulated as money, and long-term contracts were struck in terms of rice.

As a commodity, rice was relatively light, making it easier to transport than some commodities, and it could be stored up to eight or nine years. Rice could serve the monetary functions of a medium of exchange and store of value

better than most monetary commodities, which accounts for its relatively rich history as a form of money.

See also: Commodity Monetary Standard, Virginia Tobacco Act of 1713

References

Brock, Leslie V. 1975. *The Currency of the American Colonies, 1700–1764.*
Einzig, Paul. 1966. *Primitive Money.*

RIKSBANK (SWEDEN)

The Riksbank, or Bank of Sweden, the oldest central bank in the world, was the first European bank to issue banknotes. The English goldsmiths issued receipts that circulated as money, but the Riksbank was the first bank to issue paper money.

The Riksbank came into being in 1656 as a private bank split into two departments. One department was an exchange or deposit bank organized along the lines of the Bank of Amsterdam. It accepted deposits of coins and precious metals, and these bank deposits changed ownership without precious metals or coins leaving the bank. They served as money, and were backed up by 100 percent reserves of precious metals. The second department was a lending bank.

The Riksbank issued its first banknotes in 1661. Other banks had already pioneered the use of bills of exchange and transferable bank deposits that supplemented the circulation of coins. Sweden turned to banknotes as a medium of exchange because payments in copper, which served as money in Sweden, were bulky and heavy, even for domestic transactions. Sweden adopted copper as the basis for money in 1625, perhaps because Sweden boasted of the largest copper mine in Europe and the Swedish government owned a share of it. Copper mines paved the way for banknotes when, for convenience and utility, they began paying miners in copper notes that could be redeemed for copper at the mines. These notes were preferable to copper coins and traded at a premium.

In 1668, ownership of the Riksbank passed into the hands of the government, making it the oldest central bank in operation today. By the early 1700s, banknotes were no longer a rarity in Europe. The Bank of England was chartered in 1694 for the purpose of making loans and issuing banknotes, and by 1720, France was learning the disastrous consequences of issuing banknotes without discipline.

In 1789, the Riksbank began issuing government currency, and the Riksbank Act of 1897 conferred on the Riksbank a monopoly on the issuance of currency in Sweden. As late as 1873, the number of central banks in the world remained in single-digit territory, but by 1990, more than 160 central banks dotted the financial landscape, the oldest being the Riksbank.

See also: Bank of England, Bank of France, Central Bank

References

Bank for International Settlements. 1963. *Eight European Central Banks.*

Kindleberger, Charles P. 1984. *A Financial History of Western Europe.*

Samuelsson, Kurt. 1968. *From Great Power to Welfare State: 300 Years of Swedish Social Development.*

Sveriges Riksbank. 1994. *Sveriges Riksbank: the Swedish Central Bank, a Short Introduction.*

Bronze antoninianus coins, Roman, about 293–296 CE. (Museum of London)

ROMAN EMPIRE INFLATION

During the third and fourth centuries CE, inflation in the Roman Empire rose to astronomical numbers, aiding and abetting those internal forces of economic, political, and social decay that made the Empire easier prey for the barbarians.

Early in the first century, Augustus had minted full-valued gold and silver coins. In the following two centuries, the Roman emperors slowly whittled down the weight of the coins and reduced the fineness of the silver coins. In the second century, the silver content of the *denarius* sank to 75 percent during the reign of that philosophic prince, Marcus Aurelius. By mid-third century, creeping inflation had gradually lifted prices about threefold.

Early in the third century, the Caracalla replaced the silver denarius with a new silver coin, 50 percent silver in content, called the *Antoninianus*. At midcentury, this coin still contained 40 percent silver, but thereafter debasement gathered momentum at a heady pace and reached a climax under Gallienus, emperor between 260 and 268 CE. The silver content sank to 4 percent, and prices—already triple the first-century level—finishing the third century at 50 to 70 times higher than the first-century price level.

The political stage mirrored the monetary disorder, or vice versa. In a space of 40 years, starting with the assassination of Gordian in 244, 57 emperors donned the imperial purple, until the accession of Diocletian in 284 ended the revolving door for the imperial title.

The root cause of the inflation could be found in the fiscal affairs of the Roman government. The government paid its expenses in coins and had no major credit market in which to raise funds when expenditures exceeded tax revenue. Perhaps because of the inertia of tradition or political opposition, tax rates could be changed only with great difficulty. The more notorious emperors found that raising funds through taxes was not as easy as raising funds by condemning wealthy senators and citizens on trumped-up charges and confiscating their estates. The remaining alternative was debasement of the currency.

When Aurelian assumed the reins of power in 270, facing galloping inflation, he adopted a currency reform that was almost a good as printing paper money. He simply raised by about 2.5 times the nominal or face value of the silver-plated copper coins that had replaced the silver coins of the empire. Under his reign, the treasury began supplying sealed bags that contained 1,000 of these silver-plated coins. During this inflationary ordeal, the government kept the gold coins much purer, but it paid its expenses in silver-plated coins, which were legal tender.

Diocletian was the first emperor to aggressively combat the rampant inflation. He came to power in 284, amid an economy flooded with inferior coinage, and in 295, he put in place a major reform of the currency, issuing full-weight pure gold and silver coins. His *aureus* equaled one-sixtieth of a pound of gold, and his pure silver coin equaled one-ninety-sixth of a pound of a silver. His coins were comparable in weight and fineness to the coins in Nero's time, when prices were 100 times lower. Inflation continued to surge through the Roman economy and, perhaps out of frustration, Diocletian resorted to wage and price controls in 301. Raising prices above legal levels became a capital offense, and inflation may have begun to slow a bit.

Constantine became emperor early in the fourth century. He eased up the wage and price controls and continued Diocletian's policy of increasing the value of the currency. He minted a coin called the gold *solidus*, equal to one-seventy-second of a pound of gold. This coin maintained its value for 700 years, becoming one of the most famous coins in history. After making Christianity the official faith in 313, Constantine looted the pagan temples of vast quantities of gold to supply his mints. The government mints, however, continued to turn out huge amounts of the debased copper coins, and the added supply of gold may have added fresh fuel to the fires of inflation. The debased denarii continued to fall in value. By the mid-fourth century, one gold solidus in Egypt equaled 30 million denarii. By then the government protected itself by collecting taxes in gold or in kind. The mass of the population paid the penalty for the inflation while the wealthy hedged against inflation by investing in gold and land. The inflation began to decelerate toward the end of the fourth century, but by then the empire was tottering in the face of a barbarian onslaught. The Visigoths captured Rome in 410, and in 476, Odoacer the Barbarian replaced the last Roman emperor, Romulus Augustulus. Constantinople continued to mint the solidus.

See also: Inflation and Deflation

References

Duncan-Jones, Richard. 1998. *Money and Government in the Roman Empire*.

Frank, Tenney. 1940. *An Economic Survey of Ancient Rome*. Vols. I–VI.

Jones, A. H. M. 1974. *The Roman Economy*.

Paarlberg, Don. 1993. *An Analysis and History of Inflation*.

ROSSEL ISLAND MONETARY SYSTEM

Rossel Island, about 200 miles southeast of New Guinea, can lay claim to one of the most novel and complicated primitive monetary systems, one in which time was a significant factor in measuring the value of goods. The actual pieces of money had been handed down virtually unchanged to successive generations since time immemorial and allegedly were of divine origin.

Rossel money split into two variations. *Dap* money came in single polished pieces of shells, and *ko* money in sets of 10 discs made from shells. Dap money covered a larger range of values and stretched into the smallest values, whereas ko money exchanged hands in the larger transactions. These two variations bore some gender connotation, dap money was looked on as men's money, and ko money as women's money. Some goods were only priced in one type of money, and other goods in a combination of dap and ko money.

The system of denominations of shells of different values made the Rossel money unique among primitive currencies. The actual names were a bit clumsy, but 22 different values are represented. For simplification it is easiest to regard the lowest denomination as number 1, the next lowest denomination as number 2, and so on, until the largest denomination of number 22 is reached. Dap came in all 22 denominations, but ko came only in denominations of numbers 8 through 22. One denomination was not a multiple of other denominations, and no one denomination was equivalent to a fixed number of other denominations, contrary to the U.S. monetary system in which 100 pennies equal a dollar. A good costing a number 10 could not be purchased with anything but a number 10, and not in a multiple of smaller denominations.

The differences in value between denominations were based on the amount of time one denomination would have to be loaned out before repayment could be required in another denomination. If a number 10 was loaned out for a length of time, the loan had to be repaid in a number 11. A loan of a number 10 for longer lengths of time called for repayment in a number 12, or a higher denomination, depending on the length of the loan.

Transactions involved a highly elaborate system of credit. Suppose individual A sought to purchase a product priced at number 10 in dap, and this individual owned denominations below number 10 and above number 10, but not in number 10. This individual would borrow a number 10, and would repay the loan in the future with a denomination higher than a number 10, as a means of paying interest. This individual would not mind this arrangement, having the opportunity to loan out his own dap denominations and earning interest also. If a number 22 was loaned out, an initial interest payment was made in a smaller denomination, and in the future the loan was repaid with another number 22. A special class of brokers arranged these necessary transactions.

The currency units, or shells, of the higher-valued denominations (number 18 and above) were known on an individual basis by active financial traders. Only seven currency units of denomination number 22 were in existence, all owned by chiefs. The higher values were considered sacred. When a number 18 exchanged hands, the parties involved crouched down. Numbers 19 to 22 were kept enclosed, always protected from the light of day.

See also: Yap Money

References

Armstrong, W. E. "Rossel Island Money: A Unique Monetary System." *The Economic Journal* 34 (1924): 424–429.

Einzig, Paul. 1966. *Primitive Money.*

ROYAL BANK OF SCOTLAND

The Royal Bank of Scotland, like the Bank of England, began when a group of holders of public debt received a royal charter to incorporate as a banking institution. Parliament granted the royal charter creating Scotland's second public bank on May 31, 1727. The Scottish Parliament had chartered Scotland's first public bank, the Bank of Scotland, on July 17, 1695, before the unification of Scotland and England. In the Rebellion of 1715, the Bank of Scotland had appeared to stand on the Stuart side, a point frequently recalled by those who wanted to create a rival bank, the Royal Bank of Scotland. Parliament later chartered a third Scottish public bank, and also encouraged the growth of private banks. Scotland promoted competition among banks to a much greater extent than England, pioneering the development of free banking, which flourished in the United States in the first half of the 19th century.

The Royal Bank of Scotland earned a place in the history of money and banking when it developed the antecedents of overdraft privileges. In his famous book, *An Inquiry into the Nature and Causes of the Wealth of Nations*, perhaps the most famous book on economics, Adam Smith attributed this important banking innovation to the public banks of Scotland. Although he does not credit a single bank for the innovation, his description captures the spirit of the innovation in the language of the day:

They invented, therefore, another method of issuing their promissory notes; by granting what they called cash accounts, that is by giving credit to the extent of a certain sum (two or three thousand pounds, for example) to any individual who could procure two persons of undoubted credit and good landed estate to become surety for him, that whatever money should be advanced to him, within the sum for which the credit had been given, should be paid on demand, together with the legal interest. Credits of this kind are, I believe, commonly granted by banks and bankers in all different parts of the world. But the easy terms upon which the Scottish banking companies accept of repayment, are so far as I know, peculiar to them, and have, perhaps, been the principal cause, both of the great trade of those companies and of the benefit which the country has received from it. (Smith, 1937, pp. 282)

Other authors, such as Glyn Davies, confer the credit for this innovation to the Royal Bank of Scotland, and cite this innovation as the beginning of the flexible overdraft. The Royal Bank of Scotland (now called the Royal Bank of Scotland, Limited) remains one of the leading commercial banks of Scotland. In 2008, it became one of the leading beneficiaries of the United Kingdom's plan to bailout banks who had overinvested in toxic assets. In 2009, it became officially classified as a public-sector entity, because the United Kingdom's government had absorbed such a large share of its liabilities (MacDonald and Norman, February 2009).

See also: Bank of Scotland, Scottish Banking Act of 1765

References

Checkland, S. G. 1975. *Scottish Banking: A History, 1695–1973*.

Davies, Glyn. 1994. *The History of Money*.

MacDonald, Alistair, and Laurence Norman. "World News: Bank Bailouts, Sinking Revenue Fray U.K.'s Ledger." *Wall Street Journal* (Eastern Edition), February 20, 2009, p. A10.

Smith, Adam. 1937. *An Inquiry into the Nature and Causes of the Wealth of Nations*.

RUM CURRENCY

See: Liquor Money

RUSSIAN CURRENCY CRISIS

On August 13, 1998, the Russian stock and bond markets crashed amid widespread investor anticipation that the Russian government would devalue the ruble and default on its debt. The stock market lost 75 percent of its value between January and August 1998 (Chiodo and Owyang, 2002). Annual yields on ruble-denominated bonds rose above 200 percent. The expectation of crisis accelerated the crisis. On August 17, the Russian government devalued the ruble, defaulted on its debt, and declared a moratorium on payments to foreign creditors (Chiodo and Owyang, 2002). On September 2, 1998, the Russian government let the ruble float. By April 1999, the ruble traded at 22 percent of its value compared to where it stood before it began to drop in August 1998 (McKay, April 1999).

In 1997, the outlook in Russia remained optimistic. After reporting negative growth in 1995 and 1996, Russian economic growth inched into positive territory at 0.8 percent for 1997 (Chiodo and Owyang, 2002). Inflation subsided to the 11 percent range compared to over 200 percent inflation in 1994 (Chiodo and Owyang, 2002). Oil sold in the $23 per barrel range, a relatively high price at the time. Oil and nonferrous metals accounted for up to two-thirds of Russia's foreign exchange earnings. Large foreign exchange earnings from trade provide resources to keep domestic currencies strong in foreign exchange markets. Russia's credit rating was improving, and by late 1997, about 30 percent of short-term government debt belonged to non-residents (Chiodo and Owyang, 2002). Some problems remained. One vulnerable point was the public sector deficit, which remained high because of Russia's inefficient tax system.

In August 1997, speculative attacks sparked currency crises in East Asian economies. This episode alerted foreign investors to other possible soft spots in the global financial system. In November 1997, the Russian ruble came under speculative attack, causing the Central Bank of Russia to lose $6 billion in foreign exchange reserves (Chiodo and Owyang, 2002).

The Russian government was counting on 2 percent economic growth in 1998 to help pay for rising debt. As the

A security officer tries to prevent a photographer from taking pictures as a man withdraws cash from an automatic teller machine in Moscow on August 14, 1998. As a sign of Russia's unfolding economic crisis, the bank only allowed customers to withdraw money in rubles, even from accounts that were established in U.S. dollars. (AP Photo/Maxim Marmur)

price of oil and nonferrous metal fell in the wake of the East Asian Crisis, Russia's economic situation began to deteriorate. Output would actually fall by nearly 5 percent in 1998. In February, the Russian government requested an aid package from the International Monetary Fund (IMF). It was be July before the IMF approved an emergency aid plan for Russia. The IMF demanded certain reforms before approving the plan.

In April 1998, the ruble came under another speculative attack. On May 19, the Central Bank of Russia increased its lending interest rate from 30 to 50 percent (Chiodo and Owyang, 2002). With inflation in the 10 percent range, these interest rates were unusually high. This action increased the interest rate paid by ruble-denominated assets. Raising domestic interest rates tends to shore up the value of a currency in foreign exchange markets. The currency becomes a ticket to higher interest rates. On May 27, 1998, the Central Bank of Russia raised its lending interest rate to 150 percent (Chiodo and Owyang, 2002).

Missteps in public relations may have aggravated the crisis. Early in May, the chair of the Central Bank of Russia warned government ministers of a debt crisis. The warning came at a meeting with reporters in the audience. At about the same time, the prime minister of Russia stated in an interview that tax revenue was 26 percent less than targeted, and that the government was "quite poor now" (Chiodo and Owyang, 2002). When the prime minister refused to meet with a deputy secretary of treasury of the United States, regarding him as not high enough in the government, big investors became worried, and began selling Russian bonds and stocks.

Russian gross domestic product (GDP) growth recovered, growing 8.3 percent in 2000 and roughly 5 percent in 2001 (Chiodo and Owyang, 2002). The year following the crisis, Russia saw consumer prices soar 92.6 percent (Chiodo and Owyang, 2002). By 2000 and 2001, consumer price inflation had subsided to a range of 20 to 22 percent. In 2000, a world escalation of oil and commodity prices put the government's budget in the surplus column for the first time since the formation of the Federation.

See also: Currency Crises, Foreign Debt Crises

References

Chiodo, Abbigail J., and Michael T. Owyang. "A Case Study of a Currency Crisis: The Russian Default of 1998." *Review,* Federal Reserve Bank of St. Louis, vol. 84, no. 6 (November/December 2002): 7–18.

McKay, Betsy. "Ruble's Decline Energizes Russian Firms Who Manage to Win Back Consumers." *Wall Street Journal* (Eastern Edition, New York) April 23, 1999, p. B7A.

Sesit, Michael R., and Sara Webb. "Ruble's Woes Could Shake Market Anew." *Wall Street Journal* (Eastern Edition, New York) July 6, 1998, p. C1.

RUSSIAN PAPER MONEY

See: Yeltsin's Monetary Reform in Russia

RUSSIAN RUBLE

See: Decimal System, Hyperinflation during the Bolshevik Revolution, Russian Currency Crisis, Tzarist Russia's Paper Money

S

SALT CURRENCY

The word "salary" stems from the Latin word "salarium," meaning "salt money." The Romans paid soldiers, officers, and civil administrators an allowance of salt, and "salarium" came to be a term for military pay after salt was no longer used to pay soldiers.

Marco Polo in *The Travels of Marco Polo,* writing at the end of the 13th century, tells of Chinese salt money in the province of Kain-Du. In the words of Polo:

> In this country there are salt springs, from which they manufacture salt by boiling it in small pans. When the water is boiled for an hour, it becomes a kind of paste, which is formed into cakes of the value of two pence each. These, which are flat on the lower, and convex on the upper side, are placed upon hot tiles, near a fire, in order to dry and harden. On this latter species of money the stamp of the grand khan is impressed, and it cannot be prepared by any other than his own officers. Eighty of the cakes are made to pass for a saggio of gold. But when these cakes are carried by traders amongst the inhabitants of the mountains, and other parts little frequented, they obtain a saggio of gold for sixty, fifty, or even forty of the salt cakes, in proportion as they find the natives less civilized. (Polo, 1958, 187)

Ethiopia offers the most recent example of a society circulating salt as money, a practice that lasted into the 20th century in remote areas. As early as the 16th century, visiting European explorers noted the use of salt as money. Bars of salt money were called "amole," after the Amole tribe that first introduced salt money to the Ethiopians. The bars of rock salt bore a marked resemblance to a whetstone, 10 to 12 inches in length, 1.5 inches thick, and black in color, perhaps from handling. They weighed about a pound. Referring to a millionaire, Ethiopians say "he eateth salt." During the 19th century, Richard Burton visited

Harar and observed that a slave cost a donkey-load of salt bars.

20th-century reports on the value of salt bars varied, some putting the exchange rate of salt bars at less than seven bars per dollar, and others reporting as many as 48 bars per dollar. In some areas, the bars could be broken up for small change, and Ethiopians enjoyed a reputation for accurately gauging the amount to break off.

The Ethiopians are known for having a strong attraction to the taste of salt, but the black bars were not used for consumption. White salt of a finer quality met the needs for seasoning, and the black bars were reserved for monetary uses.

The use of salt as money gives added meaning to the phrase "worth his salt." In virtually every quarter of the globe examples can be found of salt circulating as money at some point in history. It is one of those commodities universally in demand. Following the inflationary chaos of the Bolshevik Revolution, salt was the main standard of value, medium of exchange, and store of value in Moscow.

See also: Commodity Monetary Standard

References

Einzig, Paul. 1966. *Primitive Money*.

Polo, Marco. 1958. *The Travels of Marco Polo*.

Williams, Jonathan, ed. 1997. *Money: A History*.

SAVINGS AND LOAN BAILOUT (UNITED STATES)

In August 1989, Congress enacted the Financial Institution Reform, Recovery, and Enforcement Act. This legislation furnished funds to redeem insured deposits at failed Savings and Loan institutions (S&Ls) and created the Resolution Trust Corporation, an agency responsibly for liquidating the assets of failed savings and loans. The bailout was expected to cost the federal government $160 billion over a 10-year period and maybe as much as $500 billion over 40 years.

Between 1988 and 1991, over 1,000 S&Ls failed, putting out of business approximately one-third of all the S&Ls in the United States. The Federal Savings and Loan Insurance Corporation (FSLIC), the agency responsible for insuring deposits at S&Ls, ran out of money to redeem insured deposits at these institutions. In effect, the S&L collapse bankrupted the FSLIC.

During the 1970s, a period of rising inflation in the United States, S&Ls faced strict legal limits on the interest rates that depositors could earn on S&L deposits. S&Ls paid low interest rates on deposits and made relatively low interest loans on home mortgages.

During the 1980s, the United States economy made the transition from an inflation economy to a disinflation economy, and the S&L industry also changed from a highly regulated industry to a deregulated industry. The deregulation of the S&Ls lifted the interest rate ceilings of S&L deposits, and allowed S&Ls to enter the business of consumer and commercial loans. Interest rates escalated rapidly in the early 1980s under the pressure of a tight, anti-inflation, monetary policy, squeezing S&Ls that held low interest mortgages while paying high interest rates on current deposits.

Savings and loans tried to save themselves by turning to riskier consumer and commercial loans that paid higher interest rates. When depression struck in the oil and real estate industry in the last half of the 1980s, S&Ls began to fail rapidly.

The S&L collapse in the United States uncovered an unsuspected weakness in deposit insurance: fully insured depositors had no incentive to favor S&Ls with conservative investment policies over S&Ls with risky investment portfolios. That is, depositors had no incentive to keep track of investment practices of individual S&Ls, allowing them free rein to finance risky business ventures.

In addition to the the Financial Institution Reform, Recovery, and Enforcement Act, Congress later enacted the Federal Deposit Insurance Corporation Improvement Act of 1991. The first act placed responsibility for insuring S&L deposits with the Federal Deposit Insurance Corporation (FDIC), the agency that before had only insured commercial bank deposits. The second act provided that the FDIC vary the insurance premiums paid by financial institutions according to the riskiness of their loan portfolios. Financial institutions carrying high-risk loan portfolios pay higher deposit insurance premiums. In 2005 Congress enacted the Federal Deposit Insurance Reform Act of 2005. This act tightened the linkage between insurance premiums and the riskiness of the institution.

See also: Depository Institution Deregulation and Monetary Control Act of 1980, Glass–Steagall Banking Act of 1933, Troubled Asset Relief Program

References

Barth, James R. 1991. *The Great Savings and Loan Debacle*.

Long, Robert Emmet, ed. 1993. *Banking Scandals: The S&Ls and BCCI*.

United States Government Accountability Office. "Deposit Insurance: Assessment of Regulators' Use of Prompt Corrective Action Provisions and FDIC's New Deposit Insurance System." GAO=07-242, A Report to Congress, February 2007.

SCEATTAS

See: English Penny

SCOTTISH BANKING ACT OF 1765

The Scottish Banking Act of 1765 established the legal foundations that enabled Scotland to pioneer the development of free banking, a system of banking that flourished in the United States before the Civil War. Under a system of free banking no one bank, usually called a "central bank," claims a monopoly on the issuance of banknotes, as the Federal Reserve System enjoys in the United States. Instead, each private bank issues its own banknotes, and maintains the convertibility of its notes into gold or silver, or other commodity, depending on the monetary standard. Under free-banking systems, the privilege to start a new bank is removed as far as possible from political processes.

The act of 1765 was entitled "An Act to prevent the inconveniences arising from the present method of issuing notes and bills by banks, banking companies, and bankers, in that part of Great Britain called Scotland." The act authorized all "banks, banking companies, and bankers" to issue banknotes, and for a century, the issuance of banknotes became the defining characteristic of Scottish banks. In England, the Bank of England had a monopoly on the privilege to issue banknotes in London. In Scotland, the Bank of Scotland and the Royal Bank of Scotland campaigned to give themselves a monopoly on the issuance of banknotes, but the public sided with the small banks wanting to maintain the privilege to issue banknotes.

The act forbade the issuance of banknotes with a face value less than 20 shillings (or 1 pound sterling, £1). The smallest note issued by the Bank of England was £5, but small note issues had circulated widely in Scotland, some as small as 5 shillings, or even 1 shilling. In Scotland, a shortage of small change created a vacuum that low-denomination banknotes filled.

The act of 1765 also forbade the so-called optional clause. In 1730, the Bank of Scotland, to protect itself from bank runs, began printing on its notes the optional clause, stating that the bank could either redeem the banknotes on demand, or defer redemption for up to six months. The clause also stated the interest rate that banknotes would earn if redemption was deferred. The notes only bore interest for the time redemption was suspended. To encourage banks to follow safer banking policies, optional clauses were banned.

Scotland's free banking system did not exactly find smooth sailing. Several banks failed in 1772, including the Ayr Bank that Adam Smith described in the *Wealth of Nations*. Notwithstanding a few bank failures, Smith sang the praises of Scotland's banking system, and noted the expansion of Scottish commerce that had coincided with the development of banking. During the Napoleonic Wars, Parliament came to the rescue of the Bank of England and Bank of Ireland by ordering the suspension of their banknote convertibility. The banks of Scotland, however, maintained the convertibility of their banknotes and never had to throw themselves on the government for protection.

See also: Bank of Scotland, Free Banking, Royal Bank of Scotland

References

Checkland, S. G. 1975. *Scottish Banking: A History, 1695–1973*.

Colwell, Stephen. 1859/1965. *The Ways and Means of Payment*.

Kroszner, Randy. 1995. *Free Banking: The Scottish Experience as a Model for Emerging Economies*.

SECOND BANK OF THE UNITED STATES

The Second Bank of the United States met the need for a central bank in the United States between 1816 and 1836. During the War of 1812, state banks suspended the conversion of banknotes into specie (gold and silver coins). At that time, each bank issued its own paper money and held specie to redeem its paper money. Today, banks issue checking accounts and hold paper money to redeem the checking accounts. When the banks suspended specie payments in 1814, six months before the war ended, the federal government had no way to pressure them to return to convertibility. The Second Bank of the United States bore a strong resemblance to the First Bank of the United States, which had lost its charter in 1811 because of constitutional questions and foreign ownership. At the time, many questioned if Congress had the authority to grant a charter of incorporation, much less sanction a monopoly. The First Bank of the United States provided monetary discipline by demanding that all banknotes deposited with it be redeemed in specie by the bank that issued them. As the government began to miss the monetary discipline enforced by the First Bank of the

United States, critics—mainly followers of Jefferson and Madison—began to soften their constitutional objections and came to support the creation of the Second Bank of the United States. Now the Jeffersonian Republicans were supporting such a bank instead of the New England Federalists.

Congress approved the charter for the Second Bank of the United States early in 1816, and President Madison signed the bill on April 10 of that year. The Second Bank was capitalized at $35 million. The government owned one-fifth of the stock and appointed five of the 25 directors. Shares of stock were sold at a price to attract broadly based ownership. Foreign-owned stock had no voting rights, and large shareholders were limited to 30 votes. Subscribers could pay as little as one-fourth in specie and the remainder in government securities.

The Second Bank got off to a wobbly start. In 1818, a House committee investigated the bank. It then had $2.4 million in specie to support $22 million in demand liabilities. The bank was on the verge of suspending specie payments itself. The investigating committee discovered that the Second Bank had extended loans to its own stockholders who used stock in the bank as collateral. This practice enabled speculators to buy stock in the Second Bank by using the bank's own money. The officers of the bank had speculated in its stock, and the Second Bank had also been slow in demanding specie payments on notes issued by state banks.

The Second Bank's poor management had consequences for the economic contraction in 1818. The bank's effort to bring its own house in order hastened the economic downturn. The Baltimore branch failed. It had made bad loans, and its officers had speculated in its stock. The

president of the Second Bank resigned, and Langdon Cheves assumed the leadership of the bank (1819). His conservative administration put the bank on firm financial footing. Nicholas Biddle succeeded Cheves in 1823. Biddle's understanding of the role of a central bank put him ahead of his time. He placed the public responsibilities of the bank above the private interests of its stockholders. In 1834, a French traveler termed the Second Bank the "banque centrale."

The Second Bank forced the state banks to maintain specie payments for their banknotes. To reduce money in circulation, the Second Bank accumulated specie. The bank increased the money in circulation by making more loans. The bank's practices made enemies of state banks in the West and South, which resented its regulation of state banknotes. These banks tended to expand the supply of banknotes in circulation beyond what their reserves of specie could be counted on to redeem.

Nicholas Biddle became president of the Second Bank of the United States in 1823. (Library of Congress)

The state banks had a powerful ally in President Andrew Jackson. Biddle and his advisors saw the hostility to the bank gathering momentum. Rather than wait for the Second Bank's charter to expire in 1836, they asked Congress for a renewal of the charter in 1832. The bill for rechartering the bank passed the House and the Senate. President Jackson vetoed the bill.

Critics charged that the bank put too much power in the hands of officials who were neither elected directly by the people nor responsible to elected officials. In addition, paper money had not yet established itself in the confidence of the voters. President Jackson himself was a "hard money" person. The public saw paper money as the culprit in depressions. In his veto message, President Jackson stated:

> Equality of talents, of education, or of wealth cannot be produced by human institutions . . . but when the laws undertake to add to these natural and just advantages artificial distinctions . . . to make the rich richer, and the potent more powerful, the humble members of society—the farmers, mechanics, and laborers— who have neither the time nor the means of securing like favors to themselves, have a right to complain of the injustice of their Government. (Schlesinger, 1945, 90)

Jackson's rhetoric may bear the stamp of the demagoguery of the frontier politician rather than the best thinking of the time. Perhaps the best-educated and most cosmopolitan of all the presidents, Thomas Jefferson, described his opinion of banks in this way:

> I have ever been the enemy of banks; not of those discounting cash; but of those foisting their own paper into circulation, and thus banishing our cash. My zeal against those institutions was so warm and open at the establishment of the [First] bank of the U.S. that I was derided as a Maniac by the tribe of bank-mongers, who were seeking to filch from the public their swindling and barren gains. (Cappon, 1959, 424)

With the establishment of the Federal Reserve System in 1913, the United States finally came to terms with the idea of a central bank. By then, the role of central banks in maintaining economic stability was better understood, and banks were better accepted than they were in Jefferson's day.

See also: Bank of England, Bank of France, Central Bank, Federal Reserve System, First Bank of the United States

References

Brown, Marion A. 1998. *The Second Bank of the United States and Ohio, 1803–1860: A Collision of Interests.*

Cappon, Lester, ed. 1959. *The Adams-Jefferson Letters.*

Meyers, Margaret G. 1970. *A Financial History of the United States.*

Schlesinger, Arthur M., Jr. 1945. *The Age of Jackson.*

Timberlake, Richard H. 1978. *The Origins of Central Banking in the United States.*

SECURITIZATION

Securitization occurs when a loan or pool of loans is transferred into a trust, and the trust then issues bonds that are rated by the large ratings agencies and sold in the bond market. The loans most often associated with securitization are home mortgages, and the bonds sold by these trusts are called mortgage-backed securities (MBS). The individual mortgages are secured by homes and property of the borrowers. The trust holds these collateralized mortgages as collateral for the bonds that these trusts issue.

Years ago, a potential homebuyer applied for a mortgage at a bank or financial institution. The financial institution that approved and funded the loan kept the loan on its own balance sheet until the borrower repaid it. Today, that financial institution is called the "originator" of the loan. The originator of the loan sells the loan to a third party. Some of the well-known third parties are Ginnie Mae, a government agency, Fannie Mae, a government-sponsored entity, and Freddie Mac, also a government-sponsored entity. The originator may also sell the loan to private sector financial institutions. The third party pools the mortgage with other mortgages and sells the payment rights to investors. The process of packaging a bundle of mortgages and selling the package to investors is called "securitization."

A bundle of packaged mortgages might take the following form. Suppose an originator has negotiated 500 mortgages averaging $200,000 each. The mortgages are all scheduled for repayment over 30 years at a fixed interest rate of 7 percent. This $100 million bundle of mortgages can act as collateral for 10,000 bonds. Each bond is worth $10,000, matures in 30 years, and pays 6.5 percent interest. Each of these bonds is called a mortgage-backed security (MBS). The interest earned on the bonds comes from the mortgage interest payments on a pass through basis. Payments made on mortgage principals go toward paying down the principal on the bonds. The mortgages charge slightly higher interest than the bonds earn because intermediates charge fees for their services.

From an investor point of view, the MBSs issued by Ginnie Mae, Fannie Mae, or Freddie Mac are safer investments than those sold by private financial institutions, which are more often based on mortgages negotiated with less credit worthy borrowers.

Private financial institutions structure securitization to meet risk-reward preferences of various investors. In the context of securitization, subordination means that issued bonds carry different bankruptcy priorities. In case of mortgage default, the subordinated classes of bonds bear the first losses. A securitization may involve up to six layers of subordination (Rosen, 2007). The senior bonds have priority in bankruptcy. The first defaults are allocated to the lowest layer of subordination. There are two other methods for controlling risk. One is overcollateralization, and the other is widened interest rate spreads between the bonds and the underlying mortgages.

The packaging and sale of an MBS is not necessarily the end of the securitization process. Bundles of MBSs are also packaged and sold. Bonds backed by securitized bundles of MBSs are called collateralized debt obligations (CDOs). CDOs can be backed by MBSs or other CDOs. Similar to the CDO is the structured investment vehicle (SIV). SIVs issue short-term and medium-term debt, whereas CDOs issue long-term debt. SIVs are also backed by bundles of assets such as MBSs or CDOs.

In 2008, the process of securitization came under scrutiny in the United States. The originators of mortgages had little incentive to be concerned about the prospects for repayment. The credit rating agencies, such as Moody's and Standard and Poor's, overrated the credit worthiness of MBSs. The mortgage default rate rose to high levels. The price of houses sank, undermining the value of the collateral backing the MBSs. Investors in MBSs discovered themselves holding illiquid assets without a measurable market value. Freddie Mac and Fannie Mae saw their stock continue to plummet in 2008 as MBSs lost all credibility. Rather than let two institutions key to home financing go under, the United States Treasury nationalized Freddie Mac and Fannie Mae. The boards of directors of the two institutions sold an 80 percent stake in each entity to the United States Treasury for 0.001 cent per share (Jenkins, 2009, p. A13).

See also: U.S. Financial Crisis of 2008–2009

References

Jenkins, Holman W. Jr. "Rethinking the Fan and Fred Takeover." *Wall Street Journal* (Eastern Edition) March 4, 2009, p. A13.

Penner, Ethan. "The Future of Securitization." Wall Street Journal (Eastern Edition), July 10, 2008, p. A15.

Rosen, Richard J. "The Role of Securitization in Mortgage Lending." *Chicago Fed Letter,* The Federal Reserve Bank of Chicago, Essays on Issues no. 244, November 2007.

SEIGNIORAGE

Seigniorage is the profit or revenue raised through coining or printing money. The word "seigniorage" stems from the French *seigneur*, a word for "feudal lord," referring to feudal manors that often exercised the privilege to mint coins in the Middle Ages. In modern societies, the rights of seigniorage belong to government.

Historically, kings, dukes, counts, bishops, or city-states exercised the privilege to coin money. The coinage usually bore the name, symbol, or portrait of the responsible ruler who guaranteed the weight and purity of the precious metal content. Originally, seigniorage was the mint's share of the coins that were struck from precious metals brought to the mint by private citizens. Some authorities define seigniorage more narrowly as the profit that mints earn from coinage of precious metals supplied by citizens.

Mints operated on the principle that private citizens brought precious metals to them, and they then tested the metal for weight and purity. A private citizen that brought precious metal meeting mint standards either received coins that had already been struck, or received the coins struck from the precious metal that he or she brought to the mint. Minted coins were worth more than equivalent amounts of precious metal because they were much more convenient for transacting business, sparing the need to weigh and evaluate the precious metal. Today, a gold coin such as South Africa's Krugerrand enjoys a market value exceeding the market value of its gold content. By adding value to the coined metals, a mint could get by with taking a cut for itself.

Early in European monetary history, governments began minting bullion brought to mints without deducting seigniorage, minting free of charge. England began the practice of free coinage in 1666. Under England's system, a citizen could bring gold bullion to the mint, wait until the mint turned bullion into coins, or take the bullion to the Bank of England and receive gold coins immediately at a discount of less than 0.5 percent.

The development of government paper money opened new opportunities for seigniorage because the face value of paper money far exceeds the value of the paper as raw material. When the government prints additional paper money, it makes the paper money already in circulation worth less. Prices rise, in effect imposing a tax on existing money balances in the hands of the public.

The dependence on seigniorage revenue varies substantially among modern governments. The United States government raises about 3 percent of government revenue from seigniorage, but Italy and Greece raise over 10 percent of government revenue from seigniorage. Seigniorage often accounts for 50 percent or more of government revenue in countries caught in a spiral of hyperinflation. The chief cause of hyperinflation is excessive government dependence on revenue from seigniorage, rather than from taxes or borrowing.

See also: Great Debasement

References

Chown, John F. 1994. *A History of Money.*

Fischer, Stanley. "Seigniorage and the Case for a National Money." *Journal of Political Economy,* vol. 90 (April 1982): 295–313.

SEIZURE OF THE MINT (ENGLAND)

The Seizure of the Mint refers to an episode in 1640 in which Charles I, reigning king of England from 1625 to 1672, intercepted the flow of coins from the mint to the government's major creditors, the goldsmiths and merchants. Minting coins had become such a booming business under Charles I that the Tower Mint could not keep up, causing Charles I to open branch mints throughout the kingdom.

The only British monarch to be executed, King Charles I ruled during the tumultuous English Civil War. (Library of Congress)

Charles I was always in need of money, despite a treaty with Spain that assured him of abundant supplies of bullion. On one occasion, Charles I forced the East India Company to sell him its entire stock of pepper on credit, payable after two years. Charles I bought the pepper at a price of 2 shillings 1 pence per pound, and then turned around and sold it for 1 shilling 8 pence per pound, raising instant cash in a roundabout credit transaction that angered the merchants of London. On two occasions, the Privy Council blocked proposals that Charles I advanced to increase the mint profits by debasing the coins, a favorite stratagem of monarchs for squeezing more resources from subjects. Debasing the coin meant reducing the precious metal content in coins with a given face value.

The machinery of public finance was a bit primitive during the reign of Charles I. The government's creditors, mainly goldsmiths and merchants, claimed freshly minted coins when they became available. In 1640, Charles I stopped the flow of coins from the mint, planning to uses the coins for his own expenditures, and instead promised to pay the crown's creditors 8 percent interest on his outstanding debt. A howl rose from goldsmiths and merchants who wanted their money immediately, causing Charles I to relent and send two-thirds of the coins to the crown's debtors. Charles I kept one-third of the coins and promised to pay his creditors 8 percent for six months.

Charles I eventually paid the creditors in full, but only after the merchants and goldsmiths had lost faith in the government's management of monetary affairs. Already there was talk of setting up a national or public bank, and the incident of the mint seizure convinced influential people that the government could not be trusted with direct power over such a bank. The Bank of England came into being in 1694 and developed as a private institution that nevertheless enjoyed close ties with the government.

See also: Bank of England, Stop of the Exchequer

References

Challis, C. E., ed. 1992. *A New History of the Royal Mint.*

Craig, J. 1953. *The Mint: A History of the London Mint from A.D. 287 to 1948.*

SHERMAN SILVER ACT OF 1890 (UNITED STATES)

The Sherman Silver Act of 1890 nearly doubled the government's monthly purchase of silver and provided for the issuance of legal-tender treasury notes in payment of silver.

The Coinage Act of 1873 made no provision for the coinage of silver dollars, an omission that became an angry point of contention as deflation and depression spread in the late 19th century and silver interest saw silver prices steadily decline. A "free silver" movement sprang up, calling for unlimited coinage of silver. The Bland–Allison Act of 1878 provided for restricted purchase of silver and coinage of silver dollars, but silver prices continued to fall, and agitation for "free silver" mounted strength. The Sherman Silver Act of 1890 extended the monetization of silver about as far as possible without embracing "free silver," and returning to a bimetallic gold-silver standard.

The act called for the treasury to purchase 4.5 million ounces of silver per month at market prices as long as the market prices did not exceed $1.29 per ounce, the historic mint price since 1837. The treasury was to pay for the bullion in treasury notes in denominations not less than $1 or more than $1,000. These treasury notes were legal tender for all debts, private and public. The act made these notes redeemable in either gold coin or silver coin, depending on the discretion of the treasury. The act only required the treasury to coin quantities of silver bullion as needed to redeem treasury notes.

The act authorized the issuance of treasury notes to save on coinage expenses. Since the market value of silver fell short of its official price, silver was preferred over gold in the payment of government obligations. Silver dollars tended to return to the treasury as fast as they were issued, notwithstanding the treasury's practice of shipping the silver coins to distant places at no cost.

Complaints were heard about the storage costs and inconvenience of the silver dollars. Before the act of 1890, the government was issuing treasury notes that were not legal tender.

The Sherman Silver Act passed the Congress after a "free silver" bill had already passed the Senate. Apparently, one motivation for enacting this legislation was to avoid what gold standard defenders saw as a worst alternative, a free silver bill.

Since the United States and the countries of Europe were on either a de facto or an official gold standard in the 1890s, gold coin was preferred over silver coin. Banks tended to ask the treasury to redeem treasury notes in gold coin, and the treasury obliged. The treasury's gold reserves dwindled, whereas silver reserves grew. Foreigners who had purchased U.S. securities with gold became fearful that these securities would be redeemed in silver, at a rate well below the market value of silver. Foreigners began to sell U.S. securities, taking payment in gold and causing a gold outflow to Europe. In 1893, after the government had to sell bonds to raise gold reserves, Congress repealed the Sherman Silver Act. The treasury stopped purchasing silver except for subsidiary coinage, and the flight of capital from the United States ceased. The Gold Standard Act of 1900 officially put the United States on the gold standard.

See also: Bimetallism, Bland–Allison Silver Repurchase Act of 1878, Crime of '73, Free Silver Movement, Gold Standard Act of 1900

References

Friedman, Milton. 1992. *Monetary Mischief.*

Hepburn, A. Barton. 1924/1967. *A History of Currency in the United States.*

Jastram, Roy W. 1981. *Silver: The Restless Metal.*

Myers, Margaret G. 1970. *A Financial History of the United States.*

SHILLINGS

See: Carolingian Reform, Ghost Money

SHINPLASTERS

Shinplasters are small-denomination banknotes or forms of paper money. The

A mock banknote parodying the "shinplasters" of the 1837 panic. Such small-denomination notes were based on the division of the Spanish dollar, the dominant specie (money in coin) of the time. Hence they were issued in sums of 6 (more accurately 6 1/4), 25, 50, and 75 cents. These fractional notes proliferated during the Panic of 1837 with the emergency suspension of specie payments by New York banks on May 10 of that year. (Library of Congress)

face value of shinplasters is usually less than $1. The name probably arose from similarities to plasters used on sore shins.

The term goes back at least to the early 19th century, when some banknotes in the United States were issued for as little as 12.5 cents. In 1834, Senator Thomas Hart Benton, a famous "hard currency" advocate who referred to himself by the nickname "Old Bullion," was heard to say, "What! Do you want a coroner's jury to sit and say, 'Old Bullion died of shinplasters?'" (Schlesinger, 1945).

Adam Smith in the *Wealth of Nations* does not mention shinplasters per se but devotes a good deal of attention to discouraging the issuance of small denomination notes. According to Smith:

> Where the issuing of bank notes for such very small sums is allowed and commonly practiced, many mean people are both enabled and encouraged to become bankers. A person whose promissory note for five pounds, or even for twenty shillings, would be rejected by everybody, will get it received without scruple when it is issued for so small a sum as a sixpence. . . . It were better, perhaps, that no bank notes were issued in any part of the kingdom for a smaller sum than five pounds. Paper money would then confine itself . . . to circulation between the different dealers [wholesalers]. . . . Where paper money is . . . confined to circulation between dealers and dealers, as at London, there is always plenty of gold and silver. Where it extends itself to a considerable part of the circulation between dealers and consumers, as in Scotland, and still more in North America, it banishes gold and silver almost entirely from the country. (Smith, 1952, 139)

In 1829, Great Britain banished banknotes of less than £5. In the United States, a treasury circular of April 1835 disallowed the acceptance of notes under $5 for payment of federal obligations. In February 1836, the treasury extended the ban to notes under $10, and prohibited banks holding U.S. government deposits from issuing such notes. In April 1836, Congress enacted legislation banning notes under $20.

In April 1862, the Congress authorized the issuance of a paper currency in fractional units of a dollar. At first, the currency took the form of postal stamp designs engraved on notes, but later took other forms. This fractional currency could be exchanged for legal-tender notes in amounts up to $5. In 1875, Congress provided for the replacement of fractional currency with subsidiary coinage.

In 1870, a shortage of silver coins led the Dominion Government of Canada to issue paper currencies in denominations of a fraction of a dollar, familiarly known as shinplasters because of their small size. The Canadian government discontinued the shinplasters in 1935 after issuing over 300 different varieties of shinplasters over the 65-year period.

The fact that history is inflationary may have put an end to shinplasters. The United States has attempted to replace the $1 bill with a coin, suggesting that the dollar bill is beginning to fall into the range of small change, in the same value range as the shinplasters.

See also: Inconvertible Paper Standard, Postage Stamps

References

Angus, Ian. 1975. *Paper Money.*

Chown, John F. 1994. *A History of Money.*

Schlesinger, Arthur M. J. 1945. *The Age of Jackson.*

Smith, Adam. 1776/1952. *An Inquiry into the Nature and Causes of the Wealth of Nations.*

SIEGE MONEY

During a siege, coins and precious metal invariably go into hiding, in secret hoards, and cities under siege have often turned to a form of fiat money, usually paper money.

In 1574, the Spanish laid siege to the city of Leyden in the Lowlands. The city needed all the metal it could muster to manufacture arms, and even collected the metallic coinage to contribute to the effort. The burgomaster of Leyden issued small pieces of paper to take the place of coinage. These scraps of paper money predate by nearly a century the permanent introduction of paper money in Europe.

Several cities issued siege notes during the wars of the French Revolution and Napoleon. In 1793, the royalists in Lyons, France, revolted and took control of the city. The republican forces laid siege. The royalists printed crude notes on cardboard with the expression "The Siege of Lyon" (Beresiner, 1977, 180) and distributed them as money. In the same year, Austria laid siege to the German town of Mainz, then under French control. The French authorities printed up a paper currency with the expression, "Siege de Mayence Mai 1793 2e de la Rep. France" (Beresiner, 1977, 180). In 1796, the city of Mantua in Italy issued a siege currency when the city came under siege by Napoleon. Colburg, Prussia, issued siege currency in 1807, under the pressure of a Napoleonic siege. Also, several Italian cities issued siege currencies during the uprisings of 1848.

In 1884, the British government dispatched General Charles George Gordon to the Sudan to evacuate Egyptian forces from Khartoum, which was about to be overrun by Sudanese rebels. Gordon reached Khartoum in February 1884, and a month later the rebels laid siege to the city. The siege lasted until January 26, 1885, when the rebels took the city and killed the defenders, including Gordon. Gordon's death after a colorful career and heroic struggle made him a martyr, and the siege of Khartoum became one memorable episode in the history of the British Empire, the stuff of Hollywood movies.

One of the less well-known aspects of the siege of Khartoum was the issuance of a siege paper money. On his arrival, Gordon found the treasury of Khartoum empty, and within a few weeks Gordon issued emergency notes. Each note bore Gordon's signature. The first 50,000 notes he signed by hand, and the rest bore his printed signature. Gordon's signature accompanied a statement on each note saying that he (Gordon) was "personally responsible for the liquidation, and anyone can bring action against me, in my individual capacity, to recover the money" (Beresiner, 1977, 179). The total value of the notes was approximately 168,500 Egyptian pounds. About 2,000 specimens of these notes have survived, mostly in the hands of collectors.

The exigencies of sieges have forced governments to experiment with fiat money, helping to make way for the ascendancy of fiat paper money in the 20th century.

See also: Inconvertible Paper Standard, Pontiac's Bark Money

References

Beresiner, Yasha. 1977. *Paper Money*.

Weatherford, Jack. 1997. *The History of Money*.

SILVER

Silver and gold were the most aristocratic of the monetary metals. Silver owes its chemical symbol, Ag, to its Latin name, *argentum*, meaning "white and shining." Ancient artisans found silver malleable, resistant to oxidation, and beautiful. It is one of the most reflective of all metals, under favorable conditions reflecting about 95 percent of the light striking its surface.

The use of silver for ornaments, jewelry, and a store of wealth stretches into the mists of ancient history. In the book of Genesis, Abraham, after returning from Egypt, is described as very "rich in cattle, in silver, and gold." The laws of Moses put a silver value on men, cattle, houses, fields, and provisions. Silver seems to have been in greater use than gold as a monetary metal among the ancient Hebrews, but gold possessed greater religious significance. Hiram, king of Tyre, furnished gold for decoration of the Temple of Jerusalem.

The practice of coinage began in Lydia in the seventh century BCE and crossed the Aegean Sea to ancient Greece, a country endowed with rich silver deposits. The Laurion silver mines furnished Athens with abundant supplies of silver, and the commercial leadership of Athens lifted the Attic silver standard to a position of dominance in Mediterranean trade. The Roman Empire debased its silver coinage, but maintained the purity and weight of its gold coinage. During the Middle Ages, the Byzantine world maintained its gold standard, but gold virtually disappeared from Europe. Silver remained an important monetary metal in India and the Far East. Given the disappearance of gold, the Carolingian reform of 755 CE put Europe on a silver standard that lasted until the end of the Middle Ages. Nevertheless, silver coinage was rare and often severely debased.

Gold coinage returned to Europe in the 13th century, but silver remained an important monetary metal. Great Britain moved firmly toward the gold standard only in the 18th century. On the Continent, silver rivaled gold as a monetary metal until late in the 19th century.

The discovery of the New World infused vast supplies of silver throughout the world-trading system. It is not commonly appreciated that 98 percent of all the precious metal taken out of the New World was silver. Silver was a favored metal in India and the Far East, and some silver was shipped directly from Latin America to China. The Spanish silver dollar became a worldwide medium of exchange, remaining legal tender in the United States until the 1850s.

In the 19th century, Europe and the United States began moving away from silver as a monetary standard, although silver continued in use as subsidiary coinage. The subsidiary coinage always kept the silver content sufficiently low to discourage melting down coins for profit. In China and India, the silver standard survived into the 20th century.

Although gold became the preeminent precious monetary metal during the 19th and 20th centuries, silver may have an even longer and more varied history as money. Silver was light enough to be carried in ships, although overland transportation favored gold, which was lighter per unit of value. Silver, however, was next to gold in value per unit of weight. Gold was too precious for many ordinary transactions, but silver, between gold and copper in value, was light enough to be carried around in values useful for ordinary transactions. In addition, silver deposits, unlike gold, were scattered all over the earth, making silver very accessible.

See also: Chinese Silver Standard, Free Silver Movement, Indian Silver Standard, *The Wizard of Oz*

References

Braudel, Fernand. 1981. *Civilization and Capitalism.* Vol. 1.

Flynn, Dennis O. 1996. *World Silver and Monetary History in the 16th and 17th Centuries.*

Jastram, Roy W. 1981. *Silver: The Restless Metal.*

Williams, Jonathan, ed. 1997. *Money: A History.*

SILVER CERTIFICATES

See: Free Silver Movement, Silver Purchase Act of 1934

SILVER PLATE

The silver plate that adorned the dinner tables of European nobility was treated as monetary reserves and frequently played that role. To help pay for the Seven Years War (1756–1763) Frederick the Great of Prussia requisitioned the silver plate from the royal palaces. He sent it to the melting pots at the mint, and minted it into 600,000 *thalers* at a rate of 21 thalers per Cologne *mark* of fine silver, rather than the usual 14 thalers. King Louis XIV of France also sent the royal plate to the mint to pay his troops.

In 1536, Henry VIII sent 20,878 pounds sterling of plate to the mint to furnish money urgently needed to pay troops. Later, in the last of the French wars, Henry VIII disgorged another 10,020 pound sterling of plate for coinage, again furnishing money to wage war. Henry also confiscated vast amounts of ecclesiastical plate and sent it to the mint.

Those further down the social scale used plate to pay benevolences, subsidies, and tithes levied against them, and the mint could convert a quantity of plate into a coinage equivalent. Nobles needing funds to finance political intrigue sent plate to the mint. Plate was the closest thing to a near-money owned by English households in the 16th and 17th centuries, and at times the mint offered a premium to attract more silver plate to be coined. The government also legally mandated a higher standard of fineness for plate than for coinage, trying to prevent coinage from being melted down and fashioned into plate. That silver plate was associated with monetary affairs is revealed in a proclamation of the English king, Charles II, in 1661. It declared: "The nation had flourished for many hundred of years, famous for her constant silver standard and renowned for her plenteous stock of monies and magnificence of plate" (Einzig, 1966, 368 footnote).

One common denominator in many types of money, whether it is human heads in Sumatra, or *manillas* in Africa, is that the money has ornamental value. Even coinage is sometimes converted into ornaments. The Argentine gauchos made leather belts a foot wide and studded with large silver coins from Peru. Although articles that serve the dual purpose of money and ornament are most common in primitive societies, silver plate in the stately homes of England was a vestige of ornamental money.

See also: Dissolution of Monasteries, Pound Sterling, Silver

References

Challis, C. E. 1978. *The Tudor Coinage.*
Cripps, Wilfred Joseph. 1878/1967. *Old English Plate.*
Einzig, Paul. 1966. *Primitive Money.*

SILVER PURCHASE ACT OF 1934 (UNITED STATES)

Under the Silver Purchase Act of 1934, the federal government purchased large quantities of silver and issued silver certificates, significantly adding to the U.S. monetary base. The act marked a renewed emphasis on silver as monetary metal, reversing a trend to demonetize silver, which had been evident since the late 19th century.

The deflation of the 1930s created fertile conditions for another silver movement, an echo of the 19th-century free silver movement. The monetization of silver appeared as a means of increasing the money stock and reinflating prices while remaining committed to precious metal money rather than fiat paper money. After the depression-driven tumble in prices of all commodities, precious metal monetary standards of any stripe held little charm for governments. The silver-producing interests, however, still had sufficient political clout to advance silver as a partial answer to the woes of economic depression.

The Agricultural Adjustment Act of 1932 (AAA) had an amendment attached, the Thomas amendment, authorizing the president to return the country to a bimetallic standard that would define the dollar in both a gold equivalent and a silver equivalent, and provide for the unlimited coinage of gold and silver. The United States had been on a bimetallic standard from 1792 until 1873, and then populist political leaders had taken up the banner of the free silver movement, advancing the idea of re-enfranchising silver as a monetary metal. By the turn of the century, gold seemed to have won a clear victory over silver as a competing monetary standard, but the Great Depression of the 1930s intervened to dethrone the much-vaulted gold standard.

After the adoption of the Thomas amendment, the United States abandoned the gold standard, and President Roosevelt showed no indication that he planned to exercise his authority under the Thomas amendment. Silverites in Congress, those favoring a return to a bimetallic standard based on gold and silver, pressed ahead with new legislative proposals, and Roosevelt finally compromised, sending a message to Congress that led to enactment of the Silver Purchase Act of 1934.

The act authorized the government to purchase silver until either the monetary value of the U.S. silver stock equaled one-third of the value of its monetary gold, or the market price of silver climbed to the monetary value of $1.29 per ounce. Under the act, the government purchased silver at market prices and made payment in silver coins and silver certificates, a form of paper money similar to Federal Reserve Notes. Soon after the passage of the act, the government nationalized domestic silver stocks at $0.50 per ounce. By 1938, the government had acquired 40,000 tons of silver, an amount that raised the issue of storage. The grounds of the West Point military academy became the home of a depository that held the silver until industry found a need for it in the 1960s.

The Silver Repurchase Agreement raised the world price of silver, and silver production increased in the United States. Rising silver prices put a hardship on the handful of countries still on a silver standard because it made the exports of these countries more expensive to the rest of the world, forcing these countries to undergo domestic deflation to remain competitive worldwide. China abandoned the silver standard in November 1935, and Mexico began exchanging its silver coins for paper. In 1936 and 1937, the United States government let the price of silver fall, but the trend toward demonetization of silver in silver standard countries had already established momentum. Because of its depression-inducing effects on silver-standard countries, the act of 1934 actually reduced the monetary demand for silver abroad, canceling long-term benefits to the U.S. silver industry. In the United States, the monetization of silver had no inflationary effects because the government retired Federal Reserve Notes to compensate for the infusion of silver certificates.

In the 1960s, the industrial demand for silver accelerated, lifting silver prices above the official price of $1.29 per ounce. The government began selling off its silver stocks. In 1963, Congress repealed the Silver Purchase Act of 1934 and authorized the issuance of Federal Reserve Notes in denominations of $1 and $2, enabling the government to retire silver certificates. The Coinage Act of 1965 allowed the government to substantially cut the silver content of its silver coinage, and thus further curtail its silver purchases. The final chapter on the demonetization of silver in the United States closed on June 24, 1968, when the right to redeem silver certificates expired.

See also: Bimetallism, Hyperinflation in China, Free Silver Movement, Sherman Silver Act of 1890, Silver

References

Friedman, Milton. 1992. *Monetary Mischief.*

Jastram, Roy W. 1981. *Silver: The Restless Metal.*

Rickenbacker, William F. 1966. *Wooden Nickels: Or the Decline and Fall of Silver Coins.*

SLAVE CURRENCY

Slaves often served as a form of wealth in primitive societies, making slaves a suitable medium of exchange, particularly for large transactions. In the modern era, Africa provides the most evidence of the use of slaves as money. In the 19th century, a slave was the unit of account in the Sudan. A standard unit was defined as a slave that met certain measurements. The value of a slave was equivalent to 30 cotton pieces, 6 oxen, or $10. In the Bagirmi country of equatorial Africa, a slave of medium qualities, defined as a standard slave, served as a standard of value for large transactions. The prices of better slaves were some multiple of the standard slave. Wealth took the form of "heads," and a successful slave raid depreciated the value of the standard, causing the prices of commodities expressed in slaves to rise. In Ghana, slave payments were made for large transactions, and slaves served as a standard of value. In Guinea, slaves were the favored unit of account in large transactions, and kings charged European ships port dues ranging from 7 to 12 slaves, depending on the number of masts on each ship. In Nigeria, slaves ran a close second to cowries as the prime unit of currency. A report in the late 19th century said of the slave: "He has been the cheque book of the country and has been necessary for all large payments. Unfortunately he has a trick of dying while passing from hand to hand" (Einzig, 1966).

The standard of value was defined in terms of a slave of a certain age, and in the course of a transaction, each slave was valued in terms of this standard slave. In Nigeria, slaves were the choice medium of exchange for large transactions, and rich men amassed wealth in slaves. In the Congo, slaves passed in payment for goods, and met the need for a standard of value. The people of this area practiced cannibalism, and the value of a slave could not drop below the value of the pounds of meat that could be gotten from the slave if the owner ate his money. In 17th-century Angola, a 20-year-old slave was a standard unit of value.

Some authors pin the blame for African slavery on the absence of a convenient currency. Slaves were mobile and often carried other forms of primitive money that was bulky and difficult to transport. Merchants brought slaves carrying other currencies on trading expeditions, and exchanged the slaves along with the other currencies for merchandise when the opportunity arose.

In early Cambodia, slaves ranked with cattle, buffaloes, horses, pigs, and elephants as an acceptable means of paying fines. In early England, values were occasionally estimated in slaves, and in Ireland,

a unit of account of one slave girl lasted well into the Christian era, long after the practice of trading human beings for goods had ended. People in western areas of New Guinea priced calico and other traded goods in terms of slaves.

The use of slave money probably began when warriors took more captives in war than they could personally use, and therefore they traded these captives for goods. From this small beginning, the practice of trading human beings evolved into the use of slaves as a type of money.

See also: Slave Currency of Ancient Ireland

References

Einzig, Paul. 1966. *Primitive Money*.
Weatherford, Jack. 1997. *The History of Money*.

SLAVE CURRENCY OF ANCIENT IRELAND

Although ownership of slaves represented wealth in slave-holding societies, and slaves were popular subjects for barter, ancient Ireland made slave girls, called "kumals" or "ancillae," a unit of account for measuring the values of goods and services. A legendary king in ancient Irish literature owned a chessboard, and each chess piece was said to equal 6 kumals in value. Queen Maeve, a figure in an epic poem dating from before the Christian era, boasted of a chariot worth thrice seven bondsmaids. During the fifth century in Ireland, St. Patrick wrote in his *Confessions*: "You know how much I have paid out to those who were judges in all the regions, which I have often visited; for I think that I have given away to them not less than the price of fifteen humans"

(Einzig, 1966). The wording suggests that St. Patrick did not pay in slaves, but was using slaves as a standard of value for reckoning what he did pay. St. Patrick would not have used slaves as a means of payment. Under his guidance, the Hiberian Synod decreed that retribution for the murder of a bishop or high prince demanded either crucifixion or payment of seven ancillae. The decree also required that if blood money was paid in specie, one-third must be in silver, a clear indication that ancillae were only a unit of account, and not a tangible means of payment.

It was probably during the second century that the kumal transformed into an abstract unit of account. The laws under King Fegus, king of Uldah, required a blood money payment of "seven kumals of silver" and "seven kumals of land" for the murder of anyone under the king's protection. These laws clearly show that land and silver were mediums of exchange, and kumals were only a unit of account. These laws were set forth in two legal texts, the *Senchus Mor* and the *Book of Aicill*, both of which contained a table legally sanctioning the kumal standard:

8 wheat-grains = 1 pinginn of silver

3 pinginns = 1 screpall

3 screpalls = 1 sheep

4 sheep = 1 heifer

6 heifers = 1 cow

3 cows = 1 kumal

The example of slave-girl money in Ireland brings to the forefront four separate functions of money. Money serves as a medium of exchange, a store of wealth, a unit of account or measure of value, and a standard of deferred payment.

The slave-girl money evolved into a unit of account only, whereas the other roles of money were filled by various commodities, land, and precious metals.

The origin of the social acceptance of the use of kumals as a medium of exchange may have stemmed from the prestige conferred by slave ownership. Also, slaves may have been regarded as the rightful spoils of war, and warriors capturing more slaves than they could employ were free to trade them for land, livestock, and goods and services that they needed. Perhaps the spread of Christianity in Ireland and the concept of Christian love helped liberate Ireland from the base practice of actually exchanging human beings in trade, making kumals less acceptable as a medium of exchange, but still sanctioned by tradition as a unit of account.

See also: Slave Currency

References

Einzig, Paul. 1966. *Primitive Money.*

Nolan, Patrick. 1926. *A Monetary History of Ireland.*

Powell, T. G. E. 1985. *The Celts,* rev. ed.

SNAKE

The so-called snake was a coordinated policy among European Community (EC) countries to constrict exchange rate variations between member countries to a narrower band than allowed by the International Monetary Fund (IMF). It was the first stage toward the monetary unification of Europe, a goal that became a reality on January 1, 1999, with the introduction of a European currency unit, the euro. The snake system began in March 1972 and remained in operation until January 1979 when the European

Monetary System (EMS) replaced the Economic and Monetary Union (EMU). The EMS and its predecessor, the EMU, were agreements of cooperation in monetary affairs between members of the EC. The EMS took a further step toward monetary unification with the introduction of the European Currency Unit (ECU).

Early in the 1970s, the IMF allowed the currencies of member countries to vary within a range of 2.25 percent above or below parity with the dollar, or 4.5 percent overall. The members of the EMU committed themselves to keeping the variation between European currencies to within 2.25 percent of each other, and fluctuations in the aggregate of European currencies was kept with the 4.5 percent band of parity with the dollar. The European currencies became known as the "snake in the tunnel" because these currencies moved up and down together relative to other currencies. When the Belgium-Luxembourg monetary union kept its own currency fluctuations within a tighter range, then the "snake in the tunnel" began to reveal a "worm in the snake." When the fixed-exchange-rate regime broke down in 1973, and the dollar floated freely, the European "snake in the tunnel" became the "snake in the lake."

The snake terminology survived in the EMS, in which a measure of exchange-rate divergence from other European currencies was treated as a warning sign or signal that intervention may be necessary. This warning sign was called the "rattlesnake."

The snake was intended to keep EC currencies fluctuating in step with each other, a preliminary measure to the complete monetary unification of Europe. The transition to a European currency unit, the euro, managed by the European Central Bank, removed the need for this sort of coordination, as the euro replaced the German mark, French franc, and several other European currencies.

See also: Euro Currency, European Currency Unit, Optimal Currency Area

References

Kenen, Peter B. 1995. *Economic and Monetary Union in Europe*.

Padoa-Schioppa, Tommaso. 1994. *The Road to Monetary Union in Europe*.

SOCIAL DIVIDEND MONEY OF MARYLAND

More than half of the first paper money issued by the colony of Maryland flowed into the economy as a social dividend, equivalent to a gift to each inhabitant over 15 years of age. Historically, the major sources of paper money have been banks that issued it on the strength of promissory notes, and governments that issued it to finance government expenditures. Often governments have issued paper money during wartime when demands on government spending are particularly heavy. Maryland's first experiment with paper money was unique for that era because its colonial government issued paper money solely for the purpose of stimulating the private economy, without feeling pressure to finance a portion of the public sector's budget.

Like other American colonies, Maryland struggled against a shortage of currency that kept the colonial economy on a tight leash, limiting trade to what could be transacted with a limited money supply. Great Britain made no special provision to supply the colonies with coins and currency, and the colonies had to get by with what could be earned from trade with the rest of the world. To infuse additional coin into the local economy, the Maryland legislature in 1729 granted a 15-percent reduction in import and export duties if they were paid with imported gold or silver.

Maryland shared with Virginia an almost exclusive dependence on tobacco, either to pay for foreign trade or as the principle medium of exchange in the local economy. In the 18th century, however, tobacco production outpaced demand and the price of tobacco on the world market steadily declined, accounting for the depression in Maryland's economy. Maryland's first proposal for issuing paper money was part of a scheme for limiting tobacco production in an effort to raise the price of tobacco. In 1731, the Maryland legislature enacted a law that provided for the issuance of £30,000 of paper money to pay for tobacco that would be taken out of production. For each 6,000 tobacco plants standing during the month of July, the owner was to burn and destroy 150 pounds of tobacco. In return for each 150 pounds of tobacco destroyed, the owner received from the colonial government 15 shillings in paper currency. For some reason, this plan was never implemented, and the paper money never issued.

The Currency Law of 1733 provided for the social dividend money issue. It authorized the issuance of £90,000, £48,000 of which were to be distributed as a "bounty of thirty shillings per tax-able." That included all citizens over 15 years of age excepting ministers of the Church of England, imported male servants, and slaves. The government issued the remaining £42,000 as loans paying 4 percent interest and secured by real estate appraised at twice the value of the loans. The government levied a tax of 1 shilling and 3 pence per hogshead of tobacco exported from Maryland. The proceeds of this tax paid for investment in Bank of England stock, creating a fund for redeeming the paper money, beginning at the end of 15 years. Within 30 years, the government planned to retire all the paper money.

The paper money issue helped finance an economic expansion in Maryland. The paper money depreciated in value moderately until 1748 when the government retired the first £30,000. After 1748, the value of the paper money stabilized. The colonial government redeemed in shillings the entire issue of the paper money at face value, making Maryland's paper money experience the most successful in the American colonies.

See also: Land Bank System, Massachusetts Bay Colony Paper Issue

References

Brock, Leslie V. 1975. *The Currency of the American Colonies, 1700–1764.*

Lester, Richard A. 1939/1970. *Monetary Experiments.*

SPANISH INCONVERTIBLE PAPER STANDARD

Spain stood aloof from the classical gold standard that brought monetary order to the world from the 1870s until 1914. In 1883, Spain abandoned convertibility of banknotes into precious metal and never returned to a metallic standard, even in the aftermath of World War I, when most of the world's trading partners adopted a gold exchange standard.

In 1868, Spain adopted a bimetallic standard along the lines of the Latin

Monetary Union. Like the Union, Spain fixed the official ratio of silver to gold at 15.5 to 1. In 1874, the government conferred on the Bank of Spain a monopoly on the issuance of banknotes. The value of silver fell as the world turned to the gold standard, raising the free market ratio of silver to gold to 18 to 1 by 1876. Gresham's law set to work in Spain. Because gold could buy more silver abroad than in Spain, gold flowed out and silver displaced gold as domestic currency. Gold currency decreased from 1,131 million *pesetas* (the monetary unit of Spain) in 1874 to 736 million in 1883. Gold reserves in the Bank of Spain increased substantially until 1881, and then dropped precipitously in 1883.

The suspension of convertibility in 1883 may have been triggered by an international financial crisis, including a stock market crash in France and a deteriorating balance of trade for Spain. When Spain's gold reserves dropped to 60 percent of their 1881 level, the government suspended convertibility.

Despite abandonment of the gold standard, Spain's prices remained relatively stable, mildly deflationary during the world depression of the 1880s and early 1890s, and rising gently in the two decades before World War I. From 1883 until 1913, the Spanish wholesale price index (1913 = 100) rose from 89.5 to 100, an annual average increase substantially below 1 percent. The exchange rate of pesetas to British pounds rose significantly during the Spanish-American War, when the government ran large budget deficits, but returned to presuspension levels by the eve of World War I. Over the same time span, the money supply grew at an average annual rate of 2 percent.

Spain eluded the severe monetary disorder many countries witnessed during experiments with inconvertible paper money. During the heyday of the classical gold standard, Spain maintained monetary stability with inconvertible paper, providing lessons that are relevant today. Despite inconvertible paper money, Spain's government engaged in only modest deficit spending, excepting the brief episode of the Spanish-American War. Spain invariably ran a trade surplus, exporting more goods and services than importing, and the Bank of Spain accumulated gold reserves, leading speculators to expect a return to convertibility. Spain's experience proved that monetary stability could be maintained without the much-vaunted gold standard.

Nevertheless, Spain paid a toll for not adopting the gold standard. The Bank of Spain kept interest rates in Spain above international levels, a necessary expedient to attract capital from countries considered safer because of the gold standard. Even with high interest rates, Spain saw a reduction in foreign capital inflows. The higher interest rates also acted to retard domestic investment in Spain, further reducing indigenous economic growth.

Spain's experience from 1883 to 1914 was unique because it occurred when the gold standard was heralded as the guardian of monetary stability. During the 20th century, Spain has shared many of the difficulties of other countries on inconvertible paper standards. In the 1970s, Spain's economy sank into the doldrums of stagflation, largely because the Bank of Spain issued banknotes to finance government deficits. In the 1980s, Spain reformed its public finance and monetary policy, and now Spain enjoys one of the best records for monetary stability in Europe.

See also: Gold Standard, Inconvertible Paper Standard, Latin Monetary Union

References

Bordo, Michael D., and Forrest Capie, ed. 1993. *Monetary Regimes in Transition.*

Martin-Acena, P. "The Spanish Money Supply, 1874–1935." *Journal of European Economic History,* vol. 19, no. 1 (1990): 7–33.

SPANISH INFLATION OF THE 17TH CENTURY

The 17th century, almost from beginning to end, saw Spain debase its silver coinage with copper and mint vast quantities of copper coins, causing inflation and shortages, punctuated with fits of deflationary policies and solemn promises of currency reform. Ironically, Spain struggled for nearly a century with debasement and inflation after exploiting vast gold and silver discoveries during the 16th century. The percent of Spain's domestic coinage made of copper rose to 92 percent, hardly believable in light of the influx of gold and silver from the New World in the 16th century.

At the beginning of the 17th century, Spain's government budget was bloated after years of financing wars and the royal pomp necessary for a great world power. Spain's revenues from gold and silver mines in the New World began trailing off, and the Spanish crown turned to minting copper coins to pay for heavy government expenditures. Spain's dependence on foreign treasure had perhaps already sapped vitality from domestic industries, rendering inflationary policies tempting in an economy that could not generate sufficient tax revenue to finance its government.

During the first quarter of the 17th century, the government's unbridled coinage of copper coins spawned a wave of inflation that drew public protest. The face value far exceeded the intrinsic value of copper coins, and the crown was reaping the difference as a profit for minting the coins. By 1627, widespread inflation aggravated public anger over wheat and livestock shortages, pressuring the government to switch to a deflationary monetary policy. The nominal values of the copper coins were cut in half without compensating the holders of the devalued copper coins. The government began a practice of making solemn promises not to tamper with the currency—promises only meant to be broken.

In 1634, the government resumed a policy of inflationary finance. To save the expense of supplying copper to the mints, the government restamped the existing copper coins, raising the face value. Coins were called in several times and restamped, often doubling or tripling nominal values. Between 1627 and 1641, copper coins were inflated three times and deflated four times. In 1641, inflation reached a peak, and silver was selling at a premium of 190 percent. In 1642, the government undertook a brutal deflationary devaluation, reducing the face value of copper coins by 70 to 80 percent.

In 1651, the government, again short of money for military outlays, called in copper coins of one denomination and restamped them, quadrupling their face values. In 1652, the government returned to a deflationary monetary policy and devalued copper coins. This time the government compensated holders of devalued copper coins with interest-bearing bonds.

Counterfeiting contributed significantly to the depreciation of copper currency. After 1660, counterfeiting was punishable with the death penalty, and burning at the stake awaited those participating in the importation of counterfeit coins.

Monetary disorder reached a climatic crisis in 1680 with silver selling at a premium of 275 percent. The government issued a decree devaluing copper currency by half, equivalent to one-fourth its 1664 value. Prices plummeted 45 percent in a few months, forcing a harsh readjustment. The government began reducing the supply of copper coins, and had ceased minting copper by 1693. Monetary stability returned to Spain and lasted throughout the first half of the 18th century.

Nearly a century of monetary disorder ravaged the Spanish economy. The woolen industry in Toledo and the number of cargo ships sailing between Spain and the Indies shrank by three-fourths, and some industrialized areas lost half their populations. Monetary chaos stifled private initiative, contributing to Spain's economic deterioration.

See also: Copper, Great Debasement, Inflation and Deflation

References

Hamilton, Earl J. 1947. *War and Prices in Spain: 1651–1800.*

Paarlberg, Don. 1993. *An Analysis and History of Inflation.*

Vives, Jaime Vicens. 1969. *An Economic History of Spain.*

SPARTAN IRON CURRENCY

In about 600 BCE, Lycurgus, the famous Spartan lawgiver, put into Sparta's constitution a provision that banned the circulation and possession of gold, silver, or other precious metals as a means of transacting business and replaced these forms of money with an iron currency, variously reported as being in the form of discs or bars. This provision was part of a plan of social reform intended to spare Sparta the evil consequences of wealth concentrated in the hands of a few citizens. According to Plutarch, Lycurgus, after effecting a land reform that spread out the ownership of that wealth, set to work reforming the currency. In Plutarch's *Lives of Noble Grecians and Romans* (1952), we read that Lycurgus:

Not content with this [land reform], he resolved to make a division of their moveables too, that there might be no odious distinction or inequality left amongst them; but finding that it would be very dangerous to go about it openly, he took another course, and defeated their avarice by the following stratagem: he commanded that all gold and silver coin should be called in, and only a sort of money made of iron should be current, a great weight and quantity of which was very little worth; so that to lay up twenty or thirty pounds there was required a pretty large closet, and, to remove it, nothing less than a yoke of oxen. With the diffusion of this money, at once a number of vices were banished from Lacedaemon; for who would rob another of such a coin? Who would unjustly detain or take by force, or accept as a bribe, a thing that it was not easy to hide, nor a credit to have, or of any use to cut in pieces? For when it was just red hot, they quenched it in vinegar, and by that means spoilt it, and made it almost incapable of being worked. (36)

Part of the motivation for the reformation of Sparta's currency may have been the discouragement of trade with foreigners, because there is no record of exchange rates between Sparta's iron currency and the coinage of other cities of the same era. It is unlikely, but possible, that Sparta was attempting to compensate for a shortage of domestic supplies of gold and silver, possessing no gold or silver mines of its own. Societies sometimes develop substitute monies when the growth of commercial activity is restricted by a shortage of money. The whole tenor of these reforms, however, seems to have been intended to limit the growth of commercial activity rather than promote it.

Lycurgus' reforms sound a familiar refrain in the ancient literature on money, variations of the Biblical warning that "the love of money is the root of all evil." The use of money first spread in the seaport cities, such as Athens, where traders and sailors of all religions and creeds met at the crossroads of international trade. Exposure to foreign creeds, morals, and traditions often weakened the hold of domestic religions on the citizens of the seaport towns. Traders from all over the world, away from home, pockets full of money, made a ready market for all sorts of vices that thrived in these cities. The inland cities such as Sparta, dependent on agriculture rather than foreign trade, sought to protect themselves from the moral chaos that they saw as a direct result of the introduction of money and the massive inequality of wealth in the seaport cities.

History, however, was on the side of the societies that made use of money, and Sparta nearly disappeared as Athens grew to a world-class city.

See also: Barter

References

Burns A. R. 1927/1965. *Money and Monetary Policy in Early Times.*

Einzig, Paul. 1966. *Primitive Money.*

Plutarch. 1952. *Lives of Noble Grecians and Romans.*

SPECIAL DRAWING RIGHTS

Special drawing rights (SDRs) are a form of fiat international monetary reserves that substitute for gold as monetary reserves in the international economy. The SDR also serves as an international monetary unit of account in the accounts of the International Monetary Fund (IMF).

SDRs were born of a shortage of international gold reserves that arose in the 1960s. Participants at the annual meeting of the IMF in 1967 at Rio de Janeiro drafted an agreement to issue SDRs. Member countries ratified the agreement in 1969, and the first allocations of SDRs came forth in 1970. Each country received allocations of SDRs proportional to its quota of funds contributed to the IMF. The IMF receives its lending resources from the contributions of member countries, which are assigned individual quotas based on such factors as national income and volume of international trade.

Physically, SDRs are bookkeeping entries in accounts with the IMF. Known in some circles as paper gold, SDRs can be created with the stroke of a pen. At first, the value of SDRs were fixed in terms of gold. In mid-1974, the gold valuation of SDRs was dropped in favor of a system that defined SDRs in terms of a "basket" of major international currencies. In 1981, the basket was simplified to five currencies, the United States dollar, German mark, French franc, Japanese yen, and British pound. The value of an SDR is based on a weighted average of the values of major international currencies. Every five years, the IMF adjusts the weights, which determines the significance of each currency that enters into the value of an SDR. The IMF last adjusted the weights in 1995.

Individual countries may draw on SDR accounts to settle international payments that could normally be settled with gold reserves or foreign exchange reserves. SDRs do not play a role in private international transactions, but, by international agreement, are accepted in intergovernmental transactions on a par with gold and foreign exchange. For example, the United States could buy French francs from France's central bank by paying for them by drawing on its SDR account at the IMF. The United States might use the French francs to buy goods and services from France or buy U.S. dollars in foreign exchange markets, propping up the value of the dollar.

The value of SDRs fluctuates on a daily basis, reflecting the daily fluctuations in the values of currencies in foreign exchange markets. The daily values of SDRs are reported in the foreign exchange tables in publications such as the *Wall Street Journal*. In time, SDRs should replace gold and the United States dollar as the principle international monetary reserve. Already

the IMF uses SDRs rather than a specific national currency as a unit of account in financial reports. Some countries define domestic currencies in terms of SDRs.

See also: Bretton Woods System, International Monetary Fund

References
Daniels, John D., and Lee H. Radebaugh. 1998. *International Business,* 8th ed.
Daniels, John D., and David Vanhoose. 1999. *International Monetary and Financial Monetary Economics.*
Snider, Delbert A. 1975. *Introduction to International Economics*, 6th ed.

SPECIE CIRCULAR (UNITED STATES)

On July 11, 1836, President Andrew Jackson issued an executive order, called the Specie Circular, requiring payment in specie (gold and silver coins) for all government lands sold to the public. The government no longer accepted banknotes in sales of government land. The Specie Circular actually came from the pen of Senator Thomas Hart Benton, who unsuccessfully advanced a Senate resolution with the same intent. Jackson and Benton were both "hard currency" advocates, and Benton had supported Jackson's veto of the rechartering of the Second Bank of the United States. As the bank war raged in the Senate, Benton thundered, "Gold and silver is the best currency for a republic, . . . it suits the men of property and the working people best; and if I was going to establish a working man's party, it would be on the basis of hard money; a hard money party against a paper party" (Schlesinger, 1945, 81).

President Andrew Jackson's imposition of the specie circular in 1837 provoked considerable negative publicity, such as this political cartoon that depicts a financially troubled tradesman and his family. (Library of Congress)

With the demise of the Second Bank, banking regulation was strictly in the hands of state governments. The proliferation of banks and the multiplication of banknotes fed a wave of inflation and a speculative frenzy in land. Banks in the East made loans on the condition that banknote proceeds were used to pay for land in the West, maximizing the chance that the banknotes would not find their way back to the lending bank for redemption. By accepting the banknotes in payment for land the government—in effect guaranteeing that banknotes could be redeemed in land—was underwriting the banking system. Benton roared in the Senate, "I did not join in putting down the Bank of the United States, to put up a wilderness of local banks . . . I did not strike Caesar to make Anthony master of Rome" (Schlesinger, 1945, 129).

The speculative frenzy hit the skids in 1837, and Jackson's Specie Circular may belong with the immediate agents that brought down an overextended banking system. By increasing the demand for specie in payment for land, the government forced banks, which now found it more difficult to maintain specie reserves, to contract banknote circulation.

See also: Independent Treasury, Second Bank of the United States

References

Atack, Jeremy, and Peter Passell. 1994. *A New Economic View of American History*.
Schlesinger, Arthur M., Jr. 1945. *The Age of Jackson*.

STATE NOTES

See: Exchequer Orders to Pay, Greenbacks, Treasury Notes

STERILIZATION

Sterilization is a market intervention undertaken by central banks to prevent inflows and outflows of capital from influencing domestic money stocks. When central banks buy and sell financial assets, whether foreign currencies or domestic bonds, domestic money stocks are affected. If a central bank purchases a government bond, the domestic money stock will increase by some multiple of the amount of the purchase. The central bank purchases the bond with newly created funds. If the central bank sells a government bond, the domestic money stock contracts. Buying and selling government bonds is the most important method central banks have for regulating domestic money stocks. The procedure is called "open market operations." When a central bank purchases foreign currency in foreign exchange markets, it again pays for the foreign exchange with newly created funds and the domestic money stock increases. It will also have an impact on the money stock in the home country of the foreign exchange that is purchased. That is, if the United States Federal Reserve Bank purchases one million British pounds, the U.S. money stock increases and the United Kingdom's money stock declines. Both the United States and the United Kingdom could undertake open market operations to cancel out the effects of the foreign exchange transaction on domestic money stocks. It is called "sterilization" when central banks undertake offsetting

open market operations to cancel the domestic money stock effects of foreign exchange intervention. Since a central bank purchase of foreign exchange increases domestic money stocks and a central bank sale of a government bond decreases domestic money stocks, the central bank can sterilize the money stock effects of the foreign exchange purchase by selling government bonds.

Issues of sterilization often come up in discussions of economic stabilization in fast-growing emerging markets. Before a U.S. investor can invest in South Korea, the U.S. investor must first use dollars to purchase South Korean currency. If there is a strong inflow of foreign capital into South Korea, foreign investors will be buying large amounts of South Korean currency, bidding up the price or exchange rate of South Korean currency in foreign exchange markets. South Korea's central bank has a choice of selling South Korean currency for foreign currency, or letting South Korea's currency appreciate in foreign exchange markets. Letting South Korea's currency appreciate will cause the price of South Korea's exports to increase in foreign markets, possibly dampening South Korea's growth. If South Korea's central bank meets the stronger demand for South Korean currency by selling South Korean currency for foreign currency, then South Korea's money supply may grow at an inflationary rate. The central bank of South Korea can sterilize the effects of the capital inflows by selling South Korea government bonds, and taking the proceeds out of circulation, cancelling the money supply growth driven by the purchase of foreign currency. Put differently, a nearly simultaneous purchase of foreign currency and sale of government bonds has a zero effect on South Korea's stock of money. Some emerging economies have had difficulty making this policy work because selling government bonds tends to push up domestic interest rates, which attracts even more foreign capital.

Some observers claim that aggressive sterilization contributed to Japan's episode of deflation. In 2004, Alan Greenspan described Japan's currency market interventions as "awesome" (Makin, March 2004). Japan was purchasing U.S. dollars in foreign exchange markets to strengthen the value of the dollar. A strong dollar lowers the cost of Japanese goods to U.S. consumers. At the time, Japan was experiencing deflation, giving Japan reason to welcome the inflationary effects of dollar purchases with yen. Instead, Japan sterilized its foreign exchange intervention by withdrawing yen from domestic money markets.

See also: Hot Money

References

Lee, Jang-Yung. "Sterilizing Capital Inflows." International Monetary Fund, Economic Issues no. 7, Washington, D.C., March 1997.

Makin, John H. "Sumo Economics." *Wall Street Journal* (Eastern Edition, New York) March 3, 2004, p. A16.

STOP OF THE EXCHEQUER (ENGLAND)

In January 1672, Charles II issued a proclamation that suspended payment on tallies and Exchequer orders to pay, an action that became known as the Stop of the Exchequer. The British treasury is called the Exchequer, because during the Middle Ages transactions with the British treasury took place in a room with tables covered by checkered cloth. The modern term "check" is a derivative of "exchequer."

During the reign of Charles II, the Exchequer discounted tallies and Exchequer orders to pay to goldsmith bankers, paying interest rates above 6 percent. Tallies were wooden sticks that represented a debt of the government, and Exchequer orders to pay were paper orders that were replacing the wood tallies, which were a holdover from the Middle Ages. The goldsmith bankers paid 6 percent interest on near-money accounts (deposits not readily available on demand, such as modern certificates of deposit) to raise funds for discounting tallies and paper orders from the government. Tallies and paper orders were similar to some present-day government bonds that are bought at a discount (at less than face value) and can be redeemed at face value at some maturity date in the future. The government pledged to redeem the tallies and paper orders in a rotating order.

When the goldsmith bankers had no more money to loan out, and were no longer able to discount tallies and paper orders, Charles stopped redemption of the tallies and paper orders already held by the goldsmiths. This Stop of the Exchequer initially caused a run on the goldsmith bankers, and many were eventually ruined by this action. Later, the government honored about half of its debt to the goldsmith bankers.

The Stop of the Exchequer reminded people of the seizure of the mint in 1640 and created more doubt about government involvement in banking. It also cast a shadow on paper money, and postponed the development of an institution such as the Bank of England for another 20 years. The credibility of government money suffered a severe setback from this experience, and in England issuing paper money became the province of banks.

See also: Bank of England, Seizure of the Mint, Tallies

References
Davies, Glyn. 1994. *A History of Money*.
Horsefield, J. K. "Stop of the Exchequer Revisited." *Economic History Review*, vol. 35, no. 4 (1982): 511–528.

SUFFOLK SYSTEM

The Suffolk System was the first effort to regulate private banking in the United States. Although banking regulation later became a government activity, the Suffolk System was born of a private initiative that saw a need to regulate country banks.

The Suffolk Bank of Boston first established the Suffolk System in 1819, and in 1824, six other Boston banks joined the system. The Suffolk System required country banks around Boston to deposit reserve balances totaling $5,000 in one or more of the seven Boston banks participating in the system. These reserve balances acted as a guarantee that country banks could always redeem their banknotes in specie.

In the pre–Civil War United States, individual banks issued their own banknotes, rather than the current practice of issuing checkbooks or debit cards to accompany checking accounts. In today's United States economy, only the Federal Reserve System can issue banknotes. Under the banking system in which individual banks issued their own banknotes, financially sound banks could always redeem their banknotes in gold and silver coinage; therefore their banknotes circulated at face value, and were accepted in trade as equivalent to gold and silver coinage or other banknotes. Bankers, however, often fell prey to the temptation to issue more banknotes than was reasonable, considering the bank's gold and silver coin reserves. This left the public holding banknotes that they could not be confident would be redeemed in gold and silver coin. These banknotes circulated below par, and anyone accepting one of these banknotes in trade risked taking a loss. Banks that often had to take banknotes as deposits were particularly vulnerable to sustaining a loss from banknotes issued by overextended banks.

The Suffolk System was designed to protect the public and Boston banks from country banks that issued more banknotes than they could be counted on to redeem in gold and silver coin. The Suffolk banks always accepted at par the banknotes of country banks that maintained reserves in the Suffolk System.

In the course of trade, banknotes issued by country banks flowed into the hands of the Suffolk banks. The Suffolk banks then immediately presented these banknotes to the issuing banks for redemption, as a way of keeping the issuing banks honest. The Suffolk banks, however, treated the banks that kept reserves within the Suffolk System with a certain amount of consideration, allowing these banks to redeem their banknotes at a steady pace over time. Country banks refusing to keep reserves in the Suffolk System often found themselves suddenly presented with a large volume of their banknotes for immediate redemption, putting an intolerable strain on reserves of gold and silver coin. Without a legal sanction, the Suffolk System was able to coerce the country banks to participate in the Suffolk System.

By 1825, virtually all New England banknotes could be converted at face value in the banknotes of any other bank, or in gold and silver coin, due in no small part to the discipline enforced by the Suffolk System. From 1825 to 1860, New England boasted of the advantages of a uniform currency, a rare accomplishment at that stage of the history of paper money in the United States. The practice of centralizing reserves in a few banks made itself felt in the development of modern central banks such as the Federal Reserve System.

See also: Central Bank, Federal Reserve System, New York Safety Fund

References

Calomiris, Charles W., and Charles M. Kahn. "The Efficiency of Self-Regulated Payments Systems: Learning from the Suffolk System." *Journal of Money, Credit, and Banking*, vol. 28, no. 4 (November 1996): 766–797.

Davis, Lance E., Jonathon Hughes, and Duncan McDougall. 1969. *American Economic History*.

Myers, Margaret G. 1970. *A Financial History of the United States*.

SUGAR STANDARD OF THE WEST INDIES

From the mid-17th century sugar became the reigning monetary standard on the Leeward Islands, and to a lesser extent on Barbados and Jamaica. Jamaica, because of its importance as a naval base as well as a favorite of the buccaneers, was always furnished with a plentiful supply of coins, but nevertheless made use of sugar money. Barbados and the Leeward Islands perennially wrestled with coinage shortages, forcing the expedient of commodity money. Before sugar rose to the forefront, tobacco met the need for a medium of exchange and unit of account in the West Indies.

A Barbados law of 1645 concerning family prayers provided that "whomsoever shall swear or curse, if a master or freeman he shall forfeit for every offense 4 pounds of sugar; if a servant, 2 pounds of sugar" (Einzig, 1966, 291). Fees and wages were also measured and sometimes paid in Muscovado or brown sugar at rates established by an act of the legislature. A rate of 10 shillings per 100 pounds of sugar prevailed for a time as the monetary standard of Barbados.

Sugar displaced tobacco a bit later on the Leeward Islands. Laws enacted in 1644 and 1688 declared that a fine of a 1,000 pounds of good tobacco in a roll awaited anyone found guilty of commerce with the heathen or Sabbath breaking by "unlawful gaming, immoderate and uncivil drinking—or any other prophane and illicious Labours of the Week-days, as digging, hoeing, baking, crabbing, shooting and such like indecent actions" (Einzig, 1966, 293).

The Leeward Islands turned to sugar as the monetary commodity after mid-century. In 1668, Montserrat paid an "able preaching Orthodox Minister" a salary of "fourteen thousand pounds of sugar or the value thereof in Tobacco, Cotton Wool, or indigo" (Einzig, 1966, 293). The going rate for sanctifying a marriage was 100 pounds of sugar or "the value thereof in Tobacco, Cotton Wool or Indigo.' (Einzig, 1966, 293). For about 30 years, the sugar standard on the islands maintained a stable parity for sugar, equating "five score pound of

Engraving of a West Indies sugar cane refinery, 1667. (Library of Congress)

good dry merchantable Muscavado Sugar" to 12 shillings and 6 pence (Einzig, 1966, 293).

By the beginning of the 18th century, metallic currency had made inroads into the Leeward Islands' monetary system. An act of 1700 provided that coinage could be substituted for commodities in payment of debts at a rate of:

> 12 shillings and 6 pence for 100 pounds of Muscovado sugar
>
> 2 shillings for one pound of indigo
>
> 9 pence for one pound of cotton wool
>
> 1.5 pence for one pound of tobacco or ginger
>
> (Einzig, 1966, 294)

Sugar played a modest monetary role in the 18th century. On August 24, 1753, the assembly of Nevis considered, but failed to enact, legislation making sugar and other commodities legal tender for debts in an attempt to ease a shortage of metallic currency. In 1751, Jamaica, which did not have a coin shortage, enacted legislation making sugar legal tender "where both parties agree for payment in sugar and other produce of this kind" (Pitman, 1917, 139). In 1756, up to two-thirds of a tax obligation in Antigua could be paid in sugar. In 1784, St. Christopher enacted revenue legislation stating that, "And whereas it may be burdensome and oppressive to the inhabitants of this Island to pay the amount in specie, be it enacted that the payment of the taxes aforesaid may be in cash, sugar, or rum at the option of the person or persons liable to pay the same" (Einzig, 1966, 294).

By the end of the 18th century, coins had edged out commodity money in the West Indies.

See also: Commodity Money, Commodity Monetary Standard

References

Einzig, Paul. 1966. *Primitive Money*.

Nettels, Curtis P. 1934. *The Money Supply of the American Colonies before 1720*.

Pitman, Frank, W. 1917. *The Development of the British West Indies: 1700–1763*.

Quiggin, A., and A. Hingston. 1949. *A Survey of Primitive Money*.

SUSPENSION OF PAYMENTS IN WAR OF 1812 (UNITED STATES)

The British attack on Washington in 1814 unnerved the public's confidence in a banking system that had overextended itself in the issuance of banknotes. Banks in the Washington area suspended payments on their obligations to redeem banknotes, touching off a round of payment suspensions that spread to every region except New England.

In the early banking system, individual banks issued their own banknotes, which they were obliged to redeem in gold and silver coin (specie). Bank customers received banknotes instead of a checking account and checkbook, and each bank held reserves of coin to redeem banknotes, just as a modern bank holds vault cash and other reserves to redeem checking accounts. A suspension of payments meant that banks no longer redeemed their banknotes with specie, putting the United States on an inconvertible paper standard. An inconvertible paper standard is a monetary system based on paper money that cannot be converted into precious metal at an official rate.

The War of 1812 contributed only part of the pressure on the banking system that preceded the crisis. From 1799 until 1811, the First Bank of the United States oversaw the banking system and made sure that individual banks could redeem their banknotes in coin. In 1811, the First Bank lost its charter from the United States government, substantially removing what regulation there was of state-chartered banks. From 1811 to 1815, the number of banks increased from 88 to 208, and the value of banknotes in circulation rose from $23 million to $110 million. The capitalization of the banking system only doubled during the same time, and most states allowed banks to issue banknotes without regard to capital or reserves. The circulation of banknotes had outgrown the supply of gold and silver, leaving the banking system floating on a thin film of public confidence. After the suspension of payments, these banknotes circulated at discounted values, usually between 10 and 20 percent, but some notes from Kentucky banks were discounted 75 percent.

The United States government encountered difficulty financing the war because its bonds not only sold at a discount, but it received payment in depreciated banknotes. In addition to interest-bearing bonds, the treasury issued $5 noninterest-bearing notes that were not legal tender but were acceptable as payment of taxes.

Congress soon regretted its decision not to renew the First Bank's charter, and in 1816, granted a charter for the Second Bank of the United States. The bank opened for business on January 17, 1817, and by February had negotiated agreements with state banks in major cities to resume redemption of banknotes in of gold and silver coins.

The suspension of payments put the United States on an inconvertible paper standard for over two years, a rather short time considering that Great Britain was on an inconvertible paper standard from 1797 until 1821. Just as Great Britain avoided the excesses of the paper money of the French Revolution, the United States during the War of 1812 avoided the excesses of paper money that arose during the American Revolution. Today, virtually all countries are on an inconvertible paper standard.

See also: Inconvertible Paper Standard, Second Bank of the United States

References

Chown, John F. 1994. *A History of Money.*

Hepburn, A. Barton. 1924/1967. *A History of the Currency of the United States.*

Myers, Margaret, G. 1970. *A Financial History of the United States.*

Timberlake, Richard H. 1978. *The Origins of Central Banking in the United States.*

SWEDEN'S COPPER STANDARD

Like most European countries, Sweden emerged from the medieval period on a silver standard. In 1625, however, Sweden monetized copper and switched to a bimetallic standard based on copper and silver. As often happened under bimetallic systems, one metal currency drove out the other metal currency, and in Sweden's case copper currency displaced the silver currency in domestic circulation, putting Sweden on a copper standard. Sweden's copper standard remained technically in effect until 1776, but its operational importance ended in 1745 when Sweden introduced an inconvertible paper standard.

Sweden turned to a copper standard not because of any perceived commercial advantage, but because copper mining was an important industry in Sweden, and the Swedish government sought to increase the demand for copper. Gustavus Adolphus, king of Sweden from 1611 to 1632, felt that drawing copper into use as circulating money would reduce the supply of copper in world markets and lead to an increase in copper prices. Spain, then the foremost power in Europe, had furnished a recent precedent for the monetization of copper when it debased its own silver coinage with a copper alloy. "Vellon" was the name given to Spain's debased silver coinage, which in the first half of the 17th century became virtually all copper in content. Spain's de facto copper standard supplied the first stimulus to the copper industry, causing the Swedish government to look to the copper industry, which it controlled, as its main source of revenue.

Because the purpose of the copper standard was to create a domestic demand for copper, it would have served no purpose to reduce the copper weight of the copper coinage relative to face value. Therefore, the copper coins were full-valued coins, with the face value of the coins close in value to the bullion value of the copper. Because copper per unit of weight was equal to about one-one-hundredth the value of silver, copper coins on average had to be about 100 times the size of silver coins, and the sheer size of the copper coins seems to have been the major drawback of Sweden's copper standard. In 1644, the Swedish government issued probably the heaviest coins in history, 10-*daler* copper plates weighing over 43 pounds each. In 1720, a Danish diplomat wrote home somewhat humorously about Sweden's copper coinage:

> A daler is the size of a quarto page . . . many carry their money

around on their backs, others on their heads, and larger sums are pulled on a horsecart. Four riksdaler would be a terrible punishment for me if I had to carry them a hundred steps; may none here become a thief. I shall take one of these dalers back to you unless it is too heavy for me; I am now hiding it under my bed. (Heckscher, 1954, 90)

The transportation of any sizeable sum of copper coins required the use of wagons, and problems associated with the transportation of the tax revenue came to the attention of the highest councils in Sweden's government.

The copper standard failed to increase world prices of copper, apparently because Sweden increased domestic copper production to meet the increased demand for copper as coinage. Nevertheless, Sweden's copper standard did lead to Europe's first peacetime flirtation with paper money. Copper mines discovered that it was easier to pay miners in copper bills, representing ownership of copper, rather that the bulky copper itself. In 1661, Sweden saw its first banknotes based on the copper coinage. These banknotes, the first in Europe, were an immediate success, being much more convenient than the bulky copper coinage. In 1656, Johan Palmstruch had received royal permission to form a bank, and five years later his bank started issuing banknotes. Paper money experiments, however, seem to be especially vulnerable to the pitfalls of success. The Palmstruch's bank overissued banknotes, the public staged a run on the bank, and the bank failed. The failed bank, however, was purchased and reorganized as the Riksbank, now the oldest central bank in Europe.

Despite the fear inspired by the collapse of Sweden's first note-issuing bank, in 1745, Sweden suspended its copper standard and issued irredeemable banknotes. Monetary disorder marked Sweden's paper-money experiment until 1776 when Sweden returned to a pure silver standard.

See also: Commodity Monetary Standard, Copper, Riksbank, Sweden's First Paper Standard

References

Heckscher, Eli F. 1954. *An Economic History of Sweden.*

Samuelsson, Kurt. 1969. *From Great Power to Welfare State.*

Weatherford, Jack. 1997. *The History of Money.*

SWEDEN'S FIRST PAPER STANDARD

Between 1745 and 1776, Europe had its first experience with an inconvertible paper standard. Sweden had been the first European country to introduce banknotes early in the 17th century, but by the mid-18th century, Great Britain and France had both made use of banknotes, and France had furnished Europe with its first example of a paper money debacle. Neither Great Britain nor France had officially adopted a paper standard when the Swedish government put Sweden on an inconvertible paper standard.

In the 18th century, Sweden had a parliamentary government, in which two parties vied for power. One party, the Hats, identified with the exporting industries, the military, the nobility, and the monarchy, and generally favored policies of foreign expansion and increased influence abroad. By 1720, Sweden had lost its Baltic empire, much to the chagrin of the Hats, who wanted to maintain Sweden as a player in European politics. The other party, the Caps, represented agricultural interests, and what might be called the commoners. The Caps preference for policies of pacifism earned them the nickname "Nightcaps," shortened to Caps, because they supposedly wanted to sleep while the great powers of Europe passed Sweden by.

Before the adoption of a paper standard, Sweden, home to vast copper reserves, had functioned on a copper standard. Copper, worth less than gold and silver per unit of weight, was bulky and awkward to transport in large monetary values, and Sweden turned to banknotes as a convenience. In the mid-17th century Sweden saw its first suspension of banknote convertibility and bank panic. Banknotes fell into disfavor at first, but the Swedish public found banknotes much more convenient than copper coinage, and banknotes returned to circulation by popular demand rather than government policy.

The Hats held the upper hand in Parliament from 1739 until 1765 and pursued a policy of inflationary war finance, a policy opposed by the Caps. Between 1741 and 1743, the financial strain of war with Russia prompted the Swedish government to look for salvation in the printing press. Because copper was bulky, the sheer cost of transporting copper enabled the government to vastly increase banknotes without triggering an export of copper coins. With copper reserves held intact, the convertibility of banknotes into copper was not immediately threatened.

The issuance of banknotes continued, partly for subsidies to manufacturers, and by 1745, the Swedish authorities imposed an inconvertible paper standard. Unlike the suspensions of payments in the 17th century, the public did not panic, but inflation rose to the forefront of economic problems. The Swedish currency depreciated on foreign exchange markets, making foreign goods much more expensive in Sweden and Swedish exports cheaper in foreign markets.

The inflationary policy irritated the Caps, who wasted no time kicking the monetary rudder in the opposite direction when they returned to power in 1765. The Caps imposed a deflationary policy. As Swedish currency appreciated in foreign exchange markets, foreign imports became cheaper in Sweden, but Sweden's export industries had to slash prices to remain competitive in foreign markets. Prices in export industries fell faster than wages and raw material prices, plunging the export industries into a depression.

Political opposition to the Caps' monetary policy mounted as economic distress defused throughout Sweden, and the Caps fell from power in 1769. The Caps' experience with disinflation policies inspired a political drama that history would see replayed again whenever democratic governments imposed deflationary policies. Unemployment, bankruptcies, and virtually every other form of economic discomfort invariably accompanies disinflation and deflationary policies, and often democratic governments find it difficult to pursue these policies for extended time periods.

The Hats regained power and reverted to inflationary policies before the Caps returned briefly to power in 1771 through 1772. The political sphere began to mirror the turbulence in the economic sphere, and in March 1772, a bloodless coup d'état engineered by the Hats, displaced Sweden's parliamentary government with a constitutional monarchy. Sweden's parliament survived, shorn of much of its power, and the parties of the Hats and Caps disappeared. In 1776, Sweden established a silver standard, completely breaking with the copper standard and putting an end to inconvertible banknotes.

Sweden's 18th-century episode of monetary disorder demonstrates how a society, exhausted with war, may find inflationary policies attractive, and how these policies are associated historically with political instability.

See also: Inconvertible Paper Standard, Sweden's Copper Standard

References

Chown, John F. 1994. *A History of Money.*

Heckscher, Eli F. 1954. *An Economic History of Sweden.*

Samuelsson, Kurt. 1968. *From Great Power to Welfare State.*

SWEDEN'S PAPER STANDARD OF WORLD WAR I

During World War I, Sweden sought to weaken the link between gold and domestic currency in an effort to tame inflationary forces. Sweden's policy was unprecedented, considering that the gold standard usually receives strongest support from those quarters where inflation is most feared. The 19th century had seen several countries abandon a silver standard to avoid currency depreciation, reacting to the depreciation of silver relative to gold, which was a stronger metal monetarily and clearly the preferred bulwark against inflation.

Sweden had adopted the gold standard in 1873. A gold standard country must stand ready to buy and sell gold at an official price in its own currency. A country's commitment to sell gold at an official price in its own currency puts a strict limit on the volume of paper money issued, acting as a guard against the issuance of inflationary levels of paper money. When a country suspends gold payments, as often happens during times of fiscal stress, such as wars, the country expects to see its currency depreciate, and domestic prices go up.

The other side of the gold standard is the commitment to buy gold at an official price, a commitment that Sweden suspended in February 1916. During World War I, Sweden supplied war materials and supplies to the belligerents and often received gold in payment. Foreign currencies sold at a discount relative to the Swedish *krone,* and gold would have sunk in value relative to the krone if the Swedish central bank had not been committed to buy gold at the official price. The influx of gold and foreign currencies would not have created difficulties if Sweden's opportunities for importing foreign goods had increased proportionately with its accelerating opportunities for export. Wartime conditions, however, favored exports over imports.

Sweden found itself faced with a swelling domestic money supply, fueled by gold inflows, and a shrinking supply of goods for domestic consumption as exports rose relative to imports. The Swedish central bank saw itself having to buy large quantities of gold that paid no interest. Also gold was sinking in price worldwide, which acted to drag down the values of gold-standard currencies, such as the Swedish krone. These difficulties converged to push Sweden into unhinging itself from the gold standard.

Freed from an obligation to buy gold at an official price and to mint all gold brought to the mint, Sweden continued to import gold, but at reduced prices, and to augment the domestic money supply. Between the first quarter of 1916 and the last quarter of 1917, the circulation of paper money increased 62 percent and prices climbed 65 percent.

Although nullifying the gold standard did not spare Sweden from a bout of inflation, it restrained the levels that inflation reached. In the Stockholm foreign exchange market, the Swedish krone rose in value relative to the U.S. dollar, the Swiss franc, and the British pound. The krone rose about 10 to 25 percent above the value it commanded when it was on a strict gold standard, and Swedish coins were worth 10 to 25 percent more than the value of their gold content.

The Swedish experience of World War I was a reminder that precious metals do not offer fail-safe protection against inflation, as Europe discovered after the influx of gold and silver from the New World.

See also: Gold Standard, Sweden's First Paper Standard

References

Cassel, Gustav. 1922. *Money and Foreign Exchange after 1914*.

Lester, Richard A. 1939/1970. *Monetary Experiments*.

SWEEP ACCOUNTS

"Sweep accounts" refer to accounts for which a computer program "sweeps" excess funds overnight from checking accounts, which must meet mandated reserve requirements, to money market deposit accounts (MMDA), which are exempt from reserve requirements. Since reserves earn no interest, depository institutions feel an incentive to minimize reserve holdings. The Federal Reserve System gets its name from one of its principle assignments, which is to insure that depository institutions (commercial banks, thrifts, and credit unions) maintain adequate reserves. Only two assets can serve as reserves, cash in the bank vault, or an account at a Federal Reserve Bank. The Federal Reserve System requires depository institutions to hold a percentage of checking account deposits in the form of reserves. Depository institutions may hold a balance directly with a Federal Reserve Bank, or indirectly through a correspondent institution, which holds deposits in a Federal Reserve Account for other depository institutions on a "pass through" basis. Checking accounts are subject to reserve requirements because these accounts undergo a high rate of daily turnover in the form of new deposits and new withdrawals. Banks must hold reserves to cover the days of heavy cash withdrawals relative to new deposits. MMDA accounts experience less activity in terms of daily deposits and withdrawals and are therefore exempt from mandated reserve requirements. To be exempt from reserve requirements, an MMDA cannot allow more than six withdrawals per month. The withdrawals can be in the form of either writing a check or a pre-authorized transfer. MMDA's attract depositors by paying interest.

Banking industry data suggest that without mandatory reserve requirements, a typical bank would elect to hold vault cash equal to roughly 5 percent of transactions accounts, and deposits at the Federal Reserve equal to roughly 1 percent of its transaction accounts (Anderson and Rache, 2001). Since the mandated reserve requirement for transaction deposits usually ranges between 10 and 20 percent, banks regard themselves as paying a "reserve tax." Reserves are assets that earn no interest, and banks must hold more reserves than they think necessary do conduct day-to-day banking operations. Therefore, banks stand eager to embrace any procedure that enables them to reduce reserve holdings within the constraints of the legal reserve requirements.

In January 1994, the Federal Reserve Board, the governing body of the Federal Reserve System, gave commercial banks the go ahead to use a new type of computer software that dynamically reclassifies balances in customer accounts from transactions deposits (demand and other checkable deposits) to money market deposit accounts. At first, the new practice caught on slowly, but after April 1995, it spread quickly.

Key to sweep accounts is the MMDA, which did not come into being until 1982. In the 1970s, when paying interest in checking accounts was illegal, banks began "sweeping" customer deposits into overnight repurchase agreements. An overnight repurchase agreement refers to a situation in which a bank sells a treasury bill to a customer overnight and "repurchases" it the next day at a higher price. Repurchase agreements were a way of indirectly paying interest on a checking account that could not legally pay interest. Only the bank's largest customers benefited from "sweeping" into repurchase agreements. The development of MMDAs in the 1980s allowed depository institutions to apply the procedure of "sweeping" to a much larger range of depositor accounts. It also relieved commercial banks of the need to keep an inventory of treasury bills on balance sheets for overnight repurchase agreements.

Sweep accounts appear to have removed the statutory reserve requirements that depository institutions face. That is, with intelligently designed software, banks can reduce required reserves to below the levels banks would voluntarily choose to hold to cover day-to-day banking operations. At first some observers feared that the spreading use of sweep accounts might force banks to turn to the federal funds market more often for overnight loans, causing more volatility in the federal funds interest rate. The federal funds rate is the key target interest rate the Federal Reserve regulates in the conduct of monetary policy. Greater volatility in the federal funds market might hamper the Federal Reserve's ability achieve its goals. Problems in this area, however, never materialized.

See also: Legal Reserve Ratio

References

Anderson, Richard G., Robert, H. Rasche. "Retail Sweep Programs and Bank Reserves, 1994–1999." *Federal Reserve Bank of St. Louis Review*, vol. 83, no. 1 (January/February 2001): 51–72.

Koretz, Gene. "Do 'Sweeps' Sap Fed Policy: A Growing Bank Practice Stirs Fears." *Business Week*, June 2, 1997, p. 26.

SWISS BANKS

Swiss banks enjoy a worldwide reputation for protecting the identity of depositors. This important characteristic helped Switzerland grow to one of the world's major banking centers in the 20th century. Another factor contributing to the growth of Swiss banking is Switzerland's position of neutrality. On May 20, 1815, the Vienna Congress established the permanent neutrality of Switzerland among the European powers—a position the superpowers of the world honored through two great wars in the 20th century.

Switzerland was not a pioneer in early European banking. Geneva was the first of the Swiss cities to become a banking center. By 1709, Geneva boasted of a dozen bankers who left a name in Swiss financial history, and Louis XIV floated loans in Geneva to finance his wars. Geneva bankers kept close ties with France and remained involved in financing French public debt until the end of the 19th century.

Basel developed a significant banking industry only in the 19th century. In 1862, the Basel Register listed 20 banks, nine of which were exclusively devoted to banking.

Financial activity of various sorts appeared in Zurich during the 16th century. In 1679, an injunction from the city council prohibited a reduction of interest rates from 5 percent to 4 percent. Merchant bankers, who accepted deposits for investment in securities, appeared in the middle of the 18th century. Zurich waited until 1786 to see the formation of a bank in the broad sense. In 1805, the official register of Zurich reported two banks devoted exclusively to banking.

By the eve of World War I, Switzerland ranked as one of the international financial centers. Six large banks—Swiss Credit Bank, Swiss Bank Corporation, Union Bank of Switzerland, Trade Bank of Basel, Federal Bank, and Swiss People's Bank—controlled a system of branches throughout Switzerland. These banks floated international loans for European governments and railroad and other industrial concerns in the United States. After World War I, inflation in the currencies of the former belligerents made Switzerland more attractive as a safe haven.

In the post–World War II era, three of the big banking houses remained in business: the Swiss Credit Bank, the Swiss Bank Corporation, and the Union Bank of Switzerland. There was also a large network of smaller banks, rural loan associations, and branches of foreign banks. In 1968, Switzerland had a population of six million people and 4,337 banking offices, which added up to one banking office for every 1,400 individuals.

In the 1930s, Switzerland enacted laws that strengthened the anonymity protection of depositors in Swiss banks. During that time, some countries prohibited citizens from holding assets abroad on pain of criminal penalties, and even sent agents into Switzerland to track down assets owed by their own citizens. On the other hand, some people wanted to keep deposits in Switzerland in case they had to make a hasty departure from their homeland for political or racial reasons. Swiss banks began opening the so-called numbered accounts, which substantially reduced the number of bank employees who knew the name of a depositor. Also, the Swiss government claimed no right to pry into bank accounts either to collect information on its own citizens or the citizens of foreign countries. Governments around the world have lodged complaints against Swiss banks for holding deposits of foreigners evading taxes. Switzerland recently has yielded to

Headquarters of the Union Bank of Switzerland (UBS) in Zurich. (AP Photo/Michele Limina)

pressure to open up information on deposits when criminal activity and tax fraud are involved.

In 1997, it came to light that Switzerland, thought to have been a neutral country in World War II, acted as a banking center for Nazi Germany, and that Swiss commercial banks had accepted three times as much gold in deposits from Nazi Germany's central bank as was originally thought. Jewish groups launched a class-action lawsuit in an effort to force Swiss banks to compensate Holocaust victims, emphasizing that Swiss banks held on to dormant accounts of Holocaust victims and laundered millions of dollars in gold stolen from Jews. On August 12, 1998, representatives of Holocaust survivors and Swiss banks announced a $1.25 billion reparation settlement to

compensate Holocaust survivors and their heirs.

Banking remains the traditional strength of Switzerland. In 2004, the *Economist* reported that Swiss banks hold one third of all private financial assets invested across borders, substantially more than any other financial center. It also reported that the financial services industry accounted for about 11 percent of Switzerland's gross domestic product (GDP).

In 2008, Swiss banks again drew the wrath of foreign governments over secret accounts. An ex-employee of Switzerland's largest bank, the Union Bank of Switzerland (UBS), confessed to a Florida court tales of smuggling diamonds in toothpaste tubes to help U.S. clients evade taxes. The ex-employee claimed that he was only a small cog in large tax-evasion operations conducted by UBS (*Economist,* July 2008).

See also: Swiss Franc

References

Bauer, Hans. 1998. *Swiss Banking: An Analytical History.*

Ikle, Max. 1972. *Switzerland: an International Banking and Finance Center.*

New York Times. "Settling Switzerland's Debts." August 16, 1998, p. 1.

Economist. "Survey: The World's Piggybank." February 14, 2004, p. 13.

Economist. "Snowed Under, Swiss Banks." July 5, 2008, pp. 79–80.

SWISS FRANC

Over the years, Switzerland developed a legendary reputation for financial probity, helping to lift the Swiss franc above the crowd of national currencies and become a symbol of strength and monetary soundness. Internationally, it is a favored currency for hoarding money, partly because Swiss banking secrecy laws protect the anonymity of depositors in Swiss banks. International pressure has steadily eroded some of the protection of anonymity afforded to depositors in Swiss banks, particularly for depositors engaged in criminal conduct.

In 1848, Switzerland adopted the French monetary system, preferring a coherent application of the decimal system. Switzerland had first tasted the French system during the Napoleonic era, when France conquered Switzerland and turned it into the Helvetian Republic.

In 1860, Switzerland debased its subsidiary silver coins to prevent the exportation of its silver coinage. In 1865, Switzerland was one of the countries attending a conference in Paris that led to the formation of the Latin Monetary Union. Switzerland argued for the adoption of the gold standard and conversion of silver coinage into subsidiary coinage. The Union agreement, however, provided for a bimetallic standard based on gold and silver. Switzerland, along with France, Italy, and Belgium, agreed to mint gold pieces only of 100, 50, 20, 10, and 5 francs. The Union members agreed to mint a fully weighted 5-franc silver piece, but lower denomination silver coins became subsidiary coinage with reduced weight. Under the Union agreement, coins from each country circulated freely in other Union countries. After Germany adopted the gold standard in 1871, the Latin Monetary Union broke down, and the member countries adopted the gold standard.

During World War I, the Swiss suspended the gold standard, and the Swiss franc appreciated relative to the currencies of the belligerents, and even relative to the U.S. dollar. Following World War I, Switzerland returned to the gold standard at its prewar parity and maintained parity through the 1920s and well into the 1930s.

During the Great Depression period, Switzerland, along with France, Belgium, Holland, Italy, and Poland, organized a "gold bloc" that sought to withstand the pressures for devaluation. Switzerland devalued the Swiss franc long after the United States and Britain had devalued their currencies, and only after France had devalued the French franc in September 1936. The French franc and the Swiss franc were devalued by 30 percent.

During World War II, the Swiss franc remained firm, but not as firm as during World War I. In July 1945, the Swiss franc traded at a 3 percent premium over the U.S. dollar. During the post–World War II era, the Swiss franc remained strong relative to the dollar and Swiss authorities had to take steps to discourage demand for Swiss francs. Under the Bretton Woods system of fixed exchange rates, slightly over 4 Swiss francs were needed to purchase a U.S. dollar. After a system of floating exchange rates replaced the fixed exchange rate system in the 1970s, the value of the Swiss franc rose relative to the dollar. In the late 1990s, about 1.5 Swiss francs were needed to purchase a U.S. dollar.

Switzerland is home to the world's largest gold market, and Swiss residents have always enjoyed unfettered freedom to hold gold, unlike citizens in the United States, where the government outlawed the domestic ownership of gold in the decades immediately preceding and following World War II. Banknotes in Switzerland are backed by a minimum of 40 percent gold reserves, suggesting that gold is still important in Switzerland, even though none of the world's major trading partners—including Switzerland—is now on a gold standard.

See also: Swiss Banks

References

Chown, John F. 1994. *A History of Money*.
Cowitt, Philip P. 1989. *World Currency Yearbook*.
Einzig, Paul. 1970. *The History of Foreign Exchange*. 2d ed.

SYMMETALLISM

Symmetallism is a type of monetary system in which a standard monetary unit is equivalent to a fixed number of ounces of gold, coupled with a fixed number of ounces of silver. The standard monetary unit becomes equivalent to a bundle of two precious metals, combined in a fixed, unchanging proportion. As an illustration, the dollar might be set equivalent to 0.0242 ounces of gold, plus 0.3878 ounces of silver. The term "symmetallism" seems to have been coined by Alfred Marshall, a prominent economist around the turn of the century who proposed a symmetallic system as an answer to world monetary woes. Symmetallic systems were not without precedent, however, because the ancient kingdom of Lydia is credited with striking the first coins from a metal called electrum, which was a mixture of gold and silver found in a natural state.

During the last half of the 19th century, the world's major trading partners engaged in a monetary tug of war between a bimetallic system, based on gold and silver, and a monometallic system relying strictly on gold. The United Kingdom favored a gold standard, which eventually displaced a bimetallic standard that France and the United States had championed without success. The bimetallic system, like the symmetallic system, made use of two metals, but it set a fixed value for each metal in terms of the other metal. Under a bimetallic system, a government might officially set the value of 15 ounces of silver as equal to 1 ounce of gold, and would stand ready to exchange gold for silver at this ratio. Because officially fixed values often varied from freely fluctuating market values, the bimetallic system worked less successfully in practice than in theory. In contrast to the bimetallic system, the symmetallic system does not fix a ratio of value between two metals, but fixes the value of a composite unit composed of a fixed quantity of each of two metals. A monometallic system circumvents the complications of two metals and fixes the value of a monetary unit in terms of a fixed weight of a single metal. Under the post–World War II monometallic gold standard, the United States officially fixed the price of an ounce of gold at $35.

The last quarter of the 19th century saw a spreading wave of mild deflation in the face of the strict discipline of a worldwide gold standard, in which the world gold supply did not keep pace with the monetary needs of an expanding world economy. Alfred Marshall held out the symmetallic system as a means of avoiding the awkwardness of the bimetallic standard, while adding to the world's stock of monetary metals, and venting deflationary pressures. He also argued that the value of a composite quantity of gold and silver would fluctuate less than the values of gold and silver separately. He advanced his proposal to the Gold and Silver Commission in the United Kingdom in 1888.

Marshall's proposal apparently made little impression on policy makers at the time, but academic economists found it a fruitful idea that could be expanded. They saw no reason why the number of commodities in the composite standard had to be limited to two, or why the commodities had to be precious metals. They extrapolated Marshall's concept into schemes that included all the commodities in the wholesale price index as part of the composite monetary commodity. These kinds of extensions of Marshall's idea surfaced in the 1980s as anti-inflation policies stood at the top of research agendas in economics.

See also: Bimetallism, Gold Standard

References

Friedman, Milton. 1992. *Monetary Mischief*.

Marshall, Alfred. "Remedies for Fluctuations of General Prices." *Contemporary Review*, vol. 51 (March 1987): 355–375.

McCallum, Bennet, T. 1989. *Monetary Economics*.

T

TABULAR STANDARD IN MASSACHUSETTS BAY COLONY

During two separate periods of rapid inflation, the Massachusetts Bay Colony put in practice a tabular standard in which debts payable in shillings were adjusted for changes in the purchasing power of the paper currency. Under the tabular standard, a 100 percent rise in the price level meant debtors owed twice as many shillings as they had borrowed. Without the protection of a tabular standard, the money that came back to creditors in repayment for loans had less purchasing power than the money they first loaned out.

The first experiment with a tabular standard occurred in 1742, when the legislature authorized a new issue of paper currency. At the same time, the legislature enacted a so-called equity law, requiring the repayment of all debts of 5 years duration and contracted after March 1742 at a rate of 6 2/3 paper shillings to an ounce of silver. The most innovative portion of the law, however, empowered justices of the Massachusetts courts, in adjudicating disputes involving debts paid in paper currency, to "make Amends for the depreciating of said Bills from their present stated Value," which was 6 2/3 shillings to an ounce of silver. That is, the justices could force debtors to pay more than 6 2/3 shillings to an ounce of silver to compensate creditors for the erosion in purchasing power of their money while it was loaned out. (Creditors often do not fully anticipate inflation and do not charge enough interest to compensate for inflation.) Every six months the purchasing power of the new bills was adjusted according to "the Rates that said Bills then commonly pass at in Proportion to Silver and Bills of Exchange payable in London."

Debtors complained that the equity law only considered the exchange ratio between paper shillings and silver, which might only reflect speculative activity, and ignored the cost of living in paper shillings, which was more pertinent to their lives. In 1747, the legislature amended the equity law to provide that "when any valuation shall be made of the bills . . . in pursuance of said act [1742] . . . regard shall be had not only to silver and bills of exchange, but to the prices of provisions and other necessaries of life" (Lester, 1939). This law did not remove all disagreement about the rate of depreciation of the bills, but it diffused the issue until 1749 when Massachusetts received from Great Britain a large reimbursement for war expenditures and began redeeming its paper money.

The colonial legislature faced similar problems during the American Revolution when Massachusetts soldiers complained that their pay, set at the time of enlistment, had lost all but a tiny fraction of its purchasing power. To encourage reenlistment, the legislature computed the original pay in terms of what it would buy in Indian corn, beef, sheep wool, and sole leather, and compensated the soldiers accordingly for the balance owed them in four bond issues, bearing 6 percent interest. The bond issues matured in 1781, 1782, 1783, and 1784, successively. Soldiers refusing to enlist received similar bonds maturing in 1785, 1786, 1787, and 1788. The legislature indexed the principal and interest on these bonds to the prices of four staple commodities. A statement on the face of these bonds read:

> both principal and interest to be paid in the then current money of said state [Massachusetts], in a greater or less sum, according as five bushels of corn, sixty-eight pounds and four-sevenths parts of a pound of beef, ten pounds of sole leather shall then cost, more or less, than one hundred and thirty

pounds current money, at the then current prices of the said articles. (Lester, 1939, 158)

The advent of fiat paper currency opened the possibility of episodes of rapid inflation that was unknown in monetary systems based on precious metal standards, such as gold and silver. Rapid bouts of inflation wiped out the claims of creditors against debtors, setting the creditors against the debtors, and making the hidden seam separating debtors and creditors a major point of social division and political discontent. Massachusetts Bay Colony demonstrated Yankee ingenuity in developing a scheme for balancing the interest of creditors and debtors at a time when inflationary finance was inevitable.

See also: Massachusetts Bay Colony Paper Issue

References
Fisher, W. C. "The Tabular Standard in Massachusetts History." *Quarterly Journal of Economics,* vol. 27 (May 1913): 417–454.
Lester, Richard A. 1939/1970. *Monetary Experiments.*

TALER

The taler was originally a German coin equal to three German marks, but the word "taler" became a common name for currency that, in various guises, appeared in other languages and countries. The English word "dollar" evolved from "taler," as did the Italian *tallero,* the Dutch *daalder,* and the Swedish and Danish *dalers.*

The first talers came from Jachymov, now a small village in the Ore Mountains in the western part of the Czech Republic. At the opening of the 16th century, Jachymov fell within the Holy Roman Empire and was administered under German authority. In 1516, the local ruler, Count Hieronymus Schlick, found a silver deposit close to his home. As early as 1519, Count Schlick, without official sanction, began minting silver coins in his castle, and on January 1, 1520, he received official approval to operate a mint. Minting silver into coins was probably more profitable than merely selling silver. Between 1534 and 1536, King Ferdinand I ordered the construction of an imperial mint in Jachymov. The building housing the imperial mint served as a museum as late as 1976.

The coins were first called "Joachimstalergulden" or "Joachimstalergroschen" after the German name for the valley, Joachimsthal, where they were minted. The names were shortened to "talergroschen," and later to "thalers," or "talers."

With the stimulus of silver mining, Jachymov blossomed into a bustling community of 18,000 inhabitants. In 1568, a plague left its mark on this mining community, but the most severe devastation was wrought by religious intolerance. Jachymov became strongly Protestant, but the Bohemian monarchy was Catholic. Religious persecution killed the community, which could only boast of 529 inhabitants in 1613, and in 1651, the government moved the official mint to Prague.

In the first year of operation, Count Schlick's mint struck about 250,000 talers. During the years of peak production, between 1529 and 1545, the mines produced enough silver to mint 5 million talers. By the end of the century, Count Schlick's mint had sent about 12 million talers into circulation.

The coinage of talers spread throughout the German-speaking world. During the 16th century alone as many as 1500 different types of talers found their way into circulation from various German states and municipalities. By 1900, as many as 10,000 different types of talers had been minted for metal currency and commemoration medals.

Maria Theresa, a famous Austrian Empress of the 18th century, gave her name to the best known, longest circulating of all talers. In 1773, the Gunzburg Mint first struck a taler bearing the image of Maria Theresa. After her death in 1780, subsequent talers were always dated 1780. After the dissolution of the Holy Roman Empire early in the 19th century, the Austro-Hungarian Empire continued to mint the Maria Theresa talers with the 1780 date. Following the break up of the Austro-Hungarian Empire after World War I, the Austrian Republic minted talers until Hitler invaded in 1937. Mussolini found Maria Theresa talers the favored coin in Ethiopia, causing Italy to mint its own talers between 1935 and 1937 to facilitate trade with Ethiopia. After World War II, the Republic of Austria resumed the coinage of talers, still bearing the date of 1780. Austria continued to mint talers until 1975.

See also: Dollar

References

Nussbaum, Arthur. 1957. *A History of the Dollar*.
Weatherford, Jack. 1997. *The History of Money*.

TALLIES (ENGLAND)

In England tallies were wooden sticks that functioned as instruments of credit and exchange in public finance. The Exchequer (treasury) began using tallies in the Middle Ages, and by the humor of

Maria Theresa taler, 1780. (Paul Cowan)

history the use of tallies survived into the early 19th century.

A tally was a wooden stick with notches denoting various sums of money. A notch the length of a man's hand denoted 1,000 pounds, and a notch the width of a man's thumb denoted 100 pounds. A simple V-shaped notch represented 20 pounds. The handle of the tally remained notchless. In a credit transaction, the notched segment of the wooden tally was split lengthwise down the middle and the handle remained with one half of the tally. The creditor kept the larger half with the handle, and the debtor kept the smaller half, called the "foil." The two halves would match or "tally." The tallies were assignable, meaning creditors could transfer ownership of tally debts to third parties. In this connection tallies circulated as money.

Tallies entered into the British public finance system in two ways. First, a citizen owing taxes to the government might hand the Exchequer a tally, signifying a debt of taxes. The government would use the tally to pay for goods and services. The recipient of the tally presented it to the taxpayer who had the other half (the foil) and demanded payment. A second use of tallies in public finance occurred when the government issued tallies in payment for goods and services. In this instance, the government was the debtor, and tallies originating from the government could be used in payment of taxes. Originally, the government pledged future tax revenue from specific sources earmarked for redemption of these tallies. Later, the government issued tallies to be redeemed from the general revenue. Tallies used as an instrument of government debt paid interest.

It was this second use of tallies that contributed to the growth of a primitive money market in London. Purveyors of goods to the government received tallies, and discounted them—that is they sold them at less than face value—to goldsmith bankers rather than using them in exchange, a practice that reached its zenith in the 17th century. The goldsmith bankers, in turn, expected the government to redeem at face value at some date in the future the tallies they had purchased. Later, the Bank of England also discounted tallies, creating an even more ready market in tallies and adding to their acceptability in exchange.

By the 17th century, tallies were already an anachronism, but they were not officially discontinued until 1834. In addition to assisting the emergence of the London money market, tallies reduced the need for money minted from precious metals and eased pressure on the English government to debase the coinage to finance excess government expenditures.

See also: Exchequer Orders to Pay

References
Davies, Glyn. 1994. *A History of Money.*
Dickson, P. G. M. 1967. *Financial Revolution in England.*
Feavearyear, Sir Albert. 1963. *The Pound Sterling: A History of English Money.*

TEA

In 19th- and early-20th-century Tibet, sheep served as a measure of value, but Tibetans used tea as a medium of exchange. Tea bricks and sheep also acted the role of money in Sinkiang.

In the 19th and 20th centuries, tea bricks displaced sheep as currency in inner Asia, and particularly Mongolia. During the 19th century, the Chinese paid Mongolian troops in tea bricks. Consumers went to the market with a sackful or cartload of tea bricks. A sheep cost between 12 and 15 bricks, and a camel between 120 and 150 bricks. Between two and five bricks could purchase a Chinese pipe. Credit transactions were negotiated in tea bricks, and reports were heard of houses purchased with tea bricks. In Burma, a tea brick was the monetary equivalent of a rupee and circulated as such.

The weight and size of tea bricks were not always consistent, but two main sizes predominated, one weighing two and one-half pounds and a larger one weighing close to five pounds. The bricks consisted of leaf stalks of the tea plant mixed with other herbs and glued with the blood of a steer or young bull. The inferior quality tea went into the production of tea bricks intended for monetary purposes, as if additional evidence was needed to validate Gresham's law. This unappetizing concoction was shaped into bricks and dried in an oven. Value per unit of weight was not a selling point for tea brick money. The transportation of a $100 worth of tea required the sturdy back of a camel.

Asiatic Russia also furnished examples of tea brick money, particularly in areas near the Mongolian border. Goods were purchased and wages were paid in tea bricks. Sugar, iron goods, tools, and arms also circulated among various tribes, and in the 1930s, jam became a favorite and circulated as a medium of exchange in these areas.

Evidence of tea money outside Asia is scanty. In medieval Russia, tea became a form of payment for government officials. Paraguay under Jesuit rule was a barter economy, but there is evidence of tea currency, including for the payment of taxes.

Stimulants and depressants, concomitants of most if not all civilizations, show up frequently as money. Tobacco, cocoa beans, and various varieties of alcohol come to mind as obvious examples. Tea shares some of the characteristics of these commodities and carries a religious significance in Buddhist cultures, rendering it a likely candidate to fill a monetary role.

See also: Commodity Monetary Standard

References
Einzig, Paul. 1966. *Primitive Money.*
Quiggin, A., and A. Hingston. 1949. *A Survey of Primitive Money.*

TOBACCO NOTES

See: Virginia Tobacco Act of 1713

TOUCHSTONE

Touchstones were stones used to test the purity of precious metals such as gold and silver. Touchstones were also called "Lydian stones," after the country of Lydia, the birthplace of precious metal coinage and the first country credited with the use of touchstones. The spread of gold coinage particularly increased the profits that could be earned from adulterating and alloying gold coinage, and touchstones offered an inexpensive and useful test for purity of gold coinage. Both individuals and governments were known to reduce the purity of precious metals by alloying them with cheaper metals.

Touchstones were cut from black siliceous stone or opaque quartz, brown, red, or yellow in color, with a smooth surface, and convenient for holding in one hand. Ancient and medieval assayers tested the purity of gold or silver by rubbing the metal across a touchstone with sufficient pressure to leave a streak. Different metals left streaks of different colors. The color of the streak left on the touchstone by a metal of unknown purity could be compared with the color of a streak left by a piece of metal of known purity. Nitric acid was put on the streaks to dissolve impurities, and sharpen the contrast between the streaks of pure and impure metal. From this comparison, an assayer rendered a judgment about the purity of a metal. Because differences in shades of color can be slight, the test involved a significant subjective component. Nevertheless, the test brought to light the more outrageous debasements and was sufficiently accurate for most purposes.

Before the development of more advanced techniques, the Goldsmiths' Company of the City of London kept test metals of known purity, called "touch needles," for use in making touchstone tests. The Company made available 24 gold needles for each of the traditional 24 gold carats. They kept similar pieces for silver.

Touchstone tests are not decisive in detecting silver alloyed with copper, but can be used to assay gold with some accuracy. By the 15th century, the Tower Mint in London was using a new method, cupellation, which makes use of the tendency of various metals to fuse at high temperatures. The new method using fire grew out of the experiments of the alchemists during the medieval era.

See also: Trial of the Pyx

References
Davies, Glyn. 1994. *A History of Money*.
Marx, Jennifer. 1978. *The Magic of Gold*.

TRADE DOLLAR

In 1873, Congress authorized the coinage of the trade dollar, a special silver dollar coin intended to facilitate trade between the United States and China, and to furnish a market demand for rising silver production in the Western states. At first, the coin was legal tender only for up to $5, but Congress later withheld its legal-tender status. The treasury stopped minting the trade dollar in 1877, and Congress officially discontinued the coin in 1887.

Trade between the United States and the Far East, particularly China and Japan, accelerated around 1869 through 1870, and a popular medium of exchange in the Pacific Basin was the Mexican silver dollar containing 416 grains of silver. The U.S. silver dollar, containing 412.5 grains of silver (before discontinuance on 1873), was not competitive with the Mexican dollar. The state of California petitioned Congress to coin a silver dollar containing 420 grains of silver, hoping to draw to California the Chinese and Japanese trade then flowing to Mexico.

The act of 1873, known in U.S. folklore as the Crime of '73, discontinued the silver dollar as a standard of value in U.S. coinage, but created the trade dollar strictly for commercial purposes with other nations. The act defined the value of the standard dollar strictly in terms of a fixed weight of gold, and silver coinage, excepting the trade dollar, remained only as a subsidiary coinage with a face value exceeding the market value of its bullion content. Apparently, Congress by accident gave the trade dollar a legal-tender status on par with the other subsidiary coinage, making it legal tender for debts up to $5. On July 17, 1876, Congress passed a joint resolution declaring that the trade dollar was not legal tender. The treasury minted nearly $36 billion of these coins, and all but about $6 million of these coins were exported.

The trade dollar was ill-fated from the outset. The traditional U.S. silver dollar remained in circulation, although new silver dollars were no longer minted. The old silver dollars, containing 7.5 grains less silver than the trade dollar, were legal tender, acceptable in payments of public debts, and the government was committed to maintaining their parity with the gold dollar. The trade dollar had more intrinsic value, but enjoyed none of these characteristics, giving rise to no small amount of confusion. Declining silver bullion prices put a tighter seal on the fate of the trade dollar, which commanded no official value and was worth only the market value of its silver content.

To put an end to an awkward situation, Congress on February 19, 1887, discontinued the coin and authorized the treasury to accept trade dollars in exchange for standard dollars or subsidiary coinage for a period of six months. Congress further provided that the treasury melt down the trade dollars received in exchange and recoin the silver content as subsidiary coinage. Over $7 million of trade dollars flowed into the treasury for exchange. As a legacy of the trade dollar, many Pacific nations, including Australia and New Zealand adopted the name "dollar" for their domestic currency.

See also: Bimetallism, Crime of '73, Free Silver Movement

References

Myers, Margaret G. 1970. *A Financial History of the United States.*

Nugent, T. K. Walter. 1968. *Money and American Society.*

Weatherford, Jack. 1997. *The History of Money.*

TREASURY NOTES

Treasury notes were interest-bearing treasury bonds that circulated as money in the pre–Civil War era in the United States. The notes were not legal tender but were accepted for payments owed the federal government, including tax obligations.

For the first two decades of its existence, the new government of the United States steered clear of the issuance of government notes that circulated as money. The hyperinflation during the American Revolution remained a thought-provoking memory of the dangers of paper money, and Alexander Hamilton stood as a staunch opponent of treasury issues of paper money.

By the War of 1812, Congress was in the hands of people without firsthand experience of the Revolutionary hyperinflation, and wartime demands for resources pressed hard on government officials. On June 30, 1812, Congress authorized the issuance of $5 million of treasury notes, redeemable within one year, and paying 5.4 percent interest. The following years saw authorizations for additional issues, $5 million in 1813, $18 million in 1814, and $8 million in 1815. The notes circulated as money and were acceptable in payment of federal government taxes.

The Constitution had strictly forbidden the states from declaring any money other than gold and silver to be legal tender and did not expressly give the federal government authority to declare any money legal tender. Most people at the time felt that the issuance of legal-tender paper money was at best against the spirit of the Constitution, and at worst unconstitutional. On November 12, 1814, Congress entertained a resolution that read as follows: "That the treasury notes which may be issued as aforesaid shall be a legal tender in all debts due or which hereafter may become due between citizens of the United States or between a citizen of the United States and a citizen of any foreign state or country" (Breckinridge, 1969).

Congress brushed aside the idea of declaring treasury notes legal tender in a decisive 95–45 vote. After the war the government retired the notes. By 1817 only 2 percent of the total issue remained in circulation.

The money panic of 1837 sent the government into a budgetary tailspin, and Congress again authorized the issuance of treasury notes. The notes were to be redeemable in one year, and pay interest no greater than 6 percent. Some of these notes paid as little as 0.1 percent interest per year. In 1838, Congress authorized the treasury to reissue treasury notes that had been paid in for taxes or other government obligations, removing an important distinction between treasury notes and circulating paper money. Congress authorized similar issues in years leading up to and including the war with Mexico from 1846 to 1848. By 1850, the government had retired the treasury note issues, but in 1857 a budget crisis once again turned the government to treasury notes to meet a budget shortfall. These notes were earmarked for retirement until the budget crisis of the Civil War overtook budgetary policy. In 1862, the government began issuing legal-tender notes that were soon dubbed "greenbacks."

The history of the treasury notes reveals how hesitant the federal government was to issue legal-tender paper money. Congress accepted without question that the issuance of treasury notes with the legal-tender function was beyond its power.

See also: Greenbacks, Legal Tender

References

Breckinridge, S. P. 1969. *Legal Tender*.

Hepburn, A. Barton. 1924/1967. *A History of Currency of the United States*.

Kagin, Donald H. "Monetary Aspects of the Treasury Notes of the War of 1812." *Journal of Economic History,* vol. 44, no. 1 (March 1984): 69–88.

Myers, Margaret, G. 1970. *A Financial History of the United States*.

TRIAL OF THE PYX (ENGLAND)

The Trial of the Pyx is a public trial or test of the purity of gold and silver coins that began in the 13th century and continues into the present day. In 1982, Queen Elizabeth II and Sir Geoffrey Howe, chancellor of the Exchequer, attended the Trial of the Pyx in celebration of its 700th anniversary. The oldest extant writ ordering a trial came at the behest of Edward I in 1282. Although similar tests were conducted at regional mints, the most meticulous and thorough tests were held for coins struck at the Royal Mint in London.

To conduct a trial, a specified sample of coins of each denomination was set aside and stored in leather bags identified by the month of coinage. In 1485, a sample consisted of 10 shillings from every 10 pounds of gold and 2 shillings from every 100 pounds of silver. These leather bags were put in a chest, or pyx. The pyx was locked with three keys, one held by the warden of the mint, a second by the comptroller, and a third by the master-worker. The crown could call for a trial every three months, but the trials were much less frequent.

To conduct a trial, the officers of the mint appeared before the Council in Star Chamber, together with the lord treasurer's clerk and officials of the Exchequer who brought the contracted specifications for the weights and fineness of coins. The pyx was unlocked before the council.

The Trial of the Pyx has always made use of the most advanced methods for assaying gold and silver, beginning in the earliest times with the use of the touchstone. A public jury of 12 lawful citizens and 12 members of the Goldsmith's Company of London actually conducted the public testing. If the jury held the coins to meet the prescribed standards, based on the fineness of the bullion sent to the mint by the crown, the master-worker received a letter of acquittance. If the coins fell short of the required weight and fineness, the master paid a penalty to the crown proportionate to the profits the master skimmed by reducing the purity of the coinage. Of course, the king was never brought before a public jury to test the purity of the precious metal he sent to the mint. Presumably the mint master assured himself of the purity of the metal supplied by the king.

The custom of the Trial of the Pyx bore witness to the ever-present danger of debasement of the coinage, either at the hands of the crown, or at the hands of dishonest mint officials. The longevity of the custom stood as a reminder of the importance certain groups in society, particularly merchants and bankers, placed on the trustworthiness of the coinage. The Trial of the Pyx helped the English crown control the temptation to debase the currency, contributing to England's reputation for sound currency and laying the foundation for England's commercial success.

See also: Touchstone

References

Challis, C. E. 1978. *The Tudor Coinage.*

Davies, Glyn. 1994. *A History of Money.*

TROUBLED ASSET RELIEF PROGRAM

The Troubled Asset Relief Program, known as TARP, was the cornerstone of the United States program to address the U.S. financial crisis that began in 2008. It came into being in October 2008 with the enactment of the Emergency Economic Stabilization Act of 2008. The legislation was commonly billed as a $700 billion bailout for banks.

The TARP plan evolved over time but originally its purpose was to buy bad loans, mortgage-backed securities, and collateralized debt obligations from banks. These assets went by the term "toxic assets" because they had no market value, and amounted to a severe threat to solvency of the banking system. At first it was thought that the government might be able to recover its investment because it would be purchasing these assets at bargain basement prices, and selling them for a profit later when the financial crisis had passed. Further consideration brought the realization that purchasing these assets at low prices undercut the capitalization of the banking system. Two weeks after the program's enactment, the secretary of treasury shifted the focus of the program to emphasize the purchase of preferred stock in banks and guaranteeing troubled assets. If a bank recovers with the benefit of the government's help, and its stock climbs, the government can sell its stake and recover at least some of the taxpayers' investment.

Citigroup was one of the large banks that benefited from the program. The United States Treasury first purchased $25 billion in preferred stock in Citigroup, and later another $20 billion. The United States government in addition guaranteed troubled loans and securities on Citigroup's balance sheet on the order of $306 billion. In return for the guarantees, the government received another $7 billion stake in Citigroup (Curran, November 25, 2008).

The government forced the top banks to participate in the government bailout. Otherwise, banks that elected not to participate would appear financially stronger, which might give a competitive advantage over the banks that did participate. For smaller banks, participation was voluntary. In the beginning, many smaller banks worried that participation in the program was equivalent to a confession of financial weakness. Once the government let it be known that it would not let banks that were fundamentally unhealthy participate in the program, perceptions changed. Banks began to fear that not applying for participation might be regarded as financial weakness.

TARP drew criticism from the outset. The government did not seem to be

Treasury Secretary Timothy Geithner announces an overhaul of the Troubled Asset Relief Program (TARP) at the Treasury Department in Washington, D.C. on February 10, 2009. (Shawn Thew/epa/Corbis)

doing enough to track how banks were using the infusions of government capital. Homeowners facing foreclosures received no relief from TARP funds. People wondered why it was more important to bail out Wall Street than to bail out families facing bankruptcy and home foreclosure. None of the TARP funds helped homeowners refinance mortgages that they could not pay. In December 2008, President Bush used his executive authority to make TARP funds available to U.S. automobile manufacturers. Both General Motors and Chrysler received TARP funds. The most controversial beneficiary of TARP funds was American International Group, a large insurance company. In January 2009, the new administration of President Obama vowed to revise the TARP plan to alleviate the rate of home foreclosures.

Bank bailouts became a global phenomenon in 2008. The United Kingdom established a plan similar in strategy and scale to the one in the United States. The Royal Bank of Scotland was the largest beneficiary of government bailout money in the United Kingdom. In 2008, Sweden announced a sweeping bailout plan to save its banking system. Belgium bailed out a large bank in October 2008. Germany and Iceland both bailed out financial institutions. Switzerland, eager to protect its status as global banking center, put together a massive recapitalization of the United Bank of Switzerland.

See also: Savings and Loan Bailout

References

Cimilluca, Dana. "The Financial Crisis: Swiss Move to Back Troubled UBS; Under Plan, as Much as $60 Billion in

Toxic Assets to be Taken Off Balance Sheet." *Wall Street Journal* (Eastern Edition), October 17, 2008, p. A3.

Curran, Rob. "Large Stock Focus: Citi Jumps on Bailout; B of A, Goldman Follow", *Wall Street Journal* (Eastern Edition) November 25, 2008, p. C6.

Kessler, Andy. "What Paulson Is Trying to Do." *Wall Street Journal* (Eastern Edition) October 15, 2008, p. A19.

Solomon, Deborah. "U.S. News: Obama Works to Overhaul TARP—Team Tries to Meld Some Paulson Ideas with Aid to Borrowers Facing Foreclosure." *Wall Street Journal* (Eastern Edition), December 17, 2008, p. A3.

Williamson, Elizabeth. "U.S. News: Rescue Cash Lures Thousand of Banks." *Wall Street Journal* (Eastern Edition), November 3, 2008, p. A3.

TURKISH INFLATION

The March 2001 edition of *Newsweek* carried an article entitled "Is This the End of Inflation? Turkey's currency crisis may be the last battle in the global war against hyperinflation." The article cited Turkey as the last major country struggling against out-of-control prices. The 1990s saw inflation rates around the world subside to the point that some observers suggested that the global economy could turn the corner from inflation to deflation. Turkey was one exception to the trend. As of 2008, Turkey had pared inflation down to single-digit territory.

Turkish inflation is more notable for its long, sustained rise in prices rather than for episodes of wild hyperinflation. Between 1964 and 2001, Turkey only saw two episodes of inflation that sent prices increasing at triple-digit rates, and even then, the inflation rates fell short of hyperinflation territory. In 1980, annual inflation soared to the 110 percent range.

In 1994, Turkey once again posted annual inflation rates around 110 percent (Leigh and Rossi, 2002). Nevertheless, average inflation rates steadily climbed. Between 1964 and 1980, annual inflation rates in Turkey averaged roughly 21 percent. Between 1981 and 1989, annual inflation rates in Turkey averaged roughly 41 percent. Between 1990 and 2001, annual inflation rates averaged roughly 72 percent (Leigh and Rossi, 2002).

The core problem appeared to be political. No one party could ever win an absolute majority, and the coalitions put together to form governments encouraged short-sighted thinking. Various governments borrowed to pay for various vote-catching programs, including substantial pay raises to public employees. An inefficient tax collection system and large underground economy compounded the problems. Subsidies to sluggish state-owned enterprises and interest on the public debt added to the deficit. Before the spike in inflation in 1994, Turkey had seen public sector borrowing as a percent of gross domestic product (GDP) rise from 3.7 percent in 1986 to 12.3 percent in 1993 (Dowden, June, 1996). Short-term borrowing from the central bank accounted for 15 percent of the government's budget (Dowden, June, 1996). When central banks purchase government bonds, they add to the money stock in circulation. The central bank also had a history of caving in to demands of ailing commercial banks for more funds.

In 2001, the IMF approved a rescue package of $8 billion to help Turkey avoid hyperinflation and debt default (*Economist,* May 2001). The $8 billion was on top of a previous $11 billion committed under a previous anti-inflation program. The package came with conditions that Turkey privatize debt-ridden state enterprises, reform a corrupt banking sector, and increase government tax collections. The IMF also required Turkey to peg the Turkish lira's value to a basket of euros and dollars. Turkey could not add to the supply of Turkish lira without increasing the central bank's holdings of foreign reserve assets.

Turkey brought down inflation with highly stringent monetary policy. As of 2006, Turkey's central bank was keeping its key lending rate steady at 22.5 percent and inflation was hovering around 10 percent (www.emerging-markets-online.com, November 2006).

Persistent inflation left its marked on the Turkish currency, the Turkish lira. Before the reform of the Turkish currency in 2005, Turkey boasted the largest denominated banknote in the world, a 20 million Turkish lira banknote (*International Financial Law Review*, 2005). The large number of zeros in figures recorded in financial statements caused technical and operational problems, particularly for banks and the treasury. The Law on the Currency Unit of the Republic of Turkey, No: 5308 became effective on January 1, 2005. This law created a new currency equal to the old currency minus six zeros. One unit of the New Turkish lira equaled 1 million units of the old currency unit. Both the New Turkish lira and the Turkish lira circulated concurrently for one year. As of January 1, 2006, the New Turkish lira became the Turkish lira. All bank accounts were converted from Turkish lira to New Turkish lira.

References

Dowden, Richard. "A Disaster that Hasn't Quite Happened." *Economist*, June 8, 1996, Special Section, pp. 8–13.

www.emerging-markets-online.com, November 13, 2006, p. 19.

Economist. "Harsh Medicine." May 19, 2001, p. 48.

International Financial Law Review. "The New Turkish Lira." vol. 24, no. 1 (January 1995): 47–48.

Leigh, Daniel, and Marco Rossi. "Leading Indicators of Growth and Inflation in Turkey." IMF Working Paper (WP/02/231) December 2002.

TZARIST RUSSIA'S PAPER MONEY

Of the European countries, only Sweden beat Russia to the punch on the issuance of government-sanctioned paper money inconvertible into precious metal. Perhaps it is no accident that Russia first saw paper money under Catherine the Great (1762–1795), whose wars broke the power of Turkey and made Russia a player among the powers of Europe. The first issue of paper money, called "roubles-assignats" appeared in 1768 to help finance the first Turkish war. Russia termed its paper money "assignats" before the French issued their own, more famous assignats during the French Revolution, which fueled one of the great hyperinflation episodes in history.

The government created two note-issuing Assignation Banks to issue the notes. The supply of assignats swelled as Catherine fought a second Turkish war and wars with Sweden, Poland, and Persia. For the first two decades, the bourse exchange rate between assignat rubles and silver rubles traded close to par. Toward the end of the 18th century, the assignat rubles were trading at a 30 percent discount, and fluctuated around that level until the Napoleonic struggles increased the government's dependence on paper money. By 1811, a silver ruble equaled 3.94 assignat rubles. The victory over Napoleon brought some improvement in confidence, but the trading range remained between 3 and 4 assignat rubles per silver ruble for the following three decades.

Between 1839 and 1843, Russia, under Nicholas I, reformed its currency and issued new silver notes convertible into silver at a fixed rate. The assignat rubles were traded for the new silver notes at a rate of 3.5 to 1.

During the Crimean war (1854), the supply of paper rubles doubled and Russia suspended convertibility of its silver notes. The value of the ruble remained uncertain and fluctuated until the period 1868 through 1875, when the government succeeded in propping up the ruble. Again, a war disrupted best-laid monetary plans during the Turkish war of 1877 and 1878.

Until the adoption of the gold standard (1897–1899), the ruble traded at a modest 30 percent discount, but fluctuated sharply in foreign exchange markets, scaring away potential foreign investment. Russia adopted the gold standard to attract foreign investors and bring in badly needed foreign capital.

See also: Inconvertible Paper Standard, Sweden's First Paper Standard

References

Crisp, Olga. 1976. *Studies in the Russian Economy Before 1914.*

Pintner, Walter McKenzie. 1967. *Russian Economic Policy Under Nicholas I.*

U

UNITED STATES EAGLE

See: Coinage Act of 1792, Coinage Act of 1834, Coinage Act of 1853

UNIVERSAL BANKS

In addition to the traditional commercial banking activities of holding deposits and extending loans, universal banks offer a full range of financial services, including underwriting, issuing new offerings of stocks and bonds, and brokering stocks and bonds. Some universal banks provide insurance. Banks that only engage in underwriting new securities, floating new offers of securities, and brokering securities are called "investment banks." Universal banks combine deposit banking of traditional commercial banking with investment banking.

In the 1800s, banks in continental Europe and Germany in particular developed along the lines of universal banks, whereas in Britain deposit banking and investment banking tended to remain separate. In the United States, financier moguls such as J. P. Morgan introduced universal banking in the United States in the last decades leading up to World War I. Congress cut short the development of universal banking in the United States with the enactment of the Glass–Steagall Banking Act of 1933. Aimed at restoring public confidence in banks, this act prohibited commercial banks from investing in the stock market or providing investment bank services. In the German model of the 19th century, universal banks purchased corporate stock for customers. In exchange, customers yielded to banks proxies entitling banks to vote the customers' shares in shareholder votes. The banks also purchased corporate stock on their own accounts. The control of a large piece of shareholder power ensured that the banks held positions on corporate boards of directors. The universal banks were also lenders to corporations. By holding seats on boards of directors, the banks had a voice in the management of companies that owed them money. In addition, they had an incentive to watch out for mismanagement at the expense of stockholders and creditors. It was an arrangement that put a large amount of power in the hands of banks.

In the post–World War II era, universal banks enjoyed the greatest legal acceptance and experienced the fullest development in Germany. German universal banks hold large equity positions in corporations, have representatives on their boards, and exercise proxy votes for customer shareholders. Japan and Switzerland also followed the universal banking model. The economic success of these countries, and particularly the rapid economic growth in Germany and Japan, began to restore confidence in universal banking. Banks in these countries help to minimize conflicts between debt and equity holders and keep corporate management under tighter rein. By ensuring access to long-term financing, universal banks shield corporate managers from short pressures from fluctuations in stock market prices.

Particularly in Germany, critics raised the issue of universal banks dominating the German stock market. It is said that rather than earning high dividends, banks were more interested in making loans to corporations on whose boards they had representation. In the 1990s, Germany experienced several corporate failures. In 1998, the German government enacted the Control and Transparency in Corporate Field Act. This act prohibits a bank holding more than 5 percent of a company's shares from controlling the proxy voting rights for its bank customers who also own shares in the company.

In the 1990s, momentum began to build to approve universal banking in the United States. Critics worried that universal banks would choose riskier investments because under a system of FDIC insurance the cost of funds to a bank does not vary with the riskiness of its investments.

In 1999, the U.S. Congress lifted the ban on universal banking with the passage of the Financial Services Modernization Act of 1999. Replacing the Glass–Steagall Act of 1933, this act allowed the integration of banking, insurance, and stock-trading. By 2007, the United States boasted three large universal banks, Citigroup Inc., JPMorgan Chase & Co., and Bank of America Corp (*Wall Street Journal,* September 6, 2007). As the subprime financial crisis of 2008 unfolded in the United States, some observers felt the financial woes stemmed directly from dismantling the wall between deposit banking and investment banking. They were referring to the repeal of the Glass–Steagall Act. At first, the universal banks seemed to fare better than the investment banks. The financial crisis could be interpreted as a symptom of the shake-out and consolidation that analysts expected from the enactment of the Financial Services Modernization Act of 1999. As the financial crisis widened, however, the stock values of Citigroup, JPMorgan Chase, and Bank of America crashed, and the future of the institutions was very much in doubt. All three of the banks received large infusions of preferred stock investments from the United States Treasury.

See also: Glass–Steagall Banking Act of 1933, Troubled Asset Relief Program

References

Esen, Rita. "The Transition of German Universal Banks." *Journal of International Banking Regulation,* vol. 2, no. 4 (2001): 50–57.

Fohlin, Caroline. "Relationship Banking, Liquidity, and Investment in the German

Industrialization." *Journal of Finance,* vol. 53, no. 5 (October 1998): 1737–1758.

Sidel, Robin. "Do-It-All Banks' Big Test; Universal Model So Far Weathers Credit Crunch, Remains Controversial." *Wall Street Journal* (Eastern Edition, New York) September 6, 2007, p. C1.

Wall Street Journal (Eastern Edition). "Glass and Steagall Had a Point." May 31, 2008, p. A10.

U.S. FINANCIAL CRISIS OF 2008–2009

The U.S. financial crisis of 2008–2009 owed its origins to a failure of institutions to adjust to rapid innovation in the home mortgage industry. The size and importance of the United States in the global economic and financial system left little doubt that the outcome would take on global dimensions.

The roots of the U.S. financial crisis go back to the aftermath of the 1990s economic prosperity. The 1990s saw the longest economic expansion recorded in U.S. history. The long expansion received its thrust from an investment boom in information technology industries. Easy credit fed the investment boom for a time. When the United States started tightening credit, a high-tech stock bubble burst, the investment boom ended, and the United States entered into recession. In a bid to resuscitate the United States economy, the government again turned to easy credit and bargain basement interest rates.

Low interest rates and easy credit between 2002 and 2005 sparked a boom in housing, creating a housing bubble comparable to the high-tech stock bubble of the 1990s. A housing bubble posed special risk to the financial system because houses are one asset that can be purchased with small down payments. Compared to purchasers of corporate stock, purchasers of houses can put in a much smaller share of their own money.

Dodd and Mills (June 2008) lay out every step in the development of the crisis. A long upswing in house prices had put creditors at ease about the risk of home mortgages. A house seemed to be bullet-proof collateral. Lenders began granting riskier loans and being less thorough in verifying the income, jobs, and assets of borrowers. Some mortgage originators went so far as to offer interest-only loans and negative amortization payment options. Negative amortization meant the borrower's monthly payment was not even covering all the interest charges, much less paying down the principal. Lenders felt that escalation in house prices assured that a house could always be refinanced for larger amounts, or sold to pay off a mortgage. Rising house prices should translate into falling loan-to-value ratios for creditors.

Another weak link in the stability of the financial situation was in the process of packaging home mortgages into financial securities. Investors buying these mortgage-backed securities had to rely on the same credit rating agencies that rated bonds. Well-established and reputable rating agencies such as Standard and Poor's and Moody's had performed well in rating bonds but had little knowledge or experience in mortgage-backed securities. Since mortgage-backed securities were new, no historical data existed to estimate past performance and risk. These agencies awarded top ratings of AAA to over 90 percent of the mortgage-backed securities based on subprime loans (Dodd and Mills, June 2008).

Investors purchased mortgage-backed securities with borrowed funds and counted on being able to trade out of these investments in a hurry to cut losses. Mortgage-backed securities, however, were sold in an over-the-counter market, and no dealers committed themselves to making a market for them. As the poor quality of the mortgages became evident, no dealers came forward willing to maintain an inventory of these securities. The market for mortgage-backed securities became a market where everybody wanted to sell and nobody wanted to buy.

The magnitude of investor losses from mortgage-backed securities would have been easily manageable if the problem had not had wider implications. Mortgage delinquencies and home foreclosures began to mount in 2006 and 2007 amid an otherwise expanding economy. It became clear that many homeowners could only make their mortgage payments if home prices continued to escalate, allowing them to refinance their homes before the teaser interest rates on their existing home mortgages expired. It was equally obvious that many loan applications had inflated measures of borrowers' income and house appraisal values. Falling home prices triggered a wave of foreclosures. Upward interest rate adjustments on adjustable-rate mortgages worsened an already bad situation.

A related casualty of the mortgage-backed securities market debacle was investor confidence in the credit ratings agencies such as Standard and Poor's and Moody's. These agencies were forced to downgrade the credit ratings of mortgage-backed securities at a much faster pace than had ever been seen for corporate bonds.

The month of July 2007 saw a significant round of ratings downgrades for mortgage-backed securities. Wall Street hedge funds began trying to liquidate large positions in these securities. In August 2007, the French bank BNP Paribas suspended withdrawals from some money market funds that were heavily invested in U.S. mortgage-backed securities. The bank claimed it had no way of putting a value on these assets. Expecting a wave of customer cash withdrawals, other money market fund managers shifted these portfolios from medium- and long-term bank deposits and commercial paper to overnight deposits. The strong demand for liquidity drained the supply of funds for short-term commercial credit instruments. The market for what was called "asset-backed commercial paper" collapsed.

The collapse of the asset-backed commercial paper market brought to the surface the role of the structured investment vehicles that a number of banks sponsored as off-balance sheet entities. Banks sponsored these off-balance sheet entities to skirt banking regulations. They amounted to a hidden banking system. These structured investment vehicles raised funds by selling asset-backed commercial paper and invested the funds in longer-term assets that paid higher interest rates. Part of the arrangement was that the sponsoring banks were obligated to provide credit to the structured investment vehicle when necessary. When the market for asset-backed commercial paper collapsed, sponsoring banks had to meet unwanted and inconvenient loan commitments.

Media and pedestrians gather in front of the Lehman Brothers headquarters in New York on September 15, 2008, the day the 158-year-old financial firm filed for bankruptcy. (AP Photo/ Louis Lanzano)

Banks, unable to raise funds by selling loans and fearful of depositor withdrawals, set to hoarding liquidity. They were caught in a squeeze between keeping loans on their books that they had planned on selling, and honoring loan commitments to hedge funds and corporate entities, commitments that they wished they had not made.

In March 2008, the Wall Street firm of Bear Stearns saw a run on its deposits that would have ended in bankruptcy if the Federal Reserve had not assisted in its acquisition by JPMorgan Chase. In September, the United States government announced a takeover of Fannie Mae and Freddie Mac, two government-sponsored enterprises concerned exclusively with the home mortgage market. Later in September, the Wall Street firm Lehman Brothers failed. The United States Treasury refused to bail out Lehman Brothers but did encourage other firms to acquire it. When no buyers appeared, Lehman Brothers went into liquidation.

Another important industry found itself drawn in to the mortgage-backed security debacle. Bond insurers usually provided investors with default insurance against municipal and infrastructure bonds. The firms had begun selling default insurance for the mortgage-backed securities. Rising mortgage delinquencies and foreclosures hammered the stocks and credit ratings of bond-insuring companies and left in doubt the ability of these companies to honor default insurance claims in the municipal bond market and the student loan market, making these investments much less attractive.

The outcome of these developments was a banking system less willing and able to make loans and demanding tighter criteria of credit worthiness. A seizing of credit markets hobbled private initiative among producers and consumers. The forces of recession gathered strength as firms across industries reported falling earnings. October 2008, stock markets around the world entered a steep slide. The world braced for a global recession. Economic policy makers assumed that the economic situation in the United States was developing along the lines of a liquidity trap. The Federal Reserve System, the central bank of the United States, pushed its policy interest rate to near zero and allowed banks to use a wider range of assets to borrow funds. The U.S. government met the crisis with plans for massive increases in deficit spending. In a liquidity trap, massive government spending is needed to offset the combined effects of strong liquidity preference and pessimistic expectations.

See also: Liquidity Trap

References

Dodd, Randall and Paul Mills. "Outbreak: U.S. Subprime Contagion." *Finance and Development,* vol. 45, no. 2 (June 2008): 14–19.

Kelly, Kate. "The Fall of Bear Stearns: Fear, Rumors Touched Off Fatal Run on Bear Stearns; Executives Swung From Hope to Despair in the Space of a Week." *Wall Street Journal* (Eastern Edition), May 28, 2008, p. A1.

Paletta, Damian, Susanne Craig, Deborah Soloman, Carrick Mollenkamp, and Mathew Karnitschnig. "Lehman Fata Spurs Emergency Session; Wall Street Titans Seek Ways to Stem Widening Crisis." *Wall Street Journal* (Eastern Edition), September 13, 2008, p. A1.

Reddy, Sudeep. "U.S. News: Fed Extends Lending Programs as Threats Persist; Move Reflects Worry Over 'Fragile' State of Financial Market." *Wall Street Journal* (Eastern Edition), July 31, 2008, p. A3.

USURY LAWS

Usury laws either prohibit payment of interest on loans or set a maximum interest rate that lenders can charge. Historically, the medieval Catholic Church disapproved of charging interest on loans. As late as 1950, Pope Pius XII felt it necessary to reassure people that bankers earn their livelihood honestly. In the late medieval period, the Church began to relent, allowing certain forms of credit involving the payment of up to 5 percent interest.

In the early history of France, the French crown often forced subjects to loan money to the crown at zero percent interest. Businesses worked around the Church's prohibition on interest. In 1311, Philip the Fair (IV), drawing a distinction between usury and trade loans made at fairs, set a maximum of 2.5 percent interest for commercial loans between fairs. (The annualized rate of this maximum equaled about 15 percent.) In 1601, Henry IV, for reasons that were unclear, issued an edict putting a 6.25 percent legal ceiling on interest rates. The edict was widely disregarded, but his government probably saw it as a way of promoting commerce. Under the regime of Cardinal Richelieu, the crown issued a royal edict (1634) further reducing the legal rate of interest to 5 5/9 percent, citing the evil effects of high interest rates that allow people to live on interest income instead of engaging in commerce.

During the time of Colbert, Louis XIV issued a royal edict (1665) lowering the maximum rate of interest to 5 percent. The discussion leading up to this edict was revealing. Feeling pangs of conscience for sanctioning the payment of interest, given the attitude of the Church, Louis XIV before issuing the edict held an informal meeting with five of the "most learned doctors" of Sorbonne to discuss the matter. The dean of the faculty spoke first and said that such a weighty matter should be discussed at a meeting of the whole faculty. The faculty took up the subject in the light of scripture, writings of church fathers, the decisions of various councils, and decrees of popes. One of the doctors reported their findings saying that "no doctor of the Sorbonne could approve the proposition that one could take interest on money or set the rate thereof" (Cole, 1964).

In 1766, a law attempted to lower the interest rates in France from 5 percent to 4 percent, but it was not obeyed, leaving interest rates in the 5-percent range until the French Revolution, when interest rate ceilings were abolished.

Even in England, the most commercialized of the European states, charging interest was a shady activity. Writing in the early 1600s, the famous English philosopher and statesman, Francis Bacon, cited arguments of his day against usury, which he defined as "interest, not necessarily excessive." It was said that "the usurer is the greatest Sabbath-breaker, because his plough goeth every Sunday . . . that the usurer breaketh the first law that was made for mankind after the fall which was . . . in the sweat of thy face shalt thou eat bread—not in the sweat of another's face" (Bacon, 1969).

Under the reign of Elizabeth I, the English government enacted a usury law condemning but allowing a maximum of 10 percent interest to be paid. The wording of this law reflected the gradual change in the meaning of the word "usury." Now the term "usury" referred to excessive interest. The legal interest rate ceiling in England remained at 10 percent from 1571 to 1624. From 1624 to 1651, the interest rate ceiling stood at 8 percent, and the period from 1651 to 1714 saw interest rates fall to 6 percent. An amendment to the usury law in 1715 reduced the ceiling to 5 percent, where it remained until the end of the 18th century. Parliament abolished the usury law in 1854. Interest rate ceilings did not apply to loans to the government.

In the United States, individual states kept usury laws on the books into the 1970s. High inflation rates in the 1970s lifted interest rates well above state usury ceilings, and states repealed usury ceilings to prevent a disappearance of credit financing. Toward the end of the 1980s, interest rates began a long downward swing that continued into the new century, easing concern about usurious interest rates. During the financial crisis of 2008, governments pushed interest rates to record low levels. Concern was expressed about what would happen if interest rates reached a natural floor close to zero and government lost its ability to push them lower. A government unable to lower interest rates would find it more difficult to revive a sluggish economy.

The view has survived into the modern era that low interest rates contribute to economic prosperity. The proper method of securing low interest rates, however, is to provide for an ample supply of credit rather than putting a legal lid on interest rates. The ample supply of credit must come from savings rather than printing up new money, which can cause inflation.

See also: Interest Rate, Medici Bank

References

Bacon, Sir Francis. 1625/1969. *Civil Essays.*

Clapham, Sir John. 1951. *An Economic History of Modern Britain.*

Cole, Charles Woolsey. 1964. *Colbert and a Century of French Mercantilism.*

Glaeser, Edward L. 1994. *Neither a Borrower, Nor a Lender Be: An Economic Analysis of Interest Restrictions and Usury Laws.*

Homer, Sidney. 1977. *A History of Interest Rates*, 2nd ed.

V

VALES (SPAIN)

Vales were Spanish paper money notes issued in the late 18th century and the Napoleonic era, the first paper money issued in Spain. During the last half of the 18th century, the gold and silver mines of Spanish America supplied the lion's share of the world's precious metals, and mints in Spain and the Indies struck most of the coins. Vast gold and silver resources were of little avail when war interrupted the flow of trade with the New World, compelling Spain to turn to the issuance of paper money.

War between Great Britain and Spain, the major colonial powers in the New World, broke out in 1779. Charles III, king of Spain, refused, perhaps out of fear, to raise taxes to fight the war. Also a history of defaults and bankruptcies damaged the ability of the Spanish government to float bond issues. A royal decree of September 20, 1780, authorized the issuance of 16,500 vales, each with a face value of 600 *vellon pesos* and bearing 4 percent interest. A syndicate of Dutch, French, and Spanish merchants had offered to extend funds to the Spanish government in return for interest-bearing notes that passed as legal-tender money.

Once a year, the vales were returned to the treasury for payment of interest, inspection for counterfeited issues, and renewal for another year. A holder of a vale endorsed it before passing it on in exchange, and the holder of a counterfeited vale was entitled to reimbursement from the last endorser.

The vales were legal tender for payment of taxes and other obligations to the crown, promissory notes and other private debts, and bills of exchange. Creditors had to accept vales even when specie had been stipulated in the contract's terms. Anyone refusing to accept vales as the equivalent of specie faced exile from Spain and exclusion from business dealings with Spain abroad. Vales had legal-tender status only for transactions equal to or exceeding 600 pesos, and recipients of salaries, wages, and pensions could refuse to accept them.

Other issues of vales followed on similar terms. The first issue drew a 10 percent commission to the syndicate supplying the funds, and subsequent issues drew a 6 percent commission.

The strains of the four-year war with Great Britain led to a modest overindulgence in paper money, and at times vales circulated at 15 to 20 percent discounts relative to specie. At the war's end, bullion and specie again flowed into Spain from the New World, and vales circulated at par again. The retirement of a portion of the vale issues further boosted their value. In 1781, the Bank of Spain was chartered partly as a means for the orderly retirement of paper-money issues, an unusual mission for the type of bank usually known for issuing paper money.

In 1793, war erupted with Revolutionary France, and the Spanish government again balked at raising taxes. At the opening of the war, vales were circulating at par and suffered little depreciation despite the 300 percent increase in the supply of vales over the course of the 28-month war.

When Spain went to war with Great Britain again in 1796 the strains of wartime finance reached the breaking point. After resisting the issuance of additional vales for the first three years of war, the Spanish increased the supply of circulating vales by 50 percent in 1799. The inflation cooker now boiled over, and vales began to depreciate relative to specie. When a government office began to redeem small amounts of vales in hardship cases, a riot ensued after people formed a long line, and some bought places in line. By 1801, vales had depreciated by 75 percent.

Monetary chaos continued in Spain as the Napoleonic struggle spread to Spain, first with occupation by Napoleon and then by the Duke of Wellington. By the war's end, the value of the vales had fallen to 4 percent of their par value. After the war, the government stopped printing vales and the inflation ceased.

See also: Bank Restriction Act of 1797, Inconvertible Paper Standard

References

Hamilton, Earl J. 1969. *War and Prices in Spain: 1651–1800.*

Kindleberger, Charles P. 1984. *A Financial History of Western Europe.*

VALUE OF MONEY

The value of money has to do with the purchasing power of a unit of money. One approach to the measurement of money value is to look at its precious metal equivalent. Under a gold standard, a dollar should be worth approximately a dollar's worth of gold. Under a gold coin standard, the value of a dollar could drop below a dollar if the government reduces the gold content of its coinage relative to its face value. Under such circumstances it might be appropriate to say that a dollar is worth only 75 cents or 50 cents, based on the value of its precious metal content.

Despite the widely hailed virtues of precious metal backing for money, the amount of precious metal a unit of money can buy is not the essential factor to individual consumers, who have to think of the cost of things they must buy to maintain themselves and their families. Furthermore, under an inconvertible paper standard such as that of the United States, where even the metallic coinage is token money, the value of money is divorced from any precious metal connection. The true measure of money value is in terms of its purchasing power.

The value of money can only be measured relative to its value at a point in time. Assume that $1 is equal to $1 in 1987. If prices double from inflation in the following decade, and in 1997 it takes $2 to buy what $1 would have bought in 1987, then it would be appropriate to say that today's dollar is worth only 50 cents.

In practice, government statisticians and economists calculate price indices, such as the wholesale price index, the consumer price index, or the gross domestic product (GDP) deflator, which show the ratio of a weighted average of prices in a given year over a weighted average of prices in some arbitrarily selected base year. If the base year is 1987, then the price index is set to 100 for that year. If prices go up 10 percent over the following year, then the price index for 1988 will be 110, indicating that it takes $1.10 to purchase what $1 would have bought the year before.

In 1998, the United States GDP deflator (base year = 1987) stood at 137.33. The value of a dollar can be calculated by dividing 137.33 into 100 (100/137.33), which equals 0.73, indicating that a dollar was worth only 73 cents in 1998. Keeping the base year at 1987, the GDP deflator for 1970 equals 34.5. The value of the 1970 dollar equals 100/34.5, or $2.90, meaning a dollar in 1970 was worth $2.90 cents relative to a 1987 dollar. In this context it would be appropriate to say that a dollar in 1970 was worth $2.90.

For a currency to be useful as a store of value and standard of deferred payment, it must maintain its purchasing power. A general rise in prices, commonly known as inflation, can be interpreted as a decrease in the value of a unit of money.

See also: Inflation and Deflation, Monetary Theory

References

Klein, John J. 1986. *Money and the Economy,* 6th ed.

McCallum, Bennet T. 1989. *Monetary Economics.*

VARIABLE COMMODITY STANDARD

Under a variable commodity standard, a currency is officially redeemable in a certain amount of a commodity, such as gold, but the authorities may vary the redemption rate, depending on other economic conditions. If the commodity is gold, the monetary authorities would vary the amount of gold the central bank stood ready to buy and sell for a unit of currency (e.g., a dollar) to maintain the value of the currency.

One of the legacies of the inflation-ridden 1970s and early 1980s was a renewed search for an inflation-proof currency. Issues surrounding the formation of the European Monetary Union and the planned development of a single European currency focused additional attention on schemes of monetary reform. In the late 1980s, numerous proposals for monetary reform surfaced that incorporated the concept of a variable commodity standard. The common theme in these proposals was the idea of a currency whose value is tied to a weighted basket of goods. The emphasis was on a currency not convertible into a fixed weight of gold, or other commodity, but convertible, at least indirectly, into a weighted basket of goods.

Irving Fisher made one of the first proposals for a variable commodity standard in 1926. He called it the "compensated dollar" and it required periodic adjustments to the rate at which dollars were redeemable into gold. The magnitude of the adjustments was based on the deviations of the current dollar value of a basket of goods from the value of the same basket of goods at a point in time. The purpose of Fisher's proposal was to stabilize the value of the dollar in terms of a basket of goods, rather than a single commodity.

More recent proposals abandoned the idea of periodic adjustments in favor of a currency indirectly convertible into a weighted basket of goods at all times. Under these plans, the monetary authorities would constantly evaluate the value of a weighted basket of goods in terms of a weight of gold or other commodity, and would stand ready to redeem a unit of currency in the amount of gold needed to purchase the weighted basket of goods.

The weighted basket of goods in these schemes would be identical with the weighted basket of goods in a price index, such as the wholesale price index (WPI). The weighted basket of goods might be viewed as a unit of a composite good composed of all the goods in the WPI, and combined in the same proportions as in the WPI. The variable commodity standard then is seen for what it is: A commodity standard that replaces gold or a single commodity with a composite of goods. If the value of a unit of currency (e.g., dollar) remained constant relative to its ability to purchase a unit of a such a composite good, then by definition the inflation rate would be zero.

The mechanics of these schemes have not been worked out satisfactorily, at least for operation over an extended period of time. Recent discussions of variable commodity standards, however, may indicate that the inconvertible paper standard may not represent the pinnacle stage of evolution in monetary standards and that in the eyes of some theoretical researchers there is room for improvement.

See also: Commodity Monetary Standard, Gold Standard, Symmetallism

References

Coats, Warren L. "In Search of a Monetary Anchor: A New Monetary Standard." International Monetary Fund Working Paper. no. 82.

Fisher, Irving. 1926. *Stabilizing the Dollar*.

Schnadt, Norman, and John Whittaker. "Inflation-proof Currency? The Feasibility of Variable Commodity Standards." *Journal of Money, Credit, and Banking,* vol. 25, no. 2 (1993): 214–221.

VEHICLE CURRENCY

A vehicle currency is a currency that individuals and businesses favor for international transactions. Individuals and businesses from a particular country do not always favor their home currency for international transactions. A business in Japan might issue bonds denominated in U.S. dollars, and a French investor might purchase one of the bonds. The transaction takes place in U.S. dollars even though no one from the United States is involved in the transaction. Bonds, short-term financial instruments, and bank accounts can be denominated in any number of currencies. A vehicle currency is the closest thing to an international currency.

The U.S. dollar emerged from World War II as the leading vehicle currency. Depression, wartime finance, and declining shares of world trade had undermined the leading European currencies. Before the U.S. dollar rose to prominence, the British pound acted as the preeminent currency in international trade.

The depreciation of the U.S. dollar and the introduction of the euro have led some observes to doubt the future of the dollar as the dominate vehicle currency. In April 2008, Iran announced that it was stopping the practice of selling oil in U.S. dollars, citing the depreciation of the dollar. The Organization of Petroleum Exporting Countries (OPEC) has always priced oil in U.S. dollars, but Iran has been lobbying within OPEC to substitute a basket of currencies for the U.S. dollar. Members of OPEC friendlier to the United States have so far resisted the change.

Criteria that define a currency as a vehicle currency included statistics such as the share of exports and imports invoiced in the currency, and the share of international bonds denominated in the currency. On the eve of the introduction of the euro, 43.6 percent of international bonds were denominated in U.S. dollars, and 13.6 percent were denominated in Japanese yen (Bank for International Settlements, 1998).

The U.S. dollar remains the dominate vehicle currency, but there is evidence that it has yielded ground to the euro, according to Working Paper no. 665 of the European Central Bank. According to this study, between 2000 and 2003, the share of Japan's exports invoiced in euro increased from 7.6 percent to 9.6 percent. Over the same period, the share of Japan's exports invoiced in U.S. dollars slipped from 52.4 percent to 48.0 percent. The importance of the U.S. dollar shows up in data for the emerging markets. Between 2000 and 2004, the share of Indonesia's exports invoiced in dollars increased from 92.7 percent to 93.6 percent. Between 2000 and 2004, Israel's share of exports invoiced in euro declined from 24.6 percent to 23.9 percent, whereas the same numbers for the U.S. dollar grew from 62.6 percent to 64.7 percent. In 2003, 33.6 percent of France's exports and 24.1 percent of Germany's exports were denominated in dollars.

Certain factors account for the emergence of a dominant vehicle currency. Firms selling goods in a global market may not want the price of their products fluctuating relative to the prices charged by competitors. Therefore, they invoice their sales in the same currency used by their competitors. This tendency is strongest among competitors producing goods that are virtually identical, such as steel or copper. This tendency is not as strong among firms producing products that do not have close substitutes.

In addition, firms and investors look for currencies that do not sharply fluctuate in value. Sellers do not want the prices of products fluctuating because prices are invoiced in a currency that exhibits wild fluctuations. Similarly, investors do not want foreign investment fluctuating in value because the investments are denominated in foreign currencies that are unstable. The U.S. dollar grew to prominence as a vehicle currency when the United States was on the gold standard, and the U.S. dollar remained equal to a gold equivalent. Inertia also appears to be a factor in helping a currency hold on to its position as a vehicle currency.

See also: Dollar

References

Bank for International Settlements, *Annual Report,* Basel, Switzerland, 1998.

Goldberg, Linda S. and Cedric Tille. "Vehicle Currency Use in International Trade." Federal Reserve Bank of New York, Staff Report no. 200, January 2005.

Kamps, Annette. "The Euro as Invoicing Currency in International Trade." European Central Bank, ECB Working Paper no. 665, August 2006.

VELLON

Originally, vellon was a mixture of copper and silver that became widely used for subsidiary coinage in Spain in the 16th, 17th, and 18th centuries. Over its history, vellon took several forms. *Calderilla*, an early type of vellon, contained a variable but modest amount of silver, and was coined mainly in the 16th century. Another type of vellon, rich vellon, was coined mainly in the 17th century and contained a token 6.95 percent silver. A pure copper vellon containing no silver or metal alloys also appeared in the 17th century.

Vellon was coined into units of *maravedis*, ranging from 0.5 maravedi to 12 maravedis. The maravedi was a large Moorish coin that emerged as the smallest unit of account in the Castile monetary system.

Vellon coinage circulated before the era of paper money in Spain. Just as paper money bears a face value far in excess of the value of the paper, vellon coins bore face values far in excess of the value of their metal content. 17th-century Spain saw one of the last great episodes of inflation before the development of paper money vastly multiplied the inflationary potential of modern monetary systems. As Spain debased vellon coinage to pure copper, vellon coins drove out silver and gold coins according to the merciless logic ordained by Gresham's law. The government called in vellon coins and restamped them at higher values, and in time vellon was carried in bags to transact business.

In 1654, the government complained that owners of calderilla had not surrendered them as requested and ordered that within a month all calderilla should be used to pay government obligations or returned to the mint for restamping. Nobles who failed to comply within the specified time faced six years' imprisonment, and commoners faced a comparable sentence to the galleys.

Like modern paper money, counterfeiters saw vellon coinage as an opportunity to profit from differences in intrinsic values, based on metal content, and extrinsic values, reflected in face values. On October 29, 1660, the government enacted a statue setting forth that: (1) counterfeiting, and efforts to import vellon counterfeited abroad, were capital offenses; (2) importing, receiving, or assisting the importation of counterfeit coins would lead to confiscation of importing vessels, forfeiture of goods, and burning at the stake; and (3) a mere failure to denounce smuggling and counterfeiting merited a sentence to the galleys and confiscation of goods.

Early in the 18th century, Spain's government limited the legal-tender status of vellon to transactions under 300 reales, and placed the practice of selling gold and silver at a premium in a category with "theft, highway robbery, and counterfeiting," with penalties commensurate with the crime. Meanwhile, economic growth had caught up with monetary policy, stabilizing the value of vellon coinage, and monetary order was for a time restored in Spain.

See also: Copper, Spanish Inflation of the 17th century

References
Grice-Hutchinson, Margorie. 1993. *Economic Thought in Spain: Selected Essays of Margorie Grice-Hutchinson.*
Hamilton, Earl J. 1969. *War and Prices in Spain: 1651–1800.*
Vives, Jaime Vicens. 1969. *An Economic History of Spain.*

VELOCITY OF MONEY

The velocity of money is the average number of times per year that a unit of currency (e.g., U.S. dollar, Japanese yen, German mark) is spent on goods and services. From a theoretical perspective, a percentage change in the velocity of money can have the same impact on prices or other economic variables as an equivalent percentage change in the money supply.

Sir William Petty (1623–1687) may have been the first writer on economics to describe the velocity of money. He advanced the plausible view that the velocity of money was determined by the frequency of people's pay periods. The famous philosopher John Locke (1632–1704) wrote on monetary economics and referred to the ratio of a country's money stock to its trade, a concept bearing a marked resemblance to velocity. By the mid-20th century, the concept of velocity was a cornerstone of monetary economics, which is the study of the relationship between the money supply and prices, interest rates, and output.

A measure of velocity can be calculated by dividing a measure of a nation's output (i.e., gross domestic product, or GDP) by a measure of the money supply. Between 1945 and 1981, one measure of velocity varied between two and seven. The stability of velocity, its tendency to fluctuate in a narrow range, remains one of the important theoretical questions in monetary economics.

Under conditions of hyperinflation, money loses its value quickly and people try to spend it faster. During the classic case of the German hyperinflation after World War I, workers were paid at half-day intervals and took off work to spend their wages before they lost their value. These are the conditions that set velocity soaring, further feeding the inflationary momentum that begins with excess money supplies.

A depression economy, particularly when coupled with falling prices, may lead households and businesses to hoard money because they are afraid that stocks and bonds are unsafe investments and perhaps because they hope to capture the benefits of falling prices. These conditions produce declining velocity, having the same effect as declining money supplies, sending the economy into a steeper descent.

Many modern economists argue that if the government stabilizes the money supply growth rate at a modest rate, perhaps 3 to 5 percent annually, velocity will also stabilize, and the growth path of the economy will mirror the stability in the monetary growth rate.

See also: Equation of Exchange, Hyperinflation in Post–World War I Germany

References
McCallum, Bennett T. 1989. *Monetary Economics.*

Sargent, Thomas. 1993. *Rational Expectations and Inflation,* 2nd ed.

VENETIAN DUCAT

During the late Middle Ages the Venetian ducat became the preferred international currency, sometimes referred to as the dollar of its time, a reference to the dominant role the U.S. dollar played in post–World War II international trade. By the 15th century, the prestige of the gold ducat of Venice made it the standard for currency reform in Islamic and Christian nations of the Mediterranean. The Mamluk *ashraftil,* the Ottoman *altun,* and the Portuguese and Castilian ducat were based on the Venetian ducat.

Venice first minted the gold ducat in 1284 at a weight and fineness of 3.5 grams of virtually pure gold (0.997 fine), a standard of purity and fineness that would be maintained until the end of the Venetian Republic in 1797. Gold coinage had disappeared in Western Europe after the eighth century, and the Italian city-states were the first European governments to renew coinage of gold.

Ducat minted under Doge Francesco Foscari (1423–1457), Venice. (Erich Lessing/Art Resource, NY)

Florence and Genoa first struck gold coins in 1252, and Venice minted its ducat at the same weight and fineness as the Florentine *florin,* a coin that commanded the prestige of an international currency before it lost credibility when the Florentine government minted issues of lighter weight. The florin also suffered from inferior imitations issued by other governments. The Venetian ducat clearly superseded the florin in the 15th century as the international currency par excellence.

Venice has been regarded as the birthplace of capitalism, a forerunner of capitalist cities such as Amsterdam and modern Hong Kong, economies whose only resources are good harbors and social and legal environments that favor commercial and financial activity. In Venice, political power and social prestige had passed from the land-owning aristocracy, which still controlled most governments, to a class of hereditary mercantile families who jealously sought to preserve the position of Venice as an international trading center. Although feudal monarchies all too easily turned to currency devaluations, debasements, and seigniorage to finance government expenses, the mercantile oligarchy that ruled Venice weighed the long-term consequences and steadfastly maintained the integrity of its currency, symbolizing Venice's commitment to fair dealings. The Venetians lodged complaints against other governments for issuing inferior imitations of Venetian ducats, and allowed only Venetian citizens to work at the mint, discouraging foreign access to stamp patterns employed to strike the Venetian coins.

Venice was on a silver standard when ducats were first struck. At first, the value of gold rose as gold was in greater demand at mints for coinage. In 1326, however, the value of gold dropped significantly, putting a hardship on debtors using gold ducats to pay debts defined in silver. The debtors, including banks needing to pay depositors and the government needing to pay bondholders, persuaded the officials to switch to a gold standard, fixing the gold price of silver at a rate that prevailed before the value of gold plummeted.

During the mid-15th century, the value of gold rose relative to silver, and Venice returned to a silver standard. The name of the gold ducat was changed to *zecchino* and the term "ducat" came to refer to a unit of account, such as dollars are a unit of account in the United States. The Venetian mint began producing silver ducats.

In 1797, Venice lost its independence as a sovereign state at the hands of Napoleon, ending the long history of the Venetian ducat (zecchino) as one of the most trusted coins in monetary history.

See also: Florintine Florin, Return to Gold

References

Cipolla, Carlo M. 1956. *Money, Prices, and Civilization in the Mediterranean World.*

Lane, Frederic C. 1973. *Venice: A Maritime Republic.*

Lane, Frederic C., and Reinhold C. Mueller. 1997. *Money and Banking in Medieval and Renaissance Venice.* Vols. I–II.

VIRGINIA COLONIAL PAPER CURRENCY

In the last half of the 18th century, the colonial government of Virginia was the last of the colonial governments to have recourse to paper currency. Paper money was not completely new to Virginia because tobacco notes, essentially warehouse receipts for stored tobacco, had circulated as money since early in the 18th century. Later, however, the Virginia colonial government issued fiat paper currency that was declared legal tender.

The circumstances that pushed Virginia to the paper currency brink were hardly rare in the history of paper money. Robert Carter Nicholas, a member of the House of Burgesses at the time and not a friend of paper money, explained the rationale as follows:

> Money, the acknowledged Sinews of War was necessary, immediately necessary; Troops could not be levied and supported without it; of Gold and Silver, there Was indeed some, what Quantity I do not know, in the Hands of Individuals, but The Publick could not command it. Did there not result from hence a Necessity Of our having Recourse to a Paper Currency, as the only Resource from which we Could draw Relief? (Brock, 1975, 465)

The crisis that led to the issuance of paper currency was the encroachment of the French in what is now western Pennsylvania. After Major General George Washington returned from an expedition against the French and reported to the colonial governor about the military situation, the Virginia House of Burgesses in February 1754 authorized the treasurer to borrow £10,000 at 6 percent interest. The treasurer reported back that there was no money to be had or borrowed. Metallic coinage, flowing out to Europe to pay for imports faster than it flowed in, was hard to come by in colonial Virginia.

At first, the House of Burgesses balked at the issuance of paper money, but in May 1755, the Burgesses authorized the issuance of £20,000 of legal-tender treasury notes for the use of General Edward Braddock. When Braddock's expedition met with disaster shortly thereafter, the Burgesses authorized another £40,000. Further issues were made in 1756. The legal-tender status of these notes drew protests, at first ineffective, from British merchants not wanting to accept depreciated paper money in payment of debts.

In 1757 the Burgesses seized on the idea of slashing government expenditures by exchanging interest-bearing treasury notes for noninterest-bearing notes. It voted to issue £100,000 in noninterest-bearing notes to retire the interest-bearing notes still in circulation. To attract additional support for the idea of noninterest-bearing notes, the Burgesses authorized the issuance of an additional £80,000 in noninterest-bearing notes to aid in the war effort. Although not paying interest, these notes were legal tender and were to be retired in the payment of taxes.

After 1762, the exchange rate between Virginia's paper currency and the British pound began to rise significantly, meaning that more of Virginia's paper currency was needed to buy British currency, usually about 40 percent more. Thus, £140 of Virginia paper currency was needed to buy £100 in British pounds. This currency depreciation forced British creditors to accept cheap paper, which was legal tender, in payment of debts owed by Virginia's colonists. As Virginia's paper currency was convertible into ever fewer British pounds, British merchants became more impatient with their losses. Parliament finally passed the Currency Act of 1764, which banned paper money as legal tender in private and public debts. The act applied only to the colonies south of New England because the Currency Act of 1751 had applied similar principles to New England. Virginia continued to issue paper money until the Constitution of the United States put the authority to issue money with the federal government.

See also: Currency Act of 1751, Currency Act of 1764, Virginia Tobacco Act of 1713

References

Brock, Leslie V. 1975 *The Currency of the American Colonies: 1700–1764.*

Ernst, Joseph Albert. 1973. *Money and Politics in America, 1755–1775.*

VIRGINIA TOBACCO ACT OF 1713

The Virginia Tobacco Act of 1713 created the most advanced form of a commodity monetary standard found in the American colonies. Under the provisions of the act, planters brought their tobacco to public warehouses, where it was weighed, graded, and stored. The planters received paper notes that were titles of ownership to the tobacco, and these notes circulated as money. Any recipient of these tobacco notes had the option of claiming the tobacco and taking possession of it.

The American colonies, struggling with a shortage of precious metal specie for transacting business, turned to several expedients, including allowing certain commodities to be acceptable in the payment of debts. Several of the northern and middle colonies had a whole list of commodities that could be used in the payment of debts at prices mandated by the government. The colony of Virginia, however, relied almost exclusively on tobacco as a medium of exchange to compensate for the shortage of specie. The government accepted tobacco in the payment of taxes and government officials and the Anglican clergy received payment in tobacco.

Tobacco as a medium of exchange, however, shared many of the defects of other commodities used for that purpose. For one thing, the quality of tobacco varied substantially and debtors always wanted to pay off debts with the lowest grade possible. Owners of tobacco also found ways to pass off lower grades of tobacco for higher grades. In 1705, the Virginia House of Burgesses enacted a law against passing off hogsheads of tobacco that had trashy tobacco packed underneath a top layer of quality tobacco. Another disadvantage of tobacco lay in its bulk and weight, which made it difficult to transport for the purposes of exchanging ownership.

The Tobacco Act of 1713 called for the construction of a number of public warehouses for the storage of tobacco. Each warehouse employed agents who weighed and graded the tobacco that a planter brought in for storage. The agents then issued to the planter notes or warehouse receipts vouching for the grade and quantity of the tobacco. These tobacco notes allowed the ownership of the tobacco to change hands without removing the tobacco. This form of tobacco money resolved many of the difficulties with the tobacco standard and decreased the inconvenience to those who received tobacco in payment of debts, effectively increasing the value of tobacco money.

The act drew strong protest from critics who were against any sort of cheap-money or paper-money plan. Because of vehement opposition, the House of Burgesses was later forced to pass a law assessing penalties for burning the newly built tobacco warehouses. In 1730, the House of Burgesses enacted additional legislation that further strengthened the government's system for inspecting and grading tobacco and providing for the rejection of tobacco that failed to meet certain quality standards. This act made Virginian tobacco more attractive in export markets.

The system of tobacco notes worked sufficiently well to delay the introduction of real paper money in Virginia until 1755, making Virginia one of the last colonies to adopt paper money. Virginia's experience with the tobacco standard demonstrates that gold is not the only commodity that may serve as a monetary standard. Any commodity that is universally in demand and acceptable in trade can serve as a standard to support paper money.

See also: Commodity Monetary Standard, Commodity Money, Rice Currency, Virginia Colonial Paper Currency

References

Brock, Leslie V. 1975. *The Currency of the American Colonies, 1700–1764.*

Galbraith, John Kenneth. 1975. *Money: Whence it Came, Where It Went.*

Nettels, Curtis P. 1934/1964. *The Money Supply of the American Colonies before 1720.*

W

WAGE AND PRICE CONTROLS

Wage and price controls freeze wages and prices at a certain point in time, and perhaps establish procedures for gradually adjusting wages and prices. Episodes of hyperinflation and wars have most often laid the groundwork for the enactment of programs of wage and price controls. Inflation is rising prices, but also can be defined as a decrease in the purchasing power of a unit of money.

In 1793, the government of the French Revolution initiated a system of price controls that became known as the Law of the Maximum. A decree of September 29, 1793, empowered district administrations with the authority to set commodity prices at rates one-third higher than the levels of 1790. The decree granted municipal authorities the responsibility for setting wages at 50 percent higher than the 1790 level. In 1794, the Committee on Provisions issued an enormous schedule of the national Maximum, or price list. Each district added transportation costs, 5 percent profit for the wholesaler and 10 percent for the retailer, and then published a catalogue of prices. Hoarding commodities to avoid selling at controlled prices was punishable by death. Despite the government's involvement in the forcible requisitioning of supplies, the controlled economy of the revolution broke down. In December 1794, the government suppressed the Law of the Maximum.

The American colonies experimented with wage and price controls to cope with shortages in commodities and labor. In 1623, the governor of Virginia issued a proclamation fixing prices and profit rates. The proclamation issued a list of prices embracing goods ranging from Canadian fish to wine vinegar. A war with Indians apparently created a shortage of goods that led to the controls. The colonial government lifted the controls in 1641. In 1630, the Massachusetts Bay Colony enacted a schedule of wages for skilled workers, coupled with a limit on the markup for finished goods. In 1633, a law banning all "excessive wages and prices" displaced the scale of wages and limitation on markups.

The colonists turned again to wage and price controls to protect themselves from the wave of hyperinflation that struck the colonial economy during the War of Independence. The Continental Congress did not have the power to impose wage and price controls and remained split on the efforts of state governments to control prices and wages. The New England colonies enacted legislation to control prices, but the southern colonies demurred. Goods flowed to regions where prices remained free to rise with market conditions, and state efforts to control prices failed.

During the U.S. Civil War, inflation surged in the northern states, and reached hyperinflation proportions in the Confederacy. Neither the North nor the South enacted a system of wage and price controls during that conflict, perhaps reflecting the ascendancy of laissez-faire economics during the 19th century.

During World War I, virtually all the belligerent powers resorted to systems of wage and price controls. By then inventions such as the typewriter had increased the administrative efficiency of governments. In the United States, wholesale prices had risen 60 percent above their 1914 level when Congress declared war on Germany. The United States government made use of as many as eight government agencies to control prices. The War Industries Board controlled the prices of many basic raw materials. The Food Administration set the prices for many staple foods, such as wheat and livestock. Inflation slowed substantially, contributing to a general feeling that the controls were a success. The controls were lifted at the end of the war amid some talk that the controls should be extended to the peacetime economy.

In 1936, Germany imposed a comprehensive system of wage and price controls that remained in effect for 12 years. This system of controls was part of Germany's centrally planned economy that was directed toward military mobilization. When the Allied occupation governments kept the controls in place at the end of World War II, black markets sprang up to meet the needs for certain supplies. Germany's rapid economic growth began after the controls were lifted in 1948.

During World War II, many countries established some form of wage and price controls to contain inflation. The United States went to a comprehensive system of wage and price regulation in 1942. The Office of Price Administration had to approve of price increases and a National War Labor Board approved of wage increases. The main effect of the controls in the United States lay in the postponement of inflation until after the war. The United States briefly turned again to wage and price controls during the Vietnam War.

The use of wage and price controls to suppress inflation runs the risk that black markets will emerge, and that producers will secretly reduce the quality of products to save money. The reduction in the quality of products, which forces consumers to buy them more frequently, defeats the purpose of the controls.

See also: Hyperinflation during the American Revolution, Hyperinflation during the French Revolution, Inflation and Deflation

References

Blinder, Alan S. 1979. *Economic Policy and the Great Stagflation.*

Rockoff, Hugh. 1984. *Drastic Measures: A History of Wage and Price Controls in the United States.*

WAMPUMPEAG

Wampumpeag was a famous currency used by the American Indians, particularly but not exclusively along the eastern seaboard, and became widely accepted by the English colonists. The name of the currency, a bit of a mouthful, was usually shortened to "wampum." "Peag" meant "beads" in the language of the Indians, and "wampum" referred to the white color of the beads. The most common color was white but some of the beads were black. Wampum rose to the status of legal-tender currency in 1643 when Massachusetts set the value of the white beads at eight to the penny and the black at four to the penny for sums no more than 40 shillings. In 1649, Rhode Island set the value of black beads at four to the penny, but reduced the value in 1658 to eight to

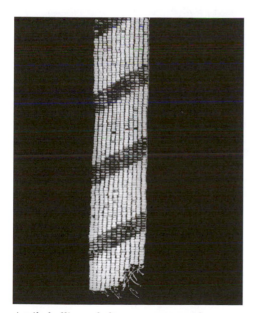

A tribal alliance belt commemorates the incorporation of the Tuscaroras (who migrated to New York from South Carolina) into the Iroquois Confederacy in 1722. (Library of Congress)

the penny regardless of the color of the beads. White beads, however, were taken in payment for taxes at six to the penny. As the white man with improved tools learned to manufacture wampum at a faster rate, the supply increased, and in 1662 Rhode Island ended the acceptance of wampum for payment of taxes.

The shells of clams and other similar bivalves furnished the raw materials for the manufacture of wampum. The estuarine rivers of the northeast of America and Canada made fertile breeding grounds for these clams and bivalves. A typical piece of wampum was a cylindrical bead about one-half inch in length, and about one-eighth to one-quarter inch in diameter. The beads were strung through a hole drilled lengthwise through each bead. The ornamental value of wampum remained an important part of its attraction as a medium of exchange. Wampum strings that traded as money were usually either 18 inches or six feet in length. They were usually counted in cubits and fathoms, but could be divided into smaller values. The black wampum usually traded at twice the value of the white wampum. Both the English and the Dutch made use of this currency. In 1644, Peter Stuyvesant, director general of New Netherland, negotiated a loan of between 5,000 and 6,000 guilders in wampum, which was used to pay workers who were building a fort in New York.

Several factors caused wampum to gradually lose its value. The stone-age technology of some of the tribes known for producing wampum had kept the supply somewhat in bounds. The colonists brought with them steel drills that substantially increased wampum production, and the colonists themselves began to manufacture wampum. Also, part of the value of wampum hinged on its usefulness in the purchase of beaver skins. As these skins declined in value, wampum lost some of its value as well. In a matter of a few years, the Indians saw the value of wampum fall by 50 percent, which they interpreted as efforts of the white man to cheat the Indian.

Nevertheless, in New England the demand for wampum remained strong into the 18th century. In 1760, J. W. Campbell built a wampum factory in New Jersey and boasted that one person could manufacture 20 feet of wampum per day. This factory remained in operation for 100 years. The manufacture of wampum still contributes to the tourist industry.

The history of wampum as money among the American colonists shows that advanced societies will find a medium of exchange when more official supplies of money are in short supply.

See also: Commodity Money

References

Hepburn, A. Barton. 1924/1967. *A History of Currency in the United States.*

Martien, Jerry. 1996. *Shell Game: A True Account of Beads and Money in North America.*

Taxay, Don. 1970. *Money of the American Indians, and Other Primitive Currencies of the Americas.*

WENDISH MONETARY UNION

From the mid-14th century to the mid-15th century, the Wendish Monetary Union maintained and guarded a common monetary standard for cities of the Hanseatic League. The Wendish Monetary Union ranks among the first of the European examples of monetary union, a distant ancestor to the contemporary European Monetary Union.

The Hanseatic League was an association of north German towns, mainly maritime towns and inland towns engaged in foreign trade, that dominated Baltic trade during the 15th century. The league negotiated trade concessions and monopoly privileges from foreign countries such as England, Norway, and Russia, often at the expense of local merchants. The league operated self-government trading compounds, called "kontors," at trading centers such as London, and these kontors were shared by the merchants who were citizens of Hanseatic towns.

The Wendish Monetary Union was formed in 1379 and officially included only four cities of the Hanseatic League, Lubeck, Hamburg, Wismar, and Luneburg. Other towns adopted the standard unofficially, making the Union influential over a broad area, including all of Scandinavia. The Union regulated the currency of northern Germany until 1569 and its monetary system was based on a silver standard.

The Union struck a silver coin equivalent to the Lubeck mark, containing 18 grams of fine silver, and bearing the coats of arms of the four member towns. The Union purchased the precious metal and supervised its coinage, including the activities of goldsmiths and the mint's employees. Compliance with the regulations of the Union was voluntary, and regular reminders issued by the Union suggest that it had a difficult time maintaining cooperation.

The spread of gold coinage in the 14th century was met with a less-than-hearty reception among the towns of the Hanseatic League. During the mid-15th century in Wendish towns the penalty for buying goods with gold was confiscation of the goods. Apparently, the Union feared the destabilizing effects of fluctuating exchange rates between gold and silver, perhaps reinforced by the Union's own unsuccessful efforts to maintain a fixed ratio between gold and silver. In 1340, Louis IV, emperor of the Holy Roman Empire, granted Lubeck the privilege to mint gold coins, leading to the introduction of the Lubeck gold *florin*, which was comparable to the Florentine florin in weight and fineness.

Unlike many feudal governments, the merchants of the Hanseatic League never sought to profit from currency debasement. Often, governments dominated by merchant princes or commercial classes displayed a strong commitment to currency integrity, perhaps to help attract commercial activity. Venice, living on an empire of trade and finance, maintained the value of the *ducat* for over 500 years, and in the 19th century, the United Kingdom became the staunch defender of the gold standard against bimetallism, which would have allowed debtors to substitute silver for gold in the repayment of debts.

See also: European Currency Unit, Latin Monetary Union

References

Dollinger, Phillipe. 1970. *The German Hanza*.

Williams, Jonathan, ed. 1997. *Money: A History*.

WHALE TOOTH MONEY IN FIJI

The case of whale tooth money on the island of Fiji shows how a commodity can become a symbol of wealth in a collectivist society in which most trade in goods takes the form of gift exchanges, omitting the need for a common standard of value. To the people of Fiji the polished ivory teeth of the sperm whale commanded a ceremonial value and sacredness that put them beyond the realm of a fixed value compared with other goods. The idea of pricing a wide range of goods in terms of whale teeth would not have occurred to the Fijians.

Captain James Cook first set forth the customs surrounding whale teeth in his *Journal* describing his voyages through the Fijian and Tongan islands in 1774. The Fijians called the whale teeth "tambua," a word that connoted a sacred sense of propriety, a positive sense of what was fitting, as well as a negative sense of what was not fitting. The negative side is captured in the modern meaning of the word "taboo."

Whale teeth served as the principle store of wealth among the Fijians and were considered precious articles to receive in gift or barter exchanges. No one left unhappy who received a whale tooth in an exchange, making it a de facto medium of exchange for large purchases. In the 19th century, a single whale tooth commanded sufficient value to barter for a large canoe. It could also purchase a bride, or serve as blood money in compensation for a murdered person. To a bride, a whale tooth bore the same symbolic significance as an engagement ring today. According to some reports the power of a whale tooth clenched any accompanying request, whether it was for a specific gift, an alliance, or a human life.

Whale teeth were constantly oiled and polished, and even in the later 19th century were preferred to gold. After Fiji became a British Crown Colony in 1874, a native Fiji official of the government asked to be paid in whale teeth, rather than sterling silver or gold sovereigns, citing the added sense of prestige and authority commanded by the sacred attributes of whale teeth in the eyes of the Fijians. The ceremonial significance of the whale teeth survived into recent times. The officials of Fiji made a formal presentation of a whale tooth to the queen of England and the duke of Edinburgh when they visited Fiji in 1982.

The native Fijians were not acquisitive in the modern sense. They traded their surplus produce for particular things they wanted, and if they did not have a partic- ular thing in mind, they let their surplus produce rot. Gold and silver coins held no charm for them when they were first introduced. Fijian whale teeth reveal pos- sible religious and ceremonial roots to the evolution of money that precede the need for a convenient medium of exchange to finance trade.

See also: Rossel Island Monetary System, Yap Money

References
Davies, Glyn. 1994. *A History of Money.*
Einzig, Paul. 1966. *Primitive Money.*

WILDCAT BANKS (UNITED STATES)

During the pre–Civil War era, wildcat banks, although technically legal, abused the banknote-issuing authority of state banks by issuing banknotes or paper money under circumstances that discour- aged or rendered impossible conversion into gold and silver specie. The wildcat banks emerged in a banking system that allowed each bank to issue its own banknotes, which legitimate banks stood ready to redeem into gold and silver specie. As security for outstanding bank- notes, state banking laws required banks to own federal or state government bonds, and keep them on file at a state auditor's office. The First Bank of the United States and the Second Bank of the United States had helped maintain an honest currency by forcing western banks and country banks to redeem their banknotes in specie.

In 1833, the demise of the Second Bank of the United States left the bank- ing system without an important safe- guard against the temptation of bankers to issue banknotes in excess of their reserves. Banknotes from distant locali- ties circulated at varying discounts, depending on the likelihood of redemp- tion into specie. Newspapers published lists of good notes and bad notes, and periodicals appeared that were exclu- sively devoted to the values of banknotes.

Wildcat banks were usually formed without buildings, offices, or furniture, and required minimal amounts of capi- tal. A group of investors would purchase bonds, often state bonds selling at a dis- count, and file the bonds with a state auditor, who authorized the investors to start a bank. The investors possessed the engraved plates and dies that were used to print the banknotes, and often printed banknotes equaling two or three times the amount of the bonds filed with the state. In practice, the legal requirement that the state auditor countersign each bill did not act as a brake on the issuance of banknotes.

Investors were known to start up wild- cat banks with only enough money to buy engraving plates and dies and pay the cost of printing up the banknotes. Investors arranged through brokers to pay for the bonds after they were deliv- ered to the state auditor's office. The investors then brought the freshly printed banknotes to the auditor's office, had them countersigned, and used them to pay for the bonds.

Although banknotes were theoretically convertible into gold and silver specie, wildcat banks were put in places difficult to find. In some cases an Indian guide was necessary to find what was no more than a shanty located on an Indian reservation. The accessibility of a wildcat bank determined the discount at which its banknotes traded. Brokers dispatched agents to find remote banks and demand the redemption of banknotes into specie. Some of the wildcat banks stationed lookouts that threatened and intimidated strangers who might be seeking redemption of banknotes.

In the early days of U.S. capitalism, the supply of capital necessarily fell short of what was needed to exploit the virtually endless supply of natural resources. The wildcat banks contributed to mobilizing much-needed capital, but they cost the banking industry a bit of credibility with the public. Understanding the history that the banking industry has had to live down helps explain why it remains highly regulated.

See also: Free Banking, Second Bank of the United States

References

Dillistin, William H. 1949. *Banknote Reporters and Counterfeit Detectors, 1826–1866.*

Dowd, Kevin. 1996. *Competition and Finance: A Reinterpretation of Financial and Monetary Economics.*

Knox, John Jay. 1903/1969. *A History of Banking in the United States.*

Rockoff, Hugh. 1975. *The Free Banking Era: A Reexamination.*

Rolnick, Arthur J., and Warren E. Weber. "New Evidence of the Free Banking Era." *American Economic Review*, vol. 73, no. 5 (December 1983): 1080–1091.

THE WIZARD OF OZ

The book *The Wonderful Wizard of Oz* by L. Frank Baum is one of the most famous American children's stories and the inspiration of a movie classic that is shown regularly on television in the United States. What is often lost to viewers of the movie is that the book, published in 1900, allegorically represented an important monetary debate in the United States in the 1890s.

The book was written against the background of the free silver movement in the United States. From 1880 until 1896, the United States saw the average level of prices fall by 23 percent, a strong downdraft of deflation that worked a severe hardship on debtors, mostly farmers of the South and West. The bankers and financiers concentrated in the Northeast benefitted from the deflation. One proposal for mitigating the hardship of

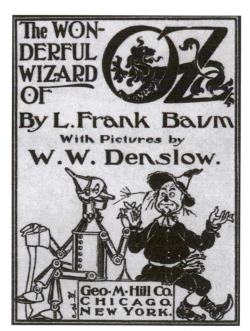

Title page of The Wonderful Wizard of OZ *by L. Frank Baum, published in 1900. (Bettmann/Corbis)*

deflation was to supplement the money supply, then tied to the gold standard, with silver, creating a bimetallic standard of gold and silver to replace the gold standard. Under a bimetallic standard, both silver and gold could be minted and circulated as money. The infusion of silver would put an end to deflation by increasing the amount of money in circulation.

The political agitation for a bimetallic standard was called the "free silver movement." Its most memorable spokesman, William Jennings Bryan, four times a presidential candidate, said in one of the epochal orations in U.S. history: "You shall not press down upon the brow of labor this crown of thorns, you shall not crucify mankind upon a cross of gold." The "cross of gold" referred to the gold standard.

In *The Wonderful Wizard of Oz*, the heroine Dorothy represents traditional U.S. values—honesty, kindheartedness, and pluck. The cyclone, representing the free silver agitation, carries Dorothy to the land of Oz, as in ounce (oz) of gold, where the gold standard reigns unchallenged. When Dorothy's house lands on the Wicked Witch of the East, the Witch dries up, leaving only her silver shoes, which become Dorothy's. The silver shoes (which were changed to ruby in the movie version) possess a magical power, representing the magical advantages of adding silver to the money supply.

Dorothy cannot find out how to return to Kansas, but learns that she should follow the yellow brick road that leads to the Emerald City. The yellow brick road represents the gold standard and the Emerald City represents Washington, D.C. On her journey to the Emerald City, Dorothy is joined by the Scarecrow,

representing western farmers, the Tin Woodman, representing the industrial worker, and the Cowardly Lion, representing William Jennings Bryan. The joints of the Tin Woodman had become rusty because the depression of the 1890s had put the industrial workers out of work.

The Cowardly Lion goes to sleep in the poppy field that represents all the issues, such as anti-imperialism and antitrust, that threatened to distract Bryan away from the central issue of the free silver movement in the 1900 presidential election.

Dorothy's group reaches the Emerald City, where everyone looks through green-colored glasses, as in money-colored glasses. Everyone in the city, including Dorothy's group must wear the glasses and they are locked on with a gold buckle, another reference to the gold standard. In other words, the financial establishment of the city required that everything be looked at from the perspective of money.

Dorothy and her friends reach the Emerald Palace, representing the White House, and Dorothy is led to her room through seven passages and up three flights of stairs, a reference to the Crime of '73, an act of legislation passed in 1873 that eliminated the coinage of silver. The next day, the group meets the Wizard, who was probably Marcus Alonzo Hanna, the chairman of the Republican Party and the brains behind President McKinley's presidency. The Wizard sends the group to find and destroy the Wicked Witch of the West, which may have been President McKinley himself. Dorothy's group finds the Wicked Witch of the West, who, knowing the magical power of the silver slippers, snatches one of Dorothy's slippers in a trick. The separation of the silver slippers, destroying their magical power, refers to the efforts of the Republican Party to diffuse the silver issue by calling for an international conference on the subject. Dorothy angrily pours a bucket of water on the Wicked Witch of the West, destroying her, and getting back her slipper.

Dorothy, with her friends, returns to the Emerald City, expecting the Wizard to tell her how to return to Kansas. The Wizard turns out to be a fraud and Dorothy seeks out the Good Witch of the South. The South is ruled by a good witch because the South was sympathetic with the free silver movement. The Good Witch of the South tells Dorothy that she can return to Kansas if she clicks her silver slippers together three times, representing the magical power of silver to solve the problems of the western farmers, made possible by the support of the South.

Despite the agitation for free silver, the United States remained on the gold standard. Discoveries of gold in Alaska, Australia, and South Africa substantially increased the world supply of gold, ending the era of tight money. From 1896 until 1910, prices rose 35 percent in the United States, diffusing the social protest that found its expression in *The Wonderful Wizard of Oz*.

See also: Bimetallism, Crime of '73, Free Silver Movement, Gold Standard Act of 1900

References

Littlefield, Henry M. "The Wizard of Oz: Parable on Populism." *American Quarterly*, vol. 16 (Spring 1964): 47–58.

Rockoff, Hugh. "The *Wizard of Oz* as a Monetary Allegory." *Journal of Political Economy*, vol. 98, no. 4 (1990): 739–760.

WORLD BANK

The World Bank, officially the International Bank for Reconstruction and Development, is the largest provider of development assistance to middle-income and low-income countries, directly financing projects and coordinating development assistance from other agencies. It also serves as a clearinghouse of ideas for promoting economic development, and publishes statistical data and research on the state of the world economy.

Aside from negotiating a fixed exchange rate system for international trade, the Bretton Woods Conference of 1944 organized the World Bank under the auspices of the United Nations. The delegates of the Bretton Woods Conference had in mind financing the reconstruction of war-torn Europe and Japan, and the development needs of the poorer areas of the world. On June 25, 1946, the World Bank opened its headquarters in Washington, D. C.

Member countries, now numbering more than 180, purchase stock in the World Bank, which also raises capital by selling bonds in private capital markets. Member governments guarantee the bonds, reducing the interest rate that investors demand and lowering the cost of capital to the bank. The United States is the largest shareholder, and the president of the World Bank has always been from the United States.

The first quarter century of the bank's existence saw an emphasis on financing basic economic infrastructure needed to support industry. Between fiscal years 1961 and 1965, electric power and transportation projects accounted for 76.8 percent of the bank's lending. The bank continued to extend substantial loans to developed countries until 1967. After Robert McNamara assumed the presidency in 1968, the bank began to channel more resources into projects that directly relieve poverty, increasing bank lending on agriculture and rural development projects from 18.1 percent in fiscal year 1968, to 31 percent in fiscal year 1981.

In 1960, the International Development Association (IDA) came into being as a division of the bank that makes soft loans and interest-free loans to the poorest countries. These countries do not qualify for loans from the World Bank, whose lending philosophy is more conservative. Also affiliated with the World Bank is the International Financial Corporation (IFC), created in 1956 to raise private capital for financing private sector projects. The loans of the IFC are structured on a commercial basis with maturities ranging from 7 to 12 years.

The World Bank is perhaps the foremost world leader on economic development issues. In 1978, the World Bank began publishing the influential *World Development Report*, combining articles on current development issues and a statistical report of economic indicators for the nations of the world.

Until the 1980s, the World Bank mainly financed public enterprises, but since then the bank has affirmed its commitment to financing private sector projects, and used its leadership to strengthen the private sector in Third World countries. The bank promotes reforms conducive to stable macroeconomic environments, and encourages privatization of public enterprises, environmental responsibility, and investments in basic health and education.

As the financial crisis deepened in 2008, critics charged that the World Bank had outlived its usefulness, that emerging and poor countries had made enough progress and no longer needed the bank. At the same time, the World Bank had won new converts. China had long regarded the World Bank as an instrument of imperialism. By 2008, China ranked among its top borrowers. China had also become a donor.

See also: Bretton Woods System, International Monetary Fund

References

Ayres, Robert L. 1983. *Banking on the Poor: The World Bank and World Poverty*.

Polak, Jacques J. 1994. *The World Bank and the International Monetary Fund: A Changing Relationship*.

Economist. "Lin's Long Swim: The World Bank." January 19, 2008, p. 59.

Y

YAP MONEY

The inhabitants of the island of Yap, one of the Caroline Islands in the central Pacific, adopted large, thick stone wheels for money, a primitive medium of exchange that survived into the post–World War II era. The inhabitants called this form of money "fei." A study of the operation of this system of currency reveals interesting insights into the nature of money that are relevant for modern monetary systems.

The stone wheels ranged in diameter from a foot to 12 feet, and the larger stones were virtually immovable. The hole in the center of the stone wheels varied with the diameter of the stone, and the smaller stones could slide over a pole and be carried. The stones were quarried from Palau, about 260 miles away, and sometimes from as far away as Guam. Stones could serve as fei only if they were made of a fine, white, close-grained limestone.

One of the interesting characteristics of this currency was that the owner did not have to take possession of it. In transactions involving these large stones, a buyer would give ownership of the fei to a seller in return for goods. The seller, however, would not actually take possession of the fei, but would leave it on the premises of the buyer of the goods. A mere acknowledgment that the seller owned the fei was all that was needed to signify its new ownership.

The logic of the Yap monetary system went so far as to acknowledge the wealth of a family on the strength of the ownership of a very large stone that had been lost at sea for several generations. According to tradition, an ancestor of this family had secured this fei and was towing it home on a raft when a storm rose, and the stone ended up at the bottom of the sea. Because all aboard the ship towing the raft testified to the size and quality of the stone, and that it was lost at no fault of the owners, the inhabitants of Yap agreed that the stone belonged to the family that lost it and that its market value remained unimpaired. Therefore, the family enjoyed the purchasing power of this stone just as if it lay on their own property.

Another interesting anecdote related to the Yap monetary system occurred after the German government purchased the Caroline Islands from Spain in 1898. The German government wanted the natives of Yap to improve the roads and make them suitable for more modern vehicles. When the natives rather obviously neglected to improve the roads, the German government was faced with finding a way to fine the natives. Since removing fei was difficult, and the stones had no value outside of the island of Yap, the German government hit on the idea of sending an agent around to paint a black cross on the most valuable stones to signify a claim of the German government. The natives of Yap immediately set to work to improve the roads. After the German government was satisfied that the roads were improved, it sent an agent around to remove the crosses, and a great rejoicing rose up among the natives.

The value of the primitive money on the island of Yap depended on the faith of its inhabitants. The idea of accepting money on faith must seem ridiculous to modern-day advocates of a gold standard as the necessary backbone of any paper-money system. The acceptance of paper money in our modern economies, shorn of the assurance of the gold standard, requires that people have faith that government will not mismanage the money supply, causing it to lose its value from inflation.

See also: Spartan Iron Currency

References
Angell, Norman. 1929. *The Story of Money.*
Friedman, Milton. 1992. *Monetary Mischief.*
Gillilland, Cora Lee C., *The Stone Money of Yap: A Numismatic Survey,* Washington, D.C.: Smithsonian Institution Press, 1975.

YELTSIN'S MONETARY REFORM IN RUSSIA

Russia opened the 1990s in monetary chaos, manifested by soaring inflation, and a currency, the ruble, that had long been shielded from the free-market forces of foreign exchange markets. In foreign exchange markets, currencies are bought and sold with other currencies, as when Japanese yen are purchased with U.S. dollars.

Under economic reforms, prices, unfettered from state controls, took off, creating a ruble shortage that left some workers unpaid for months. Wages and pensions rose, and the Russian government cranked up the printing presses on a round-the-clock basis. For the month of July 1992 alone, the government printed more rubles than the Soviet Union government had printed in its last 30 years. To expedite the process, the government increased the largest denomination of the printed ruble from the 200-ruble note to the 1,000-ruble note. Coins also became available in higher denominations. Inflation reached its peak in 1992 when monthly inflation rates ran 15 percent, and prices increased 200 percent over the year.

In 1993, the government begin to step on the monetary brakes, but in ways that threw the country into deeper confusion. In July, the government invalidated all rubles issued before 1993, and gave people only a few days to convert the old rubles into new rubles. It also put a limit on the number of old rubles that foreigners could convert into new rubles. Citizens could convert up to 35,000 old rubles into new rubles, and if they held additional rubles, these had to be put into savings accounts for six months. By the end of 1997, annual inflation had fallen to the 12 percent range, and the government announced a plan to lop off three zeros from the ruble. Effective January 1, 1998, in what was essentially an accounting reform, 1,000 rubles became 1 ruble, and all prices, balance sheets, debts, and so on, were adjusted accordingly.

One legacy of the Soviet regime was tight control over the conversion of rubles into foreign currencies. Tourists were able to convert foreign currencies into rubles at a rate close to a black market rate, but set by the Russian Central Bank. Foreign-owned enterprises earning profits in rubles faced a special difficulty. If a foreign-owned company wanted to send profits home to the parent company, those profits had first to be converted from rubles to the home-country currency at a disadvantageous exchange rate set by the Russian government. To attract foreign investment and integrate the Russian economy into the world economy, Russia had to make the ruble convertible into foreign currencies at free-market rates.

A loan from the International Monetary Fund (IMF) helped the Russian government marshal the foreign exchange reserves needed to establish a convertible ruble. On July 1, 1992, the Russian government established a single exchange rate between the dollar and the ruble at an initial rate of 126.5 rubles per dollar. The responsibility for adjusting the rate fell to the Russian Central Bank, which planned to set a rate based on twice-weekly currency auctions. After July 1993, the Russian Central Bank pegged the ruble to the dollar in a crawling peg system that avoided wild fluctuations but allowed the ruble to depreciate over time relative to the dollar. In 1996, Russia further broadened the ruble market by allowing foreigners to buy and sell Russian government bonds in secondary markets. Russian government bonds, paying over 100 percent interest at times, constitute a major demand for rubles. Rubles must be purchased before bonds can be purchased. The astronomical interest rates on Russian bonds were sometimes necessary to maintain a demand for Russian rubles. Despite high Russian interest rates, the ruble steadily declined relative to the dollar, falling to a rate of 6,200 rubles per dollar at the end of 1997. After three zeros were lopped off, the rate became 6.2 rubles per dollar.

In 1998, the Russian government again turned to the printing press to solve Russia's problems, putting pressure on the ruble in foreign exchange markets. The value of the ruble fell sharply in August of 1998, and to help cope with the crisis, the government imposed a moratorium on payments on foreign debt, significantly adding to the severity of a global financial crisis. By the end of the year, the ruble was trading at around 20 rubles per dollar. As the price of oil began to accelerate in 2000, Russia's financial difficulties began to improve markedly, and the ruble stabilized. Russia is an oil exporter.

See also: Foreign Exchange Markets, Russian Currency Crisis

References
Hanke, Steve H. "Is the Ruble Next?" *Forbes,* March 9, 1998, pp. 64–65.
Wall Street Journal (Eastern Edition). "Chaos in Russia Mounts." July 26, 1993, p. A8.

Wall Street Journal (Eastern Edition). "Russia, Facing Inflation, Plans Bigger Banknotes." January 31, 1992, p. A10.

Wall Street Journal (Eastern Edition). "Russia's Overhaul of Ruble Prompts Unease in Nation." December 31, 1997, p. A7.

Wall Street Journal (Eastern Edition). "Russia Plans to Make Ruble Fully Convertible by August 1." May 6, 1992, p. A3.

Wall Street Journal (Eastern Edition). "Soviet Printing of Rubles Soared in 11-Month Period." December 24, 1991, p. A8.

YEN

The yen is the money of account for Japan, comparable to the dollar for the United States. By the 1990s, the Japanese yen had become a major international currency, sharing the stage with the U.S. dollar, the German mark, and the European Currency Unit (ECU) as determinants of international monetary values.

The Shinka Jorei (New Currency Regulations) of 1871 established the yen as the monetary unit in Japan. The Japanese derived the word "yen" from the Chinese word "yuan," which meant "round thing," a reference to the U.S. and Mexican dollars that dominated East Asian trade at the time. The act set the yen equal to 0.05 ounces of gold, making the official Japanese price of an ounce of gold equal to 20 yen. At the time the official U.S. price of an ounce of gold was $20.67. The yen was intended to be equivalent to the Mexican dollar, the standard unit in Asian trade at the time. The yen began life as a decimalized currency; one-one-hundredth of a yen was called a "sen," and one-tenth of a sen was called a "rin."

Officially, Japan was on a bimetallic monetary system, but in practice the yen was on a silver standard. In 1877, a civil rebellion forced the government to issue inconvertible paper money to finance military expenditures. Inflation erupted, and in 1882, the government established the Bank of Japan, partly to replace inconvertible paper money with banknotes convertible into silver. Following the Sino-Japanese war of 1894–1895, Japanese received in gold a large war reparation payment from China, providing a gold reserve sufficient for Japan to establish a gold standard. In 1887 a new currency law give the Bank of Japan a monopoly on the privilege to issue banknotes, and put the yen on the gold standard.

At the beginning of World War I, most developed countries, including Japan, abandoned the gold standard and prohibited the export of gold. Following World War I, Japan, beset by economic turmoil, stumbled in its efforts to return to the gold standard. In 1930, on the eve of the Great Depression, Japan returned to the gold standard, only to have to abandon it again in 1931. The Depression dealt a serious blow to the gold standard worldwide, and Japan turned to tight government regulation of its currency, which continued through World War II.

A wave of inflation engulfed Japan following World War II, and the occupation authorities instituted a currency reform that withdrew old yen notes and issued new yen notes. In 1949, the exchange rate between the yen and the dollar was set at 360 yen per dollar. Under the Bretton Woods system, exchange rates were fixed at official rates, and the ratio of yen to dollars remained at 360–1 until 1971. Large trade surpluses enabled Japan to bolster its gold and foreign exchange reserves, paving the way for lifting all restrictions on foreign exchange transactions.

When a system of floating international exchange rates displaced the fixed-rate Bretton Woods system in 1973, the yen began an upward career of currency appreciation. In 1970, it had taken 360 yen to purchase a dollar. By 1973, it took only 272 yen, and by the end of the decade it took only 219 yen to purchase a dollar. As the yen grew stronger, it took more dollars to purchase a yen, but despite that Japanese goods constituted a major competitive threat to U.S. industries. In 1984, the world's major trading partners agreed to intervene collectively in foreign exchange markets to appreciate the yen even further. Whereas it took 239 yen to purchase a dollar in 1985, by 1988 that number had fallen to 128 yen, a substantial increase in the value of the yen.

In the 1980s, Japan took further steps to deregulate its financial system and to allow foreign firms to participate in Japan's financial markets. Japanese banks had become among the largest and most powerful in the world, and the yen emerged as a major international currency. By 1998, economic depression in Japan put downward pressure on the yen, and the yen traded at around 140 yen per dollar. On October 15, 2008, amid the U.S. financial crisis, the yen closed at 101.35 per dollar, indicating the yen had substantially strengthened against the dollar.

See also: Deutsche Mark, European Currency Unit, Dollar

References

Davies, Glyn. 1994. *A History of Money.*

Ohkawa, Kazushi, Miyorhei Shinohara, and Larry Meissner, eds. 1979. *Patterns of Japanese Economic Development: A Quantitative Appraisal.*

YIELD CURVE

The yield curve shows the relationship between the yield to maturity and the time to maturity among bonds that are identical in every respect except for varying maturities. The yield to maturity on a bond is equal to the constant annual interest rate that makes the price or market value of the bond today equal to the present value of the future payments received by the owner of the bond. The vertical axis shows the interest rate or yield to maturity, and the horizontal axis shows the time to maturity.

Usually, but not always, the yield curve slopes up from left to right. An up-sloping yield curve indicates that longer-term bonds pay a higher interest rate. Longer-term bonds have higher default risk. Since more time elapses before a longer-term bond matures, there is greater chance that economic misfortune could force the bond issuer to default on the bond. To minimize the role of default risk, a yield curve is always constructed for bonds from the same issuer. The yields on U.S. Treasury bonds are most commonly used in reporting the yield curve because the default risk on these bonds is virtually zero.

There are other risks beside default risks that favor an up-sloping yield curve. A longer time to maturity increases the chance that a wave of inflation will come along and shrink the real purchasing power of a bond's maturity value. A three-month bond bears little inflation risk because inflation can be roughly anticipated three months into the future. The longer the time to maturity of the bond, the greater the uncertainty about the average inflation rate over the life of the bond.

Another risk that accounts for an upward sloping bias in yield curves may be called the "interest rate risk." Suppose an individual purchases from the U.S. Treasury a $10,000 government bond that pays 5 percent interest. Suppose at a later date market conditions change, interest rates go up, and an individual can purchase a similar bond that pays 7 percent interest. Under these conditions, the individual owning the 5 percent bond will find that his bond will have to be sold at a discount if he elects to sell it before it matures. A bond issued at 5 percent interest is worth less the minute current market interest rates on identical bonds rises above 5 percent. The interest rate risk on a three-month bond is minimal because the time involved is too short for the interest rate to matter as much. Over the life of a 30-year bond, interest rate fluctuations can cause substantial fluctuations in the market value of a bond.

The yield curve is not always up sloping. A down-sloping yield curve is called an "inverted yield curve." If inflation is high, but expected to be lower in the future, short-term bonds will carry a higher inflation premium than long-term bonds, elevating interest rates on long-term bonds relative to interest rates on short-term bonds. In addition, central bank's tightening of monetary policy can lead to the expectation of a weaker economy, lower inflation, and lower short-term interest rates in the future. These expectations are sufficient to lower long-term interest rates. Some economic forecasters put great weight on an inverted yield curve as a sign of future economic deceleration.

Expectations exert a strong influence on the yield curve. An up-sloping yield curve indicates that financial market participants believe the economy is on a course of expansion, and that the trend for short-term interest rates is up. Borrowers will try to beat future increases in short-term interest rates by borrowing long-term, driving up long-term interest rates.

See also: Fisher Effect, Interest Rate

References

Abken, Peter A. "Inflation and the Yield Curve." *Economic Review,* Federal Reserve Bank of Atlanta, vol. 78, no. 3 (1993): 13–32.

Dueker, Michael J. "Strengthening the Case for the Yield Curve as a Predictor of U.S. Recessions." *Review,* Federal Reserve Bank of St. Louis, vol. 79, no. 2 (1997): 41–52.

Kozicki, Sharon, and Gordon Sellon. "Longer-Term Perspectives on the Yield Curve Monetary Policy." *Economic Review,* Federal Reserve Bank of Kansas, vol. 90, no. 4 (2005): 5–35.

Russell, Steven. "Understanding the Term Structure of Interest Rates: The Expectations Theory." *Review,* Federal Reserve Bank of St. Louis, vol. 74, no. 4 (1992): 36–51.

YUAN

See: Chinese Silver Standard

Bibliography

Abel, Andrew B., Ben S. Bernanke, and Dean Croushore. *Macroeconomics,* 6th ed. New York: Pearson Education, 2008.

Abken, Peter A. "Inflation and the Yield Curve," *Federal Reserve Bank of Atlanta Economic Review,* vol. 78, no. 3 (1993): 13–32.

Acheson, A. L. K. *Bretton Woods Revisited.* Toronto: University of Toronto Press, 1972.

Akhigbe, Aigbe, Melissa B. Frye, and Ann Marie Whyte. "Financial Modernization in U.S. Banking Markets: A Local or Global Event," *Journal of Business Finance & Accounting,* vol. 32, no. 7 (2005): 1561–1585.

Alesina, Alberto, and Lawrence Summers. "Central Bank Independence and Macroeconomic Performance," *Journal of Money, Credit, and Banking,* vol. 25 (May 1993): 151–162.

Allen, D. F. *Coins of the Ancient Celts.* Edinburgh, Scotland: University Press, 1980.

Allen, Larry. *The Global Economic System Since 1945,* London: Reaktion Books, 2005.

Allen, Larry. *The Global Financial System,* London: Reaktion Books, 2001.

Anderson, Clay J. *A Half-Century of Federal Reserve Policymaking, 1914–1964.* Philadelphia: Federal Reserve Bank of Philadelphia, 1965.

Anderson, Richard G., and Robert H. Rasche. "Retail Sweep Programs and Bank Reserves, 1994–1999," *Federal Reserve Bank of St. Louis Review,* vol. 83, no. 1 (January/February 2001): 51–72.

Angell, Norman. *The Story of Money.* Garden City, NY: Frank A. Stokes, 1929.

Angus, Ian. *Paper Money.* New York: St. Martin's Press, 1974.

Apcar, Leonard M. "Thrifts in Texas Scrambling for Funds, Liquidity Crisis Feared, Regulators Say," *Wall Street Journal* (Eastern Edition), June 10, 1987, p. 1.

Appleyard, Dennis R., and Alfred J. Field, Jr. *International Economics*. Homewood, IL: Richard D. Irwin, 1992.

Arestis, Philip, John McCombie, and Warren Mosler. "New Attitudes About Inflation," *Challenge,* vol. 49, no. 5 (September/October 2006): 33–52.

Aristotle. *Politics*. Translated by Benjamin Juwett. Chicago: William Benton Publisher, 1952.

Armstrong, W. E. "Rossel Island Money: A Unique Monetary System," *The Economic Journal* 34 (1924): 424–429.

Asian Development Bank. "ASEAN+3 Regional Basket Currency Bonds," Technical Assistance Report, Project Number 40030, August 2006.

Atack, Jeremy, and Peter Passell. *A New Economic View of American History*. New York: W. W. Norton, 1994.

Auerbach, Alan J., and Maurice Obstfeld. "The Case for Open-Market Purchases in a Liquidity Trap," *The American Economic Review,* vol. 95, no. 1 (March 2005): 110–138.

Ayres, Robert L. *Banking on the Poor: The World Bank and World Poverty*. Cambridge, MA: MIT Press, 1983.

Bacon, Sir Francis. *Advancement of Learning*. Chicago: William Benton Publisher, 1952.

Bacon, Sir Francis. *Civil Essays*. 1625. Reprint, New York: P. F. Collier, 1969.

Bank for International Settlements. *Annual Report*. Basel, Switzerland: 1998.

Bank for International Settlements. *Eight European Central Banks*. New York: Frederick A. Praeger, 1963.

Bank for International Settlements. "Japan's Deflation, Problems in the Financial System and Monetary Policy," BIS Working Paper no. 188, November, 2005.

Barber, Malcolm. *The Trial of the Templars*. Cambridge, UK: Cambridge University Press, 1978.

Barrett, Don C. *The Greenbacks and Resumption of Specie Payments: 1862–1879*. Cambridge, MA: Harvard University Press, 1931.

Barro, Robert J. "Government Spending, Interest Rates, Prices, and Budget Deficits in the United Kingdom, 1701–1918." *Journal of Monetary Economics,* vol. 20 (September 1987): 221–248.

Barth, James R. *The Great Savings and Loan Debacle*. Washington, D.C.: AEI Press, 1991.

Bauer, Hans. *Swiss Banking: An Analytical History*. New York: St. Martin's Press, 1998.

Baye, Michael R., and Dennis W. Jansen. *Money, Banking, and Financial Markets: An Economics Approach*. Boston: Houghton Mifflin, 1995.

Becker, William E. Jr. "Determinants of the United States Currency-Demand Deposit Ratio," *The Journal of Finance,* vol. 30, no. 1 (March 1975): 57–74.

Becket, Paul. "Banking: Glitches Trip Up Real-Life Test of Plastic Cash," *Wall Street Journal* (Eastern Edition) October 8, 1998, p. B1.

Behrman, Jere R. *Foreign Trade Regimes and Economic Development: Chile*. New York: National Bureau of Economic Research, 1976.

Belongia, Michael T., and Kevin Kliesen. "Effects on Interest Rates of Immediately Releasing FOMC Directives," *Contemporary Economic Policy*, vol. 12, no. 4 (1994): 79–91.

Benton, Pierre. *The Golden Trail*. Toronto: Macmillan, 1954.

Berdan, Frances F. *The Aztecs of Central Mexico: An Imperial Society*. New York: Holt, Rinehart and Winston, 1982.

Beresiner, Yasha. *A Collector's Guide to Paper Money*. New York: Stein and Day, 1977.

Berg, Andrew, and Edwardo Borensztein. "The Dollarization Debate," *Finance and Development*, vol. 37, no. 1 (March 2000): 38–42.

Berry, Jeffrey, M. *Feeding Hungry People*. New Brunswick, NJ: Rutgers University Press, 1984.

Betlyon, John Wilson. *The Coinage and Mints of Phoenicia: The Pre-Alexandrine Period*. Chico, CA: Scholars Press, 1982.

Beutel, Frederick K. "The Development of Negotiable Instruments in Early English Law," *Harvard Law Review*, vol. 51, no. 5 (March 1938): 813–845.

Bezanson, Anne. *Prices and Inflation during the American Revolution, Pennsylvania, 1770–1790*. Philadelphia: University of Pennsylvania Press, 1951.

Bible, The New Oxford Annotated. New York: Oxford University Press, 1973.

Bils, Mark, and Peter Klenow. "Some Evidence on the Importance of Sticky Prices," *Journal of Political Economy*, vol. 112, no. 5 (October 2004): 947–985.

Binswanger, Hans Christopher. *Money and Magic: Critique of the Modern Economy in the Light of Goethe's Faust*. Translated by J. E. Harrison. Chicago, IL: University of Chicago Press, 1994.

Birchall, Johnson. *Co-op: The People's Business*. New York: St. Martin's Press, 1994.

Birley, Robert, ed. *Speeches and Documents in American History*. vol. III. London, UK: Humphrey Milford, 1943.

Blackman, Andrew. "Family Finances: Farewell to the Float: Checks will Clear in an Instant," *Wall Street Journal* (Eastern Edition), August 1, 2004, p. 4.

Blinder, Alan. "On Sticky Prices: Academic Theories Meet the Real World." In *Monetary Policy*, edited by N. Gregory Mankiw, pp. 117–150, University of Chicago Press, 1994.

Blinder, Alan S. *Economic Policy and the Great Stagflation*. New York: Academic Press, 1979.

Board of Governors of the Federal Reserve System. *The Federal Reserve System: Purposes and Functions*. Washington, D.C., 1984.

Bogetic, Zeljko, and Zorica Mladenovic. "Inflation and the Monetary Transmission Mechanism in Belarus, 1996–2001," *International Research Journal of Finance and Economics*, no. 1 (2006): 1–20.

Bomberger, W. A., and G. E. Makinen. "The Hungarian Hyperinflation and Stabilization of 1945–1946," *Journal of Political Economy,* vol. 91, no. 5 (1983): 801–824.

Bordo, Michael, D. "The Classical Gold Standard: Some Lessons for Today," *Federal Reserve Bank of St. Louis Monthly Review* (May 1981): 2–17.

Bordo, Michael, D. *Monetary Regimes in Transition.* Edited by Forrest Capie. Cambridge, UK: Cambridge University Press, 1994.

Bordo, Michael, and Anna J. Schwartz. "Why Clashes between Internal and External Stability Goals End in Currency Crises, 1797–1994," *Open Economy Review,* vol. 7 (Supplement): 437–468.

Boughton, James M., and Elmus R. Wicker. "The Behavior of the Currency-Deposit Ration during the Great Depression," *Journal of Money, Credit, and Banking,* vol. 11, no. 4 (November 1979): 405–418.

Bradley, Harold Whitman. *The American Frontier in Hawaii.* Gloucester, MA: Peter Smith, 1968.

Bradley, Michael G., Stuart Gabriel, and Mark Wohar. "The Thrift Crisis, Mortgage-Credit Intermediation, and Housing Activity," *Journal of Money, Credit, and Banking,* vol. 27, no. 2 (May 1995): 476–497.

Bradsher, Keith. "Obscure Global Bank Moves into the Light," *New York Times,* August 5, 1995, p. A31.

Branco, Marta de Castello. "Georgia: From Hyperinflation to Growth," *IMF Survey,* Washington D.C.: International Monetary Fund, September 23, 1996.

Braudel, Fernand. *The Mediterranean.* Vols. 1 and 2. Translated by Sian Reynolds. New York: Harper and Row, 1972.

Braudel, Fernand. *Civilization and Capitalism.* Vols. 1–3. Translated by Sian Reynolds. New York: Harper and Row, 1982–1984.

Bray, Nicholas. "Future Shop: No Cash Accepted," *Wall Street Journal,* July 13, 1995.

Breckinridge, S. P. *Legal Tender: A Study in English and American Monetary History.* 1903. Reprint, New York: Greenwood Press, 1969.

Brimelow, Peter. "Going Underground," *Forbes,* vol. 162, no. 6 (September 21, 1998): 206–207.

Brock, Leslie V. *The Currency of the American Colonies, 1700–1764.* New York: Arno Press, 1975.

Brown, Marion A. *The Second Bank of the United States and Ohio, 1803–1860; A Collision of Interests.* Lewiston, NY: Edwin Mellen Press, 1998.

Broz, J. Lawrence. *The International Origins of the Federal Reserve System.* Ithaca, NY: Cornell University Press, 1997.

Bullard, James. "Testing Long-Run Monetary Neutrality Propositions: Lessons from the Recent Research," *Federal Reserve Bank of Saint Louis Review,* vol. 81, no. 6 (1999): 57–77.

Bullard, Melissa M. *Filippo Strozzi and the Medici: Favor and Finance in Sixteenth-Century Florence and Rome*. Cambridge, UK: Cambridge University Press, 1980.

Bureau of Labor Statistics. "Producer Prices." Chap 14 of *BLS Handbook of Methods*. Washington D.C., June 2008.

Burke, Bryan. *Nazi Counterfeiting of British Currency during World War II: Operation Andrew and Operation Bernhard*. San Bernardino, CA: Book Shop, 1987.

Burman, Edward. *Supremely Abominable Crimes: The Trial of the Knights Templar*. London: Alison and Busby, 1996.

Burns, A. R. *Money and Monetary Policy in Early Times*. 1927. Reprint, New York: Augustus M. Kelly, Bookseller, 1965.

BusinessWeek Online. "Did the IMF Drop the Ball in Ecuador?" January 24, 2000.

Calomiris, Charles W., and Charles M. Kahn. "The Efficiency of Self-Regulated Payments Systems: Learning from the Suffolk System," *Journal of Money, Credit, and Banking,* vol. 28, no. 4 (November 1996): 766–797.

Cameron, Rondo, ed. *Banking and Economic Development: Some Lessons of History*. London: Oxford University Press, 1972.

Cameron, Rondo, with Olga Crisp, Hugh Patrick, and Richard Tilly. *Banking in the Early Stages of Industrialization*. London: Oxford University Press, 1967.

Cantor, Richard, and Frank Packer. "The Credit Rating Industry," *Quarterly Review,* vol. 19, no. 2 (Summer/Fall 1994): 1–26.

Cappon, Lester, ed. *The Adams-Jefferson Letters*. Chapel Hill: University of North Carolina Press, 1959.

Cardoso, Eliana, A. "Hyperinflation in Latin America," *Challenge,* vol. 32, no. 1 (January–February 1989): 11–19.

Caron, Francois. *An Economic History of Modern France*. New York; Columbia University Press, 1979.

Carothers, Neil. *Fractional Money*. 1930. Reprint, New York: Augustus M. Kelley, 1967.

Carradice, Ian, ed. *Coinage in the Administration of the Athenian and Persian Empires*. Oxford, UK: B. A. R., 1987.

Carradice, Ian. *Greek Coins*. Austin: University of Texas Press, 1995.

Carstens, Agustin, Daniel Hardy, and Ceyla Pazarbasioglu. "Avoiding Banking Crises in Latin America," *Finance and Development*. Washington, D.C.: International Monetary Fund, September 2004, pp. 30–33.

Carter, Martha L. *A Treasury of Indian Coins*. Bombay: Marg Publications, 1994.

Carter, T. F. *The Invention of Printing in China and its Spread Westward*. Rev. ed. New York: Columbia University Press, 1931.

Cassel, Gustav. *Money and Foreign Exchange after 1914*. New York: Macmillan, 1922.

Cellini, Benvenuto. *The Life of Benvenuto Cellini*. 1728. Translated by John Addington Symonds. New York: Liveright Publishing, 1931.

Cellini, Benvenuto. *The Treatises of Benvenuto Cellini on Goldsmithing and Sculpture.* Translated by C. R. Ashbee. New York: Dover Publications, 1967.

Cerra, Valerie, Meenakshi Rishi, and Sweta C. Saxena. "Robbing the Riches: Capital Flight, Institutions, and Instability," IMF Working Paper (WP/05/199), International Monetary Fund: Washington, D.C., October 2005.

Challis, C. E., ed. *A New History of the Royal Mint.* Cambridge, UK: Cambridge University Press, 1992.

Challis, C. E. *The Tudor Coinage.* Manchester, UK: Manchester University Press, 1978.

Chalmers, Robert. *A History of Currency in the British Colonies.* 1893. Reprint, Colchester, UK: J. Drury, 1972.

Chandler, Lester V. *American Monetary Policy; 1928–1941.* New York: Harper and Row, 1971.

Chang, Kia-Ngau. *The Inflationary Spiral: The Experience in China, 1939–1950.* Cambridge, MA: M. I. T. Press, 1958.

Checkland, S. G. *Scottish Banking: A History, 1695–1973.* Glasgow, UK: Collins, 1975.

Cheesman, Evelyn. *Backwaters of the Savage South Seas.* London, UK: Jarrolds, 1933.

Chiodo, Abbigail J., and Michael T. Owyang. "A Case Study of a Currency Crisis: The Russian Default of 1998,"*Federal Reserve Bank of St. Louis Review,* vol. 84, no. 6 (November/December 2002): 7–18.

Chou, Shun-Hsin. *The Chinese Inflation, 1939–1949.* New York: Columbia University Press, 1963.

Chown, John F. *A History of Money.* London, UK: Routledge Press, 1994.

Cimilluca, Dana. "The Financial Crisis: Swiss Move to Back Troubled UBS; Under Plan, as Much as $60 Billion in Toxic Assets to be Taken Off Balance Sheet," *Wall Street Journal* (Eastern Edition), October 17, 2008, p. A3.

Cipolla, Carlo M. *Before the Industrial Revolution: European Society and Economy, 1000–1700.* 2nd ed. New York: W. W. Norton, 1980.

Cipolla, Carlo M. *The Monetary Policy of Fourteenth-Century Florence.* Berkeley: University of California Press, 1982.

Cipolla, Carlo M. *Money, Prices, and Civilization in the Mediterranean World.* Princeton, NJ: Princeton University Press, 1956.

Clapham, Sir J. *The Bank of England.* Cambridge, UK: Cambridge University Press, 1970.

Clough, Shepard B. *The Economic History of Modern Italy.* New York: Columbia University Press, 1964.

Coats, Warren L. "In Search of a Monetary Anchor: A New Monetary Standard." International Monetary Fund Working Paper. no. 82, 1989.

Coinage of the Americas Conference. *The Token: America's Other Money.* New York: American Numismatic Society, 1995.

Cole, Charles Woolsey. *Colbert and a Century of French Mercantilism.* Hamden, CT: Archon Books, 1964.

Colander, David, and Edward Gamber, *Macroeconomics*. Cape Town: Pearson/Prentices Hall, 2006.

Colwell, Stephen. *The Ways and Means of Payment*. 1859. Reprint, New York: Augustus M. Kelley, 1965.

Cowitt, Philip P. *World Currency Yearbook*. New York: International Currency Analysis, 1989.

Craig, J. *The Mint: A History of the London Mint from A.D. 287 to 1948*. Cambridge, UK: Cambridge University Press, 1953.

Credit Union National Association. "Will Consumers Turn to Plastic to Regain Float?" *Point for Credit Union Research & Advice,* April 1, 2005, the point@cuna.com.

Cripps, Wilfred Joseph. *Old English Plate*. 1878. Reprint, London, UK: Spring Books, 1967.

Crisp, Olga. *Studies in the Russian Economy Before 1914*. New York: Barnes and Noble, 1976.

Cummings, Richard. *The Alchemists*. New York: David McKay, 1966.

Curran, Rob. "Large Stock Focus: Citi Jumps on Bailout; B of A, Goldman Follow", *Wall Street Journal* (Eastern Edition), November 25, 2008, p. C6.

Dacy, Joe. "How to Spot Bogus Bills." *Nations Business,* vol. 81, no. 7 (July 1993): 30.

Dammes, Clifford and Robert McCauley. "Basket Weaving: The Euromarket Experience with Basket Currency Bonds," *BIS Quarterly Review,* March 6, 2006, pp. 79–92.

Daniels, John D., and David Vanhoose. *International Monetary and Financial Economics*. Cincinnati: Southwestern, 1999.

Daniels, Joseph, and David VanHoose. *International Monetary and Financial Economics*. 3rd ed. New York: South-Western College Publishing, 2004.

Daniels, John D., and Lee H. Radebaugh. *International Business*. 8th ed. Reading, MA: Addison-Wesley, 1998.

Daseking, Christina. "Debt: How Much Is Too Much?" *Finance and Development,* vol. 39, no. 4 (December 2002): 12–15.

Davies, Glyn. *A History of Money*. Cardiff: University of Wales Press, 1994.

Davis, Lance E., Jonathon Hughes, and Duncan M. McDougall. *American Economic History*. Homewood, IL: Richard D. Irwin, 1969.

Davis, Richard G. "Intermediate Targets and Indicators of Monetary Policy," *Quarterly Review,* vol. 15, no. 2, pp. 71–83.

Day, J. "The Great Bullion Famine of the Fifteenth Century," *Past and Present,* vol. 79 (1978).

De la Balze, Felipe A. M. *Remaking the Argentine Economy*. New York: Council On Foreign Relations Press, 1995.

De Vries, Margaret Garritsen. *Balance of Payments Adjustment, 1945 to 1986: The IMF Experience*. Washington, D.C.: International Monetary Fund, 1987.

Del Mar, Alexander. *The History of Money in America*. 1899. Reprint, New York: Burt Franklin, 1968.

Demiralp, Selva, and Oscar Jorda. "The Response of Term Rates to Fed Announcements," *Journal of Money, Credit, and Banking*, vol. 36, no. 3 (June 2004, Part 1): 387–405.

Dickson, P. G. M. *Financial Revolution in England*. London: Macmillan, 1967.

Dillistin, William H. *Bank Note Reporters and Counterfeit Detectors, 1826–1866*. New York: American Numismatic Society, 1949.

Dodd, Randall and Paul Mills. "Outbreak: U.S. Subprime Contagion," *Finance and Development*, vol. 45, no. 2 (June 2008): 14–19.

Dollinger, Phillipe. *The German Hanza*. Stanford, CA: Stanford University Press, 1970.

Dowd, Kevin. *Competition and Finance: A Reinterpretation of Financial and Monetary Economics*. New York: St. Martin's Press, 1996.

Dowden, Richard. "A Disaster That Hasn't Quite Happened," *Economist*, vol. 339, no. 7969 (June 8, 1996, Special Section): 8–13.

Du Bois, Cora Alice. *The People of Alor: A Social-Psychological Study of an East Indian Island*. Cambridge, MA: Harvard University Press, 1986.

Dueker, Michael J. "Strengthening the Case for the Yield Curve as a Predictor of U.S. Recessions," *Federal Reserve Bank of St. Louis Review*, vol. 79, no. 2 (1997): 41–52.

Duncan-Jones, Richard. *Money and Government in the Roman Empire*. New York: Cambridge University Press, 1998.

Dunne, Gerald T. *Monetary Decisions of the Supreme Court*. New Brunswick, NJ: Rutgers University Press, 1960.

Dupriez, Leon H. *Monetary Reconstruction in Belgium*. New York: Ding's Crown Press, 1946.

Durant, Will. *The Reformation*. New York: Simon and Schuster, 1957.

Economist. "Dearer Still and Dearer," vol. 316, no. 7668 (August 18, 1990): 2–3.

Economist. "Inflation Unbeaten," vol. 317, no. 7679 (November 3, 1990): 52

Economist. "Banking Behind the Veil," vol. 323, no. 7753 (April 4, 1992): 49.

Economist. "Galloping Towards the Brink," vol. 328, no. 7818 (July 3, 1993): 49.

Economist. "Ukraine Over the Brink," vol. 328, no. 7827 (August 4, 1993): 45–46.

Economist. "There was an old lady . . .," vol. 329, no. 7838 (November 20, 1993): 94–97.

Economist. "Cleaning up Dirty Money," London, vol. 344, no. 8027 (July 26, 1997): 13.

Economist. "Born Free," vol. 350, no. 8108 (February 27, 1999): 76.

Economist. "The Furies Wait," vol. 350, no. 8109 (March 6, 1999): 34–36.

Economist. "Wading in the Yen Trap," vol. 352, no. 8129 (July 24, 1999): 71–74.

Economist. "Special: Through the Wringer," London, vol. 359, no. 8217 (April 14, 2001): 64.

Economist. "Harsh Medicine" vol. 359, no. 8222 (May 19, 2001): 48.

Economist. "Squandering an Unlikely Recovery," vol. 360, no. 8239 (September 15, 2001): 32.

Economist. "The Americas: Defaulter of Last Resort," vol. 366, No 8314 (March 8, 2003): 56.

Economist. "Seeking the Right Medicine," vol. 367, no. 8329 (June 21, 2003): 70.

Economist. "Survey: The World's Piggybank," vol. 370, no. 8362 (February 14, 2004): 13.

Economist. "Nought to Worry About: Zeroing on Too Many Zeroes," vol. 372, no. 8390 (August 28, 2004): 67.

Economist. "The Americas: Grinding Them Down; Argentina's Debt," vol. 374, no. 8409 (January 15, 2005): 47.

Economist. "Britain: In a Spin; Money Laundering," vol. 379, no. 8479 (May 27, 2006): 35.

Economist. "Finance and Economics: Sizzling; The Big Mac Index," London, vol. 384, no. 8536 (July 7, 2007): 82.

Economist. "Lin's Long Swim: The World Bank," London, vol. 386, no. 8563 (January 19, 2008): 59.

Economist. "Finance and Economics: Selling the Family Gold; The IMF," London, vol. 387, no. 8575 (April 12, 2008): 84.

Economist. "Snowed Under, Swiss Banks," vol. 388, no. 8587 (July 5, 2008): 79–80.

Ehrenkreutz, A. S. *Monetary Change and Economic History in the Medieval Muslim World.* Aldershot, UK: Ashgate, 1992.

Einzig, Paul. *Primitive Money.* 2nd ed. Oxford, UK: Pergamon Press, 1966.

Einzig, Paul. *The History of Foreign Coinage.* 2nd ed. New York: St. Martin's Press, 1970.

Enrich, David, and Damian Palaetta. "The Financial Crisis: Walls Come Down, Reviving Fears of a Falling Titan," *Wall Street Journal* (Eastern Edition), September 23, 2008, p. A6.

Ernst, Joseph Albert. *Money and Politics in America, 1755–1775.* Chapel Hill: University of North Carolina Press, 1973.

Esen, Rita. "The Transition of German Universal Banks," *Journal of International Banking Regulation,* vol. 2, no. 4 (2001): 50–57.

Evans, A. "Some Coinage Systems of the Fourteenth Century," *Journal of Economics and Business History,* vol. 3 (1931): 481–496.

Fackler, Martin. "North Korean Counterfeiting Complicates Nuclear Crisis," *New York Times,* January 29, 2006, 3.

Fan, C. Simon, and Xiangdong Wei. "The Law of One Price: Evidence from the Transitional Economy of China," *The Review of Economics and Statistics,* vol. 88, no. 4 (November 2006): 682–697.

Fausten, Dietrich K. "The Humean Origin of the Contemporary Monetary Approach to the Balance of Payments." *Quarterly Journal of Economics,* vol. 93, no. 4 (November 1979): 655–673.

Feavearyear, Sir Albert. *The Pound Sterling: A History of English Money*. 2nd ed. Oxford, UK: Clarendon Press, 1963.

Federal Reserve Board. *Consumer Handbook on Adjustable-Rate Mortgages*. Washington, D.C.: Author, 2009. www.federalreserve.gov/pubs/arms/arms_english.htm.

Federal Reserve System. Federal Reserve Bulletin. January, 1998.

Fehrenbach, T. R. *The Swiss Banks*. New York: McGraw Hill, 1966.

Fellner, William. "The Controversial Issue of Comprehensive Indexation." In *Essays on Inflation and Indexation*. Washington, D.C.: American Enterprise Institute for Public Policy Research, 1974, pp. 63–70.

Fetter, F. W., and T. E. Gregory. *Monetary and Financial Policy in Nineteenth-Century Britain*. Dublin: Irish University Press, 1973.

Figueira, Thomas J. *The Power of Money: Coinage and Politics in the Athenian Empire*. Philadelphia: University of Pennsylvania Press, 1998.

Fischer, Stanley. "Seigniorage and the Case for a National Money," *Journal of Political Economy,* vol. 90 (April 1982): 295–313.

Fisher, Irving. *The Purchasing Power of Money*. New York: Macmillan, 1911.

Fisher, Irving. *Stabilizing the Dollar*. New York: Macmillan, 1926.

Fisher, Irving. *The Theory of Interest*. New York: Macmillan, 1930, pp. 399–451.

Fisher, W. C. "The Tabular Standard in Massachusetts History," *Quarterly Journal of Economics,* vol. 27 (May 1913): 417–454.

Fitzgerald, C. P. *China, A Short Cultural History*. London: Cresset Press, 1935.

Flynn, Dennis O. *World Silver and Monetary History in the Sixteenth and Seventeenth Centuries*. Brookfield, VT: Ashgate, 1996.

Fohlin, Caroline. "Relationship Banking, Liquidity, and Investment in the German Industrialization," *Journal of Finance,* vol. 53, no. 5 (October 1998): 1737–1758.

Fontaine, Thomson. "Currency Crises in Developed and Emerging Market Economies: A Comparative Empirical Treatment," IMF Working Paper (WP/05/13) International Monetary Fund: Washington, D.C., January 2005.

Forsyth, Randall W. "Calling London: The Fed Takes Aim at Libor," *Barron's*, vol. 88, no. 18, p. M8.

Frank, Tenney. *An Economic Survey of Ancient Rome*. Vols. 1–6. 1940. Reprint, Paterson, NJ: Pageant Books, 1959.

Frankel, Jeffrey. "The Effect of Monetary Policy on Real Commodity Prices." In *Asset Prices and Monetary Policy,* edited by John Campbell, University of Chicago Press, 2007.

Freeman, Anthony. *The Money and the Mint in the Reign of Edward the Confessor, 1042–1066*. Oxford, UK: B. A. R., 1985.

Freeman, Kathleen. *The Work and Life of Solon*. New York: Arno Press, 1976.

Freris, A. F. *The Greek Economy in the Twentieth Century*. New York: St. Martin's Press, 1986.

Friedman, Milton. *Money and Economic Development*. New York: Praeger Publishers, 1972.

Friedman, Milton. *Money Mischief: Episodes in Monetary History*. New York: Harcourt Brace Jovanovich, 1992.

Friedman, Milton. *The Optimum Quantity of Money, and Other Essays*. Chicago, IL: Aldine Publishing Company, 1969.

Friedman, Milton. "Using Escalators to Help Fight Inflation," *Fortune Magazine*, July 1974.

Gadsby, J. William. *Future of the Penny: Options for Congressional Consideration*. Washington, D.C.: The Office, 1996.

Galbraith, John Kenneth. *Money, Whence It Came, Where It Went*. New York: Bantam Books, 1975.

Garbade, Kenneth D. "The Evolution of Repo Contracting Conventions in the 1980's," *Economic Policy Review-Federal Reserve Bank of New York*, vol. 12, no. 1 (May 2006): 27–44.

Gibson, W. E. "Interest Rates and Inflationary Expectations," *American Economic Review*, vol. 62, no. 5, pp. 854–865.

Gillilland, Cora Lee C., *The Stone Money of Yap: A Numismatic Survey*. Washington, D.C.: Smithsonian Institution Press, 1975.

Glaeser, Edward L. *Neither a Borrower, nor a Lender Be: An Economic Analysis of Interest Restrictions and Usury Laws*. Palo Alto, CA: Hoover Institution on War, Revolution, and Peace, Domestic Studies Program, 1994.

Goethe, Johann Wolfgang von. *Faust*. Translated by George Madison Priest. Chicago: William Benton Publisher, 1952.

Goldberg, Linda S. and Cedric Tille. "Vehicle Currency Use in International Trade," Federal Reserve Bank of New York, Staff Report no. 200, January 2005.

Goldthwaite, Richard A. *Banks, Palaces, and Entrepreneurs in Renaissance Florence*. Aldershot, UK: Variorum, 1995.

Goldthwaite, Richard A. *The Building of Renaissance Florence: An Economic and Social History*. Baltimore, MD: John Hopkins University Press, 1980.

Gomes, Leonard. *Foreign Trade and the National Economy: Mercantilist and Classical Perspectives*. New York: St. Martin's Press, 1987.

Gorton, Gary. *Clearinghouses and the Origin of Central Banking in the U.S.*, Working paper, Federal Reserve Bank of Philadelphia, 1984.

Goswami, Gautam, Jouahn Nam, and Milind Shrikhande. "Why Do Global Firms Use Currency Swaps?: Theory and Evidence," *Journal of Multinational Financial Management*, vol. 14, no. 4/5 (October 2004): 315–334.

Gould, J. D. *The Great Debasement*. Oxford: Clarendon Press, 1970.

Green, Timothy. *The New World of Gold*. New York: Walker and Company, 1981.

Greenfield, Robert L., and Hugh Rockoff. "Yellowbacks Out West and Greenbacks Back East: Social-Choice Dimensions of Monetary Reform," *Southern Economic Journal*, vol. 62, no. 4 (April 1996): 902–915.

Greenwald, John, James Carney. "Don't Panic: Here Comes Bailout," *Time*, February 13, 1995, pp. 34–37

Greider, William. *Secrets of the Temple: How the Federal Reserve System Runs the Country*. New York: Simon and Schuster, 1987.

Grice-Hutchinson, Margorie. *Economic Thought in Spain: Selected Essays of Margorie Grice-Hutchinson*. Edited by L. Moss and C. K. Ryan. Translated by C. K. Ryan and Margorie Grice-Hutchinson. Aldershot, UK; Elgar, 1993.

Grierson, P. "The Roman Law of Counterfeiting." In *Essays in Roman Coinage Presented to Harold Matingly*. Edited by R. A. G. Carson and C. H. V. Sutherland. Oxford, UK: Oxford University Press, 1956.

Gulde, Anne-Marie. "The Role of the Currency Board in Bulgaria's Stabilization," *Finance and Development*, vol. 36, no. 3, International Monetary Fund: Washington D.C., 1999, pp. 36–40.

Haak, Bob. *The Golden Age: Dutch Painters of the Seventeenth Century*. Translated and edited by Elizabeth Willems-Treeman. New York: Harry N. Abrams, 1984.

Hagenbauch, Barbara. "A Penny Saved Could Become a Penny Spurned," *USA Today*, July 7, 2006.

Hamilton, Earl J. *American Treasure and the Price Revolution in Spain, 1501–1650*. New York: Octagon Books, 1965.

Hamilton, Earl J. *War and Prices in Spain, 1651–1800*. New York: Russell and Russell, 1947.

Hammond, Bray. *Banks and Politics in America from the Revolution to the Civil War*. Princeton, NJ: Princeton University Press, 1957.

Hammond, G. L. *Alexander the Great: King, Commander, and Statesman*. Parkridge, NJ: Noyes Press, 1980.

Hanes, Christopher. "The Liquidity Trap and U.S. Interest Rates in the 1930s," *Journal of Money, Credit, and Banking*, vol. 38, No. 1(February 2006): 163–194.

Hanke, Steve H. "The Americas: Ecuador Needs More Than a Dollars-for-Sucres Exchange," *Wall Street Journal* (Eastern Edition), March 31, 2000, p. A19.

Hanke, Steve H. "Is the Ruble Next?" *Forbes*, March 9, 1998, 64–65.

Harl, Kenneth. *Coinage in the Roman Economy, 300 B.C. to A.D. 700*. Baltimore, MD: John Hopkins University Press, 1996.

Harris, S. *The Assignats*. Cambridge, MA: Harvard University Press, 1930.

Hasegawa, Tsuyoshi. *The February Revolution: Petrograd, 1917*. Seattle, WA: University of Washington Press, 1981.

Head, Barclay Vincent. *The Coinage of Lydia and Persia*. San Diego, CA: Pegasus, 1967.

Heaton, Herbert. "Playing Card Currency of French Canada," *American Economic Review*, vol. 18, no. 4 (December 1928): 649–662.

Heckscher, Eli F. *An Economic History of Sweden*. Cambridge, MA: Harvard University Press, 1954.

Hendy, Michael F. *Studies in the Byzantine Monetary Economy*. Cambridge, UK: Cambridge University Press, 1985.

Hepburn, A. Barton. *A History of Currency in the United States*. 1924. Reprint, New York: Augustus M. Kelley, 1967.

Herodotus. *History*. Chicago: William Benton Publisher, 1952.

Hewitt, V., ed. *The Banker's Art*. London: British Museum, 1995.

Higgins, Andrew. "Twilight Economy: Lacking Money to Pay, Russian Firms Survive on a Deft System of Barter," *Wall Street Journal*, August 27, 1998, A1:1.

Hilsenrath, Jon, and Kelly Evans. "Fed Outlook Darkens on Economy," *Wall Street Journal* (Eastern Edition), January 7, 2009, A1.

Hoelscher, David, and Marc Quintyn. "Managing Systemic Banking Crises," IMF Occasional Paper 224, Washington, D.C.: International Monetary Fund, 2003.

Hogendorn, Jan S. *Economic Development*. New York: Harper and Row, 1987.

Homer, Sidney. *A History of Interest Rates*. 2nd ed. New Brunswick, NJ: Rutgers University Press, 1977.

Horne, James C. Van, and John M. Wachowicz, Jr., *Fundamentals of Financial Management*. 10th ed., Upper Saddle River, New Jersey: Prentice Hall, 1997.

Horsefield, J. K. "Stop of the Exchequer Revisited." *Economic History Review*, vol. 35, no. 4 (1982): 511–528.

Horton, Dana S. *The Silver Pound and England's Monetary Policy since the Restoration, together with the History of the Guinea*. New York: Garland Publishing, 1983.

Hull, Charles Henry, ed., *The Economic Writings of Sir William Petty*, New York: Augustus M. Kelly, 1963

Hume, David. *Essays, Moral, Political, and Literary*. New York: Oxford University Press, 1963.

Hume, David. *Writings on Economics*. Edited by Eugene Rotwein. Madison: University of Wisconsin Press, 1955.

Humphreys, C. R. *The Southern New Hebrides: An Ethnological Record*. Cambridge, UK: Cambridge University Press, 1983.

Ikle, Max. *Switzerland: An International Banking and Finance Center*. Translated by Eric Schiff. Stroudsburg, PA: Dowden, Hutchinson, and Ross, 1972.

International Financial Law Review. "The New Turkish Lira," vol. 24, no. 1, January 1995, pp. 47–48.

International Monetary Fund. "IMF Approves Augmentation and Extension of Georgia's EASF Loan," Press Release no. 99/34, 1999.

International Monetary Fund. "IMF Approves Stand-By Credit for the Republic of Belarus," Press Release no. 95/46. Washington, D.C., September 1995.

International Monetary Fund. "IMF Approves US$64 Million Tranche Under Stand-By Credit and US$829 Extended Arrangement for the Federal Republic of Yugoslavia (Serbia/Montenegro)," Press Release no. 02/25, May 13, 2002.

International Monetary Fund. "Crisis in Asia: Regional and Global Implications" *World Economic Outlook: Interim Assessment.* Washington, D.C., December 1997.

International Monetary Fund. "Lessons from the Crisis in Argentina," Prepared by the Policy Development and Review Department, October 8, 2003.

International Monetary Fund, Public Information Notice (PIN) no. 04/62, Washington D.C., May 28, 2004.

International Monetary Fund. *World Economic Outlook.* Washington, D.C., May 2000, May 2001, September 2002, April 2003, September 2003, April 2006, April 2007, April 2008, and October 2008.

Islam, Azizul. "The Dynamics of the Asian Economic Crisis and Selected Policy Implications." In *Global Financial Turmoil and Reform*, edited by Barry Herman, pp. 49–74, New York, 1999.

Israel, Jonathan I. *Dutch Primacy in World Trade: 1585–1740.* Oxford, UK: Clarendon Press, 1989.

Jackson, Kevin, ed. *The Oxford Book of Money.* Oxford, UK: Oxford University Press, 1995.

Jastram, Roy W. Silver, *The Restless Metal.* New York: John Wiley, 1981.

Jenkins, Holman W. Jr. "Rethinking the Fan and Fred Takeover," *Wall Street Journal* (Eastern Edition), March 4, 2009, p. A13.

Johnson, A. C., and L. C. West. *Currency in Roman and Byzantine Egypt.* Princeton, NJ: Princeton University Press, 1949.

Johnston, Sir Harry Hamilton. *George Grenfell and the Congo.* 1908. Reprint, London, UK: Kraus Reprint, 1969.

Jones, A. H. M. *The Later Roman Empire: 284–602.* vol. 1–2, Norman, OK: University of Oklahoma Press, 1964.

Jones, A. H. M. *The Roman Economy.* Totowa, NJ: Rowman and Littlefield, 1974.

Journal of Accountancy. "What's a Frozen ECU?" vol. 177, no. 4 (April 1994): 14.

Kagin, Donald H. "Monetary Aspects of the Treasury Notes of the War of 1812." *Journal of Economic History*, vol. 44, no. 1 (March 1984): 69–88.

Kamps, Annette. "The Euro as Invoicing Currency in International Trade," European Central Bank, ECB Working Paper no. 665, August 2006.

Karmin, Craig. "Can Asia Control the 'Hot Money'?; Even Some Investors Endorse Cash Controls to Fight Speculators," *Wall Street Journal* (Eastern Edition), April 5, 2007, p. C1.

Karouf, Jim. "Start the Presses: Euro Set to Debut," *Futures*, vol. 27, no. 9 September 1, 1988): 30.

Katz, Ian. "Capital Flight South Florida," *Business Week*, no. 4040 (June 25, 2007): 46.

Kelly, Kate. "The Fall of Bear Stearns: Fear, Rumors Touched Off Fatal Run on Bear Stearns; Executives Swung From Hope to Despair in the Space of a Week," *Wall Street Journal* (Eastern Edition), May 28, 2008, p. A1.

Kenen, Peter B. *Economic and Monetary Union in Europe.* Cambridge, UK: Cambridge University Press, 1995.

Kennedy, Ellen. *The Bundesbank: Germany's Central Bank in the International Monetary System.* New York: Council on Foreign Relations Press, 1991.

Kessler, Andy. "What Paulson Is Trying to Do," *Wall Street Journal* (Eastern Edition), October 15, 2008, p. A19.

Keynes, John Maynard. *Indian Currency and Finance.* London: Macmillan, 1913.

Keynes, John Maynard. *The Economic Consequences of Peace.* New York: Harcourt, Brace and Howe, 1920.

Khan, Mohsin, and Abbas Mirakhor. "Islamic Banking: Experiences in the Islamic Republic of Iran and in Pakistan," *Economic Development and Cultural Change*, vol. 38, no. 2 (January 1990): 353–376.

Kim, Jim. "Credit Crunch Moves Beyond Mortgages: Individuals See Higher Rates, Harsher Terms on Credit Cards and Other Consumer Loans," *Wall Street Journal* (Eastern Edition), August 22, 2007, p. D1.

Kindleberger, Charles P. *A Financial History of Western Europe.* London: George Allen and Unwin, 1984.

Kleiman, Ephraim. "Early Inflation Tax Theory and Estimates," *History of Political Economy*, vol. 32, no. 11 (2000): 265–298.

Klein, John J. *Money and the Economy.* 6th ed. San Diego, CA: Harcourt Brace Jovanovich, 1986.

Kline, Alan. "Bank in Michigan Says Check-Kiting Scheme Could Cost It $2.5 Million; '97 Profits Slashed," *American Banker*, vol. 163, no. 48 (March 12, 1998): 8.

Knee, Jonathan A. "Boutique vs. Behemoth," *Wall Street Journal* (Eastern Edition), March 2, 2006, p. A14.

Knox, John Jay. *A History of Banking in the United States.* New York: Bradford Rhodes and Company, 1903. Reprint, New York: Augustus M. Kelley, 1969.

Koretz, Gene. "Do 'Sweeps' Sap Fed Policy: A Growing Bank Practice Stirs Fears," *Business Week*, no. 3529 (June 2, 1997): 26.

Kowsmann, Patricia, and Karen Lane. "Islamic Banking Moves Into Singapore; City-State Stakes Claim in Crowing Sector; DBS, Mideast Investors Capitalize New Firm," *Wall Street Journal* (Eastern Edition), May 8, 2007, p. C7.

Kozicki, Sharon, and Gordon Sellon. "Longer-Term Perspectives on the Yield Curve Monetary Policy," *Federal Reserve Bank of Kansas Economic Review*, vol. 90, no. 4 (2005): 5–35.

Krauss, Clifford. "Commodities Relentless Surge," *New York Times*, vol. 157, no. 54190 (January 15, 2008): C1–8.

Kravchuk, Robert S. "Budget Deficits, Hyperinflation, and Stabilization in Ukraine, 1991–96," *Public Budgeting and Finance*, vol. 18, no. 4 (Winter 1998): 45–70.

Krieger, Herbert William. *Island Peoples of the Western Pacific: Micronesia and Melanesia*. Washington, D.C.: Smithsonian Institution, 1943.

Kroszner, Randy. *Free Banking: The Scottish Experience as a Model for Emerging Economies*. Washington, D.C.: World Bank, 1995.

Kumar, Manmohan S. "Deflation: the New Threat," *Finance and Development*, vol. 40, no. 2 (June 2003): 16–19.

Lane, Frederic C. *Venice: A Maritime Republic*. Baltimore, MD: John Hopkins Press, 1973.

Lane, Frederic C., and Reinhold C. Mueller. *Money and Banking in Medieval and Renaissance Venice*. Vols. 1–2. Baltimore, MD: John Hopkins University Press, 1997.

Laughlin, J. Laurence. *A History of Bimetallism in the United States*. 1896. Reprint, New York: Greenwood Press, 1968.

League of Nations. *The Course and Control of Inflation*. Geneva: League of Nations, 1946.

Lee, Jang-Yung. "Sterilizing Capital Inflows," International Monetary Fund, Economic Issues no. 7. Washington, D.C., March 1997.

Leigh, Daniel, Marco Rossi. "Leading Indicators of Growth and Inflation in Turkey," IMF Working Paper (WP/02/231) IMF: Washington, D.C., December 2002.

Lefebvre, Georges. *The French Revolution*. Vols. 1–2. Translated by John H. Stewart and James Friguglietti. New York: Columbia University Press, 1964.

Lerner, Eugene M. "Inflation in the Confederacy, 1861–1865." In *Studies in the Quantity Theory of Money*. Edited by Milton Friedman, pp. 163–175. Chicago: University of Chicago Press, 1956.

Lester, Richard A. *Monetary Experiments*. 1939. Reprint, New York: Augustus M. Kelley, 1970.

Lewis, Michael. "The Capitalist; Ruble Roulette," *New York Times Magazine*, August 13, 1995, pp. 622.

Littlefield, Henry M. "The Wizard of Oz: Parable on Populism." *American Quarterly*, vol. 16 (Spring 1964): 47–58.

Littlepage, Dean. *The Alaska Gold Rush*. Santa Barbara, CA: Albion Publishing Group, 1995.

Long, Robert Emmet, ed. *Banking Scandals: The S & Ls and BCCI*. New York: H. W. Wilson, 1993.

Lopez, Robert S. *The Shape of Medieval Monetary History*. London: Variorum Reprints, 1986.

Lowenstein, Roger. "Triple-A Failure," *New York Times Magazine*, April 27, 2008, pp 36–42.

Lucas, Robert E. Jr. "Nobel Lecture: Monetary Neutrality," *Journal of Political Economy*, vol. 104, no. 4 (August 1996): 661–683.

Luke, Jon C. "Inflation-free Pricing Rules for a Generalized Commodity-Reserve Currency," *Journal of Political Economy*, vol. 83, no. 4 (1975): 779–790.

Lumpkin, Stephen. "Repurchase and Reverse Repurchase Agreements," *Federal Reserve Bank of Richmond Economic Review*, vol. 731 (January 1987): 15–23.

Lyon, James. "Yugoslavia's Hyperinflation, 1993–1994: A Social History," *East European Politics and Societies*, vol. 10, no. 2 (March 1996): 293–327.

MacDonald, Alistair, Laurence Norman. "World News: Bank Bailouts, Sinking Revenue Fray U.K.'s Ledger," *Wall Street Journal* (Eastern Edition), February 20, 2009, p. A10.

Makin, John H. "Sumo Economics," *Wall Street Journal* (Eastern Edition), March 3, 2004, p. A16.

Manasse, Paolo, and Nouriel Roubini. "'Rules of Thumb' for Sovereign Debt Crises," IMF Working Paper, WP/05/42, International Monetary Fund, March 2005.

Mandel, Michael. "After The Binge, Who Should Suffer?" *Business Week*, October 13, 2008.

Mankiw, N. Gregory. *Macroeconomics*. 3rd ed. New York: Worth Publishers, 1996.

Marshall, Alfred. "Remedies for Fluctuations of General Prices," *Contemporary Review*, vol. 51 (March 1887): 355–375.

Martien, Jerry. *Shell Game: A True Account of Beads and Money in North America*. San Francisco: Mercury House, 1996.

Martin-Acena, P. "The Spanish Money Supply, 1874–1935," *Journal of European Economic History*. vol. 19, no. 1 (1990): pp. 7–33.

Marx, Jennifer. *The Magic of Gold*. Garden City, NY: Doubleday, 1978.

Mas, Ignacio. "Things Governments do to Money: A Recent History of Currency Reform Schemes and Scams," *Kyklos*, vol. 48, no. 4 (1995): 483–513.

Masahiro, Kawai. "The East Asian Currency Crisis: Causes and Lessons," *Contemporary Economic Policy*, vol. 16, no. 2 (April 1998): 157–173.

Mattingly, Harold. *Roman Coins*. London: Methuen and Co., 1968.

McCallum, Bennett T. *Monetary Economics: Theory and Practice*. New York: Macmillan, 1989.

McConnell, Campbell R., and Stanley L. Brue. *Economics: Principles, Problems, and Policies,* 14th ed. New York: McGraw Hill, 1998.

McKay, Betsy. "Ruble's Decline Energizes Russian Firms Who Manage to Win Back Consumers," *Wall Street Journal* (Eastern Edition), April 23, 1999, p. B7A.

McKinnon, Ronald I. "Optimal Currency Areas," *American Economic Review*, vol. 53 (1963): 717–725.

McMahon, Denis. "World News: China Vows to Crimp 'Hot Money' Flows," *Wall Street Journal* (Eastern Edition), March 10, 2008, p. A6.

Meade, Ellen E. "The FOMC: Preferences, Voting, and Consensus," *Federal Reserve Bank of St. Louis Review* (March 2005): 93–101.

Meek, Charles Kingsley. *Law and Authority in a Nigerian Tribe: A Study in Indirect Rule*. London: Oxford University Press, 1950.

Meiselman, David. *Varieties of Monetary Experience*. Chicago: University of Chicago Press, 1970.

Melitz, Jacques. "The Theory of Optimal Currency Areas." *Open Economies Review*, vol. 7, no. 2 (April 1996): 99–116.

Myers, Margaret G. *A Financial History of the United States*. New York: Columbia University Press, 1970.

Michaud, Francois-Louis, and Christian Upper. "What Drives Interbank Rates? Evidence for the Libor Panel," *BIS Quarterly Review* (March 2008): 47–58.

Miles, David, and Andrew Scott. *Macroeconomics: Understanding the Wealth of Nations*. John Wiley and Sons, New York, 2002.

Mill, John Stuart. *Principles of Political Economy*. vol. 3 of *Collected Works of John Stuart Mill*, London: Routledge and Kegan Paul, 1965.

Millett, Paul. *Lending and Borrowing in Ancient Athens*. Cambridge, UK: Cambridge University Press, 1991.

Milne, J. G. *Greek Coinage*. Oxford, UK: Clarendon Press, 1931.

Minton, Robert. *John Law: The Father of Paper Money*. New York: Association Press, 1975.

Miskimin, Harry A. *Money, Prices, and Foreign Exchange in Fourteenth-Century France*. New Haven, CT: Yale University Press, 1963.

Mittra, Sid. *Central Bank Versus Treasury: An International Study*. Washington, D.C.: University Press of America, 1978.

Moggridge, D. E. *The Return to Gold, 1925*. Cambridge, UK: Cambridge University Press, 1969.

Mollenkamp, Carrick. "U.K. Bankers To Alter Libor to Address Rate Doubts," *Wall Street Journal* (Eastern Edition), June 11, 2008, p. C1.

Mollenkamp, Carrick, and Mark Whitehouse. "Study Casts Doubt on Key Rate; WSJ Analysis Suggest Banks May Have Reported Flawed Interest Data for Libor," *Wall Street Journal* (Eastern Edition), May 29, 2008, p. A1.

Montesquieu, Charles De Secondat, Baron De. *The Spirit of Laws*. 1748. Translated by Thomas Nugent. Chicago: William Benton, 1952.

Moses, Bernard. "Legal Tender Notes in California," *Quarterly Journal of Economics*, vol. 7 (October 1892): 1–25.

Mosley, Layna. "Dropping Zeros and Gaining Credibility? Currency Redenomination in Developing Nations," Conference Paper, American Political Science Association, 2005 Annual Meeting, Washington, D.C., pp. 1–28.

Moutot, Philippe, Alexander Jung, and Francesco Mongelli. "The Workings of the Eurosystem: Monetary Policy Preparations and Decision Making-Selected Issues," *Occasional Paper Series*, no. 79. Frankfurt am Main Europe, European Central Bank, 2008.

Mundell, Robert A. "A Theory of Optimal Currency Areas," *American Economic Review*, vol. 51 (1961): 637–665.

Murphy, Antoin E. *John Law: Economic Theorist and Policy Maker*. Oxford, UK: Clarendon Press, 1997.

Myers, Margaret G. *A Financial History of the United States*. New York: Columbia University Press, 1970.

Myers, Robert J., ed. *The Political Morality of the International Monetary Fund*. New Brunswick, NJ: Transactions Books, 1987.

Nettels, Curtis P. *The Emergence of a National Economy*. Madison: University of Wisconsin, 1962.

Nettels, Curtis P. *The Money Supply of the American Colonies before 1720*. 1934. Reprint, New York: Augustus M. Kelly, 1964.

Nevin, Edward, and E. W. Davis. *The London Clearing Banks*. London: Elek Books, 1970.

New York Times. "Settling Switzerland's Debts," August 16, 1998, p. 1.

Nogaro, Bertrand. "Hungary's Recent Monetary Crisis and Its Theoretical Meaning." *American Economic Review*, vol. 38, no. 4 (September 1948): 526–542.

Nolan, Patrick. *A Monetary History of Ireland*. London: P. S. King and Son, 1926.

Nugent, Walter T. K. *Money and American Society: 1865–1880*. New York: Free Press, 1968.

Nussbaum, Arthur. *A History of the Dollar*. New York: Columbia University Press, 1957.

Nussbaum, Frederick L. *A History of the Economic Institutions of Modern Europe*. 1935. Reprint, New York: Augustus M. Kelley, 1968.

OCED Economic Outlook, Number 84, 2008. (www.oced.org/publications)

Ohkawa, Kazushi, Miyorhei Shinohara, and Larry Meissner, eds. *Patterns of Japanese Economic Development: A Quantitative Appraisal*. New Haven, CT: Yale University Press, 1979.

Oomes, Nienke, and Franziska Ohnsorge. "Money Demand and Inflation in Dollarized Economies: The Case of Russia," IMF Working Paper, Washington: International Monetary Fund (WP/05/144), June 2005.

Organization for Economic Cooperation and Development, *OECD Economic Surveys: Bulgaria*, vol. 1999, no. 9 (April 1999), OECD: Paris, France, pp. 1–111.

Paarlberg, Don. *An Analysis and History of Inflation*. Westport, CT: Greenwood Press, 1993.

Paddock, Richard C. "Russians Bank of Bartering," *Los Angeles Times*, December 28, 1998, A1:1.

Padoa-Schioppa, Tommaso. *The Road to Monetary Union in Europe*. Oxford, UK: Clarendon Press, 1994.

Paletta, Damian, and Allstair MacDonald. "World News: Liquidity-Crisis Guide Set for an Update," *Wall Street Journal* (Eastern Edition), February 22, 2008, p. A9.

Paletta, Damian, Susanne Craig, Deborah Soloman, Carrick Mollenkamp, and Mathew Karnitschnig. "Lehman Fata Spurs Emergency Session; Wall Street Titans Seek Ways to Stem Widening Crisis," *Wall Street Journal* (Eastern Edition), September 13, 2008, p. A1.

Parkman, Francis. *The Conspiracy of Pontiac and the Indian War after the Conquest of Canada*. 1899. Reprint, Boston: Little, Brown and Company, 1933.

Parrson, Jens D. *Dying of Money: Lessons from the Great German and American Inflations*. Boston: Wellspring Press, 1974.

Partner, Peter. *Renaissance Rome, 1500–1599*. Los Angeles: University of California Press, 1976.

Penner, Ethan. "The Future of Securitization," *Wall Street Journal* (Eastern Edition), July 10, 2008, p. A15.

Pereira, Luiz Carlos Bresser. *Economic Crisis and State Reform in Brazil*. London: Lynne Rienner Publishers, 1996.

Perlman, Morris. "Adam Smith and the Paternity of the Real Bills Doctrine." *History of Political Economy*, vol. 21 no. 1 (Spring 1989): 77–90.

Petrovic, Pavle, Zorica Mladenovic. "Money Demand and Exchange Rate Determination under Hyperinflation: Conceptual Issues and Evidence from Yugoslavia," *Journal of Money, Credit, and Banking*, vol. 32, no. 4. (November 2000): 785–806.

Pintner, Walter McKenzie. *Russian Economic Policy Under Nicholas I*. Ithaca, NY: Cornell University Press, 1967.

Pipes, Richard. *The Russian Revolution*. New York: Alfred A. Knopf, 1991.

Pirie, Anthony. *Operation Bernhard*. New York: William Morrow, 1962.

Pitman, Frank, W. *The Development of the British West Indies: 1700–1763*. New Haven: Yale University Press, 1917.

Plato. *The Dialogues of Plato*. Translated by Benjamin Jowett. Chicago: William Benton, Publisher, 1952.

Plutarch. *Lives of Noble Grecians and Romans*. Dryden Translation. Chicago: William Benton, 1952.

Polak, Jacques J. *The World Bank and the International Monetary Fund: A Changing Relationship*. Washington, D.C.: Brookings Institution, 1994.

Pollock, Michael. "Welcome to a Changed Muni World; Foreigners, Hedge Funds Are Among the Newcomers; One 'Hot Money' Scenario," *Wall Street Journal* (Eastern Edition), April 4, 2006, p. C13.

Polo, Marco. *Travels of Marco Polo*. New York: Orion Press, 1958.

Polo, Marco. *Travels of Marco Polo*. Edited by W. Marsden. New York: Dorset Press, 1987.

Porter, Richard D., and Ruth A. Judson. "The Location of U.S. Currency: How Much is Abroad?" *Federal Reserve Bulletin*, vol. 82, no. 10 (October 1996): 883–903.

Postgate, John Nicholas. *Early Mesopotamia: Society and Economy at the Dawn of History*. Rev. ed. London: Routledge, 1994.

Powell, Ellis. *The Evolution of the Money Market: 1385–1915*. 1915. Reprint, New York: August M. Kelley, 1966.

Powell, T. G. E. *The Celts*. Rev. ed. New York: Thames and Hudson, 1985.

Quiggin, A., and A. Hingston. *A Survey of Primitive Money*. New York: AMS, 1949.

Quispe-Angnoli, Myriam, and Elena Whisler. "Official Dollarization and the Banking System in Ecuador and El Salvador," *Economic Review* (0732183), vol. 91. no. 3 (3rd Quarter): 55–71

Radford, R. A. "The Economic Organization of a POW Camp." *Economica*, vol. 12, no. 48 (November 1945): 189–210.

Reddy, Sudeep. "U.S. News: Fed Extends Lending Programs as Threats Persist; Move Reflects Worry Over 'Fragile' State of Financial Market," *Wall Street Journal* (Eastern Edition), July 31, 2008, p. A3.

Reinhart, Carmen M., and Miguel A. Savastano. "The Realities of Modern Hyperinflation," *Finance and Development*, vol. 40, no. 2 (June 2003): 20–23.

Reiter, Seymour. *A Study of Shelley's Poetry*. Albuquerque, NM: University of New Mexico Press, 1967.

Rich, Robert, Charles Steindel. "A Comparison of Measure of Core Inflation," *Economic Policy Review*, vol. 13, no. 3 (December 2007): 19–38.

Richards, R. D. *The Early History of Banking in England*. 1929. Reprint, New York: Augustus M. Kelley, 1965.

Richter, Jean Paul, ed. *The Notebooks of Leonardo Da Vinci*. 1833. Reprint, New York: Dover Publications, 1970.

Rickenbacker, William F. *Wooden Nickels, Or the Decline and Fall of Silver Coins*. New Rochelle, NY: Arlington House, 1966.

Riley, Clint. "Help Wanted, Bank Officials to Watch Cash; Compliance Executives Are in Growing Demand As Regulation Increases," *The Wall Street Journal* (Eastern Edition), February 6, 2007, p. C1.

Ritter, Gretchen. *Gold Bugs and Greenbacks: The Antimonopoly Tradition and the Politics of Finance in America*. Cambridge, UK: Cambridge University Press, 1997.

Roberts, Richard, ed. *The Bank of England: Money, Power, and Influence, 1694–1994*. Oxford, UK: Clarendon Press, 1995.

Rock, Charles P., and Vasiliy Solodhov. "Monetary Policies, Banking, and Trust in Changing Institutions: Russia's Transition in the 1990s, *Journal of Economic Issues*, vol. 35, no. 2 (June 2001): 451–459.

Rockoff, Hugh. *Drastic Measures: A History of Wage and Price Controls in the United States*. Cambridge, UK: Cambridge University Press, 1984.

Rockoff, Hugh. *The Free Banking Era: A Reexamination*. New York: Arno Press, 1975.

Rockoff, Hugh. "The Free Banking Era: A Reexamination" *Journal of Money, Credit and Banking*, vol. 6 (1974): 146–157.

Rockoff, Hugh. "The Wizard of Oz as a Monetary Allegory." *Journal of Political Economy*, vol. 98, no. 4 (1990): 739–760.

Rogers, James S. *The Early History of the Law of Bills and Notes: A Study of the Origins of Anglo-American Commercial Law*. New York: Cambridge University Press, 1995.

Rogoff, Kenneth. "Globalization and Global Disinflation," *Economic Review*, vol. 88, no. 4 (2003, 4th quarter): 45–78.

Rolnick, Arthur J., and Warren E. Weber. "New Evidence of the Free Banking Era." *American Economic Review*, vol. 73, no. 5 (December 1983): 1080–1090.

Roover, Raymond de. *The Rise and Decline of the Medici Bank: 1397–1494*. New York: W. W. Norton, 1966.

Rose, Peter S. *Money and Capital Markets*. 2nd ed. Plano, TX: Business Publications, 1986.

Rosen, Richard J. "The Role of Securitization in Mortgage Lending," *Chicago Fed Letter*, The Federal Reserve Bank of Chicago, Essays on Issues no. 244, November 2007.

Rostovtzeff, M. *The Social and Economic History of the Hellenistic World*. vol. 1–3. Oxford, UK: Oxford University Press, 1941.

Russell, Steven. "Understanding the Term Structure of Interest Rates: The Expectations Theory," *Federal Reserve Bank of St. Louis Review*, vol. 74, no. 4 (1992): 36–51.

Ryan, John Carlin. *A Handbook of Papal Coins*. Washington, D.C.: J. C. Ryan, 1989.

Samuelsson, Kurt. *From Great Power to Welfare State: 300 Years of Swedish Social Development*. London: Allen and Unwin, 1968.

Sargent, Thomas J. *Rational Expectations and Inflation*. 2nd ed. New York: Harper Collins, 1993.

Sayers, R. S. *The Bank of England: 1891–1944*. Cambridge, UK: Cambridge University Press, 1976.

Schama, Simon. *The Embarrassment of Riches: An Interpretation of Dutch Culture in the Golden Age*. New York: Alfred Knopf. 1987.

Scheller, Hanspeter K., *The European Central Bank: History, Role, and Functions*, Frankfurt am Main: European Central Bank, 2006.

Schlesinger, Arthur M., Jr. *The Coming of the New Deal*. Boston: Houghton Mifflin Company, 1959.

Schlesinger, Arthur M., Jr. *The Age of Jackson*. New York: Book Find Club, 1945.

Schlesinger, Arthur M., Jr. *The Age of Roosevelt*. Vols. 1–3. Boston: Houghton Mifflin Company, 1957–1960.

Schnadt, Norman, and John Whittaker. "Inflation-proof Currency? The Feasibility of Variable Commodity Standards." *Journal of Money, Credit, and Banking*, vol. 25, no. 2 (1993): 214–221.

Schuler, Kurt. "Some Theory and History of Dollarization," *Cato Journal*, vol. 25, no. 1 (Winter 2005): 115–125.

Schumpeter, Joseph. *Business Cycles: A Theoretical, Historical, and Statistical Analysis of the Capitalist Process*. Vols. 1, 2. Philadelphia: Porcupine Press, 1939.

Schwartz, Anna J. "From Obscurity to Notoriety: A Biography of the Exchange Stabilization Fund." *Journal of Money, Credit, and Banking*, vol. 29, no. 2 (May 1997): 135–153.

Schwarz, Ted. *A History of United States Coinage*. San Diego, CA: A.S. Barnes, 1980.

Selgin, George A., and Lawrence H. White. "Monetary Reform and the Redemption of National Bank Notes." *Business History Review*, vol. 68, no. 20 (Summer 1994): 205–243.

Senate Committee on Finance, Wholesale Prices, Wages, and Transportation. "The Aldrich Report," Senate Report no. 1394, Part I, 52nd Congress, 2nd sess., March 3, 1893.

Sesit, Michael R., and David Reilly. "Going Global: 'Hot Money' Helps Drive Oil Volatility," *Wall Street Journal* (Eastern Edition), July 14, 2005, p. C1.

Sesit, Michael R., and Sara Webb. "Ruble's Woes Could Shake Market Anew," *Wall Street Journal* (Eastern Edition), July 6, 1998, p. C1.

Shann, E. O. G. *An Economic History of Australia*. 1948. Reprint, Melbourne, Australia: Georgian House, 1963.

Sharma, Shalendra. "The Missed Lessons of the Mexican Peso Crisis," *Challenge*, vol. 44, no. 1 (January/February 2001): 56–89.

Sidel, Robin. "American Express Drops High-Tech Payment Device," *Wall Street Journal* (Eastern Edition) March 31, 2008, p. B1.

Sidel, Robin. "Do-It-All Banks' Big Test; Universal Model So Far Weathers Credit Crunch, Remains Controversial," *Wall Street Journal* (Eastern Edition), September 6, 2007, p. C1.

Siegman, Charles J. "The Bank of International Settlements and the Federal Reserve," *Federal Reserve Bulletin*, vol. 80, no. 10 (October 1994): 900–906.

Siklos, P. L. "The End of the Hungarian Hyperinflation of 1945–46." *Journal of Money, Credit, and Banking*, vol. 2 (1989): 132–147.

Slabaugh, Arlie. *Confederate States Paper Money*. 9th ed. Iola, WI: Krause Publications, 1998.

Smith, Adam. *An Inquiry into the Nature and Causes of the Wealth of Nations*. New York: Modern Library, 1937.

Smith, Adam. *An Inquiry into the Nature and Causes of the Wealth of Nations*. 1776. Reprint, Chicago: William Benton Publisher, 1952.

Smith, R. Bosworth. *Carthage and the Carthaginians*. New York: Longman's, Green, and Co., 1913.

Smith, Vera C. *The Rationale of Central Banking and the Free Banking Alternative*. 1936. Reprint, Indianapolis, IN: Liberty Press, 1990.

Snider, Delbert A. *Introduction to International Economics*. 6th ed. Homewood, IL: Richard D. Irwin, 1975.

Solomon, Deborah. "U.S. News: Obama Works to Overhaul TARP—Team Tries to Meld Some Paulson Ideas with Aid to Borrowers Facing Foreclosure," *Wall Street Journal* (Eastern Edition), December 17, 2008, p. A3.

Solomon, Steven. *The Confidence Game: How Unelected Central Bankers are Governing the Changed Global Economy*. New York: Simon and Schuster, 1995.

Speke, J. H. *The Discovery of the Source of the Nile*. 1864. Reprint, London: Everyman's, 1906.

Spiegel, Henry William. *The Growth of Economic Thought*. Englewood Cliffs, NJ: Prentice-Hall, 1971.

Sprenkle, Case M. "The Case of the Missing Money," *Journal of Economic Perspectives*, vol. 7, no. 4 (Fall 1993): 175–184.

Spufford, Peter. *Money and its Use in Medieval Europe*. Cambridge, UK: Cambridge University Press, 1988.

Stabile, Donald R. *The Origins of American Public Finance: Debates over Money, Debt, and Taxes in the Constitutional Era, 1776–1836*. Westport, CT: Greenwood Press, 1998.

Stanley, Henry M. *In Darkest Africa*. New York: Charles Scribner's Sons, 1890.

Stewart, A. *Faces of Power, Alexander's Image and Hellenistic Politics*. Berkeley, CA: University of California Press, 1993

Stolper, Gustav. *The German Economy: 1870–Present*. New York: Harcourt, Brace, 1967.

Stuck, Hudson. *Ten Thousand Miles with a Dog Sled*. 2nd ed. New York: Charles Scribner's Sons, 1932.

Summers, Robert, and Alan Heston. "The Pen World Table (Mark 5): An Expanded Set of International Comparisons, 1950–1988," *Quarterly Journal of Economics*, vol. 106, no. 2 (May 1991): 327–369

Svensson, Lars E. O. "Escaping from the Liquidity Trap and Deflation: The Foolproof Way and Others," *Journal of Economic Perspectives*, vol. 17, no. 4 (Fall 2003): 145–166.

Sveriges Riksbank. *Sveriges Riksbank: The Swedish Central Bank, a Short Introduction*. Stockholm, Sweden: Sveriges Riksbank Information Secretariat, 1994.

Tavernier, Jean-Baptiste. *The Six Voyages of John-Baptiste Tavernier, Baron of Aubonne, through Turkey, into Persia and the East Indies*. 1677. Translated by J. Phillips. Reprint, London: Robert Littlefield and Moses Pitt, 1985.

Taxay, Don. *Money of the American Indians, and Other Primitive Currencies of the Americas*. New York: Nummus, Press, 1970.

Terranova, Anthony. *Massachusetts Silver Coinage*. New York: American Numismatic Society, 1994.

Terrell, Henry S., and Rodney H. Mills. "International Banking Facilities and the Eurodollar Market." Staff Study no. 124. Washington, D.C.: Board of Governors of the Federal Reserve System, August 1983.

Thayer, Theodore. "The Land-Bank System in the American Colonies." *Journal of Economic History*, vol. 13, no. 2 (1953): 145–159.

Thiers, M. A. *The History of the French Revolution*. Vols. 1–5. 1881. Translated by Frederick Shoberl. Reprint, Freeport, NY: Books for Libraries Press, 1971.

Thornton, Daniel L. "When Did the FOMC Begin Targeting the Federal Funds Rate? What the Verbatim Transcript Tells Us," Working Papers, 2004-015, Federal Reserve Bank of St. Louis. 2005.

Thucydides. *The Peloponnesian War*. Translated by Richard Crawley. Chicago: William Benton Publisher, 1952.

Timberlake, Richard Henry. *The Origins of Central Banking in the United States.* Cambridge, MA: Harvard University Press, 1978.

Torres, Craig. "Mexican Markets are Hit by Fresh Blows—Stock Index Sags as Rates on Treasury Bills Soar; Firm announces Default," *Wall Street Journal* (Eastern Edition), February 16 1995, p. A11.

Toynbee, Arnold. *A Study of History.* vol. 7. London: Oxford University Press, 1954.

Troxell, Hyla A. *Studies in the Macedonian Coinage of Alexander the Great.* New York: American Numismatic Society, 1997.

Ueda, Kazuo. *Wall Street Journal* (Eastern Edition), April 8, 1999, p. 1.

United Kingdom. Report of the Committee on the Workings of the Monetary System. Cmnd. 827. London: Her Majesty's Stationary Office, 1959.

Usher, Abbott Payson. *A History of Mechanical Inventions.* Rev. ed. 1929. Reprint, New York: Dover Publications, 1988.

US Fed News Service. "VOA News: Zimbabwe's Central Bank Snips 10 Zeros in Currency Redenomination," Washington, D.C., July 30, 2008.

Valdes, Juan Gabriel. *Pinochets' Economists.* Cambridge: Cambridge University Press, 1995.

Van Arsdell, and Robert D. *Celtic Coinage of Britain.* London: Spink, 1989.

Van Houte, J. A. *An Economic History of the Low Countries: 800–1800.* New York: St. Martin's Press, 1977.

Vasari, Giorgio. *Lives of the Painters, Sculptors, and Architects*, vol. 2. New York: E. P. Dutton, 1927

Vilar, Pierre. *A History of Gold and Money, 1450–1920.* Translated by Judith White. London: NLB, 1976.

Vives, Jaime Vicens. *An Economic History of Spain.* Princeton, NJ: Princeton University Press, 1969.

Vogel, Thomas T. Jr., and Michael M. Phillips. "Ecuador Leader Pegs His Political Survival to the Dollar—Currency Plan Follows Plunge and Rising Protests," *Wall Street Journal* (Eastern Edition), January 11, 2000, p. A18.

Wachter, Susan M. *Latin American Inflation.* Lexington, MA: Lexington Books, 1976.

Wall Street Journal. "Precarious Peso—Amid Wild Inflation, Bolivians Concentrate on Swapping Currency," August 13, 1985, 1.

Wall Street Journal. "In Marxist Angola, Capitalism Thrives, Using Beer Standard," September 19, 1988, 1.

Wall Street Journal (Eastern Edition). "Soviet Printing of Rubles Soared in 11-Month Period," December 24, 1991, A8.

Wall Street Journal (Eastern Edition). "Russia, Facing Inflation, Plans Bigger Bank-notes," January 31, 1992, A10.

Wall Street Journal (Eastern Edition). "Russia Plans to Make Ruble Fully Convertible by August 1," May 6, 1992, A3.

Wall Street Journal (Eastern Edition). "Chaos in Russia Mounts," July 26, 1993, A8.

Wall Street Journal (Eastern Edition). "Russia's Overhaul of Ruble Prompts Unease in Nation," December 31, 1997, A7.

Wall Street Journal. "Economic Climate Looks Good for Launch of New Currency," May 4, 1998, A17–18.

Wall Street Journal (Eastern Edition). "Amid Zimbabwe's Economic Collapse, Desperate Investors Send Market Soaring," September 15, 2000. p. A17

Wall Street Journal (Eastern Edition). "Freedom for Zimbabwe," March 21, 2008, p. A13

Wall Street Journal (Eastern Edition). "Swiss Bank Weighs Its Use of Libor," May 29, 2008, p. A12.

Wall Street Journal (Eastern Edition). "Glass and Steagall Had a Point," May 31, 2008, p. A10.

Wall Street Journal (Eastern Edition). "Many Cooks Had a Hand in Repealing Glass-Steagall in '99," September 26, 2008, p. A13.

Wang, Jian-Ye. "The Georgian Hyperinflation and Stabilization," International Monetary Fund, IMF Working Paper no. 99/65, Washington D.C., May 1999.

Watson, David K. *History of American Coinage*. 1899. Reprint, New York: Burt Franklin, 1970.

Weatherford, Jack. *The History of Money*. New York: Crown Publishers, 1997.

Weaver, R. Kent. *Automatic Government: Politics of Indexation*. Washington, D.C.: Brookings Institution, 1988.

Webb, Steven B. *Hyperinflation and Stabilization in Weimar Germany*. New York: Oxford University Press, 1989.

Weber, Warren. "The Effect of Real and Monetary Disturbances on the Price Level under Alternative Commodity Reserve Standards," *International Economic Review*, vol. 21, no. 3 (October 1980): 673–690.

Weinstein, Steve. "True Benefits." *Progressive Grocer*, vol. 77, no. 5 (May 1998): 80–86.

Weintraub, Sidney. *Capitalism's Inflation and Unemployment Crisis*. Reading, MA: Addison-Wesley Publishing Company, 1978.

Wessel, David, Paul Carroll, and Thomas Vogel Jr. "Peso Surprise: How Mexico's Crisis Ambushed Top Minds in Officialdom, Finance—As Pressure to Devalue Rose, Finance Chief Refused; Then It Was Done Badly—The Hot Money Turns Cold," *Wall Street Journal* (Eastern Edition), July 6, 1995, p. A1.

Westermann, William Linn. "Warehousing and Trapesite Banking in Antiquity." *Journal of Economic and Business History*. 1931. Reprint, New York: Kraus Reprint Corporation, 1964.

White, Lawrence J. "The Partial Deregulation of Banks and other Depository Institutions." In *Regulatory Reform: What Actually Happened?* Edited by Leonard W. Weiss and Michael W. Klass. Boston: Little, Brown, and Company, 1986.

Wicker, E. "Terminating Hyperinflation in the Dismembered Hapsburg Monarchy," *American Economic Review*, vol. 76, no. 3 (1986): 350–364.

Williams, Jonathan, ed. *Money: A History*. New York: St. Martin's Press, 1997.

Williamson, Elizabeth. "U.S. News: Rescue Cash Lures Thousand of Banks," *Wall Street Journal* (Eastern Edition), November 3, 2008, p. A3.

Willis, Henry Parker. *A History of the Latin Monetary Union*. 1901. Reprint, New York: AMS Press, 1901.

Wilson, J. S. G. *French Banking Structure and Credit Policy*. Cambridge, MA: Harvard University Press, 1957.

Wines, Michael. "As Inflation Soars, Zimbabwe Economy Plunges," *New York Times* (Eastern Edition), February 7, 2007. p. A1

Wines, Michael. "Caps on Prices Only Deepen Zimbabweans' Misery," *New York Times* (Eastern Edition), August 2, 2007. p. A1

Wines, Michael. "How Bad is Inflation in Zimbabwe?" *New York Times* (Eastern Edition), May 2, 2006, p. A1

Woerheide, Walter J. *The Savings and Loan Industry*. Westport, CT: Quorum Books, 1984.

Wu, Tao. "Estimating the 'Neutral' Real Interest Rate in Real Time," *FRBSF Economic Letter*, no. 2005-27, October 21, 2005.

Yeager, Leland B. "Stable Money and Free-Market Currencies," *Cato Journal*, vol. 3 (Spring 1983): 305–326.

Yoder, Paton S. "Paper Currency in Colonial Pennsylvania." Ph.D. dissertation, Indiana University, 1941.

Ziobrowsky, Alan, Brigitte Ziobrowsky, and Sidney Rosenberg. "Currency Swaps and International Real Estate," *Real Estate Economics*, vol. 25, no. 2 (Summer 1997): 223–252.

Glossary

Assets—Anything a household or business owns that has monetary value. A house or factory would be a real asset and stocks and bonds are financial assets.

Balance of Payments—Summary of all transactions that involve an inflow or outflow of funds relative to the rest of the world.

Bank Run—A demand on the part of a large share of a bank's customers to withdraw funds immediately.

Barter—The direct exchange of goods and services for goods and services without the use of money.

Bond—A financial device for borrowing directly from a saver rather than going through a financial intermediary such as bank. The borrower sells the bond to a lender and promises to make interest payments and repay the principal at a maturity date in the future.

Capital—Human-made goods that do not directly satisfy human wants, but help satisfy human wants indirectly by assisting in the production of goods and services. A tractor is a capital good that helps produce food.

Capitalism—An economic system in which the means of production (factories, mines, transportation facilities) are privately owned.

Capital Subscription—The dollar amount given to a company in payment for newly issued shares of stock.

Commodity—A highly standardized raw material or agricultural product. Good examples of a commodity are aluminum, crude oil, ethanol, sugar, soybeans, coffee beans, corn, and wheat.

Convertible Paper Money—Money that can always be exchanged with a government agency for a fixed weight or amount of a commodity, usually gold.

Coupon Payments—Periodic interest payments that a bond pays to its owner.

Debasement—A decrease in the purchasing power of a unit of coinage because of a dilution in its precious metal content.

Default—The inability or unwillingness of a borrower to repay a loan.

Deflation—A decrease in the average level of prices.

Depository Institution—A financial intermediary that collects deposits from various individuals and organizations, and uses the deposited funds to make loans to other individuals and organizations.

Depreciation—A measure of the amount of plant and equipment worn out in the course of producing goods and services. It can also refer to a decrease in the value of a unit of currency in foreign exchange markets.

Devaluation—A government-initiated decrease in the value of a unit of currency in foreign exchange markets.

Disinflation—A reduction or deceleration in the inflation rate.

Dividends—A share of a corporation's profit distributed to stockholders as income earned by shares of stock. Just as bonds pay interest, stocks pay dividends.

Exchange Rate—The rate at which one country's currency can be traded for another country's currency in foreign exchange markets.

Exports—The goods and services a nation produces at home and sells in foreign markets.

Federal Funds Rate—The rate of interest banks pay when borrowing reserves from each other.

Fiat Money—A money asset such as paper money that, unlike gold or silver, has no value as a commodity in its own right.

Fixed Exchange Rate—An exchange rate between currencies that is set as a matter of government policy and does not fluctuate with market conditions.

Float—A situation in which the same sum of money appears on deposit at two different institutions because of inefficiencies in check-collecting systems. In the context of foreign exchange markets, floating exchange rates are exchange rates free to adjust to supply and demand.

Floating Exchange Rate—An exchange rate between currencies that is determined by a free market.

Gross Domestic Product (GDP)—The market value of all completely processed and finished goods and services produced by an economy over a fixed amount of time.

Gross Domestic Product (GDP) Deflator—A measure of the price level in an economy that represents all the goods and services included in GDP.

Gross Domestic Product, Real—Gross domestic product adjusted for inflation. Inflation can artificially inflate market values.

Human Capital—The accumulated knowledge, skills, and experience of individuals who take time to acquire and add to society's productivity.

Illiquidity—The lack of assets that can be converted into cash. The absence of saleable assets.

Imports—Expenditures on goods and services produced in and purchased from another country.

Inflation—A rise in the general or average level of prices.

Inflation Rate—The percentage change in the level of prices.

Interest—Payment made to a lender for the use of borrowed money.

Interest Rate—The amount paid for borrowed money per hundred dollars borrowed.

International Monetary Fund (IMF)—An international lending agency that makes loans to governments who need help coping with economic and financial crises.

Junk Bonds—Bonds that pay a high interest rate in compensation for a high default risk.

M1—A measure of the money supply that is limited to paper money in the hands of the nonbank public, travelers checks, and coins. Bank vault cash is excluded.

M2—A measure of the money supply that includes all assets in M1 plus additional assets such as money market funds and money market mutual funds.

Macroeconomic—The economy as a whole, embracing all sectors and involving economic indicators such as industrial production, the unemployment rate, and the inflation rate.

Medium of Exchange—Something that everyone will accept in trade. Whatever is used as money is the medium of exchange.

Monetary Policy—The use of central banks' control over the money supply to achieve economic goals such as price stability, full-employment, and economic growth.

Money—An asset that serves as a medium of exchange, unit of account, standard of deferred payment, and store of value.

Money Illusion—A lack of awareness among individuals and businesses that their income is rising faster or slower than the prices of everything they buy. As a result, the real purchasing power of their income is either higher or lower than they thought.

Money Neutrality—The idea that changes in the money supply only affect prices and leave untouched inflation adjusted measures of economic variables such as wages, interest rates, and gross domestic product (GDP).

Money Supply—The size of the stock of money assets actually circulating in the economy at a point in time.

Open Market Operations—A central bank's purchase and sale of government bonds for the purpose of changing the money supply.

Overvalued Currency—A currency for which the official exchange rate set by the government is above its market value and therefore one that is a likely candidate for future devaluation.

Pegged Exchange Rate—An exchange rate for a currency relative to one or several other currencies that is fixed by the government and is held constant.

Rate of Return—The income from an investment that is expressed as a percentage of the investment.

Real Interest Rate—The percentage growth in the purchasing power of an interest-bearing asset. For the real interest rate to be positive, the quoted interest rate must exceed the inflation rate.

Shortage—A market situation in which the amount of a good or service producers want to make available is less than the amount that buyers and consumers want to purchase.

Solvency—A situation in which a business has enough cash and assets convertible into cash to pay its expenses and debts.

Speculative Demand—That portion of household and business money holdings that are kept as a substitute for stocks and bonds.

Stagflation—A seemingly paradoxical combination of high inflation, which suggests strong demand for goods and services, and slow growth, which suggests weak demand for goods and services.

Stocks—Ownership shares of an incorporated business. Ownership of stock allows an individual to buy part ownership of a business without the permission of the other part-owners, and to sell out part-ownership without the permission of the other part-owners.

Store of Value—An asset that preserves its monetary value over time and can be used to preserve purchasing power for a future date. Acting as a store of value is one of the functions of money.

Surplus—A market situation in which the amount of a good or service producers want to make available exceeds the amount that buyers and consumers want to purchase.

Time Value of Money—The relationship between the value of a sum of money available immediately relative to the present value of the exact same sum of money available at some date in the future. One hundred dollars payable today is worth more than one hundred dollars payable ten years from today.

Unit of Account—A unit of money (e.g., a dollar) or other commodity that can be used as a measuring rod for the value of goods and services. Acting as a unit of account is one of the functions of money.

Velocity of Money—The average number of times a dollar or other unit of currency is spent over a given period of time.

Wealth—The accumulated stock of financial assets and income-earning physical assets.

Index

About the Author

Larry Allen is a professor of economics in the Department of Economics at Lamar University in Beaumont, Texas. Dr. Allen has written *The Global Financial System: 1750–2000* and *The Global Economic System since 1945*.